Introduction to Game Systems Design

Introduction to Game Systems Design

Dax Gazaway

Addison-Wesley

Boston • Columbus • New York • San Francisco • Amsterdam • Cape Town
Dubai • London • Madrid • Milan • Munich • Paris • Montreal • Toronto • Delhi • Mexico City
São Paulo • Sydney • Hong Kong • Seoul • Singapore • Taipei • Tokyo

Cover image: Vladimir Vihrev/Shutterstock

For information about buying this title in bulk quantities, or for special sales opportunities (which may include electronic versions; custom cover designs; and content particular to your business, training goals, marketing focus, or branding interests), please contact our corporate sales department at corpsales@pearsoned.com or (800) 382-3419.

For government sales inquiries, please contact governmentsales@pearsoned.com.

For questions about sales outside the U.S., please contact intlcs@pearson.com.

Visit us on the Web: informit.com/aw

Library of Congress Control Number: 2021940285

ISBN-13: 978-0-13-744084-9
ISBN-10: 0-13-744084-7

1 2021

Editor-in-Chief
Mark Taub

Acquisitions Editor
Malobika Chakraborty

Development Editor
Chris Zahn

Managing Editor
Sandra Schroeder

Senior Project Editor
Lori Lyons

Copy Editor
Kitty Wilson

Production Manager
Vaishnavi Venkatesan/
codeMantra

Indexer
Timothy Wright

Proofreader
Betty Pessagno

Compositor
codeMantra

This book is dedicated to my game family. This includes those who raised me as a gamer, those who have been with me through this journey, and those who took me under their wing as I learned the professional trade. Thank you to everyone.

Contents at a Glance

Contents

PREFACE

This book covers the basic aspects of game system design in plain English. It uses numerous examples and analogies to help guide you through topics that might seem intimidating at first but are totally within your reach. The book focuses on learning how to use spreadsheets for system design. It covers the basics and best practices for using spreadsheets to make complex game data more manageable.

Who This Book Is For

The primary audience for this book is aspiring game designers who are new to doing system design and interested in learning more. It is assumed that anyone starting this book already understands basic mathematics. But, beyond that, there are no presumptions for prior game design learning. This book is made to guide someone with a basic high school education from being a complete novice to becoming a practicing system designer.

The following are some of the groups of people who could benefit from the methods described in this book:

- Aspiring professional video game system designers
- Game masters/dungeon masters
- Hobbyist video game designers
- Designers of pen-and-paper RPGs and other analog games
- Experienced level designers who want more system design knowledge
- Programmers/engineers who will be working with system designers
- High school educators who want to connect games with math for students
- Producers/lead designers who want to better understand systems

How To Use This Book

This book is written to be read from beginning to end if you are starting fresh, without much prior knowledge of game systems. It's also made to be a reference book that you can jump around in and pick up useful bits of information, even if you are an experienced system designer. The best method for absorbing the information would be to read through the book once, working in a spreadsheet as you go, and then come back to the book as you create your next game for guidance on the complex tasks required to fully realize your game.

This book discusses and refers to a number of existing games, and it would be helpful for you to understand these games to some extent. Before you read the rest of this book, familiarize yourself with the following games by at least watching video reviews online or finding free web apps and playing the game a few times:

- Play backgammon, chess, and the Royal Game of Ur. Pay attention to the kinds of dice rolls you make in these games, how pieces are moved, and how the mechanics of each game interact with the game objects.
- Play The Battle for Wesnoth to get a better idea of what a turn-based game is and what an RPG is. Wesnoth has attribute-driven data objects and game mechanics that illustrate many of the concepts covered in this book. Further, it is supported by an active community that keeps the game well documented and up to date.
- Play or at least watch video reviews of *Pac Man*, *Galaga*, and other classic arcade games.

The games used as examples in this book were purposefully chosen because they are easily accessible.

This book describes many methods of working with game systems in great detail. It might seem that the methods in this book are being exclusively recommended, but this is not the case. Game system designers use an infinite number of methods, tricks, and techniques to do their work. They use so many, in fact, that they could not fit into a single book. This book is designed to provide a starting point that shows a small number of sample methods that are useful for all system designers. I expect and encourage you to continue to learn more techniques from other books, colleagues, and you own personal experiences. There are as many different ways to design game systems as there are system designers, and experimenting will help you find your own style.

What This Book Covers

Here is a rundown of what each chapter in this book covers.

- **Chapter 1: Games and Players: Defined**

  This chapter defines some of the important terms used in this book and provides some clarity on some important topics.

- **Chapter 2: Roles in the Game Industry**

  The game industry includes a wide variety of disciplines and subdisciplines that can be confusing to those who are new to game design. This chapter describes the common roles in the industry.

- **Chapter 3: Asking Questions**

  Game designers must ask questions and interpret answers in unique ways, and this chapter helps you rethink how we go about it.

- **Chapter 4: System Design Tools**

  The game industry is, as you would expect, full of computer software tools. This chapter covers the kinds of tools you are likely to use and some of the most popular tools in each category.

- **Chapter 5: Spreadsheet Basics**

  Spreadsheets are ubiquitous in most work, and they are especially useful to game system designers. This chapter covers spreadsheet basics.

- **Chapter 6: Spreadsheet Functions**

  This chapter continues the exploration of the power of spreadsheets by focusing on functions.

- **Chapter 7: Distilling Life into Systems**

  When you really look in detail at the mechanics that compose any game, you find that they are analogs for aspects of real life, even if they are abstracted. This chapter explains how you use those abstractions to create the building blocks of games.

- **Chapter 8: Coming Up with Ideas**

  This chapter helps you develop your skills around being creative, specifically in regard to coming up with new ideas for games.

- **Chapter 9: Attributes: Creating and Quantifying Life**

  One of the most common early tasks system designers perform is creating attributes for game objects. This chapter covers what attributes are and how to get started creating them for a game.

- **Chapter 10: Organizing Data in Spreadsheets**

  Once you have started creating attributes for your game objects, you will need to organize them and eventually analyze them. The best place to do this is in a spreadsheet. This chapter covers how to organize your ideas in a usable format.

- **Chapter 11: Attribute Numbers**

  This chapter discusses how to quantify attributes into numbers, including a scale of numbers and what kind of number granularity best fits a game.

- **Chapter 12: System Design Foundations**

  This chapter covers attribute weights, considerations for intertwined attributes, binary searching for the correct number, and naming conventions.

- **Chapter 13: Range Balancing, Data Fulcrums, and Hierarchical Design**

  This chapter discusses methods of turning a small number of data objects into a fully fledged set of game data.

- **Chapter 14: Exponential Growth and Diminishing Returns**

  Exponential growth is one of the most powerful methods of balancing modern games. This chapter covers why we use this method and explains a formula you can use to quickly create a nearly infinite number of varieties of exponential growth in games.

- **Chapter 15: Analyzing Game Data**

  An important step in understanding a game as a whole is to evaluate all of its objects together, whether it's a small set of 10 objects or tens of thousands of objects. This chapter covers how to collect data in a spreadsheet and get started doing basic analysis.

- **Chapter 16: Macrosystems and Player Engagement**

  You can use several different styles of difficulty adjustment to make a game harder or easier or to adjust a game to a player's particular needs. This chapter provides a high-level overview of various methods and gives examples of how these methods can be used in a variety of situations to get the proper balance for a game.

- **Chapter 17: Fine-Tuning Balance, Testing, and Problem Solving**

  Much of a game designer's time is not spent designing but balancing, testing, and problem solving. This chapter covers methods of making these important tasks easier and more productive.

- **Chapter 18: Systems Communication and Psychology**

  Games can be delivered to an audience in a variety of ways. A designer must consider how a particular game gives information to players and receives information from them. This chapter covers many of the aspects of communication with players.

- **Chapter 19: Probability**

  Not everything is predictable in the world or in games. However, it is possible to understand some unpredictability. This chapter introduces you to basic methods of calculating and understanding game probability.

- **Chapter 20: Next Steps**

  This final chapter gives you some more direction toward further growth in the world of game system design.

Register your copy of *Introduction to Game Systems Design* on the InformIT site for convenient access to updates and/or corrections as they become available. To start the registration process, go to informit.com/register and log in or create an account. Enter the product ISBN **9780137440849** and click Submit. Look on the Registered Products tab for an Access Bonus Content link next to this product, and follow that link to access any available bonus materials. If you would like to be notified of exclusive offers on new editions and updates, please check the box to receive email from us.

ACKNOWLEDGMENTS

First, I must thank my wife, Melanie Gazaway, who stood by me while I lived this, encouraged me to write it down, and helped me find all my worst typos before I sent in the book for review. Next, I want to thank my children, Mazzy and Jack, who had to put up with an awful lot while I was working in the game industry. From late nights at the office to missed vacations, I was not always able to be there for them when I wanted, but they never made me feel bad about it.

Next, I want to thank my parents, Armen and Michael Gazaway, who raised me as a gamer nerd. I certainly would not be where I am today without them. Michael was my dad and first dungeon master. He was the first person I knew who designed and modified games. He taught me the fundamentals of game design before most kids even knew there was such a thing. My mom, Armen, read me *Lord of the Rings* as a bedtime story and let me skip school to see *Star Wars* on opening day. Even now we discuss games, sci-fi, and fantasy movies as a normal part of conversation.

Beyond my parents, Rick Herrick was a family friend and huge gamer influence on me. Scott Stocklin and Jesse Wise were childhood friends who introduced me to even more games and were the test subjects for some of my earliest and worst attempts at making my own games.

In college, I was in the "crucible of design" where my group of friends were constantly making and playing each other's games. It was in that time that I developed more quickly than at any other time before becoming a professional. I would especially like to thank my gaming group, including Dax Berg, Goose, Todd Meyers, Ron Mertes, Skip, Foz, the Chads, Pig Man, Sarah Lacer, Marie, Glenn, Connor, Evan, and all the Daves.

Once I became a professional, the 3DO team was a tremendous help. Special thanks in particular to the leads of the team, Jason Epps and Howard Scott Warshaw (yes, THE Howard Scott Warshaw). They guided me from being a very fresh rookie into becoming a professional game designer.

I first heard the phrase "game system designer" with the Lucas Arts Team, and once I heard Chris Ross say it, I was hooked for life. In addition, he and Dan Connors were very supportive in letting me explore this new unofficial title to figure out what it meant. I cannot thank the Gladius team enough. They were all great, and I learned a ton of what is written in this book while working on that team. Special thanks go out to the system team of Alex Neuse, Derek Flippo, and Robert Blackadder.

The Vicarious Visions Team brought me on specifically because I was a system designer, and that was the direction they wanted to take the studio. This was a massive responsibility, and I learned an incredible amount while working there. I had more friends at that studio than I can name, so I will say special thanks to my system team of Dan Tanguay, Jonathan Mintz, Alan Kimball (programmer extreme and honorary system guy), Jay Twining, Justin Heisler, Mike Chrzanowski, Brandon Van Slyke, and Jessica Lott. Thanks to Tim Stellmach for introducing me to Bad Storming.

Row Sham Bow was the last professional studio I worked at and easily the best. Every single person there was amazing. The studio set the bar so high for me that I will only ever consider working at a studio this great in the future.

I would like to thank the Full Sail team. I love teaching and sharing my experiences with enthusiastic, motivated students who are at the beginning of their game design journey. In specific, several of my colleagues encouraged me to write this book and provided valuable feedback as I did so. These include Zack Hiwiller, Ricardo Aguiló, Fernando De La Cruz, Christina Kadinger, Andrew O'Connor, Hayden Vinzant, Paul Fix, Derek Marunowski, and Phillip Marunowski. A special thanks also goes to my interns and those wonderful students who kept coming back for game days.

Finally, I want to thank all my wonderful students. Seeing their passion and enthusiasm keeps me feeling young and passionate about this profession. I wrote this book for them specifically. It took me over 20 years to accumulate the knowledge I am presenting here, and now I am passing it along to the next generation. My greatest hope is that I can make their journey easier than mine was, as all my mentors made my journey easier than theirs was.

ABOUT THE AUTHOR

Dax Gazaway was raised in a gamer family. His parents met in a Dungeons & Dragons group, and he was surrounded with games being played and made. From a very early age, Dax was fascinated by the numbers in games. He would pour over monster manuals and board game books, dissecting the rules to figure out how the systems worked.

Dax started in the video game industry in the late 1990s. During his tenure in the industry, Dax pioneered game system design at multiple independent and AAA studios, helping to refine and define the subdiscipline. In recent years, he has become a course director at Full Sail University, specializing in teaching new students the concepts and tools of the system designer. Dax has created new curriculum and multiple classes for system design students, and he teaches introduction to system design courses.

The following is a selection of Dax's game design credits:

- *Star Wars*: *Obi-Wan*, System and level designer
- *Star Wars*: *Jedi Starfighter*, System and level designer and QA liaison
- *Star Wars*: *Bounty Hunter*: System and level designer
- *Gladius*: System designer
- *Syphon Filter* franchise: Lead designer and system designer
- *Spider Man 3*: Lead system designer
- *Marvel Ultimate Alliance 2*: Lead system designer
- *Guitar Hero* franchise: System designer

In addition, Dax has been the studio lead system designer for Row Sham Bow Games and a system design consultant for multiple projects.

CHAPTER 1

GAMES AND PLAYERS: DEFINED

To begin learning any topic, it's important to agree on terminology. This chapter defines a number of terms in order to establish a common vocabulary to use throughout this book. This chapter begins by providing working definitions of *game* and *game player* and then looks at a functional definition in detail that we can use to differentiate what is a game from what is similar to a game. Furthermore, we break down the various attributes that define game players in a practical way that you can use to guide your game development.

Defining *Game*

We need to define what a game is before we can define *game systems designers* or *game data designers*. While you could philosophically argue that "Life is a game" or "The entire universe and everything in it is just a big game," for the sake of this book, we need to more narrowly focus on the activities that are commonly seen as games, and we need to look at why those activities are different from everything else.

Games are human-made creations that have a few specific attributes. Instead of trying to sum up everything that it means to be a game, it's more valuable to look at various attribute criteria that must occur in order for us to have a game. In a way, we are creating a checklist that requires all the checks be marked in order for what we are looking at to be considered a game:

- A game has agreed upon, artificial rules.
- A player can have impact on the outcome of a game.
- A player can opt out of a game.
- Game sessions are finite.
- A game has intrinsic rewards that hold no extrinsic value.

The following sections look at these attributes one at a time to build a better understanding of the term *game*.

Agreed Upon, Artificial Rules

When one animal is hunting another, that is not a game. The goals in such a scenario are to kill or survive. There are rules in the hunt, but they are dictated by biology, physics, chemistry, and many other factors. While there are physical limits to what can be done in the hunt, there are no artificial limits; there is no such thing as cheating in the hunt.

So hunting is not a game, but we can observe many animals playing hunting-like games in the wild. Bear cubs may wrestle but not attempt to hurt each other. Wolves may chase each other as they would prey—but without attacking. These, essentially, are games. We, as humans, tend to think we have the monopoly on creating games, but we certainly do not.

Now let's consider two forms of human combat: street fighting and collegiate wrestling. In a street fight, there are no rules. Street fighting is against the law, so there is not even a semblance of any rule in the activity. If one combatant is clearly larger and more skilled than the other, the fight will likely be lopsided. If one of the combatants can grab and use a weapon, he might be able to gain the upper hand. Whatever the physical circumstances of the environment allow can happen in a street fight. So, a street fight is indeed combat, and it could even be considered some form of contest, but it is not a game.

On the other end of the human combat spectrum is collegiate wrestling. It is also a very physical contest that can resemble a fight, but it is a game. So what makes it different from street fighting? The rules. In wrestling, the players are not allowed to use weapons. They are not allowed to punch each other, even though they clearly have the means to do so, and it would almost certainly be an advantage to do so.

Now let's look at a contest that involves no real physical contact, let alone combat: checkers. When two players sit down to play checkers, the goal is for one player to capture all of his opponents checkers. Although there is nothing physically stopping the player from simply reaching over to the other side of the board and grabbing his opponent's checkers, he is not allowed, by the rules, to do so. To play the game, both players have agreed that they must create a specific set of circumstances in order to remove an opponent's checker. Only when the players have followed the artificial rules of the game and one of them has created the circumstances to remove all checkers can that player be declared the winner. In the rules of checkers, the set of circumstances needed to remove a checker is exclusive—which means that any move that does not strictly adhere to the stated rule is assumed to be against the rules.

If the rules of a game were not agreed upon, the game would quickly break down and fail to function. If there is an established set of rules for a game and a player chooses to play that game, we can implicitly assume that the player has agreed to all the rules—regardless of whether that player knows or understands them.

While all of the attributes that make a game a game are important, the most important one is that a game has agreed upon, artificial rules. Without these rules, there is no game.

Players Have an Impact on the Outcome

This attribute is actually slightly controversial. A small number of people believe that a game can be a game even if players have no impact on the game. However, for the sake of our definition in this book, if a player does not have an impact on the game, she is not a player at all, and the activity is not a game. Let's take a look at a couple of examples.

In the game Candy Land, players take turns drawing a card and then moving an avatar along a linear track toward a goal. Is this a game? According to the criteria we are putting forth—that a player must have an impact on the game—it is not. A player does not have any agency in Candy Land. Imagine that one person were to play Candy Land as all four avatars. Could this player have enough influence to make a preferred avatar win? No. Candy Land would proceed in exactly the same way with one person doing all the moves for all the pawns as it would if four people were making moves individually for each pawn. It would proceed identically regardless of the desire, skill, or intent of the player.

In contrast, with chess, if a single player plays the turns for both sides, it is easy for that player to decide which side will win and which will lose. In fact, most people find it difficult to play chess against themselves because it is too easy to favor one side winning without even trying.

People Can Opt Out

So far, we have established that a game has artificial, agreed upon rules and that people involved in a game can have an impact on it. Laws fulfill both of these requirements, but clearly, they are not games, and we would not consider lawmakers to be game designers. We have a defined word for lawmakers for a reason. But what makes the law more than a set of game rules? The people involved can't opt out. Let's consider a couple of examples.

If a person is walking with a basketball and someone calls out, "That's traveling. You must be dribbling the ball while you walk," the person might respond, "I'm not playing basketball. I'm just walking, so it's okay." This is perfectly fine. People are never obliged to play a game.

On the other hand, if a person is walking across the street through traffic where there is no crosswalk, someone might say, "That's illegal. You are not allowed to jaywalk." This person can't get away with responding "I'm not playing, so it's okay." Regardless of whether they want, care about, or even know about the law, all people are required to comply with the laws of the location they are in. This is a key difference between laws and game rules: People can't opt out of laws, but they can opt out of games.

Game Sessions Are Finite

A game must have some form of ending so that participants are sometimes "playing the game"—but not always. A massive multiplayer online game (MMO), for example, may go on indefinitely, but players do stop playing from time to time. The rules of the game exist for those who are playing but not for someone who has finished a session.

With a social club, such as Boy Scouts or Girl Scouts, there are artificial rules, the members can have an impact on their status—and therefore the outcome of the membership—and the members may opt out (quit) if they want to. So, based on these three attributes, these kinds of organizations could be considered games. However, they do not have finite sessions. When you join a club or another social group, you agree to follow the rules of the group at all times—and not just during specific times. This makes social clubs, music bands, theater troupes, and many other interests distinctly different from games.

Intrinsic Rewards

Based on the attributes mentioned so far, we might consider a job a game. It has artificial rules dictating what you should be doing when and where. You can opt out, and it has finite sessions. So what differentiates a job from a game? One more aspect that distinguishes games is intrinsic rewards—that is, rewards that have value only in the game. For example, when you play checkers, it is valuable to capture an opponent's checker. However, that captured checker holds no value outside the game. At the end of the game, all checkers are returned to the set to be redistributed at the beginning of the next game. At a job, on the other hand, the reward for work is usually money. The financial reward does not lose value outside the job and can be used in the larger economic system.

Let's consider a slightly more complex example: poker. We generally recognize poker as a game, although some people play it as their profession. In this game, the players play for money that has an extrinsic value, but there are significant portions of the game that hold only intrinsic value. For example, in the context of poker, having cards of the same suit and in order is considered highly valuable. Outside the context of poker, randomly drawing five cards of the same suit in order is still very rare, but it has no value. It's the addition of intrinsic rewards that changes a task, an errand, or a job into a game.

Game Attributes Summary

By bringing together all the attributes of games we have just discussed, we create a unique definition of *game*. Every game discussed in this book has all these aspects.

Determining what is a game and what isn't can get rather complex. Jobs can have games in them. Games can have more games in them. Some activities can be called games but are missing a crucial needed aspect (such as Candy Land lacking player influence). Despite these oddities, we now have a clear enough idea of the attributes needed to call something a game that we can go forward in this book with a shared definition for reference.

PUZZLES AND TOYS

Puzzles are a large and unique game sub-genre. A puzzle has a specific correct answer. With a puzzle, you either solve it according to the rules, continue to work on it, or give up. A jigsaw puzzle, for example, has the attributes of a game, but you can't lose; you can only stop playing. When designing a large game that contains subgames and puzzles, keep in mind this distinction: If a player can fail, it's a game; if a player can keep trying, without punishment, until he solves the challenge, it's a puzzle.

Toys don't have rules, so they are easily distinguished from games. Toys are similar to games, but with a toy, you can do what you want within the bounds of physics. By this definition, many computer games and many modded computer games are toys, rather than games, because it is entirely possible to change the rules and, therefore, the outcome of the session.

Finding the Target Audience for a Game: Player Attributes

Once you know the attributes that constitute a game, it is important to consider who you are making a game for: Who will be the game player? And, more fundamentally, *what is* a game player? It could be argued that literally everyone in the world is either a current or former game player; most people enjoy and sometimes play some sort of game.

> note
>
> Don't try to define the audience you want to play your game; really, you want everyone to play it. Instead, define the audience for which you are making the game. Many players' preferences are mutually exclusive. For example, some players won't play games that have sessions that last longer than a few minutes. Other players won't play games whose sessions last less than an hour. It is literally impossible to please both of these groups, and you should not try to do it. You can, however, decide which group you want to please and make your game accordingly. So, you can accept and embrace anyone who wants to play the game you are making, but you can only attempt to lure a much narrower audience as you make the game.

To define your target audience, you can think about various attributes, much as you will do for game objects later in the book. Attributes of game players run the gamut from demographic characteristics to attitudes and behaviors. The following sections describe a number of game player attributes that are just a sampling of a nearly infinite number of ways you could describe a game player. Use this information as a starting point for your own exploration rather than as a template for what is "the right way" to define a game player.

Age

Age can most effectively be split into two major groups: adults and developing children. As children develop cognitive skills, they do so (very roughly) by age. Games made for developing children have specific requirements and face legal restrictions. As a game developer, you must take into account the cognitive development of children of different ages if you want to make games for them. There are entire fields devoted to child development and making learning activities or games for children at different stages of development. If you are planning on making a game for children, you need to do some research into the field of child development.

Adults, on the other hand, can be grouped into one large pool for the sake of game development. You can assume that all adults that you make games for can read, use a controller or keyboard, understand basic mathematics, and work out puzzles on their own. This makes the categorization of adults by specific age nearly meaningless. While there are some cultural references that generations will interpret differently, there is not much to be gained from splitting up age any further, so when defining a target audience, it is generally sufficient to say the audience is "any adult."

Gender

There is really no need to dive into the politics of gender because gender is not a particularly effective attribute for defining a gaming target audience. While a few games do target a specific gender, most don't because there is very little that has to do with belonging to a gender in most games. So, unless you have a good reason to include gender as an attribute in your game's target audience, there is no need to include it at all.

CASUAL VERSUS HARDCORE GAMERS

What is a casual gamer? What is a hardcore gamer? It's nearly impossible to define either one. For example, Garry Kasparov is a world-renowned chess champion. That should qualify him as a hardcore gamer, but what games would you build for him besides chess? You might know someone with a full arm sleeve of gaming tattoos, but she only plays specific RPGs from Japan. Is she a "hardcore gamer"? Culturally, yes, but again, the definition does not really help target that player while making a game. What about a player who buys a new video game every week, plays it for a week, and then moves on? This person sounds like a hardcore gamer, but this person is completely different from Kasparov and your tattooed friend, who could also both be considered hardcore gamers. And what is a casual gamer? Is this person just someone who plays games infrequently? Does it mean someone who plays a certain game genre?

As you can see, it would be pretty difficult to use the idea of casual versus hardcore when creating a target audience. The following sections describe several more measurable attributes you can use instead for defining the audience for a game.

Tolerance for Learning Rules

Many people hate learning new rules. If you doubt this, hand someone a thick rule book and ask her to read it. Many people would think this sounds awful, right? These people often decide it is not worth the effort to play any new games. Think of people who play chess on a daily basis but no other games. They are certainly gamers, but they're not the same kind of gamer who picks up a new game weekly just to give it a try.

On the other end of the spectrum are players who enjoy learning the rules of a game; they might even enjoy learning the rules as much as or more than playing the game itself. These people might belong to a local board gaming club, where they play a new board game every week, rarely replaying a game. The draw of the game for this group is learning new rules with the group, and the games themselves are secondary.

As you create a game, you need to decide what tolerance level for learning new rules your target audience will need to have. People basically fall into five groups when it comes to tolerance for learning rules:

- **Refusing:** Players in this group all but refuse to learn new rules. If you are making a game for this group, it is almost certainly a game based on a real-world game, or it is a sequel to an existing game, or at least it fits tightly into a very specific genre. For example, Wii Bowling was able to grab an audience of people who had no interest in video games but already liked bowling. It is fairly rare to design games for this group, and doing so is much more challenging than creating a game for a more accepting audience.
- **Resistant:** Players in this group do not like learning new rules, but they will do so occasionally so that they can play a specific game. Players in this group tend to stick to a small variety of games, or possibly a narrow genre, and tend not to explore new titles beyond what they already know. Designing games for people in this group is easy if you are doing something that would be familiar to them and takes very little ramp-up. However, members of this group are nearly impossible to reach if you are doing something unique or well outside their comfort range. Think of the "match three" genre of games, like Bejeweled. Many players play only this genre because it is easy to learn and play and is available on a convenient device, such as a smartphone. If you wanted to make a new twist on a match three game, this group might be open to giving your game a chance. However, you shouldn't expect them to wander outside of this narrow focus willingly.
- **Neutral:** Players in this group are fine with learning new rules if it is for the specific purpose of playing a new game. Many casual video game players and board game players fall into this category. This group is unlikely to read or understand all the rules; instead, they learn as they go, and they may be interested in only the rules that are needed to play the game. The neutral category is a large segment of the market. Many, many people fall into this category, and it may be worthwhile targeting them, even though getting the rules through to them can be challenging. Players in this group are the kinds of players who follow several specific franchises and buy each new installment of those games. They are also likely to buy similar competitors within the same game genre, but they are unlikely to wander outside their preferred genre to try something completely new. For example, think about players who buy every variant of first-person shooter (FPS) that is released but rarely if ever buy games from completely different genres. This kind of player might be convinced to try something new to play with a friend but would not seek the experience without that kind of prompting.

- **Accepting:** Players in this group like learning new games and new rules. They often learn more rules than the bare minimum needed to play. They sometimes seek out rules exploits and use them to their advantage. This group is also likely to have a favorite genre and stick to it mostly but also explore other genres. The accepting category is a significant market and makes up a good share of professional game developers' target market. There are far fewer gamers in this category than in the three more resistant categories, but there are enough to warrant creating large-budget console and PC games for them. This is the group that is most targeted and valued by the gaming industry, and accepting players are often flooded with a variety of games made for them. This can have an oversaturating effect on the group, and each individual game created for the accepting crowd is likely to face challenges in terms of standing out in the crowded field.
- **Enthusiast:** Players in this group love to learn new rules. They often jump from game to game, and many of them drop a game as soon as they figure out the rules completely. While it is easy to get a rules enthusiast to play your new game, it is just as hard to hold on to that player. This group is also willing to accept many more rules and much higher barriers to entry than are the other groups. While there are no exact numbers on the size of each group, sales of games with many complex rules provide significant anecdotal evidence that this is the smallest of the five groups.

Interest in Challenge

There are many varieties of challenge, but we can simplify this attribute to tolerance for failure. Most games have mechanics that allow the player to both succeed and fail. We can quantifiably measure the frequency of success versus failure and use it as a metric that defines challenge. To some players, failure is almost—or even completely—unacceptable. They want constant rewards and play games simply to feel good or pass time—and not for challenge. Other players accept or even crave high failure rates. It is possible to quantify this aspect by listing an accepted failure level as a simple ratio of the number of failures to the number of successes. Consider these two dramatically different ratios:

- **15/1:** This notation indicates an expected 15 failures for every 1 success. This is a very challenging game; it is so challenging that it will likely drive away many players, but it may attract a small devoted following.
- **1/100:** This notation indicates an expected 1 failure for every 100 successes. This would be a game that is not intended to frustrate players. Story-driven RPGs and simple puzzle games may have this type of accepted failure level. The challenge of the game is not really the point of such a game, and so challenge is heavily downplayed.

Beyond describing the player you want, this player attribute can help you determine the game's success after it is released. The success and failure rate of players is one of the easiest metrics to acquire and analyze from play tests and telemetry data. This attribute allows you to compare your expectations with the reality of the game. It can also let you know whether you need to make adjustments to the game to make it more or less challenging to better target your desired market.

Desired Time Investment

Desired time investment can be broken into two subcategories: session time and total time. Some games, such as checkers, don't have a total time, only a session time. But many games have both.

Session time is how long it takes to play a standalone session of a game or, in longer video games, to have what the player would consider a satisfying session. In some games, such as poker, a single hand could be considered a discrete session; this would be a very small session, and most poker players would consider a tournament or a night of many hands to be a discrete session. Tennis is also a well-divided game. It consists of points that make up games, which make up sets, which make up a match. So, even though you can play a game of tennis in just a few minutes, it's not considered a full session. Instead, a match is considered a full session, and a match can last an hour or more. In game design, you should consider a session to be something that a player can walk away from feeling satisfied about completing.

Total time is the amount of time it takes to "complete" a game—which can be very different for different games. Some games are never completed. Think of MMOs, match three games, and older arcade games. Players may come up with their own definitions for total time, like "hit maximum level" or "earn all achievements." So you can see that it's not necessary to have an end to game. It is, however, important to define a session and a complete game experience for the game you are making.

For each of these time investment subcategories, you need to define what you expect out of a game and what the audience wants. Some players want a quick 5-minute session with no end game; casual mobile puzzle games suit this audience. Other players want 2-hour-long sessions with a 20-hour completion time; many action and adventure video games appeal to this group. Different time investments appeal to different players. You need to know what game you are making and know how to test your game with the proper audience to get accurate and useful information about your audience.

The following are some examples of how you might quantify desired time investment for various games:

- **Checkers:** 10-minute session, no total time
- **Poker:** 3-hour session, no total time
- ***Skyrim*:** 2-hour session, 100-hour total time
- ***Mario Kart*:** 15-minute session, 50-hour total time to unlock every reward

Pace Preference

The pace of a game is difficult to quantify but is important to players. Asking someone who likes turn-based strategy games to play a high-action FPS will not likely yield good results and vice versa. You should consider multiple factors related to pace. For example, a game of speed chess is fast paced, but it is fast in a different way than a "shoot 'em up" top-down shooter is. When you want to quantify the pace preference of players, you should specify what specific type of pace you mean. For example, some games have purposeful rhythms and go through pace changes. Stealth games, for instance, often have a slow methodical buildup, an explosive fast section, and a slower-paced cool-down section.

When describing pace preference, it is important to be as accurate and specific as possible. The following are some examples of how you might quantify pace preference for various games:

- **Chess:** Slow, turn-based, thoughtful pace
- **Ping Pong:** Very fast, athletic, reflex-based pace
- **Generic computer RPG:** Alternating between slow and mid-paced action with some slower thoughtful crafting moments throughout
- **Generic deathmatch FPS:** Fast-paced, high-dexterity, with very little downtime for breaks
- **Generic 1980s arcade game:** Moderate and dexterity-based pace to start that gradually ramps up to fast dexterity until the player can't keep up; play then starts over

Competitiveness

How much do players want to be judged or compared to one another? Some games are built specifically around competitiveness, and others avoid it completely. For example, all racing games clearly rank players based on how they finished the race. Many go further and show campaign-style rankings that accurately display how well each player is doing in comparison to other players. On the opposite end of the spectrum are sandbox games, farming simulations, and other casual games. It is often hard to determine player ability in these games at all, let alone to compare one player quantitatively against another.

As with the other attributes of a game player, it is important to know who you are making a game for and what kind of feedback to provide them. For example, if you were making a highly noncompetitive game, you would want to avoid leaderboards, ranking, and maybe even visible scoring of any sort. Players who like noncompetitive games don't want to know how they are doing and just want to enjoy the experience. If you were making a competitive game, you would need to plan well in advance how to track, measure, and display relative ability to the player.

Regardless of which way you want to go with a game, it's a good idea to keep competitiveness in mind from the outset. When creating a player profile, you can use any description of the competitiveness that suits the game you are making. The following are a few examples of how you might describe various levels of competitiveness:

- **Noncompetitive:** The game has no scoring, no ability tracking, and no player-versus-player comparison. It is meant to be easy and fun to play and not make players feel bad about their current ability.
- **Competitive:** The game tracks a few key metrics on a per-session basis. At the end of a game session, players are shown a score and given a ranking for that session. However, each session is individual, and the scores are wiped clean at the end, allowing the players to feel a bit competitive without being judged overall.
- **Highly competitive:** Every possible aspect of play is tracked, measured, and displayed in detail for the player. Individual sessions are tracked and compared, and global leaderboards are dynamically maintained and shown to the player. Players are encouraged to constantly refine their skills and are driven by climbing leaderboards of different time scales (for example, weekly competitions, daily challenges, and best-ever scores).

Platform Preference

Games are available for many platforms, including PC, console, mobile, gambling table games, and VR games. (You could even consider tables and pen and paper to be platforms.) Knowing the specific hardware platform, or multiple platforms, for a game will help define your audience—though not in a deeply meaningful way. There are now games of all types on every platform, and there are audiences for each of those types of games on each platform. It is good for you as a game designer to know the strengths and weaknesses of the hardware for which you are developing. You should therefore always be thinking about platform, although it is not as important to think about console players versus PC players versus mobile players.

Skill Level

Many games require that players bring some skills with them or quickly develop those skills while playing. Like all the other attributes, requiring specific skills for a game will attract some players and repel others. When designing games for adults, you can assume that players have reading skills and basic motor dexterity skills. A game may require many other particular skills, and it's a good idea to list them early in your development process.

Consider these examples of the skills that some games require:

- **Tennis:** High degree of hand–eye coordination and physical endurance
- **Chess:** Ability to think out future moves and options
- **FPS:** High degree of hand–eye coordination and fast reflexes

- **Match three:** Pattern recognition
- **Sandbox building:** Spatial awareness
- **Poker:** Probability calculation

CONSIDERING INCLUSIVITY

Not every game player is born with or currently has the same physical and mental capabilities. Color blindness, for example, is particularly common and can severely limit a player trying to learn a new game. Taking even small steps as a game designer to think about inclusivity in design can increase the potential audience while also doing something positive for society. While the subject of design for inclusivity is too large in scope for this book, it is a topic that should at least be kept in mind right from the very beginning when designing a game.

Genre/Art/Setting/Narrative Preference

This catchall category allows you some freedom to more specifically define what your audience needs to be interested in. Some players are turned away by specific art styles. Some have a strong preference for specific settings, and some may be more interested in the story than in the mechanics and gameplay of the game. This category can also include things like outside interests and hobbies your target audience will likely have. For example, if you are going to make a game based on being a stock trader, players probably need to have some interest in stock trading.

Value Gained from Players

Another important factor to consider when designing a game is what value players are going to give to you. After all, you are going to put a considerable amount of time and effort into entertaining your audience, and you probably want some form of compensation from your audience in exchange for that experience. Money is the most obvious reward, but it is not the one answer. As discussed in the following sections, there are many types of value you can gain from players at different stages in the cycle of a game's life.

Payment

The simplest form of compensation from players is payment. This could be as simple as each player purchasing a copy of the game. Modern games, however, have much more sophisticated methods of getting payment. Each form attracts some players and repels others. Knowing the kind of payment you want to get from your players from the start is an important factor in determining how the game is built. The following sections describe a few common types of payment and some pros and cons that you should consider for each type.

One-Time Purchase

With a one-time purchase, a player buys a game and can keep it forever. This is the oldest and most straightforward method of player value. People have been making one-time purchases of board games and decks of cards for centuries—and maybe longer.

Pros

- Players pay for the entire experience up front. This is often a larger amount than is required with other types of payment.
- The game can be considered done at some point. Many modern games are in production long after they ship or are even in perpetual development. This is expensive and requires a great degree of organization. With a one-time purchase, once the player buys the game, the obligation of the developer is over.
- When the game is done, the development team can move on and fully focus on the next project.

Cons

- There is no opportunity to make more money after the initial purchase.
- There can be little incentive to fix flaws discovered after the game shipped.
- There is no opportunity for the development team to get paid to continue working on the game.
- There is no external incentive for players to return to the game for new content.

Expansions Purchase

With an expansions purchase, players buy a core game and then may buy expansions for the game at a later time to modify or expand the central game. These are usually self-contained and fairly small in number. For example, a new expansion pack may come out twice a year.

Pros

- This format potentially keeps players wanting to revisit the game, which increases other forms of value (listed below).
- It is possible to tweak balance and fix mistakes. When an expansion is released, especially in a video game, the developer has an opportunity to sneak in some bug fixes or tweak balancing flaws discovered after the game launch.
- The game can be shipped quickly and on a smaller budget since it is expected that more content will be released for the game later.
- The game can be sold for a lower price because more money is expected from players for the expansions.

- The game developers can make more money on a game they know sold well instead of taking a risk on a new game.
- Publicity is important. When an expansion for a game is released, it is a good focal point to draw in new players and to get players who have moved on to come back.

Cons

- Players may feel as though the initial game is not a full experience.
- Part or all of the team is tied up working on game expansions instead of new projects.
- Each expansion pack involves many of the same obstacles and headaches as launching a game, without the benefit of launching a new game.
- The audience is much more narrow for an expansion pack than for a new game. The audience for a new game is potentially everyone, but typically the audience for an expansion is some fraction of the audience that has already purchased the existing game.

Microtransactions

With the microtransactions model, players buy or get the game for free to start. Then, while playing the game, they can make in-game purchases of things as simple as decorative changes all the way up to new levels and mechanics.

Pros

- There is a continuing possible source of income from players.
- Games can be initially priced low, or even free, which greatly expands the potential market of players.
- Players can specifically tailor their purchases to their own taste.

Cons

- Purchasing in game can feel like cheating in a competitive game.
- Players may feel that they are being "nickel and dimed."
- The more the developer adds break points in the game to attempt to sell items to the players, the more the flow of the game is broken.
- Much of the developed content may not be used if players don't buy it.
- The base game may feel unsatisfying. Conversely, the base game may feel good enough that players decide they don't need to buy anything and, therefore, the game does not make money.
- Some players and developers have moral issues with trying to extract numerous microtransactions from players.
- There are some legal issues that need to be investigated around the use of microtransactions, depending on where the game was made and where it will be released.

Advertising

With advertising, players pay a reduced amount for the game or no money at all, and the developer makes money from in-game advertising.

Pros

- The game can be inexpensive or free for players, leading to a potentially larger audience.
- The game has a continuing source of income.
- The payment is "fair" in that players who watch advertising are not purchasing an advantage in the game.

Cons

- The player is pulled out of the game experience by the ads. Often, the developer has limited or no control of the ads being shown. The ads may have a conflicting message to the intention of the game or may even be for a competitor.
- Ad revenue tends to be rather low on a per-player basis. It takes a whole lot of players seeing a whole lot of ads to pay a development team.
- There are a few technical issues with including ads in a game, though modern game engines and platforms have greatly reduced this difficulty.

Other Forms of Value

In the end, money is the goal of professional development, but there is not always a direct path from creating a game to piles of cash. Developers can gain other forms of value from players as well. When developing a target market, it is good to list, right from the beginning, what forms of value you want to gain from your players. When thinking about the additional forms of value, it is tempting to want them all. But you should avoid this temptation and pick only one or two to focus on. Trying to target several secondary values at once is likely to water down individual efforts and weaken the chances of any of them working.

The following are a few of the ways types of value besides money that you can gain from players:

- **Word of mouth:** When players like a game and discuss it with their friends, their friends are more likely to get the game. When a game has mechanics built into it that get players to play with each other, seek out people to play with, or just talk about the game, there are more opportunities to bring in a bigger audience. When targeting word of mouth as a method of getting value, you want individuals to talk directly to other individuals because they are likely to be trusted by the people they are talking to.
- **Social media:** Social media is an even more expansive but less personal form of getting the message out than word of mouth. It essentially allows players to act as free

advertising. While social media can help a small game reach a much larger audience, there can be backlash over "spam" games in social media. If a game is constantly asking players to share scores and invitations with new people, it does reach more people but at the cost of annoying potential players.

- **Popularity contests:** "Game of the year" and similar voting contests are common across the Internet. If a small game with a motivated audience can win or even place in one of these contests, it can give the game a large amount of exposure essentially for free. Note that this is a particularly difficult method of value to plan for with a new game. It tends to occur more organically in response to a game that is already on the market.
- **Ranking sites:** Many websites have ranking lists of new games based on player scores. Games with high scores are typically more attractive to new players. Some small games have broken out and become successful simply by having a consistent and growing following of high scores on ranking sites. It might seem like ranking sites would be an obvious target for every game, but it's really not. Making a game that consistently gets high ranking scores is often expensive in comparison to making a game that gets good scores. Or, to put it another way, there is an ever-diminishing return of ranking scores based on the input of every growing effort and money put into the development of the game.
- **Content creation:** A game may allow players to create content within the game. Players can produce more content than any single development team ever could. This model tends to create an enthusiastic and dedicated player base. There are, of course, many development hurdles in creating a game that players can manipulate and expand. These hurdles may be more than many teams want to tackle.
- **Player interaction:** MMOs and other multiplayer games are good only if people play them. Simply by being in the game and playing, a player adds value to the game. Some multiplayer games need lots of players to do adequate matchmaking. With these games, too, by simply being in the pool of players, a player is adding value to the game.
- **Market numbers:** Games that are popular and have a lot of downloads or active users get attention. For this reason, some teams are willing to take a financial loss in order to encourage the largest volume of players to play the game. One of the easiest ways to become successful while selling any product is to already be popular.

Target Audience Value

Obviously, a game developer would like to gain as much value as possible from each player, but again, many of the methods listed in this section for gaining value are mutually exclusive. Having a plan upfront about the methods a team wants to use to gain value from players will help guide the team in a single direction.

For example, if the team has a small budget and no established reputation, simply getting noticed is going to be very challenging. In this case, the team might decide to get value from players by giving away the game for free, being ad supported, and trying to gain more value from encouraging players to spread the word on social media. Conversely, if the team is more developed and wants to have a gamer-friendly reputation, it may opt for an upfront cost to the game and offer expansion packs. It might at the same time target high game ranking and possibly some online awards to gain value from players.

Target Audience Composite

Once you have determined the attributes you want and don't want in the players you are making a game for, you need to do something with this information. One thing you can do is create a target audience profile. The following sections provide examples of target audience profiles for various commonly known games. These profiles were created based on games that already exist—and they show that you can examine target audience profiles after you put out a game in order to look at the kinds of players you ended up targeting.

Chess

The target audience profile for chess is as follows:

- **Learning new rules:** Resistant. This player is willing to learn a small number of unchanging rules so they can play the game repeatedly with the same or new opponents around the world.
- **Challenge level:** Variable. The player will find the right challenge level by finding the right opponent. There is no single-player version.
- **Time investment:** Sessions are around 30 minutes; there is no total time.
- **Pace:** Very slow and thoughtful.
- **Competitiveness:** Highly competitive. One player will win or lose every session. The drive to beat the current opponent is a motivating factor for playing the game.
- **Platform:** Analog board and pieces.
- **Skills required:** Very little. Only the ability to comprehend the basic rules.
- **Genre/art/setting/narrative:** None.
- **Value gained from player:** Word of mouth and player pool.

Galaga

The target audience profile for the arcade game *Galaga* is as follows:

- **Learning new rules:** Resistant. The player is not interested in learning complex controls and systems but wants to get right into the game immediately and figure out the mechanics through trial and error.

- **Challenge level:** Very high. Failure is assured with every session. The player is happy to start playing knowing that every session will end in failure.
- **Time investment:** Low. Sessions are around 5 minutes; there is no total time.
- **Pace:** Players likes to start at a moderate pace and keep playing as the pace increases to the point that they can't keep up.
- **Competitiveness:** High. Players can see their score and try and do better. A public leaderboard enhances competition at the arcade machine. Players are driven to beat their own high scores and get their initials on the public leaderboard.
- **Platform:** Arcade cabinet.
- **Skills required:** Hand–eye coordination and reflexes.
- **Genre/art/setting/narrative:** Spaceships and aliens.
- **Value gained from player:** Direct payment. A quarter gets a short one-play session.

Mario Kart

The target audience profile for *Mario Kart* is as follows:

- **Learning new rules:** Resistant. The mechanics and controls are in line with those of other racing games, so a player who has ever played any racing games will be able to quickly transition in. Further, a player who has driven a car knows the rough analogy the game is using.
- **Challenge level:** High. 5/1 failure rate. When players start, they lose against artificial intelligence (AI) most of the time. As players get better, the AI and challenge level increase consistently to keep players losing frequently. This ratio of loss motivates players to come back for more and improve their skills.
- **Time investment:** Low. Sessions are around 15 minutes. A total time of 100+ hours is required to unlock all rewards.
- **Pace:** Very high. There is no time for contemplation in any moves.
- **Competitiveness:** Very high. Players are ranked per race, and there are multiple leaderboards.
- **Platform:** Nintendo game systems exclusively.
- **Skills required:** Basic racing game skills.
- **Genre/art/setting/narrative:** Fun, bright, colorful artwork that appeals to children. Some adults may be turned off by the cartoon style.
- **Value gained from player:** Payment is primary, player interaction is secondary.

The Battle for Wesnoth

The target audience profile for *The Battle for Wesnoth* is as follows:

- **Learning new rules:** Accepting. The game is similar to many traditional turn-based strategy games but also has many unique mechanics. There are many different character classes and items to learn, and a wide variety of attributes. The player enjoys having a basic set of knowledge about the genre but also enjoys the twists and surprises the game brings.
- **Challenge level:** 1/1. Players tend to fail the first time and succeed the second on any given level. Players feel motivated by this pattern to replay a scenario multiple times and also explore new content in the game.
- **Time investment:** High. Sessions last around an hour, and there is enough content to play new sessions for hundreds of hours.
- **Pace:** Slow, thoughtful, turn-based pacing.
- **Competitiveness:** Low. While multiplayer mode is an option, most of the content is for single player mode. There is little emphasis on comparing players.
- **Platform:** PC, mobile.
- **Skills required:** Lots of reading, probability calculation, and strategic thinking.
- **Genre/art/setting/narrative:** Classic high fantasy.
- **Value gained from player:** Word of mouth, player content creation, and player interactions.

Bejeweled

For this final example, I have given the player a name and personality description to illustrate how such simple changes can humanize the target audience and help you better imagine how to make a game for those players. You can also add a few more details to help flesh out the character of your target audience. While this is not essential to get started, it can certainly help with visualization.

The target audience profile for *Bejeweled* is as follows:

- **Player name:** Chris.
- **Learning new rules:** Resistant. Chris does not play a lot of games, but she can easily figure out the basics of a match three game. She is motivated to find a few new combos and strategies as the game progresses, but she is not willing to go on forums or research a better strategy.
- **Challenge level:** Moderate. 1/10. Chris wants to be able to clear several boards of the game before the challenge starts to grow. Even at the highest challenge level, Chris can usually eke out a win and move on.

- **Time investment:** Low. Session length is around 15 minutes; there is no total length. Chris wants a game she can pick up and quickly get into and then complete a small session in just a few minutes. Chris does not want to invest large amounts of time in campaign modes or expanding mechanics.
- **Pace:** Chris enjoys slow and thoughtful turn-based moves. She does not want a game to stress her out.
- **Competitiveness:** Moderate. Chris mostly likes to play the game to kill a bit of time, but she enjoys occasionally checking the high score boards to see how she's doing compared to her friends.
- **Platform:** As many as possible, so Chris can play on any device available.
- **Skills required:** Chris is likely not color blind, but if she were, she might have a hard time with the core mechanics.
- **Genre/art/setting/narrative:** Chris likes the universal appeal of abstract decorations.
- **Value gained from player:** Chris has bought the game on some devices but plays with ads on others. Chris also likes to chat with friends about the game.

Do you feel like you can envision Chris? Maybe you know Chris or even are Chris! If you can envision Chris, and clearly see what will make her happy or upset, it's much easier to make a game that will make her want to buy the game and continue to play.

What to Do with a Target Audience Profile

You spend a considerable amount of time determining who you want to make a game for and creating a target audience profile. You can use this profile as a guide through the rest of the game-making process.

You should refer to the target audience profile often as the game is being made. Each time there is a suggestion for a new feature, system, or data, the team should consider: Will this make the audience happy? If the team is debating multiple different routes for the game, it should think about which of them the target audience might prefer. By constantly coming back to the target, the process of making the game becomes more grounded. You are not making a game just for yourself, or for some unknown people. Instead, you are making it for a person. For humans, getting this granular makes concepts make more sense.

Using a target audience profile is also a great way to ramp up new team members. As we will discuss later in this book, the game development team is rarely static from start to finish. When the target audience profile is created, it's likely that the team will still be small and in a preproduction phase. New people who are added to the team need to understand not only how the game is being made but who it is being made for. By having a single, defined target audience, it's much easier to get new people on the team to buy into the vision of the team quickly and accurately.

Further Steps

After completing this chapter, you should take some time to practice in the real world with the concepts covered here. Try these exercises to further explore the definitions of games and their players:

- Analyze several simple older games and decide for yourself if they meet the definition of a game and how. List the various attributes that make up the games specifically.
- Build several target audience profiles for your own games and other popular games. See if you can figure out why the game creators chose to target those specific target audiences.

CHAPTER 2

ROLES IN THE GAME INDUSTRY

The video game industry is relatively young compared to other creative industries. The breadth of things considered video games is also quite large: It can encompass everything from mobile games made by individuals, to AAA online video games created by teams of more than 100 people, to military simulation games, to an infinite number of other variations. Games more broadly span everything from board games, to card games, to sports, to all the other variations of games. Different games are created in different ways and require different team members.

A *game developer* (or *game dev*) is anyone who directly works on a video game, whether an engineer, a designer, or a sound tech. In some companies, only programmers are called game developers. However, this is a throwback to the early days of the video game industry, when all those who made games were programmers. Today it is generally accepted that more than just programmers are game developers.

A large game development team is likely to have a number of subdisciplines. On smaller teams, the same jobs typically need to be done, but a number of team members typically wear multiple hats. A solo developer, of course, needs to wear all the hats and do all the jobs.

A team—especially a large one—is almost never a static group whose members all work on a game from beginning to end. Throughout the course of a game development project, members are brought onto the team and moved off it. This chapter discusses a few of the roles that are common across the industry, discussing roles in roughly the order in which they come onto the team.

Core Management Team

The core management team includes the vision holder, the lead engineer, the lead artist, the lead designer, the producer, and the lead sound designer. This team tends to be consistent from the start of the project to completion.

Vision Holder

On each game development team, there is someone who is ultimately responsible for the game concept. This is the vision holder. This person either had the initial idea for the game, was assigned an idea by an outside group, or was put in charge by the team. This person must hold on to the core of the creative vision. This role is often filled by a company owner, a CEO, an executive, a producer, a creative director, or a director. The vision holder is responsible for protecting and guiding the creative vision and settling disputes in the team about the direction of the game as a whole. The vision holder is almost always the first person brought onto a team. A game may sit with the vision holder for months or years before anyone else is brought onto the team.

Especially in large studios/teams, the vision holder is the person involved the most in communication, meetings, traveling, and negotiation; this person is usually one of the team members least involved in the actual day-to-day making of the details in the game. While the vision holder owns the vision of the project as a whole, they actually have little insight into the minutia and must work with and trust the team to make a great game.

Vision holder is also one of the most senior positions in the game development industry. It takes years or even decades to climb the ranks from being a game developer on staff to being the vision holder. This position is often responsible for millions of dollars of invested money and the livelihood of an entire development team and maybe an entire company. This position would only be trusted to someone with an immense amount of experience.

Lead Engineer

Especially for video games, it's likely that one of the first people to join the vision holder is the lead engineer. The job of the lead engineer is to figure out technically how the game is going to be made. Will it be made using a third-party engine, or an engine the company has already used, or a brand-new engine? What are the scope requirements needed to make the vision come to life? Who will the engineering team need to include to create this project? These are just a few of the thousands of challenges that the lead engineer faces while creating a game.

Lead Artist

Once a game has a creative vision and has groundwork being laid in the technical department, the team needs to start establishing a look for the game. This is where a lead artist comes in. This position faces many of the same challenges as the lead engineer when it comes to determining scope, staffing, and scheduling for the art portion of the project. In addition, the lead artist sets the tone for the look of the entire game.

Lead Designer

A game needs a creative vision, and groundwork must be laid for how the game is going to be technically built and what it will look like, but none of these things actually make it a game. The team needs a lead game designer, who is responsible for determining the makeup of the design team, scoping, and scheduling. In addition, the lead designer is at the heart of creating the rules and play of the game.

Producer

Producers are the coordinators and businesspeople of the creative world. The job of a producer is to make sure the game is made on budget, on time, and with the right staffing. Producers always work with the leads, subdiscipline leads, and the development team to ensure that the whole group is working as a team.

Lead Sound Designer

The control of everything audio often is led by a single person. While a small game may have one sound designer, a large game may have an entire sound team, led by a lead sound designer.

Team Subdisciplines

Subdisciplines on a team have more specific roles than the core management team and do more hands-on work. In most cases, each subdiscipline lead (commonly called a sublead) also reports to a member of the core management group. The following sections only briefly cover the disciplines outside of design. This is, after all, a book about design.

Art

Art roles include animation, character art, environmental art, concept/2D art, interface art, and technical art.

Animation

Animators make a game move and make static objects come to life. They start with a static mesh character and manipulate it to create animations. Every action that every character takes visually is the result of an animator's work.

Character Art

Character artists specialize in character models, which are called *character meshes* in the game industry. On big games with big teams, there are artists who are so specialized that their sole job on the project is to create character meshes—and there is plenty of work for them to do.

Environmental Art

Environmental artists are, as the name suggests, responsible for the look of the environment of a game. How much they do varies depending on the needs of the game. On some teams environmental artists work closely with level designers, on other teams they have free rein with a level, and on other teams they create the building blocks that level designers use to make the levels.

Concept/2D Art

Concept artists are most closely related to traditional 2D artists in the industry. Their job can start early in the development cycle. They work with both artists and designers to come up with visualizations of conceptual ideas. They may make images to guide the art team or to help a designer express an idea; they may also make posters and promotional art for the game.

Interface Art

Interface artists specialize in the interactive interface that players use to get deeper information from the game. They work on the heads-up display (HUD) and the user interface (UI).

Technical Art

Technical artists don't just straddle the line between art and programming; they must be experts at both. This makes the position difficult to fill. Technical artists need to understand the art pipeline and must be able to program well enough to create or improve the methods artists use to get their work into the game engine.

Engineering

Engineering roles include tools engineer, gameplay engineer, scripter, network engineer, graphics engineer, and audio engineer.

Tools Engineer

Tools engineers don't work on the game directly but instead focus on building the tools that all the other disciplines use to create the game. In recent years, many more engines have been built by independent third-party companies, reducing the need for tools engineers on game development teams.

Gameplay Engineer

Gameplay engineers are mostly focused on making the game work. They work closely with the system designers and all other designers to implement features needed to bring the game to life.

Scripter

Scripters use an internal scripting language to add polish and detail to the game. Scripters sometimes fall under the engineering team and sometimes under the design team, but in either case, they do basically the same job.

Network Engineer

Network engineers focus specifically on the connectivity of computers to each other and to servers. This is an immensely difficult role that requires specific training.

Graphics Engineer

As the name suggests, graphics engineers focus on the programming that supports the visuals of the game. Whether it's making water look more realistic, creating long vista views, working out how to achieve a good frame rate, or using a new shader to create an interesting effect, graphics engineers are responsible for the underlying code.

Audio Engineer

Audio engineers do the programming that powers all of the audio in the game.

Production

Production roles are a little different from the roles discussed so far in this chapter. Under the umbrella of production, there are many roles, including assistant producers, associate producer, and production assistant. There are many variations of the titles and responsibilities in production. To add to the confusion, different studios use a variety of titles for people in production. However, production roles fall roughly into three categories: management, coordinators, and assistants.

Management

Managers are in charge of money and often staffing.

Coordinators

Coordinators are involved in the day-to-day workings of the team. They often run meetings, keep track of tasks, and check up on bugs. They also facilitate communication within the team.

Assistants

Assistants are the lowest-level producers, and they do a lot of the daily chores to free up the senior-level employees. An assistant position is usually a starting position and provides excellent insight into how games get made.

Design

The designer roles include level designer, game system designer, data designer, scripter, and technical designer.

Level Designer

Level designers create the physical space that players traverse. Depending on the team, this may be laying out rough pathways, or it could be arranging preexisting environmental assets or even roughing out the world with geometry primitives. Level designers also often do scripting and other puzzle design for their levels. They may even contribute to individual story elements. In large, open-world games, a level designer might be called a scenario designer.

Game System Designer

A game system, simply put, is a set of rules that makes a game run. In any game, the rules are what really make it a game. Game system designers deal with these rules. It is their job to create the rules of the game, organize those rules so that they are all compatible with each other, and explain those rules to the player. A very simple old game is likely to have a simple system that can be explained with a page or so of rules. Modern games often involve thousands of data objects and tens of thousands of lines of computer code that function as the rules of the game. Ensuring that all this information is organized and logical—and making sure players can digest it—is the primary responsibility of the system designer. A system designer creates AI, weapons, vehicles, and any other objects that are used throughout the game. System designers decide what attributes are assigned to the various objects and how all the systems in the game interact with each other.

Data Designer

Data designers populate the game world with characters, objects, weapons, vehicles, and every other game object. Whereas system designers decide what attributes each object will have, data designers decide the value of each of those attributes.

Scripter

As mentioned earlier in this chapter, scripters use an internal scripting language to add polish and detail to the game. Scripters sometimes fall under the engineering team and sometimes under the design team, but in either case, they do basically the same job.

Technical Designer

The term *technical designer* is currently used a couple ways in the game design industry:

- A technical designer may be an implementer who is strong at scripting/programming but does not do much of the documentation or the high-level creative design. This could potentially be a junior designer who is mostly taking direction from a senior designer.
- A technical designer may be a bridge between the engineering team and the design team, making tools or systems and using them to make the lives of the other designers easier. This would almost never be a junior designer as the skills required to do the job are simply too advanced and require too much experience.

Sound Team

The sound team is in charge of making the game sound amazing. While this seems fairly straightforward, it's one of the most difficult positions in the industry. Sound designers often need to wait until much of the rest of the game is nearing completion before they can start their job. They have to account for every bit of audio feedback the player will need, which is often vast. They also often create soundtracks, and they are increasingly adding dynamic music based on the action in the game. These are difficult, technically challenging skills to learn. Members of the sound team must have background in sound effects and music, and they are also typically much more technically savvy than traditional musicians.

QA Team

The quality assurance (QA) team, also known as testers, is in charge of ensuring the quality of the game when it is released. There is a common misconception that members of the QA team are playtesters only. This is incorrect. Playtesters are volunteers who play the game as a typical end user would and give unquantified feedback on how the game made them feel, how much fun it was, and so on. The QA team does very often play the game, but it does a lot more: It tests the game. This means doing things like bumping into every wall in a level dozens of times and from every direction to make sure the player character can't slip out between gaps in geometry and flipping back and forth between menu pages for hours to ensure that graphics and code are being properly loaded and unloaded. An average player would never do these types of activities while playing a game, but the industry has standards set high enough that all fringe cases must be accounted for. Members of the QA team include those with diverse educational backgrounds. Positions on this team are often seen as stepping stones into other career paths, most notably production and design.

Narrative Designer

The narrative designer, sometimes called an author, is in charge of the game's story. There are typically a very small number of narrative designers in a studio, and very often the role is fulfilled by those on the senior design or production team. Narrative designers have training in creative and technical writing, as well as a solid game design foundation.

Additional Roles

From human resources, to game writers, to IT, there are many more people and positions that run in the background of the game industry, making the process work. These other roles may not get a lot of press or be the face of a game at a convention, but they are every bit as important as the person credited as having "created the game."

Further Steps

After completing this chapter, you should take some time to practice in the real world with the concepts covered here. Try these exercises to further explore the roles in the game industry:

- For some of your favorite large studio games, find out what game developer roles were involved in game creation. Note how the scope of the game drastically affects the number of developers and the variety of roles on the team.
- Do some research on the websites of a few small, independent game studios and take note of what game developer roles were involved in game creation.

CHAPTER 3

ASKING QUESTIONS

Asking questions seems like a topic we all know intuitively. After all, people ask questions all the time, so why bother learning how to do this task for game development? Game designers need to ask unique questions in unique ways, and they interpret the answers to questions in a unique way. This chapter looks at how to craft theoretical questions that yield meaningful answers. For example, "Is the game fun?" is not a quantifiable or answerable question because everyone has a different and personal interpretation of what fun is. This chapter also talks specifically about how to write technical questions that seek help with problems. For example, rather than ask the lead engineer "Why does the game engine crash when I load this asset?" you need to get more granular in order to reach the heart of the issue.

How to Ask a Theoretical Question

System designers often need to ask questions about games. Specifically, they ask questions about how the game feels, how the game is balanced, and how new data objects fit into an existing system. The main goal with all of these questions is to quantify feelings. To do that, it is important to take a somewhat scientific approach, and one good way to do that is to use the scientific method.

Steps of the Scientific Method

The scientific method, as applied to game development, proceeds through the following steps:

1. Define a question for playtesting.
2. Gather information and resources.
3. Form an explanatory hypothesis.
4. Test the hypothesis by performing an experiment and collecting data in a reproducible manner.
5. Analyze the data.
6. Interpret the data and draw conclusions that serve as a starting point for new hypotheses.
7. Publish results.
8. Retest.

Step 1: Define a Question for Playtesting

If you want to know if a game is fun for a playtester, what questions do you need to ask? You could simply conduct a survey and ask players if they enjoy the game, but would that give you usable answers? Research has shown that when people agree to complete a survey, they enter the process predisposed to answer positively. After all, they were excited enough about the project to be willing to take the survey. This predisposition is called *acquiescence bias*. So by posing a question through a survey, you are unlikely to get unbiased results. Another issue with this approach is that different people have different definitions of "fun," and often these definitions run exactly counter to each other. For example, one person might find having "jump scares" in a game fun and exciting, whereas another may find jump scares to be stressful and not fun at all. So asking each of these players if a game centered around "jump scares" is fun would yield contrary results. To get meaningful results, you need to figure out how to define the feelings you want players to feel. Then you need to figure out how you can define those feelings in metrics that you can measure.

It's important to avoid asking questions that are not focused enough. Asking something as broad as "Is the whole game fun?" or "Is the entire game balanced?" or "Is the game too easy?" will not give you actionable results. Parts of the game might be fun, and others might be boring or frustrating. Asking overarching questions of large breadth leaves too much room for interpretation. When asking a question about a game, think about how focused you can make the question—for example, "Is this individual enemy character too challenging for our target player?"

Once you have narrowed your question down to the smallest unit that is practical, the next step is to quantify the question so that you can get a measurable answer. At first, it may seem that it's impossible to do this with a lot of questions. Emotions like fun, exciting, scary, and rewarding can't be directly measured. However, you can try to backward engineer a feeling based on observed data. For example, what metrics could you observe in a player who is having fun versus in a player who is bored? Play time might be a good indicator. Players who are having fun might play longer sessions, or play through a higher percentage of the game, or replay the game more often, or have a higher total time played—or maybe even all of the above. Some players find failure frustrating, so you could also track the number or ratio of failures at a given task. For example, you could say that a task is "frustrating" if the player fails at it more than 70% of the time. That is a perfectly quantified and measurable metric.

The following sections look at two more examples of transforming vague, broad questions into useful, measurable questions.

Example 1

Original question: Is level 3 exciting enough?

Quantification: You want the level to go by fast, and the designer is saying he designed it to be around 1:45 long. If players are in the level longer than 2 minutes, they are likely missing something, meaning that frustration or boredom could soon set in. However, you don't want the player breezing through because then there would be no excitement, so you want to make sure players are failing at the level and restarting it at least twice before they learn the required skills to succeed and pass on to the next level. Given these factors, you can't find out whether level 3 is exciting enough for all players. Some players will have a tougher time than others, but you do want this level to be fairly controlled. You want to target your preferred metrics for a fairly high majority; for example, you might decide that an 80% success rate indicates that you have achieved your goal.

Revised question: Can 80% of players complete level 3 in under 2 minutes, while also restarting the level at least two times but not more than five times?

The revised question is now completely quantified. While at first glance it would not appear that this question yields an answer about whether the game is exciting, through your testing, you determine that it can. You might also determine through testing that your presumed definition of exciting is incorrect. If this happens, you can revise your quantified definition.

Example 2

Original question: Is this boss battle difficult enough?

Quantification: This is a late-game boss fight, so it should have a small probability of success on the first encounter—such as 15%. The player should be using most of their acquired weapons to beat the boss; let's say 70% of weapon variations have been triggered at least once during the encounter. The battle should take a while; for example, you might want players to spend at least 5 minutes in the battle before the boss is defeated. Keep in mind that you can adjust all these numbers at a later time if you find that they don't actually represent the feeling you want.

Revised question: Do 85% of players fail the boss battle at least one time? When they are successful at the battle, do players use at least 70% of weapons available and take at least 5 minutes to complete the encounter?

Determining What Numbers to Use When Quantifying a Question

How do you know what numbers to use to quantify a question like this? Sometimes, you already have an idea for a metric in your head before you even start. For example, you might think that a challenge that is "easy" should not be failed more than 50% of the time. Other times, you don't know what metric to use. In such a case, if you already have a game to test, you can observe testers anecdotally and watch what metrics correlate with the testers' feelings. For example , if you observe a tester getting bored with a level, you want to note the time at which the player got bored. You could also observe any other metric that correlates with the tester's current observed attitude. If you don't have anything to go on, you will have to make a few guesses as you define the question and assume that you will need to adjust the numbers as you go forward with testing. At this point, it is important to do testing in which you watch and observe players while they play the relevant portions of the game.

Note that on a small scale or with individual playtesting, you can still use some subjective questions with your testers, like "How fun is the game?" You just need to acknowledge that the results you get from such a question likely won't have directionally actionable metrics. However, you can use such questions to start conversations with playtesters and eventually move toward gathering less subjective data.

Step 2: Gather Information and Resources

Once you have come up with quantifiable questions, the next step is to make observations of your players and gather information. Just as in any other field, there are several ways to do this right, and there are an enormous number of ways to do it wrong. Setting up a test incorrectly can result in ambiguous results or, even worse, misleading results. (You'll learn more about conducting tests on data in Chapter 17, "Fine-Tuning Balance, Testing, and Problem Solving.")

Step 3: Form an Explanatory Hypothesis

In this step, you need to start tying the quantified metrics you've recorded to the feelings and behaviors you observe in testers. By collecting data, you can get a much clearer definition of what characteristics such as *challenging*, *boring*, and *fun* mean for your specific game.

Step 4: Test the Hypothesis by Performing an Experiment

Once you feel that you understand how to quantify the desired emotions from players, the next step is to try to purposefully manipulate those emotions. For example, if you determine that a failure rate of greater than 70% would be frustrating, then test that. Start by performing a control test with your current data to get a baseline reaction. Next, tune the game so that testers are failing more than 70% of the time and then ask them (or observe) whether they are getting frustrated. Then do the converse and reduce the difficulty to ensure that it has a correlated effect. Through experimentation like this, it is possible to dial in on tuning to get accurate adjustments not only in numbers but also in feelings.

Step 5: Analyze the Data

This step, which needs to occur regularly throughout the process of testing, should be done using a database or a spreadsheet. This process is covered in detail in Chapter 15, "Analyzing Game Data."

Steps 6 and 7: Interpret the Data, Draw Conclusions, and Publish Results

Once you have tested, tuned, analyzed, and begun to understand the data for your game, it's time to write it all down. Ideally, you should be keeping notes throughout the entire process. It is critical to write a guide when you understand what is going in order to explain the process to teammates and your future self.

Step 8: Retest

Game testing never stops. Often games remain in a testing phase and are balanced long after the game is completed and shipped out to players.

Defining a Question for Data Analysis

When you are trying to convert players' feelings into metrics, you often have to do some guesswork and interpretation on what those feelings mean. Sometimes you need to dig through existing data and answer some questions, such as "What is the best weapon?" or "Which is the toughest enemy character?" or "How many shields could this sword defeat?" These kinds of questions don't have anything to do with the feelings of a player and often don't require any tester observation. With this type of information, you can use a spreadsheet or other calculations to determine the equation mathematically. When you ask questions like these, it is important to quantify each and every aspect of the question so that you can then write a formula to find the desired result.

The following sections look at two examples of defining questions for data analysis.

Example 1

In the game of backgammon, rolling doubles gives the player more movement. Say that you want to know the chances of a player getting the extra movement. To quantify this, you would use the question "What is the player's percentage chance of rolling doubles on two six-sided dice?"

Example 2

Say that your game has a gun that can fire a laser round 100 meters, and it loses no ability to cause damage over that entire range. You have another gun that fires bullets up to 60 meters. The bullets do more damage than lasers at point blank, but the damage the bullets can do decreases every meter they travel. To find quantitative results, you could ask, "Which is the best gun to use, from the perspective of damage, at 40 meters?" This again, would require no playtesting but would instead be done directly in a spreadsheet.

> note
>
> Methods for answering questions such as the ones posed in these examples are discussed in Chapter 15. At the early stage of development, it's more important to get comfortable asking questions than it is to find immediate answers.

How to Ask for Help with a Problem

Asking for help with a problem requires very different skills from asking a data-driven question. As discussed earlier in this chapter, you answer data questions with data results, using multiple opinions, analysis, and testing. With theoretical questions, it is likely that no one currently knows the answers, and you discover information as you pursue answers. Technical questions are much more straightforward than data-driven questions. You ask a technical question when you are unsure of something but think someone else might know the answer already. Hopefully, someone already knows the information, and they just need to know that you need it and give it to you. While this sounds straightforward, it's also easy to get it wrong, so this section examines one method you can use to increase your likelihood of getting information from someone else.

Why How You Ask Matters

In the game industry, there are constant deadlines and generally more work to go around than people or time to do it. The more responsibility a person has, generally, the more pressed for time that person is. Leads, producers, executives, and other people with big titles often have very tight schedules. Sadly, these are also the people who most often have the answers to questions you have. To complicate the situation further, the game industry is filled with many intense people who thrive under harsh deadlines and rigorous work schedules. These attributes make great workers—but not always the most patient or friendly people. A very busy, intense person might see a poorly written question as a time waster and become aggravated. Nearly every game designer in the industry would be able to tell you a story about a lead engineer giving them an earful in response to a question.

Questions that are well written, well researched, and well organized are more likely to get the attention and answers you need. Questions that are poorly written are less likely to get answered, or taken seriously, and they are much more likely to be dismissed or not answered in a constructive way. This does not mean you should keep your questions to yourself. Asking questions when you need help is vitally important. When you find that you need help, take the time and care to write a solid question, and you will have a better chance at getting the information you need.

Steps to Writing a Good Question

There are a few important steps involved in writing a good question:

1. Do your due diligence and write about the issue. When you're clear on the issue, write down your question. Try to answer your own question for 10 intense minutes. Do Internet searches, read manuals, dig through similar examples, and see if you can figure out the answer for yourself. Let the recipient of your question know the sources you have already exhausted.
2. Write reproduction steps. What exactly did you do, step by step, and how exactly did it go wrong?

> **tip**
>
> "What went wrong" is never "everything" or "something".

3. Write down attempted fixes. The person you are asking doesn't know what you have or have not tried already, so list all the things you have already tried.
4. Include a thank you with your question.
5. Before sending it, read your question as if it were sent to you and you had no knowledge of the issue until now. Can you understand it? Is all the important information there? If so, go ahead and send the question.
6. When you get an answer, assume that the answer is right, even if it seems odd.
7. Follow the answer you get *exactly*.
8. If the answer does not work, go through all these steps again and follow up. It is important to do this to prevent the person answering the question from falsely thinking that the problem has been solved by a potentially wrong answer.

As you carry out these steps, consider these additional tips:

- **Get to the point**. There is plenty of other time to chat. When you need a question answered, get right to the point without a lot of fluff.
- You may be very frustrated and angry when writing a question but remember that you are asking someone to help you. Put in extra effort to **be nice**. Also, don't act entitled or owed by the recipient, even if you are. Doing so can cause a hostile exchange, which does not set you up for getting the answers you need.
- Tell the recipient what you are trying to do and the **exact problem** you are trying to solve—not just a symptom of the problem. For example, say that you are trying to calculate the average time it takes a player to complete a game level, but each time you type your formula in Excel, the whole workbook crashes. Saying "Excel is crashing on me. Do you know why?" is not nearly as useful as saying "I am trying to calculate average player time in my level, but my formula is crashing Excel. Attached is a copy of the workbook, and this is the formula...." Knowing what you are actually attempting to do is vital information for the reader. In this example, the answer to your question might be to not use Excel because it is not the right tool for the job. But this answer can only be given in answer to a question that is trying to solve the actual problem and not a symptom.
- Be **very specific** and use detail. Consider the following:
  - When writing a technical or other difficult question, avoid using pronouns in order to eliminate one possible point of ambiguity. For instance, when you say something like, "The hero barges in on the bad guy, then he dies," how does the reader know which one died? Instead, try "The hero barges in on the bad guy, and the hero dies." This leaves no question about what exactly happened.
  - It is inadvisable to use words like *stuff*, *things*, *whatever*, *junk*, *you know*, *everything*, and *crazy*.
  - "The player character" and "the player" are different. This distinction is unique to the game industry, but it is very important. The player sits in a chair and pushes buttons. The player character is the in-game representative of the player. For example, "The player character can't see the objective" is a different problem than "the player can't see the objective."
- **Don't pretend** you know information that you don't. You may feel embarrassed about having to ask a question when you know that you should already know part of the information. It's time to come clean. Admit your lack of knowledge and just ask the question. It's not fun to do this, but it is much better than not getting the information you need.
- Use **bold wisely**. By highlighting a few key words, you can help direct a skimmer to the most important parts of your question. Don't go overboard with bold, or you will make the question look noisy and like you are screaming. No one likes to have questions screamed at them. Almost never use all caps, which tend to look like shouting. (Go back

through this list and just look at the bold words. Just based on these words, you can quickly get an idea of what is being communicated.)

- It can help to let someone know **why** you are asking them. Prefacing a question with "I know you have years of experience with C#, so I thought I would ask you how to get this script working" gives the recipient more information on what you are hoping to get. If the reason is obvious, however, it is not necessary to explain why.

Good Question Example

Take a look at the following example of an email that demonstrates the preceding advice for writing a good technical question:

Subject: Trouble adding a new row to the Time Logging Excel Spreadsheet

Hello, *Developer,*

My team and I have not been able to get the time logging spreadsheet to work properly when trying to enter new hours.

Here are the reproduction steps:

1. Open the spreadsheet in Excel 2010 on a MacBook Pro running OS X Version 10.7.5, select row 56 on Tab 1.
2. Right-click the selected row and try to select Insert New Row.

Issue: The Insert New Row option is gray, and I can't select it.

I have tried looking through the Excel help files for "Insert new row," and I have done a search on the Internet using the search term "Excel gray select new row." I read the first five search results, but none of them showed a solution for my specific problem.

I tried closing Excel and opening it again. I tried creating a blank workbook, and I could use the Insert New Row option in the new workbook.

Is there a way for me to insert a new row 56 into my workbook, or is there another workaround?

Thanks,

My Name

My Game Title, My Team Name

My Contact Info

Bad Question Examples

The following are some examples of bad questions:

- Everything in my level is broken. Can you fix it?

  This question provides no information and makes the asker sound helpless. This kind of question makes a lead engineer weep a single tear.

- "Something is wrong with my .png file, but I don't know what. What should I do?"

  This question provides too little detail. You need to tell the recipient what is wrong with the file. Does it fail to open with Photoshop CS6? Does it crash the computer when you attempt to open it with Microsoft Paint? Do the contents of the file not match your expectation? Is it something else?

- "I did what you said, but now things are different. How do I get them back?"

  There are several problems here. This question looks like it is trying to shift blame onto the person who answered it. That's not polite or constructive. The question is also lacking in specifics. What is different? Is it different in a bad way? How so?

  Here is a better way to ask this question:

  Subject: Class project Level 10 is crashing on load

  As you know, I have been working with Unity to create a level with my team. After adding a new static mesh last night, my level has been crashing.

  Here are the steps I have gone through:

  1. Open Unity and load my level on Windows 10 64-bit machine.
  2. Select the option to play my game.

  Issue: Unity crashes with no debug output or warning. The program closes completely and immediately.

  I have tried deleting the static mesh that I added last night. I have tried closing and reopening Unity. I am now frustrated and confused. Can you suggest steps for me to take to debug this issue?

  Thanks,

  My Name

  My Game Title, My Team Name

  My Contact Info

When someone's answer to a question you have asked really is your problem, say a short but polite "Thank you" either in person or via email. They need to know if it worked just as much as they need to know it didn't work, and closing the communication loop is important to show you can be trusted as an ally in finding and solving problems.

Further Steps

After completing this chapter, you should take some time to practice in the real world with the concepts covered here. Try these exercises to practice asking questions:

- Write some data-driven questions for a simple game you have made or played and then answer them. Practicing this skill takes a surprisingly large number of iterations. As you write the questions, focus on how others might misread them. You can even go so far as to try to think of all the ways the question could be misinterpreted.
- Take extra time to think about writing questions in your everyday life, as you would as a game designer. One benefit of living in a world that is full of opportunity for asking questions is that you can use these opportunities to practice. Posting questions on technical forums is a great way to get feedback from strangers and see if you are communicating your questions clearly.
- Browse through forums for examples of bad questions. This should be very easy as public Internet forums are bursting at the seams with bad questions. With subjects you understand, try to respond to questions in ways that help clarify the questions. Not only will this give you good practice writing questions, but it will also give you a chance to try to help others.

CHAPTER 4

SYSTEM DESIGN TOOLS

The game industry is, as you would expect, full of computer software tools. The needs of each team, project, and game are different, and a variety of tools are available to meet these needs. Some tools are used more often than others. This chapter discusses some of the most common categories of tools used in the game industry after taking a close look at exactly what the term *data* refers to.

What Is Data?

Throughout this and following sections, you will often see references to tools and concepts that deal with data. But what exactly is data? For the sake of this book, *data* is numbers or text used to describe something. Importantly, data is acted upon; it does not take action. Let's look at a couple of examples.

Say that a hero character has an attribute called health that has rules associated with it. Combat rules determine the amount of health that is lost during an attack or gained during healing. The hero's health score is currently 100. In this case, 100 is data. It is a number attached to the health attribute that is used by the attribute and the rules to do something. In Table 4.1 you can see several more examples of data that are attached to different attributes and rules.

Table 4.1 Examples of Data Attached to Attributes and Rules

Rule/Attribute	Data
Health	100
Weapon	Sword
Strength	50
Fuel capacity	20
Engine type	Gasoline
Is alive	True
Eye color	Green
Number of dice to roll	2

Notice that some of the data in Table 4.1 is numeric, some is binary (true or false), and some is text. Regardless of type, all the data in this table is used by rules in the game to do something. However, the data itself does not contain any rules.

Game Industry Tools

Game industry tools span a number of types of software and applications, including documentation tools, image editing tools, 3D modeling tools, flowcharting tools, databases, bug-tracking software, game engines, and spreadsheets. The following sections examine each of these tool types in detail.

Documentation Tools

Word processors are some of the oldest and most commonly used computer tools, and game developers use them constantly. Creating and maintaining documentation is the primary use for word processors. Generally speaking, each feature, level, concept, major game character, or system needs to be proposed. Once it has been proposed, or "pitched," it is discussed, clarified, and organized. All of these initial design tasks can be done quickly and safely in a word processor without fear of introducing errors into the game. Developers use a game design document (GDD) to record most or all of the concepts in the game. A GDD can be a very short document meant to keep just the core ideas, or it can be absolutely mammoth and go on for hundreds of pages. In some large teams, there is even a developer whose sole task is to organize and maintain the GDD.

Microsoft Word, Google Docs (see Figure 4.1), and Apache OpenOffice Writer are examples of popular documentation tools.

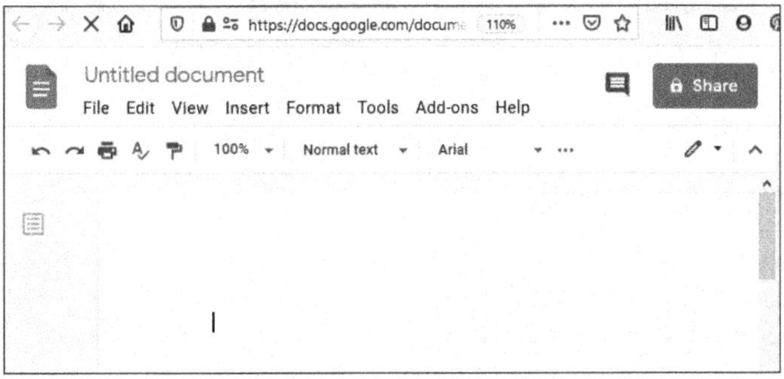

Figure 4.1 Google Docs
Screenshot of Google Docs ©2021 Google

Image Editing Tools

Everything that would have been painted or drawn in a traditional art setting is now created or modified using an image editing tool. These tools can import raw images from a camera or scanner, or they can be used to create entirely new images from scratch. Modern image editing tools are incredibly powerful and allow artists to quickly create and manipulate 2D images. Game developers use image editing tools for a myriad of tasks including creating UIs, creating textures on 3D objects, creating the skins on character models, creating concept art, and much more. Even though image editing tools are primarily the domain of artists, all developers, including designers, benefit from learning the basics of image editing.

Adobe Photoshop (see Figure 4.2) and GIMP are examples of popular image editing tools.

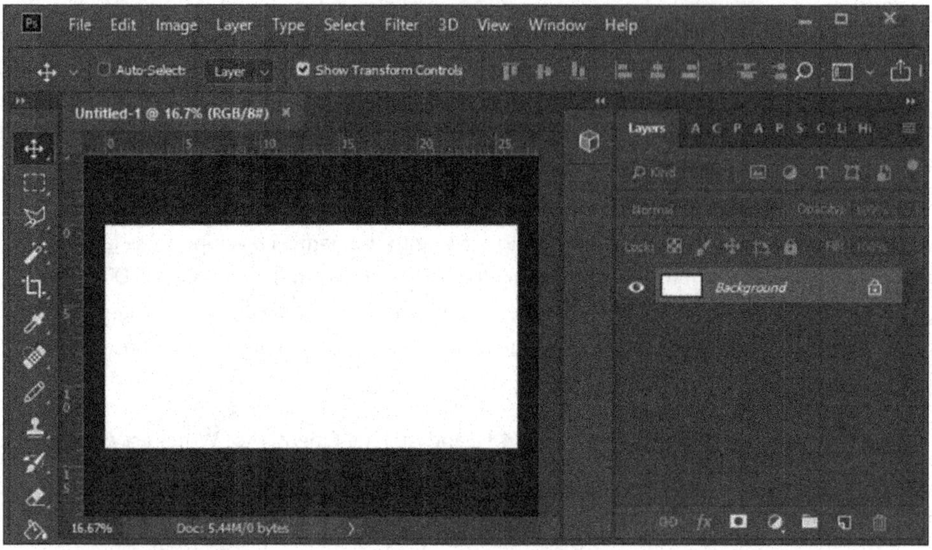

Figure 4.2 Adobe Photoshop
Screenshot of Adobe Photoshop © 2021 Adobe

3D Modeling Tools

In a 3D video game, a player can see and interact with 3D objects. Artists and designers use 3D modeling tools to make those objects. A 3D modeling tool has an interface that allows users to create 3D objects and manipulate them in simulated 3D space. Usually, a 3D modeling tool has multiple camera views that allow a user to see an object from multiple perspectives at the same time. These tools also have controls for manipulating 3D objects to do things like stretch, carve, twist, resize, divide, and attach 3D shapes. Most of these functions have very specific names in 3D modeling tools, and having a working knowledge of the jargon for the tools is highly beneficial.

Once 3D objects are created, most tools can aid the developer in making the objects textured. In games, this does not mean exactly the same thing as it does in the real world. In the real world, a texture is something you can feel. In the game world, a texture is simulated with an image. A 3D modeling tool can import an image made in an image editing tool and apply that image to the surface of a 3D object, giving it the illusion of having a textured surface.

Many 3D modeling tools can also be used to animate 3D objects. A game developer can use animation for prerendered cinematic scenes or export animations as instructions for a game engine to use in real time.

The final task of a 3D modeling tool is to export an object in a file format that the game engine can understand.

3D Studio Max (see Figure 4.3), Maya, and Blender are examples of popular 3D modeling tools.

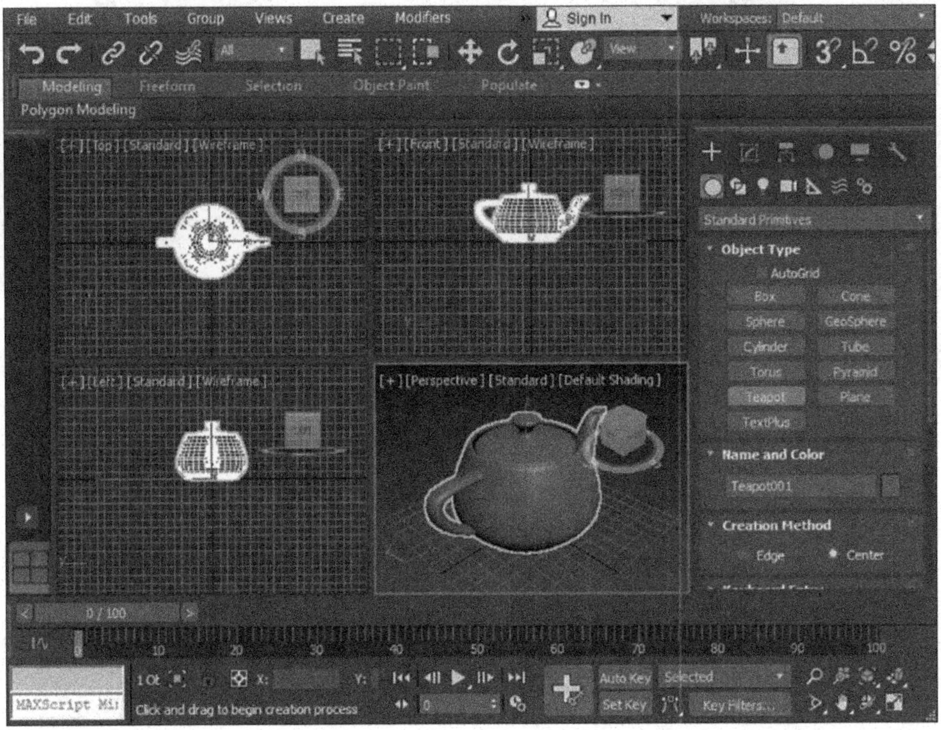

Figure 4.3 3D Studio Max

Screenshot of 3D Studio Max © 2021 Autodesk Inc.

Flowchart Tools

A flowchart, as illustrated in Figure 4.4, is used to organize ideas and show progression through a system. Unlike written text or a linear list, a flowchart can graphically display branching, loops, decision points, and terminus conditions. Very often, level designers use flowcharts to rough out the concepts of a level before they commit to the time it takes to make the level into a map or 3D model. System designers and engineers often use flowcharts to show movement through a system and to rough out concepts quickly before committing the time to create the system in the game engine.

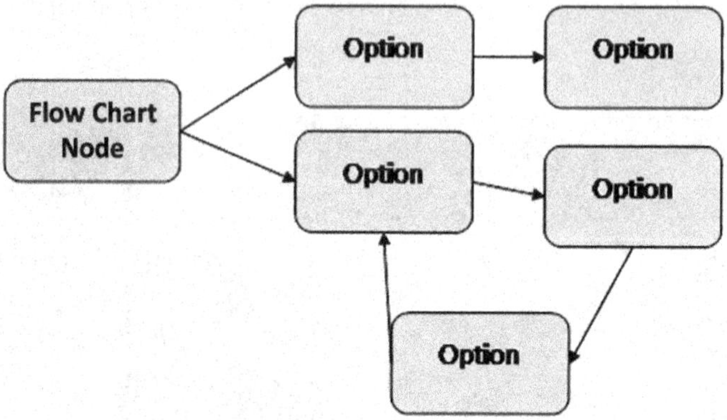

Figure 4.4 A flowchart

Google Drawings, Visio, and OmniGraffle are examples of popular flowcharting tools.

Databases

A database stores large amounts of data to be retrieved and used later on. A simple game may not need a database, but for a very large game, the amount of data that is stored can be monumental, and storing it in engine or in script can be unwieldy. System designers, in particular, need to be familiar with how to use a database as they are often the ones who manage game databases. Databases are commonly used to store weapons, armor, vehicles, power-ups, player-consumable items, AI characters, and other enemy character types. A database of objects acts as a central repository for game objects that can be used and reused, and it keeps those objects consistent across the entire game. Imagine how hard it would be to sort through all the scripts written for an MMO, looking for individual items and characters. A good analogy for a database is a file cabinet. You can go into the file cabinet, find the object you are looking for, and then either reference it for use in the game or make modifications in a central place that will affect the entire game.

A database management system provides the tools you use to actually access all the data in a database. To understand the difference between a database and a database management system, think about storing and using your music collection. On your hard drive, you might have hundreds or thousands of songs by different bands, in different genres. In this case, your hard drive is like a database, holding all your music information, including the songs themselves. In order to look at that information in a meaningful way, you could just browse through Windows file folders, but doing so would be very slow and inefficient, and you would likely miss a lot of important information. Instead, you are likely to use a music playing app, which is, essentially, a specialized database management system. You can use the app to filter for genre, or find every song by a band, or find the entire contents of a single album, or otherwise access the data. In the game development world, database management systems do a job similar to your music playing app. If you were working on a large RPG, you might want to look up every sword, or just shields, or just level 22 items that are used by knights. The database stores all the weapons, armor, and character class definitions, and the database management system allows you to access just the information you want.

Couldn't a spreadsheet handle the same tasks as a database management system? Yes, it could, and in many smaller games it does. But spreadsheets load all the data stored in them every time they are used. If you are accessing a very large amount of data, the spreadsheet will be slow. In addition, if you are only loading the items you want to edit, there is less chance of introducing errors into objects you did not intend to touch.

Microsoft Access is an example of a popular database tool, and MySQL and Microsoft SQL Server are examples of database management systems.

Bug-Tracking Software

Bug-tracking software is a specific type of database management system that is used specifically to track bugs in software. The database holds information about the bugs in the game. The management system is set up to specifically deal with the kinds of information and tasks you need to do with bugs. Unlike a generic database management system, bug-tracking software does not need to be manually configured before it is ready to be used to track bugs. You can use bug-tracking software to record new bugs, search for similar or duplicate bugs, assign a bug to a different owner, track the progression or fixes to a bug, and filter out fixed bugs.

Jira, Bugzilla, Plutora, and Backlog are examples of popular bug-tracking software.

Game Engines

A game engine is where an entire game comes together. Many of the challenges faced when making a video game are the same regardless of the specific game. Examples include rendering the graphics on the screen, detecting when objects have collided with each other, and retrieving art assets from memory. Most games need such tasks accomplished, and it would not make sense to program the functionality from scratch for each game that is made. Therefore, game teams, studios, and dedicated companies package all the common functionality needed to make most parts of the game together into a program called a game engine.

In addition to taking care of the basic functions of a game, a game engine organizes the interface for the game so that it is easy to use. For example, many game engines have a 3D view so that developers can move through 3D space to see where in the game level objects are located and adjust them or place more of them. Game engines also commonly have file management integrated so that artists, designers, and programmers can work with each other to make assets come to life in the game.

Several companies today make "middleware" engines, which are not made for any specific game or team but are instead designed to be used by anyone who needs a simple solution to game development. The upside of middleware is that it is designed to be used by as many teams as possible, so it is very flexible. The downside is that it will always be missing key components that make each game unique.

Unity 3D, Unreal Engine, CryEngine, and Cocos are examples of popular game engines.

Further Steps

After completing this chapter, you should take some time to practice in the real world with the concepts covered here. Try these exercises to further investigate game design tools:

- Do an Internet search for "Game engines for beginners." You will find articles on a large array of modern game engines and introduction videos for most of the popular engines. Take some time to watch these videos and compare the features of the different game engines to get a better sense of where the game industry is going.
- Practice using documentation tools, which have many more features than you might realize. Game designers must be comfortable using these tools, not only to type out the words but also to properly format and organize documents. Microsoft Word and Google Docs are the two most popular documentation tools.
- Make a flowchart for a game—either a game you want to make or a simple game that already exists. Use the flowchart to show the flow of the game from the beginning and through various player decisions. To get some ideas about what the flowchart needs to include, do an Internet search for "How to make flowcharts for game designers" and spend time with tutorials on the using flowcharts to design games.

CHAPTER 5

SPREADSHEET BASICS

Chapter 4 covers tools commonly used by game developers roles, but there is one tool that is the primary domain of the system/data designer: the spreadsheet. Because the spreadsheet is the primary tool you are likely to use as you design game systems, this chapter and the next are devoted to the use of spreadsheets. The spreadsheet examples in this book show Google Sheets (see Figure 5.1), which is a free and very powerful spreadsheet program. Several other spreadsheet programs are also well made and powerful. Almost everything covered in this chapter is also applicable to most other spreadsheet programs, though the interfaces may look somewhat different.

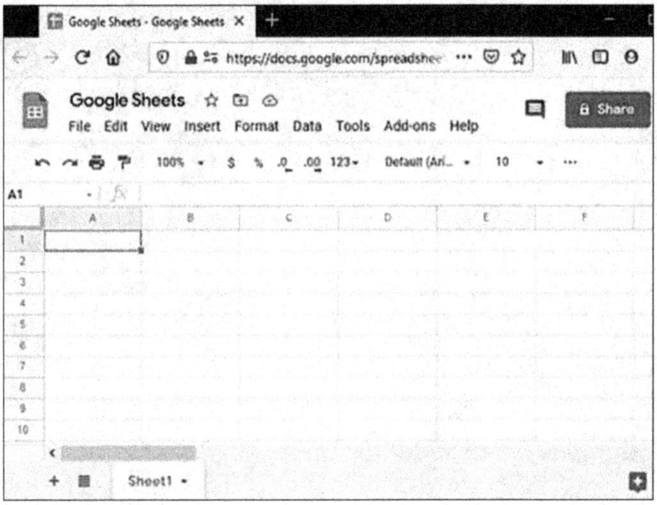

Figure 5.1 Google Sheets

Screenshot of a Google Sheet ©2021 Google.

Why Spreadsheets?

Imagine that your job involves moving ridiculously heavy things all day long every day. It is an awful, painful, and slow job. Then you learn of a giant who loves moving things and can move very heavy things all day long without complaint. It seems like your job is about to become easy quite quickly. However, the giant does not speak your language but uses his own Giantish language, and you don't know it. If you learn to speak his language, he will happily do whatever you want, and he will be able to easily do more than any human ever could. Once you learn to speak his language, you need only tell the giant what to do, and then you can sit back in the shade and watch him happily work.

In this analogy, the giant is a spreadsheet, the language is spreadsheet functions, and the heavy things are math. If you learn to speak the language of spreadsheets, you can easily perform tasks that are either impossible or completely impractical for any human to do manually. The job of a system designer is often to calculate massive amounts of data through complex formulas, but it would simply not be possible to do this manually. A spreadsheet is a perfect tool for a system designer.

Additionally, spreadsheet skills are some of the most common and transferable skills in the industry. All the other tools discussed so far in this book are in a fairly constant state of change. New game engines, art products, and team tools are added to the market regularly. In addition, many very old products are still under constant development and change. Even the mainstay Photoshop has undergone such drastic reimagining that the product is almost unrecognizable from its original form. So even if you learned older tools years ago, if you haven't used them lately, you would need to ramp up again if you wanted to use their modern incarnations.

As all the tools in the industry mature and grow, the spreadsheet remains remarkably unchanged. A stable and useful spreadsheet design popped up very early and has stuck around since then. For example, Figure 5.2 shows VisiCalc, which is the very first program that is considered a fully functioning consumer spreadsheet.

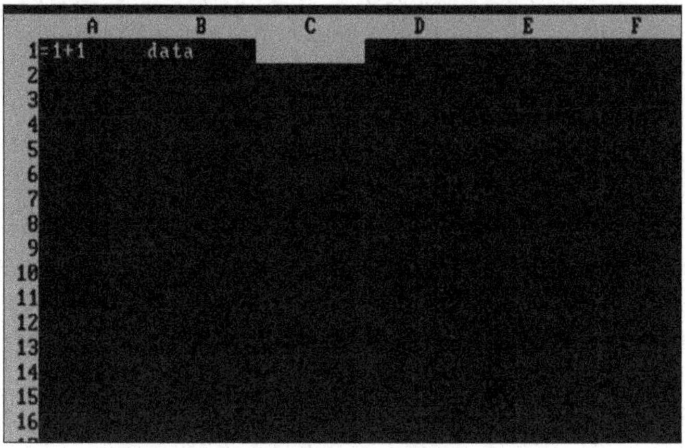

Figure 5.2 VisiCalc

Screenshot of VisiCalc © Copyright 1999-2018 by Daniel Bricklin.

Even though VisiCalc was released in 1979, you can pretty easily see all the same basic components that are present in a modern spreadsheet. Over the years, spreadsheet programs have added a lot of new functionality, but even a spreadsheet built in the late 1990s would have the vast majority of functionality available in a modern program. As spreadsheets have matured, the rate of change has actually slowed, whereas with many other tools the rate of change has increased. Learning to use spreadsheets is likely to be one of the most long-term game tool investments you can make. Popular examples of spreadsheet tools include Microsoft Excel, Google Sheets, and OpenOffice.org Calc.

Whereas game engines, 3D modeling tools, and many other game development tools tend to be pretty unique and require the user to learn specific skills, modern spreadsheet programs are very similar in usage and functionality. If you learn one, it is trivially easy to pick up any other spreadsheet tool. It is also possible and even fairly easy to convert data files from each of the programs to the others. This is another unique benefit of a spreadsheet. Most other game design tools have specific file formats that are difficult or impossible to transfer from tool to tool.

What Is a Spreadsheet?

Basically, a *spreadsheet* is a group of data containers that can communicate with each other. We use spreadsheets to gather and contain data. We also use spreadsheets to organize, manipulate, and calculate this data so that we can find meaningful information. From a practical standpoint, this means we take a whole bunch of raw data that is hard or impossible to understand, and we let a spreadsheet do the heavy work of cleaning up the data and answering questions we have about the data. We can then further use the tool to manipulate that data individually or en masse to make it behave the way we want it to.

Spreadsheet Cells: The Building Blocks of Data

This section discusses the common elements of all the spreadsheet tools. Each tool may have additional features unique to that program, but once you know the common elements, it is fairly easy to learn the unique ones. As you read through the following sections, it would be very helpful to open a new spreadsheet and follow along in it, re-creating the examples provided. If you don't have a spreadsheet program already, you can get the free Google Sheets program, which is available on any modern web browser.

> note
>
> This chapter explores spreadsheets as they pertain to game system design. There are many great resources in other books and online that cover spreadsheets in much greater depth for other disciplines.

Cells

The smallest unit of data container in a spreadsheet is called a *cell*. When you first open a spreadsheet and look at the grid, what you are seeing is a series of cells. The cell is the foundation on which all spreadsheets are built. Cells can hold data, retrieve data, calculate data, or perform more complex functions. Cells can also communicate with each other to perform even more complex tasks. Each individual cell can also contain many different types of information. The following sections examine the most common aspects of a cell.

Cell Address

A spreadsheet uses *cell addresses* to organize and refer to individual cells. Every cell, even an empty one, has an address that can't be removed or modified. A cell address is based on the intersection of the column and row where the cell resides; it consists of a letter (for the column) and a number (for the row). Both numbers and letters start at the top left of the sheet and increase by one for every cell they move from the top left. For example, the top-left cell in a spreadsheet has the address A1. The cell directly to the right of that one is cell B1, and the cell directly below A1 is A2. Figure 5.3 shows cell B2 highlighted and selected.

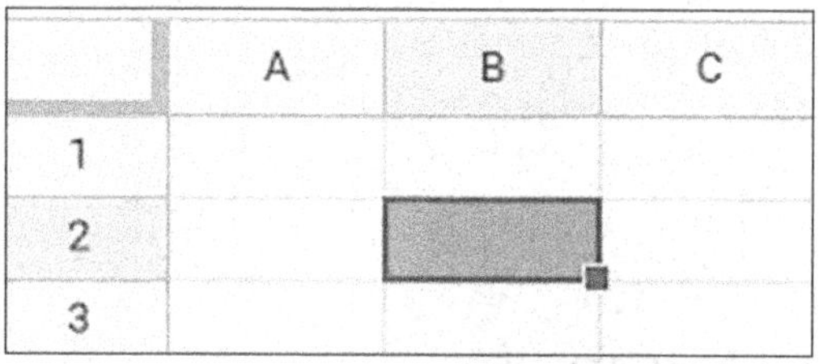

Figure 5.3 Cell B2

By knowing the address of a cell, you can access the contents of that cell. This is one of the most valuable aspects of a spreadsheet and what really distinguishes it from a calculator. By using the cell address to reference information in another cell, you can perform not one but a series of calculations, building in complexity, while leaving the original cell data unchanged.

Cell Value

If you select any cell in a spreadsheet, you will notice a cursor flashing in it. When you see the flashing cursor, you can type pretty much anything you want into the cell. You can store basic text, numbers, and many other forms of data in a cell. For example, if you were to type HELLO in a cell and then press Enter, the value of that cell would become HELLO. You could, for example, store a list of items by typing a different item into each of a series of cells to create a list.

A cell value can be any kind of data, and it specifically refers to what you see in the cell after you press Enter. It is important to know that what you see in a cell and what you type in the cell may be different. What you see in the cell is always referred to as the *value*.

Cell Formula

Whereas a cell value can be seen as a noun, a cell formula is more like a verb. A cell formula is a calculation you enter in a spreadsheet when you want the spreadsheet to calculate an answer (which it displays as a value).

The Formula Bar

Directly above the grid of columns and rows in a spreadsheet is the formula bar. You can spot it by the distinctive *fx* symbol, which is called the *function symbol* (see Figure 5.4). The formula bar shows what is happening inside the cell, regardless of what the cell is displaying. You can enter information directly into a cell or inside the formula bar.

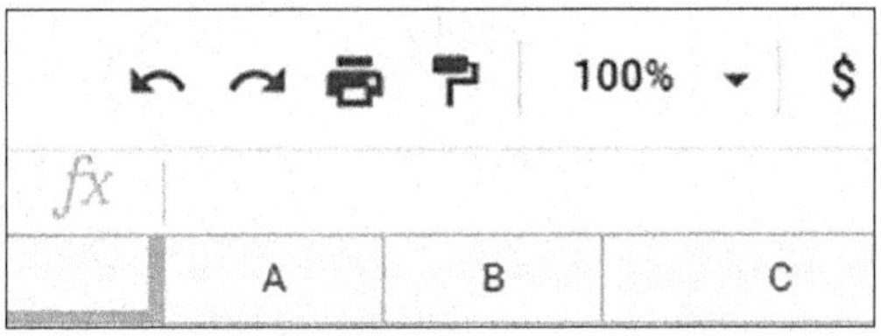

Figure 5.4 The formula bar

Spreadsheet Symbols

Spreadsheets use a wide range of symbols for a host data of manipulations and calculations. The following sections describe the basic symbols that are used most often.

Equal Sign

Spreadsheets can do both simple and sophisticated calculations in cells. To communicate with a spreadsheet that you are going to enter a formula—and not just enter a data value—you need a special code. In this case the code symbol is = (the equal sign). In a spreadsheet, the equal sign does not mean what it means in written mathematics when used to start a formula. In a spreadsheet, it's used as a special symbol that means "do something." When you use an equal sign in a spreadsheet, it is as if you were saying, "I want this cell's value to equal the result of the formula I am about to type."

Unlike in basic math, where the equal sign is between the parts of an operation (for example, 1 + 1 = 2), the equal sign appears first in a spreadsheet cell that contains a formula, function, or reference. An equal sign is the most important symbol used in a spreadsheet, as it unlocks the use of all the rest of the symbols. Without an equal sign at the start of a cell, the spreadsheet cannot do calculations.

For example, if you type =1+1 in a cell, the cell will display the value 2. If you type in just 1+1, the cell will display the value 1+1. In Figure 5.5, note that cell A1 is selected, and the contents of that cell are shown in the formula bar. Also note that the display of =1+1 in the formula bar is not the same as what is displayed in cell A1 in the spreadsheet, which is 2. Technically, both are correct; remember that the formula bar always displays what you have typed in, whereas the cell (by default) displays the value—the result of what you have typed in.

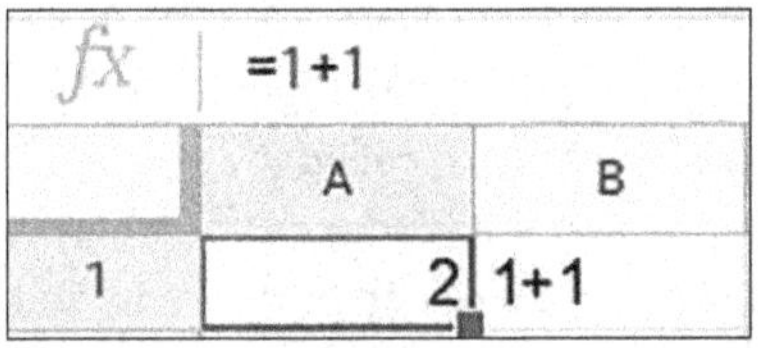

Figure 5.5 The formula bar showing a formula and cell A1 showing the result of the formula

Formulas can get very complex and powerful. You can, for example, use the equal sign in conjunction with a cell address to tell the spreadsheet to access the contents of the designated cell. In Figure 5.6, for example, cell B1 is referencing cell A1.

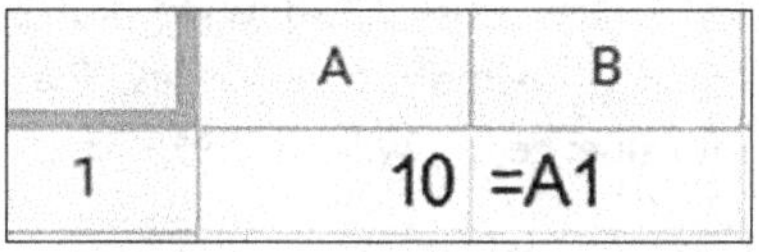

Figure 5.6 Cell B1 referencing cell A1

The calculated value for cell B1 in this case will be the same as the calculated value for A1 (see Figure 5.7).

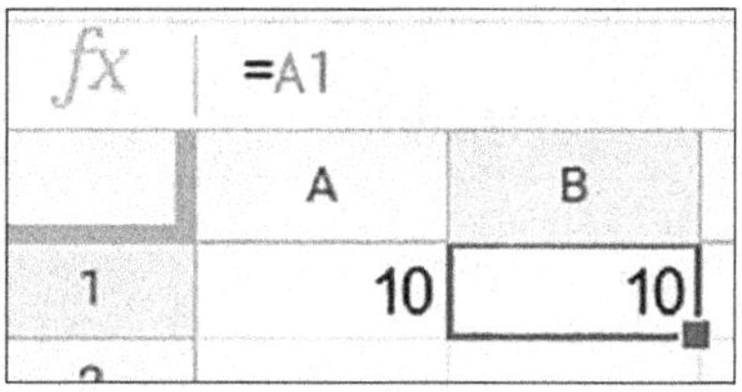

Figure 5.7 A1 is the same as B1

A spreadsheet can use a cell reference to perform simple and complex calculations. In the example in Figure 5.8, cell B1 is adding 5 to the reference of cell A1.

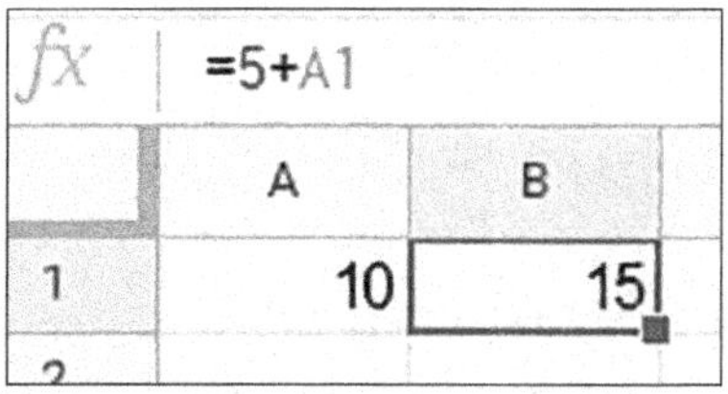

Figure 5.8 A reference modified with a formula

> **note**
>
> You may at times include multiple formulas or functions in the same cell, but the equal sign is needed only as the first character in the cell. You do not, and should not, type an equal sign in front of multiple formulas and functions in the same cell. Starting a cell with = is like flipping a switch that lets the spreadsheet know it is going to perform an active task in the cell, as opposed to holding passive data.

Parentheses

Parentheses work in a spreadsheet in a very similar manner to the way they work in mathematical notation, but they can also do even more. At their most basic, parentheses denote order of operation. Any calculation inside a matched set of open and close parentheses will occur before outside operations occur. Figure 5.9 shows formulas in cells A1 and B1 that are the same except that the version in B1 includes parentheses. These parentheses cause the cell to return a completely different value: cell A1 will return 10.75, and B1 will return 2.75.

> **note**
>
> By default, the spreadsheet will only display the formula result in the cell, but the formula itself will always be displayed in the formula bar.

	A	B
1	=2*5+6/8	=2*(5+6)/8

Figure 5.9 Formulas with and without parentheses

You can also use parentheses in conjunction with cell references, as shown Figure 5.10. In cell A1, the value of 10 is a static numerical value that is being referenced by cell B1 to use in a formula.

fx =(5+A1)*3

	A	B
1	10	45
2		

Figure 5.10 Using parentheses in conjunction with a cell reference

Beyond denoting order of operations, parentheses act as containers for functions, as discussed later in this chapter.

Quotation Marks

Quotation marks in a spreadsheet, like in many programming languages, denote text. A spreadsheet reads anything inside quotation marks as nonfunctional and nonnumeric. For example, in Figure 5.11, the cell starts with an equal sign, as it should, but the calculation is enclosed in quotation marks, so the spreadsheet returns the display value of the calculation (that is, 1+1) instead of returning the calculated value (that is, 2).

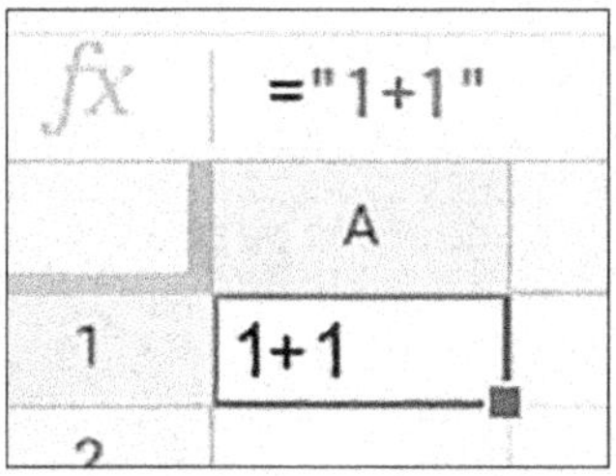

Figure 5.11 Using quotation marks to turn numbers into text

Other Mathematical Symbols

Standard mathematical symbols that work in a calculator also work in spreadsheet formulas:

- +: Addition
- *: Multiplication
- /: Division
- -: Subtraction
- ^: Exponentiation (to the power of)

Any of these symbols can be applied to a formula or reference. In Figure 5.12, for example, cell B1 is adding together the contents of cells A1 and A2 and then multiplying that result by 5.

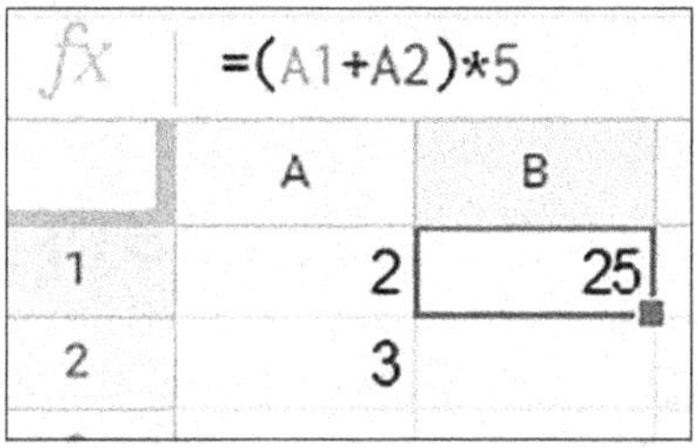

Figure 5.12 A formula with multiple references in cell B1

Ampersand

The ampersand (& symbol) represents concatenation—which basically means sticking text together. With concatenation and quotation marks, a spreadsheet can take several different pieces of text and numbers and create a complete phrase with them. In Figure 5.13, for example, cell B2 references information stored on column A and concatenates all of it together to form a larger piece of text.

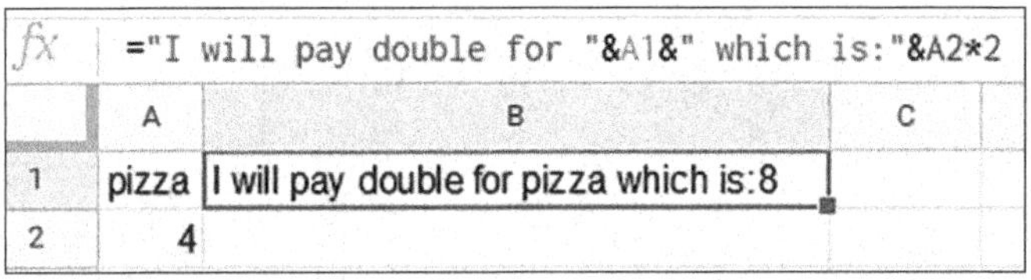

Figure 5.13 Concatenation in cell B1

Because of the cell reference, the formula in cell B2 is considered *live*, or *dynamic*, which means the same formula produces different results when the data it references changes. In Figure 5.14, for example, pizza has been switched to sushi, and the value has increased.

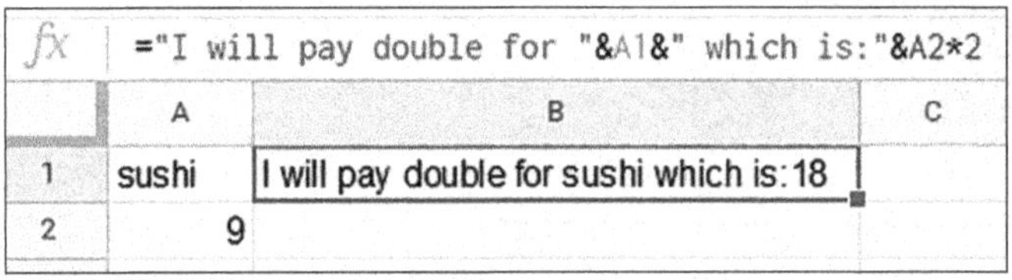

Figure 5.14 A dynamically updated cell

Writing complex calculations that dynamically change based on data allows you to use a spreadsheet to do many sophisticated tasks quickly without the need to rewrite evaluations and create new formulas.

Data Containers in Spreadsheets

Spreadsheets are made up of collections of cells in columns and rows. On a larger scale, columns and rows make up a grid, which is the spreadsheet. In modern programs, users are able to make multiple spreadsheets connected to each other and all open in memory at the same time. This is called a *workbook* and contains all sheets as tabs, which can be seen below the current sheet.

Columns and Rows

Rows and columns are the next largest groupings in a spreadsheet after cells. A row contains a series of cells that runs horizontally across a sheet, and a column contains a series of cells that run vertically down a sheet. Both columns and rows are used to organize data. You can access individual cells in a column or row and edit them, or you can select an entire column or row and do group editing. In the example shown in Figure 5.15, the user has clicked on the row header labeled 2, which selects all of row 2 at once. Rows are always labeled with numbers, starting with row 1, and the rows are always laid out horizontally. Columns are always labeled with letters, starting at A, and they are laid out vertically. To help remember this, think of columns in Greek architecture, which are vertical structures. Conversely, farmers plant rows of crops on the ground, and they go back and forth horizontally like rows in a spreadsheet.

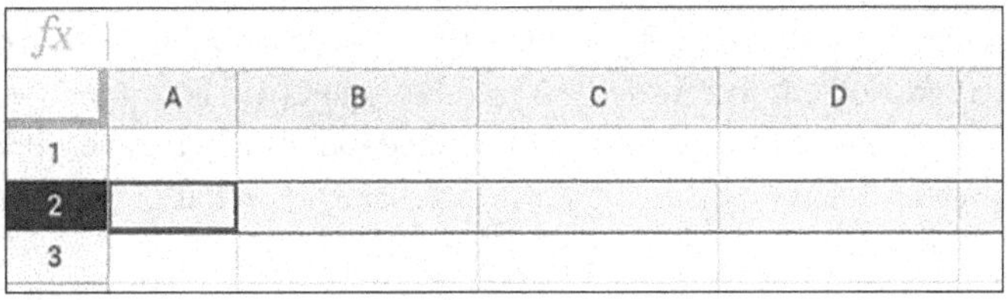

Figure 5.15 Highlighting row 2 by selecting its row header

Sheets

The next largest grouping after columns and rows is the sheet. A sheet contains a series of rows and columns in a grid. When someone speaks of working in a spreadsheet, this is most likely what they are referring to. However, it is possible and useful to have more than one sheet. All sheets are identical when it is created; a sheet always contains the same series of lettered columns and numbered rows. As discussed in the preceding section, it is possible to select everything in a column or row by clicking on the header of that column or row. To select everything in an entire sheet, you can use the select all button, which is at the very top left of the sheet, between the column A header and the row 1 header (see Figure 5.16). By clicking the select all button, you select every cell in the sheet and can then do operations on all cells at once.

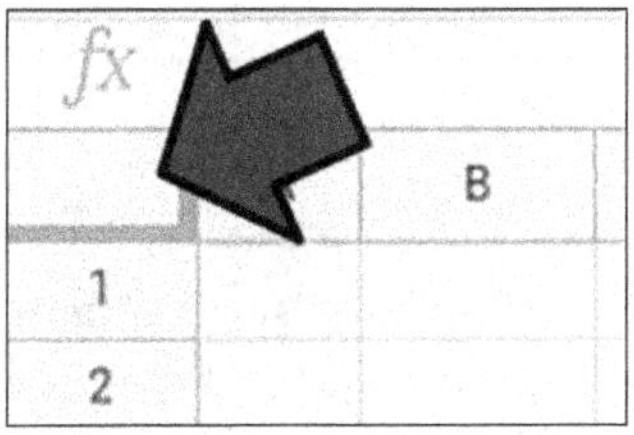

Figure 5.16 The select all button

Workbooks

When you open a spreadsheet program and load up what most people refer to as a *spreadsheet*, you are actually opening a *workbook*. The term *workbook* is also the name of a spreadsheet file that resides on your hard drive or in the cloud (in Google Sheets, for example). This term is a holdover from the days when people would manually write down figures on sheets of paper and bind them into a workbook. It also serves as a good analogy for how we work in spreadsheets. It is completely possible to create many different, individual sheets to do all of your work in different files, but there are two distinct advantages to grouping sheets together in a workbook instead:

- **Spreadsheet organization:** When sheets are grouped together in a workbook, it helps you keep game data organized. If you know that a project is going to have characters, weapons, armor, loot, and monsters, for example, you can make a sheet for each of these different types of data but keep them all contained together in a single workbook for the game as a whole. That will help distinguish the characters in this game from characters in another game.
- **Spreadsheet connections:** When multiple sheets are contained in a workbook, they are all loaded into memory every time the workbook is opened. This means that any sheet has full and immediate access to the data on every other sheet. It is possible to access data from different workbooks, but this access involves more overhead and complications. In general, it's better to use more sheets in a single workbook if the data is related than to create separate workbooks.

To create a new sheet in a workbook, you look below the bottom of the grid of cells, where you see a gray bar there with a single tab (by default). This tab is the current sheet you are working on. In Google Sheets, it is called Sheet1 by default (see Figure 5.17).

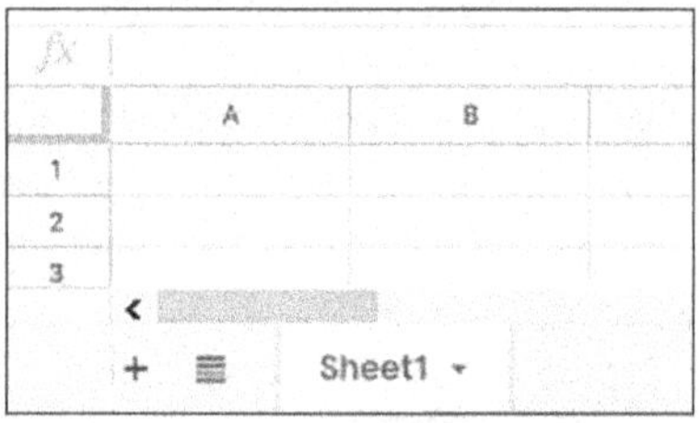

Figure 5.17 A sheet tab

To the left of all the sheets is a button that shows several horizontal lines. That is a list of all sheets. In very large workbooks, this symbol is handy because you might have more sheets than the program can display at once, and clicking this button gives you quick access to all sheets without having to scroll through them.

On the far left of the bottom tab is a + button, which you click to add a new sheet. If you click this button, the program adds a new sheet, with a new tab for the sheet, and gives it a default name; Figure 5.18 shows that a new sheet called Sheet2 has been added. You can click on the new sheet tab to change your view from the original sheet to the new one.

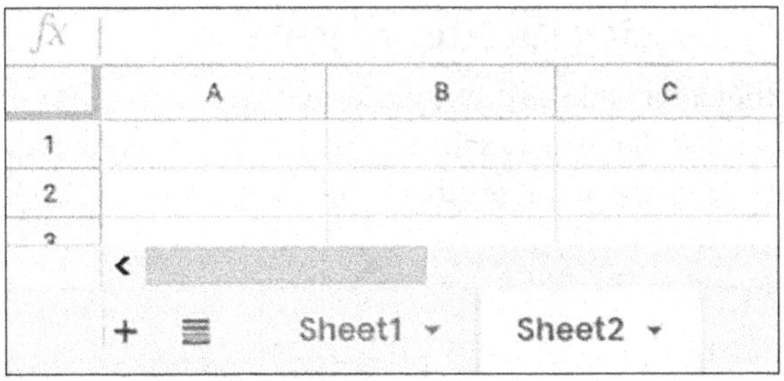

Figure 5.18 A new sheet tab

> **note**
>
> It is important to note that when a workbook is open, all the data on every sheet of the workbook is open and in memory.

When a new sheet is created, it is advisable to rename the sheet to suit the contents of the sheet (see Figure 5.19). If you want, you can also color code the sheet tabs to better organize the workbook, although the colors do not give the sheets any special functionality.

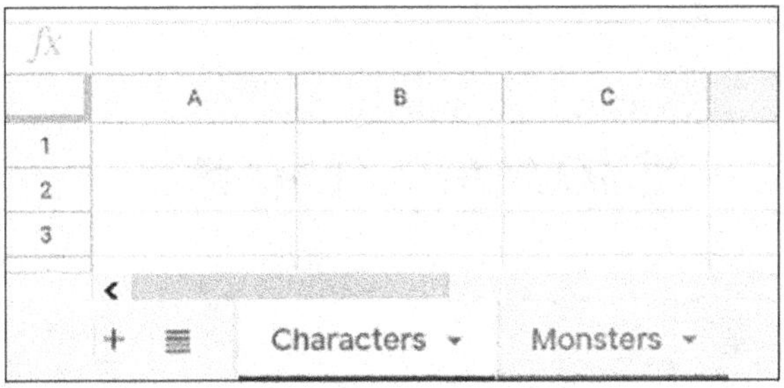

Figure 5.19 Renamed sheets

You can move a sheet tab left or right, delete it, and duplicate it, and in some programs you can move it to another workbook. You can also hide it or protect it, as discussed in more detail later in this chapter.

Spreadsheet Operations

This section focuses on tasks you can perform with spreadsheets, such as referencing and hiding data, freezing portions of a sheet, using comments and notes, filling a form, and using filters.

Referencing a Separate Sheet

When a workbook contains multiple sheets, you need to be able to reference the data from one sheet in another sheet. Figure 5.20 shows a sheet for characters and a sheet for monsters. On the Monsters sheet, you can see that there is an ogre whose strength is 10.

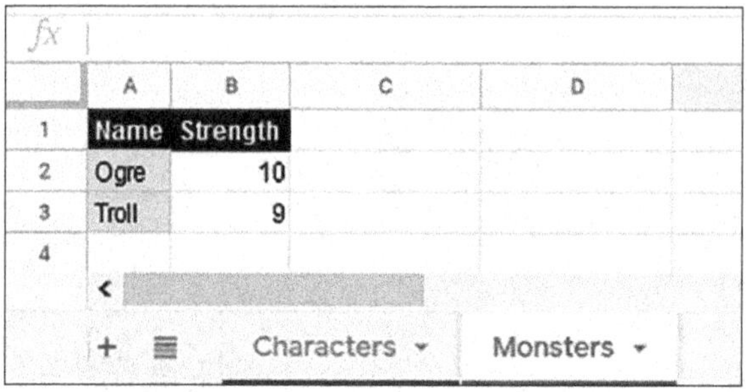

Figure 5.20 Organized sheet names

Say that on the Characters sheet, you would like to do a comparison between the "Soldier" character and a reference to the "Ogre Strength" in cell C2. We can see in the Monsters sheet, that the data for the ogre strength is in cell B2 of that sheet (see Figure 5.21).

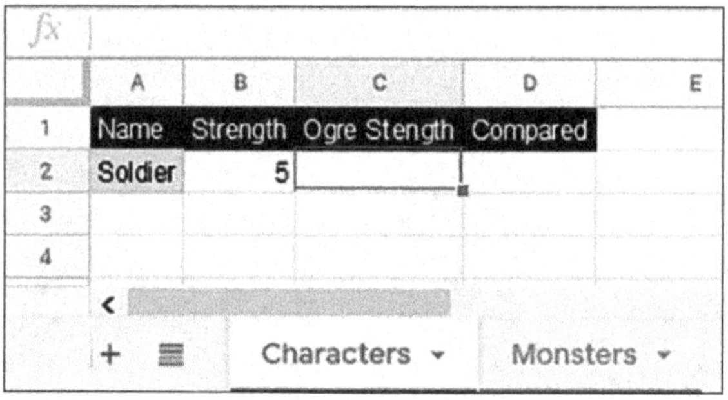

Figure 5.21 A cell for doing a comparison

You can't simply write a formula that points to B2, however, because B2 on the Characters sheet contains the soldier's strength, not the ogre's. In this case, you need to use a special symbol to access a separate sheet: the ! operator.

To access data in a separate sheet, the spreadsheet needs to know where you are looking to retrieve the data. To make this clear, you need to use the name of the sheet. However, because a sheet can be given any name, the spreadsheet does not know whether what you are typing is the name of a sheet, a function, a variable, or just plain text. The ! in a spreadsheet allows you to contain a sheet name in a format that the spreadsheet can understand. When you place an ! at the end of the name, the spreadsheet recognizes the sheet name and enters that sheet. For example, to refer to the Monsters sheet, you would start by writing the following:

=Monsters!

After the ! is found at the end of the name, you can write the rest of the expression as if you were working on that sheet. In this example, if you were on the Monsters sheet and wanted to refer to ogre strength, you would write =B2. Because you want to access that same cell from a different sheet, however, you need to add the name of the sheet at the beginning of the expression with the ! to designate that it is a sheet, and then you can add the reference after that. In this example, the final expression would look as shown in Figure 5.22.

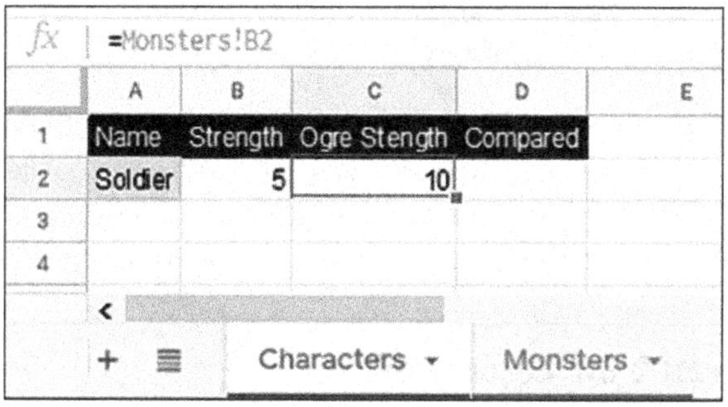

Figure 5.22 Sheet-specific reference

Now that the cell on Monsters!B2 has been referenced, the data it contains can be used as if it resided on the current sheet.

Hiding Data

In a spreadsheet, you often want to have information on a sheet or in a workbook, but you don't need users to see that information. For example, it's a common practice to separate out building blocks of complex operations into separate cells. While these intermediate steps are important, they do not need to be in view at all times. In such cases, you can use the built-in functionality called *hiding*. You can hide rows, or columns, or entire sheets. To hide a row or column, you click on what you want to hide to select it and then right-click on the header and choose Hide Column. Once the column or row is hidden, it is no longer visible on the sheet, but it can still be accessed by formulas or functions. In the example in Figure 5.23, the strength of monsters has been hidden, but the selected cell is referring to a hidden cell and showing the result.

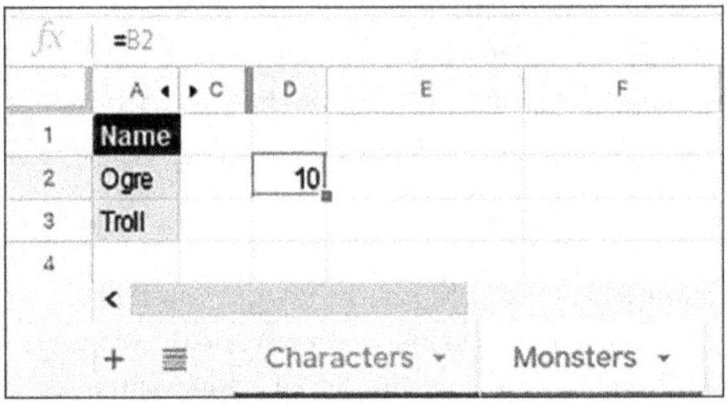

Figure 5.23 Referenced cell

Note that when a column is hidden, you can no longer see its header letter. Hidden columns are all collapsed and replaced with a single set of arrows. To make the hidden information visible again, you can click on the collapsed arrows and all hidden columns open up.

Similarly, you can hide entire sheets. To do so, you right-click a sheet tab and select Hide Sheet. Again, the information is still there and loaded into memory, but it is not visible. You might want to hide a sheet, for example, if it contains mountains of information that would clutter the workbook without providing important information for the user.

Freezing Part of a Sheet

Sheets often contain more data than can fit on a single visible page. While a spreadsheet can handle the extra information without issue, humans have a hard time reading such a spreadsheet because they have to scroll to make more information visible. In Figure 5.24, for example, there is a large set of data, and you can see only some of the data that's partway down the sheet.

What are the values listed in this example? It's impossible to tell because the labels for the attributes are at the top of the sheet, above the part of the sheet you can see here. On very simple sheets, this might not be an issue, but as the data becomes more complex, it's more important to be able to see data labels along with the data at all times. To alleviate this problem, you can freeze columns or rows. This simply means making a column or row visible, regardless of what other portion of the sheet is visible. To freeze the column, for example, you select the row, select the toolbar option View, select the Freeze menu option, and then select First Row. There are multiple options in the Freeze menu: You can freeze the top row, the first column, and more. In our example, you can see that freezing the top row, which includes the column headings, makes the data clearer (see Figure 5.25).

25	Swamp Man	m	5	5	25	2	2	4	3	4	1	Wood	y	1
26	Mummy	u	10	4	20	6	2	2	3	4	2	Cloth	y	1
27	Giant Scarab	a	8	5	15	9	2	4	3	4	1	Stone	y	1
28	Razorback	a	6	6	15	6	3	5	4	4	1	Skin	y	1
29	Serpent	a	6	6	15	6	6	4	4	4	1	Skin	y	1
30	Giant Scorpion	a	6	5	15	9	4	5	4	4	1	Stone	y	1
31	Black Bear	a	7	6	15	6	4	6	4	4	1	Skin	y	1
32	Harpy	m	6	8	15	6	5	7	4	4	2	Cloth	y	1
33	Gargoyle	m	7	5	15	6	5	6	5	4	1	Stone	y	1
34	Stone Golem	m	8	5	25	8	3	4	5	4	1	Stone	y	1
35	Giant Crab	a	8	5	15	12	5	6	5	5	2	Stone	y	1
36	Gorilla	a	9	7	15	3	3	4	6	5	1	Skin	y	1
37	Iron Golem	m	9	5	30	10	3	4	6	5	1	Iron	y	1
38	Hill Troll	m	12	4	20	5	1	4	6	5	2	Stone	y	1
39	Sasquatch	m	9	6	15	4	6	5	6	5	1	Wood	y	1
40	Cave Gobbler	a	10	8	3	1	1	4	7	5	2	Stone	y	1
41	Sabertooth	a	10	6	20	7	5	6	8	6	2	Skin	y	1
42	Giant Spider	a	8	7	15	6	5	6	8	6	1	Stone	y	1

Figure 5.24 Viewing part of a table of data

	A	B	C	D	E	F	G	H	I	J	K	L	M	N
1	Character Type	PLR	STR	DEX	HP	AV	D	MV	LVL	XP	Loot Cards	Loot	Use?	Deck
25	Swamp Man	m	5	5	25	2	2	4	3	4	1	Wood	y	1
26	Mummy	u	10	4	20	6	2	2	3	4	2	Cloth	y	1
27	Giant Scarab	a	8	5	15	9	2	4	3	4	1	Stone	y	1
28	Razorback	a	6	6	15	6	3	5	4	4	1	Skin	y	1
29	Serpent	a	6	6	15	6	6	4	4	4	1	Skin	y	1
30	Giant Scorpion	a	6	5	15	9	4	5	4	4	1	Stone	y	1
31	Black Bear	a	7	6	15	6	4	6	4	4	1	Skin	y	1
32	Harpy	m	6	8	15	6	5	7	4	4	2	Cloth	y	1
33	Gargoyle	m	7	5	15	6	5	6	5	4	1	Stone	y	1
34	Stone Golem	m	8	5	25	8	3	4	5	4	1	Stone	y	1
35	Giant Crab	a	8	5	15	12	5	6	5	5	2	Stone	y	1
36	Gorilla	a	9	7	15	3	3	4	6	5	1	Skin	y	1
37	Iron Golem	m	9	5	30	10	3	4	6	5	1	Iron	y	1
38	Hill Troll	m	12	4	20	5	1	4	6	5	2	Stone	y	1
39	Sasquatch	m	9	6	15	4	6	5	6	5	1	Wood	y	1
40	Cave Gobbler	a	10	8	3	1	1	4	7	5	2	Stone	y	1
41	Sabertooth	a	10	6	20	7	5	6	8	6	2	Skin	y	1
42	Giant Spider	a	8	7	15	6	5	6	8	6	1	Stone	y	1

Figure 5.25 Frozen row

You can now see each column label, even when you scroll down the sheet.

Using Comments and Notes

Cells that contain data, formulas, or functions don't have much meaning on their own. This is why you often take extra time to add a label row or column. Frequently, however, individual cells need even more information than a column or row label can provide. It is sometimes possible to add information in an adjacent cell, but often it isn't, or there is too much information to be visible in the cell. Further, if you are not entirely sure how the flow of reference works, adding text to cells in a shared spreadsheet can potentially break functions and formulas. To solve all of these problems, modern spreadsheets provide two options that can help: comments and notes. These two options work similarly to each other but have a few differences that make each the better choice in some circumstances.

> **note**
>
> With both comments and notes, the information you input can't be accessed by other cells in formulas or functions. It is added "on top of" the spreadsheet and not as active content within the sheet.

Comments

A comment is meant to be a temporary "call to action" in a spreadsheet. To add one, select the cell you would like to comment on, right-click, and select Add Comment (which is near the bottom of the context menu). A dialog pops up next to the designated cell, showing the name of the user adding the comment, a small picture of the user taken from their user profile, a text box to add the comments, and Comment and Cancel buttons (see Figure 5.26).

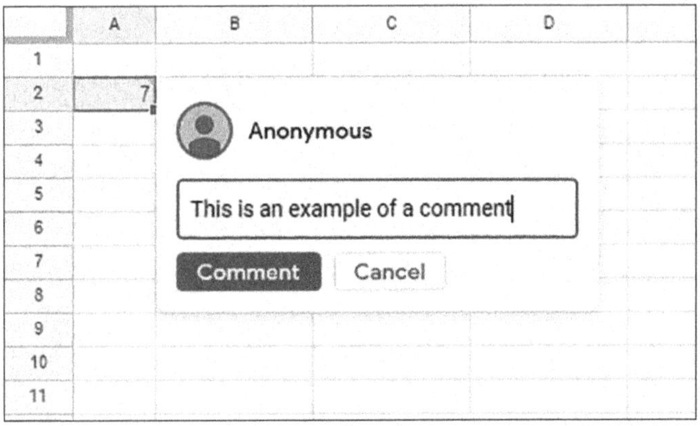

Figure 5.26 Comment dialog

In general, you should be logged on to a current account when adding comments. When you are, other users can reply to your comment, and Google Notes notifies you by email when the comment has been updated. However, adding comments anonymously, as shown in Figure 5.26 , still allows you to add useful comments. When you have the comment dialog box open, you can type or paste in the information you want to add to the cell. A comment is attached to a particular cell, to help others understand something about that cell's contents. Comments are meant to be temporary, so you should not add background or explanatory information. The following are some examples of the types of information you might include in comments:

This formula is referencing the wrong data.

We may need to update this value when we hear back from the programming team.

What is this formula supposed to be doing?

Can we delete this sheet?

When your comment text is complete, you can click the Comment button to commit the comment to the sheet. After that, there are a few indicators on the sheet that have changed. For example, notice in Figure 5.27 how the cell with the comment, A2, now has a little orange triangle in the top-right corner. This is a *flag*, which provides an indication that there is a comment for the cell that a user can see by hovering over the cell with the mouse pointer. Also notice that on the sheet tab there is now a small word balloon with the number 1 in it. This balloon shows the number of comments on the sheet.

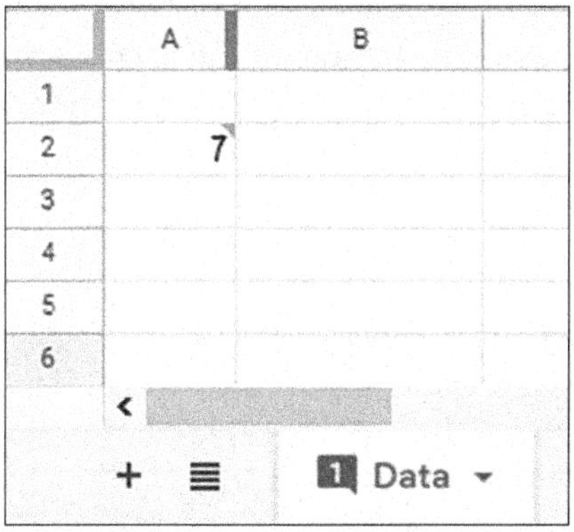

Figure 5.27 Comment flag

The purpose of comments is to grab the attention of a user and direct them to the comment. When a user navigates to a sheet containing the comment and hovers the mouse cursor over the flagged cell, the comment pops up, as shown in Figure 5.28.

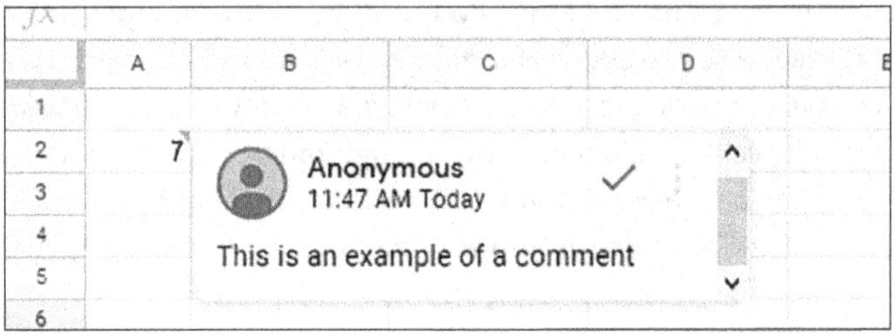

Figure 5.28 Comment

The user can read the comment and close it by clicking the checkmark at the top right. Google Sheets sends an email to the creator of the comment to indicate that the comment has been read.

Additionally, users can reply to a comment and start a conversation. In Google Sheets, this sends an email to the person you are replying to, allowing them to reply back.

Notes

Whereas comments are made to be temporary calls to action, notes are made to provide extra information over the long term. Unlike comments, notes do not indicate who added them, prompt emails to users, or allow for conversations. They also aren't marked by notifications on sheet tabs. Instead, notes operate very much like Notepad text files that are embedded in cells. A note is distinguished by a black flag in the top-right corner (see Figure 5.29). Notes are generally meant to be used to further explain the contents of a cell without cluttering the sheet.

In Figure 5.29, you can see a solitary 7 typed in a cell with no surrounding context. This would be confusing for anyone who happened on the sheet, including the future self of the person who typed it. This is a great example of a place to add a note: The note can explain why that 7 is there and what it does.

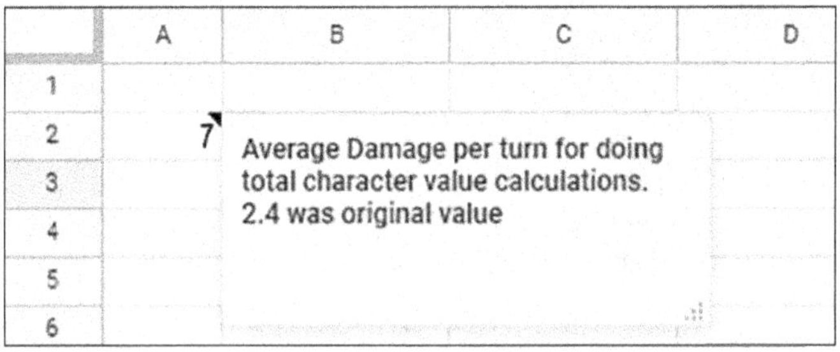

Figure 5.29 Note

In the example in Figure 5.29, the note explains the use case for the 7 in the cell and also explains a little history on why that number is there. Notes are excellent for both of these uses. In addition, notes are great for adding the following kinds of information:

- Maximum and minimum expected values for a cell
- Game rules that explain the formula in a cell
- The owner of the data in the cell
- The source of the data or formula
- Usage notes on specific functions or formulas
- Expiration dates for data that may not be valuable anymore
- Any other small snippet of information that might be helpful

The best way to use both notes and comments is to use them frequently. Adding comments on cells allows you and others to better understand the intention and usage of what might otherwise be very confusing data.

Using Formfill

One of the major advantages of using a spreadsheet is that data can be spread out over many cells. In addition, formulas can be spread out and repeated over many cells. In the example in Figure 5.30, several players have played a game three times. Each time they finished the game, they entered their final scores.

	A	B	C	D	E
1	Player Name	Score Game #1	Score Game #2	Score Game #3	Total
2	Adam	37	58	49	
3	Bob	55	81	10	
4	Carl	67	32	54	
5	Dave	11	79	25	
6	Ed	56	12	89	
7	Fred	63	87	32	
8	Gary	22	86	15	
9	Herb	73	37	46	

Figure 5.30 Recorded scores for players

Say that you want to get the total of each player's scores. This requires a simple formula (though it could be done with a function as well, as discussed later in this chapter). In cell E2, you would write the formula =B2+C2+D2 to get Adam's total score, which turns out to be 144. Next, you would do exactly the same thing for each additional player. Rewriting the same formula seven more times would be slow and prone to error. Instead, you can use the formfill feature of the spreadsheet to let it do all the work for you.

To start using formfill, write the desired formula in a single cell. Writing the formula in the topmost cell makes the process a bit easier, although it's not required to start in this cell. Once the formula is written and behaving as intended, you can select the cell you want to copy (see Figure 5.31).

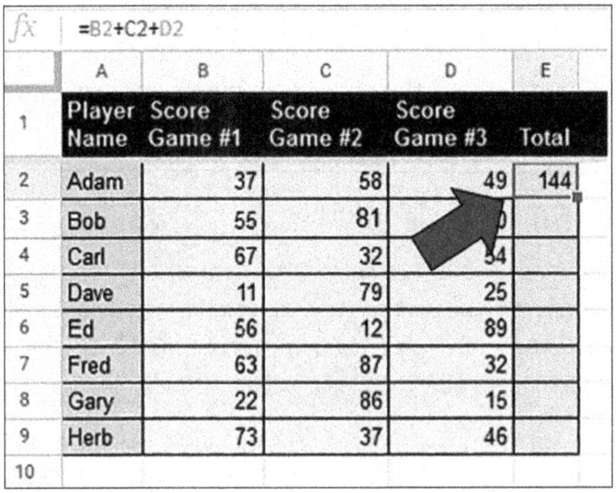

Figure 5.31 A template cell is selected to formfill

If you zoom in, you can see that the border around the cell has changed: It has become thicker, and the color has changed to blue (see Figure 5.32). In addition, there is a little blue box in the bottom-right corner of the selection. That is the formfill widget. When you move the mouse cursor over the widget, the cursor changes from the default arrow to a crosshair. which indicates that you can use the widget. To use it, left-click on the widget and drag your mouse down the page in the column until you reach the end of cells into which you want to copy the formula, and then let go. This tells the spreadsheet to copy and paste the formula from the first cell into all the other selected cells and update the formula to match each new selection. Alternatively, you can double-click the formfill widget to instruct the spreadsheet to copy the current cell down until it finds a blank cell one column to the left. This may seem confusing, but trying it in a spreadsheet a couple times makes this useful option completely clear.

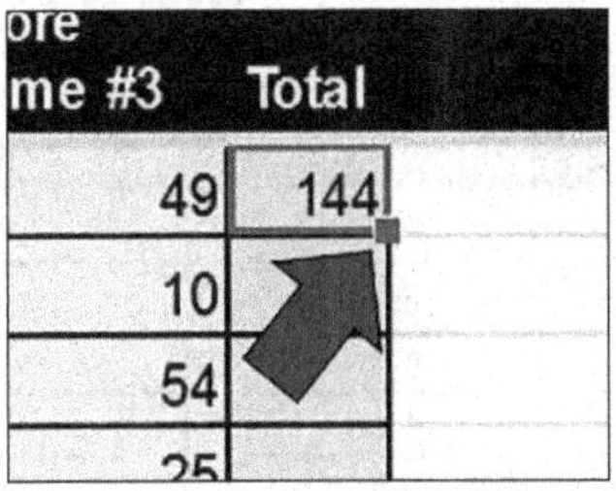

Figure 5.32 Formfill widget

Figure 5.33 shows the result of using formfill. Notice that the spreadsheet knew to update the row references for the entries in column E as the formula was copied down. This is called *relative referencing*, and it allows you to write a formula a single time and then copy it down or over to do the same calculations in a series. It is a powerful tool in a spreadsheet, but it also has some limitations and drawbacks.

	A	B	C	D	E
1	Player Name	Score Game #1	Score Game #2	Score Game #3	Total
2	Adam	37	58	49	=B2+C2+D2
3	Bob	55	81	10	=B3+C3+D3
4	Carl	67	32	54	=B4+C4+D4
5	Dave	11	79	25	=B5+C5+D5
6	Ed	56	12	89	=B6+C6+D6
7	Fred	63	87	32	=B7+C7+D7
8	Gary	22	86	15	=B8+C8+D8
9	Herb	73	37	46	=B9+C9+D9

Figure 5.33 Result of formfill

The biggest drawback of relative referencing is that you don't always want to update every cell reference. To better show this, let's consider another example (see Figure 5.34).

Say that you now want to compare each player's score with the score you expected the player to get on the three attempts. You might also want to change the expected score at some time in the future, so you can't assume that a given number, 130 for example, will always be the desired number.

	A	B	C	D	E	F
1	Player Name	Score Game #1	Score Game #2	Score Game #3	Total	Minus Expected
2	Adam	37	58	49	144	
3	Bob	55	81	10	146	
4	Carl	67	32	54	153	
5	Dave	11	79	25	115	
6	Ed	56	12	89	157	
7	Fred	63	87	32	182	
8	Gary	22	86	15	123	
9	Herb	73	37	46	156	
10						
11	Expected Score	130				

Figure 5.34 Static number that needs to be referenced

> note
>
> It is not advisable to put variables like "expected score" on the same sheet as the data, but it is done in this example for ease of display in the book.

To calculate column F, the "score minus expected" value, you need to subtract the expected score from the total listed for each player in column E. It is straightforward to write the first formula in cell F2 as a single calculation, but in this case, you need to write it in such a way that it can be formfilled down. If it is written the same way as the formula in cell E2 was written, it looks as shown in Figure 5.35.

fx =E2-B11

	A	B	C	D	E	F
1	Player Name	Score Game #1	Score Game #2	Score Game #3	Total	Minus Expected
2	Adam	37	58	49	144	14
3	Bob	55	81	10	146	
4	Carl	67	32	54	153	
5	Dave	11	79	25	115	
6	Ed	56	12	89	157	
7	Fred	63	87	32	182	
8	Gary	22	86	15	123	
9	Herb	73	37	46	156	
10						
11	Expected Score	130				

Figure 5.35 A selected cell

This would work well for cell F2, but what happens when it formfilled down? Each of the references in the formula is then updated to a new row (see Figure 5.36).

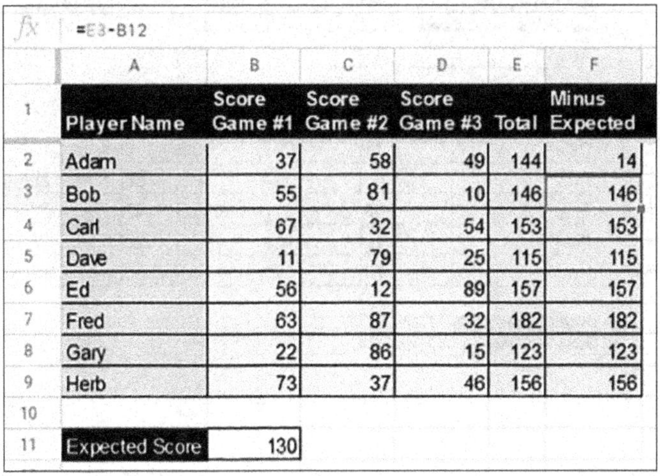

fx =E3-B12

	A	B	C	D	E	F
1	Player Name	Score Game #1	Score Game #2	Score Game #3	Total	Minus Expected
2	Adam	37	58	49	144	14
3	Bob	55	81	10	146	146
4	Carl	67	32	54	153	153
5	Dave	11	79	25	115	115
6	Ed	56	12	89	157	157
7	Fred	63	87	32	182	182
8	Gary	22	86	15	123	123
9	Herb	73	37	46	156	156
10						
11	Expected Score	130				

Figure 5.36 A row that has been formfilled

In Figure 5.36, notice how, starting in cell F3, the expected score of 130 is no longer being subtracted. In the formula bar, you can see that the new formula does correctly reference Bob's total of 146 in cell E2, but now the formula is pointing to cell B12 instead of B11 for the expected score. While it makes intuitive sense that you would want to update each row for each new player but not update each row past the expected score, this does not happen automatically with the spreadsheet. Instead, you need to instruct the spreadsheet that some cell references need to be updated and changed as they are formfilled and others do not. To instruct the spreadsheet to do this, you have two options:

- **Use a relative reference:** You can use a relative reference for any cell reference that you want to change as the formula is formfilled. This is the default state for any reference and requires no changes to the reference in the original cell to make it work.
- **Use an absolute reference:** You can use an absolute reference for any cell reference that you want to remain the same regardless of whether the formula is formfilled. To designate this, you need another special character. In this case, you use the dollar sign ($) to signify that a reference is absolute and should not be changed. It is important to note that when using $, column and row references are independent. So, if you want an absolute reference to a single cell, you need to place a $ in front of both the row and the column label. In this example, the expected score in cell B2 is not going to be updated, so you would enter $B$2 to indicate that the spreadsheet should be referencing that cell exactly, regardless of where the original cell is formfilled to. With this in mind, Figure 5.37 shows the example updated to show the new formula using the proper forms of absolute and relative referencing.

fx =$E2-$B$11

	A	B	C	D	E	F
1	Player Name	Score Game #1	Score Game #2	Score Game #3	Total	Minus Expected
2	Adam	37	58	49	144	14
3	Bob	55	81	10	146	16
4	Carl	67	32	54	153	23
5	Dave	11	79	25	115	-15
6	Ed	56	12	89	157	27
7	Fred	63	87	32	182	52
8	Gary	22	86	15	123	-7
9	Herb	73	37	46	156	26
10						
11	Expected Score	130				

Figure 5.37 An updated formula using absolute and relative referencing

The formula shown in the formula bar is now ready to be copied. Because the total for each player is always in column E, the cell reference has been changed to be absolute toward column E. But you want the sheet to update the reference to each new row after row 2, so this reference is left as relative. You also know you want the reference for cell B11 to never change, so both the column and row are converted to use absolute references in respect to column and row. When the formula is formfilled down the rest of the rows, it now produces the desired calculation. To provide a bit more clarity, Figure 5.38 shows the same sheet with all the formulas visible.

	A	B	C	D	E	F
1	Player Name	Score Game #1	Score Game #2	Score Game #3	Total	Minus Expected
2	Adam	37	58	49	=B2+C2+D2	=$E2-$B$11
3	Bob	55	81	10	=B3+C3+D3	=$E3-$B$11
4	Carl	67	32	54	=B4+C4+D4	=$E4-$B$11
5	Dave	11	79	25	=B5+C5+D5	=$E5-$B$11
6	Ed	56	12	89	=B6+C6+D6	=$E6-$B$11
7	Fred	63	87	32	=B7+C7+D7	=$E7-$B$11
8	Gary	22	86	15	=B8+C8+D8	=$E8-$B$11
9	Herb	73	37	46	=B9+C9+D9	=$E9-$B$11
10						
11	Expected Score	130				

Figure 5.38 Showing formulas for all cells

Relative and absolute references are some of the less intuitive features of spreadsheets. It takes time and considerable practice to understand when to use one and when to use the other.

Using Filters

In addition to giving you the built-in columns, rows, sheets, and workbooks, spreadsheets enable you to build your own defined selections of cells with the filters feature. To use a filter, you first enter your data as discussed earlier in this chapter. Let's look at an example that continues the previous example of players playing games and tracking scores (see Figure 5.39).

	A	B	C	D	E	F
1	Player Name	Score Game #1	Score Game #2	Score Game #3	Total	Minus Expected
2	Adam	37	58	49	144	14
3	Bob	55	81	10	146	16
4	Carl	67	32	54	153	23
5	Dave	11	79	25	115	-15
6	Ed	56	12	89	157	27
7	Fred	63	87	32	182	52
8	Gary	22	86	15	123	-7
9	Herb	73	37	46	156	26
10	Adam	73	37	46	156	26
11	Bob	67	32	54	153	23
12	Carl	37	58	49	144	14
13	Dave	11	79	25	115	-15
14	Ed	56	12	89	157	27
15	Fred	63	87	32	182	52
16	Gary	55	81	10	146	16
17	Herb	22	86	15	123	-7
18						

Figure 5.39 Data to filter

To use a filter, you select all of your data, including the headers, and then click the Create Filter button (which looks like a funnel) from the far-right end of the toolbar (see Figure 5.40).

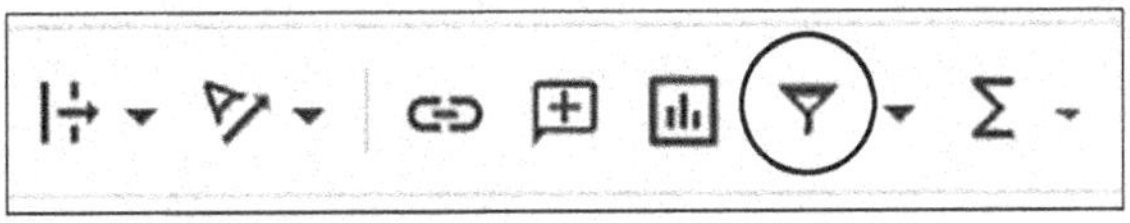

Figure 5.40 The Create Filter button

When you click this button, the spreadsheet applies filters to your entire selected data range, which opens up an entire suite of new options. The data also visibly changes. The column headers change to a shade of green, and new triangular buttons appear in the first row (see Figure 5.41).

	A	B	C	D	E	F
1	Player Name	Score Game #1	Score Game #2	Score Game #3	Total	Minus Expected
2	Adam	37	58	49	144	14
3	Bob	55	81	10	146	16
4	Carl	67	32	54	153	23
5	Dave	11	79	25	115	-15
6	Ed	56	12	89	157	27
7	Fred	63	87	32	182	52
8	Gary	22	86	15	123	-7
9	Herb	73	37	46	156	26
10	Adam	73	37	46	156	26
11	Bob	67	32	54	153	23
12	Carl	37	58	49	144	14
13	Dave	11	79	25	115	-15
14	Ed	56	12	89	157	27
15	Fred	63	87	32	182	52
16	Gary	55	81	10	146	16
17	Herb	22	86	15	123	-7

Figure 5.41 A table with filters applied

Clicking on the triangular filter button in cell A1 brings up a new filter dialog that looks as shown in Figure 5.42.

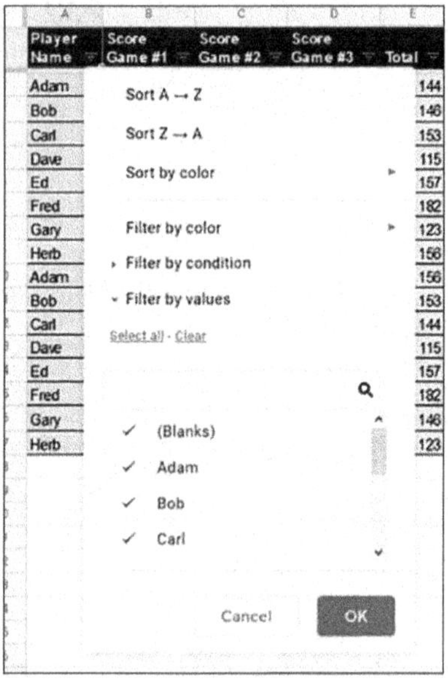

Figure 5.42 Filter dialog

Most of the options in this dialog are fairly self-explanatory. You can sort the entire set of data alphabetically or by color for the selected column, or you apply a filter based on many different conditions. The filtering options in this dialog are as follows:

- **Filter by color:** Shows only cells with the specified background color.
- **Filter by condition:** Allows you to filter numbers below or above a number you want, or based on many other variations of ranges.
- **Filter by values:** Shows a list of all the values listed in that column. In the current example, this would be the names of players. This list is dynamically generated by the spreadsheet for each column to have all the current values. From here, you can check or uncheck each value individually, or you can select all or clear all.

By selecting the desired filters, you can keep a lot of information in a single sheet but display only the rows you want to see at any given time. For this example, say that you want to filter down to seeing only Adam and Bob, as shown in Figure 5.43.

	A	B	C	D	E	F
1	Player Name	Score Game #1	Score Game #2	Score Game #3	Total	Minus Expected
2	Adam	37	58	49	144	14
3	Bob	55	81	10	146	16
10	Adam	73	37	46	156	26
11	Bob	67	32	54	153	23

Figure 5.43 Filtered data

When filters are applied, only the rows you want to see are visible, but all the other data remains in the spreadsheet. You can tell the rows are still there by looking at the row headers. Notice in Figure 5.43 how the row numbers skip from 3 to 10. Rows 4 through 9 are currently being hidden by the filter.

Another important thing to note is that the columns that are causing the filter to be applied have now replaced the triangle with a funnel icon in the header cell (in this case, cell A1). If you ever open a spreadsheet and find that much of the expected data is missing, you should check to see if any filters are applied. Look across the header row for any funnel icons, which indicate that the columns are being filtered. To remove a filtered view, right-click the funnel icon and undo any filters by selecting them or choosing Select All from the context menu. You can also remove all filters by selecting all cells and clicking the filter button in the toolbar.

Data Validation

By default, users can input any kind of data they want into any given cell of a spreadsheet. This is great for creating new workbooks with a vast array of variation, but once a workbook is created and you have a better idea what kinds of data you want in a cell, being able to input anything becomes a liability. If there are formulas or functions in the sheet that need to do mathematical equations on referenced cells, then it is vital that the cells contain the correct kind of information. For example, say that you want to find the total number of siblings a group of people has, and you ask everyone to enter that information in a cell on a spreadsheet. The following is a sample of the kinds of responses you might get:

2

Three

A brother

Only child

Sally and Dave

My parents keep having kids

2, but also a stepbrother

If we were to put this list into a spreadsheet and add the cells, you would get the result shown in Figure 5.44.

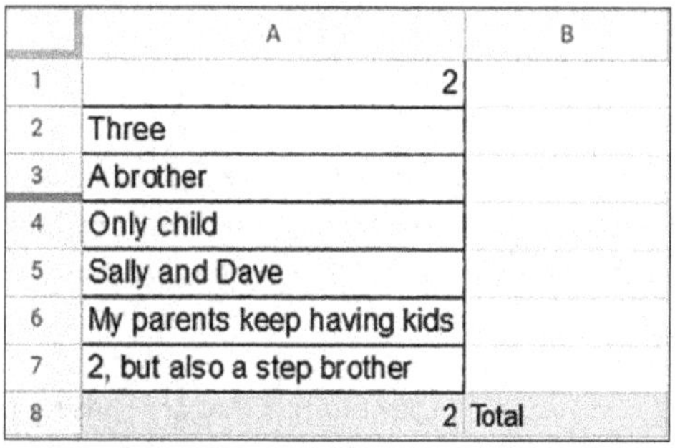

	A	B
1	2	
2	Three	
3	A brother	
4	Only child	
5	Sally and Dave	
6	My parents keep having kids	
7	2, but also a step brother	
8	2	Total

Figure 5.44 Badly entered data

This spreadsheet calculates the answer to be 2, although you know this answer is incorrect. Unfortunately, you don't know what the real answer is and can't know from the information listed. Row 6 does not even give an answer that can be turned into a number. The list is filled with *improperly formed*, or *invalid*, data. Getting this invalid data is an almost universal problem with collecting and analyzing data. To solve this problem, you need to take away some power from users and limit what they are allowed to enter in cells. To do this, you use data validation. Data validation allows you to specify exactly what a user is allowed to enter in any given cell. To start using data validation, you select a cell that you want to limit. You can remake the list from the siblings example and label it better for easier use, as shown in Figure 5.45.

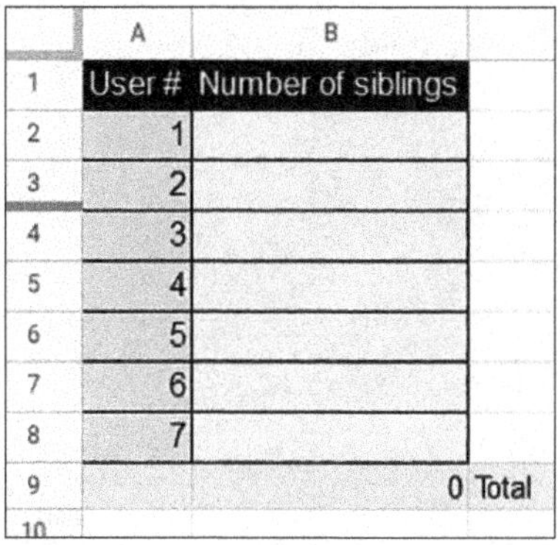

Figure 5.45 An organized entry list

Now the sheet is formatted in a way that will provide some clues about what to enter, with color coding and proper labeling of the input column, including an instruction. To take it further and guarantee that only numeric values are entered, you need to select the range of cells that should be limited—in this case, from cell B2 through cell B8. To select a range in a spreadsheet, you first click on one end of the range (in this case, B2), hold down the Shift key, and select the other end of the range (in this case, B8). When you do this, the entire range is selected and surrounded with the same box that has shown cell selection on all other operations (see Figure 5.46).

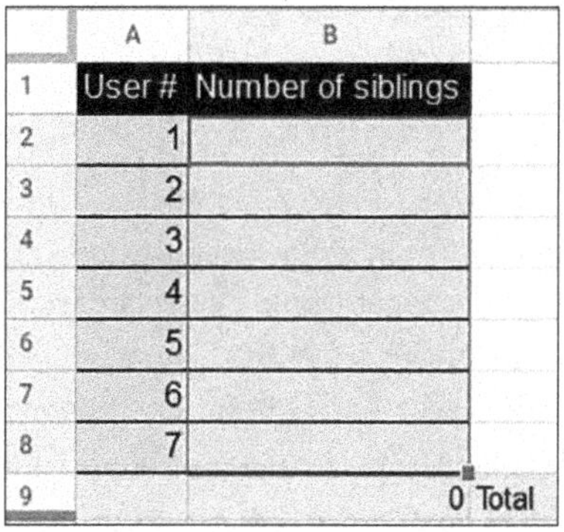

Figure 5.46 A selection of cells

The Data Validation Dialog

Once the range you want to limit is selected, you can right-click inside the range. scroll down the menu until you find Data Validation (near the bottom of the list), and click it. The Data Validation dialog, shown in Figure 5.47, pops up.

Figure 5.47 Data Validation dialog

The Data Validation dialog has several options for limiting selections:

- **Cell Range:** This is the list of cells you want to limit. Notice that in Figure 5.47, Cell Range is set to Siblings!B2:B8. This is a reference to a range of cells. It does not list out each cell individually but instead uses a colon (:) to show that there is an entire range of cells between the first listed cell, B2, and the last, B8. This method of defining a range is available for all operations in spreadsheets.
- **Criteria:** By default, Criteria is set to List from a Range, as shown in Figure 5.47. In this case, you know you want numbers, so you need to change this setting. To change how the cell is limited, click Criteria and choose which method you want to use, such as Number. As shown in Figure 5.48, when you select Number, more options appear.

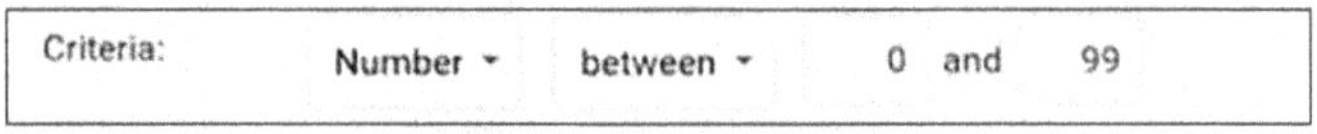

Figure 5.48 Validation Criteria

For this example, you want any number between the minimum and maximum possible siblings. Because it's hard to say what would be the largest number you could receive, you should choose a number that is larger than you would expect. If you want very specific minimum and maximum values, then use those numbers.

- **On Invalid Data:** This option lets you either warn a user they are putting in questionable data but allows them to do so anyway or rejects the data. For our example, an incorrect response should be rejected.
- **Appearance:** This final option allows you to write a helpful note to users.

After all the options have been adjusted, the Data Validation dialog should look as shown in Figure 5.49. When it looks as you want it, click Save.

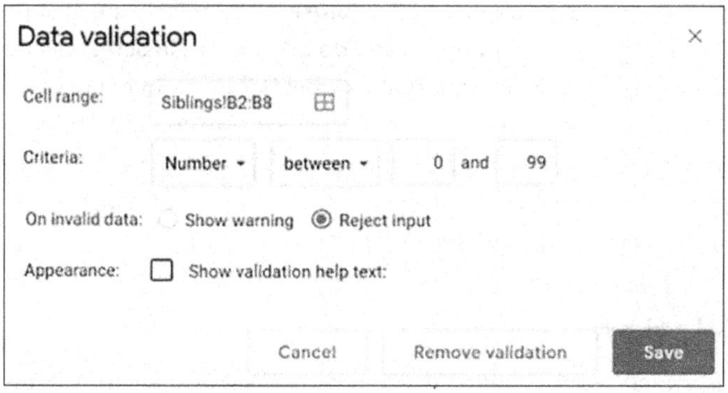

Figure 5.49 Completed Data Validation dialog

With these rules now in place, users are not allowed to enter invalid data.

Time Validation

Data validation works not only for numbers but for many other forms of data as well. In particular, dates are troublesome. The recording format of dates and times has been problematic since the first computers tried to use dates. The scales we use for time don't match up with how computers calculate time. Further, different regions and organizations use a vast array of formats for dates and time. For example, midnight on January 1, 2000, could be written in any of the following formats—and more:

2000/1/1 12am

00/01/01 midnight

1,1,2000 12

1-2000-1 0:00

All of these formats cause havoc when trying to do calculations. To prevent this issue, spreadsheets use a single date and time format for calculations:

Month/Day/Year Hour:Minute:Second

For midnight January 1, 2000, this format looks as follows:

1/1/2000 0:00:00

Strangely, if you type this date into a cell and then reformat the cell to show as a number, you see this:

36,526.000

While this number might seem strange, it is not broken. This is the value that the computer uses to store this date. Because computers can't do calculations in actual calendar time, they convert every time into a single number. That number is the number of days that have passed since 12/30/1899 0:00:00. Hours and minutes are converted into partial days as decimal values. So midnight on January 1, 2000, happened exactly 36,526 days after the beginning of "computer time" began. We rarely if ever look at dates in this format, but it is valuable to understand what is going on behind the scenes.

List Validation

List validation is a great tool for limiting user input and also for speeding up the job of a data designer. With list validation, you create a drop-down list in a cell that is populated with any items you want. You can manually input a list of items, or you can refer to a range of data.

Named Ranges

A named range is a collection of cells that have a user-defined reference name. Named ranges are not required for setting up a sheet, but they are a powerful tool that gives you easier access to stored data or values. A named range can be as simple as a single cell, or it can include multiple cells or rows or both. A selection of any size that can be made in a sheet can become a named range.

While named ranges are not technically needed, they help in simplifying references to existing data. We can see this with the monster list from earlier in this chapter. If you wanted to use data validation to make a drop-down list populated with all the possible monsters, you could select Data, Named Ranges to open the Data Validation dialog and select the range, as shown in Figure 5.50.

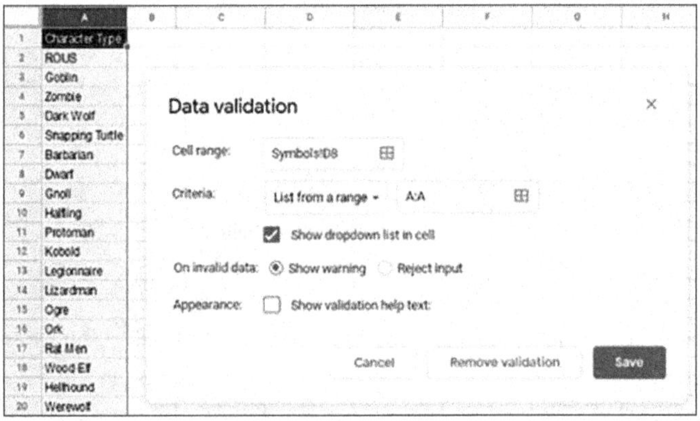

Figure 5.50 List validation

When you make the selections shown in Figure 5.50, you get a drop-down list in cell D8. However, when you review the Data Validation dialog, you must remember what some of the information refers to (such as column A:A in Figure 5.50). Sometimes, it will be obvious, such as when the information is on the same page and fully visible. However, if the data is on another sheet or if it is hidden, it can take some digging to discover what A:A actually means. Because every sheet has this same range, there is no built-in clue about what is stored in that range. To prevent this kind of confusion, you can give a range a name that is more recognizable and informative to humans (such as MonsterNames in this case). When you then see that name in the future, you will understand what data is being referenced.

To define a named range, you select the cells you want to include in the named range. Then you go to Data, Named Ranges, and you see the dialog shown in Figure 5.51.

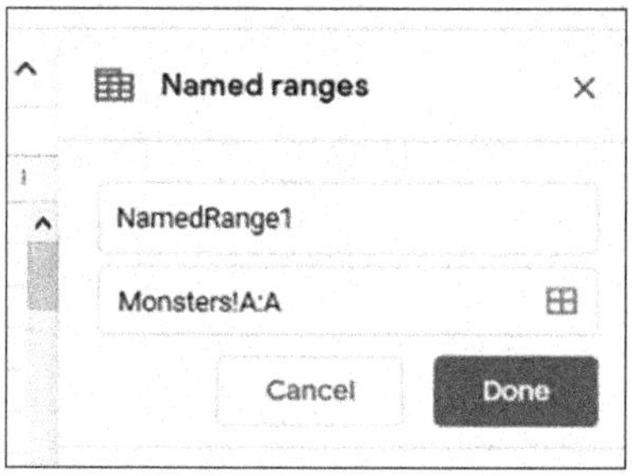

Figure 5.51 Named Ranges dialog

Because you selected the data you wanted included, the spreadsheet automatically populates the selected range for you. Note that you can modify the range in this interface, or you can even select the Mouse Select option to choose an entirely different range. These same rules for accessing other sheets also apply to this interface. Above the selection is the actual name of the range. By default, Google Sheets applies a placeholder name. It's a good idea to replace this placeholder with a more meaningful name, as the whole point of named ranges is to make the selection of areas more intuitive. In the current example, a name like MonsterNames works better (see Figure 5.52).

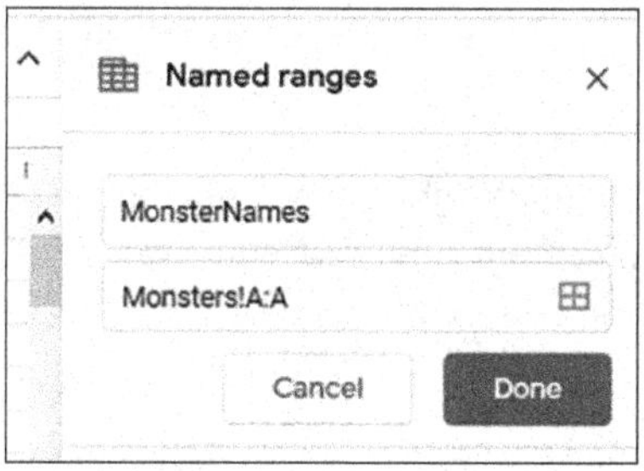

Figure 5.52 Renamed range

> **note**
>
> After the name of a range and the range itself have been defined, you can click Done to create the range. It is possible to go back and rename or redefine a range at any time after this by accessing the same named range interface from the Data menu.

After the range has been named, you can use the name of the range anywhere you want to access the data in the range. For example with the example of using data validation to create a list from monster names instead of referring to Monsters!A:A, you can simply refer to the named range MonsterNames to get this functionality (see Figure 5.53).

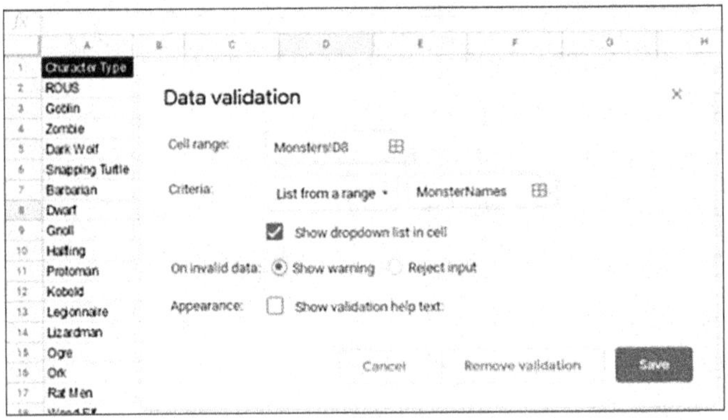

Figure 5.53 Validation with a named range

Named ranges can also be used in formulas or as variables in functions. Named ranges are particularly powerful when it comes to storing complex or long numbers. For example, if you had a cargo van in a game that could hold 1,480 pounds, it would not be particularly easy to remember that large number or to do math with it. Further, what if through the process of testing you found that the capacity needed to change? If you memorized 1,480 and typed it in manually everywhere that the number was needed, you would be left with the challenge of hunting down that number in numerous formulas and functions. Instead of going through this, it would be much easier to make a cell on a reference sheet, type in 1,480 and give that cell a name, as shown in Figure 5.54.

From this point on, the name CargoWeight can be used instead of the number. It is easier to remember than the number and dramatically easier to update. In a formula, it would look as shown in Figure 5.55.

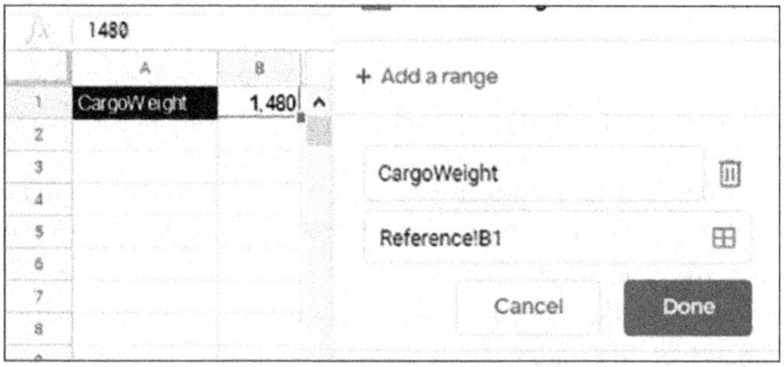

Figure 5.54 Named range cell

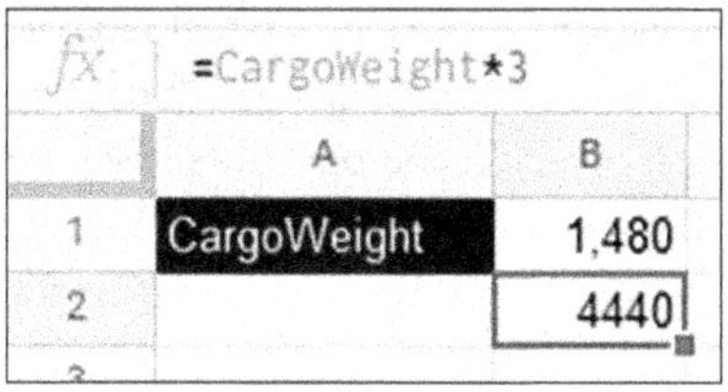

Figure 5.55 A named range in a formula

Keep in mind the following important notes about named ranges:

- Named ranges can be used from anywhere in a workbook (and so they are *global*), and they can be accessed from any sheet without requiring a reference to the sheet itself. So, for example, you can access MonsterNames and CargoWeight anywhere in the workbook by simply using those names.
- Named ranges are dynamic. If the contents of the cells they contain change, then anything referencing the range will also change. The same exception for drop-down validation also applies to named ranges: The list changes in the drop-down, but changing data in the list does not update any data elsewhere.
- A named range must have a unique name. Because they can be accessed globally, the spreadsheet needs to have distinct names for the named ranges.
- A named range's name can't contain a space. In a spreadsheet, a space denotes a new term, such as a new variable or new sheet name. You can use an underscore instead of a space in the name of a named range, or you can use camel case (for example, Monster_Names, or MonsterNames).
- Named ranges are not case sensitive, so CargoWeight, Cargoweight, and cargoweight are all treated as exactly the same name.

Further Steps

After completing this chapter, you should take some time to practice in the real world with the concepts covered here. Try these exercises to further investigate spreadsheet basics:

- The best way to learn to use a spreadsheet is to use spreadsheets a lot! Start thinking about ways that a spreadsheet might be useful. Making a budget is a common use, but there are also many more. You could, for example, use a spreadsheet to make an inventory of a home or an office. Or you could use a spreadsheet to track exercise numbers, weight change over time, or other health-related data. Spreadsheets are great for organizing catalogs of music, movies, and games.
- Spreadsheets can and should be used for game development. To get an idea of how helpful they are, find some game data for a game you like. Most popular games have fan sites or even official sites that show some form of data that you can copy and paste into a spreadsheet and then manipulate. By practicing with data that others have created, you can see some best practices in action and possibly some pitfalls to avoid when you start making spreadsheets with your own data.

CHAPTER 6

SPREADSHEET FUNCTIONS

Spreadsheets can calculate more than simple formulas; they can use *functions*, which are prewritten bits of code, each of which does a specific task. End users, including game system designers, use functions to quickly perform complex tasks without needing to know exactly what the underlying code does. Every function has a function name and parameters. The function is what should happen, and the parameters accept bits of data called *arguments* and tell the function what data to use as it performs the function.

Grouping Arguments

Computer programs do not know English intuitively as humans do, so you must write functions and input data in a format that the computer can understand without any ambiguity.

For example, consider the English language phrase "Pesto butter toast." Does this phrase mean pesto and butter and toast? Or does it mean "pesto butter" and toast? Or does it mean pesto and "butter toast"? Or does it mean toast that has been coated with a pesto-infused butter mixture? As English speakers, we can use context and custom to figure out the meaning of words, but computers cannot. For a human, they could take vocal cues of emphasis, or visual clues related to what they see in front of them, to figure out the intended meaning. For a computer, you need to spell out what you mean in exacting detail. When inputting data into a function, each piece of data is called an *argument*, and you use commas to separate multiple arguments. The way you group the arguments has meaning for the computer. For example, you could write "pesto butter toast" in several different ways to communicate the exact items you want the spreadsheet to understand. Here are several ways you could break it down for the computer, and how the computer would interpret each one:

- (pesto butter toast) is one item: toast with pesto butter on it.
- (pesto, butter toast) is two items: One is pesto, and the other is buttered toast.
- (pesto butter, toast) is two items: One is mixed pesto butter, and the other is plain toast.
- (pesto, butter, toast) is three items: Each ingredient in the list is separate.

Function Structure

Functions are, in behavior, much like machines in the real world. Things go into a machine, the machine does a preset operation on the things, and the machine returns the things changed in some way. To better understand how functions work, an analogy to using real-world machines can be helpful.

For example, consider a blender, which, as its name suggests, is a machine that blends up food. You, as the user, can place a wide variety of food items in the blender, and then the blender does what it says it does and returns a new product to you. Imagine that the blender is a spreadsheet function. Much like a blender, the function needs a machine, a container, and ingredients in order to do its job. For a spreadsheet, the "machine" is the name of the function, the "container" is a set of parentheses, and the "ingredients" are data, in the form of comma-separated arguments.

As you can see in Figure 6.1, the blender is standing in for the name of the function. It is followed by the container full of ingredients. In this case, multiple ingredients ("any item") can be placed in the container.

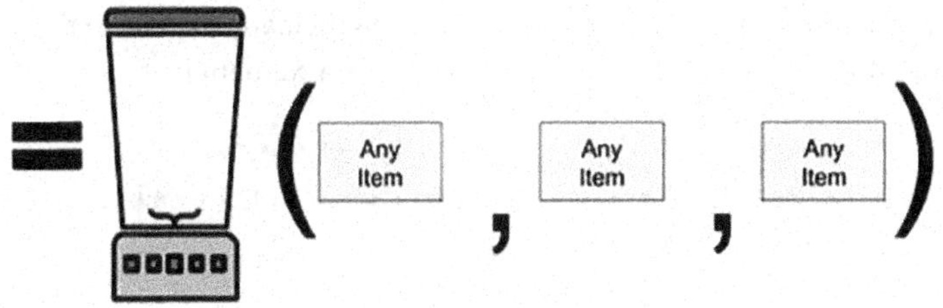

Figure 6.1 A blender as a function

Figure 6.2 A blender with ingredients

Figure 6.2 shows tomato, basil, and garlic placed inside the blender as the data. Once the blender is turned on, it processes these three ingredients to form an output—in this case, tomato sauce. Figure 6.3 shows the same function but with different data.

Figure 6.3 A blender with different ingredients

Again, the blender performs its job and blends together the ice, pineapple, and spirits to form a new output—in this case, a fruity drink. This is a completely different output from the same function because the data input is different.

We can break down a spreadsheet function in much the same way we've just broken down the blender ingredients. Let's consider the function SUM. Just as its name suggests, SUM is a function that adds together any data that is placed inside the function container. Here are a few examples:

=SUM(1,1) returns the value 2.

=SUM(1, 1+1, 5, 2) returns the value 10.

Functions allow for formulas or even other functions in their arguments. In the second example above, for instance, SUM would add 1+1 in the argument first, and then it would add the other arguments to get a total of 10.

In the example in Figure 6.4, SUM is adding up the contents of two cells. Each cell is referred to in the arguments by the cell address.

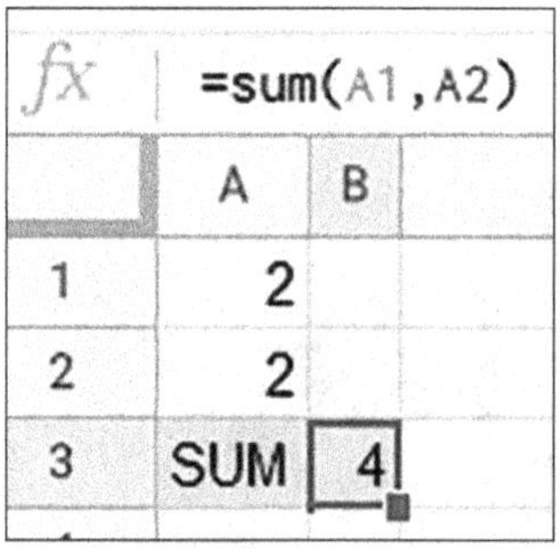

Figure 6.4 A sum or a reference

In the example in Figure 6.5, SUM is adding the contents of a range that goes from A1 through A6. The colon (:) indicates to the spreadsheet that every cell in the range should be included in this argument. Notice also that different numbers of arguments have been used in this example. Some functions allow the user to input as many or few arguments as they want; SUM is one of them.

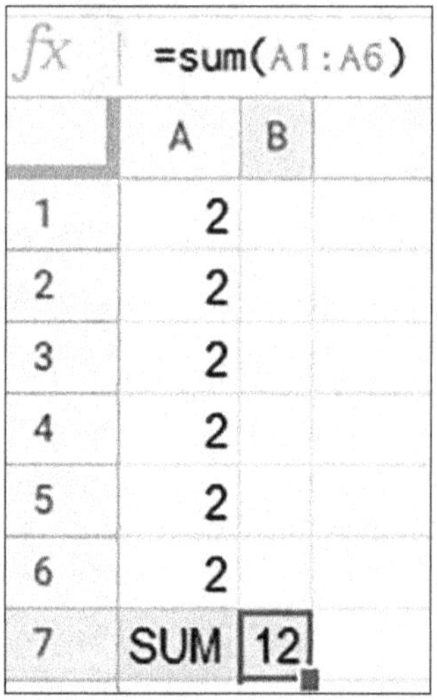

Figure 6.5 The sum of a range

When working with any function for the first time, it is a good idea to look at the help file for the function to see what arguments are allowed and expected. This is called the *syntax*. For SUM, the help file shows the syntax illustrated in Figure 6.6.

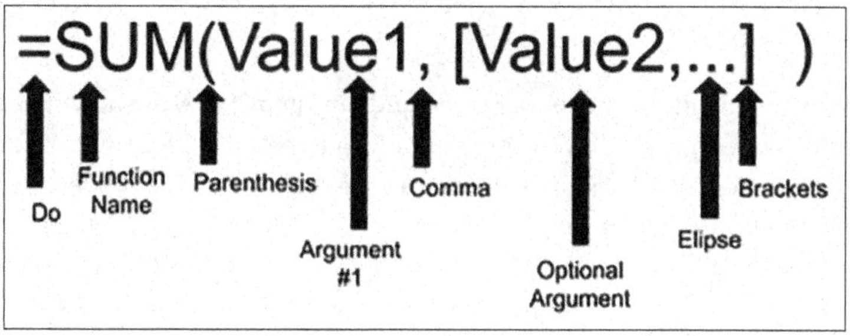

Figure 6.6 Syntax of a function

Each of these elements means something important in the context of the function:

- **Do:** Every function must start with = so the spreadsheet knows the cell is active.
- **Name:** To use a function, you need to reference it by name. In this example, the function name is SUM.
- **Parentheses:** These are the data "containers" that hold all the data arguments.
- **Argument 1:** In this function, there is only one required argument.
- **Comma:** A comma separates two individual arguments.
- **Brackets:** In the syntax of a function, brackets indicate that more arguments can be added, but they are not required. For example, SUM can be used to add together any quantity of numbers.
- **Ellipsis:** The ellipsis indicates that there could be more than one optional argument. For SUM, you are allowed to add as many arguments as you want, and the function will simply add them all together.

More Complex Functions

Like machines in the real world, some functions are more complex than others. They require that only specific types of data go in specific arguments. If you use the wrong number of arguments or the wrong type of data, the function breaks. You can see this in a real-world analogy of a car. In a simplified example of a car, it has three containers: one for gasoline, one for coolant, and one for the trunk. It would look as shown in Figure 6.7 if it were a function.

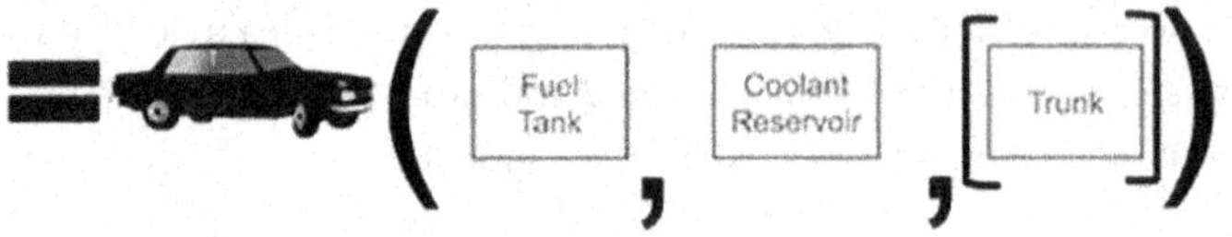

Figure 6.7 A car as a function

Notice that the arguments are no longer the vague "any item"; they are now specific items. Also, the trunk is optional (which you know because it is in brackets), as there does not need to be anything in the trunk. In Figure 6.8, you can see the car with the proper arguments, running as it should.

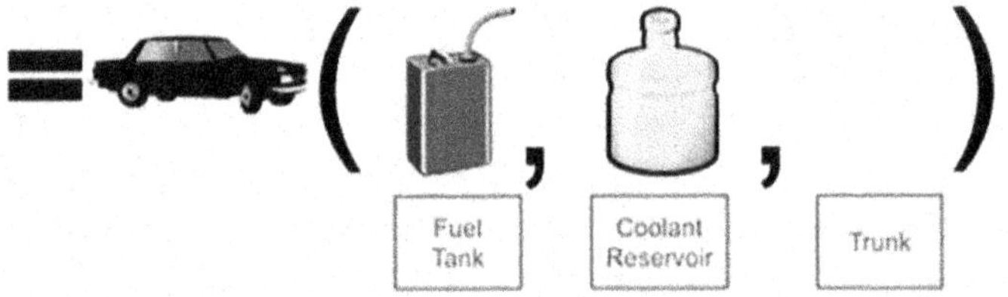

Figure 6.8 Materials in the proper places

This example shows gas in the fuel tank, water in the coolant reservoir, and nothing in the trunk. These are the correct data types, and they are placed in the correct argument spaces, so everything is working as it should. Anything could be placed in the trunk, but in this case, it is empty. (It would work with something in it as well.)

In Figure 6.9, the data types have been switched. What happens to the car now?

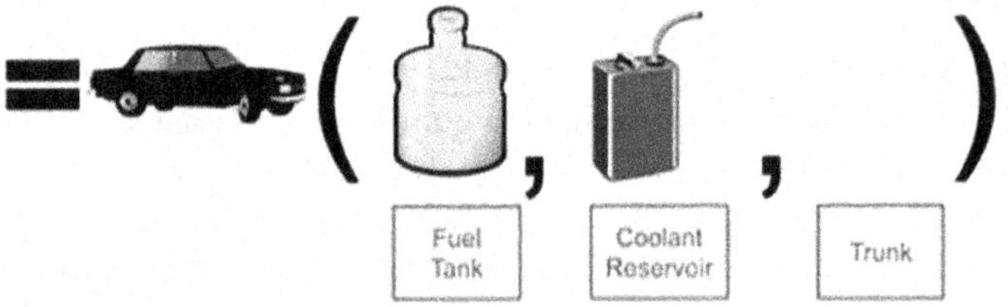

Figure 6.9 Correct materials in the wrong places

With the coolant in the fuel tank and gas in the coolant reservoir, the car does not run. Many spreadsheet functions work the same way: Not only do they require data to go in the arguments, they require specific types of data to go into the arguments. For example, the COUNTIF function has the following syntax:

COUNTIF(*range, criterion*)

This function "returns a conditional count across a range." This means that you must give it a range and then what you are looking for. For example, if you have a list of people who are signing up to volunteer, and you want them to type "Here" when they arrive, you get a list that looks like the one in Figure 6.10.

	A	B
1	Name	Check In
2	Charlotte	no
3	Ethan	no
4	Evelyn	Here
5	Mia	no
6	Elijah	Here
7	Amelia	Here
8	Isabella	no
9	Emma	Here
10	Benjamin	no

Figure 6.10 A list of people

Now that you have this list, you need to write a function to look through the list and count up the spaces where individuals have marked themselves as "Here." For the function, this means the range is all of the cells in column B, starting at B2 and ending at B10. Within this range, the function needs to look for the word "Here" and count up how many times it appears. After the function runs, the spreadsheet looks as shown in Figure 6.11.

Importantly, with the function COUNTIF, the order of arguments must be exact, and the arguments must contain the correct kind of information. Argument 1 must contain a range, and argument 2 must contain something to check for. If the order is reversed, the function will not work. If anything but a range is in argument 1, again, the function will not work.

When learning new functions, the help files are absolutely invaluable. Modern spreadsheets have both a small quick-reference help file and a larger more in-depth help file for every function available. By referencing the help file, you can see what arguments are needed and in which order, and you can see what types of data are allowed in each.

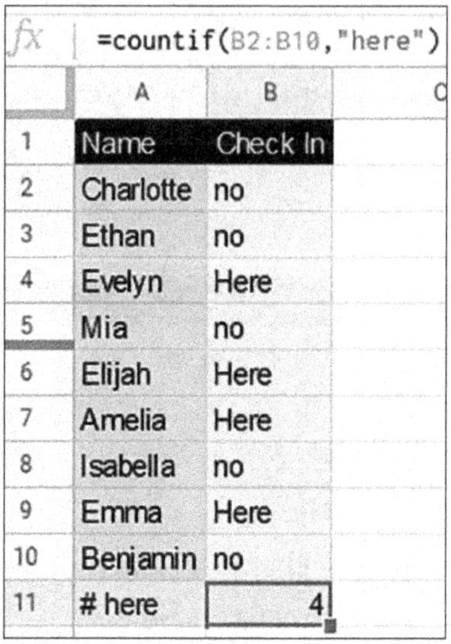

Figure 6.11 Using COUNTIF

Functions for System Designers

There are hundreds of functions available in spreadsheets, but most of them were created to solve specific problems for specific professions. This means that many of the available functions are not typically useful for a game system designer. This section focuses on the functions that are truly essential to a system designer. If you learn and understand the functions described in the following sections, you will know how to do the vast majority of the tasks that a system designer does every day.

> **note**
>
> For general information on how these functions work, see the help files for your spreadsheet program. The following sections focus specifically on how to use these functions in game system design.

SUM

SUM is one of the most simple and useful functions for a system designer. As mentioned earlier in this chapter, it adds up whatever you give it. SUM can add up numbers you type into the function as arguments, or it can add up a range of cells that contain numbers—or both. Figure 6.12 shows SUM being used to add up the total STR (short for Strength) attribute in a list of monsters.

	A	B
1	Character Type	STR
2	Goblin	3
3	Zombie	4
4	Dark Wolf	4
5	Snapping Turtle	6
6	Barbarian	7
7	Dwarf	6
8	Gnoll	3
9	SUM	33

Figure 6.12 Using SUM

AVERAGE

The AVERAGE function finds the mean or average value of a list of values. Game system designers use this function constantly when analyzing data. Figure 6.13 shows AVERAGE being used on the same range as in Figure 6.12 to find the average STR.

	A	B
1	Character Type	STR
2	Goblin	3
3	Zombie	4
4	Dark Wolf	4
5	Snapping Turtle	6
6	Barbarian	7
7	Dwarf	6
8	Gnoll	3
9	AVERAGE	4.7

Figure 6.13 Using AVERAGE

MEDIAN

The MEDIAN function serves as a good counterpoint and check against the output of the AVERAGE function. The median is the central score in a data distribution. It can provide similar information to the average, depending on the distribution of the data. However, if a set of data has extreme outliers, the average will be considerably different from the median, and knowing that there is a difference should prompt you to explore the data further. In the example in Figure 6.14, for instance, the median is lower than the average. As you can see here, you can use MEDIAN in the same places as AVERAGE, and you can use both of these functions on the same data to get deeper insights into the data.

	A	B
1	Character Type	STR
2	Goblin	3
3	Zombie	4
4	Dark Wolf	4
5	Snapping Turtle	6
6	Barbarian	7
7	Dwarf	6
8	Gnoll	3
9	MEDIAN	4.0

Figure 6.14 Using MEDIAN

MODE

Depending on the data set, the MODE function may or may not be useful. The mode is simply the most frequently appearing value in a data set. With data that is very granular and that has a large amount of variance, the mode doesn't provide much insight. However, if a data set has a lot of repetition, the mode can expose trends in the data. The example in Figure 6.15 is multimodal (that is, more than one value is equally the most common), and the spreadsheet returns the first candidate.

	A	B
1	Character Type	STR
2	Goblin	3
3	Zombie	4
4	Dark Wolf	4
5	Snapping Turtle	6
6	Barbarian	7
7	Dwarf	6
8	Gnoll	3
9	MODE	3.0

Figure 6.15 Using MODE

MAX and MIN

MAX returns the largest entry in a range of numbers. MIN returns the smallest number in a range. In Figure 6.16, you can see that the highest STR value is 7, and the lowest STR value is 3.

	A	B
1	Character Type	STR
2	Goblin	3
3	Zombie	4
4	Dark Wolf	4
5	Snapping Turtle	6
6	Barbarian	7
7	Dwarf	6
8	Gnoll	3
9	MAX	7
10	MIN	3

Figure 6.16 Using MAX and MIN

RANK

The RANK function can show the order of items in a distribution. In Figure 6.17, for example, you can see that it also lists ties as having the same rank and then skips the next rank; for example, in this figure, two characters are tied for second, so they are both ranked 2, and no characters are ranked 3. RANK by default ranks items in order from largest to smallest, but it can also be reversed to find smallest to largest.

fx =rank(B2,$B$2:$B$8)

	A	B	C
1	Character Type	STR	Rank
2	Goblin	3	6
3	Zombie	4	4
4	Dark Wolf	4	4
5	Snapping Turtle	6	2
6	Barbarian	7	1
7	Dwarf	6	2
8	Gnoll	3	6

Figure 6.17 Using RANK

COUNT, COUNTA, and COUNTUNIQUE

COUNT, COUNTA, and COUNTUNIQUE are slightly different versions of a function that counts entries in a range:

- COUNT counts only entries in a range that are numbers.
- COUNTA counts the total number of entries.
- COUNTUNIQUE counts how many entries in a list are unique.

In the example in Figure 6.18, the range A:A has a mix of words, numbers, and some duplicate words and numbers. With this example, COUNT finds any number, COUNTA counts any cell that is not blank, and COUNTUNIQUE counts only cells in the range that have unique entries.

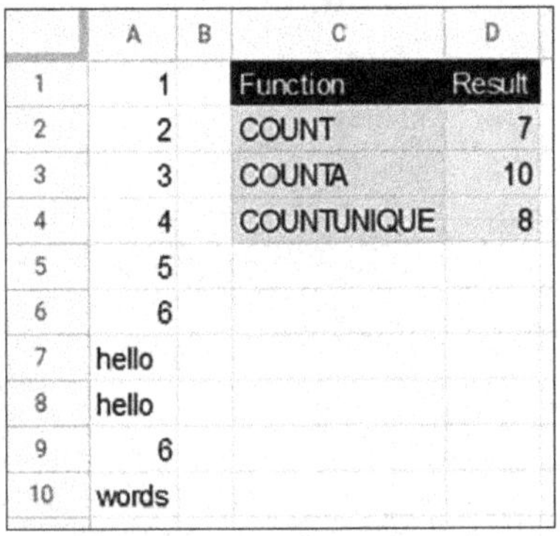

	A	B	C	D
1	1		Function	Result
2	2		COUNT	7
3	3		COUNTA	10
4	4		COUNTUNIQUE	8
5	5			
6	6			
7	hello			
8	hello			
9	6			
10	words			

Figure 6.18 Using COUNT functions

LEN

The LEN function counts the number of characters in a cell. This might seem like something system designers would rarely use, but it is used quite frequently. In game design, many times the user interface for a player, dialog for characters, of text for instructions must fit in a designated space. To ensure that the text that is written will fit, without having to test each and every line in the game individually, teams often put all the text for a game into a spreadsheet. Then, using LEN, they can do a quick initial check and make sure no dialog is too long. In the example shown in Figure 6.19, a historical quote is being checked for length to ensure that it can be quoted by an in-game character.

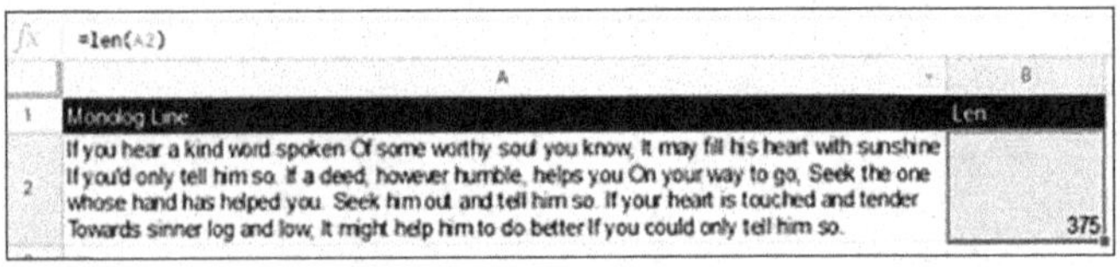

=len(A2)

	A	B
1	Monolog Line	Len
2	If you hear a kind word spoken Of some worthy soul you know, It may fill his heart with sunshine If you'd only tell him so. If a deed, however humble, helps you On your way to go, Seek the one whose hand has helped you. Seek him out and tell him so. If your heart is touched and tender Towards sinner log and low, It might help him to do better If you could only tell him so.	375

Figure 6.19 Using LEN

IF

IF is a very powerful and highly adaptable function. It evaluates a *logical expression*, which is basically a statement, and calculates whether the expression is true or false. Based on this calculation, the function returns one of two different outcomes. System designers use IF all the time to do a wide variety of conditional checks. In the example in Figure 6.20, an IF statement checks whether the quote from Figure 6.19 is too long for the game (where 350 is the maximum character length for text).

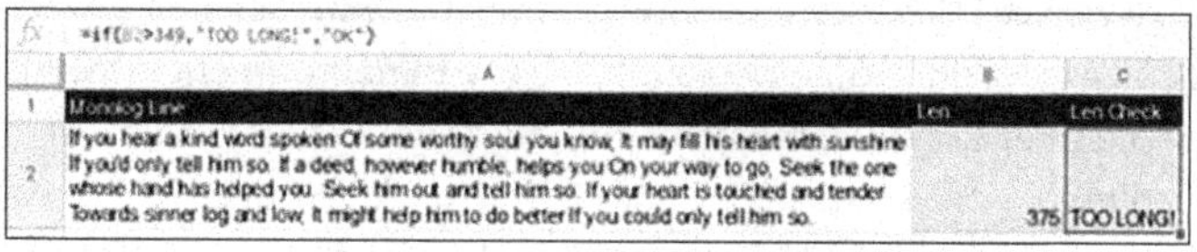

Figure 6.20 Using IF

COUNTIF

The COUNTIF function, as its name suggests, combines features of the IF and COUNT functions you have already seen. With COUNTIF, you can apply a conditional to a counter and see how many items in that list match the conditional. In the example in Figure 6.21, COUNTIF is being used to find out how many characters in the list have a STR value that is larger than 3.

	A	B
1	Character Type	STR
2	Goblin	3
3	Zombie	4
4	Dark Wolf	4
5	Snapping Turtle	6
6	Barbarian	7
7	Dwarf	6
8	Gnoll	3
9	More than 3	5

Figure 6.21 Using COUNTIF

VLOOKUP

VLOOKUP is a slightly more sophisticated function than the ones presented so far. VLOOKUP dynamically searches a table of data and retrieves elements from it for use. You typically use it when you have lots of data in a very large spreadsheet but you want to focus on only a small part of it at one time. In the example in Figure 4.80, the spreadsheet is looking for the Barbarian character in the list and returning the value it finds in the STR column.

With VLOOKUP, the first argument is what you are looking for, which can be text (in quotation marks) or a reference. The second argument is the table that contains everything you want to search and everything you want to return. The third argument is the offset of the return. In Figure 6.22, for example, the goal is to return not the first column, which is names, but the second column, which is the STR value. The final argument is optional and designates whether you want the spreadsheet to estimate (find the value nearest to the search term) or to use only an exact match. In this case, you want it to find only an exact match, so the argument is set to FALSE, which indicates "don't estimate."

fx =VLOOKUP("Barbarian",A1:B8,2,false)

	A	B	C	D
1	Character Type	STR		
2	Goblin	3		
3	Zombie	4		
4	Dark Wolf	4		
5	Snapping Turtle	6		
6	Barbarian	7		
7	Dwarf	6		
8	Gnoll	3		
9	Barbarian STR	7		

Figure 6.22 Using VLOOKUP

FIND

You use the FIND function to locate specific text within a large block of text in a cell. You use it to pull out key information from larger blocks of text. In its default use, FIND returns the character position where the text starts. In Figure 6.23, for example, the spreadsheet is finding the position of the word *spoken* in the large block of text.

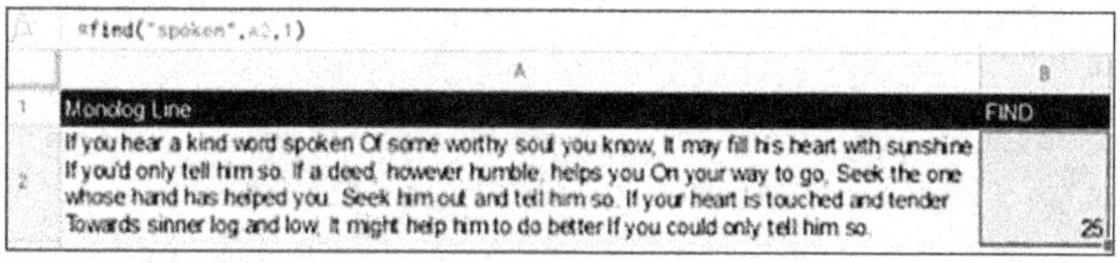

Figure 6.23 Using FIND

MID

The MID function serves nearly the opposite purpose of concatenation. When you use the & character to concatenate text (as described in Chapter 5, "Spreadsheet Basics"), you combined small pieces of data to make a larger text. On the other hand, MID extracts smaller pieces of data from a larger block. In the example in Figure 6.24, MID is extracting all the characters up to the word *spoken*, and then it stops one character short of the first letter in *spoken*. (Figure 6.24 is also a good example of a compound function that uses another function, FIND, as an argument.)

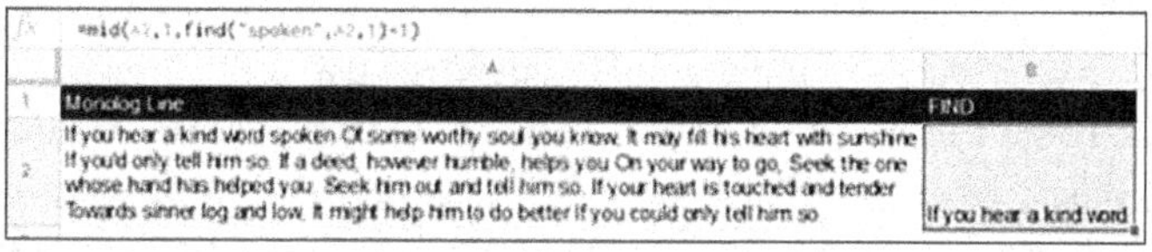

Figure 6.24 Using MID

NOW

NOW is a bit of a strange function, in that it is not very useful on its own. If you type =now() into a spreadsheet cell, the spreadsheet returns the current time. Each time a cell is updated, the function again retrieves the current time and displays the new time. Essentially, it works as a clock that updates only when the sheet updates. The computer already has a clock, so what good is the NOW function? On its own, the NOW function does not have much use, but when combined with a static time, it becomes much more useful. By using validation or copying and pasting values only from a cell containing the NOW function, you can get a static time. When the spreadsheet has a static (unchanging) time, the NOW function can be compared against it to find out how much time has passed since previous times or how long until future times will happen. In the example in Figure 6.25, cell A1 is using the function NOW, cell A2 contains a static time value, and cell A3 is measuring the distance between them.

> **note**
>
> To make times in a spreadsheet easier to read for humans, it's important to change the formatting of the times (as discussed in Chapter 5) so that times are formatted as times and the distance between times is formatted as duration.

fx =A1-A2

	A	B
1	9/18/2020 16:28:15	Now function
2	9/17/2020 14:02:22	Static time
3	26:25:53	Duration

Figure 6.25 Using NOW

RAND

The RAND function produces a random number between 0 and 1 to a very large number of decimal places. This is another odd function, in that it updates every time the spreadsheet is updated, including when any cell is changed. Much like NOW, RAND is more useful when the result of the function is copied and then pasted as value only, to eliminate the underlying function and keep the randomly generated number. Because RAND produces a long decimal number, it is also not entirely useful for random numbers in games, which tend to avoid long random decimal numbers. However, RAND, like all other functions, can be used in other functions or as part of a formula to manipulate the default output number into something more useful, such as a number between 1 and 100. Figure 6.26 shows raw output from RAND. Notice that this output, on its own, does not provide much information.

fx =RAND()

	A
1	0.54187400504263900000

Figure 6.26 Using RAND

ROUND

The ROUND function does exactly what it sounds like it does: It rounds off any given number to a specified number of decimal places. You often need to use this function to make long decimal numbers more digestible by players or even your own team. Figure 6.27 shows the ROUND function being used in combination with the RAND function in a simple formula to generate a more useful random range of 1 through 100.

> **note**
>
> Functions are not case sensitive in spreadsheets. Whether you use capital letters, lowercase, or a mix of both, the spreadsheet will read any function you type in the same way. It will also update your writing to be all capitals.

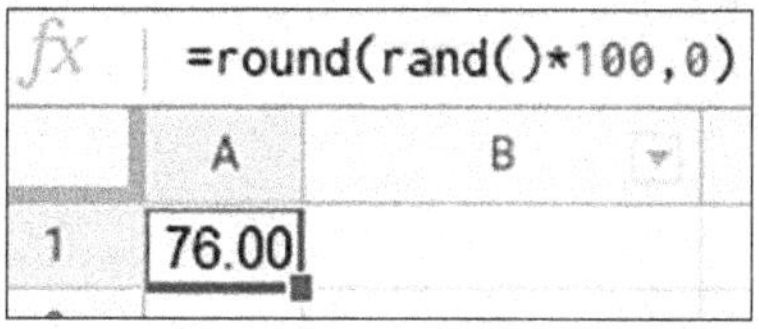

Figure 6.27 Using ROUND

RANDBETWEEN

For many applications, you don't want a random number that is between 0 and 1 or some multiple of that because you have a specific range in mind already. In such cases, you can use the RANDBETWEEN function to specify minimum and maximum values, and it randomly generates numbers within that designated range. In the example in Figure 6.28, the sheet is showing the generation of random numbers between 10 and 20. Note that RANDBETWEEN, like RAND and NOW, is often best used when the result of the function is copied and then pasted as value only.

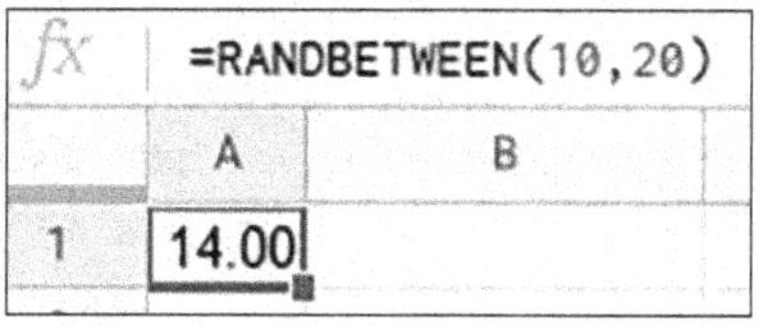

Figure 6.28 Using RANDBETWEEN

Learning About More Functions

While there are many hundreds more functions in every spreadsheet, the ones listed here are the ones that system designers most commonly use. If you take time to learn these functions thoroughly, you will be able to use them to do the majority of work needed to make a game.

To find even more functions, you can click on the function symbol (the Greek letter sigma) in the toolbar (see Figure 6.29). Then, if you select Learn More, you will see an list of every function available in the spreadsheet program. Don't be overwhelmed by how many of them there are. There may be hundreds of functions, but most of them are designed to be used for very specialized professions and can be ignored by everyone else.

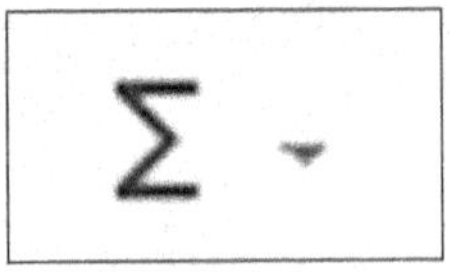

Figure 6.29 The function symbol

How to Choose the Right Function

You should practice with the functions described in this chapter to become more familiar with how they work. As you continue to work on spreadsheets as you make games, you are likely to run into situations where you know what you want to do, but you don't know what function can make it happen. This is a very normal problem that's even common for experienced professionals. The following steps can help you determine what function to use:

1. **Make a plan.** Think of what you want to do and then write it out in great detail. After you have written out exactly what you want the spreadsheet to do for you, parse each word of the plan and think about what it would mean exactly.
2. **Do it manually once.** When you know what you want the spreadsheet to do for you, go ahead and do it manually once. This might mean adding up numbers in your head or searching through large sheets of data with your eyes.
3. **Write down your exact steps.** As you did your task manually, did you need to click on another sheet? Did you use the mouse wheel to scroll down the page to find something? Did you add things up? Take all the steps, one at a time, and write down all the steps in exact, excruciating detail.
4. **Extract keywords.** Look at the steps you just wrote. What keywords stick out? Look for words like *searched*, *added*, *counted*, and *averaged*. Extract these keywords into a short list.

5. **Do some research.** Go to an Internet browser window and type in "google sheets" and one or two of your extracted keywords. It is quite possible that someone else has tried to do exactly what you are doing and asked about it. It is also possible that someone else has already answered that question and given clear instructions on how to do it. In spreadsheets, functions are often named intuitively based on what they do, so if you search your spreadsheet program's help file for your keywords, you might find that a function that does exactly what you already exists. If it does not, then you might find functions that get you part of the way there and that can be combined with other functions for exactly the effect you want.
6. **Ask questions.** If doing research and trying the functions you find is not giving you the results you want, you can use the steps you wrote down in step 3 to ask either someone you know or people on the Internet for help. There are multiple forums that discuss spreadsheet usage, and the people on those forums tend to be very helpful to those who ask questions clearly. See Chapter 3 for information on how to ask a question.

Further Steps

After completing this chapter, you should take some time to practice in the real world with the concepts covered here. Try these exercises to further practice asking and refining questions:

- Create several spreadsheets and practice using the formulas and functions shown in this chapter. If you completed the exercises in the "Further Steps" section of Chapter 5, you already have game data in a spreadsheet. Think about how each function can be used on that data to get an interesting result. (It is a good idea to create this spreadsheet now if you haven't already as it will come up again in later chapters.)
- Read the help files in your spreadsheet program. This chapter discusses some important functions in enough detail to get you started, but you can find a lot more information in the help files. Functions are also updated occasionally, so it is a good idea to look at the help files in the program of your choice to make sure you understand the current working version of each function.

CHAPTER 7

DISTILLING LIFE INTO SYSTEMS

Now that you understand the fundamentals of creating and using spreadsheets, it's time to start populating a spreadsheet with new game data. When you're creating a new game, where does game data come from? Obviously, the data is generated from game systems and, more generally, from games. This means, to generate data, you need systems, and to create systems, you need to start actually making a game. This chapter covers the basics of coming up with game ideas completely from scratch and then building them out with systems and data.

The first concept to understand is that no game is created in a vacuum. When you look closely at the mechanics that compose any game, you find that they are analogs for aspects of real life, even if they are abstracted. This similarity to real life helps explain why humans (and other animals) play games.

Life is complicated, messy, random, and unfair. It is more complex than we as a society can understand. Life is constantly changing, and for the most part, it's out of our control. "Solving" life is impossible, but humans like to solve things. We like to figure out systems and understand them in total. We also like to have a full grasp of rules and completely understand them. We like to have agency in our surroundings and make decisions that have meaningful consequences. Although it is impossible to have all these things in life, it is completely possible in a game. If you remove the vast majority of systems from life and distill a game down to just a small number of mechanics, you can get a grasp of the systems and how they interact, as well as what the game means. You can also do something else in games that is not possible in life: You can make games fair. To illustrate the complexities and how we distill a system of the real world, let's take a look at two examples.

First, Figure 7.1 shows a picture of a city street. Before reading on, start thinking about all the systems you can see in this single image.

Figure 7.1 A picture of a city street

Here is a small selection of systems represented in this single image:

- **City layout:** People have decided where all the buildings go.
- **Architecture, engineering, and construction:** Beyond deciding where all the buildings are located, many different groups have come up with complex systems for how each individual building is designed, constructed, and maintained.

- **Plumbing:** Each building has pipes that bring water from a centralized location to places throughout the building. Each building also has pipes that remove dirty water from the building and the streets and move it to a centralized location for treatment.
- **Electrical system:** Each building has an electrical system, as does the city street.
- **Traffic:** People are walking and driving in designated locations and according to rules. Without these systems, transportation would be nearly impossible.
- **Plant life:** You can see that a few trees are growing on this street. The decision about where to plant trees is a system, as are the trees themselves. Beyond the trees you can see that there are smaller plants growing here and there.
- **Weather and beyond:** You can see the sky in the background, which contains a multitude of weather and air systems. In addition, the rest of the entire universe is actually out there, though it's out of sight.
- **People:** Each individual person in the image is made up of a multitude of complex systems.
- **Clothing:** Everyone in the image is wearing clothes, and complex systems govern how those clothes are designed, created, purchased, and worn.
- **Society:** Taken as a whole, we humans have complex societal systems that influence everything we do.
- **Commerce:** There are multiple sophisticated economic systems in play anywhere there are large numbers of people.
- **Law:** Beyond basic societal rules, there are more rigid rules of law in place everywhere.
- **Advertising:** We can see advertisements throughout the street. Each of these obeys complex rules of law and advertising tactics to entice consumers.
- **Parasites:** It is strange to think of it, but almost certainly in an image of this many people, at least one of them has some form of parasite, whether it's lice, worms, or a case of athlete's foot. This illustrates how quickly we can go deep with systems. We could spiral into these kinds of details endlessly.

This is just a brief overview of the uncountable array of systems, rules, and interactions taking place in this single image. No game has ever gotten close to this kind of detail in its rules, and this is absolutely on purpose. Would you really want to simulate parasites in an RPG? Probably not. Would you want to address building zoning permits in a car racing game? Absolutely not. Instead, you want to make a game a very simplified impression of the world, so players can recognize it for being an abstraction of the world but without all the tiny details they don't care about within the game.

Now let's look at an abstracted version of a city street (see Figure 7.2).

In this abstracted image of a city street, we can also see various systems: people, trees, utility poles, roads, sky, and buildings.

Figure 7.2 An abstract image of a building

This list is smaller than the earlier one, and it's missing all the detail of that list. In fact, if we get very literal, we can see that this image is actually a few strokes of paint. The people in it are just a few paint blobs with paint circles slightly above them. The road is just a smudge of gray, and the trees are a few longer strokes of brown and green paint. If we were to look at any single part of the painting in total isolation, it would be difficult to even identify what the object was supposed to represent. However, when we take a casual look at the first and second images, we can easily describe each of them as showing a city view with some people on a road. In the painting, our mind fills in all the tiny details that are missing, or we simply ignore them because they aren't important to what the image is trying to communicate.

The difference between the photograph and the abstract painting is akin to the difference between real life and a game. To create a game, we look at life and then pull out a few key elements and present them to players in such a way that the players understand the impression of what we are presenting without being bogged down by the myriad details.

A game mechanic can be as simple as pattern recognition. For example, in tic-tac-toe, the goal is to make either three X's or three O's in a row. Tic-tac-toe has a very simple mechanic and a very simple set of rules. While tic-tac-toe is so simple that it is not particularly compelling for adults, it is appealing in that we can fully know all the rules. Even small children can grasp all the rules of the game. And, unlike in real life, in tic-tac-toe, players are never surprised or disappointed by unexpected rule changes midgame. Even simple interactions in real life can have unpredictable results that we don't fully understand. In tic-tac-toe, we are never denied an X because it is lost or never lose the game because our opponents bought another turn. These kinds of chaotic events happen in the real world whether we like it or think it's fair, but in the reality of the game, we do have control over these kinds of elements. We can decide what is fair and enforce it for the game. This gives games and their rules a kind of purity we never see in the real world—and that is inherently appealing to many humans.

If we take this discussion to a simple extreme, we can pull out just a few simple elements from a real-life scenario to make a well-known game. If you have ever tightly loaded a vehicle or packed things into a storage space, there is a good chance that it reminded you of a game. When you look closely at the details, you see that it's actually much more complicated than that. Figure 7.3 shows a packed car, and Figure 7.4 shows a Tetris-like game. They bear an obvious resemblance to one another, and some of the basic mechanics are the same.

Figure 7.3 A packed car that resembles a game

Figure 7.4 A Tetris-like game

In both instances, the "player" is trying to pack as many objects into a given space as possible, leaving as few empty spaces as possible. This underlying mechanic drives the game of Tetris, and even though the mechanic is abstracted, the inspiration is clear: The main mechanic of Tetris arises from the same built-in feeling of satisfaction we, as humans, get when we efficiently pack a space.

Now, let's look at some major differences between the packed car and the Tetris-like game. In the car, you can see small gaps between some of the items, and it might be possible to slip very small items in there. Some of the boxes might be fragile and best placed near the top of the car. Some might be very heavy and best placed at the bottom. In addition, it's important to consider whether all the items are going to be secure when the car moves. And is the car insured properly? Hopefully none of those containers have anything perishable or living in them that will not survive the trip. Such concerns are real and directly applicable to the real-life activity of packing up a bunch of items into a fixed space.

The game Tetris eliminates a lot of the car-packing concerns. Why did the designer decide to exclude those aspects of the real-life analog? Mostly because they aren't fun, and they distract from the core mechanic the designer wants the player to focus on: fitting shapes together in a confined space. Notice also that Tetris does things that are not possible in real life, such as eliminating a row when it is complete. The game designer has looked at the real world, recognized a mechanic, and distilled that mechanic and added to it in an abstract way to make it more enjoyable for players. This is the essence of good game design and one of the reasons Tetris has been so successful for such a long time.

An Abstract Example

Now let's take a look at a more sophisticated set of abstracted mechanics that we can later rework to make them into a popular game. For this example, we are going to look at paleolithic hunting techniques. Humans lived in that phase of existence for a very long time, and many of our most deeply held instincts were developed then. The following sections look at a few of paleolithic hunters' greatest strengths.

Throwing

Paleolithic hunters often need to throw things, such as rocks, accurately. Let's examine the mechanic of throwing things. Humans, unlike other animals, can accurately and quickly throw objects heavy enough to kill even large animals. This gave humans an enormous advantage in paleolithic hunting. By attacking with a disposable object from a safe distance, they could do damage to a target without being in immediate peril. Humans developed their throwing ability further and further, to the point that throwing things is a deeply ingrained human instinct. Just watch small children playing: They don't need to be taught to throw things, and, in fact, parents often have a hard time stopping them from throwing things. This happens across all countries and cultures, so we can clearly say that it is a built-in instinct and not something learned through observation.

Sticks

Paleolithic humans also learned how to use sticks and other tools to gain an advantage while hunting. Unlike any other animal, humans are able to accurately and strongly swing a stick to hit something. If the stick is damaged during this activity, that's fine by us because it is easily replaced, and using a stick allows us to maintain a safer distance while attacking a target. Again, waving around sticks is something all children all over the world pick up naturally, showing just how deeply connected we are to the activity as a species.

Running

Most animals run, but humans are particularly good at it. We have evolutionary adaptations that allow us to run long distances, particularly in hot weather. Running fast is also deeply ingrained in people as an inherently good thing. Again, watch children anywhere in the world and in any society, and you will find that running is valued in some form of sport. This is a feature of humans that has been used in hunting since before we were even fully human.

Teamwork

Finally, humans in the paleolithic began to work in groups. Other animals also work in groups and do so effectively, but humans are very much specialized in doing all the things we do together.

Putting Together the Mechanics

If we distill all the abstracted mechanics just discussed, rework them a bit, and combine them, we can use this information to create a game for modern humans that's based on hunting activities of paleolithic humans.

One game that is an abstraction of paleolithic hunting techniques that springs to mind is baseball (see Figure 7.5). It is highly unlikely that anyone making the rules for baseball, rounders, or any related games thought about this, but they did not need to. Instead, what they most likely did was think about activities that were fun and compelling for them and their friends. They observed what kids were doing while out playing at the park. The activities that are characteristic of baseball and paleolithic hunting are fun and compelling because they are deeply embedded in the human mind as being fun and compelling. These feelings reach back a very long way into human development. So it's actually not surprising that we would make games that include the same mechanics that are involved in paleolithic activities. It's also unsurprising that many of the same mechanical themes pop up in games across cultures and across times.

Figure 7.5 Baseball

Credit: Rob Marmion/Shutterstock

Distilling mechanics from life for use in a game does not need to be a conscious or purposeful activity. If you look closely at any game and really start studying the mechanics of the game, you can find analogs in the real world.

Story in Games

This is not a section about how to write stories for games. Writing stories for games is not in the domain of a system designer. It is certainly possible that a system designer might also be a narrative designer, but in that case, the single person would be fulfilling two different roles. Instead, this section is about how system designers create stories based on what someone else has written. Think about the following statement:

> It's not the story we put in the game that matters; it's the story the players get out of the game that matters.

Consider what this statement actually means. It does not try to invalidate the work done by narrative designers but instead shows how we as system designers use a different method to get stories into our players' heads. Also, of important note, the two methods of creating stories are not mutually exclusive. Developers can spend a great deal of time creating fantastic backstories and character arcs. System designers want to use the game itself to enhance—or even completely create—the narrative for the players. Let's look at some examples.

Poker has absolutely no story built into the rules of the game. The "character backgrounds" are those of the players; none have been written. There is no narrative arc in the rules, and there is no background narrative, but many thousands of stories have come out of poker. Poker stories have been created for movies, books, and comics, and many stories have been told to friends about amazing poker games. Poker stories contain tales of heroes and villains, of triumphs so large as to change a person's life, and of defeats devastating enough to affect the economy of a town. How do all of these stories happen when no narrative designer crafted them? The systems of the game created fertile ground for those stories to grow. This is the domain of the modern system designers. As a system designer, it is your job to create possibilities for players to craft their own dramas within the bounds of the rules.

Think about any game you have played that has really stuck with you. There might have been some well-written narrative embedded in the game, but it is highly likely (especially if you are reading this book) that there was something more. Something happened to you that has not happened before, and it was amazing. It was hard to describe the event to friends, especially those who are not familiar with the game. This is a unique domain of games. Movies play out for everyone the same way. Books have the same beginning, middle, and end, no matter who reads them. But games are interactive and provide unique experiences for their players. Further, they give players agency in what happens over the course of the game. No other medium does this.

As a system designer, you should be constantly thinking of mechanics and systems that allow your players to create their own stories. Keep this thought in mind as you read the following chapters. Consider how you can make your game in such a way that players can tell their own unique stories with it.

Further Steps

After completing this chapter, you should take some time to practice in the real world with the concepts covered here. Try these exercises to further games as abstractions of the real world:

- Analyze several old games and look at the mechanics involved. What are the analogs in those games to human activities?
- Go a step further and break down individual game mechanics in classic games and in your favorite modern games. What abstractions are being used for just those mechanics and not the game as a whole?
- Observe the world around you and pick out several mechanics from the real world that you have not commonly seen in games. Could you turn those mechanics into a game? Could you build those mechanics on to an existing game to improve it?
- Study several modern games and, instead of looking at the mechanics they included and how they were abstracted, think about what they excluded. What mechanics were left out of the games that are present in the real world? Why do you think the designers left out those features?

CHAPTER 8

COMING UP WITH IDEAS

Coming up with ideas can be hard. Even more difficult is coming up with new ideas or new modifications for ideas. Harder still is coming up with new ideas that work well, can be made into reality, and actually please people. There is a common notion that some people are creative and others are not. Like so many other aspects of what people do, however, creativity is a skill; it is not just an innate talent. Much like learning to play an instrument, drive a car, play a sport, draw, dance, or sculpt, being creative is partly talent, but mostly it is a learned skill. People who appear to be very creative were likely born with some degree of natural talent, but it is guaranteed that they continued to develop their natural talent with hard work and a plan.

This chapter describes methods and practice exercises you can use to develop your skill at being creative, specifically in regard to coming up with new ideas. If you feel that you are not naturally creative, you should read this chapter carefully and work through the exercises in earnest. All game system designers are expected to be fountains of ideas. Your challenge should be to choose which of your overflowing ideas to use rather than to come up with a single idea. Don't worry if it feels difficult and unnatural at first; this is to be expected. Like any other learned skill, using your mind in new ways will, at first, seem unnatural. Just as with learning any other skill, the only way to get better is to practice. Keep working on these methods and doing the exercises until they start to feel comfortable or even natural. You will likely find that the ideas start coming easier and faster, eventually to the point that it is hard to stop them from popping out constantly.

Idea Buffet

Every game designer, and creative person in general, should develop and keep an idea buffet, which is basically a list of ideas and short descriptions. It can be game ideas, or characters, mechanics, weapons, vehicles, level setups, or anything else you want. Eventually, you will probably want to organize these ideas into loose categories to make finding the ideas easier when the buffet becomes very large.

I use the word *buffet* to describe this list because it should act much like a real-world buffet. The idea is to have more ideas laid out in front of you than you could possibly use. Many of the ideas will not go well together. But you can pop in to the idea buffet when you need inspiration and pick and choose the options that suit your needs at that moment.

Sample Idea Buffet

The following is a snippet of an idea buffet. As you can see in the following example, your idea buffet can include general ideas, bits of ideas, questions, and anything else you want. There is no strict format for how to record the ideas in your idea buffet. Note that most of the ideas are just brief descriptions. They are not meant to be full explanations or even be useful on their own. The only intention with lists like this is to help with memory and trigger new ideas when looking through the list. Typically these lists should be many pages long.

Game Ideas

- Bouncy physics-ish game. Jelly Stacker.
- Jenga with odd shapes or physics. Mobile or VR.
- "Military survival manual"–based game. Serious game.
- Knot-tying game based on real knots. VR? Race through tubes made of knots?

- Parimutuel betting: Monster fights, dog races, and so on.
- Decision-making game from the perspective of animals. Start with very low forms of life and very simple decisions. As the forms of life get more complicated, so do the decisions and controls.
- Choose your own adventure in a puzzle game.
- Slide puzzle combined with a platformer.
- Real-time rock paper scissors.

Mechanics

- Mixing colors to match an enemy color. Lasers?
- Traveling salesperson puzzle in an RPG.
- Bad camera controls is the challenge.
- Glass breaking in unpredictable ways to be used by a player.
- Giving a dog commands through a simple set of symbols.
- An enemy that takes damage only if you don't hit him.
- Play as an NPC in someone else's game.

Running a Brainstorming Session

Brainstorming can take many forms, and it can be used in a very particular way in making games. This section discusses how to run a brainstorming session and methods you can use to dislodge ideas that are not flowing freely.

Having Goals

It is important to have goals for every brainstorming session. These goals should be written down and shown to everyone in the group prior to the session. They should be simple, one-phrase goals that are easy to understand but don't restrict the creative thought process. Here are a few examples of goals that system designers might have for a brainstorming session:

- New character classes that complement our old ones
- New mechanics for vehicle interactions with the world
- Better weapon/armor combinations
- Environment mechanics that set our game apart from others
- How to use the new controller for our target console

Once you have a short list of goals (for example, one to three goals), you can get started with your brainstorming session.

> **note**
>
> Goals should not contain topics like "solve this problem" or "make a final decision." Those topics are not in the domain of a brainstorming session. A well-run brainstorming session should be for the singular purpose of generating ideas, not implementing, critiquing, or judging ideas.

Gathering the Troops

One person should be the moderator for a brainstorming session. While you can brainstorm all by yourself—and it is often done that way—brainstorming as a group is even better. People in the session should be familiar with the problem but need not be experts. New perspectives are a great thing. Two people is enough for a group brainstorming session, and five is about the maximum number of participants for a useful session. Having more than five people in a session makes it hard for everyone to participate and creates issues with coordination. When more than five people need to be involved, it would be better to run separate sessions with smaller groups than to run one big one.

It is important for everyone involved to have time completely cleared for the session. It is also important to eliminate all distractions and interruptions. Ringing cell phones are a complete mood killer in a brainstorming session. No one should be on any screen or other media for the duration of the session. The only exception could be for a note taker to have a document open for typing session notes. Distractions destroy creativity.

It's best to have a small set of ground rules for the session written on a white board or another viewable area. Here is an example of such a list:

- Session is 1 hour long, from 2 p.m. to 3 p.m.
- No screens, headphones, or calls.
- Door is shut; no one leaves or enters during the session.
- No ideas are bad ideas.
- No person is wrong for coming up with new ideas.
- Have fun and be silly.
- Participate.
- Goals: (list session goals).

Giving Yourself a Block of Time

A brainstorming session should have defined start and end times. One hour is a good amount of time for a new group. As you continue sessions, the group will gain more endurance—but not indefinitely. More than 2 hours is probably too long. Under 30 minutes is too short to get into the proper mindset for most groups. The start time needs to be firm. Everyone in the group needs to be committed. It badly hurts the process if one person shows up partway into a brainstorming session. The latecomer is prone to repeat ideas, fail to understand the mood of the room, or want to impose their own current mood on the room.

The end time should be firm but not inflexible. If ideas are really flowing and progress is spilling out, then you can keep going for a little bit. If the mood of the room is bad, and there is more negativity than creativity, then the session might need to end early. If this happens, the issue needs to be addressed with the group before the next session. Leave some designated time at the end of the session for note gathering and for planning future steps. If people try to start planning during the session (which is very common), the moderator should gently remind them that there will be time for planning at the end.

Don't Accept the First Answer

One of the biggest traps in brainstorming sessions and the creative process in general is the temptation to accept the first answer. Let's look at a quick example. Say that you have been given some red buttons, blue buttons, a piece of grid paper, and two dice (see Figure 8.1). The goal for the session is to come up with game ideas that use these objects. Think about it for a few seconds before you continue reading.

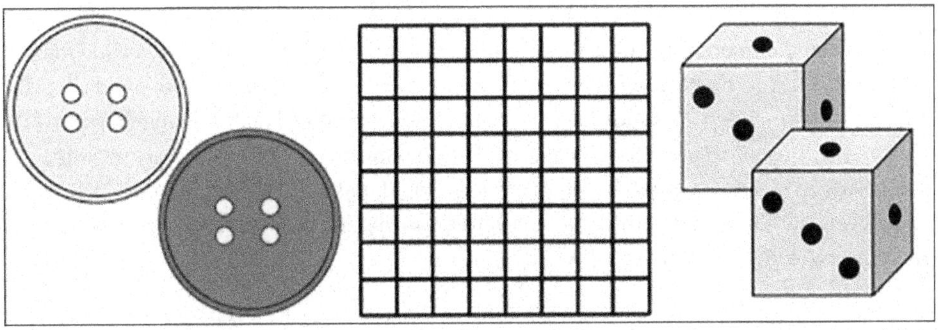

Figure 8.1 Game Pieces

Your first answer might be to create a game like checkers but with random dice movement. This simple challenge has been issued to countless hundreds of prospective designers, and that is by far the most common answer given. However, in a brainstorming session where the goal is to come up with new ideas, you don't want to go with the obvious answer. There is a big temptation in brainstorming sessions to latch on to the first idea that someone blurts out and fixate on it. You need to fight that urge. The moderator should say "great idea, keep going" to every answer.

You can try this now with the buttons and dice example: Write down your first idea and then come up with 10 more. Make sure those 10 answers are completely different from each other. For example, make sure you should have several ideas where the buttons and grid are not used together, several where combinations of items are used together in a novel way, and several that make no logical sense at all. Most of these ideas will be bad, but that's fine. You don't need tons of ideas in the end but are mining for a precious few among all the rest.

In some cases, the first idea suggested may end up being a diamond. That's great! The additional time coming up with more answers is still not wasted. Getting a great idea out of a session is a win no matter what, and you can feel more confident that it's the best when you can compare it to all the others. In brainstorming, it doesn't matter whether the best idea is first, fifth, or one hundredth. What matters is finding the best idea you can.

Avoiding Criticism

The goal during a brainstorming session is always to add ideas and never to eliminate them. As technical developers who want to produce quality products, it is in the game developers' nature to be very critical. When doing production work, especially near the end of a project, this is a good thing. During a brainstorming session, however, it is a disaster. Criticism forces people into a defensive mindset, where they are thinking about defending a single idea more than coming up with new ideas. Hearing criticism also discourages participation, which is crucial to success.

It is important for a brainstorming session moderator to keep a close eye out for criticism and address it. Since combativeness is also destructive to the creative process, one good way to address criticism when it's spotted is to say something like "I see you have found a potential flaw, but let's focus on a solution." Additional good phrases are "That idea may not work, but what's an idea that would?" and "Okay, how could that idea be even better?" By being obsessively positive and guiding others toward positivity, the moderator can help the session produce more ideas of better quality.

Keeping on Topic (Kind Of)

If the goal of a brainstorming session is to come up with character ideas, but the session produces only new game ideas, the session is of limited usefulness. However, staying too focused can stifle creativity. A moderator needs to let the group flow and bounce ideas without wandering too far away. Think of it like herding puppies through a field back to home. The moderator wants to get them all home but also wants to let them run and play in the field to get all that energy out. The moderator should let participants wander off a bit and let them be silly and riff off each other but should then gently bring them back. The moderator should be sure not to be critical or tell anyone they are doing it wrong but gently steer participants back toward the goal. A statement like "Let's get back on track" can be stifling. Instead, the moderator could say something like, "I hear some very creative ideas here. How can we relate that all back to our goal?"

Capturing the Creativity

A brainstorming group should be capturing ideas as they come out, using a white board, paper, or a computer. It's best if all participants can see the ideas as existing ideas often spawn more ideas—and that is just what you want. Don't worry about typos or organization; instead, focus on getting ideas recorded. In a good session, ideas will be coming out fast and often, and it is important not to slow people down or stop them from producing new ideas. If needed, have more than one person jot down ideas. Plan for time near the end of the session to do cleanup. Building in this cleanup time helps very organized types of people relax a bit. When you see someone erasing and rewriting ideas during the session, gently remind them that time at the end of the session is allocated to cleanup, so they need not do it quite yet.

Don't erase anything as you go. If, at the end of a session, you find some ideas that are gibberish, or if everyone in the meeting has now forgotten what those ideas mean, go ahead and remove those. But any ideas, bad or good, that you can still understand should be recorded.

After the session, you can organize all of the generated ideas into an idea buffet.

Keeping Expectations Reasonable

Brainstorming sessions are tough. Generating new ideas is very hard. Don't expect that one session will produce every answer you need—or even any answer. Try not to get frustrated. With patience and practice, your results will improve.

Percolating

When a brainstorming session is over, there is still more to do. At this point, you should have rivers of good, creative, silly, or plain bad ideas flowing through your head. In the hours and days to come, your mind will continue to churn on all these ideas and new, possibly great ideas will pop out when you least expect them. Be ready for this by having a recording device handy. It is not uncommon for designers to remain in this phase once they enter it. You can generate ideas and solutions at any time. Your creative mind doesn't care about your schedule or whether you're in a brainstorming session; it does what it wants when it wants. After a brainstorming session, your job is to be vigilant in waiting for those ideas to surface and then to capture them.

Methods to Force Creativity

Creativity does not always come easily, and sometimes (maybe even often) it stalls completely. If, as a moderator or a brainstorming session participant, you find a session prematurely slowing down, or if you are completely stuck, you can reach for a few methods to break through the barrier and get the ideas flowing again. Note that the methods discussed in the following sections are best used when the natural ebb and flow of a session has stalled. In a good session, none of them will be needed at all, and the moderator will just direct traffic and keep the group moving forward.

Bad Storming

This method is a great session opener. People tend to be reluctant to come up with bad ideas, which makes them hesitant to come up with any ideas at all—for fear that the ideas will be considered bad. To combat that, force the issue by bad storming. The goal of this exercise is for everyone in the session to purposefully come up with a bad idea.

For example, here's a very bad idea for a game with the buttons, grid, and dice example: The first of two player sticks two red buttons up in her nose and then sneezes as hard as possible, shooting both objects onto the grid paper. Both players then secretly set the dice to a wager. The second player then stuffs the blue buttons up his nose and sneezes, attempting to shoot the buttons out, hit the red buttons, and knock the red buttons off the grid. If the second player succeeds, he wins the amount of his wager; if not, he loses the amount the first player wagered. Is this a good idea for a game? Absolutely not. Did it make you chuckle? Maybe. Did it make you think about your items into a completely different light? You bet!

Requiring everyone to come up with bad ideas tends to get more creativity going because the participants don't have to obey any inner preconceptions about "right" answers. This also gets people loosened up. After they have had the courage to say one really bad idea, their fear of saying more decreases or even vanishes completely.

Jokes

Encourage jokes and joke ideas. This technique is an extension of bad storming. When an idea is phrased as a joke, there is less pressure for it to be a good idea. As a tension breaker, have participants start saying the idea with a phrase like "I've got a crazy idea. Here goes!" While the joke idea may not be a winner, it might inspire other ideas that are more serious. In professional settings, many times the best answer springs out of a joke. Jokes also keep the mood light and help the team flow together. While excellent craftsmanship can come from somber discipline, fun and creative ideas cannot.

Building Blocks

One of the best methods to start generating ideas, especially for system designers, is to break down objects or concepts into their smallest pieces. We will discuss this technique further in Chapter 9, "Attributes: Creating and Quantifying Life," but it is noted here because it is also an excellent exercise to perform in a brainstorming session. The first phase involves breaking down an idea into the smallest-sized components possible. This will likely generate a large list. The next phase involves changing one of those components to something else and then guessing what would happen to the system as a whole with that one change.

For example, think about a toy wagon that has a metal bed, four wheels, two axles, a handle, and a handle hinge. What would happen if you were to change one of those aspects into something else? For example, say that you give the wagon skis instead of wheels. Now you have a sled. What if you exchange the metal bed for a boiling vat of soup? Now you don't have a wagon but a mobile food source for a frozen tundra. By changing the smallest building blocks of a concept, you can dramatically change the concept as a whole. Again, none of the ideas generated in this way may be winners, but the thought process of breaking down an object into components may produce a winner.

Future Past

The future past method is best used when you have a specific problem that needs a solution. With this technique, you state the problem, and then someone blurts out a vague, random, or even purposefully wrong solution. The exercise then is not to determine whether the solution works but instead to imagine that you are in the future, and it turns out that the solution did work. Now you need to figure out how it worked. People tend to think too much about *whether* ideas will work or not, which keeps them from focusing on *how* ideas can work.

The future past method is particularly powerful and can be applied more broadly to problem solving in many aspects. Let's say you have a goal of growing your company from a garage-sized startup to a prosperous indie studio. One way to get started with solving that problem would be to imagine it is the future, and you now work for that thriving studio. How did you get there? Think about the steps you might have taken to go from where you were to where you wanted to be. Reframing the question from "Is this possible?" to "How is this going to be possible?" can dramatically change your insights on a problem.

Iterative Stepping

In an iterative stepping exercise, you start with a known idea and then consider the question "What's close to that?" In a group setting, you would hand off the question from one person to the next. It's best not to dwell on the iterations but to blurt out the first thing that comes to mind. This technique can meander into odd places, but it produces interesting results.

For example, say that you start with the idea horse. Your iterative stepping could go something like this:

1. Horse power
2. Muscle car
3. Mussels (the clam-like critters)
4. Seafood pasta
5. Dinner with mom
6. Family drama
7. Family comedy
8. TV
9. Ratings

You could carry on indefinitely.

Iterative stepping is also a great method to use when you want to break free from tropes. If the group is stuck on a tired idea, then iterating away can knock that loose, starting with small changes from the idea and eventually moving to fresh new ideas. Let's look at another example that is more closely related to games. We can start with the tired trope of breaking pots to find treasure. The iterative stepping might go like this:

1. Smoking pot to find treasure
2. Smoking beef jerky to find treasure
3. Smoking beef jerky to find yourself
4. Finding treasure to find yourself
5. Questioning why you need treasure at all
6. Questioning why you break pots
7. Is it morally okay for a hero to break a peasant's pots?
8. Punishment and repayment for broken pots
9. Balancing broken pot punishment with treasure pot reward

This is a very silly list, but that's okay! There are many interesting interactions listed here. Maybe none of them will be the idea you are looking for, but the clue to what you want may very well be in there somewhere. At the very least, you are not defaulting to a boring old trope.

Halfway Between

You can use the halfway between method when you have two very different ideas. It's sort of the opposite of the iterative steps. In this exercise, the goal is not to diverge from a point to somewhere unknown but to find an imaginary, nonexistent point between two known ideas.

When you have a pair of wildly differing concepts among the ideas generated in your brainstorming session, you can consider the mismatched pair and try to figure out what would be halfway between the two ideas.

Here are a few example of pairs of ideas that you can practice with:

- A first-person shooter and a farming game
- A race car and a racehorse
- A sword and a shield
- A crafting system and a damage system

Try it! If needed, solve each pair more than once with different answers. You could even have each participant write down a different answer and then have everyone reveal their answers at the same time to see how much variation there is. It is likely that new or interesting ideas will come up as you consider what might be halfway between each pair.

As with all the other methods listed in this chapter, the deeper you dig using the halfway between technique, the more likely you are to find a diamond of an idea.

Opposite Of

With the opposite of method, you start with a topic and try to come up with the opposite of that idea. You then take the new idea and come up with the opposite of that idea, with the caveat that you can't choose the first item again. This is challenging to do, but it yields some very interesting results. In function, it is similar to translating some text though several languages (using Google Translate, for example) before translating it back to English. You rarely end up with what you started with; the results are often funny and also often very different and interesting.

For example, say that you start using opposite of with the idea of a gun. Here's what you might get in four passes:

1. Flower (peace instead of war)
2. Sheep (plant eater instead of plant)
3. Nails (spikey instead of soft)
4. Hammer (drives nails instead of being driven)

You could keep going as long as you like.

Again, this technique generates a lot more ore than diamonds, but that is not what matters. Getting that one diamond by any means necessary is what matters.

Random Connections

Classic random word association is another technique that can help you get unstuck during a brainstorming session. Start with one of your generated ideas or topics and then pick a random word by using a random word generator or an old-fashioned dictionary. Now list the ways those ideas are similar and how they are different. Get specific. This technique doesn't always yield diamonds, but it often produces surprising results.

Stream of Consciousness Writing

If you're still having trouble generating ideas after using the methods described, or if you just want more ideas (there are never too many), you can try stream of consciousness writing. To do so, get pencil and paper and set a timer for 2 minutes. This might seem like a very short amount of time, but when you are in the middle of it, it will feel much longer. When the timer begins to run, start writing. You can write anything. Ideas are best, but nothing is off limits. The only rule is that you must be actively writing for the entire 120 seconds, with no pauses, no breaks, no corrections, no reflection, and no talking. Just write for a solid 2 minutes. If no thoughts are coming to your head, write that down. Try to change tracks in your mind as often as possible and don't get stuck writing lists of items that are all related. By the time the timer is finished, hopefully a few nuggets have popped out. You can expect that most of your writing will not produce anything useful, but that's fine. When you are mining for diamonds, you may need to dig through a lot of ore.

> **note**
>
> All the methods listed in this section can be useful by helping break up a stalled session and getting people thinking of ideas again. Keep a list of these methods handy. If you notice that a session has stalled and needs a nudge, you can try one of these methods to get it going again. However, it is also important to use these methods with some constraint. You do not want your brainstorming session to feel like a bunch of party games meant for killing time rather than generating ideas. If a session is going well and ideas are flowing right from the start, sit back, gently guide the flow when needed, and enjoy. In an experienced team, the moderator may not need to do much at all, and this is a great thing!

Further Steps

After completing this chapter, you should take some time to practice in the real world with the concepts covered here. Try these exercises to further explore brainstorming methods:

- Perform a solo brainstorming session. Pick a narrow topic, such as a game mechanic you are working on, and go through all the steps of brainstorming to see what you get out of it.
- Perform a group brainstorming session. Find a few friends and go through the method outlined in this chapter. You can pick any topic, but a game-related one will be most beneficial. In many brainstorming sessions, it's not necessary to go through all the steps and try all of the forced creativity activities, but for your practice session, do so anyway. This will allow you to get familiar with each step and method, without the pressure of needing to produce any results.

CHAPTER 9

ATTRIBUTES: CREATING AND QUANTIFYING LIFE

One of the most common early tasks system designers perform is to create attributes for game objects. We can define *game object* as any individual object in a game that does something. It could be something as simple as a block of ground that has a texture and collision, all the way up to a character that has a vast array of attributes, animations, 3D meshes, and more.

Mechanics Versus Attributes

Game objects can be defined using attributes and mechanics. Simply put, *mechanics* are rules that govern usage, and *attributes* are values that influence those rules. In a practical sense for video games, mechanics require some amount of encoding, whereas attributes are represented as values (data). In a board game, mechanics require rules, or combinations of rules, and attributes are represented as values.

Let's look at a simple analogy that illustrates the relationship between mechanics and attributes. In a game, data objects and attributes function as nouns function in writing, and mechanics function as verbs. We can take this analogy further and say that microsystems function much as written sentences, macrosystems function as chapters, and games function as stories. The basic building blocks always come back to the nouns and verbs or, in the case of games, data and mechanics.

Think of the game chess. You could say that each square on the board is an object. There are rules about what pieces can be placed on each square to begin the game. In addition, each piece is also an object. All of these objects have their own mechanics and attributes.

A king and a queen in chess both have the mechanic that they can move in any of eight directions on a turn. However, the king may only move one space if the path is clear, whereas the queen may move up to eight spaces if the path is clear. So we could say that the king has a movement attribute of 1, with the mechanic being that the space must be clear, and the queen has a movement attribute of 8, with the same movement mechanic. The king also has additional mechanics regarding check and checkmate, but neither of these has an associated attribute; each is just a simple mechanic.

Let's now consider a slightly more complex example: the classic arcade game *Galaga*. A player's spaceship has several mechanics: It can move side to side, it can fire projectiles at enemy ships, and it takes damage when it collides with an enemy ship or projectile. A player's spaceship also has a few attributes that drive these mechanics, including moving speed, firing rate, and hit points. Without changing the mechanics, you can dramatically affect game play by manipulating the attributes. Imagine what would happen if you slowed down the player character (the PC) and allowed it to move only half as fast as before. How much harder would the game be? Now imagine if the PC could shoot 10 times as fast as usual. Each of these attribute changes would not require a change in the rules of the game but would have a dramatic impact on game play.

Listing Attributes

For a very simple game, a game object may have only one or even no attributes. Checkers, for example, has no functional attributes since all of the pieces behave in exactly the same manner. For more complicated games, game objects may have dozens of attributes—some seen by the player, some hidden, and some derived with calculations.

The first step in creating attributes for an object is to take a very close look at the object you want to define. This can be done even before you have mechanics and might inform what mechanics you want. You need to think about all the facets of that object that might be different from instance to instance.

Let's look at an example of creating attributes for an object—in this case, the very generic "person" shown in Figure 9.1.

Figure 9.1 A generic human character

Initial Brainstorming

The first step in coming up with a list of attributes is to just write down what comes to mind quickly. What attributes can people have that change among instances of people? The following are some very obvious attributes you might come up with off the top of your head:

- Height
- Weight
- Waist size
- Wingspan
- Shoe size
- Hat size
- Blood pressure
- Heart rate
- Age

- Body fat percentage
- Strength
- Dexterity
- Speed
- Intelligence
- Wealth
- Dancing ability

Blue-Sky Brainstorming

After you've listed the very obvious attributes—the ones that spring quickly to mind—you enter the "blue sky" phase of attribute brainstorming. During this phase, you should be open to any and all contributions, even silly ones. In this phase, you might add the following attributes to your list:

- Magic aptitude
- Magnetic personality
- Humor
- Stench
- Clumsiness
- Luck

In this phase of creating attributes, you want to come up with as many attributes as possible. Quantity is more important than quality. A little later on, you can weed out what you don't want or what does not fit your game. While going through the process of defining objects, people tend to get more closed-minded and focused. It is therefore especially important to take advantage of this very early blue-sky phase to be as creative and open to new ideas as possible. You can use the techniques covered in Chapter 8, "Coming Up with Ideas," during this phase of attribute development.

Researching Attributes

Once you have a large list of both basic attributes and more creative attributes, you can move on to the next phase of creation, which is research. It is highly recommended to do this phase after the creative phase because research will form a construct in your mind about what these objects "should be," based on what others have observed. While it is good to be grounded in reality and to have a working knowledge of objects similar to your own object, expectations tend to stifle creativity. So you should do research only after you have exhausted your own internal creative well.

For a generic person object, you would want to research two things: attributes that define people in the real world and attributes that others have used to define people in previous games.

Researching Real-World Attributes

The Internet is a valuable resource for this type of research. For example, when researching a person object, you might look at sites that provide statistics for individual people, such as exercise and diet sites, medical reference sites, education sites, and demographic studies. At this point, you are not concerned with the results obtained by any of those sources; instead, you are concerned with what attributes they are studying. In addition, you probably don't need attributes as detailed as the ones you might find in medical textbooks, so you can simplify them.

When you research attributes from real life, you might come up with the following:

- Blood oxygen level
- Bench press weight
- Biceps curl weight
- Squat weight
- Pancreatic function
- Kidney function
- Stomach pH
- Neurons in the brain
- Hearing ability
- 100-meter dash time
- Marathon time
- Baseball pitching speed
- Football kicking distance
- Eyeglasses prescription

This list could get absolutely enormous. As a system designer, you can choose the level to which you want to simplify and how much you want to include. A good rule of thumb is to include at least twice as much on this list as you think you might need. This will create a large pool of choices for you to pick from when you decide on a final list.

Researching Attributes in Past Games

Next, you can research past games to see what attributes they use to define a person; when you find any that you have not yet included on your list, write them down. For this research, you should start with games in similar genres that include objects that are the same as or similar to objects that you are creating. This step intentionally occurs late in the brainstorming process because it is the step that is most likely to narrow your creative focus. It is easy to copy what others have done and very tempting to stop there. In doing this step late in the process, you ensure that you have already come up with new and creative ideas before delving deep into what others have done.

When you research attributes from games, you might list the following attributes for your generic person:

- Constitution
- Wisdom
- Acrobatics
- Arcana
- Insight
- Intimidation
- Spirit
- Melee
- Ranged accuracy
- Leadership
- Movement rate
- Encumbrance

Referring to Your Own Personal Attribute Bank

The final step in the process of listing attributes is to refer to your own personal "attribute bank." When you are new at listing attributes, you won't have such a bank yet, but it will grow quickly. Every system designer, whether formally or informally, has a bank of attributes that they refer to whenever creating new objects. This is a list of attributes that the designer has used multiple times for different objects across many games. Since there are no specific criteria for what attributes go into your personal bank, it is likely that most of them will not be applicable to any given new object you are trying to define. However, some of them may be, and it is a useful final step to refer to an attribute bank to make sure that you have not forgotten any attributes that you know work well.

> **note**
>
> An attribute bank is similar to an idea buffet and could even be included in the same document. However, the attribute bank includes only attributes and not ideas in general.

Defining an Attribute

Notice that in all of the attributes lists so far in this chapter, each attribute is a single word or a very short phrase. This is what you want when coming up with new ideas, as trying to define every attribute during the brainstorming phase would slow down the process and likely stifle creativity. To make attributes useful, however, you must go further and define them.

So how do you define an attribute? For example, what is strength? This seems like a pretty straightforward question. By looking at different people, you can often guess whether one person is stronger than another. When you get into the realm of designing game mechanics and attributes, however, you must be exact. For the sake of making a game, you must also abstract the concept because a real-world attribute is likely to be too complex to contain in a single value.

As of this writing, the world bench press record, set by Kirill Sarychev, is 738.5 pounds. Obviously, Sarychev is very strong. The world squat record, set by Jonas Rantanen, is 1,268 pounds. Obviously, Rantanen is also very strong. But which one is stronger? Sarychev can't squat as much weight as Rantanen, and Rantanen can't bench press as much as Sarychev. So there is not one simple attribute that measures strength. In a game, you need to decide what exactly the attribute strength means.

To flesh out the definition of the attribute strength for a game, you need to know what the attribute is being used for in the game. Let's say that in your game, characters are doing a caber toss (see Figure 9.2). A caber tosser needs strong legs but is even more reliant on upper body strength. When you define the strength attribute, you need to define it specifically as it pertains to the game. In this example, you might define strength as follows:

> The maximum weight of a caber that the player can successfully flip.

This definition is fairly short because the game is very simple and mechanically limited in scope. With a more complex game involving more interactions, you would need to further define the attribute and how it interacts with the mechanics of the game. In this simple game, however, you want to keep the definition of the attribute as simple as possible.

You can now use your definition of strength to determine which of two characters is strongest. For example, if you wanted to compare Sarychev and Rantanen using this definition of strength, you would consider that although both of them are very strong, the one with the stronger upper body, Sarychev, would be more successful in a caber toss. With this in mind, you might give Rantanen a strength rating in your game of 99 out of 100 (again, he is very strong), but you would give Kirill a 100 out of 100 because he is the strongest at the designated game mechanic. If the game were changed to focus on pushing heavy things with the legs, these players' attribute scores would likely be flipped.

Figure 9.2 Caber toss
Credit: Vineyard Perspective/Shutterstock

Considerations When Defining an Attribute

Through your brainstorming and research, you might discover dozens or even hundreds of attributes that could be assigned to a data object. Early in the process of listing attributes, you want to come up with as many attributes as possible. When the list of possibilities is fleshed out, it's time to start being more selective about which attributes are actually going into the game.

- **Every attribute should have a use.** Every chosen attribute should do something in the game. In Chapter 7, "Distilling Life into Systems," I said that games are abstractions of life. Attributes are also abstractions and simplifications of life. Therefore, many attributes that could be listed for a given object are unneeded for the specific game being made.

A simple test to check attributes is to consider what a specific attribute will be used for in your specific game. For example, if you are making a car racing game, you could assign an attribute for the volume of the trunk, but would that ever be used? Probably not, so it is not needed in the game and should not be included. This is the first and most important test to apply to all proposed game object attributes. The intended mechanics usage of the attribute should also be formally listed in the description of the attribute.

- **Attributes should be intimately related to mechanics.** Every attribute should have related mechanics. For instance, if you have a character with a strength attribute, you need to relate that attribute to the mechanics that will use it, which might be combat, encumbrance (that is, ability to move heavy loads), endurance, or resistance to damage. When narrowing your list of possible attributes down to the final list, it's a good practice to tie each proposed attribute to the mechanics that will use that attribute in the game. In fact, you can often generate more attributes by thinking about what attributes you need to drive your mechanics.

Grouping Attributes

Once you have finished listing and defining attributes, you are likely to notice that many of the definitions and attributes are redundant, and you don't need them all for your game. The next step in the process is not to eliminate the attributes you don't need but rather to group them. This way, you get a much clearer idea of what your abstracted attributes actually mean.

For a very simple action game, you might want to deal with very few attributes to make it easier for the player to comprehend the game. Say that you decide to use just the following attributes:

- Strength
- Dexterity
- Health
- Speed

You can now go through all of your earlier research and decide which attributes will be grouped. Your list might come out something like this:

- Strength
  - Bench press weight
  - Biceps curl weight
  - Squat weight
  - Baseball pitching speed
  - Football kicking distance
  - Melee
  - Encumbrance

- Dexterity
  - Hearing ability
  - Eyeglass prescription
  - Acrobatics
  - Ranged accuracy
- Health
  - Blood pressure
  - Heart rate
  - Blood oxygen level
  - Pancreatic function
  - Kidney function
  - Stomach pH
- Speed
  - 100-meter dash time
  - Marathon time
  - Movement rate
- Unused
  - Height
  - Weight
  - Waist size
  - Wingspan
  - Shoe size
  - Hat size
  - Age
  - Body fat percentage
  - Intelligence
  - Wealth
  - Magic aptitude
  - Magnetic personality
  - Humor
  - Stench
  - Clumsiness
  - Luck
  - Neurons in the brain
  - Constitution

- Wisdom
- Arcana
- Insight
- Intimidation
- Spirit
- Leadership

Note that the attributes listed under "unused" are not bad attributes, but they don't fit our current needs. It would be a good idea to put them in your attribute bank for later use in other games.

Something else to notice in this final list is that the attribute melee (that is, the ability to perform hand-to-hand combat) is listed in the strength category, and the attribute acrobatics (that is, the ability to jump, flip, and otherwise move) is in the dexterity category. In the real world, these two attributes are actually fairly closely related. Many melee moves require acrobatic-like ability, and many acrobatic moves are very similar to those you would see in a melee combat. So, why are they grouped into two separate categories? When creating and organizing object attributes, you often encounter conflicts like this. The real world is very complex, and often even simple activities can be categorized in multiple ways. As a system designer, you often have to make calls about how attributes are categorized. When making a game, you are creating your own little universe of rules, and you are the deity of that universe. If you were to try to be perfectly accurate in organizing attributes, you would have an endless task that would make no practical sense for your game. As a system designer, you have to make calls on how to abstract elements of life into a game.

Further Steps

After completing this chapter, you should take some time to practice in the real world with the concepts covered here. Try these exercises to further explore the process of creating attributes for games:

- Analyze the attributes of several games in a similar genre, such as RPGs or FPSs. List every attribute for every character and item. Which attributes show up the most? For unique attributes, why do you think the designers felt the game needed them?
- Do a practice brainstorming session to create attributes for some game objects. This could be any objects of your choosing, but here are a few examples to get you started: a cow, a stick, a spaceship, and a banana.
- Start your own attribute bank with the attributes you found in the preceding exercise. Write a short definition of each attribute and how various mechanics may be able to use it in a game. Keep this bank in a place you can easily access from now on and continue to expand it as you come up with more ideas.

CHAPTER 10

ORGANIZING DATA IN SPREADSHEETS

As you create attributes for your game objects, you need to organize and eventually analyze them. The best place to do this is in a spreadsheet. A very small board game may not require the use of a spreadsheet, but even slightly more sophisticated games can almost always benefit from having their data organized and analyzed in a spreadsheet. By following some best practices when creating and using a new workbook, you can make the process of creating game data much less painful. This chapter discusses several of these best practices.

Create a Spreadsheet to Be Read by an Outsider

One of the biggest mistakes that new designers make when they create a new spreadsheet workbook is to dive in headfirst, making large lists of characters, weapons, vehicles, or other objects without thinking about how the spreadsheet will be viewed by others (or even themselves in future). By taking a few moments to plan what you want to do with a spreadsheet and decide how it will be used, you can save many hours later sorting out masses of data that have become a jumbled mess.

One way to know that you are on the right track in making a usable workbook is to think of it from the perspective of an outsider. If you brought on someone new to the team, how would they view the workbook and data it contains? Would they understand what data is in it? Would they understand why the attribute numbers are what they are? By taking the time to organize your data as you go, you can reduce the confusion others experience when they look at the spreadsheet. When someone is seeing your spreadsheet for the first time, you don't want them to see a list of unlabeled names and numbers or, even worse, multiple data tables for different kinds of objects patched together on a single sheet.

Avoid Typing Numbers

When possible, use references in spreadsheets and avoid typing in numbers. For example, let's say that in your current game, there is a gravity setting. Each time you refer to any momentum of a character jumping, or a projectile traveling, or a vehicle moving, it is affected by the gravity setting. Even if the variable for gravity is a simple single-digit number that is easy to remember, you shouldn't type in that number for all the listed calculations. Instead, put the variable in a labeled cell somewhere, such as on a reference sheet (see the section "Reference Sheet," later in this chapter). Then, everywhere that variable is needed, refer to the variable by name. By doing this, you can guarantee that if the number associated with the variable changes, all the equations that use it will be updated automatically. Also, don't fool yourself into thinking that number will never change. Through the process of testing and iterating, pretty much any number in any game may have to change for some reason or another. It's better to be prepared to change it and not need to than to need to change it and not be prepared to.

In addition, avoid doing calculations—even simple ones—in your head. For example, say that you have a goblin who has a strength of 2. You also have an ork, whose strength should be double that of the goblin. It might be tempting to type 4 in as the strength attribute for the ork, but don't do it! Instead, take the extra few seconds to write a reference for the goblin strength attribute and a formula that multiplies goblin strength by 2. If possible, go a step further and create a cell that contains an "Ork to goblin strength multiplier" with the value 2.

Then you can multiply the contents of the multiplier value cell by the goblin strength to arrive at the ork strength. Taking the extra time to use references will ultimately make the process of revising data dramatically faster and less prone to error.

When you do a first pass on data, it is highly unlikely that it will be the final pass. A system designer should expect to revise and iterate data five or more times; revising and iterating over a dozen times is quite common. If you have to go back into your data and find every variable that is affected by new updates, you will face a cascade of numbers becoming out of date, branched, or just plain broken. Therefore, using the extra few steps of references and labeled variables as described above will have some initial investment time, but will save great amounts of time in the revision and iteration process.

Label Data

Figure 10.1 shows a difficult situation you might face when trying to debug a problem. You can see that something is wrong with this formula, but what is it? What is this formula trying to do? What part of the data is it used for? Is this formula actually useful?

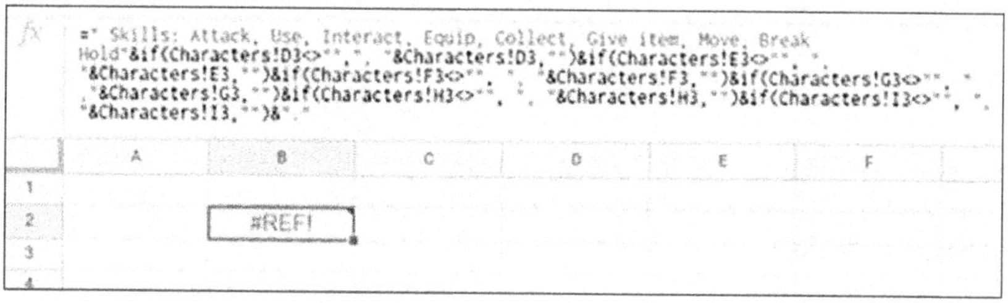

Figure 10.1 A run-on nested function

There are multiple reasons this formula is problematic. First, the cell B2, which holds the problematic formula, is not labeled. It could have been labeled in A2 or C2, or with a note, or even with a comment. The label could have provided much-needed context to help figure out why it is returning a "REF!" error—or at least what it was intended to do in the first place.

Second, there is way too much going on in a single cell. Any one of the many parts of this formula could be the culprit, but it is hard to debug all of them at once. The spreadsheet can only tell you if the formula or function in total is correct; it cannot let you know about individual parts. To debug a giant run-on formula like this, you need to either do a lot of trial and error or break it up into pieces and test each one. By breaking the formula into parts and labeling them, you could make it much easier to debug problems with each of the individual cells. You would then also be able to get better feedback from the spreadsheet to help pin-point the locations of problems.

> **note**
>
> Remember that, if needed, you can always hide intermediary columns or rows and show only the final calculation.

Validate Your Data

As much as you can, validate your data. For example, if you have character names listed in a column, you can validate the data in that column by ensuring that cells accept only text. If you have a column for the strength attribute, you can validate the data in that column by ensuring that it accepts only numbers. Ideally, you should go even further and make sure the strength column accepts only numbers within the range of numbers you have determined work for the strength attribute. If you can equip a character with a named weapon, you can validate that cell with a list built from the names of the weapons. It is incredibly easy to misspell words or to slightly rephrase them in a way that looks correct but that won't work for analyzing the data later. Validating the data in a spreadsheet can help you avoid problems that occur with such errors.

Validation is needed if you are making all the data for a game yourself, and it is even more important if you are working on game data with a group. It is vital that all the people entering data know what is expected in any given cell and that they are limited to inputting only technically acceptable data. While this can't completely eliminate typos and bad data entry, it can help reduce the number of times that entire data sheets need to be reworked or that single mistyped attributes cause the game to crash.

Use Columns for Attributes and Rows for Objects

Figure 10.2 shows a list of attributes for a selection of fantasy creatures. Note that column A contains a list of the creatures, which are the data objects. Each column starting with B lists an individual attribute (abbreviated for the sake of organization in this sheet).

While it is completely possible and mechanically sound to put the data objects in columns and the attributes in rows, it is not advisable to do so. The reason for this is simple tradition. Some time ago, likely in the 1980s, game designers started using computer spreadsheets to keep track of data objects. The intention was to eventually print out those data tables on paper. Most games made in those days had more data objects than they did attributes per data object. It made sense to organize the sheet so that each data object got its own row and could flow down onto multiple portrait-orientation pages, with attributes limited to a page width. This tradition stuck, and since then, it has been common practice to put data objects in rows and attributes in columns, even though modern computers are completely capable of working either way. In addition, as game engines developed to import data objects into a game, they used the existing convention of rows for objects in their importers, cementing this tradition as the "right way" to do it. This means that while there is no technically right way to lay out a spreadsheet, there is a practical right way: with data objects in rows and attributes in columns.

	A	B	C	D	E	F	G	H
1	Character Type	PLR	STR	DEX	HP	AV	D	MV
14	Lizardman	y	3	7	7	2	4	7
15	Ogre	y	8	3	17	5	1	3
16	Ork	y	6	4	10	5	1	5
17	Rat Men	y	2	8	8	2	8	8
18	Wood Elf	y	3	8	8	1	6	6
19	Hellhound	n	5	4	12	3	3	6
20	Werewolf	n	7	5	7	1	1	5
21	Blob	n	7	3	20	7	2	2
22	Giant Ant	n	6	5	10	6	2	5
23	Warg	a	7	4	8	3	3	6
24	Clay Golem	m	7	5	12	6	3	4
25	Swamp Man	m	5	5	25	2	2	4
26	Mummy	u	10	4	20	6	2	2

Figure 10.2 Game data

Color Coding

There is no official color coding method or game industry standard for spreadsheets. Because color coding isn't exported into game engines, it is just something you can use to help organize and visualize your data. Because there is no official standard for color coding, you have to come up with your own rules for color coding.

The most important factor with color coding for a spreadsheet is that it be labeled and consistent. Figure 10.3 shows one example of a color coding scheme, but keep in mind that this is just an example. Many color coding schemes can be effective. As long as you set up a color coding scheme in the early stages of building the workbook and stick to it, yours is likely to work.

	A	B
1		
2	White on Black	Headers
3	Tan	Input data here
4	Green	Formula, DO NOT input data
5	Blue	Sub-label
6	Black on White	Static Text
7		

Figure 10.3 Sample color coding scheme

Figure 10.3 shows a color coding scheme in which only a few colors provide the level of detail needed for most games. Let's look more closely at the scheme used in this example:

- **White on black for headers:** Headers, which usually run along row 1, are the major labels for attributes or categories. White on black is very visually distinct, and it renders well on a black-and-white printer.
- **Tan for input data:** Data input cells are meant to be changed for the purposes of tuning. The data in these cells is always numbers or text and never formulas or functions.
- **Green for formulas:** In this scheme, green cells contain formulas or functions that refer to data in other locations in the workbook, or can do standalone calculations, like NOW(). Typing over data in these cells will break the calculations.
- **Blue for sublabels:** Sublabels are used for minor categories. The names of individual data objects are often color coded blue in column A to help the viewer distinguish the name from the rest of the data.
- **Black on white for static text:** Static data has often been brought in for reference from somewhere else. It should not be changed for tuning or any other purpose. For example, if you needed a list of mountain heights around the world, you could pull in static data. It would not be tan because you can't change it, and it would not be green because it is not formulas.

Figure 10.4 shows this color coding scheme in use. In this example, the color coding makes it possible for a viewer to tell, at a glance, roughly what is happening in the sheet:

- Row 1 is formatted as headers. The first header is for character type, and the rest of the headers are for attributes that govern all the characters in the game.
- The individual character names in column A are color coded as sublabels.
- Next, there is a group of attributes that you can change to balance the data, all colored tan.
- A number of analytical calculations are done on each character to get a weighted balance. Since these formulas are driven by the attributes, they are color-coded green.
- Finally, the column "Loot Cards" was copied from another data source. Although it is not a formula, it should not be changed, so it is coded as static text.

1	Character Type	STR	DEX	HP	AV	D	MV	LVL	XP	Loot Cards	DPT	APT	TTK	DPT VAL	TTK VAL	MV VAL	Total VAL
2	ROUS	3	3	3	1	5	3	0	1	0	0.90	0.5	0.32	1.80	0.39	1.35	21.27
3	Goblin	3	4	5	1	3	5	0	1	1	1.20	0.3	0.62	2.40	0.64	2.25	21.77
4	Zombie	4	2	6	0	0	2	0	1	1	0.80	0	0.60	1.60	0.75	0.90	24.50
5	Dark Wolf	4	4	7	2	3	6	0	2	0	1.60	0.6	0.74	3.20	0.93	2.70	40.99
6	Snapping Turtle	6	4	10	10	2	1	1	2	1	2.40	2	1.25	4.80	1.56	0.45	45.88
7	Barbarian	7	3	13	2	4	5	1	3	1	2.10	0.8	1.41	4.20	1.77	2.25	51.30
8	Dwarf	6	4	13	3	2	4	1	3	1	2.40	0.6	1.38	4.80	1.73	1.80	53.97
9	Gnoll	3	7	8	4	6	6	1	3	1	2.10	2.4	1.05	4.20	1.32	2.70	54.29
10	Halfling	3	7	6	1	8	5	1	3	1	2.10	0.8	0.65	4.20	0.82	2.25	53.59

Figure 10.4 Color coding example

Avoid Adding Unneeded Columns or Rows or Blank Cells

Another best practice is to avoid the temptation to add blank lines, rows, or cells to visually divide information in a table of information. In the example in Figure 10.5, the designer wanted to show a difference between playable creatures and monstrous creatures. To make the distinction, the designer added a blank row and colored it black. This should be avoided for several reasons.

1	Character Type	STR	DEX	HP	AV	D	MV	LVL	XP
14	Lizardman	3	7	7	2	4	7	1	3
15	Ogre	8	3	17	5	1	3	1	3
16	Ork	6	4	10	5	1	5	1	3
17	Rat Men	2	8	8	2	8	8	1	3
18	Wood Elf	3	8	8	1	6	6	1	3
19									
20	Hellhound	5	4	12	3	3	6	2	3
21	Werewolf	7	5	7	1	1	5	2	3
22	Blob	7	3	20	7	2	2	2	3
23	Giant Ant	6	5	10	6	2	5	2	3

Figure 10.5 Unneeded row separator

The first problem with the blank row in this example is that it breaks the computational flow of the spreadsheet. Even if they are blank, those cells are recognized by the spreadsheet. If you try to formfill down a column in this spreadsheet (as described in Chapter 5, "Spreadsheet Basics"), the blank line will halt the operation. If you try to filter a column in the spreadsheet, those rows will be filtered out, making them meaningless. The blank line also throws off visual counts. If we have 20 data objects, the last one should be 20 rows after the header. With a bunch of blanks, the last object will appear in an arbitrary row number. Finally, blank lines don't translate into data. If this sheet were exported into a game, those blanks would mean nothing to the engine and might even cause errors.

To distinguish between playable creatures and monstrous creatures, you should instead use another attribute in its own column, as shown in Figure 10.6.

	A	B	C	D	E	F	G	H	I	J
1	Character Type	PLR	STR	DEX	HP	AV	DI	MV	LVL	XP
14	Lizardman	y	3	7	7	2	4	7	1	3
15	Ogre	y	8	3	17	5	1	3	1	3
16	Ork	y	6	4	10	5	1	5	1	3
17	Rat Men	y	2	8	8	2	8	8	1	3
18	Wood Elf	y	3	8	8	1	6	6	1	3
19	Hellhound	n	5	4	12	3	3	6	2	3
20	Werewolf	n	7	5	7	1	1	5	2	3
21	Blob	n	7	3	20	7	2	2	2	3
22	Giant Ant	n	6	5	10	6	2	5	2	3

Figure 10.6 Adding an attribute column for the type of character

Now, not only is it possible for humans to see that there is a difference between the character types, it is possible for the computer to distinguish playable creatures from monstrous creatures. This setup will allow you to filter based on the PLR attribute if you want, and it will also allow you to export the PLR attribute so that a game engine can use it. In Figure 10.6, you can see that the column labeled PLR is color coded white. This means the data in this column is static and should not be changed for tuning purposes.

Separate Data Objects with Sheets

There is a temptation to mash all the data objects for a game into a single giant sheet so that all the data can be seen and accessed at once. While this is technically possible from the perspective of the spreadsheet, it would make using the data much more difficult. Instead, you should separate the data objects by type. Data objects that have different attributes should go on different sheets. While some differing data objects will share some attributes ("cost of item" is a classic example), if they have significantly different sets of attributes, the data object types should be separated onto different sheets. For instance, weapon and armor data objects should most likely be on separate sheets.

You can use a number of particular type of sheets to separate data objects, as discussed in the sections that follow.

Reference Sheet

In most games, the same variables are used over and over again in many different calculations. The best way to store these variables in a workbook of game data is to put them all into a single reference sheet (often called a *ref sheet*). The ref sheet is a bank of inputs that you plan to use multiple times on multiple sheets. You can also use a ref sheet to store variables needed for a single sheet that would otherwise clutter the sheet.

A ref sheet can contain variables like the following:

- Attribute weights
- Minimum and maximum attribute values
- Conversion numbers, such as game engine units per meter
- An overarching damage multiplier for difficulty adjustment
- Maximum and minimum character counts per level

Figure 10.7 shows a ref sheet that provides notes to help the user understand what a number of acronyms stand for. This ref sheet contains various multipliers, weight scores, and other globally used numbers, as well as descriptions.

	A	B	C	D	E	F	G	H
1								
2	DPT Weight	2.00						
3	TTK Weight	1.25						
4	MV Weight	0.45	Move value weight for calculating character total value					
5	Total Val Weight	6	gets the numbers closer to 100pt scale					
6	Ave DPT	10	Average Damage per turn for doing total character value calculations. 2.4 was original value					
7	LVL Mult	10	Affects how spread out level advancement is					
8	LvL variance	40	normalizing level weights so the difference between levels is larger					

Figure 10.7 Reference sheet

Ref sheets can look different in different situations. The best way to start one is to simply create a blank ref sheet when you create a new workbook for game data. As you work through the game, you may notice that you are typing the same referenced number repeatedly. When you find this happening, you can convert this number from something you manually type to a named variable and store it on the ref sheet.

Introduction Sheet

If a workbook is going to be shared by multiple people, or even if only you will use it, but you anticipate that it will become complex, you might want to use an introduction sheet. An introduction sheet is a sheet to the very beginning of the workbook that is labeled "Instructions" or "StartHere" or "Help." On this sheet, you can show your color coding, explain what each of the sheets is for, and record any instructions needed for use.

Figure 10.8 is an introduction sheet from a workbook made to create and track teams in the game *Blood Bowl*.

Worksheets:	Description and usage:
Roster	The main page of the workbook. It's the roster for your team and is set up to print all needed information for a game. You will need to make a copy of this workbook to make changes and create your own roster
Log	Keep track of your games played. The results are also updated on the Roster sheet
Ledger	When you make purchases for your team, use the ledger to track what you are purchasing
Inducements	If you are playing against a team with a higher rating, go to this page to get inducements (which help you)
Skill Descriptions	Skill descriptions from LRB5. The "improvement" column indicates if a player on your team has that skill, including star players or mercenaries. You can filter by this column and print all skills that are relevant to your team to have as reference during a game
Passing	Chart that shows passing range
Color Code	Reference for how to color code your team positions so everyone knows who is who
Hidden Sheets	Don't change anything on any of these sheets as it is imported from a source document and any changes will break this entire workbook
Notes on usage	General note: Don't type in any cell that is not light tan, like this one. Many cells contain formulas that will break if you type in them. The tan indicates a field that it is expected you will fill out
	Note 2: Many cells have a drop down arrow next to them. Use this! Lots of formulas are based on the exact text entered and all the values in the drop down are accurate. If you type in invalid values, many formulas will break!!!

Figure 10.8 Introduction sheet

This introduction sheet provides instructions for using the workbook as a whole and notes on individual tabs. It is a help sheet in a workbook created for novices, so it is more thorough than would be needed for a workbook used by a professional team.

> note
>
> The instruction sheet in Figure 10.8 provides clear instructions on what new users should be changing and what they should be leaving alone. It is relatively easy to break a spreadsheet, so giving clear instructions to new users is very important.

Output/Visualization Sheets

Once you have made large masses of data objects, you will almost certainly want to analyze the data by using functions and formulas or visualize it by using charts. In general, it's better to create charts on separate sheets than to try to add them on the same sheet as the data in different rows or columns.

In the rather complex example shown in Figure 10.9, the probability of combat outcomes for the game *Blood Bowl* has been calculated using character attributes in conjunction with the rules for combat. This chart illustrates how large and cumbersome data analysis charts can become. Having these kinds of tables on the same sheet as the game data makes both aspects much more difficult to use and much more likely to break. Chapter 15, "Analyzing Game Data," provides much more information on how to handle such analyses. For now, the import takeaway is that you should separate the data from the analysis.

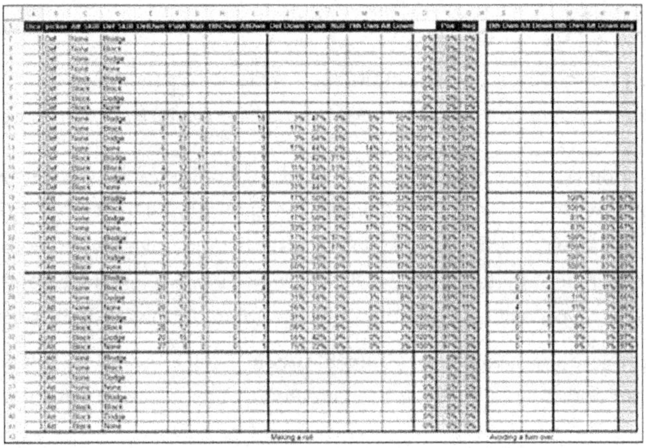

Figure 10.9 Complex analysis

Scratch Sheet

Very commonly while laying out data objects or working in spreadsheets in general, you will need to do quick one-off calculations. To keep your workbook tidy and organized, it's best to confine all those messy bits in a single place. You can create a scratch sheet at the very far right of all the other sheets for such bits. It is okay to delete or overwrite anything on the scratch sheet. If you find that you are using a calculation from the scratch sheet frequently, you should pull it over to the ref sheet or make a new sheet that can act as a permanent container for the information.

Spreadsheet Example

If you follow the best practices described in this chapter, when you create a new workbook, you will ensure that it contains several sheets right from the beginning: help, ref, data, analysis, and scratch sheets. Figure 10.10 shows an example of what this might look like. By starting with a solid structural framework, you set up the flow of data from idea to reality in a cleaner and more organized way.

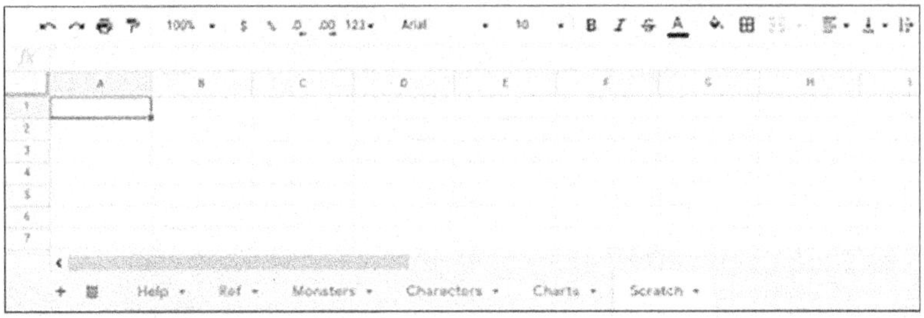

Figure 10.10 Best practice spreadsheet organization

Further Steps

After completing this chapter, you should take some time to practice in the real world with the concepts covered here. Try these exercises to further explore data organization:

- For many modern games, you can find a lot of data online. Take some time to look up the data for your favorite games and see how it is organized. What attributes did the game designers use? In what order are the objects listed? How have the game designers separated out their data object types? By reviewing how others have done this for several different games, you will gain a better understanding of how to do it yourself.
- Create a template spreadsheet for yourself. Create a color coding system and record it in an introduction sheet. Once you have created this template and ensured that it works well, you can use it to create new workbooks and be ensure that they are properly formatted from the start.

CHAPTER 11

ATTRIBUTE NUMBERS

So far in this book, you have created objects and their attributes. You have also created a spreadsheet to organize all your data. The next step in bringing your game ideas to life is to start putting in numbers for all of those attributes.

Getting a Feel for Your Attributes

Before trying to assign numbers to attributes, you should start by getting a feel for what you want to get from those attributes. For example, if you were making a racing game and wanted to create the speeds and acceleration attributes for three different vehicles, you could start with some descriptions of what the speed and acceleration feel should be:

- **Sports car:** Good acceleration and good top speed
- **Muscle car:** Fastest top speed but with less acceleration than a sports car
- **Motorcycle:** Fastest acceleration but lowest top speed

While you have assigned no numbers to these attributes yet, you now have a guide that will help in determining what numbers fit the feel you want.

Determining the Granularity for Numbers

After you come up with attributes for game objects, you need to assign numbers to the attributes. Because you are making up all the attributes and numbers for your game, technically you could use any numbers you want. The granularity of the numbers you use can have a dramatic impact on how a player perceives the game. The following sections provide some to help you determine the granularity of your numbers.

Numbers Should Relate to Probability

Numbers should have a visible impact on the game. The larger the possible outcome of a random event, the larger the corresponding numbers of the game must be. For example, if a character has 10 HP, it doesn't matter if the character receives 11 damage or 5,000 damage, as either one will be a one-hit kill. Say that you know a character is rolling 1D6 (a single six-sided die) for damage, and you always want the character to survive at least three hits. In this case, the minimum hit point value would be 111.

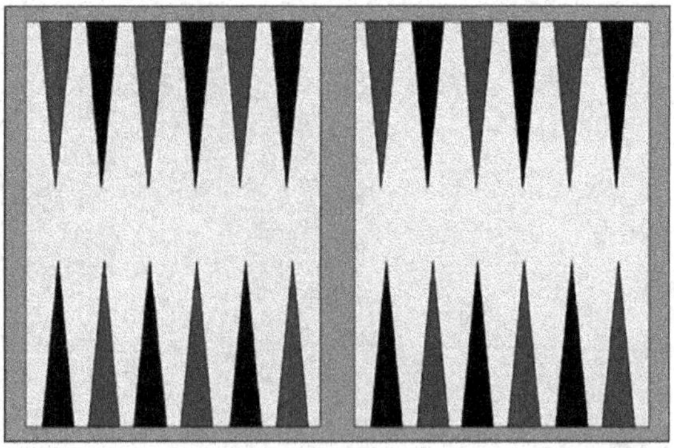

Figure 11.1 Backgammon board

Let's consider backgammon as an example. (Do a search for "official backgammon rules" if you need to familiarize yourself.) In backgammon, the maximum number of moves a piece can take at one time is 24. The maximum is 24 because even the largest roll possible can have a use and not be wasted. In addition, 24 is the number of spaces on the board (see Figure 11.1). The relationships between the number of needed movement spaces and the potential outcomes of the dice are intertwined. If you were to expand the board, you would likely need larger potential rolls to keep the game moving. Conversely, if you were to shrink the board, you would want to reduce the amount of possible movement.

Some Numbers Need to Relate to Real-World Measurements

Some numbers, such as height, weight, and speed, are analogs of the real world. The scale of those numbers has already been decided for you. Even if it is better for your game to use three-digit numbers than to use smaller numbers, you can't decide that every person in your game is going to be measured in hundreds of feet (or meters) in height. Players have incoming knowledge of fixed scales and expect you to play along with the real world. So, if being taller in your game is better, then you will need to adjust your scale. There are a few ways to do this:

- Use a smaller unit of measurement so you get larger numbers.
- Adjust your scale of numbers to fit a fixed attribute.
- Convert the real-world scale to a game scale.

For example, you might list attributes for a basketball player as follows:

Example 1

Strength: 150

Height: 6 (feet)

Speed: 220

Dexterity: 180

This looks odd because the height attribute is a single digit, while the rest of the attributes are triple-digit numbers. In addition to looking odd, this would create the need to use fractions or decimals. Here's another example of attributes for a basketball player:

Example 2

Strength: 150

Height: 182 (centimeters)

Speed: 220

Dexterity: 180

This scale is much better. All the attribute numbers are triple-digit numbers and within a similar range.

Here's another example of attributes for a basketball player:

Example 3

Strength: 50

Height: 72 (inches)

Speed: 73

Dexterity: 60

This scale is also better than the first one. Changing to a more granular measurement of inches and switching all attributes to be two-digit numbers makes them line up nicely.

Now consider this final example of attributes for a basketball player:

Example 4

Strength: 150

Height: 165 (game units)

Speed: 220

Dexterity: 180

This scale also works because you have ditched reality and made your own scale that enables the attributes to all be three-digit numbers in a similar range. Making up your own units may lead to a bit of confusion as a player won't initially know how to picture a height of 165 game units, but you can overcome this difficulty with art.

User Smaller Numbers for Easier Calculations

A player needs clear numbers for each individual calculation and for repeated calculations. If you are asking players to do calculations in their head in the game, then you need to limit the complexity of the numbers. Further, if you are asking players to do many calculations or frequently recurring calculations, you need to further restrict the complexity of those calculations. It is easiest for players to process simple numbers—that is, small whole numbers.

In very old games, attribute numbers are all very small. The number of pieces a player has, the faces of the dice, and total points for a game tend to be no more than two digits. Often they are single digits. Old games use small whole numbers to make the numbers easier for players to remember and use in calculations in their heads. The more frequently a player is required to do calculations, the simpler the calculations tend to be and the smaller the numbers involved are.

Think again about backgammon, for example. Players need to be able to calculate rolls and results in their heads, and complex systems of multiplication or addition would cause unneeded confusion. For each turn in backgammon, a player rolls 2D6 to determine how much movement their pieces get for that turn. A player gets double that movement with a roll of doubles. (Rolling double 6s, for example, allows the player to move a total of 24 spaces.) On every turn, the player uses the individual rolls of the dice, or adds together the rolls of two six-sided dice, and turns go by in a matter of seconds. Fortunately, adding together the rolls of two six-sided dice is a very easy calculation and does not slow the pace of the game. In addition, the results are all small numbers. The results also tie into the physical space of the game. The board contains only 24 spaces, so any more movement than that would be useless.

Let's now consider scoring in the game spades. Spades has a rather sophisticated scoring system, where players guess their score at the beginning of the game and then, at the end of the game, compare their final results to their initial guess. They then use a scoring system to interpret their results and calculate the final score. This is a somewhat complex calculation, and players often use paper or a calculator to do the scoring—but it is only done once during a game. The numeric results are also much larger than in backgammon, with scores in the hundreds or even up over 1,000. Because this calculation occurs only once a game, it's an event and can even build some tension as a game is calculated, but if it were done every turn, it would completely bog down the game.

Early and even many modern tabletop games and pen-and-paper RPGs continue to use attribute numbers in the single digits and low double digits. For example, a sample fifth edition Dungeons & Dragons character could start with the following attribute scores:

STR 10 DEX 13 CON 14 WIS 19 CHA 14

Note that all of these numbers are in the low two-digit range. Also, while this is a modern, fairly sophisticated game, it is working under the same limitations as backgammon in that the players are needing to do calculations in their head. Whereas in backgammon, players do calculations every few seconds, in an RPG they do calculations every few minutes.

As you can see from these examples, the less frequently calculations are made, the more complex they can be and the larger the numbers involved can be. When assigning numbers to attributes, you should think about how much calculation you expect your players to do in their heads. The more calculations, the smaller the numbers should be for attributes. The more frequent the calculations, the smaller and simpler the calculation and numbers must be.

Use Larger Numbers for More Granularity

If small numbers are easier for players to understand, why not use single-digit numbers for everything? Small numbers do not allow for much granularity or variety. Say that you are assigning strength to five fantasy characters. These are the five characters, and the feeling you want to convey through the strength attribute for each of them:

- **Human:** Middle-of-the-road guy
- **Ogre:** Much stronger than anyone else

- **Ork:** Stronger than humans but significantly weaker than ogres
- **Goblin:** Weakest by far, but not so weak that they can be ignored
- **Dwarf:** Stronger than humans but notably weaker than orks

Here's how you might turn these feelings into numbers if you want to constrain the numbers to 10 and below:

- **Human:** Middle of the road leads you to choose the halfway point, which is 5.
- **Ogre:** Because this is the strongest character, it is 10. Note that there is no longer room on the scale for stronger characters like dragons or giants. While this might be fine within the scope of your game, it does limit your ability to expand the game.
- **Ork:** You might assign an ork a strength of 7 because an ork is much weaker than an ogre but is not that much stronger than a human.
- **Goblin:** A goblin is the weakest character, so you assign it 2, but 2 might be too weak.
- **Dwarf:** You are now stuck. If you assigned a dwarf 6, then this character would be stronger than a human but not notably weaker than an ork.

As you can see, even with just five characters and a few criteria, you start running out of space in the scale to properly translate your feelings about character strengths into numbers. As you add more characters and more criteria, the scale will get even more crowded, and characters will start to feel too similar. To fix this, it is tempting to make all the values considerably larger, allowing more granularity to work with.

Very Large Numbers Are Confusing

Given the problems discussed so far with small numbers, it might seem like a good idea to go to the opposite extreme in a computer game. If you were to use four- or five-digit numbers, you would have plenty of space to make a large variety without ever crowding your range. Further, given that the computer will be doing all the calculations, you don't need to worry about players doing lots of math on big numbers, as they would need to do with a board game. But calculations are not limited to just what a player must do to make the game progress; they also tie in to how well the player can understand what is going on in the game. We humans are, in general, not designed to calculate large numbers in our heads. For example, try to calculate the final hit point score for each of the following scenarios in your head:

- 5 hit points, taking 2 points of damage
- 100 hit points, taking 27 points of damage
- 34863298 hit points, taking 456321 points of damage

It's clear that the smaller the numbers, the easier the calculations.

The takeaway is that you need to find the right amount of granularity for your game. In general, you want to use numbers that are just large enough to accommodate all needed variety but no larger than absolutely necessary.

Humans Hate Decimals and Fractions, but Computers Don't Mind Them

It is exceedingly rare, outside of educational math games, to ever show a player a decimal score or a fraction. It's not that they aren't valid numbers, but people just don't like seeing or (worse) calculating them. Games typically show players only whole numbers.

However, behind the scenes, computers have absolutely no problem calculating decimals. This means you can feel free to use as many decimal places as you want for computer calculations as long as you can present whole (rounded) numbers to the player in a way that is not confusing.

Numbering Example

Figure 11.2 provides an example in which each column presents a pair of values: one for Attribute A and one for Attribute B. In each pair, the ratio of A to B is the same: 94%. Because each pair has the same ratio, for a computer, they would all work exactly the same way. However, players would be able to comprehend some of these numbers easily and others with great difficulty. If the players are going to see the numbers, you should use just the two-digit numbers, if possible, or the three-digit ones.

Attribute A	1.230769231	16	160	4592
Attribute B	1.307692308	17	170	4879
Ratio	94%	94%	94%	94%

Figure 11.2 Number granularity example

The Tension Trick

There is a trick that systems designers can use to cause a wide variation of tension in a game by manipulating a few related numbers. The basic rules for tension are as follows:

- Using numbers that are not easy to calculate creates dissonance for players.
- Dissonance creates tension, fear, and other heightened negative emotions.

- These emotions can heighten an experience, if used properly.
- Using numbers that are easy to calculate creates calmness for players.
- Use easy-to-calculate numbers to give the players a calm, easygoing experience and use numbers that are difficult to calculate to cause more heightened emotions.

For example, say that a player character (PC) has 20 HP, and an enemy character should kill the PC in 4 hits. You could assign these numbers for the least tension:

> Enemy does 5 damage per hit, so the PC is at 5 HP after 3 hits and at 0 HP after 4 hits.

You could assign these numbers for the most tension:

> Enemy does 6 damage per hit, so the PC is at 2 HP after 3 hits and at 0 HP after 4 hits.

In both of these cases, the PC is alive after 3 hits and killed on the fourth, so functionally they are the same. But they can feel very different to a player. Why?

Let's look at it graphically and then break it down further. Imagine that the PC has taken 3 hits. Figure 11.3 shows two options for the health bar for the PC at this point.

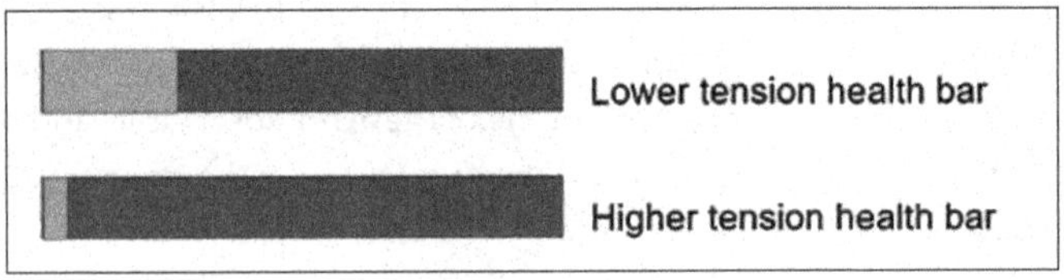

Figure 11.3 Lower- and higher-tension health bars

In both cases, the PC will be killed with the next shot, but which one looks scarier? Players know that more red on a health bar is generally a bad thing. The fact that the lower of the two bars is more red signals to the player, subconsciously, more danger, even though numerically the danger is identical with the two health bars.

Let's look at another example. Say that, in a farming game, the player plants a field that is 20 square meters in 1-square-meter units, so there are 20 total spaces in which to plant. The player has the following resources:

> 5 corn
>
> 10 beans
>
> 5 wheat
>
> 10 rice

In this example, it is fairly easy for a player to calculate the division of crops to plant. All the numbers are easy to grasp and can easily fit in 20, which is also the total number of squares.

Young or inexperienced players should be able to quickly figure out what to do in this scenario, with little stress.

To increase the tension in the same farming game, you can change the units to something more difficult to grasp and also change the amounts to numbers that are more difficult to calculate. This time, say that the player has 2.5 acres to plant and plants in units of 100 square yards. This alone makes the calculations much more difficult for anyone who is not already familiar with converting square yards into acres. In this case, the player would have 121 things to plant. The player has the following resources:

37 corn

63 beans

58 wheat

29 rice

In this revised example, it is very difficult for the player to do the planting calculations in their head. This difficulty will cause a sense of stress and tension. In an action game, this can heighten the player's experience, but in a farming game, it might create stress in what should be a relaxing activity.

There are no universal right or wrong answers about inducing tension in a game through use of numbers, but there are situational rights and wrongs based on the feeling you want the player to have at any given time.

Searching for the Right Numbers

Once you decide on the granularity of the numbers you are going to use, it's time to start plugging in numbers. If you have already described the feel you want with the numbers and determined the number of digits and ratio you want to use, you can do a rough pass immediately.

Keep in mind when doing a first pass at data numbers that they will almost certainly not be what you end up with. This is okay and to be expected. Until a game is tested, it is impossible to know the exact effect numbers will have on the game. Don't think of this as failure; instead realize that you can take the pressure off the first pass. If you approach the first pass knowing that the numbers will be wrong, you don't have the stress of trying to guess right the first time. Instead, you can just get some numbers in there. Use the targeted number of digits and rough ratios for each object and just plug them in.

Let's go back to our racing game example from the beginning of the chapter. Say that you want to make a very simple, new-audience-friendly game, so you want to stick to single-digit numbers. This is what you came up with earlier for what the speed and acceleration should be:

- **Sports car:** Good acceleration and good top speed
- **Muscle car:** Fastest top speed but with less acceleration than a sports car
- **Motorcycle:** Fastest acceleration but lowest top speed

Based on this list and the fact that you want to use single-digit numbers, you might assign the numbers shown in Table 11.1. Are these numbers right? Almost certainly not. But they're a start.

Table 11.1 Basic data table

Car	Acceleration	Top Speed
Sports car	8	8
Muscle car	6	10
Motorcycle	10	6

When testing numbers, it's a good idea to go beyond reasonable, expected numbers. To find the extents of a range, you must exceed those extents during testing. You want to try making something with too much acceleration or a speed that's too low; for example, you might experiment with your numbers as shown in Table 11.2.

Table 11.2 Experimental data

Car	Acceleration	Top Speed
Sports car	8	8
Muscle car	1	15
Motorcycle	200	10

These numbers are undoubtedly wrong—and, again, that's fine and expected. You are not trying to get the numbers right at this point. Instead, you are trying to understand your game and game engine. Can the engine handle an acceleration of 200? Does this number cause the game to crash? Does collision still work? By testing unreasonable numbers, you can understand the game and engine better, which will make it more likely that you will find interesting and exciting new results.

The great news is that with game data, there is nothing you can do in testing that can't be undone. You can use this aspect of game making to your advantage for wild and interesting tests. Once you have broken the game in interesting ways and understand the mechanical workings better, it's time to home in on the balance you truly want.

The next step is to test and test and test—and then tune and test more and then do more tuning and testing. On this first round of testing, the goal is to get the numbers to emulate what you wrote in your original list of what you feel you want from the numbers. Does that motorcycle feel like it has great acceleration? Does the sports car feel like it has slower acceleration but can eventually top out at the highest speed? Eventually you will find the right balance with the numbers.

Further Steps

After completing this chapter, you should take some time to practice in the real world with the concepts covered here. Try these exercises to further explore the numbers that populate game data:

- Look online for data for your favorite games—in a variety of genres—and analyze the scales used in those games. Take note of the kinds of numbers used for each game and how the games compare with each other in terms of the numbers.
- Take the preceding exercise a step further and redo the values for each of the games by changing their values proportionally. Try doubling them, or multiplying by 10, or multiplying by 0.1 Describe how the feel of the game changes when you change the scale of the data numbers.

CHAPTER 12

SYSTEM DESIGN FOUNDATIONS

Once you have decided on the attributes you want to quantify and the scale of numbers you would like to use, it's time to look at more factors in creating a mass amount of data objects. In the next steps, you learn how attributes of different quality get different numbers and how to properly name all the data objects you create.

After you have assigned numbers to every attribute, it is a good idea to add them all up so you can compare the different data objects against each other. By getting a total score, you can start to get some insights into the balance of all the data objects in comparison with each other.

Attribute Weights

This section shows how to find attribute weights for the racing example from Chapter 11, "Attribute Numbers." Table 12.1 shows how you would get a total score for each car, based on its attributes (refer to Table 11.1).

Table 12.1 Adding the attributes for each car

Car	Acceleration	Top Speed	Total Value
Sports car	8	8	16
Muscle car	6	10	16
Motorcycle	10	6	16

Now, you need to test these numbers in a game. For this example, you would race all three cars several times and find out which one wins most often and by what margin. Let's say that in this testing, the muscle car wins every race by a significant margin. You are now seemingly stuck: The data is clearly not balanced if one car is winning every time. But if you lower either attribute value for the muscle car, its total won't be as high as the totals for the other two cars, so you will no longer be able to compare them in the spreadsheet.

This kind of situation happens with game data all the time. It's actually fairly rare for attributes to add up across balanced game objects to be the same. It often turns out that one attribute is simply more important in the context of the game than others are. In the case of our racing example, the more important attribute appears to be top speed.

If we add one more attribute to our cars, we can get an even better idea of how badly skewed raw attribute numbers can be. Table 12.2 shows an additional attribute, horn sound, and one more car.

Table 12.2 An additional car and an additional attribute

Car	Acceleration	Top Speed	Horn Sound	Total Value
Sports car	8	8	4	20
Muscle car	6	10	4	20
Motorcycle	10	6	4	20
Clunker	1	1	30	32

If you simply look at the total raw scores for the car, it seems like the clunker is far and away the best vehicle. However, when you look at the attributes in the context of what they do in the game, you see a very different picture. This is a racing game, so the loudness of the horn is not important to the game, even if it is an attribute you can control. The problem is that attribute value is throwing off the total value of each car.

The solution to this problem is to use attribute weights. An *attribute weight* is a multiplier you apply to each attribute that compensates for some attributes being more important than others. When setting up the data at first, using 1.0 is a nice neutral starting point. It indicates that all attributes are equally important and lets you get through the data entry process more quickly. When you begin testing, you are likely to find that the attributes are not of equal value, and they need to be modified with weights. In the racing example, testing shows you that top speed is more important than acceleration, and horn loudness is not very important at all. You can use these observations to inform your first pass with weights, which might look something like this:

- **Acceleration:** 1.0 (Neutral. Not very important but not unimportant.)
- **Top speed:** 1.5 (Top speed is therefore 150% as important as acceleration.)
- **Horn sound:** 0.0 (This essentially removes horn sound from the total value equation since it is not an important factor for the game.)

You can now recalculate the weighted total for each car, as shown in Table 12.3.

Table 12.3 Weighted attributes

Car	**Acc**	**Speed**	**Horn**	**Acc**	**Speed**	**Horn**	**Total Value**
Weights	*1.0*	*1.5*	*0.0*	*Weighted*	*Weighted*	*Weighted*	
Sports car	8	8	4	8	12	0	20
Muscle car	6	10	4	6	15	0	21
Motorcycle	10	6	4	10	9	0	19
Clunker	1	1	30	1	1.5	0	1.5

With the new weights applied, the total value looks a lot more like the test results you see in the actual game. The muscle car always wins because it has a better total real value in game. The goal of the weights should be to represent the effect of each attribute in the game as realistically as possible.

The next step is to go back to the data and adjust it so that each car has the same total weighted value while retaining its own unique character. Given these goals, you can adjust the attributes on the other vehicles as shown in Table 12.4 to make them feel different from each other, hit your intended goals for the feel of the game, and use balance attribute weights.

Table 12.4 Modified attributes

Car	Acc	Speed	Horn	Acc	Speed	Horn	Total Value
Weights	*1.0*	*1.5*	*0.0*	*Weighted*	*Weighted*	*Weighted*	
Sports car	8	8	4	8	12	0	20
Muscle car	5	10	4	5	15	0	20
Motorcycle	11	6	4	11	9	0	20
Clunker	1	1	30	1	1.5	0	1.5

With these new numbers, it appears as though you have reached all your goals—but there is only one way to find out. After doing a balancing pass with weights, you need to go back and test the feel of the game. If the game now feels more balanced, you can conduct some specific tests to find out how many times each car wins and by what margin. When you have that information, you can be more confident that your game is more balanced, and you will be able to add new objects to your spreadsheet and quickly get them into balance before ever actually placing them in the game.

One more factor we need to look at here is that the clunker is still way out of balance. This type of imbalance is not always a bad thing or something that needs to be fixed. This might be a joke car that was placed in the game, or it could be a punishment for a player who wrecks a car too often that will set up the player for almost certain failure. It could even be a challenge car that a very good player might pick to show that, even with the quantifiably worst vehicle in the game, they can still win. These are just some of the valid reasons to have data objects that are well out of balance. It is just as important that you know they are out of balance and by how much.

It is important to note that weighting can require some counterintuitive thought. In Table 12.4, you can see that speed is weighted 1.5 and acceleration is weighted 1.0, which means that speed is more important than acceleration in this game. It also means that the raw numbers for speed are likely to be smaller in total than the raw numbers for acceleration.

Let's consider a more extreme example. Say that you are making an archery game where each archer has the attributes power and accuracy. Because a missed shot does no damage, you have determined that accuracy is twice as valuable as power. In this case, your attributes would get the following weights:

- **Accuracy:** 2.0
- **Power:** 1.0

This means two equal archers would have raw attribute numbers where the power attribute is higher than accuracy in most cases. It's only once the weight is applied to the raw values that you can see which of the players is the better archer. For example, look at Table 12.5.

Table 12.5 Archer attributes

Archer	Power	Accuracy
Archer 1	10	10
Archer 2	20	5

At a glance, if you don't know the weights, Archer 2, who would have a higher total attribute summed score, looks like the overall better archer. But when you apply the weights, you can see that the two archers are, in fact, balanced (see Table 12.6).

Table 12.6 Weighted archer attributes

Archers	Power	Accuracy	Power	Speed	Total Value
Weights	*1.0*	*2.0*	*Weighted*	*Weighted*	
Archer 1	10	10	10	20	30
Archer 2	20	5	20	10	30

Be patient when searching for proper weights. It can take dozens of tests—or more—in varying circumstances with multiple playtesters to determine the proper final weights to apply to your attributes. While this process should start very early in the production of data objects, it's likely that it will continue throughout production and almost up to the end.

DPS and Intertwined Attributes

Very often, a single attribute tells only part of the story of the in-game interaction. The most common example of this is damage per second (DPS), where a series of characters have both a damage attribute and an attack rate attribute. Each of these has its own scale, with a minimum and a maximum. However, looking at only one part of the pair—that is, looking at only damage or only attack rate—does not explain accurately how powerful the character is. For example, say that you have a pair of weapons—a dagger and a battle axe—which have the damage scores shown in Table 12.7.

Table 12.7 Weapon damage scores

Weapon	Damage
Dagger	6
Battle axe	14

Which one of these weapons does more damage? Without any other context, the answer is fairly clearly the battle axe, but let's look a little deeper. Table 12.8 shows how often each weapon can attack in a minute.

Table 12.8 Weapon damage per minute

Weapon	Damage	Attacks per Minute
Dagger	6	17
Battle axe	14	7

Now which weapon do you think does more damage? While individual hit damage has not changed, the total accumulation of damage output has changed considerably. Instead of asking how much damage each weapon does, it would be more helpful to consider how much damage each weapon does in a single minute. When you take into consideration both the amount of damage done and the frequency at which damage is done, you can get a much clearer idea of which weapon does more damage in a practical setting in the game. Because video game combat goes fast—usually in seconds rather than in minutes—we commonly express this value as DPS (damage per second).

But how do you determine DPS for two weapons that can't attack every second? To do this, you need to take an intermediate step and calculate using a scale at which both weapons can do damage multiple times. For this example, we can use minutes, but any amount of time will work, as long as it's enough for both data objects to have multiple attacks. To get the value, you need to multiply the damage of each shot by the frequency:

$$\text{Weapon damage} \times \text{Attacks per minute} = \text{Damage per minute}$$

Table 12.9 shows the results for the dagger and battle axe example.

Table 12.9 Damage per minute calculation

Weapon	Damage	Attacks per Minute	Damage per Minute
Dagger	6	17	102
Battle axe	14	7	98

You can now clearly see that the dagger does slightly more damage over time. To translate damage per minute to DPS, you divide the damage per minute value by 60, using this formula:

$$(\text{Weapon damage} \times \text{Attacks per minute} = \text{Damage per minute})/60$$

Table 12.10 shows the results for the dagger and battle axe example.

Table 12.10 DPS values

Weapon	Damage	Attacks per Minute	DPS
Dagger	6	17	1.7
Battle axe	14	7	1.6

With this calculation, you can now compare two weapons meaningfully, and in Table 12.10, you can see that over time the dagger will do slightly more damage than the battle axe. Note that the final DPS value has a decimal portion, so it is likely going to be used only for internal evaluation. If you wanted to represent this to players, it might be better to leave it as damage per minute or show it graphically as a bar chart.

The calculation becomes slightly more complicated when the frequency is measured in delay, as opposed to attacks per time. For example, for the dagger and battle axe, you might have a cooldown delay between attacks. To convert a cooldown into a per time measurement, you divide 60 seconds by the cooldown to determine how many times the cooldown can trigger in a minute. For example, a 3-second cooldown would be 60/3 = 20 attacks per minute.

While DPS is the most common intertwined set of attributes used in games, it's far from the only one. The good news is that any given set of intertwined attributes can be treated in the same way as DPS for the sake of comparison. Let's look at one more example that at first seems to be quite different. Say that you have forklifts that can carry pallets. In this game, quickly moving pallets is advantageous, so you want a forklift that can carry a lot of pallets. The other part of the equation is how many trips the forklift can take in a minute. The more trips, the better. Table 12.11 summarizes the capabilities of two forklifts.

Table 12.11 Forklifts

Forklift	Pallet Capacity	Trip Duration, in Seconds
Speedy	5	20
Big Brutus	9	30

Which forklift is the better one in terms of this game mechanic? To compare the two, you need to first calculate how many trips per minute each can make:

Speedy: 60/20 = 3

Big Brutus: 60/30 = 2

These are now your trips per minute scores. Next, you need to multiply the capacity by the trips per minute to get a total pallets per minute score. This gives you a final comparison that looks like what is shown in Table 12.12.

Table 12.12 Compared attributes

Forklift	Pallet Capacity	Trip Duration, in Seconds	Pallets per Minute
Speedy	5	20	15
Big Brutus	9	30	18

In this case, Big Brutus is the better of the two forklifts over the long run.

When using intertwined attributes, you often use the final DPS comparison score to evaluate weight in the total comparison of data objects instead of the individual attributes.

Binary Searching

Binary searching is a mathematical method of searching that enables someone to find an exact unknown number in the fewest possible guesses. Why is this important to you as a game system designer? You are constantly trying to find the right numbers for your data objects. By using binary searching, you can home in on the number you need more quickly, saving valuable time when creating large amounts of data.

How Binary Searching Works

The way binary searching works is slightly unintuitive, but once you understand how it works, it becomes simple and fast to use. To perform a binary search, you need just a few pieces of information:

- **Range of viable numbers:** For a strict binary search, you need to know the largest and smallest possible numbers that could be correct. There are workarounds for this, as discussed later in this chapter, but they don't fit the strict definition of binary searching.
- **Feedback response:** This lets you know if your current number is too high or too low. Without knowing this, you really are flying blind. But if you can at least get this one clue, binary searching can work.

Let's consider a basic example of a higher/lower guessing game. This guessing game starts with someone saying, "I'm thinking of a number between 1 and 100. Guess a number, and I will tell you if the actual number is higher or lower." This game is the basis for all binary searches, and there is a "correct" answer to this opening question: In this case, the correct answer is 50. Why is this the correct answer? This is where the method becomes slightly unintuitive. The goal for the guess is not actually to find the right answer. The odds of doing that on the first try are 1%, which are far too low to use this as a viable method. Instead, the goal is to eliminate as many wrong answers as possible. To see why there is a correct answer, let's look at two scenarios involving the same guessing game:

- **Scenario 1:** You are trying to guess the right number, so you guess a favorite (or maybe random): 88. The response to this guess is "lower." From this, you can deduce that no number in the range 88–100 is the correct answer. So you have eliminated 13 of 100 options, leaving a possible 87. Using a random guess method, you have no idea how many options you might eliminate and, therefore, how many options will be left. The goal of the game is to get the list of options down to 1—or as few as possible—so you can guess correctly. The fewer options left in the list, the higher the probability that the next guess will be correct.
- **Scenario 2:** Instead of guessing a random or arbitrary number, you can divide the total possible pool by 2, which means you guess 50. This way, if the answer comes back as "higher," you have eliminated 50 options. If the answer comes back "lower," you have also eliminated 50 options. By always guessing exactly in the middle of the remaining options, you can always guarantee that you will eliminate 50% of the incorrect options. You also might get lucky and guess correctly, which would save even more time, but that is not the goal.

By using the method described in Scenario 2, you can tackle even very large numbers of options with very few guesses. Let's take the above example to its conclusion:

Range: 1–100

Guess 1: 50

Response: Lower

New range: 1–49

Guess 2: 25

Response: Higher

New range: 26–49 (where the halfway point is 36.5, which is not a whole number)

Guess 3: 36 (though 37 would also be a valid choice here)

Response: lower

New range: 26–36

Guess 4: 31

Response: Higher

New range: 32–35 (where the halfway point is 33.5, which is not a whole number)

Guess 5: 33 (though 34 would also be a valid choice)

Response: Higher

New range: 34 and 35

Guess 6: 35 (though at this point you can guess either and know that there is only one more option)

Response: Lower

Guess 7: 34

In this example, out of 100 possibilities, where no guesses were lucky enough to be correct, it was possible to find the exact answer in seven guesses. This is the maximum number of guesses possible for this range using a binary search. Using this method is dramatically faster, on average, than guessing arbitrary numbers in the range, and it saves over 90% of time needed to guess through the possibilities. If you apply binary searching everywhere you possibly can in a game, you are likely to find the answer you need in as little as one-tenth the amount of time it would take to guess the right answer.

Table 12.13 shows the range of possible guesses and the maximum number of guesses needed for that range when using a binary search.

Table 12.13 Binary searching guesses for various ranges

Options	Maximum Guesses
1	1
2	2
4	3
8	4
16	5
32	6
64	7
128	8
256	9
512	10
1,024	11

You can see in Table 12.13 that adding twice as many options to the range increases the number of guesses needed by only 1. The more options there are to guess from, the more powerful the binary search method becomes.

How does binary searching apply to system designers? You actually play the higher/lower game at work all the time When tuning data numbers, you are constantly guessing what data numbers are right for each attribute given to the data objects. The higher/lower feedback you get comes from the feel of the changes in testing.

Binary Searching Example: Boss Fight

Let's say you are designing a boss character for a difficult fight that is going to take place in a game. You know what hit points the player character has and how much damage the player character can do. This gives you a frame of reference for how difficult to make the boss character. You also know how often you want players to fail at the fight. This provides the frame of reference for whether you have guessed too high or too low. So you can guess a range of total hit points that you might want the boss to have, from a minimum you would safely know is too weak to a maximum you can safely know is way too much. Then you apply the binary search method to make a guess and test. If players are beating the boss too often, this equates to the response "higher." If the players are losing more often than you want them to, you have received the feedback "lower."

Binary Searching Example: Jump Distance

One of the most classic mechanics in platformer games is having the player character jump over a pit to get to the other side. If player characters are easily able to jump the pit each attempt, the pit loses its challenge and becomes a chore; on the other hand, if the player characters are not able to clear the pit in a jump, the game becomes impossible to complete and breaks testing. The difficulty in this case shows you the range. The minimum is the smallest amount of jump distance needed to clear the pit by only a pixel. The maximum is the jump distance that so easily clears the pit that players fail to see any challenge in the obstacle. With this range, you can again apply a binary search and find the exact amount of jump distance that allows players to feel challenged by jumping over the pit without being frustrated by it.

Lacking a Viable Range

For a true binary search, you need to have the exact minimum, exact maximum, and accurate higher/lower feedback. However, you don't always get all these factors when trying to find the right numbers for data, but you can still apply the principles of binary searching to situations where you have very little information. If you don't know the minimum or maximum of a range, you can still test for the feeling of too much or too little, and you can use the rule "double it or halve it."

For example, say that you are working with brand-new game data, and nothing has been tuned yet, so you don't have a point of reference for determining a range that is too low or too high. You have an archer that you want to be able to shoot targets from far away—but what does "far away" mean? You have no idea to start with, but you do have an attribute variable called shot momentum that tells the physics engine how much momentum to apply to the arrow when the bow is fired. At this point, you would want to dig for any possible clues to what a good range might be. How big are the levels? How far away are enemy targets? You might or might not have answers to these questions, but for the sake of making the challenge more difficult, let's say you have none of this information at all.

To solve this challenging problem, you can start by making a very quick test level in the game engine with a single archer and a single target. Take some time walking the character up to the target and then further away. How far away feels like a practical distance? All modern game engines have methods for measuring game distance, and you can feel out the possible distances and make notes about them. At some point, the target will be too far away to render onscreen, and that is likely too far. Take the extra time to work out the variables that are available to try to find some kind of range. When you know that range—or at least have a guess—you can move on to shooting at the target.

Because in this case you have no idea what your units of "shot momentum" actually mean to the game engine, you have to take a completely wild guess. Say that you guess 100, knowing you will certainly be far off, and then try it out to see what happens. In this example, imagine that you put in the value 100 and take a shot, but the arrow barely goes a meter. Now, you have some information to work with, and you double the shot momentum to 200 and test again. This time the shot goes further, but it is still too short. You double again to 400. This time the shot flies out of the game world. Congratulations! You have found your range and can now use a binary search between the known too-low value 200 and the known too-high value 400.

Taking the other possible branch in this example, you can put in the value 100. The arrow flies out of the world, far into the distance. For your next guess, you cut the value in half, to 50, and try again. Again, the arrow flies out of the world. Next, you cut the value in half again, to 25, and repeat. By doing this task repeatedly, it is entirely possible that you will find that the shot momentum was intended to be a decimal number, and your actual range might end up being 0.01 to 0.2.

Both of these very nebulous scenarios show how to use binary searching when you don't know the top and bottom bounds to quickly home in on an appropriate range of values. As long as it is possible to test to see if a value is too large or too small, you can use binary searching to quickly determine what numbers will fit in your attribute range.

Naming Conventions

When making even moderately complex games, you will generate numerous game objects—and which could easily get into the hundreds and possibly into the thousands. One of the most basic requirements of any game object is that it needs a name. Coming up with hundreds or thousands of names for objects can be a tedious task if you don't have a standardized convention. Even more complex is tracking down and then working with a specific object that you have previously created that is floating in the sea of game objects. Even more challenging than that is finding and working with a specific object that someone else on the team has made. Try to imagine sifting through hundreds of objects that are numbered or named gibberish to try to find the one you are working on. It sounds awful—and it is awful. Now imagine doing this dozens of times a day, every day, for several months or even years. If you don't have a good naming convention, this task becomes miserable and dramatically slows down work on the game.

You know what the problem is, but what is the solution? In the end, the most important thing about naming is to have one naming convention—and only one—for the team. There are many ways to name game objects, and many conventions can work. The important fact is that the entire team needs to agree to the rules of the naming convention it uses.

Let's look at a naming convention that is data designer centric. It is made to help a data designer, who is usually the person most often modifying the data objects, find what they need quickly and keep the entire group of objects organized. To understand the system, first let's talk about the English language a bit. English is inherently ambiguous in the way it describes objects. Let's start a sentence in English as an example:

> My game object is a big...

This is the start of a description, but it is not enough to give someone an idea what the object is. Let's add another more:

> My game object is a big, fast...

This is still not enough for someone to know what the object is; it could be any of millions of different things. Let's add another word:

> My game object is a big, fast, blue...

We are now three words into the description of the game object, and although we're narrowing down the range of possibilities, it's still impossible to know what the object is. One final word clears it all up:

> My game object is a big, fast, blue narwhal (see Figure 12.1).

Aha! Four words into the description, and we finally have it: We are talking about a narwhal. The English description "big, fast, blue narwhal" does allow someone to picture what the object is, but it would not work well as a name in data design. Given that files automatically sort alphabetically on a computer, and most databases sort alphabetically by default, this name would sort by the first adjective, instead of by what the object is. Therefore, a basic English description like this won't work very well as a name in a game.

In a very large collection of game objects, you would usually want to start names with a parent category. For example, you might start with the category sea mammals or, if you were playing the game as a narwhal, character. It is common to shorten the category name to a few letters for the sake of brevity and easier reading. If all category names are three letters long, for instance, then everyone knows that the object name starts at the fourth character. For this example, say that you are going to be playing as a narwhal, and you want to use the category prefix Cha (for character).

Figure 12.1 A narwhal

The following are some of the game object categories that are commonly used in games:

- **Cha:** Character, for playable characters
- **Npc:** Nonplayer friendly characters
- **Bad:** Enemy characters
- **Pow:** Power-ups, or useful boost items
- **Wep:** Weapon items
- **Amr:** Armor item (Note that this category name is Amr, not Arm, because *arm* is already a real word with a meaning.)
- **Vhc:** Vehicles

One of the first jobs of a system designer to create game objects is to create and maintain the names and definitions of object categories. Any lengths or convention will work, but for ease of reading, try to keep names fairly short and easy to understand. In creating a naming system, you want to find a good balance between getting very specific (with too many categories) and being too vague (and lumping together too many objects).

If your naming convention is for a large game with thousands of objects, you might follow the category with the subcategory. In this case, let's assume the game is smaller and follow the category abbreviation with a noun that describes the game object. If the object is a narwhal, its name might therefore look like this:

ChaNarwhal

or

Cha_Narwhal

These two naming methods—using CamelCase and using an underscore—are both valid. CamelCase tends to be a bit shorter, but underscores can be a bit easier to read. For a small game, you don't really need to worry that your game object name lengths will get out of hand, so you can use underscores. Both CamelCase and underscores work well, so you can choose either one; the important thing is to stick with the convention you choose.

> **note**
>
> Why don't you just use a space in an object name? While many game engines can handle spaces in names, some can't. When referring to game objects in code, spaces can actually break many coding languages, and the compiler will interpret the space to indicate a new object. Therefore, you should avoid using spaces in any names as a generally good practice.

If you are making a rather simple game, the object name Cha_Narwhal might be good enough. If, for example, there is only one type of narwhal, you would not need to go any further. However, say that you are creating a game that has several narwhal objects to choose from. In this case, you need more information to distinguish them from each other. At this point, you need to decide exactly how much granularity you need in order to describe your set of data. For the sake of this example, say that you have more than a dozen narwhals, so you need a name that is quite detailed. In this case, the next part of the name should be one word that describes the most important attribute of the object. It's important that it be a description, and not a value, because it's very likely that attribute values will change multiple times. You would not want to rename all your objects each time an attribute value changes. Instead, you want to describe objects in a relative manner. For this example, say that you have two class sizes of narwhal: big and small. For an object in the larger class, the name might now look like this:

Cha_Narwhal_Big

Now you can add the next most important attribute in the game. For this example, you might determine that speed is the next most important attribute and split the group into two classes: fast and slow. For a big narwhal character in the fast group, the name would now look like this:

Cha_Narwhal_Big_Fast

> **note**
>
> How do you know which attributes are the most important? That's up to you as the system designer to determine. In many games, it is obvious which attributes are most important. For example, in a racing game, speed is likely to be the most important attribute. However, there are a lot of ways you could go that would not be wrong. The important thing is to make a decision and then stick to it.

The name is now very close to a full description, but in this game, the characters can come in a variety of colors, so you want to add a final descriptor to make each name unique. For a blue narwhal with all the preceding characteristics, the name looks like this:

Cha_Narwhal_Big_Fast_Blue

This name may not, and likely will not, reflect all the attributes associated with this object. For this naming convention, you are not trying to cram in each and every attribute; instead, you want to pick just enough of the most important attributes to distinguish the specific game objects from each other. Cha_Narwhal_Big_Fast_Blue is quite a different name than the original description "My game object is a big, fast, blue, narwhal," but it contains the same information, presented in a way that is easier for computers and data designers to work with. The order that this naming convention makes possible becomes apparent when you look at a larger group of objects, all names using this naming convention:

Cha_Narwhal_Big_Fast_Blue
Cha_Narwhal_Big_Fast_Green
Cha_Narwhal_Big_Fast_Red
Cha_Narwhal_Big_Slow_Blue
Cha_Narwhal_Big_Slow_Green
Cha_Narwhal_Big_Slow_Red
Cha_Narwhal_Small_Fast_Blue
Cha_Narwhal_Small_Fast_Green
Cha_Narwhal_Small_Fast_Red
Cha_Narwhal_Small_Slow_Blue
Cha_Narwhal_Small_Slow_Green
Cha_Narwhal_Small_Slow_Red
Cha_Whale_Small_Fast_Red
Cha_Whale_Big_Fast_Blue
Cha_Whale_Big_Slow_Green
Cha_Whale_Small_Slow_Red

This naming convention groups together all the narwhal characters so they're separate from the whales. The fast ones are separated from the slow ones, the big ones are separated from the small ones, and so forth. Having a strict naming convention like this makes it dramatically more efficient to find the information you need and then to pass that along to anyone else who might need it on the team.

> **note**
>
> Although we have not talked about what the characters in this game actually do, the names provide some pretty big clues. In addition, the names give you enough information to allow you to think about how this theoretical game might play. You can guess that it's likely not a racing game since speed is not the most important attribute. You can guess that it's not a color-matching puzzle game since color is the least important of the attributes listed. Looking at just the name, you might guess that this is a game about surviving at sea or possibly some form of battle. In both of these cases, size would be very important, with speed coming in a close second.

This is just one example of many different ways to form a good naming convention, and it is a solid starting point from which you can create the right convention for your game. In the end, the most important thing about a naming convention is that your team has one and that all the team members stick to it strictly.

Naming Object Iterations

Static, single-use names are not the only names in a game. Many objects need to have new names as they are revised. To properly organize all those names, you need to include a system of naming specific iterations of objects. It might be tempting to label a new version of an object *new*, but doing so is highly problematic. The good news is that there are better ways to get the desired effect.

The Problem with "New"

When a designer remakes an object, there is a temptation to name the new object with the word *new* (for example, New_Cha_Narwhal_Big_Fast_Blue or Cha_Narwhal_Big_Fast_Blue_New). The problem is that there is also a very real possibility that this overhaul will be repeated, perhaps many times. What happens when you redo an object whose name was already changed to include the word new? Do you name it New_new, new2, or something else? Such options are not clear, so it's best to avoid using the word *new* in names altogether. Instead, it's better to use a system of iteration notation, if needed.

> **note**
>
> Many source control software packages handle iteration naming for you. For example, Perforce keeps track of multiple iterations of an object with the same name by using timestamps.

> **note**
>
> Just as you should avoid using *new* when naming iterations, you should avoid *rework, modified, updated, changed,* and any other description that is vague.

Iteration Naming Method 1: Version Number

Many programs do not keep track of timestamps and do not keep old iterations of objects or files. What if you want to keep an older object or file but use a newer version? The easiest way to iterate an object or file in this scenario is to add a numeric suffix that indicates the version of the object. For example, if you were to rebuild your fast blue narwhal character three times, you might end up with the following game objects:

Cha_Narwhal_Big_Fast_Blue_01

Cha_Narwhal_Big_Fast_Blue_02

Cha_Narwhal_Big_Fast_Blue_03

By using this method, you can keep the old versions for reference but use the most recent version. You can also clearly explain to anyone on the team which version of the object you are referring to by using its number. This method works well if you are planning on doing a small number of versions over the course of a project.

Iteration Naming Method 2: Version Letter and Number

If a project is going to be large and the object or file in question is likely to get remade many times, you can use a more detailed versioning method than the version number method just described. For this method, you use a letter that represents major changes and a number that represents minor changes. *Major change* is a subjective term that you need to define for a specific project, but it generally means a big, potentially problematic change that should stand out at a glance through a list. If you were to take a character in a new direction or delete mechanics from a weapon or completely rebalance a vehicle, these could be considered large changes that warrant new letters. Small value tweaks or superficial changes would get new numbers. Using this method, you could get this list of iterations:

Cha_Narwhal_Big_Fast_Blue_a01

Cha_Narwhal_Big_Fast_Blue_a02

Cha_Narwhal_Big_Fast_Blue_a03

Cha_Narwhal_Big_Fast_Blue_a04

Cha_Narwhal_Big_Fast_Blue_b01

Cha_Narwhal_Big_Fast_Blue_b02

Cha_Narwhal_Big_Fast_Blue_c01

Cha_Narwhal_Big_Fast_Blue_c02

Cha_Narwhal_Big_Fast_Blue_c03

Cha_Narwhal_Big_Fast_Blue_c04

In this example, it is easy to spot where major changes occurred. This is helpful in tracking the changes made to an object, and it is also helpful if problems arise in a major change. Instead of sorting through versions, you would know to look back at the last major revision, such as c01, to start your search for the culprit.

Special Case Terms

Special case terms are used for temporary objects or files during testing or development. Some special case terms illustrate the purpose of the keyword.

Deleteme

You can probably guess what the special case phrase deleteme means. You are likely to very often need to make game objects or files in order to run tests or sketch out ideas. You don't want those objects hanging around forever, taking up space or causing confusion, so it is a good idea to name them in a way that clearly illustrates their temporary nature. Many game designers use deleteme for this purpose. For example, if you wanted to test the idea of a giant character for the narwhal game, you might name it like this:

Cha_Narwhal_Gaint_Fast_Blue_deleteme_a01

Many other keywords would work just as well as deleteme, but this word also has instructions for use built in, so it does a fantastic job of being short and clear.

Deprecated

Like deleteme, the special case word Deprecated also means exactly what it says. However, whereas deleteme indicates that the object or file is a temporary file that should be deleted, Deprecated indicates that this file or object has been replaced by a newer version, and you want to keep it around (perhaps as a backup). For example, if you updated your narwhal completely, you could eliminate all other parts of the naming conventions and use this:

Cha_Narwhal_Deprecated

Test

Another special case word that you can use in object names is test, which also does what it says. Test works in a similar fashion to deleteme, but it does not indicate that the object should be deleted. When you see the word *test* in an object name, you know that you should keep the object but should not refer to it for any finalized information.

Date or Time

In some instances, you might want to add the date to an object to show a progression of iterations at specific times. In such cases, you can add the date at the end of the name. How specific you get with the date depends on how exactly you need to know when the object was created. Regardless of the specificity you choose, you should present a date in descending order, starting with year and working down through smaller and smaller units of time (such as month, day, hour, minute). Doing so ensures that dates will be ordered properly when sorted. For a test narwhal object created October 2, 2020, you might use this name:

Cha_Narwhal_Test_2020_10_02

Using the Handshake Formula

After you start creating game objects, you need a method of comparing them. For very simple games with few objects, this is simple: You take each variation of an object and compare it to every other variation. For example, if you were making a fighting game, you would have the characters fight against each other to ensure that they are all balanced in a fair way. If you were making a car racing game, you would race each car against all the other cars. If you were making an action game, you would want to compare each enemy AI type against every other enemy. This method of "brute force" testing and balancing works fine for very small games with a small number of variations. However, problems start cropping up when the number of game objects you create increases. Doing a full round of testing and balancing between two objects can take an hour or more for even a simple pairing—and that's just for one round of testing. Making a full game often involves dozens of rounds of testing, tweaking, balancing, and rebalancing.

The first step in knowing how to deal with testing, tweaking, balancing, and rebalancing is knowing just how big the problem is. This is where the handshake formula comes in. The name *handshake formula* is based on an old mathematical riddle that goes like this: "A group of doctors are in a room together. To say hello, each doctor needs to shake the hand of every other doctor. How many handshakes does it take for any given number of doctors to shake every hand needed?"

You might wonder what this riddle has to do with balancing game objects. If you think of the handshakes in the riddle as a metaphor for how you test and balance objects against each other, it might start to make sense how useful this formula is to game designers. We can rephrase the riddle into language that is closer to home for game system designers: "A group of combatants are in a fighting game. Each combatant must fight every other combatant in the game to determine who is the best." or "A group of cars need to race against each other to determine which is the best car. How many races would it take for all cars to race against each other?" While the outcome of the handshake formula might, on the surface, seem like nothing more than a bit of trivia or a curiosity, it is something system designers do constantly.

The handshake formula can be extended to larger examples (three-way races, group combat, and so on), but for now, we will focus on just two parties at a time. You need to think about how you will use the formula not for a single specific number but as a formula that you can apply to any number.

Any time you need to compare a number of objects to a group, you need to start with the size of the group. For the current example, let's start with four. To compare any two of the group of four, how many combinations would you need? The very simple way to find the answer would be to combine each of the four with all four. This, mathematically means, squaring the number. You can also do this graphically in a spreadsheet, as shown in Figure 12.2; this is called a *possibility grid*.

	A	B	C	D	E
1		1	2	3	4
2	1	X	X	X	X
3	2	X	X	X	X
4	3	X	X	X	X
5	4	X	X	X	X

Figure 12.2 Possibility grid

Here you can see that if you list all objects in a row and also in a column, you can check off how many combinations there will be; this is the same as multiplying the number times itself, or finding the square. In this case, 4 squared is 16, so there are 16 combinations. This seems like a lot of combinations needed to do a comparison with just 4 objects, and indeed it is. There are several redundancies in the simplistic view of squaring the number that you can immediately eliminate. The first of which is a game object compared to itself. You don't need to compare identical cars to know that they are the same, for example. If you look at every point where you would compare an object to itself, you find the clear pattern illustrated in Figure 12.3.

	A	B	C	D	E
1		1	2	3	4
2	1	X	X	X	X
3	2	X	X	X	X
4	3	X	X	X	X
5	4	X	X	X	X

Figure 12.3 Unneeded combinations

Object 1 is compared to itself in cell B2, Object 2 is compared to itself in cell C3, and so on in a diagonal pattern through the chart. In a fighting game, you know that Combatant 1 will be equal to Combatant 1, so you can eliminate the need to test that combination. Therefore, you can eliminate every point on the graph where an object would be compared directly to itself. In the case shown in Figure 12.3, this is 4 combinations. In fact, for any comparison, the number of eliminations will equal the number of objects you are comparing. So, if you were to compare 6 objects, you could eliminate 6 combinations, and if you were to compare 1,000 objects, we could eliminate 1,000 combinations. With this in mind, you need to update your formula to get rid of those unneeded combinations. This is the update formula:

$$(\text{Number of game objects})^2 - (\text{Number of game objects}) = \text{Unique comparisons}$$

or:

$$G^2 - G = \text{Unique comparisons}$$

or, in this example:

$$4^2 - 4 = 16 - 4 = 12 \text{ unique comparisons}$$

While this formula removes the redundancy of comparing objects to themselves, there is one more step you can take to make your comparisons fully efficient. In a fighting game, if you compare Combatant 1 with Combatant 2, do you then need to compare Combatant 2 with Combatant 1? No. You already did that comparison, but in the opposite order, and because order doesn't matter in the comparison, you can eliminate any combinations that you have already done in the opposite order. Figure 12.4 shows this graphically in a spreadsheet.

	A	B	C	D	E
1		1	2	3	4
2	1		X	X	X
3	2	X		X	X
4	3	X	X		X
5	4	X	X	X	

Figure 12.4 Redundant combinations

Both highlighted cells in Figure 12.4 are making the same comparison because they are both comparing object 1 with object 2, and you need only one of these comparisons. You need to know mathematically how many of these redundant comparisons are left in the chart. Because you are comparing every object with every other object, and all the objects are listed in both dimensions of the chart, you will get twice as many matchups of each object as needed. For every time Object 1 is compared to Object 2, Object 2 will be compared to Object 1. The same goes for each other pairing. This means you can eliminate half of the pairings because they are comparing the same two objects but in the opposite order. Figure 12.5 shows the redundant comparisons that you can eliminate.

	A	B	C	D	E
1		1	2	3	4
2	1		X	X	X
3	2	X		X	X
4	3	X	X		X
5	4	X	X	X	

Figure 12.5 Removing redundancies

Because all the highlighted cells in Figure 12.5 are redundant, you can remove them from your count of combinations that you need to test and balance. Mathematically, this means you can divide your total combinations by 2. This leads to the final formula:

$(G^2 - G)/2$ = Total combinations to test

or, in this case:

$(4^2 - 4)/2 = 6$

To validate that the formula is working, you can count the number of *X*s in your chart after eliminating all redundant combinations (see Figure 12.6).

	A	B	C	D	E
1		1	2	3	4
2	1		X	X	X
3	2			X	X
4	3				X
5	4				

Figure 12.6 Valid remaining combinations

As you can see, 6 is indeed the number of valid combinations remaining. Now that you have the needed formula, you can input any number into it and find out exactly the number of combinations you need to compare your entire set of objects. As one more example, Figure 12.7 shows 20 objects and the combinations you need to test.

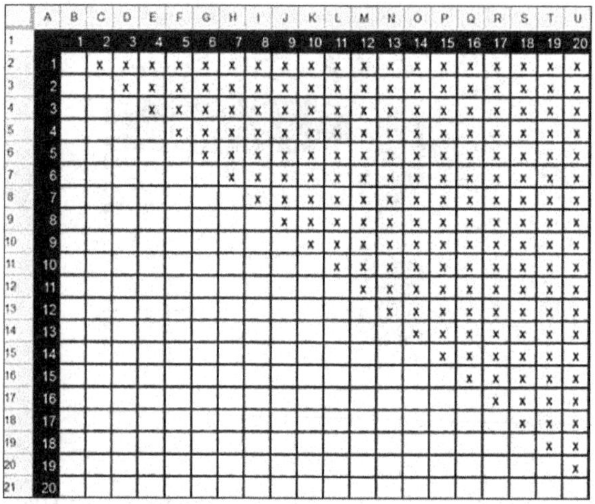

	A	B	C	D	E	F	G	H	I	J	K	L	M	N	O	P	Q	R	S	T	U
1		1	2	3	4	5	6	7	8	9	10	11	12	13	14	15	16	17	18	19	20
2	1		X	X	X	X	X	X	X	X	X	X	X	X	X	X	X	X	X	X	X
3	2			X	X	X	X	X	X	X	X	X	X	X	X	X	X	X	X	X	X
4	3				X	X	X	X	X	X	X	X	X	X	X	X	X	X	X	X	X
5	4					X	X	X	X	X	X	X	X	X	X	X	X	X	X	X	X
6	5						X	X	X	X	X	X	X	X	X	X	X	X	X	X	X
7	6							X	X	X	X	X	X	X	X	X	X	X	X	X	X
8	7								X	X	X	X	X	X	X	X	X	X	X	X	X
9	8									X	X	X	X	X	X	X	X	X	X	X	X
10	9										X	X	X	X	X	X	X	X	X	X	X
11	10											X	X	X	X	X	X	X	X	X	X
12	11												X	X	X	X	X	X	X	X	X
13	12													X	X	X	X	X	X	X	X
14	13														X	X	X	X	X	X	X
15	14															X	X	X	X	X	X
16	15																X	X	X	X	X
17	16																	X	X	X	X
18	17																		X	X	X
19	18																			X	X
20	19																				X
21	20																				

Figure 12.7 Large set of combinations

You can see that no matter how large or small the number of objects, the pattern repeats. If you plug in the new number to the formula, you get the following:

$(20^2 - 20)/2 = 190$ combinations

If you wanted, you could count the number of *X*s in the chart and arrive at the same answer to verify, but doing so would take more time than using the combination formula. There is another way to do this formula that takes a little longer but that shows a very interesting pattern. To illustrate, let's solve for the numbers 1 through 20 (see Table 12.14).

Notice that if you add the number of objects with the number of combinations, you get the number of combinations for the next greater count of objects. This means that if you know the formula for any number, you can quickly figure out the result for the next larger number by adding the number of objects to the number of combinations. If you wanted to extend this chart up to 21, therefore, you would add 20 to 190, for a result of 210 combinations.

When you know the number of combinations you are dealing with, you can use this information to more accurately calculate how much effort will be needed to check and balance these combinations. For example, if you know that it takes an hour to properly test and tune a single combination, you can figure out how many hours you need to account for in total.

Table 12.14 Possible combinations

Objects	Combinations
2	1
3	3
4	6
5	10
6	15
7	21
8	28
9	36
10	45
11	55
12	66
13	78
14	91
15	105
16	120
17	136
18	153
19	171
20	190

In addition to using the combinations formula for testing and balancing, you can use it in the following ways:

- To make a round-robin tournament where every player plays every other player
- In a fighting game, to create a special victory animation for each combination of combatants
- In a racing game where a voiceover announcer says a unique line for each pairing of cars before the cars start the race
- In a superhero game where two of heroes combine their powers to form a special power that is unique to that combination of characters
- In a fantasy RPG, where each combination of character classes has a unique bonus when played as a team
- In a combat game, to create a special animation for each combination of attack and defense

In addition to using the combinations formula to manually figure out how many combinations you need to test, you can use a spreadsheet shortcut function that does this math for you. This function, COMBIN, takes two arguments: the number of objects in the dataset and the number of objects in a combination. For all of the examples in this section, that second argument has been 2 because we have been combining only two objects at a time. However you can combine more than two objects with one another to get a significantly larger number of total combinations. Using a spreadsheet formula makes it possible to easily calculate these larger numbers of combinations.

Further Steps

After completing this chapter, you should take some time to practice in the real world with the concepts covered here. Try these exercises to further explore concepts covered in this chapter:

- For some real-world examples of game objects, list their attributes and try to assign weights to those attributes. Try to do this for a variety of different objects and use the objects that you have created from previous chapters.
- Create a naming convention for game objects—either objects you have made or preexisting games objects. Take the time to figure out how many attributes need to be contained in a name and in what order they should appear.
- Use the handshake formula to determine the number of combinations in several actual scenarios (for example, your favorite upcoming sport or a game tournament you follow).

CHAPTER 13

RANGE BALANCING, DATA FULCRUMS, AND HIERARCHICAL DESIGN

This chapter covers three very important data concepts: range balancing, data fulcrums, and hierarchical design.

With these concepts, you can start creating a larger amount of data objects that are balanced and ready to go into your game. By learning these foundational principles first, you will be able to avoid many of the most common pitfalls that new data designers experience when building their first set of data.

Range Balancing

Many numbers you use for data object attributes have physical or virtual constraints. For example, miles per hour and weight in pounds (or kilograms) are known measurements that are well entrenched in our audiences. You want players to easily understand the measurement of attributes in your game, so you are likely to use such known systems of measurement when displaying an attribute of a data object instead of using abstract measurements.

On the other hand, using your own scale that meshes well with your systems and spreadsheets can help you, as a game system designer, do your job more quickly and effectively. For example, if you want to express the weight of an MMA (mixed martial arts) combatant, you can take either of the two following approaches:

MMA combatant: 105–265 pounds

or:

MMA combatant: 0–100 in game "weight units"

Pounds are much easier for players to grasp than "weight units" because players are used to the real-world analog of "weight class" in the sport. However, using pounds makes doing calculations on the scale of weight more cumbersome. Where is the middle? You don't know. What is a mid-high value? You don't know that either. You could use a spreadsheet to calculate these values, but it's not very easy for us to visualize the scale from the least to the most and see how each score will compare to other data objects.

If you use an in-game unit with a standard scale of 0 to 100, you can much more easily do calculations. Where is the middle? It's 50. What is a mid-high value? It's 75. What is a mid-low value? It's 25. You can easily find all these values in your head very quickly. The problem with using game units, as mentioned earlier, is that they do not have meaning to the player. How much does a man weigh if he is 25 in game units? Will this make sense to a player?

An ideal system would allow you to use a standardized range such as 0–100 internally to do calculations and comparisons and provide a different scale that more closely matches a real-world analog for the player—and the two would work well together. Fortunately, this type of ideal system exists, and it is called *range balancing*. Range balancing provides a bridge between the two methods of numbering, and it also has several other benefits:

- Normalizes numbers so they are easier to work with in spreadsheets
- Works around odd units of measurement that are difficult to work with (such as radians and force)
- Eliminates "ripple effect" balancing

- Decouples the work of the system designer and data designer(s)
- Makes balancing easier on a larger scale

How Range Balancing Works

Range balancing starts by finding the data range in the player-facing scale. This range can have any minimum and any maximum, and the range may at some point change. At first, all you need is an educated guess about the range. For example, if you were making a racing game and you wanted to find the top speed of race cars, you could simply estimate that the slowest race car might go around 110 miles per hour and the fastest would go 190 miles per hour. Don't worry about being accurate at this time, as one of the benefits of range balancing is that you can change it painlessly later on.

After you estimate the minimum and maximum, subtract the minimum from the maximum to find the data range. You can now express every attribute value as a percentage of this range. Let's dive in a bit deeper to better understand all the concepts involved in range balancing.

To better understand the data attribute range, let's look at a very simple example of the height of ogres. Say that you want a variety of ogres in your game, and you want them to be of various heights so they seem more dynamic and natural. However, it would not make sense for this game to have very tiny ogres, and the levels can only hold ogres up to a certain size. For the player-facing portion of this, you can use a real-world unit, the foot, as your measurement. Through discussion with the team, you have estimated that the smallest ogre that can still feel "ogre like" would be 6 feet tall. That is a very small ogre, but it is big enough to be a viable ogre. While the game engine and levels could technically handle smaller ogres, you simply don't want them because anything smaller than 6 feet would feel odd and out of place. So you choose an ogre minimum height of 6 feet.

On the upper end, you need to keep in mind some technical constraints. For example, the level designers have been making doorways with a minimum height clearance of 8 feet. You want ogres to be able to fit through the doors without any special crouching animations, so this can guide you on the maximum height. This also works well with your vision of what a big ogre is, so there is no need to add further complications to production. Finally, if you look at your existing hypothetical hierarchy you find that level geometry ranks above secondary monster AI for this particular hypothetical game. This seals the deal: If ogre height might conflict with level geometry, it is on you to limit the ogre instead of asking for geometry changes.

Once you have the minimum and maximum ogre height as 6 feet and 8 feet, you can get the total range of ogre height by subtracting the minimum from the maximum—in this case, 2 feet. So you know all ogres in the game will fall somewhere in this 2-foot range. You can see this illustrated in the graph in Figure 13.1.

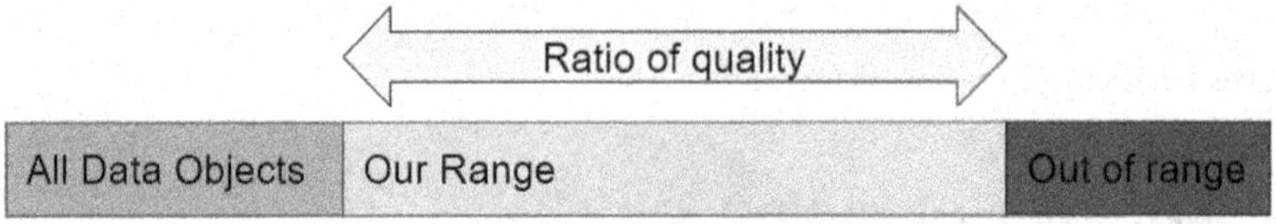

Figure 13.1 Range of acceptable numbers

The next step is to turn this range into a number that is normalized and easier to work with behind the scenes. The most commonly used range is 0% to 100%, and you can stick with this unless there is a good reason not to (see Figure 13.2).

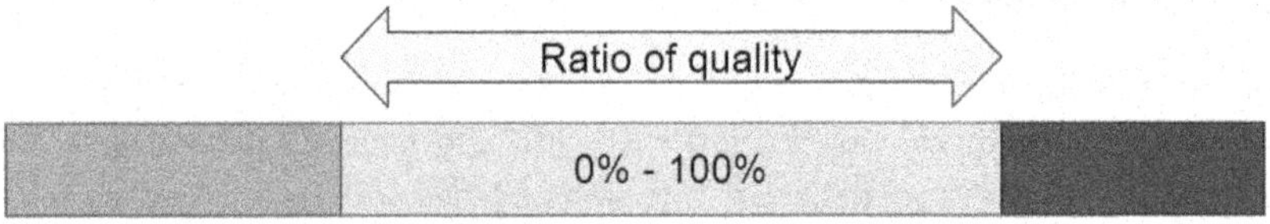

Figure 13.2 Range illustrated as percent

Knowing the maximum, the minimum, the range, and the scale, you now have all the information required to make a wide variety of ogres that fit within your goals. To use this information together for a translation, you need to apply a single formula, and then you can reuse the data many times. The formula for translating between developer scale and user scale is as follows:

$$((\text{Max} - \text{Min}) \times \%) + \text{Min} = \text{Numeric value}$$

This might seem like a complex algebraic formula, but it is much simpler than it looks. Let's break it down using the ogre example. We can start with a very simple example of an ogre that is rated at 50%. You already know the rest of the values:

Percentage = 50%

Range = 2 (feet)

Max = 8 (feet)

Min = 6 (feet)

Value = ((8 – 6) × .5) + 6

or

Value = 7 (feet)

Thinking of this intuitively can help to clarify what is happening. If you have a linear range of ogres from 6 feet up to 8 feet, then an ogre exactly in the middle is 7 feet tall, as in Figure 13.3. When doing this intuitive calculation in your head, you are actually going through the range balancing formula. It's likely that you have used this formula countless times in your life but never actually broken it down into parts to examine how it works.

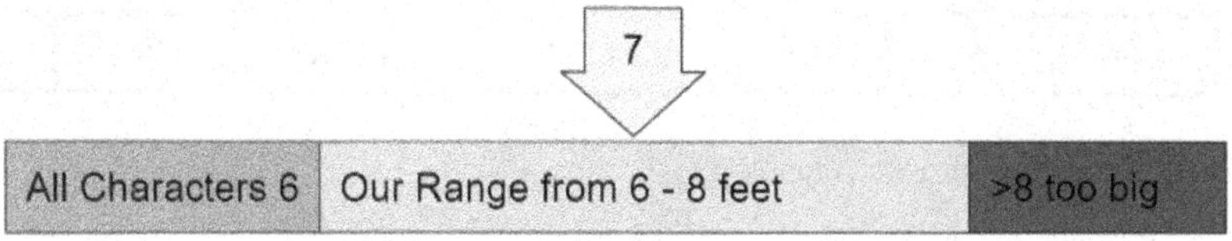

Figure 13.3 Example Ogre height range

To get deeper into the range balancing formula, let's use a larger, more sophisticated example. This example shows how to balance the run speed attributes of several different kinds of people. In this example, you start with descriptions that don't have literal numbers, as shown in Figure 13.4.

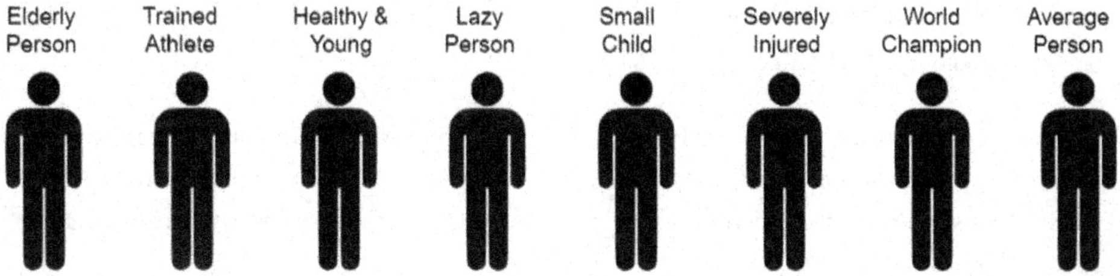

Figure 13.4 Example character types

In Figure 13.4, you can see a wide variety of characters that will have a wide variety of top run speeds. Next, you need to quantify them. Take a moment before moving on and read the descriptions of each of the characters and think about how fast each could run. Write down a percentage from 0% to 100% for each of them, indicating how fast you think they would be in comparison to each other. Importantly, while you can think about this question in terms of miles per hour if it helps, you shouldn't write down actual miles per hour; just consider the relative percentages for the characters for now. When you have your numbers written, take a look at Figure 13.5, which shows the percentages I assigned.

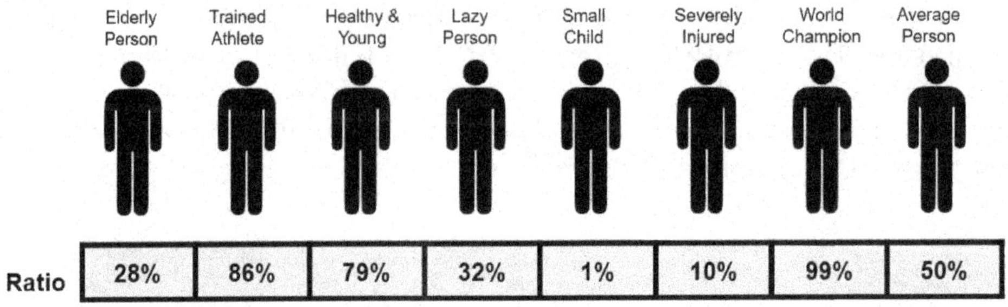

Figure 13.5 Character types with ratio listed

Do you agree with these numbers? Did they closely match yours? More importantly, did you use the same rank order from slowest to fastest? If not, don't worry; you did nothing wrong. There is really only one character here who has what could arguably be a "correct" answer: the average person, at 50%.

While doing this exercise, you might have had questions such as these:

- "Severely injured how? On the legs or arms?"
- "How lazy is this lazy person?"
- "What kind of elderly person?"

If you did, congratulations: You are thinking like a system designer! Translating vague concepts into numbers is a difficult thing to do, and it always involves ambiguity. When groups of system designers go for lunch on a workday, they often bicker and debate these exact topics, which is part of how they do their jobs well.

In some cases, asking follow-up questions is exactly what you want to do. If a level designer asks you to put in character design for a "lazy person," you may want to ask "Lazy how? Physically out of shape? Low motivation? Something else?" Other times, you very well might be handed a vague list like this and be expected to fill in the gaps yourself. Fortunately, this system is flexible, and you can go back and tweak it later.

After all the thought and debate, when you have a set of percentages recorded for the characters, it's time to apply the range balancing formula to these percentages to see what they translate to. To do this, you need a minimum and a maximum. Just making a guess at it, you could say that a very slow person could move at 3 miles per hour. That's very slow. Next, we could estimate that a very fast person might be able to run up to 20 miles per hour. Very few humans have ever run faster than that in the real world. When you assign your slowest runner the lowest value (min = 3) and your fastest runner the highest value (max = 20), you have all the data you need to apply the formula. Your spreadsheet can easily and quickly calculate the speed, in miles per hour, for all the other characters based on the min, the max, and the percentages. In this case, you get the set of numbers shown in Figure 13.6. Once you have these numbers, it's time to test them.

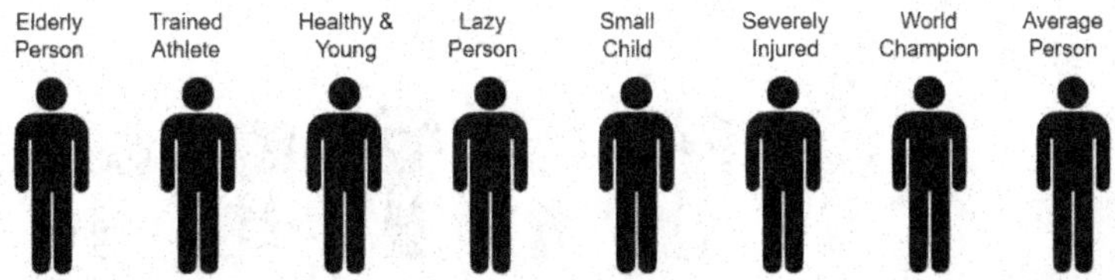

	Elderly Person	Trained Athlete	Healthy & Young	Lazy Person	Small Child	Severely Injured	World Champion	Average Person
Ratio	28%	86%	79%	32%	1%	10%	99%	50%
Min= 3, Max = 20	8	18	16	8	3	5	20	12

Figure 13.6 Example character with ratio and real value

Who Adjusts What

Once the data objects go into the testing phase, it becomes possible to break up the responsibility for data tuning into two separate tasks:

- **Systemic balance:** Systemic balance controls the feel and function of the entire set of data objects, without bogging you down with the minutiae of individuals.
- **Individual balance:** Individual balance is responsible for making each data object feel just right, while staying within the confines of the system as a whole.

On small projects, a single person can handle individual balance, but for a large game, it would be impossible for a single person to do all the work of balancing all the data objects. For example, an MMO might have hundreds of different characters and thousands of objects. In such situations, range balancing can help dramatically. When you have the min and max separated out from the individual data, you can adjust them independently of any individual data object. This can have a huge impact on the game and the actual production life of the team.

Say that you are working with human run speed, and testing has revealed that all the characters feel slow. It turns out (and this is actually true in video games) that for the game to feel right, many actual physical traits need to be heightened to unrealistic levels. Even in realistic games, characters run faster, jump higher, hold their breath longer, take more damage, and do many other superhuman feats regularly—and this is what "feels right" to players. What this means, practically, is that there is one person responsible for the minimum and maximum value, since those two values alone drive the feeling of all the objects in the game. This is typically the lead system designer, whose job is to ensure that the game as a whole feels balanced. Say that your testing group finds that the numbers are simply too low. By doing some more in-game testing, you discover that better numbers for minimum and maximum are min = 5 and max = 40. Using the range balancing formula, you can tweak the min and max numbers, and instantly all of your humans' run speeds are updated to new numbers (see Figure 13.7).

	Elderly Person	Trained Athlete	Healthy & Young	Lazy Person	Small Child	Severely Injured	World Champion	Average Person
Ratio	28%	86%	79%	32%	1%	10%	99%	50%
Min= 3, Max = 20	8	18	16	8	3	5	20	12
Min = 5, Max = 40	15	35	33	16	5	9	40	23

Figure 13.7 Example character with modified ratio

In Figure 13.7, you can see the original percentages, the first pass at numbers, and the newly updated values that you arrived at through testing. There are several things to notice in this example:

- Numbers at the bottom of the scale did not change nearly as much as did numbers at the top. This is fine and accurately reflects that the bottom of the range did not change much.
- Numbers at the top of the scale changed a lot. Clearly, this is where the testers had the issue. They might have been okay with an elderly NPC hobbling about or characters having special conditions (such as severely injured) that make them slow. But when players heard that a character was a trained athlete, they wanted to see the character zipping around the level.
- The world champion has a percentage of 99% but has 100% of the max value. This discrepancy is due to rounding all the numbers displayed to players. As mentioned in Chapter 9, "Attributes: Creating and Quantifying Life," you should avoid showing decimals or fractions to players. You might want to reconsider the percentage for the world champion character as well. He is a world champion, but might there be someone even better out there, lurking in the shadows? By giving this character a perfect score, you have not left any room for improvement.

When the team is happy with the limits of the system, the data designers can further tune and revise individuals. In terms of the game, the min and max always sit above individual characters, and individuals need to be adjusted to fit the scale. The good news is that most of this is done automatically as characters maintain their relative comparisons to each other, regardless of any changes to the min and max. Note that this tuning can now—and forevermore—be done independently of the data range as a whole. Large teams of data designers can work in concert and the lead system designer to create massive amounts of data that all naturally fall within the bounds of the desired system. For example, a level designer who asked for an elderly person might come to the data designer and explain that they want her to be very elderly and barely mobile. With this request, the data designer can easily change the one percentage variable from 28% all the way down to 0%. This still works within the designated range, requires no adjustment of the min or max, and satisfies that level designer.

I'd like to drill this concept home with one more example: In the early days of large-scale video games, every data object attribute had to be entered manually, and there was no such thing as a range balancing system. Imagine being a data designer on a game with thousands of characters and being asked to speed them all up. This would require you to work in a database multiple days, doing individual calculations or guesswork to add a few points to each. If someone then thinks you went too far, and wants you to slow them all down a bit again, you would have to do all the tedious work again. This was the reality for years in the game industry; a few companies continue to do it this way today.

Data Fulcrums

The ancient Greek mathematician Euclid said, "Things which are equal to the same thing are also equal to one another." The same method of thinking can be applied to large groups of data objects. If we try and compare data objects to a single, fixed example, we can in a way, compare all of the objects to one another without having to manually do so.

In Chapter 12, "System Design Foundations," you learned about the handshake formula and saw that adding new objects creates an ever-increasing number of combinations. Creating more combinations requires more effort. Maybe even more importantly, having more combinations means much more testing and balancing time is needed for each iteration. So how are game designers able to make large sets of objects? How can an RPG have 100+ character classes? How can racing games have dozens of cars? Using brute-force creation and testing methods would require an army of system designers to keep up. This type of creation is impractical for even the biggest team, and it is completely impossible for smaller teams. However, many medium and small teams make large varieties of objects in their games. How do they do it? Again, there are many methods, but most of them can be boiled down to variations of a single philosophy: the use of fulcrums.

What Is a Fulcrum?

The dictionary definition for a fulcrum is "a thing that plays a central or essential role in an activity, event, or situation." In game design, a *fulcrum* or *data fulcrum* is something you use as a single point of comparison so you can avoid needing to use the handshake formula method to create large numbers and varieties of objects. Any time you have more game objects than you can balance with simple brute-force testing, there is another good opportunity to include a fulcrum. A fulcrum is a game object that is going to be the center point of comparison for all other objects of its type. Often, this object doesn't even actually appear in the game but is used exclusively as a balancing tool for the designer behind the scenes.

What's most important about the fulcrum object is that it is the balancing center. It should not be the best or the worst. It should not be special in any way. That is, in fact, the entire point of the fulcrum object: It's the most basic example of a creation (or an object or item) to which you can compare every other object in the group.

For example, if you were making a large variety of swords, the fulcrum would be a basic sword. It would not be the best or the worst but the most central, average sword you could create. Some swords might be large and powerful but slow. Other swords might be smaller and faster than most. The fulcrum sword is right in the middle. Some swords might be enchanted or cursed. But the fulcrum sword is neither; again, it is right in the middle.

As another example, in a racing game, you might have cars that are fast but have poor handling. Other cars might have great handling but lower top speed than average. Some cars might be fast with great handling but very expensive. Still other cars might be cheap but slow and might have poor handling. The fulcrum car would be right in the middle of all of these things: moderate speed, handling, and cost. If you had a 0 through 100 weighted rating on all of these aspects—speed, handling, and cost—the fulcrum would be 50, 50, 50.

> note
>
> Most games have more than one fulcrum. In a fantasy RPG, there might be fulcrums for swords, shields, armor, characters, magic spells, and so on.

Creating a Fulcrum

Once you have decided what needs a data fulcrum, it's fairly straightforward to make one. Start with every attribute in the middle of the expected range. For example, if the game you are working on has strength, dexterity, and intelligence attributes for all characters and the expected range is 0–100, the fulcrum character would have the following attribute values:

- **Strength:** 50
- **Dexterity:** 50
- **Intelligence:** 50

But keep in mind that this is just a starting point. It may turn out, for your game, that all 50% attributes are not actually balanced or fun. This is just where you start and not where you finish.

Testing a Fulcrum

Once you have the initial numbers for a fulcrum in place, it's time to test. You should think of the most common situations in which this object will be used and test them. These situations will, of course, vary for different kinds of games, but we can look at an example to illustrate.

For a game that is centered around characters in combat situations, like an RPG or action shooter, then that's the best place to start testing. Put your fulcrum character into a large variety of combat scenarios. If the game is multiplayer, test the fulcrum against itself. Let's say you made an eight-player death-match shooter with one test level. You would need a fulcrum character and a fulcrum gun. You would then use that character and gun eight times—once for each of the players—and play a game session. This session will probably not be the most interesting version of the game, but it should work, and it should also start to show some slightly interesting gameplay. It's likely that it won't even work on the first test. However, it is easy enough to redesign the single fulcrum character and test again.

You need to keep iterating on this fulcrum character until you achieve the goals of having a working game and slightly interesting combat. It's not uncommon for a fulcrum to take a dozen or more iterations to get to a working state. Say that you have a character with these stats:

- **Strength:** 50
- **Dexterity:** 50
- **Intelligence:** 50

During playtesting, you might find that dexterity of 50 is just too low for anyone; characters are constantly missing, and the battle is a slog. You might discover that the actual scale of standard usable range is 70–100, with anything below 70 reserved for special cases like injuries. In this case, you would change the fulcrum character to have dexterity of 85 because that is the halfway point in the 70–100 range. This might or might not be your final number, but it's a good starting guess.

After you adjust the fulcrum, you need to test again. Take note of what has changed and what has stayed the same. It is advisable to change only one attribute at a time so you can more easily see the effects of changing that attribute. You may need to repeat this process many times. Getting the feel of the fulcrum is very important as it is the basis for all other data objects to come. Don't worry if determining the fulcrum takes much more time than you have allotted to balancing an individual object; it is likely to take far longer to get the fulcrum right than it will take to nail down the other objects.

It is also important to test your fulcrum in as many different conditions as possible. For example, you might want to see how the fulcrum does in a one-on-one battle, with three players, with four players, and so on. You should also check different environments, if possible. What's the smallest area? What is the largest? Does the fulcrum work equally well in these areas? What is the most wide-open area you are going to have? What about the tightest area? Try to test the fulcrum in isolation in as many different situations as you can. Doing this testing helps you work out any balance issues not only with that data object but with the game environment. Testing often uncovers limitations in game systems.

Locking a Fulcrum

After you do testing for days, weeks, or even months, a clear picture of what the game is and how the game objects will work should start to emerge. This is rather exhausting, tedious work, but doing it will yield dividends in the end. Once your team feels the fulcrum object is rock solid and you understand the basic mechanics of the game, it's important to lock down the fulcrum, which means making no more changes to it. Unless there is a catastrophic bug or a major change to the project, the fulcrum needs to be locked before anything else is created.

A locked fulcrum serves a few very important purposes. First and foremost, it is the measuring stick for every other object of its type. So, if you are making a cart-racing game, you will be comparing each new cart with your fulcrum. If it's a fighting game, each new character will be compared to the fulcrum. If it's a weapon, each new weapon will be compared to the weapon fulcrum, and so on.

A locked fulcrum also acts as a reference for other aspects of the game. For example, if you have a game that allows players to mix and match characters with weapons, you can use a fulcrum character to even the playing field for weapons testing. Conversely, you can use a fulcrum weapon to test how each character uses the weapon. Finally, you have the set standard of a fulcrum character armed with a fulcrum weapon; you have a benchmark for the middle.

Finally, you need a locked fulcrum for testing everything around it. With an arena shooter, for example, you can give level designers a rock solid character to play in each of their new level designs. They can be confident that they are building levels that will work with the types of characters being built for the game. You, as system designer, can also be confident that the level design team knows what to expect from the characters you are building and that they will make levels that conform to the needs of the systems. This can be done long before you have all the data done for the game, which means the level design team gets a huge head start. This is also the time to have discussions with the team about expectations. It's better to get everyone on the same page now than to wait until vast arrays of data objects and levels have been created.

Using a Fulcrum for Data Creation

Once the fulcrum object is locked, it's time to start working on all the rest of the data. Let's look again at the arena shooter example. After much tweaking and tuning, say that you have a fulcrum character with the following stats:

- **Strength:** 40
- **Dexterity:** 85
- **Intelligence:** 50

For this design, let's say you have 19 more characters to make. You have already gone through the process described in Chapter 11, "Attribute Numbers," and decided what kinds of adjectives to use:

- **Bruiser:** Strongest, very slow, very low intelligence
- **Sniper:** Weak, good dexterity, good intelligence
- **Medic:** Weak, poor dexterity, best intelligence

To start building these characters, you have determined that the bruiser will be your highest priority, and we will start by giving him an attribute score. Here's what you use on the first pass:

- **Bruiser**
  - **Strength:** 40
  - **Dexterity:** 85
  - **Intelligence:** 50

It may seem surprising that the first pass is identical to the fulcrum, but this is the best way to start: Literally copy and paste the same attributes from the fulcrum into every other data object. Now that your bruiser has stats, you can start to test and tweak them. But first, you need to test the bruiser with just the copied numbers. You need to make sure that he behaves exactly like the fulcrum. It's entirely possible that some unanticipated factor might change the object's behavior. The model mesh, animations, a material, some code error, or any number of other factors can cause bugs at this stage. The great thing about using the fulcrum numbers first is that doing so enables you to more quickly isolate the problem because you know the intention of the attribute numbers you have assigned to the character. Once you have tested the bruiser with fulcrum numbers and he checks out, you can start to deviate. These might be the numbers you test next:

> note
>
> At this point, it becomes increasingly important to keep referencing the bruiser to the fulcrum.

- **Bruiser**
  - **Strength:** 90
  - **Dexterity:** 73
  - **Intelligence:** 20

If you are making an eight-player death match, you should use seven fulcrum characters and one bruiser for your test on the first set of deviation numbers. How does the bruiser perform?

Test again and make sure the results are consistent. If the bruiser fares on par with the fulcrum, then you have successfully deviated without causing an imbalance. Once this test is done, it would be a great idea to mix it up and do a few more tests, such as two bruisers and six fulcrum characters or four of each or seven bruisers and one fulcrum. It is important to do tests like this to make sure small deviances don't add up and become large imbalances on a larger scale.

When the testing cycle for the bruiser is complete, it's time to make more adjustments to the attributes and test again against only the fulcrum. This can take several iterations, but the process should go much faster than the original tuning of the fulcrum.

Remember that the goal in all of this is a fair fight between the bruiser and the fulcrum. They should have an equal chance of winning. If the bruiser is dominant, then he needs to be adjusted down; conversely, if he is constantly losing, he needs to be adjusted up. But remember that you never adjust the fulcrum once you've locked it.

When the bruiser has numbers that work well against the fulcrum in all the test situations, you can set him aside. Next, you need to repeat the process with the sniper. Importantly, we do not initially test him in comparison to the bruiser. This is where having a fulcrum character really starts to pay off in time savings. Because you know the bruiser is balanced against the fulcrum, you can make a fair assumption that the sniper will be balanced against the bruiser if you balance the sniper against the fulcrum as well.

When you have finished with the sniper, you can set him aside and work on the medic. Again, you need to test the medic only against the fulcrum, and not against the bruiser or the sniper. You continue this process for all the remaining characters. Your testing and tuning phase turns from an ever-expanding slog into a simple linear test. When you add another character, you don't need to test it against every other character; you only need to test it thoroughly against the fulcrum.

Unavoidable Cross-testing

After completing all 20 characters and testing them against only the fulcrum, you have to do the unavoidable: test them in many combinations. A vast number of combinations are possible in this situation. To find out how many, you can use the spreadsheet function COMBIN that was introduced in Chapter 12. To determine how many combinations of 20 characters you can have in an 8-player game, you use the following formula:

```
=COMBIN(20,8)
```

This formula gives you a result of 125,970 possible combinations. It would be impossible to test this many combinations internally at a studio. The good news is that you don't have to test all of them; for the most part, because you tested all the characters against the fulcrum, everything should be balanced from the very first test.

Because you did the extra prep work of making the fulcrum, locking it, and using it to balance all the characters, they will naturally be close to balanced already. Therefore, instead of testing all the characters against each other, you only need to test some combinations, based on human intuition. The system designers and a good QA team should try combinations they think might be problematic. This is a necessary step in finding the final balance. (In Chapter 17, "Fine-Tuning Balance, Testing, and Problem Solving," we further discuss how to go about finding the right balance in game data.)

> **note**
>
> On large teams, developers may be able to use automated testing AI or other algorithms in lieu of brute-force testing.

Fulcrum Progression

Up to this point in the chapter, we have been discussing a single slice of game objects, but in more complex games, this might not be enough. If a game has the concept of leveling up or another form of progression among data objects, developing a single fulcrum won't be enough. For example, a player might start out as Level 1 and fight against Level 1 orks, improve to Level 2 and fight against bigger and tougher Level 2 orks, improve to Level 3, and so on. In such a case, the fulcrum character needs to be made for all versions or levels before the rest of the data objects can be built and stratified across the levels.

Which level of fulcrum should be created first? There could be an argument made for starting at the lowest, at the highest, or in the middle. When in doubt, starting in the middle is the safest bet. For example, if your game has objects that go from Level 1 to Level 9, you might first create the fulcrum at Level 5. Once the fulcrum feels good in isolation at Level 5, you can strip away power from the object until it is weak enough to be considered Level 1. After that, you can add power to the fulcrum character until it is at its maximum, Level 9. (For further details on increasing power, see Chapter 14, "Exponential Growth and Diminishing Returns.")

Once the boundaries and center point have been established, you can test those objects against each other. Is Level 5 better enough than Level 1 that players will be able to feel the progression? Similarly, there should be clearly large amounts of improvements in the fulcrum character at the very top level.

After the fulcrum is created with lowest point, a highest point, and a midpoint, you can create all other objects at the same middle progression, knowing that they will be balanced against the central fulcrum. Once all the levels for the fulcrum are calculated and the central points of all other data objects are established, you can use the same gradient built for the fulcrum to apply changes to the rest of the data objects. In the end, you will have a series of data objects in their own lines of progression that should be running parallel to each other from lowest to highest, as illustrated in Figure 13.8.

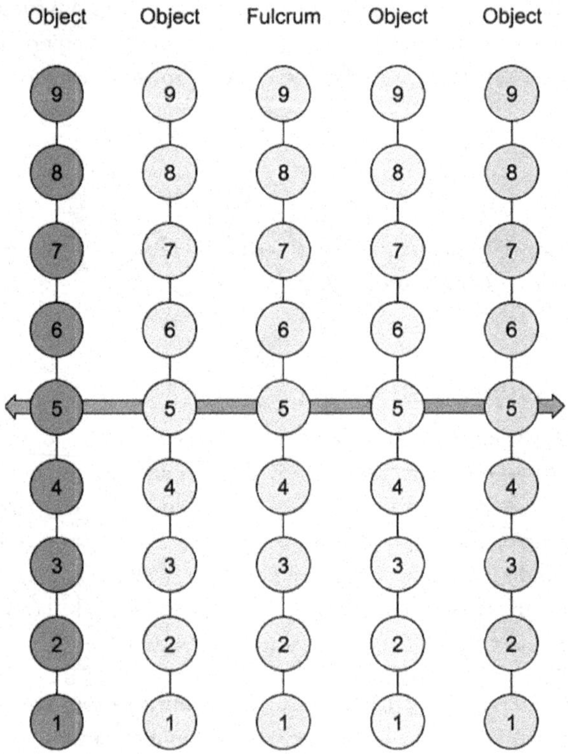

Figure 13.8 Fulcrum in progression

As you can see in Figure 13.8, the center of the data world is the fulcrum object that runs up the middle. At the central point of progression—in this case Level 5—all the other data objects are created and balanced. Then, each additional data object has its own line of progression that runs in lock step with the fulcrum as it increases in level.

Hierarchical Design

There is a common problem that occurs not only in games but in any complex system that contains multiple variables that can all be tuned. Which variable do you tune? For example, if you are working on a game where the player character is doing battle with a monster, and you decide that the monster is too difficult, how do you make the monster easier to battle? Assuming standard RPG combat attributes, you could make the monster do less damage, attack less frequently, or start with fewer hit points. Conversely, you could make the player character do more damage, start with more hit points, or hit more frequently. You could also use any number of combinations of any of these adjustments. But which one should you change? Which ones should be left the same? As discussed earlier, the data fulcrum should be locked by the time you get to balancing characters, so that should not change. What else governs which value to change? This answer will be slightly different for every game, but there is a method you can use for any game to make the decision easier: hierarchical design.

The basic method of hierarchical design is very easy: Write a linear list of the elements in the game from most important at the top to least important at the bottom. Then, if two features conflict with each other, check where each lies on the list. Change the feature that is the lowest on the list. When in doubt, start with the most globally affecting features at the top and work down to the most local features at the bottom. As a general rule, you should tune local features to fit with the global design—and not the other way around.

Starting the Hierarchy

At the very beginning of the game-making process, you can begin to form your hierarchy. Start with very broad concepts like the following:

- Core game vision
- Game engine
- Console platform
- Game controls
    - Game camera
    - Control input buttons
- Game user interface
- Player character
    - Attributes
    - Mesh
    - Animations
- Level design constraints
    - Fulcrum level with max ceiling height, door width, and so on
- Fulcrum enemy character
    - All other enemy characters
- NPC fulcrum character
    - All other NPC characters
- Power-ups

- Individual levels
    - Geometry flow
    - Interactive setups
    - Macro system rewards
- Sound
    - Music
    - SFX

With this basic example of a hierarchy, you already have the answer for part of the earlier question: The player character should not change, but the monster should. Imagine changing the player character's attributes to make this one monster fight better. What might that do to the rest of the game? It is highly likely that it would throw off the balance of combat in many or all other monster fights. That would require other designers to go back and tune them again, and they might even want to change the PC again. This would cause an endless cycle of rebalancing the PC to try to fit a multitude of situations. On the other hand, if you change the monster, all the other fights between the PC and other monsters would remain the same. The changes would remain as local as possible, which is a key to keeping rework time accurate and fast.

To determine which attributes to change on the monster, you could use the fulcrum monster as a guide because it is higher in rank than this individual monster. After that, there could be a sublist of attributes that are in order as well, or an individual designer could be given leeway to make a judgment call at this lower level.

Advantages of Hierarchical Design

There are several reasons for a team or even an individual developer to build a game hierarchy:

- It helps solve disputes. Being able to point at a definitive list makes it easier to make a decision and stick with it.
- It facilitates communication. If the whole team has access to the hierarchy and knows what is most important, team members can better work together, without stepping on each other's toes.
- It makes priorities in production clearer. In the hierarchy example you just saw, the game camera is very high on the list. This means that work on the game camera should start and even finish much earlier in the project than items lower on the list, such as level geometry. These two aspects in particular are often at odds with each other during development, so locking down the higher of the two early on will translate into less rework time.

- It can be a living document. Notice that the example above is rather vague, only listing categories of game features. As the game is developed, the hierarchy should grow to match. Each individual monster or power-up could be listed, if needed.
- It's flexible in scope. While you could list every feature and data object in the game, getting this granular is usually not needed. Working through the project, starting with a high-level overview and adding more detail when needed, the team can organically find the level of granularity that works best for the project. On a very large project with hundreds of developers and thousands of data objects, the hierarchy might need to get very big and detailed. Conversely, on a solo project or small team, the high-level example shown earlier in this section might be enough for the entire project.

Once the initial hierarchy is created, it should be discussed within the team. Everyone needs to know where the features they work on lie in the list. There may be some friction among developers about the "importance" of their features. It's better to have these conversations early than let them go unspoken until a real problem arises.

Further Steps

After completing this chapter, you should take some time to practice in the real world with the concepts covered here. Try these exercises to further explore the hierarchical design and range balancing:

- Create a spreadsheet with either characters from your own game or a favorite game of yours. Bring in their attribute values and calculate the min and max values. Then use these numbers for a range and do range balancing on the characters.
- Create a new fulcrum character for either a game you are working on or an existing game. Look at all the characters that exist and try to calculate what the exact center values should be for each attribute.
- Create a game hierarchy for a project you are working on. Start with the broadest strokes first and then start adding specific details about your project and see how you need to adjust the rankings as the project develops. It can be very eye opening to see your own project laid out this way.

CHAPTER 14

EXPONENTIAL GROWTH AND DIMINISHING RETURNS

In an exponential growth system, a linear set of steps calls for an ever-increasing amount of input or output. A good real-world example of this is in the speed of cars. In general, a faster car costs more money. But the speed and cost of cars almost never increase at the same rate. Instead, you must pay ever-increasing amounts of money to get a car that is only slightly faster. So for each mile per hour faster you want to go, the speed gets increasingly more expensive. This type of increase is called *exponential growth*. On the flip side, the top speed of the car you are paying for gets smaller per dollar. Such a decrease in the marginal (incremental) output of a production process as the amount of a single factor of production is incrementally increased while the amount of all other factors of production stay constant. This is called *diminishing returns*. These two concepts work together.

Simple games—such as chess, backgammon, and checkers—don't need to use an exponential or diminishing returns system. It's not until you start to make campaign-style mechanics that you need growth systems at all. In game systems, exponential growth is consuming ever-increasing resources and giving back only linear incremental change. Diminishing returns is the flip side of this same coin. A simple and common example is earning experience points to level up a character. In an exponential growth system, it takes ever more experience points to increase the characters level by one more level.

Game system designers make exponential growth systems for several reasons:

- They can "hook" the player into the game by providing early reward cycles.
- They can entice the player to play for longer periods of time and form a deeper relationship with the game in the later phases of the game.
- They allow developers to introduce new, simple mechanics quickly to expand play possibilities.
- They make it possible to pace out later rewards at intervals that fit the development and mechanical goals.

Anything that levels up or gets more difficult over time or space can make use of exponential growth charts. The following are some examples:

- Difficulty of progressive levels in a coin-operated arcade game
- Quality of weapons compared to cost
- Speed of a vehicle compared to cost
- Experience needed to level up
- Time played to earn an achievement
- Number of enemies defeated to complete a quest line
- Number of daily pushups done over the course of exercise training
- Number of material items collected to make better-crafted equipment

Linear Growth

Before trying to understand exponential growth it's good to have a point of comparison in linear growth. *Linear growth* simply means that as a number of iterations gets larger, so does a total amount. For example, if after each turn in a game you add 2 points to a total, then after 10 turns, you would have 20 points, and after 100 turns, you would have 200 points. The chart in Figure 14.1 illustrates this type of growth.

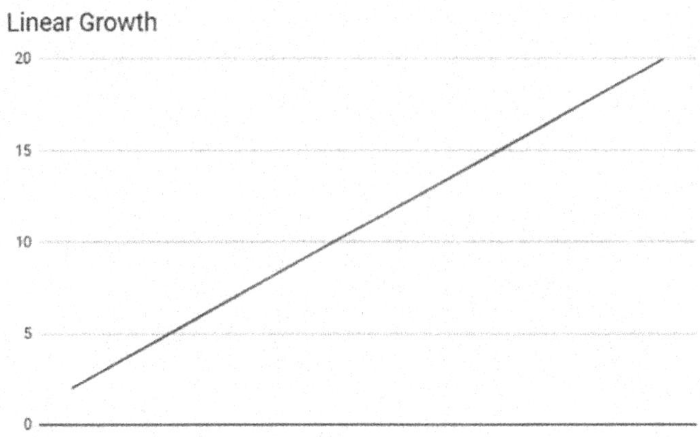

Figure 14.1 Linear growth chart

You use linear growth in games where you want a simple, steady progression. Game designers turn to exponential growth and diminishing returns in more complicated games. These two concepts are flip sides of the same coin, and game designers constantly use both of them.

Exponential Growth

As mentioned earlier in this chapter, *exponential growth* is growth whose rate becomes ever more rapid in proportion to the growing total number or size. Figure 14.2 shows a graph with a curve illustrating exponential growth. There are an infinite number of ways to create exponential growth in a game, and each has strengths and weaknesses. Because this is an introductory book, the formula we discuss here is a great formula to start with; throughout the book, we refer to this formula as the *basic exponential growth formula*. By starting with a simple formula and then testing it with your game, you will likely find ways to tweak and tune it to exactly fit your needs.

> **note**
>
> To get the most out of this chapter, open a spreadsheet and work through all the examples as you read.

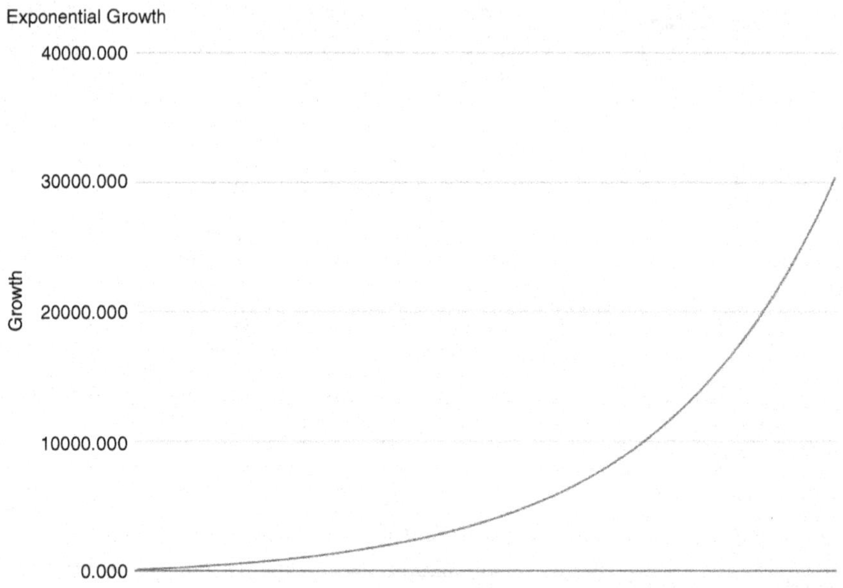

Figure 14.2 Basic exponential growth chart

Parts of the Basic Exponential Growth Formula

There are only a few adjustable parts of the basic exponential growth formula, but making even slight changes in them can create a vast multitude of variations of growth. These are the adjustable parts:

- Number of iterations
- Initial starting value
- Iteration additive value
- Iteration multiplier value

With just these four variables and a single formula, you can create a curve in a spreadsheet. To start, open up a blank spreadsheet and add some labels for the needed variables, as shown in Figure 14.3.

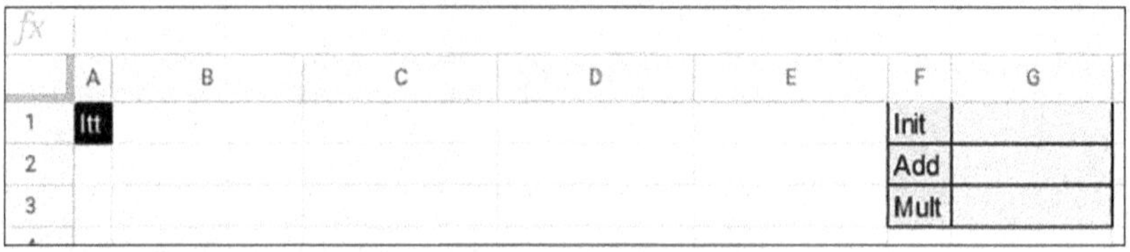

Figure 14.3 Basic input variables

In this example, the variable names have been shortened to fit on the page better. Itt, which stands for "number of iterations," needs to be a column header because it is going to get a lot of entries. Init (initial starting value), Add (iteration additive value), and Mult (iteration multiplier value) have been color-coded as sublabels and have individual variable cells next to them. The blank columns in this spread sheet leave room for you to add computational columns later.

> **note**
>
> In a game example, you could change "iterations" to "player" level to find the experience required to level up.

The first decision that needs to be made to fill out the spreadsheet is how many iterations, or "steps," are needed. This could be how many levels the player can go through until they max out. Or it could be the cost of different swords that a player can buy, or power levels of spaceships, or anything else that should have exponential growth. The basic exponential growth formula is purposely generic enough that it can fit in a wide multitude of applications. In the example in this chapter, you are going to use 100 iterations to see the growth over a long curve. In your own game, you might use a curve that is much smaller or even larger.

To add iterations, start by typing 1 in cell A2 and then formfill down (as discussed in Chapter 5, "Spreadsheet Basics") until you have a list of numbers that matches your needs. Next, you need some placeholder numbers for the remaining variables (Init, Add, and Mult); you can input 1 for each of them for now. Your spreadsheet should now look as shown in Figure 14.4.

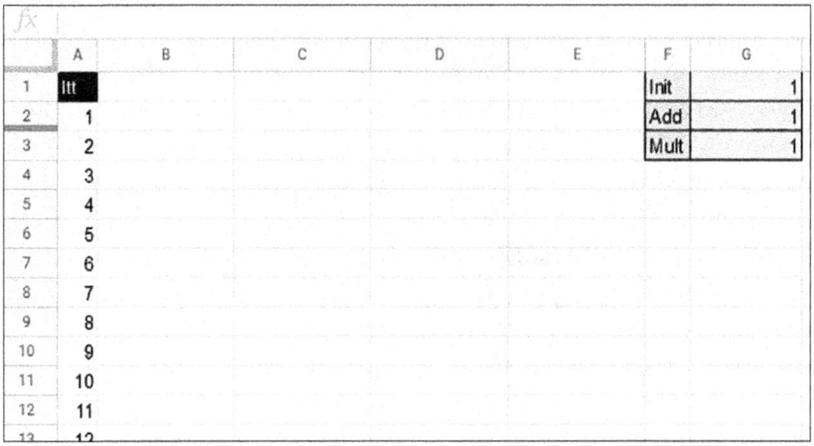

Figure 14.4 Creating iterations

Next, you need to add a calculated value for the result of each step. You can start this in cell B2. The very first step will be identical to the value of Init, so you should set cell B2 to reference cell G1 in this case. You should also add the title Value to column B because it will show the calculated value for each step. Then, in cell B3, you can start entering the formula that will govern the entire exponential curve, as described next.

Building Blocks of the Exponential Growth Formula

In each step of the basic exponential growth formula, the previous step is multiplied by the iteration multiplier value, and then the iteration additive value is added to the result:

(Previous step × Iteration multiplier value) + Iteration additive value = New step

This formula is repeated for the number of iterations desired.

Figure 14.5 shows a spreadsheet with this formula applied for the first time.

	A	B	C	D	E	F	G
1	Itt	Value				Init	1
2	1	=G1				Add	1
3	2	=(B2*$G$3)+$G$2				Mult	1
4	3						

Figure 14.5 Applying the basic exponential growth formula

Notice in Figure 14.5 that the reference to B2 is relative, which means it will be updated with each iteration as it is formfilled down the list. Also notice that the references to the iteration additive value and the iteration multiplier value are absolute, as denoted by the $ in the cell reference. Because the location of these values never changes, the references need to be locked and unchanging as well. After you enter this formula as shown in Figure 14.5, you can formfill it down to create values for the iterations. With the placeholder numbers you already have in the spreadsheet, you will get a very uninspiring list of numbers from the formula, as shown in Figure 14.6.

fx =(B3*$G$3)+$G$2

	A	B	C	D	E	F	G
1	Itt	Value				Init	1
2	1	1				Add	1
3	2	2				Mult	1
4	3	3					
5	4	4					
6	5	5					
7	6	6					
8	7	7					
9	8	8					
10	9	9					
11	10	10					
12	11	11					

Figure 14.6 Step calculations

This is not quite exponential growth yet because the multiplier is at value 1. Because any number multiplied by 1 is itself, using a multiplier of 1 actually gives you a linear growth chart and not an exponential one. To see this visually, select column B and insert a line chart. You should see a chart that shows basic linear growth, as in Figure 14.7.

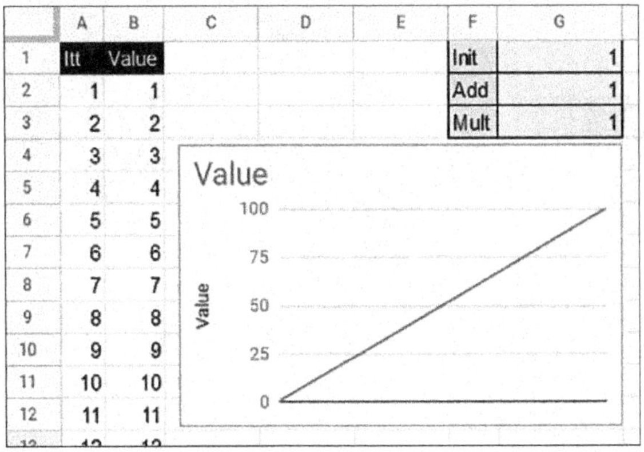

Figure 14.7 A chart showing linear growth

This is not what we ultimately want in this example, but all the needed components are now in place. The key to exponential growth is the multiplier. Without a multiplier, there is no exponential growth. But what number should you enter for the multiplier? Keep in mind that the player will likely never see this variable, so you don't have to worry about it being an integer or anything that is accessible at all. It may be surprising, but over the course of a long iterative run like this, very small multipliers are needed. You can test this yourself by typing in values for the Mult variable (in cell G3) and noting what happens to the chart. With even a modest integer, like 3, the graph shoots off the scale in the later iterations, with numbers so large they can be displayed properly only with engineering notation (see Figure 14.8).

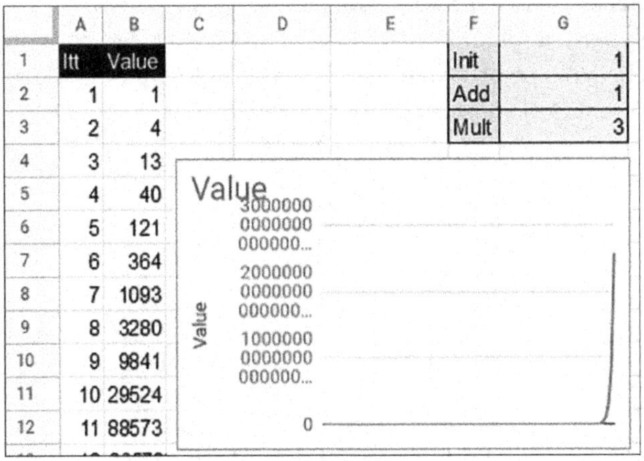

Figure 14.8 Broken growth with 3 as the multiplier

You can think of the multiplier as a percentage—and a small one at that. To get started, 2% growth is a nice middle ground that is not very steep but clearly shows growth over iterations. To write 2% as the Mult value, you would use 1.02; this multiplier yields the graph shown in Figure 14.9.

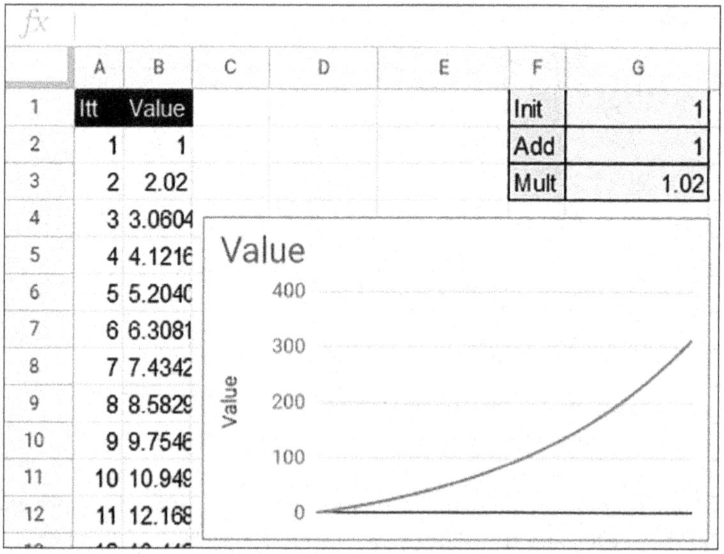

Figure 14.9 Smooth growth with 1.02 as the multiplier

At this point, the graph is showing exponential growth; technically, you could stop here. However, there are some practical problems with this growth. To see the first problem, observe the values in column B and imagine them in the game context of experience points needed to reach the next level. The player would start at Level 1 and be told to gain 1 XP (experience point) to level up. At Level 2, the player would be told to gain 2.02 XP. Here is the first problem: You never want to display decimals to the player. One way to solve the decimal issue is to create a derived value (or "display" value), where the decimal value is rounded using a function to make it more digestible for the player. Figure 14.10 shows a column added for display value (column C).

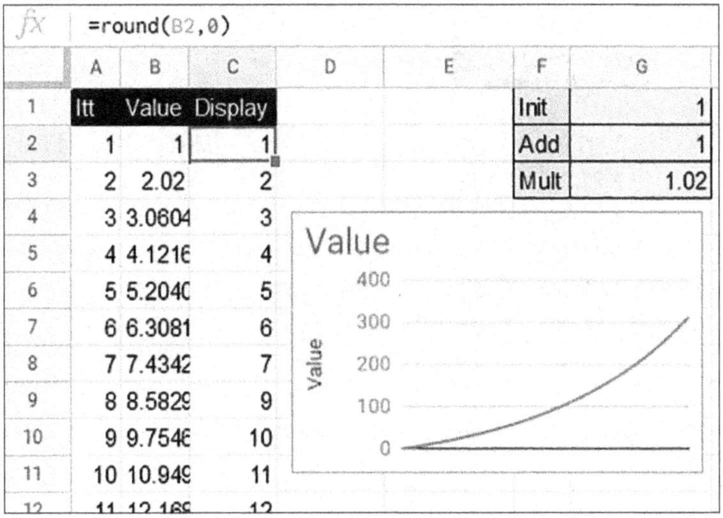

Figure 14.10 Adding a column for display values

The Display column now presents numerals that players can work with more easily, but it exposes another problem with the list. At the early levels, the iterations provide nearly linear growth—which can lead to player confusion and, even worse, present some difficult math problems for systems designers.

For example, in a racing game, to level up a race car, you might have the number of XP needed listed in the Display column. And you might allow the player to earn XP by doing a very simple race to gain 1 XP or a tougher, higher-failure-rate race to gain 2 or more XP. With the values as listed in Figure 14.10, the player would gain levels very quickly and would not be encouraged to ever take on the tougher, higher-failure-rate races. It would be easy to "grind" the easy race repeatedly because the increase per level is so small.

While it would be possible to fix this issue by increasing the multiplier, doing so would lead back to the same problem of very large numbers at the end of the list. Instead, you want to have steady, noticeable growth at the beginning and larger, exponential growth at the end. To accomplish this, you can change the Add value. Because it is additive, it does not affect the shape of the growth curve, but it changes the increments at the start of the curve. For example, changing the Add value to 10 results in the graph shown in Figure 14.11.

	A	B	C	F	G
1	Itt	Value	Display	Init	1
2	1	1	1	Add	10
3	2	11.02	11	Mult	1.02
4	3	21.240	21		
5	4	31.665	32		
6	5	42.298	42		
7	6	53.144	53		
8	7	64.207	64		
9	8	75.491	75		
10	9	87.001	87		
11	10	98.741	99		

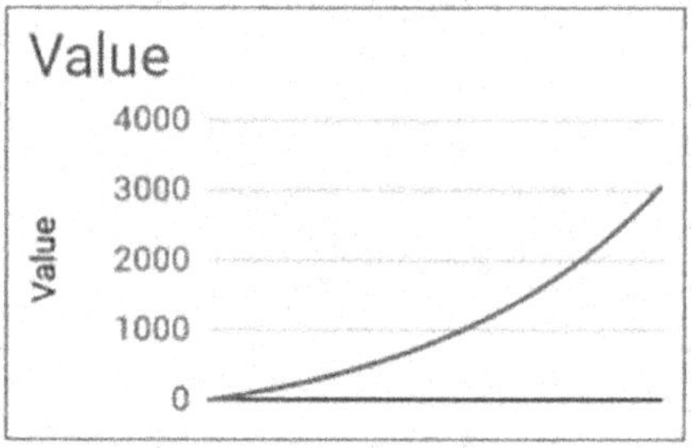

Figure 14.11 Rounded numbers

At this point, the curve is still showing a comfortable growth rate, but the early levels show distinct growth for each iteration. The growth is enough that the players can clearly notice it intuitively, and it will be enough to encourage players to perform tasks to gain more of the resources needed (XP in this example). There is one more problem hidden in here. To see it better, scroll down to the bottom of the iterations and look at the kind of growth shown near iteration 100 (see Figure 14.12); compare this growth to the growth shown in the first 10 levels.

	A	B	C
1	Itt	Value	Display
91	90	2419.127153	2419
92	91	2477.509696	2478
93	92	2537.05989	2537
94	93	2597.801088	2598
95	94	2659.75711	2660
96	95	2722.952252	2723
97	96	2787.411297	2787
98	97	2853.159523	2853
99	98	2920.222713	2920
100	99	2988.627168	2989
101	100	3058.399711	3058

Figure 14.12 Growth near the end of the iterations

If you are unable to spot the problem, that's fine: It may not be obvious to you unless you see it as a curve or put it into a game and test it. But you can expose the issue here in the spreadsheet by doing one more check: You can determine the growth of each iteration as a percentage of the last iteration. That is, you can determine the size of jump in needed XP for each level. Is it even across the entire run, or does it spike?

To visualize this, you can take the previous value of each iteration and divide it by the new iteration value. This will show, as a percentage, how much of a jump there is in the value needed to level up. Compare the top of the iterations list (shown in Figure 14.13) to the bottom of the list (shown in Figure 14.14).

fx =B3/B2

	A	B	C	D
1	Itt	Value	Display	
2	1	1	1	
3	2	11.02	11	1102.00%
4	3	21.2404	21	192.74%
5	4	31.665208	32	149.08%
6	5	42.29851216	42	133.58%
7	6	53.1444824	53	125.64%
8	7	64.20737205	64	120.82%
9	8	75.49151949	75	117.57%
10	9	87.00134988	87	115.25%

Figure 14.13 The top of the iterations list

	A	B	C	D
1	Itt	Value	Display	
91	90	2419.127153	2419	102.42%
92	91	2477.509696	2478	102.41%
93	92	2537.05989	2537	102.40%
94	93	2597.801088	2598	102.39%
95	94	2659.75711	2660	102.38%
96	95	2722.952252	2723	102.38%
97	96	2787.411297	2787	102.37%
98	97	2853.159523	2853	102.36%
99	98	2920.222713	2920	102.35%
100	99	2988.627168	2989	102.34%
101	100	3058.399711	3058	102.33%

Figure 14.14 The bottom of the iterations list

As this check shows, to go from Level 2 to Level 3, there is 1102% increase in needed XP! This is a huge increase and will likely cause problems in assigning XP values because so much is needed to move up in these first levels. Compare this with the values at the end of the list, where the final iteration is a 102.33% increase. Notice that this increase very nearly matches the growth multiplier, which means the additive value is no longer having a significant effect.

To fix this issue, you need the amount of added growth per iteration to be a smaller percentage of the initial value. Because the initial value is still sitting at the default 1, and the additive is at the relatively larger amount 10, the percentage increase is dramatically affected. Because you already changed the additive to get it where you want it, the final tweak to make is to adjust the initial value so that it is large enough that the additive value does not create the dramatic percentage increase at the start of the curve. For this example, you can plug in 100 for the Init value and see what happens (see Figure 14.15).

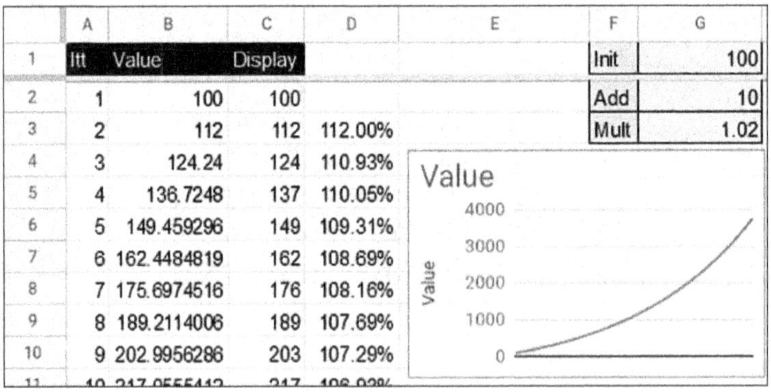

	A	B	C	D	E	F	G
1	Itt	Value	Display			Init	100
2	1	100	100			Add	10
3	2	112	112	112.00%		Mult	1.02
4	3	124.24	124	110.93%			
5	4	136.7248	137	110.05%			
6	5	149.459296	149	109.31%			
7	6	162.4484819	162	108.69%			
8	7	175.6974516	176	108.16%			
9	8	189.2114006	189	107.69%			
10	9	202.9956286	203	107.29%			

Figure 14.15 Basic input values for each of the variables in the growth formula

The percentage increase has now dropped to 112% at the most and is 102.27% at the last iteration. This might seem like it is still a bit large, but look at the display numbers. The first iterations go from 100 to 112 to 124. A player would not notice a large percentage increase in the number because the actual number is relatively small, at just 12 more points for the second step. This last change has now solved the final common problem of basic exponential growth curves. With these numbers, you have a solid start to work from for almost any exponential growth curve imaginable.

Tweaking the Basic Exponential Growth Formula

You could easily branch off from what you have learned to this point by tweaking these four variables to get a wide array of effects. The best way to learn how to do this is to play with the values in a copy of this spreadsheet. Leave up all of the values as they are here and tweak the iterations, initial value, additive, and multiplier. Also take some time to go further than common sense would warrant. Put in very large numbers for the variables and see what happens. Put in decimals. Then go even further and put in negative numbers, formulas, exponential powers, and anything else you can think of. By interactively playing with the variables and observing the results, you can quickly learn how to get effects you want and avoid those you don't.

A Note on Iterations

In the example in this chapter, you did not change the number of iterations, but this variable is important. There is a basic rule you should keep in mind for the number of iterations: The more iterations in a chart, the smaller the multiplier must be. To illustrate this, Figure 14.16 shows exactly the same list of iterations as in Figure 14.15, but the chart includes only the first 10 iterations.

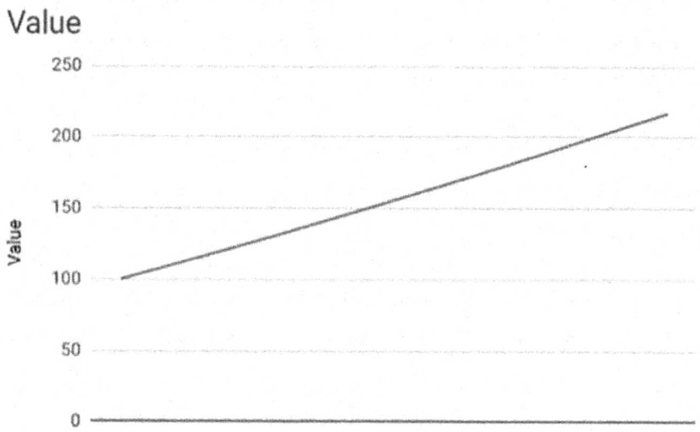

Figure 14.16 Using short iterations

Notice that this curve looks almost completely linear. The 2% growth does not have enough iterations to start to take significant effect over the course of the chart. As you can see, it is important to know the number of iterations needed for total growth before building a chart like this. Fortunately, it's also easy to change the variables quickly to account for any change of iterations.

Exponential Charts and Game Hierarchy

It may be fast and easy to completely change the character of a game by adjusting an exponential growth chart, but doing so also has dramatic ripple effects for the rest of the game. By changing a single variable in the chart, it is quite possible to completely change the balance of every level and every encounter in the game. Because of this, it is highly recommended to place each needed growth chart high in the game design hierarchy (as discussed in Chapter 13, "Range Balancing, Data Fulcrums, and Hierarchical Design") and to lock them down early in the game development process.

Further Steps

After completing this chapter, you should take some time to practice in the real world with the concepts covered here. Try these exercises to further explore the Exponential growth charts in all of their many variations:

- Create a spreadsheet and make the exponential growth chart shown in Figure 14.15. Be sure to use the chart functionality to visualize your data. Start by making 200 iterations and using 100 as the Init value, 1.02 as the Mult value, and 10 as the Add value. This chart will provide a good starting point that you can use to start experimenting.
- After you create the chart described in the preceding exercise, make a copy of the sheet in the same workbook and label the copy "Play." On the Play , change the input values until you break the chart. (Really, that's the goal here.) Try putting in very large or very small numbers. Put in negative numbers, or decimals, or even formulas and functions. Keep trying the most bizarre and creative things you can think of and observe what happens to your chart. Can you get it to make a cone? How about a solid bar? Can you get it to look somewhat like a chart of a heartbeat on a medical device? Only by pushing systems beyond their intended bounds can you find where the true bounds are. Note that even when you are purposefully breaking the data, you are not actually doing any damage. Because you made a copy and are not working on the original, your data and structure are completely safe. This is one of the great benefits of working in the digital world.
- When you are comfortable breaking the data, make another copy of your original sheet and see if you can come up with a few varieties of charts that you might like. How gentle can you make the curve before it is functionally linear? How steep can you make it before it breaks? Again, getting comfortable with doing these extreme exercises will help you know what your boundaries are.

CHAPTER 15

ANALYZING GAME DATA

Up to this point in the book, we have been focusing on making data objects one at a time and then evaluating them individually against other data objects. The next step in understanding a game as a whole is to evaluate all the objects together, whether it's a small set of 10 objects or tens of thousands of objects. You can do this for data as it is created or with existing game data that is fully complete—or anywhere in between.

There are many ways of viewing and analyzing game data, but this chapter focuses on two methods to provide an introduction. The first method is overview analysis, which involves clues and characteristics of the data setup. The second method is comparison analysis, which involves comparing two different data objects and analyzing them in more depth.

Overview Analysis

Overview analysis involves looking from a high level at trends in data to get a larger picture of what is happening. A standard way of getting a high-level view is to find an average of values. However, on its own, an average does not provide much information—and it can actually provide misinformation. Let's look at a simple example of how averages can go wrong. What is the average of the following list?

10

10

10

10

10

10

10

10

10

999,910

The average is 100,000.00. But does 100,000 actually give insights into what is going on in this list? No, it doesn't. If you look at the list, you intuitively understand that most numbers in the list are low numbers (10), but a single number is huge and throws off the average in the data as an outlier. In the end, 100,000 is too small to represent the outlier and too large to represent most of the data points, so it does not give much true insight into how this data works. In order to counterbalance this problem, you can find both the average and the median and then compare those two values. In this example, the median is 10. So this is what we know about the list:

Average: 100,000

Median: 10

By looking at these two numbers, you know that something strange is going on in the data. In a uniform and even distribution of numbers, the average and median are fairly close together, but in this example, they are different orders of magnitude. When analyzing data, this difference would warrant a deeper dive into the data to find out what is going on.

Table 15.1 shows a scenario that you might encounter in making a game: a list of fantasy creatures, each of which has a set of attributes.

Table 15.1 Creature data

Character Type	STR	DEX	HP	AV	DG	MV
Goblin	3	4	5	1	3	5
Zombie	4	2	6	0	0	2
Dark wolf	4	4	7	2	3	6
Snapping turtle	6	4	10	10	2	1
Barbarian	7	3	13	2	4	5
Dwarf	6	4	13	3	2	4
Gnoll	3	7	8	4	6	6
Halfling	3	7	6	1	8	5
Protoman	6	4	9	3	3	5
Kobold	3	8	5	3	5	6
Legionnaire	4	6	10	1	5	5
Lizardman	3	7	7	2	4	7
Ogre	8	3	17	5	1	3
Ork	6	4	10	5	1	5
Rat man	2	8	8	2	8	8
Wood elf	3	8	8	1	6	6
Hellhound	5	4	12	3	3	6
Werewolf	7	5	7	1	1	5
Blob	7	3	20	7	2	2
Giant ant	6	5	10	6	2	5
Warg	7	4	8	3	3	6
Clay golem	7	5	12	6	3	4

Character Type	STR	DEX	HP	AV	DG	MV
Swamp man	5	5	25	2	2	4
Mummy	10	4	20	6	2	2
Giant scarab	8	5	15	9	2	4
Razorback	6	6	15	6	3	5
Serpent	6	6	15	6	6	4
Giant scorpion	6	5	15	9	4	5
Black bear	7	6	15	6	4	6
Harpy	6	8	15	6	5	7
Gargoyle	7	5	15	6	5	6
Stone golem	8	5	25	8	3	4
Giant crab	8	5	15	12	5	6
Gorilla	9	7	15	3	3	4
Iron golem	9	5	30	10	3	4
Hill troll	12	4	20	5	1	4
Sasquatch	9	6	15	4	6	5
Cave gobbler	10	8	3	1	1	4
Sabertooth	10	6	20	7	5	6
Giant spider	8	7	15	6	5	6
Gorgon	6	9	20	4	6	4
Minotaur	10	7	20	5	6	5
Crocodile	10	7	20	8	3	4
Grizzly bear	10	8	20	7	5	6
Tigerman	11	8	18	7	6	6
Lionman	11	8	15	7	6	6
Rhinoman	13	7	20	9	3	4
Cave bear	12	8	20	8	5	6
Hydra	12	6	30	9	6	5
Cyclops	11	8	30	9	7	5
Treeman	15	5	50	20	3	1
Dragonling	11	7	40	10	7	10

Let's look at one individual attribute from this table—STR (strength)—and do an overview analysis of it. The simplest way to get an overview is to get the average of the STR values for all of the characters. After that, you can find the median and compare it against the average. Figure 15.1 shows these two calculations.

	A	B
	Attribute	STR
	Average	7.42
	Median	7

Figure 15.1 Finding the average and median of the STR attribute for a list of characters

This comparison provides a little bit of insight. You can see that the average and median are less than one whole point off from each other, so it is likely that there is a somewhat even distribution of values for this attribute (although that is not guaranteed to be the case). You can also get a feeling for the attribute numbers this list probably contains; in this case, medium to large single-digit numbers are likely.

The next step in understanding the data is to know the size of the data set (that is, the number of items in the data set). For this, you can use the COUNT function to count the number of STR attribute values included in the data set (see Figure 15.2).

	A	B
1	Attribute	STR
2	Count	52
3	Average	7.42
4	Median	7

Figure 15.2 Finding a count of items in the data set

Now you know how big the data set is, and you can make a few determinations based on this knowledge. The smaller the data set, the more outliers will affect the data. If you only have a list of 10 items, for example, even 1 being an outlier will easily throw off the results, but if you have 10,000 items, the data set is so large that a few outliers are likely to go unnoticed. In this example, the count of 52 means that large outliers would likely be visible in the comparison of average to median, but small ones might not.

Another observation you can make in this comparison is that the average is indeed a bit larger than the median. This means there are likely a few more large numbers in the data set, or there may be one or more rather large numbers that skew the results. You have already gleaned quite a bit of information from only three checks.

To dig even deeper, it's useful to know what number comes up in the data the most frequently. This is the *mode*, and you can find it with the MODE function. The mode also has some limitations, so let's look at one more small example before applying it to the RPG characters. In the following list of numbers, what is the mode?

1	8	14
2	9	15
3	9	16
4	10	17
5	11	18
6	12	19
7	13	

This example is simple enough that you can figure it out without a spreadsheet. The number that appears most frequently in this list is 9—but it is also the only number that is duplicated. So, is knowing that 9 is the mode important for understanding this list? Probably not. The list contains only a few numbers, and almost all of them are unique. The mode can be useful, but as with the average, you typically need another check to determine how much of a statement the mode value is making. In this case, you want to know what proportion of the numbers in the list are the mode. If very few are the mode, then the mode value is not particularly important. If the percentage of values that are the mode is higher, then the mode is a more important factor to watch. In the case of this simple list, 2/20 numbers are the mode; this works out to 10%. This percentage is small enough that the mode is not a very important factor when evaluating this data. Figure 15.3 shows a number of formulas applied to the RPG character data.

	A	B
1	Attribute	STR
2	Count	52
3	Average	7.42
4	Median	7
5	Mode	6
6	CountMode	10
7	Mode %	19.2%

Figure 15.3 Several of the most typical methods of doing high level analysis.

In Figure 15.3, you can see that the mode is smaller than the median and average. You can also see that 19.2% of the characters in the game have a STR value of 6. While 19.2% is not a huge percentage, it does provide some information. In this case, it shows that a sizable portion of characters have a STR value that is lower than the average or median, signaling that there are likely a few higher outliers in the data.

Next, you need to find the extent of outliers that exist in the data. To do this, you can find both the minimum and maximum values for that attribute. To take it one step further, you can do a count of how many are the minimum value and how many are the maximum value. Figure 15.4 shows a set of functions you can use to get helpful numbers from the character data, which is on another sheet.

	A	B
1	Attribute	STR
2	Count	=counta(ChaData!B2:B)
3	Average	=AVERAGE(ChaData!B2:B)
4	Median	=MEDIAN(ChaData!B2:B)
5	Mode	=mode(ChaData!B2:B)
6	CountMode	=countif(ChaData!B2:B, B5)
7	Mode %	=B6/B2
8	Max	=max(ChaData!B2:B)
9	Max Count	=countif(ChaData!B2:B, B8)
10	Min	=min(ChaData!B2:B)
11	Min Count	=countif(ChaData!B2:B, B10)

Figure 15.4 Functions used for this calculations; exposed

Figure 15.5 shows the results of these functions. In these numbers, you can see how common the most extreme outliers are.

	A	B
1	Attribute	STR
2	Count	52
3	Average	7.42
4	Median	7
5	Mode	6
6	CountMode	10
7	Mode %	19.2%
8	Max	15
9	Max Count	1
10	Min	2
11	Min Count	1

Figure 15.5 Adding Max, Min, and counts of values for a deeper dive

When you look at all the information provided in Figure 15.5, the picture of what is going on in the data becomes a bit more clear. You can make some commonsense observations like the following:

- This attribute has a fairly wide possible distribution, but most of the numbers are clustered around 7.
- The mode, 6, belongs to 10 characters, where the minimum and maximum each only have 1. This suggests that there is likely to be a bell curve, where most of the values fall in the center of the range, and just a few are at the high and low ends.
- Given that the average is only a little bit larger than the median, but both are much smaller than the maximum, it's likely that there are very few characters at the upper end.

All these observations together paint a picture of a fairly standard set of characters where most are around average, and there are a few stand outs on the high and low ends.

The final step, which is also the most important step, is to go back to the raw data and observe it. The STR attribute, at least, should start to make a lot more sense when you scroll through that data. It doesn't really matter that you don't yet know what the attribute actually does in the game. This is also a great time to start pairing names (and possibly descriptions) with the data. What names of characters are associated with larger numbers, and which ones are associated with the smaller ones? By doing this type of analysis, you can start to form a picture of what each of these character types will be like in the game.

By doing so much analysis for STR, you have created a format to do the same type of analysis for each of the other attributes. If you run the same functions shown in Figure 15.4 for all the other attributes, you get the results shown in Figure 15.6.

	A	B	C	D	E	F	G
1	Attribute	STR	DEX	HP	AV	DG	MV
2	Count	52	52	52	52	52	52
3	Average	7.42	5.77	15.81	5.50	3.90	4.90
4	Median	7	6	15	6	3.5	5
5	Mode	6	5	15	6	3	6
6	CountMode	10	11	12	9	13	15
7	Mode %	19.2%	21.2%	23.1%	17.3%	25.0%	28.8%
8	Max	15	9	50	20	8	10
9	Max Count	1	1	1	1	2	1
10	Min	2	2	3	0	0	1
11	Min Count	1	1	1	1	1	2

Figure 15.6 Expanded attribute analysis

From this view of the data, you can make even more observations:

- HP is on a larger scale than the other attributes. MV and DG are on a smaller scale.
- All of the attributes are tending toward middle-sized single-digit numbers, and there are some outliers.
- The average and median scores for all attributes are close together, indicating a consistency in the spread of character data for this game.
- The mode is more telling for some attributes than for others. There is likely an in-game reason that so many characters have 6 MV. When games use single-digit numbers or small digit integers, it's likely that the mode will be a higher percentage of the data objects because there simply are not enough numbers at that scale to have large amounts of variation.
- None of the min count or max count values have many instances. This indicates that most of the character attributes cluster more closely toward the center, and a few attributes stand out as being extreme.

For a basic high-level view of a game, this analysis might be enough. This is the level of data analysis that would work for playing a game at a serious level or evaluating a simple game. In some cases, you need to do further analysis, as described next.

Next-Level Deep Analysis

For more complex or larger games, you may need to dig in a bit deeper. The next step in this research is to find the numbers that are involved specifically for each attribute. The goal of this analysis is to find out what numbers are being used for each attribute and how often each of them is being used. You can find this information by using a spreadsheet and the functions SORT, combined with the function UNIQUE. This compound function can look at a list of repeating numbers and pull out only one instance of each number and sort those instances into an ascending list. Figure 15.7 shows how you use this compound function to find the STR attribute distribution in column B of the ChaData sheet.

```
fx  =sort(unique(ChaData!B2:B),unique(ChaData!B2:B),true)
```

	A	B	C	D	E	F	G	H	I	J
1	Attribute	STR	DEX	HP	AV	DG	MV		STR	STR#
2	Count	52	52	52	52	52	52		2	1
3	Average	7.42	5.77	15.81	5.50	3.90	4.90		3	6
4	Median	7	6	15	6	3.5	5		4	3
5	Mode	6	5	15	6	3	6		5	2
6	CountMode	10	11	12	9	13	15		6	10
7	Mode %	19.2%	21.2%	23.1%	17.3%	25.0%	28.8%		7	7
8	Max	15	9	50	20	8	10		8	5
9	Max Count	1	1	1	1	2	1		9	3
10	Min	2	2	3	0	0	1		10	6
11	Min Count	1	1	1	1	1	2		11	4
12									12	3
13									13	1
14									15	1

Figure 15.7 Using SORT and UNIQUE to create a list

You already knew from the earlier checks that the maximum value is 15, and the minimum is 2. The procedurally generated list also finds the same thing. Notice also that there is no 14 in the list because no character had an attribute value of 14. In this list, all of the same things are apparent as in the first breakdown of the attribute in column B, but this time you see more granular results. In column J, you see a COUNTIF function that does a check for how many times each of the possible values shows up in the entire list of data. Just as you would expect, 6 is the most common value; you already knew that from the mode. Interestingly, you can see that this is not exactly a uniform bell curve distribution. There are very few 5s and 4s, and there are more 3s. On the upper end, the numbers taper off more, as expected, with a few minor exceptions. Figure 15.8 shows this data charted.

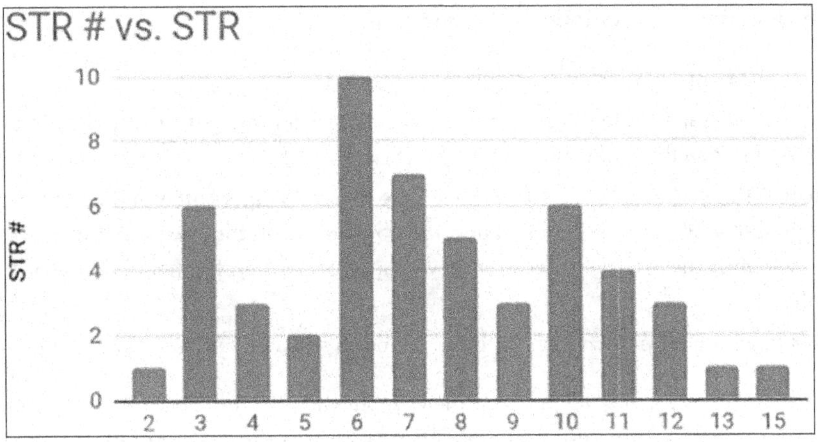

Figure 15.8 Chart of data

The chart gives you even more insights into how the data works in the game. It looks like there are three peaks of frequency that then taper off into the next peak. This indicates that there might be "classes" of STR among characters—perhaps low, medium, and high or weak, average, and strong—with variations in those groups. You can apply similar analyses to all the attributes to get a full readout of the distribution of each attribute value set (see Figure 15.9).

fx =countif(ChaData!B$2:B,I2)

	A	B	C	D	E	F	G
1	Attribute	STR	DEX	HP	AV	DG	MV
2	Count	52	52	52	52	52	52
3	Average	7.42	5.77	15.81	5.50	3.90	4.90
4	Median	7	6	15	6	3.5	5
5	Mode	6	5	15	6	3	6
6	CountMode	10	11	12	9	13	15
7	Mode %	19.2%	21.2%	23.1%	17.3%	25.0%	28.8%
8	Max	15	9	50	20	8	10
9	Max Count	1	1	1	1	2	1
10	Min	2	2	3	0	0	1
11	Min Count	1	1	1	1	1	2
12							
13							
14							
15							
16							
17							
18							

	H	I	J	K	L	M	N	O	P	Q	R	S	T
1		STR	STR #	DEX	DEX #	HP	HP #	AV	AV #	DG	DG #	MV	MV #
2		2	1	2	1	3	1	0	1	0	1	1	2
3		3	6	3	3	5	2	1	6	1	5	2	3
4		4	3	4	10	6	2	2	5	2	7	3	1
5		5	2	5	11	7	3	3	6	3	13	4	13
6		6	10	6	7	8	4	4	3	4	4	5	14
7		7	7	7	9	9	1	5	4	5	9	6	15
8		8	5	8	10	10	4	6	9	6	9	7	2
9		9	3	9	1	12	2	7	5	7	2	8	1
10		10	6			13	2	8	3	8	2	10	1
11		11	4			15	12	9	5				
12		12	3			17	1	10	3				
13		13	1			18	1	12	1				
14		15	1			20	10	20	1				
15						25	2						
16						30	3						
17						40	1						
18						50	1						

Figure 15.9 Expanded attribute analysis

With this fuller picture, even more patterns emerge:

- You can see that MV has a very tight grouping around 5.
- DG has one value, 3, that seems to be very important for this game because it is much more common than the other numbers.
- AV has a more traditional peak in the middle and then tapers off, but it has one very high outlier on the high side and one very low outlier on the low side. It would be easy to miss these outliers because they counterbalance each other in the full list of values.
- DEX has a weaker pattern than the other attributes and a more linear distribution.

You could easily keep going deeper with analysis, but with just the tools used so far, you already have a much better understanding. Also, the deeper the analysis goes, the more individual it becomes to the game, the data, and the attributes. The methods discussed so far can apply to any game that has lists of data objects that have attributes.

Practicing Data Analysis

If you had a hard time following along with the observations in the previous sections, keep in mind that those observations are the most difficult part of analysis. The good news is that it is fairly easy to practice making such observations.

One of the best ways to practice is to try out the previous methods of analysis on games you already know. Both official websites and fan-made sites are full of data sheets containing lists of data objects and their attributes. You probably want to start with a game whose feel you already know. Then you can do an analysis of the game and note what patterns in the game caused that feeling to emerge to you as the player. What mechanics and technical limitations do you already know about the game that may have driven the numbers you find in the data attributes? By going through this process for several games, you might start to see the connections between what the data is doing and what the game feels like.

Comparison Analysis

With complex games that have large lists of data objects, it can be helpful to focus on a comparison of two objects in isolation. For example, with the earlier example of the RPG characters, you might want to look at two characters at a time and compare their stats directly. To do this, you can use data validation (as described in Chapter 5, "Spreadsheet Basics") to create a drop-down list of all the data objects and then use VLOOKUP to pull up each of the attribute values for the two data objects. Figure 15.10 shows an example of this.

fx =VLOOKUP($B2,ChaData!$A:$G,7,false)

	A	B	C	D	E	F	G	H
1	#	Character	STR	DEX	HP	AV	DG	MV
2	1	Zombie	4	2	6	0	0	2
3	2	Barbarian	7	3	13	2	4	5

Figure 15.10 Using VLOOKUP for Data object comparison

Here you can see the zombie character in direct comparison to the barbarian character. Once you have this comparison set up, it is easier to go further and more closely examine the data. The following are a few examples of what you might want to look at:

- A difference in attributes between the objects
- A plot of where each character falls in comparison to the minimum and maximum
- Charts that further show detailed comparisons between the objects.

When you isolate a small number of data objects for analysis, you can further expand the depth of analysis done for each of them. Each game calls for unique analyses, so take the time you need to think about what comparisons would be most useful to run on various pairs.

Canaries

There is a common problem when analyzing new or very foreign data: You don't always know when you have made a mistake. When you don't know the expected results of the analysis, you can't know for sure if the generated answer is right or wrong. This is a difficult problem to completely eliminate, but there is a tool you can use to help safeguard against it: a data canary. If the canary finds that something is wrong with your data, then you know there might be a bigger problem.

> **note**
>
> The idea of the data canary is based on the canaries coal miners used to determine if the air in parts of a mine was safe to breathe.

To see how a data canary works, consider the list of percentages in Figure 15.11. You know intuitively that the sum of all percentages is 100% in most cases. So, is the list in Figure 15.11 correct? It's very difficult to tell just by looking at the list. This type of problem can appear anywhere that there is data analysis: It may look like all the results are correct, but it's hard to tell for sure if they are.

	A	B
1	Things	Percent
2	Thing 1	11.00%
3	Thing 2	2.00%
4	Thing 3	15.80%
5	Thing 4	3.00%
6	Thing 5	4.00%
7	Thing 6	2.50%
8	Thing 7	2.00%
9	Thing 8	4.50%
10	Thing 9	3.10%
11	Thing 10	1.00%
12	Thing 11	0.04%
13	Thing 12	6.00%
14	Thing 13	3.00%
15	Thing 14	12.00%
16	Thing 15	4.00%
17	Thing 16	6.00%
18	Thing 17	7.00%
19	Thing 18	3.50%
20	Thing 19	1.00%
21	Thing 20	8.20%

Figure 15.11 Do these percentages total 100%?

The canary is a calculation for which you already know the result, either because it is intuitive—such as 100% being the sum of percentages—or because you can double-check it by calculating the same result in two different ways (for example, using the function AVERAGE and then using SUM and COUNT to get the average). Redundancy and checks like this can reduce mistakes to a great extent (although mistakes may still happen). In the list of percentages in Figure 15.12, you can see that there is a mistake of some sort because the total is less than 100%.

	A	B
1	Things	Percent
2	Thing 1	11.00%
3	Thing 2	2.00%
4	Thing 3	15.80%
5	Thing 4	3.00%
6	Thing 5	4.00%
7	Thing 6	2.50%
8	Thing 7	2.00%
9	Thing 8	4.50%
10	Thing 9	3.10%
11	Thing 10	1.00%
12	Thing 11	0.04%
13	Thing 12	6.00%
14	Thing 13	3.00%
15	Thing 14	12.00%
16	Thing 15	4.00%
17	Thing 16	6.00%
18	Thing 17	7.00%
19	Thing 18	3.50%
20	Thing 19	1.00%
21	Thing 20	8.20%
22		
23		
24	Sum	99.64%

Figure 15.12 Mistake found

To examine a slightly more sophisticated example, let's revisit the RPG characters. This time, say that you want to double-check the distribution of attribute values. You know that the count of attributes is 52, and you can do a quick sum of attribute counts for a single column of distributions to make sure it comes up as 52 as well (see Figure 15.13).

fx =sum(J2:J14)

	A	B	C	D	E	F	G	H	I	J	K	L	M	N	O	P	Q	R	S	T
1	Attribute	STR	DEX	HP	AV	DG	MV		STR	STR #	DEX	DEX #	HP	HP #	AV	AV #	DG	DG #	MV	MV #
2	Count	52	52	52	52	52	52		2	1	2	1	3	1	0	1	0	1	1	2
3	Average	7.42	5.77	15.81	5.50	3.90	4.90		3	6	3	3	5	2	1	6	1	5	2	3
4	Median	7	6	15	6	3.5	5		4	3	4	10	6	2	2	5	2	7	3	1
5	Mode	6	5	15	6	3	6		5	2	5	11	7	3	3	6	3	13	4	13
6	CountMode	10	11	12	9	13	15		6	10	6	7	8	4	4	3	4	4	5	14
7	Mode %	19.2%	21.2%	23.1%	17.3%	25.0%	28.8%		7	7	7	9	9	1	5	4	5	9	6	15
8	Max	15	9	50	20	8	10		8	5	8	10	10	4	6	9	6	9	7	2
9	Max Count	1	1	1	1	2	1		9	3	9	1	12	2	7	5	7	2	8	1
10	Min	2	2	3	0	0	1		10	6			13	2	8	3	8	2	10	1
11	Min Count	1	1	1	1	1	2		11	4			15	12	9	5				
12									12	3			17	1	10	3				
13									13	1			18	1	12	1				
14									15	1			20	10	20	1				
15													25	2						
16									canary	52			30	3						
17													40	1						
18													50	1						

Figure 15.13 Using a canary to check the accuracy of the results

By consistently using canaries in this way, you can have a much greater degree of confidence that most or all of your data is doing what you expect it to do.

Further Steps

After completing this chapter, you should take some time to practice in the real world with the concepts covered here. Try these exercises to further explore the concepts of data analysis in both a high-level overview and in more detailed review.

- Create a spreadsheet and either import or copy and paste in data from a favorite game. Take some time to clean up the data and ensure that it is arranged in a way that is easy to evaluate (for example, ensuring that each attribute has its own column and that each data object has its own row).
- When you have data imported and tidied up, use the methods presented in this chapter to do an analysis of the data. After you use all the basic methods described here, look to see if the game you have chosen lends itself to any other form of analysis. Which type of analysis works best with your game—a broad overview of all data or a more detailed comparison of individual objects?
- Start to draw conclusions about how your chosen game plays, given the data. After doing this exercise on a game, you should understand much more deeply why the system designers made the game the way they did. Also while doing this, keep an eye out for mistakes or loopholes. It's not common for them to slip through in modern games, but it does occasionally happen.

CHAPTER 16

MACROSYSTEMS AND PLAYER ENGAGEMENT

You can use several different styles of difficulty adjustment to make a game harder or easier as a whole or to adjust it to a player's particular needs. You will often find, especially in larger games, that you can use multiple methods at the same time to get a better balance. This chapter discusses balancing the game at a very high level, across all the integrated systems.

Macrosystem Difficulty Adjustment

Difficulty adjustment is quite easy to implement in games, and it is often used for encouraging high levels of competition. The following sections discuss these broad categories of difficulty adjustment:

- Flat balancing
- Positive feedback loop
- Negative feedback loop
- Dynamic difficulty adjustment
- Layered difficulty adjustment
- Cross-feeding

Flat Balancing

A flat balanced game is inherently fair and never adjusted for either side.

> note
>
> Flat balancing is the oldest form of balancing, and it is used for most sports games. It is also used for many old games like chess and backgammon. Here's what it's good and bad for:
>
> - **Good for:** Serious competition
> - **Bad for:** Fun, accessible games

With flat balancing, it does not matter what either player does, what position the players are in, or how well or poorly they're doing: The game runs without adjustment.

For example, if two players play chess and Player 1 wins, you can assume that Player 1 is better. You know that the game has not done anything to make Player 1 have a better chance or worse chance of winning. The downside of this is that if Player 1 is considerably better than Player 2, then Player 2 will never win. Player 1 will always win, and the game will soon be boring for both sides. It's not particularly fun to play a game when you know you're always going to lose or always going to win. Part of the fun of playing games is the mystery of the outcome, and if the outcome is not mysterious in any way, then it's not interesting.

Flat balancing is really good for competitions where you want to find out who is the best, such as sports. In sports at the professional level, you don't want to see a close game each time; you want to see which side is better at the game. On the other hand, if you want a game to be competitive and fun, which is generally the goal with consumer-facing games, you don't want to use flat balancing.

Positive Feedback Loops

In addition to flat balancing, another common type of balancing is a *positive feedback loop*; it is also sometimes called a rich *get richer, poor get poorer* mechanic or a *divergent curve*. Figure 16.1 provides an illustration of the concept of a positive feedback loop.

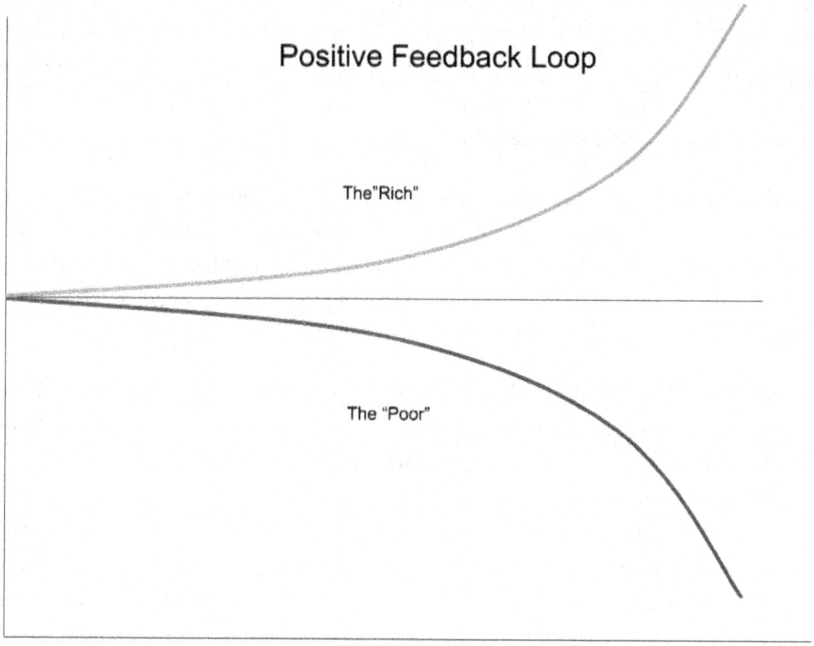

Figure 16.1 Positive feedback loop

> **note**
>
> Positive feedback loops are used in poker and bowling. Here's what they're good and bad for:
>
> - **Good for:** Breaking a stalemate, where scores are consistently too close
> - **Bad for:** Allowing players to catch up and fun, not-so-serious serious games

A positive feedback loop works by diverging players to give the better players an advantage and put the worse players at a disadvantage. It is easy to implement this type of balancing in a game: All you have to do is reward players who are doing better with a reward that makes the game easier. If players do better and get better rewards, they are probably going to continue to do even better. In the same vein, you can also use this form of balancing to punish players for doing poorly. Both methods can cause a positive feedback loop.

For example, say that in an FPS, every time you get a successful shot, you are given a better gun that does more damage and has better accuracy. Conversely, every time you miss a shot, your gun gets worse. This would very quickly lead to the better players becoming completely unstoppable and the worse players having no ability to compete. In general, this may seem to be a bad thing because you don't want players to be completely divergent from each other. If you find that someone is continually getting better and you're continually getting worse, the game is going to cease to be fun.

However, you can use this mechanic for a few good effects. One of the reasons you would use a positive feedback loop is when a game tends to get stuck in a stalemate. If games are consistently very close or go back and forth, you can break the stalemate with a positive feedback loop. By rewarding a player who is doing slightly better, you will enable the player to pull away and bring the game to a conclusion.

Bowling is a really good example of a game where a positive feedback loop can be used well. In bowling, the most pins you can knock down with a single ball is 10. You get 10 chances to knock down all the pins, so a total score of 100 would seem to be the natural maximum. Once players start to develop skill at bowling, however they are able to get 10 pins each attempt much more often. If the maximum score were 100, game scores would be very close and often tied. At the professional level, players would score around 96 to 98 points each and every game. This would leave little mystery in the progression of the game and would make the game less fun to play and watch. To keep things interesting in bowling, each time a player knocks down all 10 pins on the first attempt, it is considered a strike, and the frame is scored 10 plus the total of the player's next two frames. This allows a good player to get up to 30 points for a single frame and allows the top score to be up to 300 points. Because a single missed attempt can lead to a massive reduction in points, the scores diverge much further than it seems they would over a few missed pins—and the game becomes less predictable.

Another example is the classic game Monopoly. In Monopoly, the better you roll, the more properties you are able to own and the more money you get, which allows you to buy more properties, so you can get more money, more properties, and more money. This cycle continues until one player inevitably wins. If it were more difficult for players to get more money and property, the game would go on forever. Given that the game already takes a long time, a further extension of gameplay would likely cause severe boredom in players.

Negative Feedback Loop

Negative feedback loops are sometimes called *rubber banding* because a player who does well gets more penalties and fewer rewards. Conversely, a player who is doing poorly gets more rewards and fewer penalties. This acts like a metaphorical rubber band that holds back the leading player and pulls forward the trailing player. Figure 16.2 illustrates this concept.

The idea of a negative feedback loop is fairly unintuitive, because you would think you would want to reward good play and punish bad play, but it really depends on the kind of game you're creating. If you're creating a very competitive game, a negative feedback loop would be a bad thing as it tends to make the outcomes between better and worse players closer than they otherwise would have been. But often you want to make games more inclusive of more players. This could be a style choice to make a family-friendly game or implemented to grow the game's audience. Leveling the playing field allows better players to compete with lesser players and still have some mystery in terms of the outcome of the game.

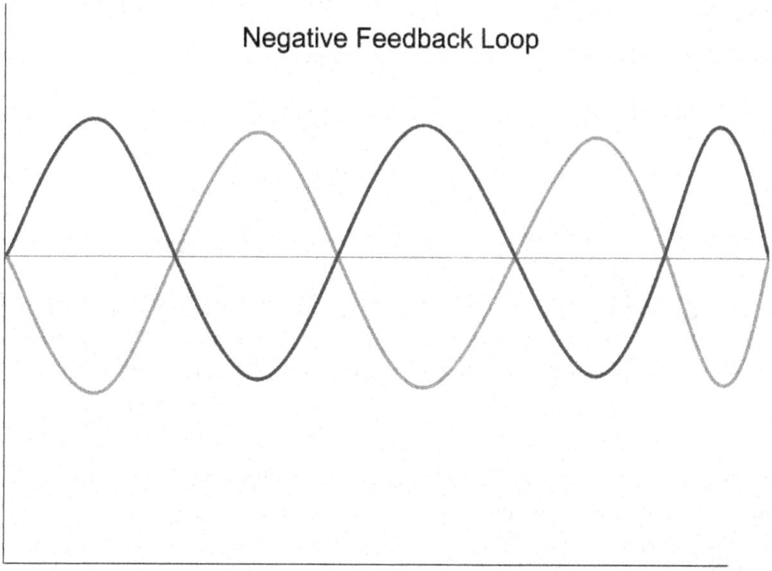

Figure 16.2 Negative feedback loop

> **note**
>
> Cart-racing and party games typically use negative feedback loops. Here's what they're good and bad for:
>
> - **Good for:** Light-hearted, fun games
> - **Bad for:** Highly competitive games

One of the most obvious places this form of balancing is used is in mass-market cart-racing games—that is, games where players are racing around and can get little power-ups that can help a little bit or a whole lot. Classically, in these games, the further behind you are, the better the power-ups you get, which allows you to catch up. Conversely, the further ahead you are, the worse the power-ups you get, which makes you fall back. This type of balancing tends to pull everyone toward the middle. This can be frustrating for very competitive players because it seems like the game rewards bad behavior and punishes good behavior—and this is exactly the case. Negative feedback loops are used in light-hearted games to make sure players of different skill levels all feel like they have a chance to win.

Negative feedback loops are commonly used for *handicapping*—that is, giving extra points to players with lower skill levels. Handicapping is used in the real world in bowling, golf, and horse racing. Let's look at an example of a handicapped bowling video game. In bowling, recall from earlier in the chapter that the highest score a player can get is 300. Say that two players have the following averages:

Player 1: 100 points average

Player 2: 200 points average

Each player receives a handicap score that is the maximum score possible minus their average score:

Player 1: 300 max score – 100 points average = 200-point handicap

Player 2: 300 max score – 200 points average = 100-point handicap

The next time the players bowl a game, they each get to add their handicap score to the score they bowled on the most recent game. The less skilled player now has a handicap of 200 points, and the better player now has a handicap of 100 points. If these players were to play against each other with no handicap, and they were consistent, the first player would always lose and the second player would always win. With flat balancing, neither of them would go into the contest with any mystery about the outcome. In a high-level competition, this would be good, but for a friendly game, you want some mystery.

Now let's say these players face off against each other, and each of them scores 150 points in this game. To update the handicap for each of the players, you add up each player's most recent score and handicap. To Player 1's score of 150 you add the handicap of 200, so Player 1 now has 350 points—even though this is a higher total than is possible in bowling without a handicap. (When using a handicap system, you often see scores that are higher than naturally possible.) For Player 2, you also start with 150 and then add this player's handicap, which is 100, so Player 2 now has 250 points. Or, to put it more simply:

Player 1 handicap 200 + score 150 = 350 points for this game

Player 2 handicap 100 + score 150 = 250 points for this game

In this game, Player 1 wins even though both players bowled the same score. This may seem unfair, but handicapping levels the playing field by comparing a player against their average play instead of directly against their opponent. The scoring system is metaphorically saying "on this day, Player 1, who is a worse player in general, was having a good day. Player 2, who is a generally better player, was having a bad day. Therefore, today, Player 1 wins because they had a relatively better day." In this way, you can compare each player on the day, which creates some mystery in the outcome of the game.

Dynamic Difficulty Adjustment

Dynamic difficulty adjustment (DDA) is an interactive method of adjustment that relies on either human or AI decisions to adjust difficulty within the game in real time, depending on conditions.

> note
>
> Examples of DDA include freemium mobile games and modern AAA action games. Here's what they're good and bad for:
>
> - **Good for:** Ensuring a consistent experience among large numbers of players
> - **Bad for:** Giving players unique or individual and controlling scope

One way DDA was commonly used before the advent of computers was by arbiters—and arbiters still use this balancing method in games today. A dungeon master or a game master can dynamically change the scenario based on intuition. The game master monitors the players and guides them through a scenario. A game master who finds that a scenario is too difficult for the players can, on the fly, make some changes and adjust the difficulty so that it is more fun for the group as a whole. A game master who finds that the players outsmart a scenario or are too good at it can also adjust the difficulty. Throughout a game, the game master may find that some sections are too difficult for the group and others are too easy, and they can adjust the difficulty in both directions. This is an analog form of dynamic difficulty adjustment.

Computers that run video games are the intelligence behind the flow of the games. We've gotten good enough at making games that we can program artificial intelligence to make the same kinds of adjustments that human game masters make. Computers, without human intervention, can adjust the difficulty of a game in real time to provide dynamic difficulty adjustment. For example, if there is a boss in a game that a player tries to defeat multiple times without success and then, on the next attempt, the boss feels much easier, it is likely that some numbers have been changed behind the scenes to ensure that the player does not get frustrated and quit. The game changes in a quantified way, like reducing the hit points of the boss or reducing the damage output.

It's appropriate to use DDA when you want to provide a consistent experience for all of your players throughout a game. One of the big problems in creating mass-market games is that players' abilities vary widely. Some players do not have very good hand–eye coordination, and others have amazing hand–eye coordination. Some players are not very good puzzle solvers, and others are incredibly good. How do you get all these players through the same game and give them the same consistent experience? You can do dynamic difficulty adjustment behind the scenes to monitor the progress of players and adjust the difficulty so their experience feels similar. For the boss battle example, let's say that a player is not very good at the game and doesn't have very good hand–eye coordination. A second player is a professional-level video game player. As a designer, you want to have both players experience the boss battle, lose once or twice, and then get through the battle on the third or fourth try. You would encode into the game the desired metrics, such as the rate at which the boss is losing hit points compared to the player, the number of tries the player has attempted to beat the boss, and the time the player has spent fighting the boss. Then you set up trigger thresholds. For example, on the first attempt, if the boss is losing HP three times as fast as the player, this condition can trigger an increase in difficulty. Conversely, if this happens on the player's fourth attempt, it can trigger a decrease in difficulty.

It is sometimes not advisable to use DDA. For example, you typically don't want to use this form of balancing when you want each player to have a unique experience based on their ability and choices. If you think players of different skill levels should have different experiences in a game, then you absolutely would not want to use DDA. Big open-world RPGs are good examples of where you would not want to have much DDA because players are meant to be able to choose their own experience. Similarly, in sandbox games, you let the player choose their own experience and you let their ability take them where it does. You would also avoid using DDA when you need to limit a game's scope. Defining each of the metrics and coding the triggers for DDA can be very difficult and can take nearly as long to do as making the game in the first place. You should count on spending at least half again as much time adding even light DDA to a project as you spent creating it.

note

Different types of gamers have very different reactions to DDA. Some gamers who are out to prove their skill or create a unique experience will reject a game wholesale if they suspect any DDA in the game. On the flipside, many gamers who are more interested in the experience and smooth flow of going through a game to completion are attracted to DDA.

Layered Difficulty Adjustment

If you've ever played a game that has easy, medium, and hard modes, you've experienced layered difficulty. Layered difficulty adjustment simply means allowing players agency in adjusting difficulty on their own.

> **note**
>
> Here's what layered difficulty adjustment is good and bad for:.
>
> - **Good for:** Letting players make their own choices
> - **Bad for:** Giving players a consistent experience and controlling scope

Very often in games you will see that there's one path you can progress along that will give more rewards but involves more dangers. Then, there's another path you can take that is simpler to complete but presents fewer rewards. However, rewards don't even necessarily have to be tied to layered difficulty. A particular path or mode might just be more difficult for the sake of being more difficult. In fighting games, when you can choose an opponent, and you choose more and more difficult opponents, that is also layered difficulty.

The benefits of layered difficulty are that it gives players a lot of choice, and it gives players agency over their choice. They feel in control and empowered.

In the games industry, a particularly difficult game might be called "90s hard." In the 1990s, games were made almost exclusively for experienced gamers. There was an inflation of difficulty going on, where gamers kept getting better, so games kept getting harder—and the cycle continued. In those days, if you started a game and you couldn't progress, that was the end of the game. Today, not allowing a player to go any further in a game would be seen as mostly unacceptable in mass-market games. Game makers want to get as many players through as much of the experience of the game as possible.

If a player is playing a game without layered difficulty and gets stuck, this often causes frustration. Very often, the player's frustration is targeted at the game, the design team, or even the individual designer of the scenario. We hear comments that a game is "unfair" or "cheating." However, if a game has layered difficulty and a player chooses to play on hard mode, the response is different. It is much easier for the player to accept that the difficulty may be their own fault. They know they have agency to adjust the difficulty down.

As another example, in an open-world game, say that you are encountering a creature in a lair. It's a very difficult scenario, but you can easily walk around the area. If you choose to attempt the scenario and it's very difficult, you can leave and come back later if you wish. You might feel frustrated at the difficulty of the scenario, but you may stop feeling frustrated pretty quickly, when you find another scenario that is a better match for you. If there were no option to stop a particular scenario and move on to another one, your frustration would likely continue to grow.

You should avoid layered difficulty when a game's scope is an issue. Adding layered difficulty is not simply a matter of adding a multiplier to difficulty, as you'd do with damage outputs or health. In fact, it is significantly more difficult than simply changing a few universal numbers. Not only do you have to rebalance the entire game to make a different difficulty level, it's usually not a linear change. Similarly, if there are areas of a game that a player can opt out of, then those areas of content—which the team dedicated time and resources to making—go unused.

Cross-Feeding

Cross-feeding is a method of balancing that allows the players to use different skills to complete the same task. Cross-feeding is often used in stealth combat games and RPGs with multiple classes.

> note
>
> Here's what cross-feeding is good and bad for:
>
> - **Good for:** Offering player choice and unique stories
> - **Bad for:** Balancing difficulty and providing a consistent player experience

A classic example of cross-feeding is being able to defeat an enemy boss in various ways. For example, one way might be to take extra time to get very powerful gear that allows you to defeat the boss even if your skill at combat is lacking. Another way to defeat the boss might be to attack the boss directly with poor gear and rely on your ability at combat. In one scenario, the player is good at finding gear but is not particularly good at combat. In the other scenario, the player is good at combat but does not like searching for more powerful gear. With cross-feeding, you allow the player to tackle the task in either way.

Cross-feeding is most applicable when you have a large game with lots of interrelated mechanics. Giving the player a variety of ways to complete challenges makes the game feel very personal and allows the player a great deal of agency. It can lead to conversations between players where they discuss and debate the strengths of their own preferred method. For us as designers, this is one of the highest compliments we can get from players in regard to the way we created our systems.

One downside of cross-feeding is that it is not possible in very simple games. Another downside is that it can be difficult to balance individual scenarios when the designer does not know how the player is going to tackle the presented challenge. Another problem that can arise with cross-feeding is that when there are several ways to tackle a scenario, one of them might be clearly the worst. In some games you might find that there are mechanics you can use but that don't seem to be very useful. It's quite likely that they were designed to be a cross-feeding balance mechanics, but the mechanics were not fully balanced and ended up being useless.

Poorly implemented cross-feeding can lead to wasted game-creation effort and player dissatisfaction. Consider, for example, a shooter who has lots of different varieties of guns. If the designer created 50 different styles of guns but 1 of them is clearly better than the rest, players will all gravitate to the overpowered gun and ignore the other 49 guns. This means that the designers and the art team who made those guns and the QA team who tested those guns wasted their time on those guns. Even worse, players will say the game is boring and lacks variety even though it has a large variety built into it.

Balancing Combinations

As games get more sophisticated, they are likely to use multiple methods of balancing in combination. They may implement negative feedback loops in the player-versus-player competitive mode and dynamic difficulty adjustment in single-player mode, for example. They may use flat balancing in certain areas in order to present the game fairly to all players, and they may use layered difficulty adjustment in other areas. The important takeaway is that the balancing methods described in this chapter can be used in combination with each other.

Further Steps

After completing this chapter, you should take some time to practice in the real world with the concepts covered here. Try these exercises to further explore the various methods of balancing discussed in this chapter.

- Pick several games that you enjoy from a variety of genres (for example, video games, tabletop or board games, sports). Go through the rules of the games and identify what specifically in the rules causes each of the types of balancing listed in this chapter to happen in that game. Some games use only a single method of balancing, and others use multiple balancing methods together.
- After identifying the balancing methods in the games you choose, try to switch them in the rules and think about what would happen. Here are a few hypotheticals to get you started:
  - Basketball with a positive feedback loop
  - Monopoly with a negative feedback loop
  - Mario Kart with cross-feeding

CHAPTER 17

FINE-TUNING BALANCE, TESTING, AND PROBLEM SOLVING

Most of a system designer's time is actually not spent designing. Most of a system designer's time is actually spent tuning, testing, and problem solving. This chapter discusses some of the specific methods that make this very large task more manageable.

Balance

Balance, in terms of game design, refers to massaging game data so that players feel that they have agency. Throughout a game, you want a player to constantly consider questions such as these:

- Does my RPG hero use a sword or an axe?
- Does my racing car use front-wheel or rear-wheel drive?
- Does my farmer plant corn or wheat?

In a good game, the answers to questions such as these are not always obvious. In addition, different players should have different opinions, and different situations in the game should have different solutions. You can consider a game's data to be balanced when there is a time and place or playstyle for every system and data object, and thought is required to make the right choices.

It is not enough to feel as though a game is balanced. You need evidence, based on clear and quantifiable guidelines. Some of this evidence will need to be observational in testing, but other aspects can have actual numbers applied that can be analyzed either with live testers or with telemetry.

Why Balance Matters

Players play games to have agency. *Agency* in a game means that the player has a real influence on how the game progresses. If you only offer players false options in a game, and they have no real agency, they will no longer have a reason to spend time on the game.

For example, say that you are playing a game and gearing up to fight the toughest battle you have yet dealt with. You are at the armory, choosing a weapon, and you have two choices:

- **The Sword of Destruction:** It hits 100% of the time and does 100 points of damage.
- **A ham sandwich:** It hits 2% of the time and does 1 point of damage.

This is not a legitimate choice. Not many players would choose the sandwich. Such "choices" are really chores. The game makes you select the armory and makes you click on a weapon, but it is clear which one you should pick, so you are simply going through the motions. You're not likely to feel a connection to the game or have an investment in your choice.

A more balanced choice that actually gives the player some agency might look like this:

- **The Sword of Destruction:** It hits 100% of the time and does 25 points of damage.
- **The Sword of Kapow:** It hits 5% of the time and does 500 points of damage.

If you work out these choices mathematically, you find that they both do, on average, 25 points of damage per hit in the long run. (Refer to Chapter 9, "Attributes: Creating and Quantifying Life," for information on attributes.) But practically, they will feel very different. With the Sword of Destruction, you know you can take down the opponent in regular chopping shots that do consistent and predictable damage. The Sword of Kapow, on the other hand, is a big gamble. You might be able to take out the opponent with a single shot and be done with it, or you might be swinging and missing for ages. Is this a gamble you want to take? There is not a clear choice. The choice really depends on the player's personality. Individual players may be clearly drawn to one choice or the other, and there will be disagreement between players. Even an individual player may need to ponder this decision for a while. This is exactly what you want in your game. Regardless of which choice the player makes, they feel as though they have had agency in the game and decided what is personally best for them. This strengthens the player's investment in further choices and the game as a whole. It can also strengthen the development of the player community. A "Team Destruction" and a "Team Kapow" could defend and argue for their weapon preferences. Getting a game in balance matters deeply to game designers because it gives players agency and encourages them to invest in the game.

Let's look at one final weapons choice example to illuminate another balance issue:

- **A ham sandwich:** It hits 2% of the time and does 1 point of damage.
- **A broken stick:** It hits 1% of the time and does 2 points of damage.

Mathematically, this is a balanced decision, but the problem is obvious: These are both terrible choices. Giving players false agency while also setting them up to fail is one of the best ways to frustrate them. In the end, you want players to have multiple balanced and viable options to choose from.

Another practical reason balance matters comes down to allocation of team resources while building a game. If you spend the time and resources to build and test 20 cars for a racing game, but players only ever choose 2 of them, then you have wasted time building and testing the other 18. This is clearly not what anyone wants. By making all 20 choices viable, you give more agency to the player and allow for a broader spectrum of players to feel investment in the game. You also fully allocate the time of the developers. There are many stories in the industry of developers reviewing telemetry to find out portions of the game they worked very hard on were viewed by only a tiny portion of the audience. This is a terrible feeling for any developer.

General Game Balance

While there is not an exact formula or set of criteria that can definitively prove that a game is balanced, there are several indicators that can be measured objectively and tracked. Theoretical numeric balancing can help you start balancing a game, but you don't really know whether you have achieved balance until the testing stage . When doing tests, you can look for the following indications that the game is getting close to or has achieved good balance:

- **Head scratching:** When a player understands the game and faces a choice, notice how quickly they make the choice. The choice may be picking between a sword or an axe before a battle. It could be the choice of using a sports car or a muscle car when racing on a new track. It could also be choosing between planting corn or wheat in a farming game. Any time there is a choice, you should be especially observant of the time testers take to make the choice and their commitment to the choice. If all the testers choose the axe within a second, then that is an indication of imbalance. On the other hand, if many of the testers pause, go back and forth between the options, ponder, and possibly ask questions before making a decision, this is a good indicator that the decision is balanced. It is important to note, however, that this pausing and asking questions can also indicate player confusion. It is important to make sure your testers are doing the head scratching because they are trying to come up with the best solution and not because they are confused or frustrated.
- **Disagreements among players:** It is important to let testers who made different decisions discuss why they made them. If there is disagreement—and, ideally, passionate defense of the different decisions—you are doing great balancing the game. Even if it is a group of only two testers, each with their own bias, this is a good sign. With this kind of feedback, you know you have done something to make both options feel viable to at least one person. On the other hand, if all testers quickly come to the same consensus, there is possibly an imbalance. This would be a great opportunity to ask the testers about the reasoning behind their decisions and look for clues about how to solve the imbalance.
- **Even distribution of choices selected:** When you work with a large pool of testers, you can begin to see patterns in the distribution of their choices. These patterns can emerge during the playtest stage, and they really start to show with telemetry. If you present players with five options, and each option is chosen roughly 20% of the time, you could not ask for anything better! Such an outcome is not likely, though, even with the most balanced games, as there are always some external factors involved that can influence players. It's not critical that all variations are chosen in exactly equal proportions, but it is important that they are all chosen at least some of the time.
- **Changing game conditions:** If players change objects or preferences throughout the game based on conditions, that is another excellent indicator of balance. This one is fairly easy to enforce artificially with concepts like damage types (for example, in the land of fire, only ice weapons do damage). Beyond the artificial forced changing of items and tactics, there are more natural, organic, forms of changing. Players' preferences change based on the conditions they see and the choices available. As long as players have

multiple legitimate choices for each decision, and players don't all agree on an outcome, having players also change due to conditions is a great expansion of balance.

- **Rock paper scissors combinations:** Another good sign of balance is when any given option has a clear use and an Achilles heel, much as in the game rock paper scissors. Such combinations are often purposely built in to game mechanics but can also occur naturally as a game develops.
- **Change in lead:** Change in lead—one player or team taking the lead from the other side—can be a sign that a game is balanced. It is not always a perfect indicator but can offer some clues to balance in multiplayer games in particular. If a game has measured competition, watch for frequency of change in lead. This also applies to real-world games. Watch any given sporting event and pay attention to change in lead. In games where there is a high number of changes in lead, observers will more often consider the game to be exciting.

Breaking Your Data

When you have gone through the full gauntlet of tests and are starting to see the kinds of responses you want, it is tempting to stop—to "cash out" with a minor win. But don't give in to this temptation. Instead, keep making changes. The more time you have, the more experimental your changes should be. You want to purposely break the bounds of the systems to see what happens. You should do this type of experimentation in isolation, safely away from the shippable game. During this important phase, game data can go from technically acceptable to truly innovative.

Problems with Balancing Judged Contests

If you have ever screamed at a referee or judge, you already know there are problems with judged contests. In many cases, people disagree with judgment calls and feel that contests are not fair. A game that is seen as unfair may be greatly diminished in the eyes of its players and audience. While older games may be able to get away with seeming unfair because they are embedded in cultural tradition and have been accepted for a long time, new games are at great risk of failure if they are seen as unfair.

There are two primary ways to deal with problems with judged contests:

- **Playing to the judge:** This is an elegant solution because it sidesteps the problem altogether. If the goal of a cooking contest is to make the judge happy, then that judge can fairly determine which dish makes them the happiest. Whether the judge's pick is objectively the best dish can't really be argued because the judge is not expected to be impartial. Instead, bias is built in to the contest as a mechanic. The biggest negative to this system is that it only determines the winner in the eyes of the judge; the judge doesn't determine who is objectively better at something. For example, the judge might pick the winning dish because it is loaded with an ingredient he likes. The dish might not be the best designed or executed dish, but it contains something that plays well to that specific judge. The result of the contest really only shows the preference of the judge and not the ability of the contestants.

> note
>
> Playing to the judge comes up all the time in the game industry in pitch sessions. If you are fortunate enough to be able to pitch a game idea to an executive or investor, you do not want to spend that time trying to prove that your game project is the best; instead, you want to show that your game is the best for them. An investor is fully allowed to be biased and may choose what you feel is an inferior project because they like it better. There is nothing wrong with this. Investors are free to invest where they want in what they want.

- **Quantification:** The other method of handling issues with judged contests is by clearly quantifying criteria that the judges use to minimize inconsistency. In video games, you have a massive advantage in doing this. Because the entire game universe is programmed by your team and fully under your control, you can set up exact and perfectly quantifiable criteria for literally every situation that needs it. For example, in a fighting game, unlike in MMA or boxing in the real world, you can 100% guarantee that there will be no illegal shots in the game. All you need to do is program the game so that it does not allow them. In the real world, there are always going to be gray areas.

  If you are designing an analog game or sport, there are further measures that you can take to make sure all situations are quantified. Officials in games such as tennis used to have a difficult time judging exactly where a ball landed and whether it was in or out. Today we have high-speed cameras with computer controllers that watch over a game and can clearly show the state of the ball at any moment—and arguments over line judgment have been drastically reduced. Similar cameras are used in races to impartially prove, almost without any doubt, exactly who won.

  The recommendation for an analog game would be to minimize—or ideally eliminate—any situation that could be interpreted differently by different people. A good way to determine whether you have properly quantified judged actions is to ask several qualified judges to observe several judged situations and then give their opinions. If all judges consistently come to the same conclusion, then you can be sure that the mechanic has been properly quantified and is ready. If judges disagree, on the other hand, you know you have a problem with the mechanic.

How to Start Balancing Data

To balance a game, you need to do a lot of testing. To fully test video games, you can't just jump right into testing. First, you need a code base, an engine, data structures, systems, placeholder art, and much more. But you can start testing for balance before any of that.

Prototyping

One way to approach balancing is with prototyping. *Prototyping* involves making a small piece of a game with the specific intent to gain knowledge from it. Prototypes are intended to be as cheap and fast to make as possible. They are also designed specifically to be thrown away after they have served their purpose.

> note
>
> Do not make the mistake of slapping together a prototype and then falling in love with it and wanting to keep it. Make it with the clear intention of discarding it after use.

A concept related to a prototype is a *vertical slice*—an early version of a partially completed game. A vertical slice has many or even all the mechanics in place, much of data, and much of the art.

A vertical slice should include as much of the game as possible so you can see how the game as a whole is trending. With prototyping, on the other hand, you purposely exclude as much as possible so you can focus on a single aspect in detail.

The following sections provide a few examples of where you can use prototypes.

Crafting Prototype

Say that you have created a crafting system for an exploration video game. Instead of building it in a full game engine, you are going to build some of the data in a spreadsheet and then make rules and actions into physical notecards. You plan to make a temporary analog set of rules that mimic how the mechanics work, and then you will test the system. You will leave out as much as possible, including harvesting mechanics, leveling mechanics, graphics, and UI elements. You want to focus on just one factor with the prototype: how the materials stack up and get exchanged for completed items.

As you play this prototype, you should be looking for items that are used all the time or none of the time. Are there certain combinations that turn out to be the obvious choice in most situations? Are there items or combinations that never get used? Finally, if you find a weakness, you need to figure out whether it is a symptom of the game data or whether it is more likely a symptom of the prototype. Keep in mind that you can't port all data into a prototype easily, so you can't have 100% certainty that everything in a prototype will be analogous in the finished game.

By focusing on just these aspects, you can get started prototyping before a single line of code is written or a game engine is chosen. Often, it takes only a few hours to go from a prototype idea to a completed test. If you are lucky, you might find that this prototype is actually fun. It may even spawn a spinoff idea. This has happened several times in the industry. But don't worry if it does not. You are not trying to make a completed game; you just need to focus on a single factor.

Leveling Up Prototype

Say that you have an RPG that allows characters to choose new skills from a skill tree after earning XP. Again, you can go fully analog and test this system for a specific purpose—in this case, to find the best pace of XP gain to fuel the leveling system. Again, you can use notecards to represent the skills. You can draw out skill trees with stats on a white board or paper. You can even give out XP as poker chips, coins, or using some other proxy. You won't be able to tell a whole lot about the game as a whole from this prototype, but you will be able to drill down on one single aspect and work out many of the details before the game is built. While it is likely that there will need to be some tweaks to the system once it is integrated with the rest of the game, the prototype will at least give you a starting point to work from. It is possible, with some practice, to build all the systems exterior to the game and fairly accurately predict how they will operate once integrated.

Jumping Prototype

Now say that you are going to make a classic platformer. Instead of creating levels for the game, you can create an empty level in an off-the-shelf engine (such as Unity or Unreal) with just a floor, no enemies, no power-ups, and no goals. This is called a *proxy test* because you won't be using your actual game engine but rather a stand-in or proxy engine. It could be any engine or system you can modify enough to find the information you are looking for. Many game engines can be easily modified and used as proxy engines for prototyping. When you are planning to discard a prototype test, you don't need to worry about licensing, hardware constraints, and other baggage that come with using an engine for a full game.

Once your proxy game is set up, you can make your main character and put in numbers for their jump—velocity, direction, controls, and so on— but just the smallest attribute set possible to get the character jumping around. Then you can write down an outcome—something like "Find the jump height that feels best." Next, you need to playtest the game...a lot. Jumping around in an empty room would be a very boring game, but with the prototype, you are not looking for fun. Instead, you need to focus on the jump mechanic in isolation, considering the size of the character onscreen and the portion of the screen the character should cover in a single jump.

By the time the prototype test is over, you should have some good numbers to start with. This test will likely lead you directly into a new prototype test as well. Once you get the jump feeling the way you want it, for example, you might be ready to give the player character a box to jump over. Then you can test again. The cycle repeats, the tests get slightly more complex, and your focus becomes more clear. By the time the real game engine, character models, and animations are ready for use, you will have excellent starting guesses for your data attribute values.

Macrosystems Prototype

Say that you plan to build a large-scale war game in which players have battles in small locations that have ramifications on a larger battle map. You want to determine how to deal with the information from the small battles on the large map. In this case, you can use a combination of analog and proxy prototyping. For the small battles, you might choose a preexisting game that is in roughly the same ballpark as the game you want to build (even if it is not a perfect fit). You can then play out battles in that game and take the results to a fully analog board game map you create on paper. So part of the testing is done in another game, and part of the testing is done on a large sheet of paper.

> **note**
>
> Using any combination of proxy, analog, and any other methods to move on to testing as quickly as possible will get you test results faster and allow for more iteration. Some teams have even gone as far as using action figure toys, rubber bands, and miniature models to quickly lay out scenarios and test game mechanics. The prototype phase is the best time in the life cycle of game development to get creative and crafty. It also gives the system and data designers something to do while the core engine is being built and prevents them from being idle while waiting out the lag time.
>
> Remember that your first iteration will be the worst, so you should just get it out of the way and move on to the next one quickly.

Performing Playtests

Playtesting is much more testing than playing. Depending on the phase of game creation and the desired outcome, different kinds of playtests can be used. Playtesting tends to start with minimum viability testing and then moves to more types of testing as the game progresses. As testing expands, the early types of testing remain constant, and the scope of testing increases.

When choosing testers, keep in mind that you only get fresh eyes once. So if you have a limited pool of testers, you shouldn't use them all for the first tests. If possible, you should trickle in new testers with every new round of tests, always holding back a few of them for later tests. Someone who has never seen the game before is going to have a very different perspective than someone who has already had some exposure to the game. Further, testers who see early versions of the game are going to have a unique bias. They will be able to mentally compare what they saw in the first version they experienced with what they see now. Your full audience will not have this bias, so it makes those testers, in some ways, less valuable for measuring how the game will be received once it ships. For example, if a tester at an early phase complains about a specific level and then that level is changed, the tester is going to be much more likely to artificially praise the change, regardless of whether the game is now better, because they feel a personal connection in asking for the change and seeing it made. This is not to say that testers are useful only once. Sometimes, having a tester who is already ramped up and familiar with the game is a great asset. It saves time with instructions, and you know the tester is at least enjoying the experience enough to do another test voluntarily. It is mainly important to keep in mind that experienced testers will behave differently from fresh testers and to adjust your expectations accordingly.

The following sections discuss the primary divisions of playtesting:

- Minimum viability testing
- Balance testing
- Bug testing
- User testing
- Beta/postlaunch telemetry testing

Minimum Viability Testing

Minimum viability testing is usually done directly by the game creator, and it should be done constantly. As you make changes to a game, you must test them. During the minimum viability testing phase, you want to ensure that any change you have made works as intended. It's much better to err on the side of too much testing rather than not enough. For a video game, this means (possibly) compiling the game in the engine and then playing quickly to see if the change worked. For changes in mechanics or code, this type of testing should be done every time a single change is completed.

If you are planning to add a lot of changes, it might not be feasible to test each and every data unit. For example, if you have just built 200 different weapons for a game in a spreadsheet and are ready to port them over to a game engine, it would not be practical to check each one as it is imported. Instead, at this point, it is advisable to do a test of the first one, without any others. To do a thorough check, you need to consider questions like the following:

- Can the hero equip the weapon?
- Does the weapon do the amount of damage intended?
- Does the weapon hit as often as possible?
- Does the weapon work with existing animations?

Once the first data object—usually the fulcrum—is implemented and tested, you can move up to a small batch, such as five data objects. Are you able to successfully implement five in a batch and then have one or two of them pass the same tests? If so, you can do a bigger batch, each time spot testing to see if the data is importing properly. You should never assume that if you set up one thing and it works, it will work properly every time.

Once minimum viability tests are successful and you have enough data that you can do more exhaustive scrutiny, it is time to move on to balance testing.

Balance Testing

After data has been entered into a game, it's time to start balance testing. If the data has been compared against a fulcrum, then balance testing should go quickly. As mentioned in Chapter 13, "Range Balancing, Data Fulcrums, and Hierarchical Design," you need to start by testing the fulcrum against itself. Then you can pick the data objects that are furthest from the fulcrum and test them against each other, as this is the most likely place to find imbalances.

For example, let's say you are working on a fantasy RPG, and you made the knight your fulcrum. Orks, goblins, kobolds, barbarians, Vikings, and soldiers are all fairly similar characters, but when you built archers, you gave them ranged weapons instead of melee weapons, and when you built giant spiders, you gave them poison for attacking. So the archers and giant spiders are quite different from your fulcrum character and from each other, and even though you already balanced them against the fulcrum, you would want to plan to spot check this combination individually. The more special and unique a data object is, the more important it is to test it thoroughly.

The next step is to have someone else play with the new data. As the creators of the data, your team will have insights no one else would, and you will likely create the data in such a way that you know how to use it to its fullest potential. Other players won't know any of this, and it's important to get fresh eyes on a test. When doing a balance test with others, it's okay to coach them on expectations. At this early point, you can explain controls, context for the test they might not know, and other information that is important for them to do the test the way you want it done.

While testing for balance, encourage your testers to speak a lot—and find talkative testers, if possible. A nonstop stream of consciousness from a tester is a great thing, especially at the balance stage. Ask testers to talk about their feelings a lot. Do they feel surprised? Annoyed? Puzzled? Do these feelings align with what is desired? When you hear statements such as the following from testers, you know you need to pay close attention:

- I don't know what to do.
- This one feels way better than the other one.
- I know what to do, but I'd rather do something else.
- I am debating which of these options is best.

Statements like these during a balance test are gold. Be sure to take note of important statements like these and what prompted them.

Finally, you should be sure to balance test others' work. You will get better at running your own test when you know what it is like to be a tester under the microscope. When you are a tester, you should aim to be a good tester. As you will learn when you run balance tests, you really don't want to hear comments like "It's okay" and other vague, noncommittal statements that provide very little actionable information. When you are testing for others, be as specific as possible and use language that is as direct as possible.

Bug Testing

After a game is in production, it is common to bring on an independent quality assurance (QA) team. While the members of this team can certainly help with balance testing, their job is to find bugs. Their ultimate goal is to save the company money. If a large game goes to a publisher with game-breaking bugs, it will be rejected. This might push back release dates, make a publisher miss an advertising window, and in other ways increase the cost of the project. To avoid such problems, a QA team needs to do a very deep dive into a game to ensure that it is in good enough shape to go to the publisher.

As a game system designer, you need to be in communication with the QA team about your game, your systems, and your data. System and data designers in particular are often able to make content faster than they can test it themselves. You should start writing a plan for a QA test as soon as systems are built. QA team members can also be great balance testers. They are, after all, highly trained game players who play games all day every day. If possible, hang out with the QA team while they are testing portions of your work. They also tend to be very open about criticism (unlike typical game players). Be ready for harsh and direct feedback and embrace it when you get it. It does not feel good to hear all the ways you did something wrong, but it is by far the best way to get better.

User Testing

User testing comes into play as a game gets closer to completion. The goal of user testing is generally to find out how the users are interacting with the game, how the balance is working, and whether users are having fun.

Finding good test subjects at this stage is much more important than in previous rounds of testing. Ideally, the testers should closely match the target audience for the first few rounds. When asking for testers, specify the kind of tester you are looking for. You do not have to develop a profile as thorough as the target audience profile, but you should write a good enough profile to eliminate some people from your test pool. Not every player is going to be right for the game, and it is important to have the right testers. The following are some examples of calls for playtesters that specify the types of testers:

- Testers needed. Must enjoy fast-paced FPS games.
- Testers needed. Must enjoy free-to-play mobile games and be willing to play for an hour.
- Testers needed. Fans of anime and JRPGs are ideal, but any RPG players are welcome.

Note the jargon and acronyms in these calls. For user testing, this type of language is fine because players who don't understand it probably won't be the tester you want. Make your call for testers short, simple, and directly to the point. Don't worry if it will reduce the tester pool for now; getting the right kinds of testers at this stage is more important than getting a large number of testers.

For each user test you should outline a goal ahead of time. However, in most cases, you should not communicate this goal to the testers. You want them to have as little external information going into the test as possible. Here are a few examples of user test goals:

- How long does it take players to learn the controls?
- How well are players able to navigate the main menus and go through the tutorial?
- Do players tend to pick one character class over the others?
- What points in the game are most likely to confuse new players?

Feel free to collect as much information as possible, even if it is outside the framework of the stated goal. Pay particular attention to the testers as they go through the experience to get better insight into the stated goal.

For a user test, you may want to create a script for the proctor to read to a tester before the test begins. If the test is for the beginning of the game, the script might be something like this:

> Please start the game and comment on anything you notice. The test will run for 30 minutes. Keep in mind we will not be answering any questions until after the test,

> but please ask them anyway. We will take down notes and make sure you understand everything clearly after the test.

Not only does a script like this help you stay organized, but it can be handed off to someone else. If you are using the same testers now and also later in the game cycle—which is a very common practice—you might need a little bit more in the script. You would want to describe where the tester has been placed in the game and what has come before, but that should be about it.

> **note**
>
> To eliminate bias, some teams purposely use a proctor who has no personal attachment to the game. The proctor can then assure the testers at the start of the test that they are not involved with the game, and nothing the testers say will hurt their feelings.

The most important thing a user test proctor can do is observe. If possible, the proctor should be absolutely silent once the test starts and make observations only. As the game is nearing completion, it is critical for the game to be able to speak for itself. If at any point in the test the proctor must intervene, you know there is a rather large issue that needs to be addressed before more user testing can proceed. If the error is bad enough, it might be time to shut down the test for now, thank the tester for their time, and go about fixing the issue. If a tester gets too far off in the weeds with errors, the team can't get good information from the test.

While testing, it is common to make video recordings of the testers while playing the game and the game as it is being played. When a tester really gets into the game, the notes can come faster than they can be written. A tester's face may also give great feedback that may be missed in an "over the shoulder" observation. When possible, you should have a camera pointed at the tester's face and also record the game at the same time. On larger projects, game developers can even record and play user input through the controller. Being able to go back and review all of these aspects of the testing in detail can provide feedback that would likely be missed otherwise.

After a user test, it is a good idea to conduct a conclusion interview with the tester and use prepared questions, but you can also dig more deeply into any comments the tester makes. A tester who is doing the testing in person and has volunteered their time is much more likely to give positive feedback than is a common audience, and it is important to remember this. It certainly feels good to hear a glowing review, but honest constructive criticism is more useful.

> **note**
>
> Playtesters should not be professional QA folks (unless that is the target market of the game). Amateur playtesters do not have the same training or ability to communicate as professionals. This is not said to discredit them but as an important factor that the proctor must consider.

When formulating final interview questions, a proctor should avoid open-ended, ambiguous, and leading questions like "How did you like the game?" This particular question is both leading—in that it assumes the player did like the game—and too easily leads to the most dreaded answer a proctor can receive: "It was pretty good." This kind of feedback provides developers with almost no actionable information. It also shuts down the conversation. Instead, the proctor should phrase questions in a way that encourages testers to offer up insightful information. Let's look at a couple of sample questions that ask basically the same thing but are phrased in subtly different ways.

Original question: "Did you find any of the levels you played confusing?"

This question often leads to answers like "No" or "Not really" that give you nothing to work with. If the tester says "Yes" or "Kind of," that's better, but the proctor will still need to do much more digging to get some good information.

Revised question: "Of the levels you played, which was most confusing?" and, after the first question is answered, "Why was that?"

See how this question gently seeks out more information? Instead of prompting for a binary yes/no question, this wording prompts the user to mentally rank the levels in order of confusion and pick one. It can also open up great follow-up questions such as "Which was easiest to understand?" or "Besides the most confusing, what other levels also confused you?" You can see that this is a fruitful cycle of communication with the tester.

Let's look at another interview question that needs revision.

Original question: "What improvements could we make in the game?"

This is a very unfair question to ask a playtester. A tester is probably not a game designer and may have no idea what would improve a game. It's also very open-ended and begs for the response "Nothing." If the tester does offer up improvements, either in response to such a question or impromptu, you need to listen! Keep in mind that testers have no clue what is going on in the game internally, and they may say things that are totally unrealistic, but that's fine. You want to hear what they are thinking. When listening to this kind of feedback, it's important for the team not to think about whether it is possible but instead to think about whether it would help the game and whether there is something else that could address the essence of the improvement.

> **Revised question:** "We are thinking of these three improvements to the portion of the game you played. Which do you prefer?"

This question frames the answers you get the way you want them. You already know what is possible, and you know the kinds of answers you are looking for at this phase. This wording encourages the tester to go beyond thinking in a binary yes/no way and to think of simple options that are much easier to digest because they are limited.

One good way to handle questioning is to make contrasts (for example, "What was the best aspect of this character class, and what was the worst?"). Even great games have best and worst aspects. A question framed as a contrast invites the playtester to give more honest feedback.

Consider these final notes on proctoring playtests:

- Thank the testers and be nice. They are doing you a service, not the other way around.
- Never disagree with a tester unless they are factually wrong. Any feedback they give is good feedback. If a tester says something wild and completely unrealistic, a simple response like "Thank you for that feedback. I'll write it down" helps you move past it and get to more useful information.
- Call back good testers. Most games take more than a single session to complete, and having experienced testers is often not only wanted but really needed.
- Don't call back bad testers. If a tester gives little or no feedback or clearly has an agenda of changing the game into something else, then there is little more to learn from that tester. While such a person is playtesting, be polite but note that they will not be needed for further tests. You may even need to go as far as to throw out the data generated from a bad tester. If you have a tester who is purposely playing the game in a way that was not intended or is clearly uninterested in learning the game, it's not likely that they are going to be a good representative of real players. Almost all data from testers is good data, but in extreme cases it's not.
- Get a variety of testers from within or near your target audience. Find a variety of ages as well as gaming and social backgrounds. It's also a good idea to get a few testers who are well outside your target market, just to get a fresh perspective. Characteristics of testers should be noted so their feedback can be judged accordingly. If a parent brings in a young tester, that parent becomes a great possible outsider tester.
- Don't expect gold from any single tester. Everyone has different opinions, desires, and play styles in a game. It's more likely that as the game matures and tests are conducted, you will receive less actionable feedback and more repetition of the same themes.
- Look for repetition. If one tester has a piece of feedback, that is valuable. If many or most have the same feedback, then that is critical feedback that should not be ignored.

After you run user testing and review of all the notes, it's important to bring your team into the process and let them know how it went. In particular, the design team needs to understand what happened during tests and why changes are being made as a result of testing. If possible, show designers raw footage of testers playing the game. It is humbling but very informative to see a new player struggling through something you have spent a lot of time and effort crafting.

Beta/Postlaunch Telemetry Testing

Telemetry testing is, as the word implies, done at a distance. While the full scope of telemetry testing is massive and beyond what this book can cover, it is worth noting that most video games use some form of it today. Even smaller games made by individual developers can do some light forms of telemetry data collection. Every mobile platform, console, and PC game has the capability to do at least a little of it.

Data Hooks

Doing telemetry testing involves inserting data hooks into a game and then sending information to the team from everywhere the game is being played. A data hook can be as simple as a single line of code that records a variable to be sent. For example, each time the player character dies, you can add that to a variable "total PC deaths" and send it off. The team can then capture this data and tally it in a database. Some studios have entire teams whose only function is to evaluate these hooks and use them to determine how to make the game better. On smaller teams, this task often falls to the system designers, who are, after all, the spreadsheet people. On any team of any size, system designers are heavily involved in the design of the hooks and the analysis of the data.

The following are some examples of a nearly endless possible set of data hooks you might want to implement in a game:

- Player time in game
- Player session time
- Time in main menu
- Time per level
- Amount of in-game currency earned per level
- Number of times the PC died/failed
- Usage of a character class, specific vehicle, or other item
- Game completed
- Amount of XP or currency earned using different methods
- Number of players in a multiplayer game
- Best and worst scores in a competitive match

- User screen size
- Operating system
- Geographic location
- Default language
- How much money the player has spent in game

For each of these hooks, there needs to be a snippet of code that collects the data as described. For each hook, the data needs to be fully quantified. To record player session time, for example, you need to define the start and end of a session. To define telemetry hooks, you use the same methods you use when asking data questions, as described in Chapter 3, "Asking Questions."

When all the hooks are encoded in the game, and the game has been sent out to testers (or even customers), the code sends back regular updates on all the hooks. As you might expect, this process can generate a very large amount of data. While it can occasionally be useful to drill down to a single user or session, it usually is better to try to look at the data as a whole for patterns that you can take action on to improve the game.

Telemetry Considerations

Telemetry data is not a magic bullet or cure-all. It can provide massive amounts of information and can yield some otherwise invisible insights, but real humans are required to interpret it properly. When making telemetry hooks, it's tempting to put in a hook for everything you can think of, but it is important to avoid creating noise and not useful information. Therefore, when designing hooks, you should think of the kinds of information that will actually have an effect on the way the game is being made.

While your data sample is low, watch for outliers. Even when the sample gets large, you should keep a keen eye out for discrepancies in data. This ties back to the section on analyzing data. Don't simply rely on averages or the minimum and maximum values you find in the data. Those types of data provide great starting points but can easily distort the results. The following two examples from the game industry illustrate why this is so important.

Telemetry Example 1: Time in Tutorial

A simple mobile puzzle game had a tutorial. The team found through playtesting that players got bored with tutorials after about 5 minutes, so they designed their tutorial to be well short of this, at 4 minutes. They put in a data hook to calculate the amount of time it took for players to complete the tutorial and launched the game into a small set of beta tests. After the game ran for a day, the team evaluated the time players were spending in the tutorial, and the result was a shock. Their average time was over 2 hours! What could have gone so horribly wrong? If you think back to Chapter 15, "Analyzing Game Data," the answer is pretty obvious: There were some huge outliers. By digging more deeply into the game and the hooks that already existed, the team was able to discover that some players started the tutorial and then set their phone aside for the night and went to bed; they came back and finished the tutorial some time the next day. In response, the team simply discounted any time over 20 minutes and used other methods of measurement, such as median, to get a more accurate picture of what the data meant. When looking at the data this new way, the team found that the tutorial was taking most players roughly the correct amount of time to complete. The team found that many users who spent longer than this on the tutorial did not speak the language. This informed the team that they needed to take the primary language of the player into consideration as well.

Telemetry Example 2: Abandoned Levels

In another game, a large team of designers was each assigned to a set of levels. Each designer was primarily responsible for making sure their level was great. When the game shipped, it had a hook in it that tracked when players started the level, how long it took them to complete, and whether they quit the level. After the game had been out a few weeks, the levels were analyzed to determine which of them were the most often abandoned. It turned out that all of the most abandoned levels belonged to the same designer. Just looking at the surface of this data, it seemed clear that the designer was not very good at his job. However, the team knew that this was the best designer on the team. He was brought on very late in the project and was purposely given all the most broken and unbalanced levels to salvage as best he could in the very limited time that was left before the game shipped. Again, it was very important to look past the raw data and get deeper into the meaning of the numbers before drawing a conclusion.

> note
>
> Telemetry is an amazing and useful tool for evaluating games with large numbers of testers in an unbiased way, but it is a tool that is only as good as the person using it. Therefore, it is a good idea to plan for and use telemetry in every game possible but not to put too much faith into every result that comes from the data.

Solving Problems

Making games involves solving a lot of problems. Coming up with initial ideas can happen quickly. Implementing ideas also becomes fairly fast with experience. However, but the process of solving problems with ideas and implementation is a slow one—and it always will be. Figure 17.1 provides a rough breakdown of the time spent on making a game.

To solve problems in a highly technical system, such as a game, you follow many of the same steps you use to create a game system in the first place but in a more condensed structure.

A series of steps go into solving problems. What you do in each step depends on the problem, but the steps remain relatively the same in any case:

1. Identify the problem.
2. Eliminate variables.
3. Come up with solutions.
4. Communicate with the team.
5. Prototype and test.
6. Document the changes.

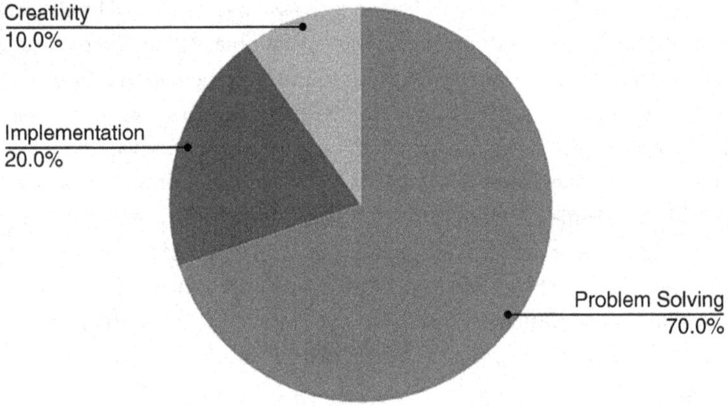

Figure 17.1 Designer time spent making a game

Identify the Problem

This is the first and arguably the most important step in the process of solving a problem. It's not as obvious as it sounds, though. When doing this step, there is a big temptation to identify symptoms, but what you really need to do is identify the problem. For example, the initial problem statement might be "How do we keep players beyond Level 3?" This is not actually the problem but a symptom. There is no switch to adjust to make players stay longer. When identifying a problem, it's important to identify aspects that are under your control. If, for example, players are quitting early because of low batteries in their cell phone, this is not something you can fix. You need to dig deeper to find the problem that is causing the perceived symptom. In the cell phone example, it might be that your game is taxing the hardware too much, causing the battery to drain. This is something that is in your control and can yield a good problem statement. Players are likely quitting on Level 3 because something is poorly designed in this level. A better problem statement would be "Investigate Level 3 to discover why players' phone batteries are consistently dying at this level."

Eliminate Variables

Once the problem has been identified, the next step is to eliminate variables. What variables might be causing the problem? Which ones are under your control? The best way to find a problem variable is to isolate it and test it individually.

In the cell phone game example, you would want to look at what processes are running during the game and separate them out and test them individually. If the levels are empty, do they still drain the battery? If the AI and game objects are in an empty box level, devoid of geometry, do they drain the battery? If one does and the other does not, then you have gotten closer to finding the actual problem. Continue to break down large chunks of suspect areas in the game into smaller ones until you can identify the exact location of the problem.

Come Up with Solutions

Coming up with solutions is very much like coming up with new ideas, and you can use the same methods listed in Chapter 8, "Coming Up with Ideas," to generate solutions. The only real difference is that the problem, instead of a conceptual idea, defines your brainstorming session.

Communicate with the Team

At this later point in the game-making process, it's important that the affected team know that a problem exists and that they may need to be part of the solution. While it is not always possible to get universal buy-in for every solution, it should be the goal to get as much team agreement as possible. At this point, the team should be relying on the game hierarchy, discussed in Chapter 13, "Range Balancing, Data Fulcrums, and Hierarchical Design." If more than one system can be changed to solve the problem, then it is important to change the system as far down on the hierarchy as possible and account for further trickle-down effects.

Prototype and Test

Before injecting a large change into a complex project like a game, you should test the solution in isolation, if possible. If needed, make a test level, character, weapon, vehicle, or whatever is being changed and test it in full isolation from the game. This process should work in a very similar fashion to the way new features are rolled out as discussed early in this chapter.

Document the Changes

After a suitable solution is found, be sure the changes are well documented. This documentation helps the team understand what change needed to happen and can serve as reference in the future if a similar problem crops up.

Further Steps

After completing this chapter, you should take some time to practice in the real world with the concepts covered here. Try these exercises to further fine-tuning data, testing, and revising data.

- Develop and run some playtests on either a simple game you have made or a very simple game that is new to your testers (such as backgammon or checkers). Observe the actions of your testers and note how many of the indications listed in the section "General Game Balance" you observe. Do the testers do a lot of head scratching? Is there change in lead? Do the players disagree on optimal strategy?

CHAPTER 18

SYSTEMS COMMUNICATION AND PSYCHOLOGY

Unlike books, movies, songs, paintings, and other forms of artistic expression, games have communication going in multiple directions. When a movie plays on a screen, it unfolds the same way every time, regardless of what the audience thinks or does about it. This makes games different from other art forms in ways that are important to acknowledge. The player has agency to change the outcome of the game, and the game has influence on how the player reacts; together, they form a communication circle.

Games are, in some ways, similar to human communications. Interpersonal communication is a reciprocal cycle between two or more people. Many studies have been done on this subject, and some of them are directly applicable to games. This chapter highlights some of the concepts from human communications that most directly apply to game making, especially game systems.

Games as Conversations

You can think of a single-player game played between a human and a machine as a conversation. You can similarly think of a multiplayer game as a conversation between multiple people. In both these analogies, the game is the language. For example, it is possible for two people who do not speak the same language to play a game of chess. They can play a complete game, get to know each other's gaming personality, and conclude the game all without needing to know a common language—beyond the rules of the game.

In single-player games, the rules to start the game open the dialog with the player. The designers of a game make a set of rules they want the player to understand and use to communicate their thoughts to the game or to another player (see Figure 18.1).

Figure 18.1 Player learning rules

Figure 18.2 illustrates a fairly standard video game communication loop. The game includes images and sounds that the player interprets. The player then communicates back to the game what they want to do, based on their interpretation of what they experience in the game. The game interprets the information from the player according to the game rules and sends the player feedback through audio and visuals on the screen. The loop repeats constantly throughout the game, much like a conversation between two people.

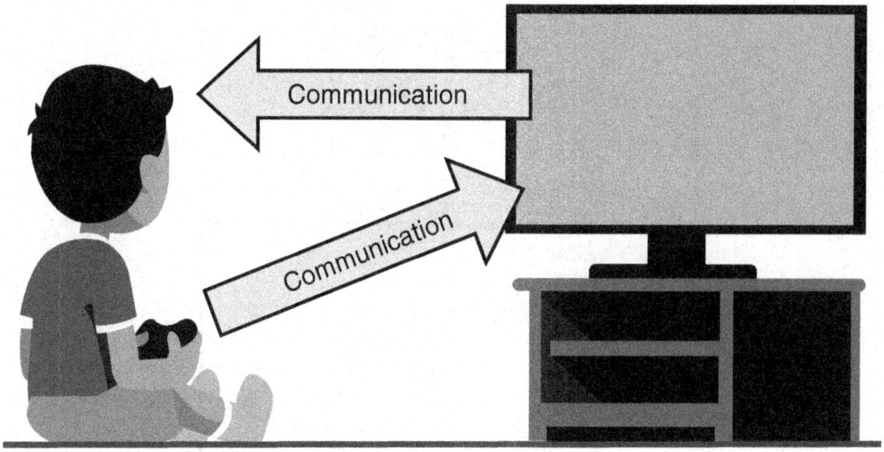

Figure 18.2 Example of a player and a game communication loop

Word Meanings

Language is inherently imperfect, and it is important to keep this in mind when writing rules for a game. The high-level goal of language is to convey an idea from the mind of one person to the mind of another, but language simply can't be precise enough to always do this effectively. For example, consider the following sentence:

> The dog likes eating meat.

It seems like a straightforward sentence, right? Do you imagine a dog eating meat in your head? Does what you imagine look like any of the images shown in Figure 18.3?

Figure 18.3 The dog likes eating meat

All of these images fit the description, but they are completely different from each other. Which one of them is most like what the author of the sentence intended? We can't know.

To complicate the imprecise language problem, pronouns—which serve as nice shortcuts in casual conversation—can cause a great deal of misunderstanding in written works, especially in rules. Consider the following rule:

> When the player character hits the enemy with the Staff of Purity, he becomes immune to poison.

Who becomes immune: the player character of the enemy? It is impossible to tell because of the way this rule is written: We don't know who the pronoun *he* refers to.

Dealing with the meanings of words is a difficult challenge that all humans face, and game designers need to be particularly careful with their wording because of the importance of having clear rules in a game. There is also, sadly, no quick trick to solve this problem. There are methods you can practice to get better at more clearly getting the ideas from your head into the head of the audience. You may have heard the saying "Show, don't tell." This is a tactic you can use in games—and you also have a number of other tools at your disposal.

The following are some of these tools, listed in order from most effective way to communicate concepts to least:

- **Interact:** Show the player what to do. Have them do it and correct them if they do it wrong. Test to make sure the player has a good grasp of what is and is not allowed before letting the player move on. In video games, this function is often called a *gatekeeper*. For example, if a core mechanic of a game is for players to shoot a bow and arrow, you can present a player with a locked door that the player must open by hitting an easy target with an arrow in a low-stress situation before she can move on. Once you understand the concept of gatekeepers, you will start to see this mechanic pop up in video games everywhere.
- **Show:** If it is not possible to explain rules interactively, show the player the rules by using video and audio. You might, for instance, have a helpful NPC doing the action you want the player to do or use a cut scene that takes control away from the player to show how the player character can do the desired action. Or, as illustrated earlier in this chapter with the meat-loving dog, you can show a simple picture—such as a map or a diagram—that illuminates what you want the user to do.
- **Tell:** If it is not possible to use any type of video means to instruct the player, you can use clear audio instructions with good audio feedback.
- **Write:** Players are generally less likely to absorb directions that are written than directions presented using the above-mentioned methods, but if it is not possible to interact with, show, or tell the player how a particular rule works, you can provide written instructions. It may be beneficial to add written instructions along with using the methods listed above. A user might, for example, want to refer to written information to quickly get a refresher on the rules.
- **Hint:** If it is not possible to give the player written instructions, you can provide hints such as iconography to help players understand what is expected. You could use cracks in a wall, for example, to provide an iconographic hint to players that they should attack those walls to find that it crumbles, revealing a secret door. In some situations, you might want to use more blatant hints, such as an arrow painted on a wall, telling the player where to turn.

> note
>
> For many game mechanics, hinting is actually the preferred method of communication because part of the fun for a player is figuring out what to do. The design team should purposely think through where to use hints. What parts of the game do you want to require the player to figure out, and what parts of the game do you want the player to intuitively understand? Old video games made players figure out basically everything on their own. This method is now considered primitive and frustrating for modern audiences, and game designers pick and choose which mechanics belong at various levels of communication.

- **Guess:** The most frustrating—and least advisable—way to have players figure out the rules is to have them guess and punish them if they guess incorrectly. In general, you should avoid this method. If you find that testers are guessing about rules, consider using one of the methods listed above to make sure they don't need to guess.

Noise

From the perspective of communication theory, noise is not just background sounds. Noise is anything that can impede communication or lead to misunderstandings (see Figure 18.4). In games, this can be many things, including game controllers, understanding of the rules, the physical setup of the game, literal audio noise, visual noise on a computer screen, or anything else that can cause communication to be interrupted. Noise is inevitable any time there is communication, and a designer needs to acknowledge that and minimize it as much as possible.

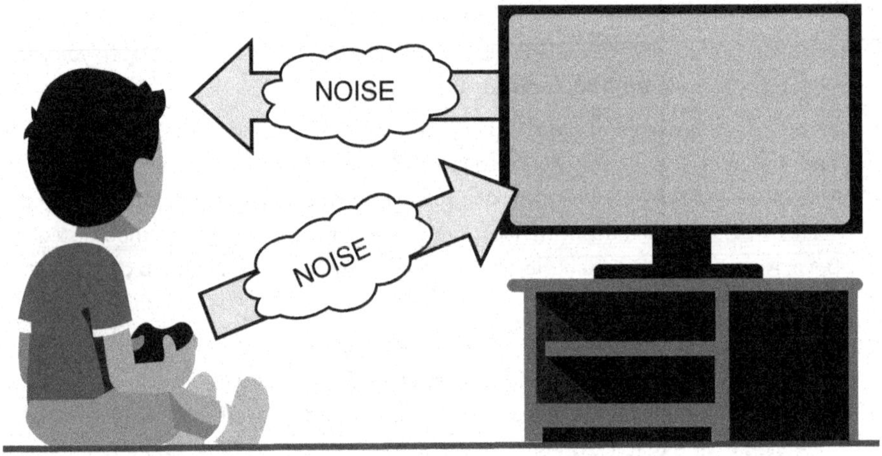

Figure 18.4 Noise in the communication loop

When you write or code rules for a game, you know what you want the player to experience and how you want them to communicate, but the players don't have that knowledge, so the conversation starts out quite lopsided. Whether you teach rules in a book, in a video, or in an interactive tutorial, you must battle noise to get your idea from your head, into the game, communicated to the player, and into the brain of the player.

Even if you have the most well-written set of game rules ever made, if the player experiences noise while learning the rules, they will have a diminished experience. Noise can be injected into the system at many points on the side of the game or on the side of the players. Some of the most common points of noise are as follows:

- **Unclear rules:** If the rules are poorly written or communicated, they are bad, regardless of how well they were intended. You have likely experienced a moment playing a game where you found out about a rule of the game that you had previously not known. Once you took in that rule, you probably thought about how that rule would have drastically changed decisions you had made up to that point. Such misunderstandings cause a large amount of frustration in players. Testing is the best way to find unclear or ambiguous rules. Ask your testers what the rules of the game are. Challenge them (nicely) with fringe case rulings and see if they know how the game should play. Ask your testers about what circumstances in the game would break the rules and see if their answers are right. The design team is responsible for ensuring that all of the rules they come up with are clearly communicated.
- **Technology limitations:** Even with today's powerful computers, there are limitations to what you can show onscreen. You might have a play area that is too big to fit on a screen. You might not be able to do what you want to do with a controller. You might not have the ability to produce enough distinct sounds to properly signal to players. This is another place where designers need to take responsibility. No system will ever be perfect, and it is a designer's job to acknowledge the limitations of hardware and build communication with the player out of what is available.
- **Visual limitations:** Even if the screen on which you are displaying a game is capable of displaying every aspect of the game you want, it might not be digestible by the players. Think of very complex MMOs that have more than 50% of the screen filled with various UI elements. To an audience that is fluent in the language of the MMO, this is acceptable, but to new players, it looks like chaos. This can be a difficult problem to solve, and we will talk more about it in the next section, "Reciprocity."
- **Controller limitations:** Humans have arms, legs, fingers, eyes, and a mouth to communicate in person. We have all spent our entire lives learning to use these tools as subtle or blatant forms of communication. However, when playing a video game, players can't use any of those tools. They must, instead, use a game controller. Modern controllers have a multitude of buttons and joysticks with various degrees of pressure and motion sensitivity. A controller provides a special form of communication pathway for the player to use with the computer. This can be very intimidating to new players because they have not spent their entire life learning to use a controller the way a game designer wants them to. Over the past 30 or so years, designers have come up with many conventions for using controllers for games. For the most part, this is a good thing as it offers a shortcut to reduce noise related to controllers. This is also one place where creativity may not always

be the best idea. If you are finding that players are frustrated with the controllers as they play your game, you should look at what other games are doing with controllers. Do you think you need to have a unique interaction? Would it be better to go with convention for the sake of noise reduction? While it is certainly possible that your game has a mechanic that really does require the player to use the controller in an unorthodox way, keep in mind that this novelty will inevitably create noise when players are learning. Take extra steps to ensure that any controller usage has been thoroughly researched and tested against what your target audience expects.

For example, if you were making an FPS that required a keyboard and mouse, you could research the traditions of other FPS games that also use a keyboard and mouse. If you don't currently use WASD keys for player movement, why not? There may be a good reason, but is it worth fighting expectations and introducing noise?

While these are some of the most common forms of noise and miscommunication in games, they certainly are not the only ones. The key to reducing noise is to identify it through testing and questioning of testers. Once a source of noise is found, the design team needs to figure out how to minimize it.

Reciprocity

There is a communication theory called *reciprocity* that is part of the greater idea *social penetration*. The very high-level explanation of the theory of reciprocity is that people start more reserved when they meet someone new, revealing very little about themselves at first. As people get to know and trust each other, slowly, layer by layer, they expose more of themselves to each other. Only with complete trust in each other do they finally disclose their innermost thoughts and feelings. What does this have to do with games? Games and players are building a sort of relationship with each other. As discussed earlier in this chapter, there is a great amount of communication between them. In the relationship between humans and games, the game asks the player to perform tasks of ever increasing difficulty and in return gives the player rewards both virtually in the game and in entertainment value derived from the game. Players ask the game for instructions on how to perform the tasks and, in return, performs the needed tasks. This is reciprocity. The following sections provide a few examples of problems with reciprocity.

Overstepping Bounds

A player who is first beginning to play a game tends to be reserved in their willingness to commit to the game. The player wants to get some positive feedback from the game before being willing to commit more time and effort to the relationship. If the game asks too much of the player too early, the player is likely to see the game as overstepping its bounds; this is a form of rudeness toward the player that is off-putting.

Say that two people meet for the first time. The first one says, "Nice weather." The second says, "I was in a house fire as a child. I still wake up crying about it every night." Whoa. You may have had a conversation in your life like this and know how awkward it feels. The second person's feelings and experiences are not invalid, but they have overstepped the bounds of societal norms by exposing so much of their inner feelings upon first meeting. This is too much to ask of someone you do not know.

Now say that a player picks up a new video game and boots it up on their computer for the first time. The game has large text onscreen that says "Read and memorize the 63-page user manual before beginning the game." Whoa again! The player does not know if they are going to like this game and if they are willing to invest time memorizing 63 pages of a user manual to find out. The game has overstepped the bounds of what it can ask from a player upon first meeting. It is completely possible that over the course of playing the game, the player might happily read 63 or even more pages of instructions—if they know that their time investment is worth it and that the game is willing to reciprocate the player's effort with rewards in entertainment.

Shallow Relationship

If a game fails to gradually ask more and then give more to the player in return, the player may feel as though the relationship is shallow.

For example, say that two old men have known each other for 50 years. The wife of the first old man asks him what the second old man's favorite dinner is. The first old man says, "I don't know. We never really talk about anything except the weather." You would think that people who know each other for such a long time would pick up a bit of information about each other. When a relationship has been going for a long time, it is expected to advance at least somewhat. If it does not, it is considered a very shallow, unfulfilling relationship.

A player has been playing an MMO for years and has invested many hours playing and studying how the game works. The player logs in for the newly launched quest line and goes through the needed steps to launch the quest. At this point, the quest giver says to the player, "Hail adventurer! We are overrun by Level 1 goblins. Please go kill two Level 1 goblins to complete the quest." What a letdown! All that hype, all that time invested, all that work and planning...and the game asks the player to do something trivial. While the player has held up their end of the bargain, the game has shown itself to be shallow in the relationship.

Right Balance

Now let's look at a couple examples that strike the right balance in terms of reciprocity. First, say that two strangers meet at a party and spend the evening chatting about movies. They find that they like many of the same movies, so they go see new movies together. As time goes by, they start to have deeper conversations about relationships, family, work, and social life. After many happy events together, they slowly come to trust each other enough to reveal inner secrets, wants, and fears that they would not trust anyone else to know.

Now say that a player picks up a game, and the game immediately welcomes her. The game then lays out a very simple task, such as "Pick up that sword on the ground by pressing A." When the player does this, she is rewarded with a nice sound and the message "You now have a sword!" As the player progresses, the game places slightly more difficult challenges in front of her. Because the first reward felt good, she is now willing to invest a little more time and effort into completing this more difficult challenge, trusting that the game will reward her fairly for the effort. After many hours of play, with ever-increasing challenges, the player is faced with a "boss level" that is significantly difficult. She will fail often and may have to go away to better equip and come back. She is ready and willing to take on this challenge because the game has established a deep level of trust with her that the reward for completing the challenge will be worth it.

As you can see from these examples, by knowing about reciprocity and planning it into game systems as you build a game, you can better develop the kind of relationship you want your games to have with players. By purposely taking steps to establish trust with a player in the beginning and by handing out rewards in a methodical way, you can create more willingness in players to commit themselves to your grand vision of the game, regardless of how deep or sophisticated you make it.

Reward Expectations

Players' reactions to rewards can differ dramatically, depending on the expectations they have for the rewards. As discussed in the preceding section, if players keep giving more of themselves and the game does not respond, the players may become disillusioned with the game. There are also other ways to disappoint players. One is setting misleading expectations of reward. In general, the rule should be to underpromise to players and overdeliver. Let's look at an example.

Say that a game tells a player that if they complete the next quest, they will receive a special prize that is worth up to 100 gold pieces. The player completes the quest and claims the prize, which turns out to be 50 gold pieces. The player is now disappointed because when they heard "Blah blah blah...100 gold pieces reward," they tuned out everything except "100 gold pieces" and immediately set their expectations for that. Anything less is a disappointment, so even though the player has been rewarded, they are dissatisfied with the result and possibly also dissatisfied with the output of effort required to get the reward.

Now let's look at the same circumstances but rearrange the example just a bit to see a very different effect. In this revised version, the game tells the player that if they complete the quest, they will receive a prize worth at least 40 gold pieces. They complete the quest and claim the prize, which ends up being 50 gold pieces. Even though this is exactly the same reward as in the first example, in this case the player is very happy instead of disappointed. She was already happy enough with the reward that she was willing to take the quest, and she would have been happy with a reward of 40 gold pieces. When you give players an extra reward, they are happily surprised on top of already being happy with the original deal. They are likely to take on even more tasks in the game, thinking there could be more potential rewards hidden throughout.

If you think back through your own game-playing experience, I bet you could think of more than one time that a game overpromised and underdelivered rewards. This might happen, for example, with a hyped named prize object like The Amazing, Flaming Sword of the Ancient Gods! that turns out to be a sword that is basically like every other sword, but it's orange.

To avoid overpromising and underdelivering rewards, purposely make a plan to slightly underpromise and overdeliver whenever possible. Also keep a close eye out for this during the testing phase. The look on the face of a tester who has just been rewarded can be revealing. Players are often at their most emotive when they are disappointed.

Further Steps

After completing this chapter, you should take some time to practice in the real world with the concepts covered here. Try these exercises to further explore the concepts of player communication theory.

- For a game that you are working on, write a list of possible noise barriers that the player might face. Then list mitigation steps you are planning to take to ensure that these factors do not disrupt the player's experience.
- Make a purposeful plan for reciprocity in a game. Determine how deep each mechanic is and what you expect from the player before you expose that mechanic to them.
- Find an example of a game that you feel oversteps bounds and an example of a game that provides a shallow relationship. How could each of these games be improved to make a well-balanced relationship with the player?

CHAPTER 19

PROBABILITY

Not everything is predictable in the world or in games. However, it is possible to understand unpredictability. By examining basic probability, you will understand how existing games use random chance to manipulate players. Further, you can learn techniques that allow you as a system designer to allow random, unpredictable events while maintaining control over the flow of the game. But what is random?

Random is more difficult to define than you might imagine. There are entire fields of study dedicated to randomness and probability. This book covers many of the most basic concepts of probability, but it stops well short of providing full explanations; you can find books and other resources dedicated to those subjects.

For the purposes of this chapter, I define *random event* as follows:

> Any event for which the player can't accurately predict the outcome with the information they have at the time.

Randomness is not binary. Events don't have to be either all random or not random. For example, think about golf. If a player is about to drive the golf ball toward the green, it is impossible to know the exact position where the ball will come to rest. However, this does not make the event totally random. You could estimate an approximate location where the ball will likely land. Based on what you know of the player, the shot, and the conditions in the environment, you might be able to make a somewhat accurate prediction, but you can never be completely accurate.

Basic Probability

This section covers the absolute basics of probability, including how it is written and how it is calculated.

Probability Notation

Probability notation is surprisingly easy, and you are likely already familiar with it even if you don't know that you are. A probability calculation has only two variables: the total number of outcomes and the number of outcomes considered success. To break this down with a simple example, we can look at flipping a coin. Say that you want to know the probability that a coin flip will be heads. There are two sides of the coin: one heads and one tails. Of the two sides, only one is heads. This means the coin has heads on one out of two possible sides; therefore the chance, or probability, that the coin will land on heads is 1 out of 2, or 1/2. Based on the fact that the probability of an event equals the number of successful options out of number of total options, we can create the following formula:

> Probability = Successes / Total options
>
> P = S/T

In the case of a coin toss landing on heads, we can use this notation:

> 1 chance of heads out of 2 possible outcomes
>
> 1/2 = chance of heads

We use this final notation throughout this chapter to further explain probability.

Real and virtual dice are often used to determine outcomes in games. Special notation is used for the probability of dice rolls. With dice, we use the notation *XDN* to express the count of the number of options on a die (*N*) and the number of dice that are being rolled (*X*). For example, the notation for rolling a single six-sided die is 1D6. The notation for rolling two six-sided dice and adding them together is 2D6. The notation for rolling four two-sided dice is 4D2. You could also use this notation to represent coins, which are, in effect, two-sided dice.

Calculating One-Dimensional Even-Distribution Probability

Spreadsheets are fantastic tools for doing probability calculations, but they need to be set up correctly. In this section, we begin to look at calculating probability, and we again use the coin example—but this time we bring it into a spreadsheet. This section shows how to start building a framework for doing complex calculations in a spreadsheet.

> **note**
>
> As you read this chapter, I strongly recommend that you follow along in a spreadsheet and build this framework yourself.

To get started, you need to enter a few pieces of data. You know the type of die you are using, 1D2, and you know that this die has a heads side and a tails side. Figure 19.1 shows how you would lay this out in a spreadsheet.

	A	B	C
1	1D2	Event	Count
2		Heads	1
3		Tails	1

Figure 19.1 1D2 probability

As you can see, you want to include in the spreadsheet the label 1D2, an Event column for outcomes you want to calculate, and a Count column that lists the possible successful outcomes. For this example, you are going to calculate the probability of each event in a simple coin toss—1 head and 1 tail—so we need two more pieces of information immediately. First, to get the number of successes out of the total possible, you need a total count of all events.

Then you need to divide each event count by that total. Your spreadsheet needs to look as shown in Figure 19.2.

	A	B	C	D
1	1D2	Event	Count	Chance
2		Heads	1	50.0%
3		Tails	1	50.0%
4		Total	2	100.0%

Figure 19.2 Labeled probability table

Figure 19.3 shows the same spreadsheet, with all the needed formulas and functions to do the proper calculations.

	A	B	C	D
1	1D2	Event	Count	Chance
2		Heads	1	=C2/$C$4
3		Tails	1	=C3/$C$4
4		Total	=sum(C2:C3)	=sum(D2:D3)

Figure 19.3 Probability formulas

There are a couple things of note about the spreadsheet in Figure 19.3. First, notice that some of the references are absolute and others are relative. You need both absolute and relative references to make the formula ready to formfill down. When you use relative references pointing toward the count and an absolute reference pointing to the total, as the formula is copied down, it updates properly for all the cells. Second, notice that in cell D4, the percentage chances of all the events have been summed to give a total of 100%. This seems unnecessary, but it is a very good practice to total your percentages with complex calculations, so you can ensure that they indeed add up to 100%. You know intuitively that percentages should add up to 100%, and when you see in a spreadsheet that the percentages do, in fact, add up to 100%, you have confirmation that you have correctly done all the calculations in all the other cells that feed this final check. This is an example of a data canary, which helps you know when you have a problem in your data (refer to Chapter 15, "Analyzing Game Data").

Now that you have a very simple probability spreadsheet laid out, it's time to increase the complexity. Let's jump up to using a standard six-sided die, or 1D6. For the most part, this is going to be very similar to the 1D2 spreadsheet but longer and with different chances. To get started, you should set up your formulas so that they behave basically the same as those for 1D2 but with a longer Event list. In formula view, your spreadsheet should look as shown in Figure 19.4.

	A	B	C	D
1	1D6	Event	Count	Chance
2		1	1	=C2/$C$8
3		2	1	
4		3	1	
5		4	1	
6		5	1	
7		6	1	
8		Total	=sum(C2:C7)	=sum(D2:D7)

Figure 19.4 1D6 table

Cells D3 through D7 have not been filled out in Figure 19.4, but cell D2 has been written in such a way that you can use formfill to drag it down and complete all the rest of the cells without writing a new formula. Once that is done, you should have a spreadsheet that looks as shown in Figure 19.5.

	A	B	C	D
1	1D6	Event	Count	Chance
2		1	1	16.7%
3		2	1	16.7%
4		3	1	16.7%
5		4	1	16.7%
6		5	1	16.7%
7		6	1	16.7%
8		Total	6	100.0%

Figure 19.5 1D6 table completed

The spreadsheet now shows the basic probability events for a single six-sided die. This information is useful for making a classic board game that relies on getting specific roles with a six-sided die. If you were to graph this probability distribution, it would look as shown in Figure 19.6.

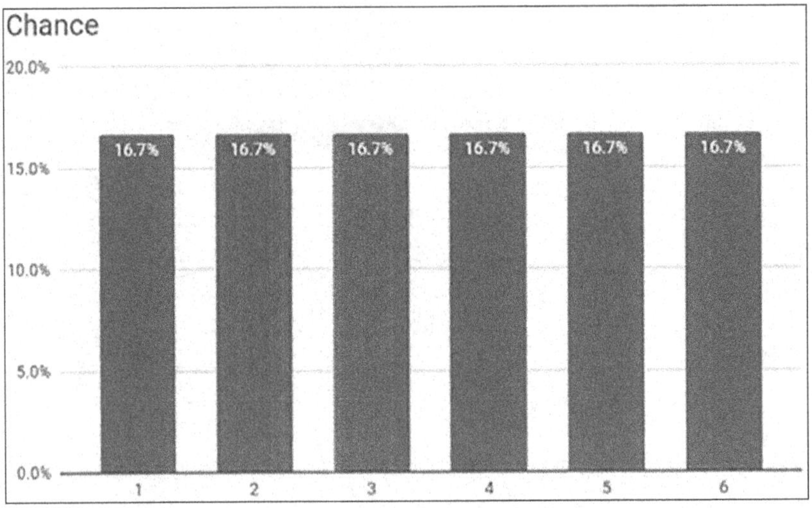

Figure 19.6 Chart of 1D6

This is not a particularly interesting chart, but keep it in mind for comparison with future charts that you make later on. Notice, in particular, that the heights of all the bars are the same, forming a level line across the chart. This is the shape of an even distribution in a chart.

In many games, specific rolls are not always required for success. Often in analog and video games, a player can be successful with a range of rolls. For example, a player may need to roll a 3 or higher to score a point. In such a case, you can't simply look at a single-series chart to find the probability of rolling 3 or higher. To get this probability, you need to add another calculation to the chart to get a cumulative probability, which is also called a *running total*. To set it up, you need to think about what exactly is going on with the probability. What is the probability of rolling a 6 or better on a six-sided die? This seems like a trick question because there is no number higher than a six. When you start to look at cumulative probability for rolling a number or higher, you can safely calculate the highest number in the list: It is the same probability as rolling that number independently. In this case, the chance of rolling a six or better is equal to the chance of rolling a six. You need to add the new column and calculation shown in Figure 19.7 to include this information.

	A	B	C	D	E
1	1D6	Event	Count	Chance	Or Higher
2		1	1	=C2/$C$8	
3		2	1	=C3/$C$8	
4		3	1	=C4/$C$8	
5		4	1	=C5/$C$8	
6		5	1	=C6/$C$8	
7		6	1	=C7/$C$8	=D7
8		Total	=sum(	=sum(D2:D7)	

Figure 19.7 formulas for calculating each event of a 1D6 probability roll

This first cumulative probability calculation is the easy one, and it holds regardless of how many events you are calculating. Next, it's time to start doing the cumulative probability. Fortunately, this is not nearly as difficult as the name makes it seem; you need only a single formula to do it. However, before we can use that formula, we need to take a small detour and look at *cumulative lists*, also known as *running totals*. Examine Table 19.1, which shows numbers and payments made each week.

Table 19.1 Pay schedule

Week	Payment
1	$10
2	$10
3	$10
4	$10

Without even using a calculator, you can quickly tell that by week 3, $30 has been paid. By week 4, the total paid is $40. What process do you use in your head to do these calculations? You look at the first payment on week 1 and know that it stands alone. For week 2, you know that you already got the week 1 total, and now you need to add the week 2 payment to it, for a total of $20. On week 3, you add another $10 to the previous total, for a new total of $30. In this way, you figure out the running total—which is exactly the same thing you do with the probability. The only differences for our probability example is that you are adding up the percentage chance, rather than dollar amounts, and you are going from the bottom to the top. Now that you know all this, it's time to write the formula for calculating the entire list of cumulative probability.

In cell E6, you need to add your running total, which starts in E7, to your new addition, which in this case is the probability that is calculated in D6. The formula and spreadsheet should look as shown in Figure 19.8

	A	B	C	D	E
1	1D6	Event	Count	Chance	Or Higher
2		1	1	=C2/$C$8	
3		2	1	=C3/$C$8	
4		3	1	=C4/$C$8	
5		4	1	=C5/$C$8	
6		5	1	=C6/$C$8	=D6+E7
7		6	1	=C7/$C$8	=D7
8		Total	=sum(	=sum(D2:D7)	

Figure 19.8 Beginning to calculate 1D6 cumulative probability

By adding the chance in the cell below to the chance of the current event, you can calculate the running total of probability. After calculating the first running total as shown in Figure 19.8, you can formfill the contents of E6 up through the entire range of events to complete the running total. Your spreadsheet should now look as shown in Figure 19.9.

	A	B	C	D	E
1	1D6	Event	Count	Chance	Or Higher
2		1	1	16.7%	100.0%
3		2	1	16.7%	83.3%
4		3	1	16.7%	66.7%
5		4	1	16.7%	50.0%
6		5	1	16.7%	33.3%
7		6	1	16.7%	16.7%
8		Total	6	100.0%	

Figure 19.9 Completed "or higher" cumulative probability spreadsheet

Now you can take a look at the probabilities in the cumulative odds columns (column E) to gain more insights into how the game is going to work. Recall that we began this journey trying to figure out the probability of rolling a 3 or better. Looking at the spreadsheet, you can see that the answer is 66.7% (which is technically 66.6666% repeating). This makes sense if you look at it from a slightly different perspective as well: You know that to calculate probability, you are really looking for the chances of success compared to the total chances possible. In this case, success means rolling a 3, 4, 5, or 6—which is four possible total options out of 6 total options. This means that the probability calculation here is 4/6. You can simplify this fraction to 2/3—which is the same as 66.7%—so all the numbers check out.

> **note**
>
> With a single six-sided die roll, any individual number is not a rare occurrence. That is, 16.7% chance of something happening or 82.3% chance of that something not happening is not a rare occurrence. Often, players get wrapped up in the psychology of there being only a single 1 on a die and think they roll a 1 more than they should. Part of this is due to selective perception, as rolling a 1 (especially if it is a bad result) stands out more than rolling the other numbers. However, the main factor is that rolling a 1 is just not that rare.

Calculating One-Dimensional Uneven-Distribution Probability

This section builds on the principles covered in the previous sections and looks at calculating probability in an uneven distribution. Take a look at the spinner shown in Figure 19.10. It has eight spaces with seven different colors. We can assume that a spin has the same chance of landing on any of the eight spaces.

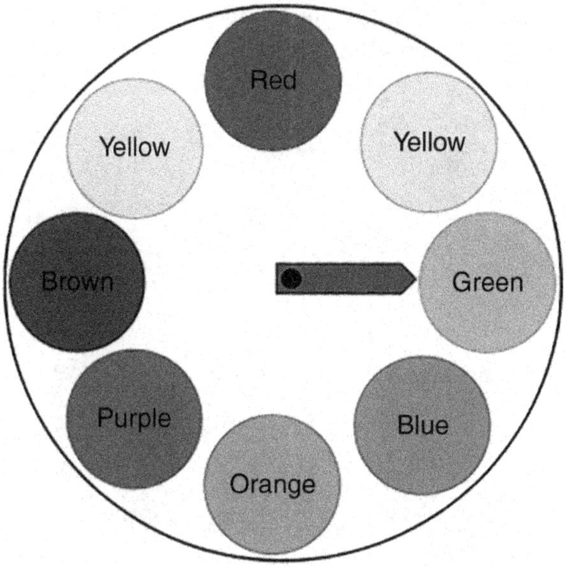

Figure 19.10 Spinner

It might seem like the calculations in this case will be complex, but they are exactly the same as for the 1D6 example. The only differences between this spinner example and the six-sided die example is that there are more possible outcomes with the spinner, one event has higher probability than the others, and it is not possible to do cumulative calculations. The fastest way to do the new calculation in a spreadsheet is to duplicate the 1D6 sheet and make the minor modifications needed. The spreadsheet should look as shown in Figure 19.11.

	A	B	C	D
1	Spin	Event	Count	Chance
2		Red	1	12.5%
3		Orange	1	12.5%
4		Brown	1	12.5%
5		Yellow	2	25.0%
6		Blue	1	12.5%
7		Green	1	12.5%
8		Purple	1	12.5%
9		Total	8	100.0%

Figure 19.11 Unequal-distribution spreadsheet

By using this method, you can calculate probability for any given list, no matter how long or short.

You can use the data from Figure 19.11 to create a chart that provides a visualization of the distribution, as shown in Figure 19.12. As you can see in this figure, most of the probability is evenly distributed, but yellow gets a double share. Therefore, the bars in the chart are level except for the yellow bar.

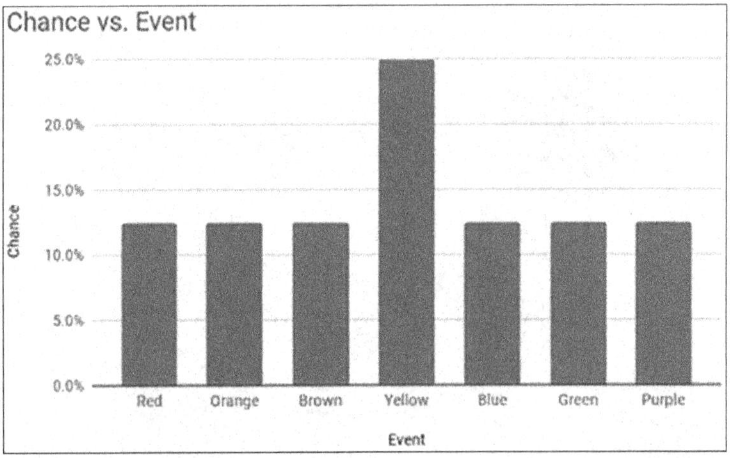

Figure 19.12 Unequal distribution chart

Calculating Compound Probability

One-dimensional probability tables can calculate a great variety of probabilities, but they are limited to a single dimension and a single event. In other words, they are missing some key probability modifiers, such as "and" and "or." One of the simplest and most common places you encounter compound probability is when you add together the rolls of two dice. When rolling 2D6, there is no longer a single event that determines the outcome. Instead, there are two events that are then added together, each having independent probability. To account for these multiple events, you need a more sophisticated method of determining probability. When calculating one-dimensional probability, you lay out your events in a line, which is a one-dimensional object. To illustrate this, Figure 19.13 shows a line overlaid on top of the 1D6 events.

	A	B	C	D
1	1D6	Event	Count	Chance
2		1	1	16.7%
3		2	1	16.7%
4		3	1	16.7%
5		4	1	16.7%
6		5	1	16.7%
7		6	1	16.7%
8		Total	6	100.0%

Figure 19.13 Linear events

With compound probability, you add another dimension. So instead of having a single line going in only one direction, you need to have two lines running perpendicular to each other to represent all of the possible events.

> **note**
>
> This is very similar in concept to the difference between linear feet and square feet. When measuring a straight line, such as a rope, you do the measurement in linear feet. When you measure an area in two dimensions, such as a field or the floor of a room, you use square feet.

When you add the new dimension to the data, it is going to run exactly perpendicular to the first set, starting at the same origin point. The lines the events make will end up looking as shown in Figure 19.14.

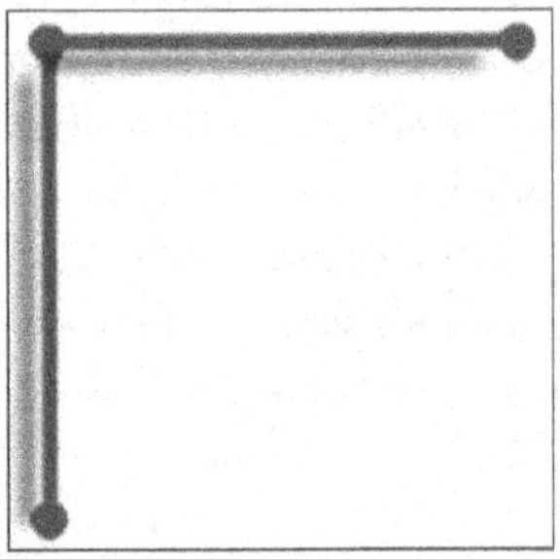

Figure 19.14 Two-dimensional events

To actually start adding data to your spreadsheet, first you can tackle two two-sided dice—which are really coins—where for each coin you can roll either a 1 or a 2. To begin, you can enter all the events of one coin in a single column, as shown in Figure 19.15.

	A
1	2D2
2	1
3	2

Figure 19.15 2D2 table of possible events

To add the second dimension, you need to enter the same numbers from column A into row 1 (see Figure 19.16). With this addition, you now have a two-dimensional spreadsheet.

	A	B	C
1	2D2	1	2
2	1		
3	2		

Figure 19.16 2D2 two-dimensional spreadsheet

The next step is to fill in the grid. You should first do this manually in your head. Since it is a very small spreadsheet, it should be fairly easy. In B2, you add the 1 from A2 and the 1 from B1 to get 2. You follow a similar procedure for each of the other squares in the grid. The result will look as shown in Figure 19.17.

	A	B	C
1	2D2	1	2
2	1	2	3
3	2	3	4

Figure 19.17 2D2 two-dimensional spreadsheet with probabilities calculated manually

It is easy to see that this simple example has a single 2, two 3s, and a single 4. The next step is to write a scalable formula that will calculate all the cells in the grid, regardless of how many there are. To do this, you need to fully understand mixed reference formulas. In each two-dimensional probability grid, there is a header row and a header column. In this case, the header row is all of row 1, and the header column is all of column A. Regardless of where the formula is copied, it always needs to refer to the header row and column. When locking a reference as absolute, you need to ensure that there is a $ in front of the portion of the reference that is to be absolute. In this case, you know that row 1 is absolute, so when writing the formula, you need to place a $ in front of the reference to row 1. The same goes for column A. On the other hand, you need the reference to move up and down row 1 and side to side on column A because the even values change in their respective axes. This means that portions of the reference must not be absolute and can't have a $ in front. When you use these rules to create the master formula that will populate the entire grid, you get a formula that looks as shown in Figure 19.18.

	A	B	C
1	2D2	1	2
2	1	=$A2+B$1	
3	2		

Figure 19.18 Two-dimensional formula

You can now use this formula to formfill the entire grid. You could further use it to formfill any two-dimensional probability grid of any size. As a result, you get the same numbers you calculated in your head earlier (see Figure 19.19, which looks just like Figure 19.17).

	A	B	C
1	2D2	1	2
2	1	2	3
3	2	3	4

Figure 19.19 2D2 table completed with a formfilled formula

When the grid is complete, you have a list of all the possible options that can happen in this event, and you can move on to calculating the probability. To do this, you use exactly the same method you used earlier to determine the linear probability calculations. When you do, you get the result shown in Figure 19.20.

	E	F	G	H
1	2D2	Event	Count	Chance
2		2		
3		3		
4		4		
5		Total		

Figure 19.20 2D2 complete table

Notice that this is the first spreadsheet in this chapter where the data does not start on A1. Remember that you need to keep the 2D2 grid around so that it can be referenced in this new calculation. Also note that 1 is not listed in the Event column—because it is not possible to get a 1 when combining two dice this way. (This is the case any time two dice are added together.)

After you lay out this spreadsheet, you need to populate the Count column. To get the counts manually, you can look at the 2D2 grid and count how many of each number appear in the grid. Although it's possible to do this manual counting with this simple example, it would quickly become very difficult to do the counting this way. Instead, you should set up the spreadsheet to do this counting automatically. When you know how to do this in a simple case like this example, you will be able to use it easily later in more sophisticated computations.

Think for a moment what formula or function you would use to do the counting in this example. Which of the functions that described spreadsheeting in Chapter 6, "Spreadsheet Functions," would be most applicable? When learning how to use spreadsheets, one of the best ways to determine what function to use is to think about what you do manually to get the answer. In this case, you look at the grid in B2:C3, and each time you see a 2, you count up by 1, for a total of 1. Then, you look for 3, count up by 1, and get a total of 2. Finally, for 4, you get the result 1. So what you want a function to do is look in a specific group of cells and count each time it finds what you are looking for. The function that would do this for you is COUNTIF. To set it up to do the counting calculation, you start by entering the function in cell G2, reference the 2D2 grid, and have the function look for the event listed in F2. The function should end up looking as shown in Figure 19.21.

	E	F	G	H
1	2D2	Event	Count	Chance
2		2	=countif($B$2:$C$3,F2)	
3		3		
4		4		
5		Total		

Figure 19.21 COUNTIF formula made to look in a probability table

When this formula is formfilled to the rest of the cells, the accurate counts of the events are automatically calculated, as shown in Figure 19.22.

	A	B	C	D	E	F	G	H
1	2D2	1	2		2D2	Event	Count	Chance
2	1	2	3			2	1	
3	2	3	4			3	2	
4						4	1	
5						Total		

Figure 19.22 2D2 count of events, completed

To fill out the rest of the cells, you use exactly the same methods used to calculate 1D2 to get total and a chance for each event. After all that is done, the sheet should look as shown in Figure 19.23.

	A	B	C	D	E	F	G	H
1	2D2	1	2		2D2	Event	Count	Chance
2	1	2	3			2	1	25.0%
3	2	3	4			3	2	50.0%
4						4	1	25.0%
5						Total	4	100.0%

Figure 19.23 2D2 chance complete

The biggest difference between the probability of 2D2 and 1D2 is that not all events have the same chance. Even though both dice have the same number of sides and have the same values on each of those sides, the count for 3 comes out higher than the count for either 2 or 4. This is the natural effect of adding separate random numbers together. The distribution is uneven. To further explore this concept, we can move on to six-sided dice.

You use exactly the same method to calculate 2D6 as you use to calculate 2D2. Again, you should make a copy of your 2D2 sheet and expand it out to accommodate the larger 2D6 grid. Because you already set up all the formulas and functions to be automatic, they automatically expand and formfill not only 2D6 but any two numerical combinations that make a grid. Figure 19.24 shows a completed 2D6 event grid.

	A	B	C	D	E	F	G
1	2D6	1	2	3	4	5	6
2	1	2	3	4	5	6	7
3	2	3	4	5	6	7	8
4	3	4	5	6	7	8	9
5	4	5	6	7	8	9	10
6	5	6	7	8	9	10	11
7	6	7	8	9	10	11	12

Figure 19.24 2D6 event grid

At first, this may seem like a large field of arbitrary numbers, but take a few moments to look for patterns. You can see at the top left that there is a single 2, and then, on the diagonal, there are two 3s, then three 4s, four 5s, five 6s, and six 7s. Then the pattern shrinks back down as the numbers get larger, ending with a single 12. To illustrate this further, the spreadsheet in Figure 19.25 shows the same numbers but has conditional formatting applied so that the largest and smallest numbers are highlighted with deeper colors.

	A	B	C	D	E	F	G
1	2D6	1	2	3	4	5	6
2	1	2	3	4	5	6	7
3	2	3	4	5	6	7	8
4	3	4	5	6	7	8	9
5	4	5	6	7	8	9	10
6	5	6	7	8	9	10	11
7	6	7	8	9	10	11	12

Figure 19.25 2D6 conditionally formatted event grid

The conditional formatting graphically highlights the patterns in the grid. To go from a nice visualization to mathematical clarity, you can use exactly the same method shown for 2D2, which is also the same method used for 1D6. List all the different events, use COUNTIF to find the exact count in the grid, and use those counts to calculate the chance of each number coming up. The spreadsheet should end up looking as shown in Figure 19.26.

	I	J	K	L
1	2D6	Event	Count	Chance
2		2	1	2.78%
3		3	2	5.56%
4		4	3	8.33%
5		5	4	11.11%
6		6	5	13.89%
7		7	6	16.67%
8		8	5	13.89%
9		9	4	11.11%
10		10	3	8.33%
11		11	2	5.56%
12		12	1	2.78%
13		sum	36	100.00%

Figure 19.26 2D6 probability calculation

Figure 19.27 shows what it looks like when all this spreadsheet's functions and formulas are exposed.

	A	B	C	D	E	F	G
1	2D6	1	2	3	4	5	6
2	1	=$A2+B$1	=$A2+C$1	=$A2+D$1	=$A2+E$1	=$A2+F$1	=$A2+G$1
3	2	=$A3+B$1	=$A3+C$1	=$A3+D$1	=$A3+E$1	=$A3+F$1	=$A3+G$1
4	3	=$A4+B$1	=$A4+C$1	=$A4+D$1	=$A4+E$1	=$A4+F$1	=$A4+G$1
5	4	=$A5+B$1	=$A5+C$1	=$A5+D$1	=$A5+E$1	=$A5+F$1	=$A5+G$1
6	5	=$A6+B$1	=$A6+C$1	=$A6+D$1	=$A6+E$1	=$A6+F$1	=$A6+G$1
7	6	=$A7+B$1	=$A7+C$1	=$A7+D$1	=$A7+E$1	=$A7+F$1	=$A7+G$1

	I	J	K	L
1	2D6	Event	Count	Chance
2		2	=countif($B$2:$G$7,J2)	=K2/$K$13
3		3	=countif($B$2:$G$7,J3)	=K3/$K$13
4		4	=countif($B$2:$G$7,J4)	=K4/$K$13
5		5	=countif($B$2:$G$7,J5)	=K5/$K$13
6		6	=countif($B$2:$G$7,J6)	=K6/$K$13
7		7	=countif($B$2:$G$7,J7)	=K7/$K$13
8		8	=countif($B$2:$G$7,J8)	=K8/$K$13
9		9	=countif($B$2:$G$7,J9)	=K9/$K$13
10		10	=countif($B$2:$G$7,J10	=K10/$K$13
11		11	=countif($B$2:$G$7,J11	=K11/$K$13
12		12	=countif($B$2:$G$7,J12	=K12/$K$13
13		sum	=sum(K2:K12)	=sum(L2:L12

Figure 19.27 2D6 formulas exposed

note

In Chapter 10, "Organizing Data in Spreadsheets," I recommended not using blank columns or rows to separate data in a table. It might seem like I have broken that rule in Figure 19.27 because column H is blank. However, there is a distinction. On this sheet, there are two different tables: a grid of results on the left and the analysis of those results on the right. So column H is between the tables, not within a table. To create the cleanest spreadsheets possible, it would be ideal to separate those two tables into two separate sheets. However, I have shown them on a single sheet here to more clearly show all the information together in one image. There are times when having multiple small tables on a single sheet is an advantage. When in doubt, though, separate data into individual sheets.

Of course, it's not enough to create a big grid of numbers without taking the time to evaluate them and make observations that have practical effects on games. By looking at the chance of each event in the 2D6 grid, you can see the same patterns emerge as in the 2D2 grid and in the conditionally formatted 2D6 event grid. The numbers near the center of the list are more likely to occur than are those at the corners. To illustrate this further, you can load the data into a chart (see Figure 19.28).

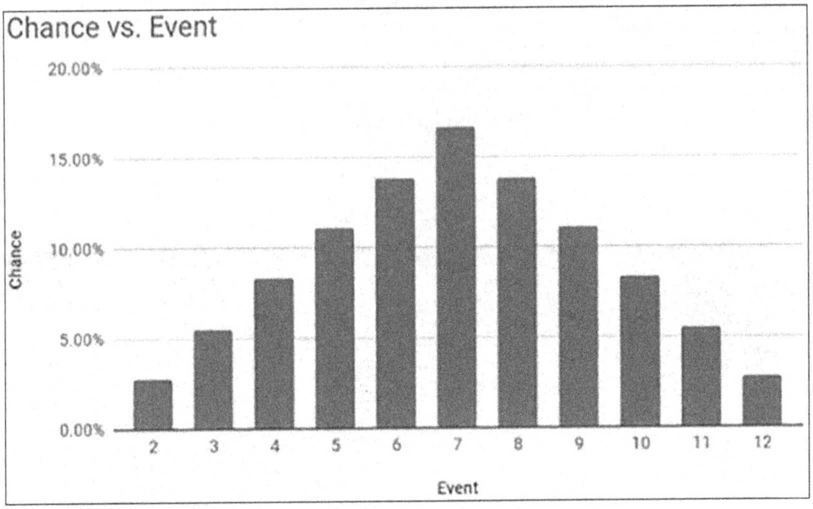

Figure 19.28 2D6 distribution chart

The layout of the bars in this chart is very different from the layout of the bars in any of the charts created for linear probability. This is called *bell curve* probability because it makes a smooth curve from each end up to the middle, similar to the shape of a bell. The distribution in a bell curve is unique in a number of ways:

- The high and low ends are quite rare. In our 2D6 example, rolling either a 2 or a 12 has less than a 3% probability.
- The central point has a very high relative probability. In the case of 2D6, it is 16.67%. It is five times more likely that you will roll a 7 than that you will roll either a 2 or a 12.
- The probability of rolling the central number, in this case 7, is the same probability of rolling any given number on a 1D6. This holds for any bell curve distribution, so if you were rolling 2D8, the probability of rolling a 9 would be the same as rolling any individual number on 1D8.
- The central point is one higher than the count of a single die. If you have 2D6, the center is 6 + 1, or 7. The central, or most common, number for 2D13 would be 14, for 2D14 would be 15, and so on.
- The distance between any two adjacent chances (called the *step*) is the same as the probability of rolling a number at one of the ends of the curve. For example, there is a 2.78% chance of rolling a 2 on 2D6. The probability of rolling a 7 is also 2.78% higher than that of rolling a 6. This holds true for any other bell curve distribution.

Calculating 2D6 "Or Higher" Cumulative Probability

Once the distribution of 2D6 is in a spreadsheet, you can use exactly the same method used for 1D6 to find the distribution of rolling any given number or higher on 2D6. Again, you start at the highest number and write a single formula that adds up each new probability and provides a running total. The spreadsheet should look as shown in Figure 19.29.

2D6	Event	Count	Chance	orHigher
	2	1	2.78%	100.00%
	3	2	5.56%	97.22%
	4	3	8.33%	91.67%
	5	4	11.11%	83.33%
	6	5	13.89%	72.22%
	7	6	16.67%	58.33%
	8	5	13.89%	41.67%
	9	4	11.11%	27.78%
	10	3	8.33%	16.67%
	11	2	5.56%	8.33%
	12	1	2.78%	2.78%
	sum	36	100.00%	

Figure 19.29 2D6 "or higher" cumulative probability spreadsheet

When graphed out, the distribution looks as shown in Figure 19.30.

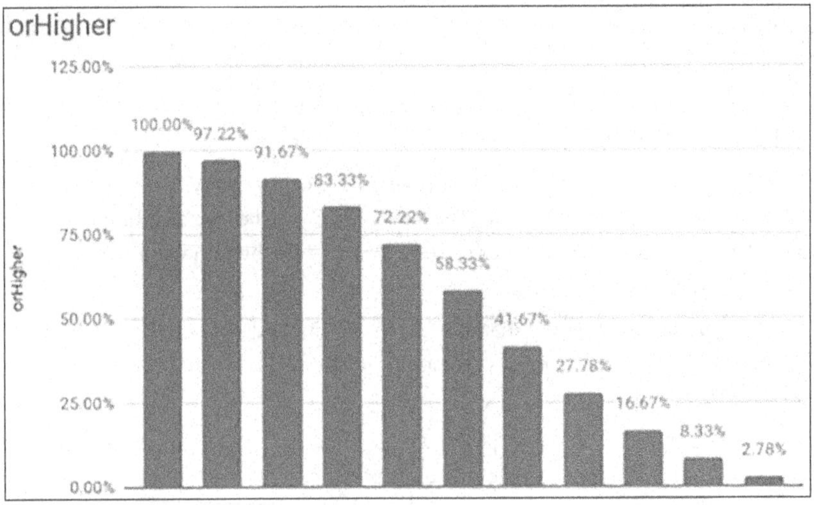

Figure 19.30 2D6 "or higher" cumulative probability chart

Consider the following important observations about the cumulative probability distribution of 2D6 that work with any two-dimensional probability table:

- The steps in between numbers at the top and bottom of the chart are small, but the steps between numbers in the center of the chart are very large. For example, a player who needs to roll an 11 or better has a 5.56% greater chance of succeeding than if they need to roll a 12 or better. In contrast, a player who needs to roll a 7 or better has a 16.67% greater chance of succeeding than if they need to roll an 8 or better; the increase in a single step is three times greater in the middle of the chart than in the ends.
- Exactly the same probability applies to "or worse" charts as to "or higher" charts—but in the reverse order.

Calculating the Probability of Doubles

In many games, rolling doubles—that is, the same number on two dice—holds significance. To help you understand how to calculate the probability of rolling any given doubles, Figure 19.31 shows the same 2D6 spreadsheet as before but now with shading applied to the doubles.

2D6	1	2	3	4	5	6
1	2	3	4	5	6	7
2	3	4	5	6	7	8
3	4	5	6	7	8	9
4	5	6	7	8	9	10
5	6	7	8	9	10	11
6	7	8	9	10	11	12

Figure 19.31 Doubles table

You can see in Figure 19.31 that the pattern of doubles runs diagonally through the chart in the opposite diction from the 7s, and the count is exactly the same: There are 6 ways to roll doubles, and there are 6 ways to roll a 7. Because there are 6 ways to roll doubles out of 36 possible outcomes for 2D6, there is (yet again) a 16.67% chance of rolling doubles.

> note
>
> You may have noticed that 16.67% keeps popping up when dealing with 1D6 and 2D6 probabilities. This is not a coincidence. The chance of an occurrence of any single result will be embedded throughout the probability of the roll: You can find the probability of doubles on any two dice roll by finding the probability of rolling a given number on one of those dice.

Calculating a Series of Single Events

With the calculations described so far in this chapter, you can figure out the probability of a vast array of different dice rolls, but those are all individual events. What do you do with a series of events? You know the chance of rolling a 1 on a one-sided die, and you have calculated the chance of rolling a 1 on each of two six-sided dice. This is the start of a series. Now, let's take this series further with a few examples.

What is the probability of rolling a 1 on 1D6 three, four, five, or more time in a row? To create a series of probability events, you must multiply the probability of the current event by itself for each new step. This may seem unintuitive, but a graphic example can help explain. Let's say you have a whole pizza. If you were to eat half of it, how much would be left (see Figure 19.32)?

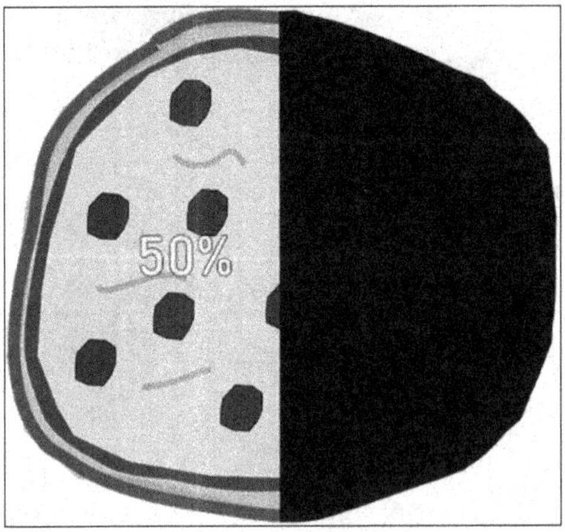

Figure 19.32 Half a pizza

You would have one-half (or 1/2 or 50%). This is easy enough to calculate. What if you again eat half of the remaining pizza? How much is left now? You don't subtract half of the whole, or you would be left with 0%. Instead, you would subtract half of the half, so you end up with 25% (see Figure 19.33). You can apply the same method to any series of probability events.

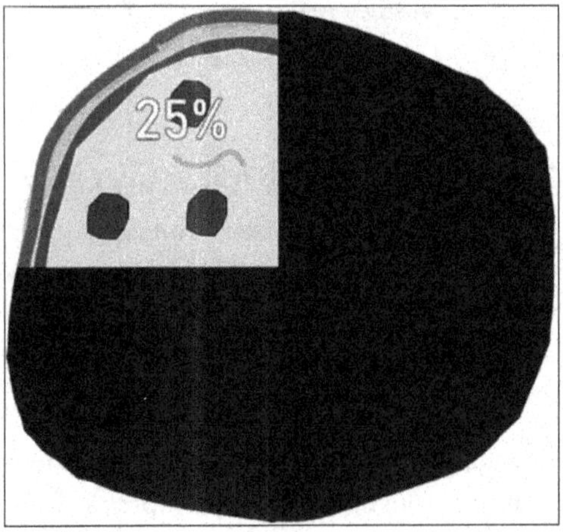

Figure 19.33 A quarter of a pizza

Now let's think about rolling a 1 on 1D6 again. In a spreadsheet, you can set up a formula starting in the first iteration with the odds 1/6 (see Figure 19.34). For all iterations down the sheet, you multiply the previous iteration by 1/6 again.

	A	B
1	In a row	Odds
2	1	=1/6
3	2	=B2*(1/6)
4	3	

Figure 19.34 Probability series formula

After you write the formula in B2, you can formfill it down to produce the odds of a 1 being rolled any number of times. As you can see in Figure 19.35, the chance of this happening is incredibly small, but it will never reach zero.

	A	B
1	In a row	Odds
2	1	16.666667%
3	2	2.777778%
4	3	0.462963%
5	4	0.077160%
6	5	0.012860%
7	6	0.002143%
8	7	0.000357%
9	8	0.000060%
10	9	0.000010%
11	10	0.000002%

Figure 19.35 Probability series

This kind of spreadsheet works well for a one-time calculation of a series. You can also go a bit further and make a dynamic spreadsheet that will allow you to input any probability numbers you want, and the spreadsheet will automatically figure out the probability of the series. The variables you need, just as before, are number of events and number of successes. With those two variables, the spreadsheet does the rest. Figure 19.36 shows all the related formulas exposed.

	A	B	C	D	E
1	In a row	Odds		Possible	6
2	1	=E3		Successes	1
3	2	=B2*$E$3		Probability	=E2/E1
4	3	=B3*$E$3			
5	4	=B4*$E$3			
6	5	=B5*$E$3			
7	6	=B6*$E$3			
8	7	=B7*$E$3			
9	8	=B8*$E$3			
10	9	=B9*$E$3			
11	10	=B10*$E$3			

Figure 19.36 Variable-driven series calculation

Once this spreadsheet is set up, you can change the "possible" and "successes" numbers and cause the probability of each item in the series to be recalculated.

Now let's look at an atypical example. The spreadsheet in Figure 19.37 shows 7 possible successes out of 11 possibilities. (You are very unlikely to find these probabilities on dice, but you might find them in cards or with a video game loot table.)

	A	B	C	D	E
1	In a row	Odds		Possible	11
2	1	63.6364%		Successes	7
3	2	40.4959%		Probability	63.6364
4	3	25.7701%			
5	4	16.3992%			
6	5	10.4358%			
7	6	6.6410%			
8	7	4.2261%			
9	8	2.6893%			
10	9	1.7114%			
11	10	1.0891%			

Figure 19.37 Series output

This kind of formula can be applied to any set of probability to find the likelihood of the event happening. The same formula can be used in inverse as well. Let's say you have a game where you roll 2D6, and if you get a 12, you automatically lose; otherwise, you can continue rolling. In this case, you are not trying to figure out the odds of rolling a 12 multiple times in a row; instead, you are trying to figure out the odds of *not* rolling a 12. While this may seem more complex, it is exactly the same calculation but with one additional step. You know that the odds of rolling a 12 on 2D6 are 1/36, or 2.78%. This means that the odds of not rolling 12 are 100% minus the odds of rolling 12: 100% – 2.78% = 97.22%. You can then substitute these numbers into the original formula. To adapt the spreadsheet to account for this, as shown in Figure 19.38, you can add one more calculation below Probability, for Not, and you can add one more column, Inverse, which is the probability of the event not happening a number of times in a row.

	A	B	C	D	E	F
1	In a row	Odds	Inverse		Possible	36
2	1	=F3	=F4		Successes	1
3	2	=B2*$F$3	=C2*$F$4		Probability	=F2/F1
4	3	=B3*$F$3	=C3*$F$4		Not	=1-F3
5	4	=B4*$F$3	=C4*$F$4			
6	5	=B5*$F$3	=C5*$F$4			
7	6	=B6*$F$3	=C6*$F$4			
8	7	=B7*$F$3	=C7*$F$4			
9	8	=B8*$F$3	=C8*$F$4			
10	9	=B9*$F$3	=C9*$F$4			
11	10	=B10*$F$3	=C10*F			

Figure 19.38 Underlying formulas for series and inverse

Note that with both formula series, there are mixed absolute and relative references. In the series, the references need to be relative so that they will update with each iteration of the series. When the formulas are pointing to the root variables, they need to be fixed because those variables don't change as the formula is formfilled down. With these formulas in place, the final odds should look as shown in Figure 19.39.

	A	B	C	D	E	F
1	In a row	Odds	Inverse		Possible	36
2	1	2.778%	97.222%		Successes	1
3	2	0.077%	94.522%		Probability	2.78%
4	3	0.002%	91.896%		Not	97.22%
5	4	0.000%	89.343%			
6	5	0.000%	86.862%			
7	6	0.000%	84.449%			
8	7	0.000%	82.103%			
9	8	0.000%	79.822%			
10	9	0.000%	77.605%			
11	10	0.000%	75.449%			

Figure 19.39 Inverse series of events output

You can now see that the chance of rolling 2D6 10 times in a row without ever getting a 12 is slightly over 75%. Those are pretty good odds!

Let's look at a final example of calculating the inverse. This time, say that you want to find the likelihood that a player will not roll a 6 on 1D6. Based on basic intuition, many people assume that if you roll a 1D6 six times, it should be nearly inevitable to roll a 6 at least once. But Figure 19.40 shows what the actual probability is.

	A	B	C	D	E	F
1	In a row	Odds	Inverse		Possible	6
2	1	16.667%	83.333%		Successes	1
3	2	2.778%	69.444%		Probability	16.67%
4	3	0.463%	57.870%		Not	83.33%
5	4	0.077%	48.225%			
6	5	0.013%	40.188%			
7	6	0.002%	33.490%			
8	7	0.000%	27.908%			
9	8	0.000%	23.257%			
10	9	0.000%	19.381%			
11	10	0.000%	16.151%			

Figure 19.40 Odds of NOT rolling a 6 on a six-sided die in a series

As it turns out, there is more than a 33% chance that you *won't* roll a 6 on a six-sided die after six rolls. It's actually quite possible that you might go 10 rolls in a row and still not see a 6. The reason for this is that each event is independent.

Calculating More Than Two Dimensions

Up to this point, we have only been discussing one- and two-event probability. A spreadsheet has two dimensions, so it is a natural fit for one or two dimensions. When you move up to calculating three dice or three dimensions, you must get a bit more creative. With this many dimensions, you need to list the pairings of two of the dice in the vertical dimension and use the horizontal dimension for the third die. That is, you use the first two columns of the spreadsheet to list every possibility for the first two dice, by repeating the first die in increments in the first column and adding each combination with the second die in the second column. Figure 19.41 shows how to do this manually for 3D4.

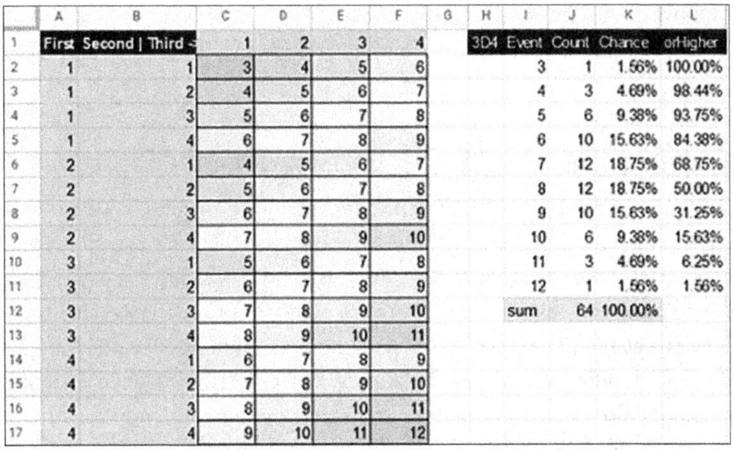

	A	B	C	D	E	F	G	H	I	J	K	L
1	First	Second | Third →	1	2	3	4		3D4	Event	Count	Chance	orHigher
2	1	1	3	4	5	6			3	1	1.56%	100.00%
3	1	2	4	5	6	7			4	3	4.69%	98.44%
4	1	3	5	6	7	8			5	6	9.38%	93.75%
5	1	4	6	7	8	9			6	10	15.63%	84.38%
6	2	1	4	5	6	7			7	12	18.75%	68.75%
7	2	2	5	6	7	8			8	12	18.75%	50.00%
8	2	3	6	7	8	9			9	10	15.63%	31.25%
9	2	4	7	8	9	10			10	6	9.38%	15.63%
10	3	1	5	6	7	8			11	3	4.69%	6.25%
11	3	2	6	7	8	9			12	1	1.56%	1.56%
12	3	3	7	8	9	10			sum	64	100.00%	
13	3	4	8	9	10	11						
14	4	1	6	7	8	9						
15	4	2	7	8	9	10						
16	4	3	8	9	10	11						
17	4	4	9	10	11	12						

Figure 19.41 3D4 spreadsheet of 3 dimensional probability

In this example, you can see in column A that there are four 1s followed by four 2s and so on until all possible numbers on the first die are complete and copied as many times as there are possible outcomes on the second die (four). Column B then cycles through each of the options on the second die to show the unique combinations between each of the first two dice. Finally, the rest of row 1 is used to list all the possible options on the third die. Each cell in the range C2:F17 adds up the first, second, and third dice. After that, the Event, Count, Chance, and higher values are calculated in exactly the same way that 1D and 2D combinations are calculated. This same method can be applied with more columns for more dice, although it does get rather complex. Once all the 3D4 probabilities are calculated, you can create a chart with the data; you should see that the chart is much higher in the middle and also more concentrated toward the middle (see Figure 19.42).

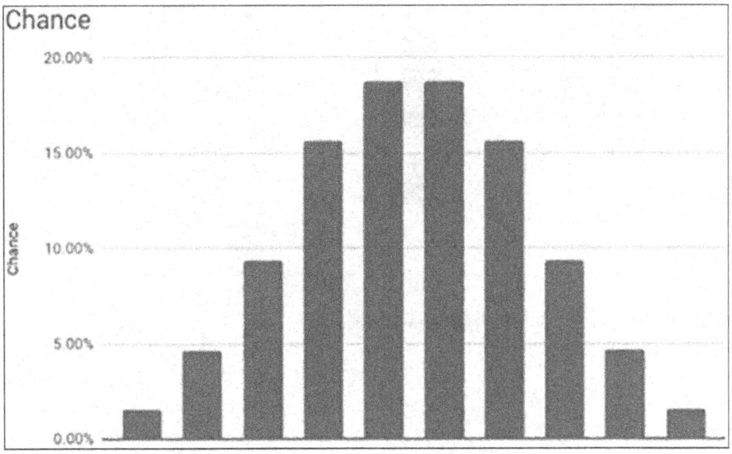

Figure 19.42 3D4 chart showing a steep bell curve in the center of probability

For each die added as a new dimension, this trend continues to grow stronger. The more dice in a pool, the more rare the chance of one of the ends occurring and the more likely it is that one of the most central possibilities will occur.

Calculating Dependent Event Probability

In every calculation of probability discussed so far, any given result has had no effect on any other given result. Rolling a single die has no effect whatsoever on the next die roll, and getting any color on a spinner has no effect on the next spin. These are the easiest kinds of probability events to track and calculate, but there are plenty of probability events that do change based on previous events. The most common is the draw of multiple cards from a deck of cards. Another event with dependence is the draw of a colored tile from a pool of colored tiles. A game might also have a loot pool of items that are removed from the pool as they are collected by players. The common feature that all of these events have is that the occurrence of the first event affects the probability of the next. Instead of using an axis to calculate these kinds of events, you use branching because each event creates a new set of probability.

As a very simple example, let's say you have 2 circles and 1 square. What is the chance that, in a completely random draw, you would get a circle? In exactly the same fashion as we calculated for dice earlier in this chapter, you would note 3 possible outcomes and 2 possible successes, or a 2/3 chance of success, which equates to 66.66% probability. Now let's say that you have drawn one of the shapes, and you draw again from the remaining two shapes. There are no longer 3 circles but 2, so the odds have changed. If you select 1 of these remaining 2 circles, you have 1 shape remaining. It is possible to graph the possibilities with each of these selections as shown in Figure 19.43.

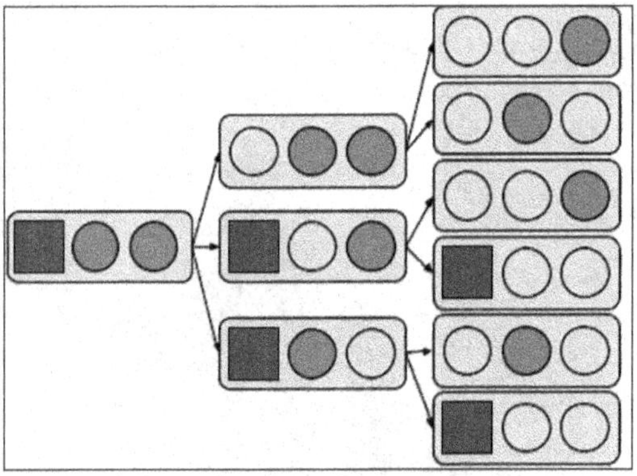

Figure 19.43 Probability tree with all possibilities still open

On the far left in Figure 19.43, you can see that the first event has 3 possible outcomes, and each of those 3 possibilities has 2 possible outcomes. In this scenario, with just 3 shapes, there are 6 possible outcomes:

Square then circle

Square then circle

Circle then square

Circle then circle

Circle the square

Circle then circle

Now that you know how many events there are and how many possibilities are generated, you can calculate the probability of lots of different possibilities. For example, if you wanted to find the chance of a square being the last shape drawn, you would look at the third column and count the total possibilities as 6 and the successes as 2 (where squares remain) and get 2/6 (which simplifies to 1/3), or 33.3% chance of a square being the last remaining shape. Much as with a series of dice, you could also calculate the chance of each event along the way.

For example, if a circle is drawn first, what is the chance of a square being drawn second? In this case, you focus on just the branches where a circle is drawn first, as illustrated in Figure 19.44.

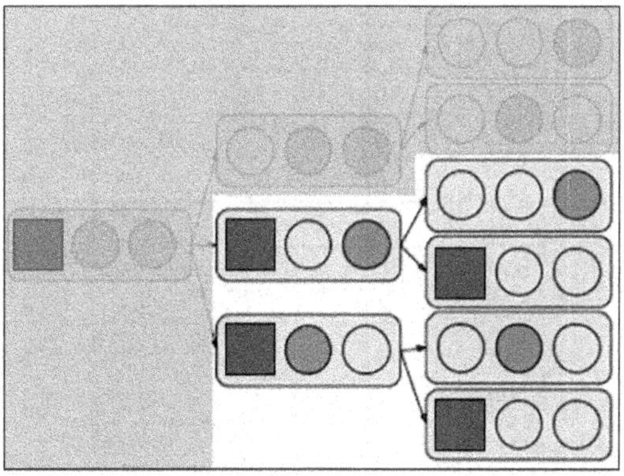

Figure 19.44 Probabilities of drawing a circle first

When you look at the remaining events in the right column, you can see that there are 4 possible outcomes, and in 2 of them, squares are drawn, so the probability is 2/4, or 1/2, or 50%.

Calculating dependent probability is certainly more complex than calculating independent probability, but it is well worth exploring because games use it often.

As another example, consider a deck of 52 cards that is divided into 4 equal suits of 13 cards: hearts, spades, clubs, and diamonds. What is the probability of drawing a heart? What is the probability of drawing 2 hearts in 2 draws? To find this answer, you would use a similar method as with the checkers, but this time you can focus on a single branch of the tree.

For the first draw, 13 of 52 cards would be successful draws—that is, 13/52, or 1/4, or 25%. In the second draw, however, there are only 12 hearts remaining, and there are 13 each of the other suits. The probability of a successful draw would now be 12/51 (remember that the total is also lower now), or 23.53%—which is slightly lower than it was on the first draw. You use a spreadsheet to calculate this single branch of the tree by iterating the remaining hearts and the remaining total cards (see Figure 19.45).

C2 fx =A2/B2

	A	B	C
1	Hearts	Total	Chance to draw
2	13	52	25.00%
3	12	51	23.53%
4	11	50	22.00%
5	10	49	20.41%
6	9	48	18.75%
7	8	47	17.02%
8	7	46	15.22%
9	6	45	13.33%
10	5	44	11.36%
11	4	43	9.30%
12	3	42	7.14%
13	2	41	4.88%
14	1	40	2.50%

Figure 19.45 Series of probability of card draws

note

Note that this example follows only one branch of the immense number of possible branches available when drawing cards from a deck. When calculating dependent probability, it's often not possible to graph out the entire tree of possibilities, as it would be too large for any practical use. Instead, you can calculate a branch of it, as was shown here, to get a sample of what is going on in the data.

Calculating Mutually Exclusive Event Probability

In the previous section, we looked at the odds of drawing a certain suit from a deck of cards in a series. You saw that drawing two hearts in a row involves dependent events because the draw of the first card has an influence on the probability of the second draw. Another type of probability you might have to calculate at some point involves mutually exclusive events. *Mutually exclusive events* are events that cannot occur together: When one event happens, the other can't happen.

For example, say that you are calculating the probability of drawing the ace of spades from a card deck. On the first try, it would be 1/52, or 1.92%. If the ace of spades is not drawn on the first attempt, then on the second attempt, the odds improve slightly because the pool of cards has been reduced from 52 to 51. The odds of drawing the ace of spades on the second attempt would be 1/51, or 1.96%. But what if the ace of spades is drawn on the first attempt? In this case, the odds of drawing the ace of spades on the second attempt would be 0% because there is no ace of spades left in the deck. Similarly, if you were to draw two cards at once, what would be the odds of drawing the ace of spades twice? Again, 0%. This is what it means to be a mutually exclusive probability event. If one of the events happens, the other event can't happen.

Calculating Enumerated Probability with an Even Distribution

Not all random events happen with fixed-quantity variables such as dice and standard card decks. Many modern games have customizable, variable-sized card decks, loot tables, and other methods of randomizing among an indeterminate list of items. For such pools of items, you must calculate enumerated probability. Calculating enumerated probability works very much like the methods already discussed. For example, let's look at a small loot table for an RPG (see Figure 19.46).

Name	Sell Value
Small Coin Purse	10
Coin purse	15
Small Chest	30
Treasure Chest	50
Weak Health Potion	5
Minor Health Potion	15
Health Potion	30
Strong Health Potion	50
Cloth	1
Healing Potion	60
Mesmo Scroll	10
Book of Knowledge	10
Cloth Armor	5
Troll Ring	10
Treasure Map	0
Rabbit Foot	15

Figure 19.46 Loot table enumerated probability with an even distribution

This list includes several different items, each having a value. If a player were to get an item each time they opened a chest, it would be easy enough to calculate the probability of each item coming up by using the same method used earlier in this chapter for dice: You would add up the total—in this case 16 items—and specify 1 as the chance of each item coming up. From a mathematical standpoint, this is exactly the same as 1D16 and should be treated the same. So each item would have 1/16 chance, or 6.25% probability of being drawn. Calculating enumerated probability with an even distribution works the same way regardless of how long the list of items and regardless of whether it is done with a spinner, a deck of cards, or a computer.

Calculating Enumerated Probability with an Uneven Distribution

While calculating the probability of a list of items is useful for simpler games, in even mildly complex games, there is often an uneven chance of events from a list occurring. With the RPG loot list, for example, you might want the small coin purse to be the item most commonly drawn and for some of the better items to be much more rare. There are a few ways to handle, and two of the most common are by using percentages and by using probability weights.

To use percentages, you list the percentage chance of each event in the list occurring. This is really all there is to it. The upside of using percentages is that the chance of each event occurring is clearly shown. The downside of using percentages is that you as the data designer must ensure that the list of percentages always adds up to 100%, or the probability will not be accurate. This means any change made to the chance of any item on the list occurring can cause a cascade effect of percentages changing, requiring constant rebalancing.

Using probability weights, on the other hand, does not initially seem possible, and there is no fixed scale of probability to start with. You, as the designer, must decide what the smallest weight is and what the largest is, and then you distribute weights to all the items on the list. For the RPG loot example, Figure 19.47 shows each of the items on the list now been given a probability weight.

	A	B	C
1	Name	Sell Value	Weight
2	Small Coin Purse	10	60
3	Coin purse	15	20
4	Small Chest	30	20
5	Treasure Chest	50	10
6	Weak Health Potion	5	30
7	Minor Health Potion	15	50
8	Health Potion	30	20
9	Strong Health Potion	50	10
10	Cloth	1	40
11	Healing Potion	60	10
12	Mesmo Scroll	10	10
13	Book of Knowledge	10	10
14	Cloth Armor	5	10
15	Troll Ring	10	10
16	Treasure Map	0	10
17	Rabbit Foot	15	10

Figure 19.47 Loot table enumerated probability with an uneven distribution

In the spreadsheet in Figure 19.47, why is the smallest weight 10 and the largest 60? Whoever designed this example wanted the most common item to occur 6 times as frequently as the rarest, based on balancing goals for the game. The smallest number was decided as 10 to leave room in the weighting scale in case the team forgot about some items that should be of even lower weight or needed to make adjustments to put an item rarity between two weights that are already listed. One of the upsides of using arbitrary probability weight values is that there is no minimum or maximum. Each team can determine what scale to use for a specific game. Another large benefit is that the list does not need to add up to 100. It can add up to anything and still work.

Once each item in the list has a weight assigned, you can calculate the probability of each event in exactly the same way you calculated probability for 2D6. First, you get a sum of the weights (in column C in Figure 19.48), and then you divide each event weight by the total.

fx =C2/$G$1

	A	B	C	D	E	F	G
1	Name	Sell Value	Weight	%		Total	330
2	Small Coin Purse	10	60	18.18%			
3	Coin purse	15	20	6.06%			
4	Small Chest	30	20	6.06%			
5	Treasure Chest	50	10	3.03%			
6	Weak Health Potion	5	30	9.09%			
7	Minor Health Potion	15	50	15.15%			
8	Health Potion	30	20	6.06%			
9	Strong Health Potion	50	10	3.03%			
10	Cloth	1	40	12.12%			
11	Healing Potion	60	10	3.03%			
12	Mesmo Scroll	10	10	3.03%			
13	Book of Knowledge	10	10	3.03%			
14	Cloth Armor	5	10	3.03%			
15	Troll Ring	10	10	3.03%			
16	Treasure Map	0	10	3.03%			
17	Rabbit Foot	15	10	3.03%			

Figure 19.48 Loot table enumerated probability with an uneven distribution, using probability weights

Once the weights are set up for calculation into a percentage chance, you can change any of the raw weight values, and the entire list will automatically update. To illustrate this, let's say that the healing potion has occurred as a result too often. To fix this, you can simply lower the individual weight for that item, and the spreadsheet will instantly recalculate all the probability chances for the entire list, as shown in Figure 19.49.

	A	B	C	D	E	F	G
1	Name	Sell Value	Weight	%		Total	325
2	Small Coin Purse	10	60	18.46%			
3	Coin purse	15	20	6.15%			
4	Small Chest	30	20	6.15%			
5	Treasure Chest	50	10	3.08%			
6	Weak Health Potion	5	30	9.23%			
7	Minor Health Potion	15	50	15.38%			
8	Health Potion	30	20	6.15%			
9	Strong Health Potion	50	10	3.08%			
10	Cloth	1	40	12.31%			
11	Healing Potion	60	5	1.54%			
12	Mesmo Scroll	10	10	3.08%			
13	Book of Knowledge	10	10	3.08%			
14	Cloth Armor	5	10	3.08%			
15	Troll Ring	10	10	3.08%			
16	Treasure Map	0	10	3.08%			
17	Rabbit Foot	15	10	3.08%			

Figure 19.49 Loot table adjusted weight

With this basic setup, a list of any size with probability weights in any range can be balanced and calculated instantly. If a game engine needs a percentage chance, those numbers are available for export. Similarly, if you want to show the chance to players, you could add one more column for rounded display values.

Calculating Attributes Weights Based on Probability

In Chapter 12, "System Design Foundations," you learned applying weights to attributes based on usefulness in game. However, there is yet another layer to finding the value of attributes that are influenced by chance. In the RPG loot table example, what is the value of loot that the player receives on a given draw or on an average draw? To make this somewhat complex calculation a bit easier to digest, let's start with a very simple example. Say that you have 10 items, each with an equal chance of happening, at 10%. Nine of those items have a value of 0, and 1 item has a value of 100 (see Figure 19.50).

	A	B	C	D
1	Items	Value	Weight	Chance
2	a	100	1	10.00%
3	b	0	1	10.00%
4	c	0	1	10.00%
5	d	0	1	10.00%
6	e	0	1	10.00%
7	f	0	1	10.00%
8	g	0	1	10.00%
9	h	0	1	10.00%
10	i	0	1	10.00%
11	j	0	1	10.00%

Figure 19.50 Even weight distribution in an enumerated list

In this scenario, what is the average payout for a draw from the loot table? In this case, there is a 10% chance of a payout of 100, so on average, the payout would be 10% of 100, or 10. You could do this calculation in the spreadsheet as shown in Figure 19.51.

fx =sum(E2:E11)

	A	B	C	D	E	F	G	H
1	Items	Value	Weight	% Chance	% Value			
2	a	100	1	10.00%	10.0		Total % Value	10.0
3	b	0	1	10.00%	0.0			
4	c	0	1	10.00%	0.0			
5	d	0	1	10.00%	0.0			
6	e	0	1	10.00%	0.0			
7	f	0	1	10.00%	0.0			
8	g	0	1	10.00%	0.0			
9	h	0	1	10.00%	0.0			
10	i	0	1	10.00%	0.0			
11	j	0	1	10.00%	0.0			

Figure 19.51 Returned value of all enumerated items

For each event, the percentage chance of occurrence is multiplied by the value of the event. The average value for a draw is then calculated by adding up the percentage chance values of all the events. In this case, it is 10.

To move up in complexity, we can return to our RPG loot table example. Here, the events have different weights and values, so how do you calculate the expected value per draw? You use the same method just shown and also use two additional evaluations:

- **Total Weights:** Determines the chance based on weight.
- **Average Sell Value:** The value that each draw would be if there were no weights applied to the events.

The formulas for the entire chart look as shown in Figure 19.52.

	A	B	C	D	E	F	G	H
1	Name	Sell Value	Weight	% Chance	% * Value			
2	Small Coin Purse	10	60	=C2/$H$2	=D2*B2		Total Weights	=sum(C2:C17)
3	Coin purse	15	20	=C3/$H$2	=D3*B3		Ave sell value	=AVERAGE(B2:B17)
4	Small Chest	30	20	=C4/$H$2	=D4*B4		Event Ave Value	=sum(E2:E17)
5	Treasure Chest	50	10	=C5/$H$2	=D5*B5			
6	Weak Health Potion	5	30	=C6/$H$2	=D6*B6			
7	Minor Health Potion	15	50	=C7/$H$2	=D7*B7			
8	Health Potion	30	20	=C8/$H$2	=D8*B8			
9	Strong Health Potion	50	10	=C9/$H$2	=D9*B9			
10	Cloth	1	40	=C10/$H$2	=D10*B10			
11	Healing Potion	60	5	=C11/$H$2	=D11*B11			
12	Mesmo Scroll	10	10	=C12/$H$2	=D12*B12			
13	Book of Knowledge	10	10	=C13/$H$2	=D13*B13			
14	Cloth Armor	5	10	=C14/$H$2	=D14*B14			
15	Troll Ring	10	10	=C15/$H$2	=D15*B15			
16	Treasure Map	0	10	=C16/$H$2	=D16*B16			
17	Rabbit Foot	15	10	=C17/$H$2	=D17*B17			

Figure 19.52 Returned value formulas

And the results of using these formulas look as shown in Figure 19.53.

	A	B	C	D	E	F	G	H
1	Name	Sell Value	Weight	% Chance	% * Value			
2	Small Coin Purse	10	60	18.46%	1.846		Total Weights	325
3	Coin purse	15	20	6.15%	0.923		Ave sell value	19.75
4	Small Chest	30	20	6.15%	1.846		Event Ave Value	14.892
5	Treasure Chest	50	10	3.08%	1.538			
6	Weak Health Potion	5	30	9.23%	0.462			
7	Minor Health Potion	15	50	15.38%	2.308			
8	Health Potion	30	20	6.15%	1.846			
9	Strong Health Potion	50	10	3.08%	1.538			
10	Cloth	1	40	12.31%	0.123			
11	Healing Potion	60	5	1.54%	0.923			
12	Mesmo Scroll	10	10	3.08%	0.308			
13	Book of Knowledge	10	10	3.08%	0.308			
14	Cloth Armor	5	10	3.08%	0.154			
15	Troll Ring	10	10	3.08%	0.308			
16	Treasure Map	0	10	3.08%	0.000			
17	Rabbit Foot	15	10	3.08%	0.462			

Figure 19.53 Table calculation

You can see that the chance of each event occurring will affect the outcome of the calculated value, as events with a smaller chance of happening will contribute less to the average than events that have a high chance of happening. You can see here that if unweighted, a draw would, on average, have a monetary value of 19.75, but with weights, it has been dropped to 14.892. This makes sense because the more valuable items are also the rarest and will be drawn far fewer times than will the cheaper, more common items. By doing calculations like this, you can better predict the player experience throughout the game. You know, for example, that if you want the player to have a minimum average draw of 45 gold coins by the end of a scenario, three draws from the loot table will, on average, not be quite enough to hit that goal. Using this information, you could then adjust the scenario to allow a fourth draw from the loot table.

Calculating Imperfect Information Probability

Up to this point, this chapter has discussed only events that are clearly and measurably random. However, games are full of other events that are both random and not random, based on perspective. Rock, Scissors, Paper, is a classic example. Each player chooses an option, so it would seem that it would not be random. However, each player does not know what the opponent is going to do, so their choice of options is based on unknowable outcomes—and this is the definition of random. In this case, the events are both random and not random.

In games, you also face many other similar scenarios. For example, in an FPS, there is no way to know for sure where opponent players will be at any given moment, which makes their appearance seemingly random—or unpredictable—to a player who is ambushed. This is not true randomness but instead *imperfect information*.

Trying to do calculations of probability based on imperfect information is impractical at a theoretical level, but it can be measured during testing through observation and telemetry. You could, for example, run hundreds of tests to determine what is the most commonly chosen option in rock paper scissors, or you could track players in the FPS to determine most likely paths taken.

Perception of Probability

Another very important concept that all system designers must be aware of is that players do not perceive probability of events in games in a realistic way. There is a psychological phenomenon called *optimism bias* which roughly states that players think they are less likely than they really are to receive a negative event. In game systems, if a player has a 40% chance to get lucky and receive a random reward, because of the optimism bias, they will expect that reward far greater than 40% of the time. This does not make logical sense, but it's the way that humans think.

As another example, if a player has a 70% chance to hit a target, the player is likely to get frustrated at the game if they miss 3 out of 10 tries—even though the game has clearly stated the 70% chance of success, which implicitly means a 30% chance of failure. So what can you do about this? Some games blatantly lie to the players. They show the player far lower chances of success than are running in the background of the video game. Other games make the odds of everything happening high and deal with the ramifications. Other games leave everything as is and learn to deal with grumpy players who all feel they have terrible luck.

Probability Uncertainty

When learning the methods of predicting probability discussed so far in this chapter, there is a natural tendency to feel as though you can predict probability with some certainty. While this is true, there is a very important caveat you need to understand: All the methods described here represent mathematical hypotheticals and not real-world data.

For example, think about an 1D2 coin. What are the odds of getting a heads? As discussed earlier, the odds in this case are 1 chance out of 2 possible, or 1/2, or 50%. You might assume that if you flipped a coin 4 times, it would come up heads 2 times and tails 2 times. It might, but it also might not. The 50% chance is not a cosmic certainty that forces all coin flips to be distributed perfectly. Instead, the 50% is an average that often has little effect on short-term events. It would be entirely possible to flip a coin 4 times and get 4 heads.

To take this one step further, if you were to roll 1D6 1,000 times, you would expect each number to come up 16.67% of the time, or 167 times. It is highly unlikely that events would unfold this way, but the more iterations done on the random event, the closer you are likely to get to the average expected probability outcome. So you could easily see a range from 127 to 207 rolls of any given number, and it would be highly unlikely to see 900 rolls of a given number (although it would not be impossible).

Mapping Probability

As you start to develop a game, it is a good exercise to map the probability of events in the game. As a system designer, you should have a good understanding of what kinds of randomness your players will be facing. You can use this information to purposefully create scenarios and feelings that are appropriate for the game. While it is not necessary, or even possible, to graph every random event that happens in a game, it's a good practice to create a large sample of graphs to get better insights into the function of randomness in the game. This is similar, in theory, to graphing sentences for children as they learn to read and write; it's not necessary to graph every sentence written to make graphing sample sentences useful.

Attributes of a Random Event

Each random event has several attributes that change its effect on a game. These attributes can be charted for any individual random event and will create patterns that more deeply inform how that event will affect the game.

The following sections discuss these attributes of a random event:

- Computation use
- Measure of random result
- Type of randomness
- Probability distribution
- Outcome dependency

Computation Use

Computation use measures whether and how a random result can be calculated and manipulated for mathematical functionality. This is important to use as game designers to know if we are able to use the generated random result as a starting point for mathematical manipulation. For example, being able to add dice together.

- **Numeric:** A finite, known range of numbers. Results can be used for mathematical functionality.

  Examples: 1–6 on a die, 1–36 on a roulette wheel, 1–13 in a suit of cards (when treating face cards and the ace as numbers), distance from a target in inches

- **Enumerated list:** A finite, known list of results that can't be used to perform mathematical functionality.

  Examples: Loot tables, Magic the Gathering cards, Settlers of Catan tiles, colors on a spinner
- **Non-enumerated result:** An infinite, unknown result that can't be used to perform mathematical functionality.

  Examples: Curtain prizes on a game show, random unknown loot box, thrift store grab bag

Measure of Random Result

Random result data is produced by random events. This is used to determine what a designer can do with the result and how predictable the result will be. Discrete results are far more predictable than nonlinear, for example.

- **Discrete:** Discrete random results have finite and listable results.

  Examples: A coin toss, die roll, or roulette wheel spin
- **Continuous linear:** Continuous linear random results have infinitely variable but measurable results.

  Examples: Golf shot distance, prediction of the height of a child when grown, final score of a basketball game, tomorrow's exact temperature
- **Continuous nonlinear:** Continuous nonlinear random results have infinitely variable and nonquantifiable results.

  Examples: Curtain prizes on a game show, random unknown loot box, grab bag

Types of Randomness

For each random event in a game, there can be one or more methods of creating randomness. Each of these types of randomness informs how the game is played and how the designer can track the output. For example, in Pure random, the chance should not change based on players, but in the performance-based type, it is heavily dependent on the players in the game.

- **Pure chance:** Designed specifically to be unpredictable. All players have equal probability of all results.

  Examples: Dice, lottery machine, cards, spinners, lava lamps, scattered coins
- **Performance variation:** Players have some amount of influence on the outcome but not total control.

  Examples: Darts, pool, baseball batting, golf, bocce, parimutuel betting
- **Obscured knowledge or incomplete information:** One or more people possess knowledge that the other player does not have. This may or may not be chosen by another player.

  Examples: Guess the number, rock paper scissors, poker

Probability Distribution

There are many different variations of probability distribution. For games, the following are some of the most popular probability distributions:

- **Equal distribution:** Every outcome has the same probability of occurrence.

  Examples: Deck of cards, single die, roulette wheel, lottery numbers
- **Bell curve distribution:** When random results are added together, a bell curve distribution results.

  Examples: 2D6 and other multidimensional probabilities
- **Exponential:** Many results are possible on one side, and increasingly few are possible on the other.

  Examples: "Or greater" dice probability, pounds of weight lifted by an athlete, score on *Donkey Kong*
- **Uneven distribution:** Results vary widely in the distribution of probability among events.

  Examples: Loot tables, curtain prizes, carnival game prizes

Outcome Dependency

Outcome dependency is an attribute that indicates whether the current random event is affected or limited by other events. Based on the type of outcome dependency the event has, the type of probability calculation you will need to evaluate it will change. For example, independent is linear, and dependent is a form of bell curve.

- **Independent:** An independent random event stands on its own and has an equal chance to each other event.

  Examples: Dice roll, roulette wheel spin, throw of a single dart
- **Dependent:** A dependent result is affected by past events and can affect future events.

  Examples: Drawing a card from an unshuffled deck, hitting a scoring space in darts
- **Mutually exclusive:** When one result occurs, it makes other results impossible.

  Examples: Drawing the ace of spades in a series of card draws, choosing a path in a maze

Mapping Probability Examples

By using the attributes listed above, you can describe nearly any random event that happens in a game. By sampling some of the events that most commonly happen in a game, you can get better insights into how that game works and what the character of the game will be to the players who play it. To graph an event, you first need to pick a very specific event. The smaller the event you pick, the more specific information you will be able to observe in it.

Let's look at a backgammon example. In the scenario illustrated in Figure 19.54, it is red's turn.

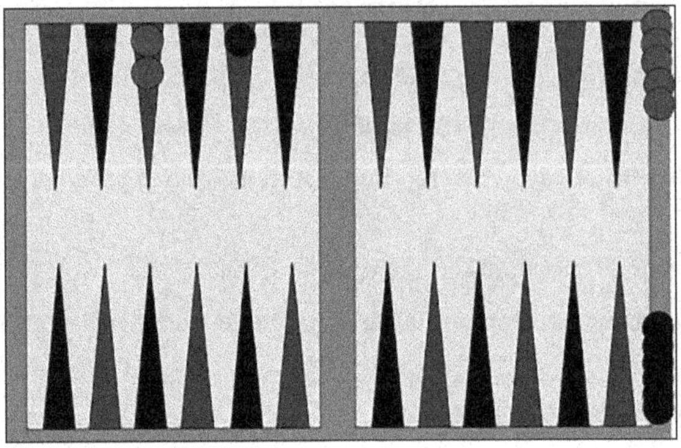

Figure 19.54 Backgammon move

On their turn, red will roll a pair of dice to determine movement points available. You could describe this event as follows:

- **Name:** Backgammon move
- **Computation use:** Numeric
- **Measure of random result:** Discrete
- **Type of randomness:** Pure chance
- **Probability distribution:** Bell curve
- **Outcome dependency:** Independent

Now let's look at a completely different type of probability event: a carnival game where the player throws a dart at a wall of balloons (see Figure 19.55). The dotted balloons are empty, but the other colored balloons contain small toys or other prizes.

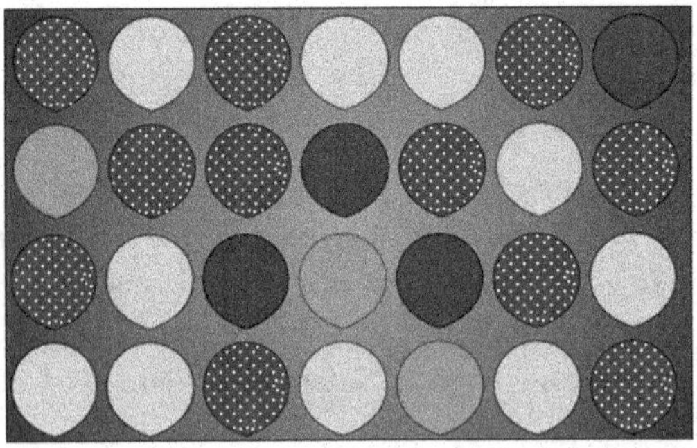

Figure 19.55 Balloon pop game

You could describe this event as follows:

- **Name:** Balloon pop, first dart
- **Computation use:** Non-enumerated result
- **Measure of random result:** Discrete
- **Type of randomness:** Performance variation
- **Probability distribution:** Uneven distribution
- **Outcome dependency:** Independent

This list of attributes is quite different from the list for backgammon, although the games do have two attributes in common. By comparing the two lists, you can see some characteristic differences between the two games. In backgammon, players have no control over the dice but a high level of control over what they do with the results of the dice. Players can also make predictions about the dice based on bell curve probability. With the balloon pop, on the other hand, the player has some agency in choosing which target to aim for but not complete control. Once a target is hit, the player has absolutely no agency in what to do with the result. These differences cause two different characteristics in the game. In backgammon, players are not as interested in what the individual dice rolls are as they are in playing the odds of what they can be and reacting appropriately to the results. In the balloon pop game, players are most interested in trying to target a desired balloon, knowing that once the dart leaves their hand, the rest of the game is out of their control.

While working on a game, you need to think about the kinds of events and attributes you want to happen in your game. It may be a useful exercise to examine the random events and attributes in similar games or in a competitor's game and then use that information to inform the design of your game as you build it. Think about the events and attributes you see in other games and what feelings players, especially testers, have associated with them.

As a game project develops, you can come back to listing events and attributes if a problem arises. If playtesters are getting frustrated with the rewards from a random loot table, for example, you can list the attributes of the event to see if any aspects of the event might be changed to fix the problem. With some creative thinking, a designer can change individual aspects of an event to get dramatically different feelings from very similar events.

Let's look at one more example. What happens if you combine the previous two examples by mixing and matching their lists? Think about what that would mean for a game with these attributes:

- **Name:** Hybrid graph
- **Computation use:** Numeric
- **Measure of random result:** Discrete

- **Type of randomness:** Performance variation
- **Probability distribution:** Uneven distribution
- **Outcome dependency:** Independent

What might this list of attributes look like as a game mechanic? It could be manifested in several ways, which is great for designers. By simply thinking about the relationships of the attributes, you are likely to encounter new ideas. In this case, one possible outcome could be a backgammon type of game, but instead of rolling dice, the players throw two darts at a board with squares representing dice results. It might look something like the game in Figure 19.56.

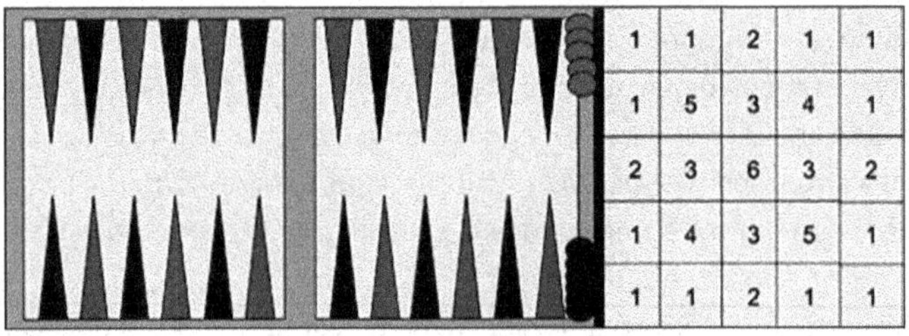

Figure 19.56 Hybrid backgammon/darts game

This random event now combines aspects of the two previous games to create something completely new and very different in feel from either of the other games.

Measuring Luck in a Game

For complex games, unfortunately there is no single algorithm you can use to determine whether a game is pure luck, luck dominant, luck influenced, or pure ability. In fact, there have been several famous lawsuits pertaining to this exact topic. Pinball was once made illegal because it was considered gambling. Poker has been argued as both a luck-based game and a skill-based game in courts of law. There are many factors involved with complex games that may make a game appear to be more or less luck based than it is, but you can look for signs that a game—or even part of a game—relies on luck.

In terms of the influence of luck, games fit into four broad categories:

- **Pure luck:** Player decisions have little or no impact on the activity. At this point, the activity does not meet the criteria for being a game.

  Examples: Candy Land, war (card game), roulette, lottery

- **Luck dominant:** Player decisions impact the game, but the outcome of the game can't be predicted based on the ability of the player. Better players win slightly more often than worse players in the long run, but there is no way to accurately predict a winner of an individual session based on player ability.

Examples: Bingo, blackjack, video poker, solitaire

- **Luck influenced:** Player decisions have a major impact on the game. Players with more ability at the game win more frequently, but players who are close in ability will have less predictable results when paired against each other. This variable also takes into account uncertainty that is not random. For example, a player attempting to hit a golf ball into the hole may miss unpredictably but not randomly.

  Examples: Royal Game of Ur, backgammon, poker, golf, Tetris, pool

- **Pure ability:** There is no inherent randomness built into the game. The player with the better ability at the game or the player who is having a better day will be more likely to win. In other words, the outcome of the game is not affected by any mechanism in the game that is outside of the players' full control.

  Example: Chess, Go, 100-meter dash

Testing for Pure Luck

You can test for pure luck by carefully reading and understanding the rules of the game. Does the player have agency? is the only question you need to answer. If there are no mechanics that give the player agency to affect the outcome of the game, then the outcome is a matter of pure luck, and the activity ceases to be a game (refer to Chapter 1, "Games and Players: Defined"). Another way to think about it: Does there need to be a player? Candy Land, for example, is a four-player game, but one player can handle all the turns for all the players, and exactly the same outcome will result as if the four players all perform their own turns.

Testing for Luck Dominant

You can do some simple tests to determine if a game is luck dominant. In a game that is luck influenced or even luck dominant, part of the outcome of the game is determined by luck, and another part of the game is determined by player ability. The easiest test to perform to determine whether a game is mostly based on luck is to purposefully try to lose. In a single-player game, this is straightforward. The player should make what they think is the worst possible decision at every opportunity. In a multiplayer game, one of the players is designated the winner, and the others as the losers. The designated losers attempt to purposely lose at the game. In games with some degree of skill, the outcome of the game should be clear. For example, imagine playing a game of chess in which one side is trying to lose and the other side is trying to win. It would be a fast and decisive game every single time. Even games that are heavily luck influenced—like The Royal Game of Ur, backgammon, and Parcheesi—become absolutely lopsided blowouts under this test.

If players are unable to consistently cause a predetermined losing player to lose, the game can be considered luck dominant. Blackjack is a good example of a game that is luck dominant. There is skill involved in the game, and it is certainly possible to make better or worse decisions. A player who tries to lose certainly will, but for those who play using perfect strategy, the outcome is still far from predictable. In blackjack, even when playing with perfect strategy, a player can still expect to lose slightly more often than they win. This game is considered luck dominant.

Testing for Luck Influenced

Luck influenced games are by far the largest category of modern games. Even many old games of chance are still more skill than luck but heavily luck influenced. Backgammon and poker are excellent examples. In these games, large levels of disparity in player ability are obvious. For example, a poker pro will absolutely dominate children playing poker nearly all the time. A professional backgammon player will defeat a novice with a very high percentage of wins.

With luck-influenced games, an important factor to look at is how close in player ability players need to be before the outcome of the game is unpredictable. In chess, players need to be almost identical in skill level for the outcome to be unpredictable. With backgammon, players of similar skill levels have unpredictable outcomes. In most cart-racing video games, players of a fairly large spectrum of ability will produce unpredictable outcomes. Individual instances of luck-influenced games don't provide usable results. Instead, with games like this, trends over a large number of instances start to provide a clearer picture of player ability.

Getting the measure of player quality and win percentage is not particularly easy. Because it takes many iterations of games with players of varying skill levels all playing against each other to determine long-term trends, you need a rather big system. This is where player ranking systems become useful. Systems like Elo rating, TrueSkill, Tournaments, and player ladders can be used to assess and compare players to determine ability.

Adjusting the Influence of Luck

Once you have done testing on your game to determine what kinds of randomness or luck-based mechanics influence it and to what level the game is randomly determined, you may find that you want to adjust the amount of influence luck has. Unfortunately, it is not as straightforward as adding or subtracting some dice rolls. You need to determine how much impact luck should have on the game. As a general rule, the more luck involved in a game, the more inclusive the game is. This is why games with heavy randomness are perennial family favorites. When playing spades, dominoes, and party-style video games, everyone knows going in that they have a chance to win. This means that seasoned experts can play with relative novices. In a family setting, this means grandma who has been playing the game for 70 years and knows the rules by heart can play with the grandkids who just learned the rules, and they can all feel competitive in the game.

Two major factors to think about when adjusting luck in a game are the frequency of random events and the amount of impact that individual random events have. Intuitively, it may seem like a game with a large number of random events would be more random, but this is not always the case. Let's look at a modified version of backgammon as an example.

In the standard rules of backgammon, each player rolls 2D6 before their turn and then may move pieces that number of spaces. All movement in the game is randomly determined, so it would seem that the game would be dominated by luck. We know, though, that this is not the case with backgammon. If you want to test this for yourself, look online for a backgammon simulator with advanced AI. Play against the best AI the game has and notice how incredibly good the computer is at the game. Even very seasoned backgammon players have a very difficult time beating the AI. How is this so? Based on the list of backgammon random event attributes you saw earlier in this chapter, you might guess that because there are so many random events, the results of a series of games would eventually average out to roughly 50% won against the AI. It works out like this precisely because there are so many random events, each having only a small impact on the game, and the game allows a high degree of player choice in using the random events. Because there are numerous random events, the curve of probability for the game tends to even out. Any given player will get mostly middle rolls, around 7, with just a few at the extremes, 2 and 12. This means that if the players are getting roughly the same distribution of rolls each game, player skill is actually having an impact on the game.

To see this more clearly, let's change the rules of backgammon a bit and imagine how the game would play out. In the standard rules, a player starts with 15 pieces and attempts to bring all of them home, moving based on the values of rolled dice. In our changed version, let's say that there are no more random rolls. All the movement has been predetermined and is visible to both players in a list that is equal for both players. The list of example moves would look something like this:

1. 3, 4
2. 1, 6
3. 4, 4
4. 2, 5

So you have now eliminated the traditional dice rolls from the game. However, you are going to add in a single roll at the very beginning. At the start of the game, each player rolls 2D6. The player may then remove from the board a number of pieces equal to that roll and place them home instantly. Think about what that would mean for the game. If the first player rolled a 12 and the second rolled a 2, it would be virtually impossible for the second player to win. If you went through many games like this, it would become clear that the die roll at the beginning is all that actually matters in the game. Even though there is much less rolling of dice in this new version, it is actually driven by luck far more than the standard rules for backgammon.

The other factor that determines luck is the amount of impact that each random event has on the game. Let's look at an extreme example of modified darts to see how it differs in terms of luck from a regular game of darts.

In our changed version of darts, on every turn, before a player throws their darts, they roll a 1D20. The result of the roll is the active space. Players only score points by hitting the active space for that turn. The game goes for 20 turns, scores are added, and a winner is determined. In this game, there is a lot of dice rolling. A die is rolled each turn for 20 turns, but is the game luck dominant? No. If anything, the game has no more luck in it than a standard game of darts. The player who can hit the target more often will win more often, regardless of what dice rolls occur. In this case, we would say that even though there are dice rolls, they have little impact on the game. This is in contrast to the change in backgammon in the previous example. In that example, there is only one roll of the dice, but it had an extremely large impact.

All this means that when you modify a game to make it more or less luck influenced, you need to think about not just the number of random events but how much impact those events have. If you find that your game is too luck dominant, you shouldn't just remove some random events. Instead, you should look at how the random events you have add up and average out, and you should consider what impact each one has on the game. You may actually find that adding more random events makes the game less luck dominant overall.

Chaos Factor

Even in games of pure ability, there is no way to 100% guarantee the outcome. If the outcome of a game were certain, there would be little point in actually playing the game. Players can have a bad day. Exceptional streaks of probability do happen. External factors can be involved. Bugs in video games can have a dramatic effect. You should therefore never run a test and make a sweeping assumption based on any given set of data. As much as this book has tried to guide you to making logical, fact-based decisions, when it comes to the feel of a game, human intuition will always be required.

Further Steps

After completing this chapter, you should take some time to practice in the real world with the concepts covered here. Try these exercises to further explore the concepts of probability in games.

- List some real-world game examples of probabilities you can calculate. Loot tables, chance to hit, and so on are good candidates. Use the graphing system explained in this chapter to graph each of these events. What patterns do you see emerge?
- Pick a game that involves some random events and change the way the probability works. For example, how would backgammon work with cards instead of dice? How would it work with 1D12 instead of 2D6?
- In your own games, do some experiments with multiple random event attributes. Be sure to test thoroughly as initial results could easily be probability outliers.

CHAPTER 20

NEXT STEPS

Now that you are at the end of this book, where should you go from here? This book is designed to be an introduction to many different subjects but not a definitive resource for any individual topic. I put a lot of effort into covering as many subjects as possible and showing you the basics, but the goal of the book was not to cover each subject in great depth. Given that, it's important that you see reading this book as the first step in your journey into game system design. This brief chapter describes a few next steps that you should take to continue the journey.

Practice

Many of the concepts in this book are more than basic facts that can be memorized and understood. The techniques described in this book need to be actively performed and practiced multiple times to be fully understood. I highly recommend that you go through each of the chapters again and actively practice using the concepts described. Then try taking each concept further. For example, experiment with modifying the exponential growth formula to see what happens. Try combining multiple concepts covered in the book, such as graphing and communication noise, and see what happens. By taking the concepts from the book further, you can be sure you actually understand the concepts and are not just able to copy what you have read.

Analyze Existing Games

What are your favorite computer and analog games? What games that you love make heavy use of game systems? Go back and play those games with your newly gained knowledge and see what aspects of the games you notice now that you never have before. Start analyzing your favorite games as if they were your own. By analyzing complete games that have already been through the development and testing process, you can start to see the correlation between how the game feels as you play it and how the systems were created to induce that feeling.

Play New Games

Another valuable exercise is to play new games, ideally in genres that you don't know well, and observe how you learn the systems. Take some time to record your feelings before you play a game for the first time and then after the first play and again after multiple plays. Notice how the systems go from being completely mysterious to being systems that you understand. To take this exercise a step further, find a game that you have never played and do some data analysis on it before playing it even a single time. Guess how the game should feel, based on what you see in the data. Finally, play the game and note how the game actually plays and feels.

Modify Existing Games

There are a few published games (such as the RPG The Battle for Wesnoth) whose data is in a state that can be modified. Seek out these games and study them thoroughly. When you understand their systems, try to modify them for a specific result. Doing this kind of exercise is a very fast and easy way to learn about modifying systems without the required overhead of building your own game. The existing game gives you a stable base to start with. Its code and game engine are fully functioning, and when you edit them, you can see what changes your edits cause. Once you are comfortable changing the data of an existing game in simple ways, try causing strange and experimental results. As with testing, you often can't know how far to take a change until you have gone too far. An existing game gives you a very easy way to do these kinds of experiments.

Work on Your Game

If you have completed this book, I presume that you are interested in creating a game or some systems within a game. There is no such thing as starting to work on a game too early. Take what you have learned in this book and apply it to the game you are working on. Whether your game is a video game in full production or a board game that is currently just an idea, you can start to apply the techniques outlined here to move your game forward.

Keep Learning

This book provides a basic introduction to game system design, but there is much more you can learn. From this point on, it's likely that you will need to study a number of subjects in more depth to really learn how they work. For example, you might seek out one of the many good books on using spreadsheets at a more advanced level. Similarly, you might look for books on game theory, psychology, and probability. By doing Internet searches, you can find much more and deeper information on each of the subjects introduced in this book.

INDEX

Numerics

A

B

C

D

E

F

G

H

I

J-K

L

M

N

O

P

Q-R

S

U-V

W-X-Y-Z

EXAMPLES & EXPLANATIONS

Remedies

Fifth Edition

EXAMPLES & EXPLANATIONS

Remedies

Fifth Edition

Richard L. Hasen
Professor of Law and Political Science
University of California, Los Angeles

ASPEN
PUBLISHING

To contact Customer Service, e-mail customer.service@aspenpublishing.com, call 1-800-950-5259, or mail correspondence to:

Aspen Publishing
Attn: Order Department
1 Wall Street
Burlington, MA 01803

Printed in the United States of America.

1 2 3 4 5 6 7 8 9 0

ISBN 979-8-8890-6633-0

Library of Congress Cataloging-in-Publication Data

SUSTAINABLE FORESTRY INITIATIVE
Certified Chain of Custody
At Least 10% Certified Forest Content
www.sfiprogram.org
SFI-01028

About Aspen Publishing

Aspen Publishing is a leading provider of educational content and digital learning solutions to law schools in the U.S. and around the world. Aspen provides best-in-class solutions for legal education through authoritative textbooks, written by renowned authors, and breakthrough products such as Connected eBooks, Connected Quizzing, and PracticePerfect.

The Aspen Casebook Series (famously known among law faculty and students as the "red and black" casebooks) encompasses hundreds of highly regarded textbooks in more than eighty disciplines, from large enrollment courses, such as Torts and Contracts, to emerging electives, such as Sustainability and the Law of Policing. Study aids such as the *Examples & Explanations* and the *Emanuel Law Outlines* series, both highly popular collections, help law students master complex subject matter.

Major products, programs, and initiatives include:

- **Connected eBooks** are enhanced digital textbooks and study aids that come with a suite of online content and learning tools designed to maximize student success. Designed in collaboration with hundreds of faculty and students, the Connected eBook is a significant leap forward in the legal education learning tools available to students.

- **Connected Quizzing** is an easy-to-use formative assessment tool that tests law students' understanding and provides timely feedback to improve learning outcomes. Delivered through CasebookConnect.com, the learning platform already used by students to access their Aspen casebooks, Connected Quizzing is simple to implement and integrates seamlessly with law school course curricula.

- **PracticePerfect** is a visually engaging, interactive study aid to explain commonly encountered legal doctrines through easy-to-understand animated videos, illustrative examples, and numerous practice questions. Developed by a team of experts, PracticePerfect is the ideal study companion for today's law students.

- The **Aspen Learning Library** enables law schools to provide their students with access to the most popular study aids on the market across all of their courses. Available through an annual subscription, the online library consists of study aids in e-book, audio, and video formats with full text search, note-taking, and highlighting capabilities.

- Aspen's **Digital Bookshelf** is an institutional-level online education bookshelf, consolidating everything students and professors need to ensure success. This program ensures that every student has access to affordable course materials from day one.

- **Leading Edge** is a community centered on thinking differently about legal education and putting those thoughts into actionable strategies. At the core of the program is the Leading Edge Conference, an annual gathering of legal education thought leaders looking to pool ideas and identify promising directions of exploration.

To Deborah, Shana, and Jared
With love, for a bright future

Summary of Contents

PART III. RESTITUTION

PART IV. OTHER IMPORTANT REMEDIES CONCEPTS

Contents

PART II. EQUITABLE REMEDIES

Acknowledgments

This book owes an intellectual debt to two exemplary scholars and teachers. In 1997, Laurie Levenson, then Loyola Law School's associate dean, agreed to let me come as a visitor to teach Remedies, a course I had never taught before. I was anxious to get back to Los Angeles, and I was willing to come even if it meant teaching a course I did not especially want to teach. Now, having taught the course numerous times, it has become one of my favorites. I get to pull together interesting tidbits from all parts of the first-year curriculum, and it allows me to move back and forth between theory and practice with seasoned law students.

The other scholar to whom I owe a debt is Doug Laycock, whose Remedies casebook is a tremendous teaching tool and a wonderful resource. That casebook (and its teacher's manual) was my bible in 1997, and it has guided me in understanding Remedies both in and out of the classroom. Doug also has been consistently responsive to e-mail questions I have peppered him with over the years. Anyone familiar with Laycock's book will see the influence his view of Remedies has had on mine. I also owe a debt to my Remedies students, beginning with my 1997 guinea pigs. I was assigned the 8:10-10:10 p.m. slot twice a week for the course. I expected a group of tired, graduating students with little interest in the course. To my pleasant surprise, the students were intellectually engaged, serious, and blessed with an understanding of the real world that only evening students have. For my Remedies students through the years, the course is really a nice capstone, bridging the law school and real worlds. I have learned a great deal from my students.

Doug eventually asked me to join his Remedies casebook, and you will see the influence of his casebook throughout these materials. We are also co-Reporters on the ongoing project of the American Law Institute, Restatement, Third, Torts: Remedies. Some of the already-approved sections are discussed in this edition of the book.

This book is much stronger because of the excellent assistance I have received across the five editions of the book. Thanks to my terrific research assistants: Jim Buatti, Denny Chan, Danielle De Smeth, Rachel Ettinger, Sam Hall, Justin Martin, Tony Sain, Vince Shang, Christina Wang, Joel Yanovich, and Sammy Zeino. Thanks for the excellent library assistance of Lisa Schultz and the Loyola Law School library staff and Christina Tsou and the University of California, Irvine Library staff. Sam Austin-Docampo, Sara Galloway, Carla Heidlberg, Betty Kinuthia, Stacy Tran, and Valda Hahn of the Loyola, UC

Irvine, and UCLA faculty support staffs provided wonderful administrative support.

None of my work would be possible without the love and encouragement of my wife, Lori Klein, who supports me in all that I do. This book is dedicated to our three most successful joint ventures: Deborah, Shana, and Jared.

I continue to receive insightful questions and comments from book users. If you have questions or suggestions, or see an error (no one is perfect!), please send an email to hasen@law.ucla.edu, and I will use those comments to improve the next edition.

I am grateful to the American Law Institute for granting permission to quote from its publications:

For Restatement material:

Restatement of the Law Second, Contracts © 1981;
Restatement of the Law Third, Restitution and Unjust Enrichment © 2011;
Restatement of the Law Third, Torts: Intentional Torts to Persons © 2019;
Restatement of the Law Third, Torts: Liability for Physical and Emotional Harm © 2010, 2012;
Restatement of the Law Third, Torts: Liability for Economic Harm © 2020;
Restatement of the Law Third, Torts: Remedies © 2022, 2023

Los Angeles, California
July 2023

How to Use This Book

No matter how your professor starts this course, you should begin with Chapter 1. It sets forth some basic terminology and ideas that are used throughout the book, including the important "rightful position" standard. After Chapter 1, you can begin at the beginning of Part I (on damages), Part II (on injunctions and other equitable remedies), Part III (on restitution), or Part IV (presenting the remedies topics of punitive damages, declaratory judgments, ancillary (or helping) remedies, and remedial defenses). Within each Part (except for Part IV), I expect that you will begin with the first chapter in each part, which defines basic concepts and sets the stage for what comes next.

You should save the last chapter, Chapter 19, for the end of the course. It will help you with issue spotting and choosing remedies skills that you cannot test until you master the material in the first eighteen chapters.

For the most part, this book follows standard Bluebook citation format. However, I usually avoid putting in pin cites in an effort not to clutter up the text, and I don't always note when I've deleted internal citations or footnotes. Before quoting any material in this book, be sure to check the original source. There are two sources that I cite so often that I just use a short form. I cite DAN B. DOBBS & CAPRICE L. ROBERTS, LAW OF REMEDIES: DAMAGES-EQUITY-RESTITUTION (3rd ed. 2013) simply as DOBBS & ROBERTS § ___. I cite DOUGLAS LAYCOCK & RICHARD L. HASEN, MODERN AMERICAN REMEDIES: CASES AND MATERIALS (5th ed. 2019) simply as LAYCOCK & HASEN p. ___.

How to Use This Book

EXAMPLES & EXPLANATIONS

Remedies

Fifth Edition

CHAPTER 1

Read This Chapter First: Why Remedies? What Remedies?

1.1 WHY SHOULD A LAW STUDENT CARE ABOUT REMEDIES?

Students may have many reasons to take a course in Remedies. In places such as California, for example, Remedies is heavily tested on the bar exam, and many students feel obligated to take a "bar course." Even in states that do not test Remedies independently on the bar, it is a good bar preparation course because much material from the first year of law school—particularly from Constitutional Law, Contracts, Property, and Torts—gets covered, albeit from a different angle. Other students may take Remedies because they like the instructor teaching it, or because it fits into their schedule. I have run into very few students (though there are some) who take Remedies out of an intrinsic interest in the subject.

Fortunately, however, many students complete a course in Remedies with their (admittedly low) expectations exceeded—there are some intellectually interesting issues related to Remedies, many of which are covered in this book. Consider these examples:

- Jane steals Bill's idea for an invention and makes millions of dollars selling it. Should a court award Bill a sum of money equal to his loss (perhaps the amount of money he would have charged Jane to use his intellectual property), or to Jane's gain (some or all of her profits from the invention)? In some cases, there can be huge differences between these two figures.

- Gary makes repeated defamatory statements about Roxanne, injuring Roxanne's business reputation. May a court order Gary to shut up about Roxanne, or does such an order run afoul of the First Amendment?
- Phillip fraudulently induces Hector to enter into a contract. Can Hector have the court rewrite the contract more to his liking, or must the contract be cancelled, with Hector entitled to nothing more than a return of his consideration?
- Tomorrow Acme Wrecking Company is going to bulldoze what the Main Street Preservation Society believes is a building of historical importance protected by state law. How should a court decide, in the face of much ignorance on the merits of the Society's case because there is no time to get up to speed fully, whether to issue an order temporarily preventing the demolition?
- From 1850 to 1950, the State of Pacifica discriminated against African Americans in educational and housing opportunities. Since 1950, there has been no official state discrimination, but African American residents of Pacifica still lag behind in education, and much of the state's housing market remains unintegrated. What remedies, if any, can—or should—a judge order against Pacifica today to assist Pacifica's current African American residents, many of whom were born after the period of official state discrimination?
- Sarah and Larry rob a bank together, agreeing to split the loot equally. Sarah doesn't give Larry his half. Should courts allow Larry's suit against Sarah to go forward, or should the suit be barred because of Larry's bad conduct?

If the intellectual feast in store to answer these questions does not convince you that Remedies is a course well worth your attention, there is an even more compelling reason for a student to take a course in Remedies: your future clients want you to do so.

1.2 WHY SHOULD A LAWYER CARE ABOUT REMEDIES?

Ask a practicing lawyer what clients care about the most, and the answer typically is "the bottom line." The client's attitude is often: Don't talk to me about abstractions—problems of proximate cause, supplemental jurisdiction, or the Statute of Frauds. Tell me what I have to lose or gain in this case. How likely is it that I'll prevail? If I prevail, how much will I get? Or if I lose, how much will it cost me?

In that sense, clients care about remedies mostly because remedies translate abstract legal rules into concrete consequences. Suppose that even if Bill has a good case for prevailing on the merits against Jane for her misappropriation of Bill's invention, it may not be worth bringing suit if Bill could only get money equal to his loss. On the other hand, if Bill has a chance of capturing Jane's "ill-gotten gains" (through the law of restitution), it may make economic sense for Bill to sue. Indeed, if Jane has a good chance of losing her profits to Bill, she might be more likely to settle her case than if all that is at stake is paying Bill's losses. A good lawyer must think not only about substantive law—the legal basis for Bill's claim that Jane has wronged him—but also about the range of available remedies. Similarly, just as it is not always obvious what substantive law addresses a particular legal dispute, there is often much up in the air about available remedies. Part of a lawyer's job, whether as a litigator or as a transactional lawyer, is to figure out the range of potentially applicable remedies in a given case.

EXAMPLE

Example 1

Abbott and Costello are entering into a contract for the sale of widgets. You represent Abbott, the seller. What remedies issues might you wish to address in the contract?

EXPLANATION

Explanation

Good transactional lawyers will consider many remedies issues that could arise should something go sour between the parties to the contract. Here are a few remedies issues for Abbott's lawyer to consider:

- Should the contract contain a provision allowing the winning party to obtain attorney's fees in the event of a dispute under the contract? Would it be permissible to draft a provision allowing only Abbott to get attorney's fees in the event that such a dispute arises and Abbott wins?
- Should the contract specify the amount of damages in the event of a breach? If so, how can the clause be written so that it is an enforceable "liquidated damages provision" rather than an unenforceable contractual penalty?
- Should the contract exclude certain remedies, such as consequential damages?
- Which state's law should apply to contractual disputes? (Chapter 4 explains that for some contracts governed by the Uniform Commercial Code, the choice of state's law may not matter much because the law is the similar in most states.) Might there be some state whose remedies law is more advantageous to Abbott?

1.3 REMEDIES AS THE LAWYER'S TOOLBOX

Some have compared remedies to the "lawyer's toolbox." Just as a carpenter carries around a number of tools and decides on the right tool to use for a particular project, a good lawyer does the same (whereas a bad lawyer, like a bad carpenter, can commit malpractice by failing to use the right tool for the job). If the legal rules allow for the recovery of either Bill's losses or Jane's gains, and Jane's gains are substantially larger than Bill's losses, Bill's lawyer must be in a position to seek the more lucrative recovery, and doing so requires knowing when restitution might be the better tool than damages. Jane's lawyer, too, must keep an eye not only on the choices of remedies that Bill's lawyer might pull out of the toolbox, but also on Jane's own possible remedial defenses. For example, if Bill waited a long time to sue, Jane's lawyer should consider if the action could be barred by the defense of "laches," a doctrine which bars some suits because of unreasonable delay.

The toolbox analogy doesn't exactly hit the nail on the head (sorry—you can expect bad puns like this throughout the book), because it suggests that the choice of remedies is rather mechanical: everyone knows, for example, that one uses a hammer and not a screwdriver to put a nail through a piece of wood. There is a lot more creativity, however, involved in choosing an appropriate remedy than in choosing whether to use a hammer or screwdriver. Good lawyers can come up with creative arguments for or against the use of particular remedies in particular cases, just as good lawyers may make creative arguments for creative application of the underlying substantive law. But there are some constraints on creativity.

One particular constraint involves plaintiff's *choice of remedies*. Bill at some point will be forced to choose between recovering his losses or Jane's gains. We usually don't let him get both—and courts sometimes are reluctant to allow plaintiffs to change their minds after electing to seek a particular remedy. In addition, certain remedies might violate a constitutional right, such as the right to a jury trial, or the remedy might be precluded by statute or be limited for reasons of public policy (think of Larry's suit to get his share of the bank robbery loot from Sarah). One of the most important rules in choosing a remedy, as we will see, says that court orders (often an injunction) are commonly unavailable when a damages remedy would be "adequate" in redressing plaintiff's concerns.

Even within classes of remedies, however, there is room for lawyerly creativity. If Bill is only entitled to his losses, how do we measure his losses? If he is entitled to Jane's gains, how do we measure Jane's gains? As we shall see, sometimes damages are awarded for losses we expect a plaintiff to incur *in the future*, which creates its own complications.

EXAMPLE

Example 2

Mary causes a serious automobile accident, permanently disabling Fred, a 50-year-old white male. Fred will need round-the-clock nursing assistance. This year, his nursing care cost $100,000 per year. How much should a court award for nursing care that Fred could need 10 years from now?

EXPLANATION

Explanation

There may be considerable uncertainty over how much medical care Fred will need in 10 years—or whether Fred even will be alive then. But even if we overcome these problems about Fred's condition, the jury will have to consider issues related to the costs of goods and services in the future (a topic explored in Chapter 2.5.2). In cases where enough money is at stake, lawyers will need to bring in experts, including economists, to make predictions about the future economy. These experts will have their depositions taken and, in cases that go to trial, they will be subject to examination and cross-examination on their economic assumptions driving the "bottom line." That means that good lawyers will have to understand rudimentary economic principles applicable to these kinds of problems. I know that many of you chose law school because you hate the sight of blood—thereby precluding medical school—and because you hate math—thereby precluding business school. Unfortunately, however, for the innumerate, good lawyers need to understand some mathematical content beyond that which is necessary to bill clients in six-minute increments. Also, I hope the amount of blood you see in your job is minimal.

So suppose that the jury believes that Fred will need exactly the same medical care in 10 years that he needs today, and today it costs $100,000 to provide this care. Economists will have to make assumptions about medical technology and the costs of medical goods and services to predict how much the care will cost in 10 years. Economists will have to make further predictions about how much money we would need to give Fred today to invest so that it will yield the right amount of money for Fred to pay his bills 10 years from now. This is the issue of *present value*, discussed in Chapter 2.5.2.

1.4 THE CATEGORIES OF REMEDIES

Remedies teachers usually divide the major remedial tools into three categories:

- Damages—an amount of money awarded to a wronged party from the party who committed the wrong to *compensate* for that wrong.

- Injunction—a court order to a defendant to do or not to do something in relation to the plaintiff. Sometimes this category is referred to as "Equity," because injunctions were the most important of a class of remedies once issued by courts of equity (as opposed to courts of law). That distinction sounds historical and perhaps unimportant, but, as we will see, that history has real-world consequences, even today.
- Restitution—money awarded to a wronged party from the party that committed the wrong, measured by *the gain to the party that committed the wrong*, and not by the loss to the wronged party.

These tools do not form the complete universe of remedies, but they serve as useful organizing principles for much of the material in the course, and they are covered in the first three parts of this book. The final part of this book covers other important remedies, including punitive damages, declaratory judgments, and ancillary (helping) remedies (including attorney's fees). It also considers remedial defenses.

Thinking about the "Why" in Remedies. In some Remedies courses, it is all trees and no forest. The course moves from remedial tool to remedial tool, much like the carpenter who teaches the trade tool by tool. "This is a screwdriver. You use the screwdriver by turning it clockwise in the following situations . . ." Other Remedies courses are more theoretical, looking for connections among remedies and differences in form and function. These courses also focus more on the "why" of remedies: what purpose do particular remedies serve, and how can one with a particular theoretical orientation (say, to maximize economic efficiency) choose the right remedies?

I have written this book to help students whose instructors focus only on trees, only on the forest, or on a mixture of forest and trees. All students need to understand how remedial tools work. For some students, those remedies are all they will need to understand. Other students will need to understand the more theoretical questions, which are explored in the appropriate chapters. While students who have "tree" professors might be tempted to skip the more theoretical part of the reading, I hope that these students keep reading—not only because this material is interesting, but also because developing a deeper understanding of remedies will help these students think creatively as lawyers.

The most important concept in the Remedies course is the "rightful position" standard, a term coined by Professor Douglas Laycock. It serves as a benchmark for judging various remedies. *The rightful position standard says to choose the remedy that puts the plaintiff back (or keeps the plaintiff) in the position that she would have been in but for the defendant's wrong.* Embedded within this definition are assumptions about the ability of courts to identify plaintiff's position before and after the wrong, as well as about remedies that restore plaintiff to (or keep plaintiff in) the rightful position. But there are also broad philosophical issues behind the rightful position standard. What social purpose is served by the rightful position standard? Under what circumstances would it be better (from whatever normative point of view) to give plaintiff more or less than the rightful position? Some remedies, at least in theory, try to tailor themselves to the rightful position standard while others do not.

One argument in favor of the rightful position standard comes from the law and economics school, where at least some scholars, such as Judge Richard Posner of the Seventh Circuit, have argued for legal rules—like the rightful position standard—which seek to maximize overall social wealth (and not worry about distribution of that wealth—who wins and who loses under different legal rules). This efficiency standard is sometimes referred to as "Kaldor-Hicks efficiency," after two economists who had discussed the concept. Further, the theory of "efficient breach" (discussed in Chapter 4.2) provides that courts award damages for breach of contract that are measured by what the non-breaching party would have stood to achieve had the contract not been breached, placing the non-breaching party in the position she would have been in but for the contract breach. These damages therefore are tied to the rightful position. Posner likes this remedy not because it helps plaintiffs (remember, economists don't care about distribution), or because it is morally right, but because he believes it best promotes economic efficiency.

Other jurisprudential theories also have much to say in favor of the rightful position standard. Philosophers going back to Aristotle have advocated forcing defendant to restore what had been taken from plaintiff as a matter of *justice*. Indeed, Aristotle's restoration principle ties justice to the rightful position standard.

The law often deviates from this rightful position standard, however. Suppose Alice steals $100 from Bob's wallet, runs to the casino, gambles, and walks away from the table with $1,000. If a court awards Bob a sum of money equal to Alice's gains rather than his losses, it has chosen a (restitutionary) award not tied to the rightful position. Consider Figure 1.1, measuring Bob's financial situation.

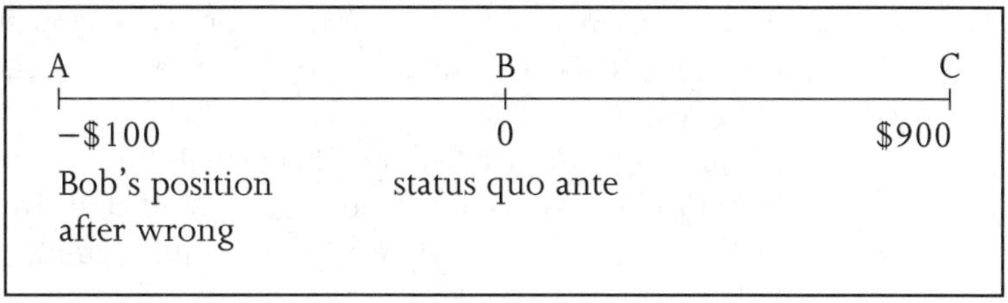

Figure 1.1

We might think of Bob at Point B, the status quo ante, or 0, before he ever meets Alice. When Alice steals his money, we can think of him as moving to Point A, −$100, his position after the wrong. A damages remedy tied to the rightful position standard says that giving Bob $100 will move him back to the status quo ante (Point B) and restore him to the rightful position. (Of course, this is an oversimplification because it ignores Bob's costs of finding an attorney, the lost value of money over time, and other factors that we will consider in due course. But for now let us say that $100 perfectly moves Bob back to 0.)

If we give Bob a choice, however, between damages and a restitutionary remedy that gives him Alice's gain of $1,000, we can see why Bob would choose restitution. That remedy moves him from −$100, Point A, to Point C, or $900. (Why does it not move Bob to $1,000? Although Bob would receive $1,000 from Jane, he is already out $100 from the initial theft, so he now has in his wallet only $900 more than he had in the past.)

Sometimes the law allows for the recovery of gains, and when it does so, it deviates from the rightful position. In our case, the rightful position is Point B, but restitution leaves Bob at Point C, better than his position before the wrong. Why might the law decide to give Bob what appears to be a windfall? Should it have something to do with the wrongfulness of Alice's conduct? To test your thinking about this question, consider whether we should still give Bob the choice of damages or restitution if Alice took the $100 honestly believing it was her money.

These are issues we will take up in later chapters. The point now is that the rightful position standard serves as a useful benchmark in evaluating the choice of remedies. We can use it when considering how to use remedies to reach (or at least approximate) the rightful position standard, and also when it is appropriate to allow litigants to deviate from the rightful position.

With this introduction, you are ready to move forward. How you should proceed depends upon how your instructor has organized the course. You can begin at the beginning of Part I (on damages), Part II (on injunctions and other equitable remedies), Part III (on restitution), or Part IV (presenting the remedies topics of punitive damages, declaratory judgments, ancillary (or helping) remedies, and remedial defenses). Within each part (except for Part IV), I expect that you will begin with the opening chapter, which defines basic concepts and sets the stage for what comes next.

You should save the last chapter, Chapter 19, for the end of the course. It is provided to help you with issue spotting and skills in choosing remedies that you cannot test until you master the material in the first 18 chapters.

EXAMPLE

Example 3

Frank punches Javier in the nose, breaking Javier's nose and causing him to miss work for a week. What is Javier's rightful position, and how would a court go about putting Javier back in the rightful position?

EXPLANATION

Explanation

Even this simple example of a punch in the nose shows the gap between the theory of the rightful position and its implementation. In theory, we want to move Javier from Point A in Figure 1.1, his position after the punch in the nose, back to B, the status quo ante. But how do we do so? Certainly, Javier will have some losses that will be easy to quantify. For example, we can look at his doctor's bills to know how much Javier has paid out of his pocket for medical care, and we can look at a recent pay stub to see how much money Javier would have earned had he not needed to miss work for a week of recuperation. But other costs will be harder to measure, the most important of which are his pain and suffering. We do not know exactly how to quantify in dollars this kind of emotional distress damage, and it may be that there is no amount of money that Javier would have willingly exchanged for the punch in the nose. So the law sometimes engages in a fiction that money can in fact put the plaintiff back to the position he would have been in but for the wrong.

EXAMPLE

Example 4

Same facts as in Example 3. A jury awards Javier damages for his hospital bills and lost work, and an additional $5,000 in punitive damages (damages which are intended to punish and deter Frank and people like Frank). Do the punitive damages restore Javier to the rightful position?

EXPLANATION

Explanation

If compensatory damages were perfect at putting plaintiff in the rightful position, punitive damages would put plaintiff in a better position than would apply had there been no wrong. In terms of Figure 1.1, the compensatory damages would move Javier from A (below 0) to B (0, or the status quo ante). The punitive damages would then move Javier beyond C, to +$5,000, or $5,000 better than where Javier would have been had Frank never punched him. This potential "windfall" to plaintiff troubles some opponents of large punitive damages awards.

The analysis in the last paragraph assumed that compensatory damages were perfect at compensating Javier. But the explanation to Example 3 tells us that the compensatory damages might *under*compensate Javier by underestimating his emotional distress damages. Javier also might be undercompensated because Javier will likely incur some attorney's fees (because this is a torts case, Javier will likely give up a percentage of his recovery from Frank to his lawyer under a contingency fee arrangement). Punitive damages, therefore, might be justified as making it more likely that plaintiff in fact is put back in the rightful position. There are other justifications for punitive damages as well, as we shall see in Chapter 15.

PART I

Compensatory Damages

CHAPTER 2

Introduction to Damages: Show Me the Money

2.1 COMPENSATORY DAMAGES AS SUBSTITUTIONARY RELIEF

One of the most common remedies given by courts to a complaining plaintiff is an award of compensatory damages. We refer to the award of damages as *substitutionary* relief because money substitutes for the thing that has been lost or damaged.

Why would a plaintiff want substitutionary relief? Sometimes, substitutionary relief is all that is available because it is not physically possible to restore to the plaintiff that which defendant has lost or destroyed. When Alex burns down Barbara's house while carelessly playing with matches, there is no way for Barbara to get her house back. The same principle applies when Carly breaks Dan's arm while rollerblading. Money substitutes for that which plaintiff would really want: the house as it stood before the fire or the unbroken arm.

Sometimes, it is possible to give plaintiff back the very thing that was taken, or to prevent threatened harm to the plaintiff from occurring. We call such a remedy *specific* relief. When specific relief is available, a plaintiff may not want damages. For example, if Erica steals Franny's bike, Franny may want to bring an action to have the bike returned, at least if the bike is undamaged. Such an action may be in the form of replevin, discussed in Chapters 7 and 13. As we shall see, we don't give Erica the option of keeping the bike and paying Franny damages if Franny wants her bike back.

In addition to the bike, Franny may want damages to compensate for any losses she suffered by being deprived of the use of the bike between the time of Erica's theft and the time of its return.

The fact that damages are substitutionary raises a whole host of measurement problems. When Erica returns the bike undamaged, we don't have to worry about how to value it. That is an advantage for the courts in granting specific relief. But even in cases of specific relief, some amount of substitutionary relief will also be necessary. In Franny's case, a court may have to come up with a measure for the value of the loss of use of the bike during the period it was in Erica's possession. How is the court to do so?

Valuation problems pervade awards of compensatory damages. When Alex burns the house down, valuation problems immediately emerge: How much would it cost Barbara to rebuild the house? What about money to replace the lost contents of the house? Suppose Barbara has an old but reliable refrigerator in her kitchen. Does she get the market value of that fridge (very low) or the cost of a new replacement (much higher)? Suppose the fire destroyed some sentimental one-of-a-kind photographs. How should those be valued?

The measurement problems are even more profound when it comes to personal injury. Consider Dan's broken arm. Some of the costs associated with the break will be easy to measure; think, for example, of the bill from the emergency room. But what about damages for the loss of use of the arm for a specified period? And what of emotional distress/pain and suffering? Should such damages be compensable, and if so, how should they be measured?

Even more easily measured costs such as hospital bills can create valuation problems. Suppose Dan is reimbursed by his health insurer for the hospital bill. Can he recover again from Carly? Do we measure the hospital costs by what the insurer paid or what the hospital billed? Or suppose Dan doesn't get a damage award from Carly until two years after the accident. Is he entitled to interest on his money?

We will consider these questions in this chapter or in later chapters, but the point now is that substitutionary relief creates valuation problems for the courts, problems that don't exist with specific relief.

Example 1

Gary owns a 1966 Thunderbird convertible in excellent condition. He received the car as a gift from his mother, who was the car's original owner. The original purchase price of the car in 1966 was $3,000. Its current market value as a collectible is $30,000, and Gary recently turned down an offer to sell his car for $50,000 to a collector. Heidi, who works for Acme Construction Company, accidentally flattens Gary's car with a steamroller that she was driving down Gary's street as part of a paving project. Gary is devastated by the loss of his car, and he sues Heidi and

Acme for negligence. Will Gary ask for specific or substitutionary relief? If Gary asks for substitutionary relief, how do you think his loss *should* be measured in monetary terms?

Explanation

The first question is a no-brainer: Gary will want substitutionary relief because specific relief (in this case, the return of the car in its original condition) is not available. Returning a flattened car to him is of no use; he will want a sum of money to compensate him for his loss. The money *substitutes* for the car and therefore damages are a kind of substitutionary relief. The harder question is: how to value the loss? Before you continue with the rest of the chapter (and the other chapters on damages) to see how the law answers this question, ask yourself the normative question of what *should* be the proper measure. Is the original purchase price relevant? The fact that Gary received the car as a gift? The current market price? What about the emotional loss he may feel from the loss of a car he loved that came from his mother? Whatever answers you give to these questions, ask yourself another question: if Gary receives the sum that you think is the right one, does that sum truly "substitute" for the destroyed car? And reconsider your answer after you have completed the material in this chapter.

2.2 COMPENSATORY DAMAGES AND THE RIGHTFUL POSITION STANDARD

We have discussed how compensatory damages are substitutionary, but we have thus far ignored the "compensatory" label. The label is significant in that it gives a possible *baseline* for a court to determine the amount of damages. Such damages should *compensate*: "make satisfactory payment or reparation to; recompense or reimburse." American Heritage Dictionary of the English Language 376 (4th ed. 2000). Under this definition, and according to most courts, compensatory damages are oriented toward plaintiffs' losses (unlike restitution, which, as we shall see, is oriented toward defendants' gains), and they require a payment that is "satisfactory" to repair the loss suffered by the plaintiff. In this way, they are different from (at least the conventional understanding of) other kinds of damages we will discuss later: nominal damages, which serve a declaratory function, and punitive damages, which serve punishment and deterrence functions.

The idea that damages should serve a compensatory function traces far back in history. Aristotle, for example, wrote of the need for "corrective justice" in his Nicomachean Ethics, Book V. As Professor Weinrib explains,

> Corrective justice . . . features the maintenance and restoration of the notional equality with which the parties enter the transaction. This equality consists in persons' having what lawfully belongs to them. Injustice occurs when, relative to this baseline, one party realizes a gain and the other a corresponding loss. The law corrects this injustice when it re-establishes the initial equality by depriving one party of the gain and restoring it to the other party. Aristotle likens the parties' initial positions to two equal lines. The injustice upsets that equality by adding to one line a segment detached from the other. The correction removes that segment from the lengthened line and returns it to the shortened one. The result is a restoration of the original equality of the two lines.[1]

In this way, the corrective justice understanding of damages lines up with the *rightful position* standard, discussed in Chapter 1: ideally, awarding a plaintiff compensatory damages puts the plaintiff back in the position she would have been in but for the defendant's wrong.

To see how compensatory damages can serve to restore the plaintiff to the rightful position, consider again Alex's burning down Barbara's house. Let's make two unrealistic assumptions: first, we can perfectly compute the value of the loss to Barbara (we will set it at $100,000); and second, Alex, after burning down the house, instantaneously makes a payment of compensatory damages to Barbara (thereby eliminating questions about the relationship of time and money discussed in section 2.5.1 below).

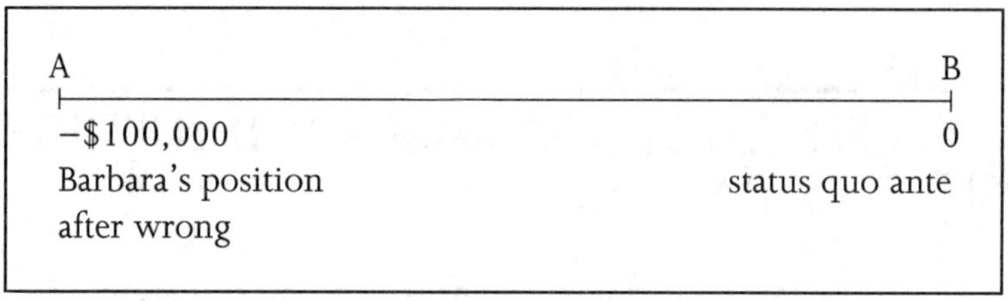

Figure 2.1

The money line in Figure 2.1 measures Barbara's position before and after Alex's wrong. Before the wrong, Barbara was at Point B, or at zero in relation to Alex. After the wrong, Barbara is at −$100,000. If Alex pays Barbara $100,000 instantaneously, she can use it to "buy" her way back to B, the status quo ante. In that way, compensatory damages return the plaintiff to the rightful position. (Mathematically, the court awards Barbara (B − A), or (0 − (−100,000)), or $100,000 [remember, convert the two minus signs into a plus].)

---

1. Ernest J. Weinrib, *Corrective Justice in a Nutshell*, 52 U. Toronto L.J. 349, 349 (2002) (footnote omitted). Aristotle writes of a situation where plaintiff's loss equals defendant's gain, which, as we shall see in the chapter on restitution, is not always the case.

The money line also nicely illustrates how valuation problems can threaten the rightful position. Imagine that Barbara really suffers $100,000 in losses (putting her at Point A), but the court underestimates her damages at $80,000. In that case, as Figure 2.2 shows, Barbara is not returned to the rightful position. Instead, she is brought to place B–, which is at –$20,000. The damages award does not put her in the place she was at before the wrong. She will need another $20,000 to restore her house to its previous state.

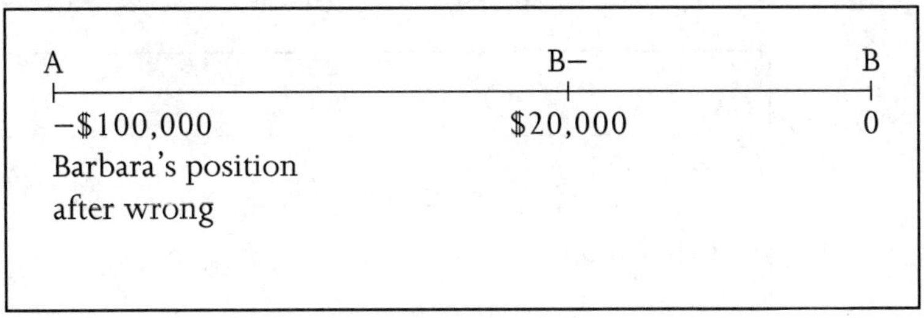

Figure 2.2

Valuation problems don't necessarily work against plaintiffs. So again imagine that Barbara really suffers $100,000 in losses (putting her at Point A), but this time the court *overestimates* her damages at $150,000. In that case, as Figure 2.3 shows, Barbara is brought to a position better than the rightful position. She will be at position B+, which is at +$50,000. (Do you see why? The first $100,000 of damages moves Barbara from A back to B, and then the next $50,000 moves her into positive territory on the money line to $50,000.) In this scenario, Barbara is actually *better off* than she was before Alex burned her house down. Even after paying to get her house back into the same shape it was in before the loss, she has an extra $50,000 in her bank account.

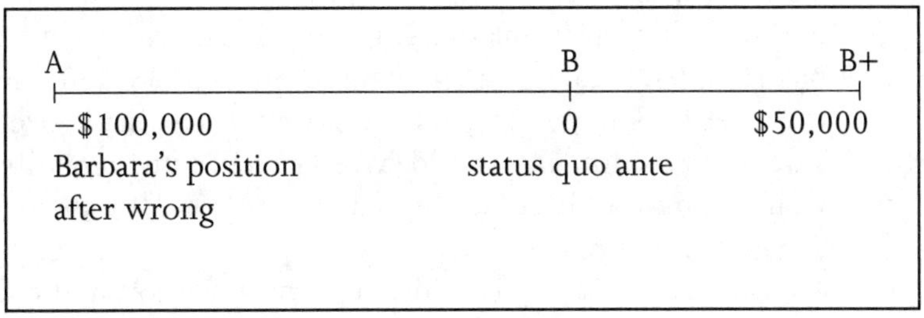

Figure 2.3

Figures 2.2 and 2.3 show that courts will need to value accurately the position that plaintiffs would be in but for the wrong, in order for compensatory damages to satisfy the rightful position standard.

In the typical torts case, such as Barbara v. Alex, the rightful position means accurately measuring the plaintiff's losses, which will necessarily be somewhere in the region less than B, or 0. In typical contracts cases, however, the rightful position means accurately considering *the gains that plaintiff failed to realize* because of a defendant's breach of contract. So imagine that Irina was going to buy a valuable painting from Juan at a cost of $25,000. The market price of the painting is $35,000. They had a valid binding contract and Irina paid in advance. Juan decided not to sell to Irina after he realized he could make more money selling to someone else. He sells the painting to another buyer for $35,000.

Consider in Figure 2.4 how we might represent the rightful position:

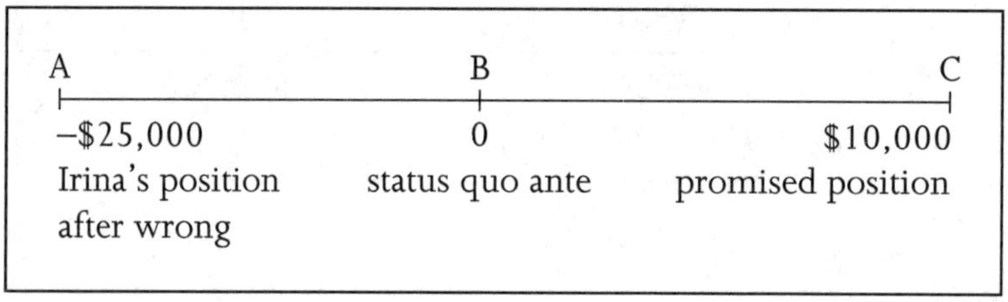

Figure 2.4

Before Irina entered into any contract with Juan, she was at position B, the status quo ante (or zero). When Irina paid Juan in advance and received nothing, she landed at position A, −$25,000. At first blush, it might appear that giving Irina $25,000 would put her back in the rightful position by restoring her to the status quo ante position. But remember that the rightful position is the position that the plaintiff would have been in *but for the defendant's wrong*. In this case, had Juan not breached the contract, Irina would have spent $25,000 for an item that she could then turn around and sell for $35,000, yielding a profit of $10,000 (putting aside the costs of entering into the two transactions and other complexities that we will discuss later) and placing her in position C, +$10,000. To place her into the position she would have been in without Juan's breach (think of a list of her assets with a net balance increase of $10,000), Juan is going to have to pay her $35,000: the first $25,000 takes her back to 0, and the next $10,000 puts her above the status quo ante, the position she would have been in but for the breach (a court would compute these damages as C − A, or 10,000 − (−25,000), or $35,000).

Later chapters will consider how and why tort and contract damages typically differ in this way, with tort damages usually geared toward restoring the status quo and contract damages usually geared toward giving the plaintiff the benefit of the bargain. Chapter 5 considers some exceptions to this rule, especially for fraud cases in tort. For now, keep your eye on the general point: if we value gains and losses correctly, compensatory damages can put the plaintiff into the rightful position.

One final point on the rightful position standard and compensatory damages: while corrective justice adherents such as Aristotle focus on the rightful position as a means of *compensating plaintiffs*, some adherents of the economic analysis of law focus as well on how compensatory damages affect *the incentives of defendants*.[2]

Consider, for example, the incentives facing Juan, who is wondering whether he should breach the painting contract with Irina. Suppose Juan has another willing buyer who will pay $35,000 for the painting. Would Juan—assuming he cares only about the immediate bottom line and not about any moral obligation to keep promises made in a contract or about his long-term reputation—decide to breach? He likely would not decide to do so if he is going to have to pay that $35,000 over to Irina as compensatory damages (though he might if the measure of damages were the under-compensatory $25,000 measure).[3] Think also of Carly, who was not careful and collided into Dan in a rollerblading accident, breaking Dan's arm. The possibility that Carly will have to pay damages if she rollerblades carelessly and injures someone will motivate Carly to take the right amount of care. In this way, damages can serve to influence the behavior of defendants. (In the economic model, the possibility of recovering damages also influences the behavior of plaintiffs. Think of the extra precautions Dan might choose to take if he knew that Carly or others could injure him and not have to pay anything.)

Accurate valuation is important for the economic view of compensatory damages as well. Recall the example (illustrated in Figure 2.2) in which Barbara really suffers $100,000 in losses (putting her at Point A), but the court underestimates her damages at $80,000. For purposes of the economic analysis, if courts consistently underestimate losses or, equivalently, if too many plaintiffs who should win their lawsuits end up losing their lawsuits, then damages might not create sufficient incentives for defendants not to wrong plaintiffs. Indeed, for this reason, some economists say that the possibility of a plaintiff's recovery of additional punitive damages might be necessary to provide the "efficient" amount of deterrence.

To sum up to this point: compensatory damages aim to put the plaintiff in the rightful position, the position the plaintiff would have been in but for

---

2. Economists care about this question because they want courts to choose legal rules that promote "Kaldor-Hicks efficiency," or maximizing overall social wealth for society. Creating the right incentives for defendants and plaintiffs is part of a court's task in promoting efficiency. For an introduction to the concept of Kaldor-Hicks efficiency and economic analysis in general, see Richard A. Posner, Economic Analysis of Law 14-17 (9th ed. 2014).

3. He also would choose to sell to a new buyer if he found a buyer willing to pay $40,000. Remember, the market price is $35,000, which forms the basis for Irina's compensatory damages. In the case of a new buyer willing to pay over the market price, Juan could pay Irina the $35,000 and still end up with a $5,000 profit. Economists call this idea "efficient breach," and it is one to which we shall return in Chapter 4.2.

the wrong. There are both philosophical reasons and economic arguments in favor of utilizing compensatory damages to bring plaintiff to the rightful position, and both views depend on courts being able to accurately value plaintiff's losses. It is to this valuation process that we turn next.

Example 2

One day after Laurent bought a new chocolate Labrador retriever puppy from a breeder for $1,000, Kira stole it. The market price for similar puppies is $2,000. Kira sold the puppy to Mary, who has left the country with it. Laurent sues Kira. Would compensatory damages put Laurent in the rightful position? If so, how much should the compensatory damages be?

Explanation

Laurent might have become emotionally attached to his new puppy (though he's only had it for one day), and it may be hard to value any emotional loss. However, dogs are not one-of-a-kind items, and presumably Laurent could use compensatory damages to buy a replacement dog. There should be some amount of money that puts him in the position where he was before the wrong, possibly setting aside the emotional distress. As for the *amount* of damages, absent evidence that Laurent could buy another dog for half the market price and putting aside any emotional distress, it is going to take $2,000—and not merely $1,000—to put him into the position he was in before the wrong: owning a new puppy. That is what it takes to get substitutionary relief.

Example 3

Nina enters into a binding contract with Olivia for the sale of a rare coin. Nina agreed to pay $1,000 for the coin. The market price for this type of coin in the same condition is $700. Olivia breaches the contract because she has misplaced the coin. Nina has paid nothing in advance. Would compensatory damages put Nina in the rightful position? Is so, how much should the compensatory damages be?

Explanation

This looks like a lucky break for Nina. Had Olivia held up her end of the contract, Nina would have purchased an item worth $700 for $1,000. On an imaginary ledger of Nina's net worth, we would say after the purchase her net worth would have declined by $300. Thus, because this is a losing contract, compensatory damages are not going to be helpful in putting Nina in the rightful position. As we will see in Chapter 11.4, in the case of losing contracts, plaintiffs sometimes seek the remedy of restitution rather than compensatory damages because there are no damages. If Nina still wants the coin, she should be able to purchase it from another seller for the market price of $700. Because the market price of the coin is lower than the contract price, Nina has suffered no damages, except perhaps the costs to locate a substitute coin.

2.3 VALUING COMPENSATORY DAMAGES

2.3.1 Damages in a Well-Functioning Market

Let's return to Barbara and her home (burned down by Alex) to begin our exploration of valuation for purposes of compensatory damages. Consider first the structure of the home itself, rather than its contents. How should the home be valued? Initially, we must choose between an *objective* measure of damages (such as market value) and a *subjective* measure of damages (such as the value that Barbara would place on her home).

For example, suppose that a competent builder would charge $50,000 to rebuild a home for Barbara of the same general size and quality as the one that burned down. This market value is an objective measure; though the parties can disagree about how much competent builders charge to build such a home, the court can resolve this dispute through the taking of evidence from experts in the construction market in Barbara's area, and by using data about the type of home Barbara had before the fire. Alternatively, we might ask how much Barbara *personally* valued her home. Suppose that this was her childhood home, and that it had great sentimental value to her. Indeed, imagine that Barbara had recently turned down an offer for the purchase of her home and land for $400,000—many times the fair market value of the land and home—because she loved it so much. In other words, a person's subjective valuation does not necessarily line up with objective market value.

Generally speaking, when there is a well-functioning market (meaning that there are many buyers and sellers), courts use an objective market measure for calculating a plaintiff's compensatory damages. "Determinations based on value are pervasive in damage measures. Familiar damage measures include the value of the property taken or destroyed, the difference between the value of property before damage and the value after damage, and the difference between the contract price and the market value of property promised but not delivered." LAYCOCK & HASEN p. 22. In Barbara's case, the portion of damages for the loss of her home is going to be measured by the objective market cost to replace the damaged home, and not by Barbara's subjective value.

Objective market measures of value will be undercompensatory when plaintiffs subjectively value items more than the market does.

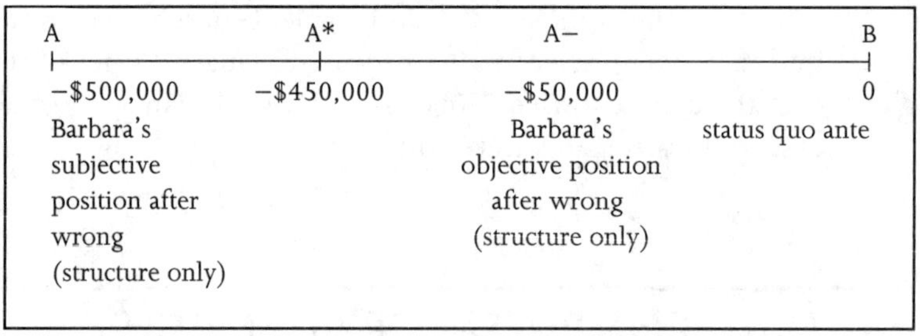

Figure 2.5

Imagine that Barbara would not have moved from her house unless someone paid her $500,000 (plus more money for the land, but we'll ignore that complication). Figure 2.5 shows how the use of objective market value will undercompensate her in this instance. If Barbara is truly at position A (−$500,000) after the fire, it will take a $500,000 damages award to move her back to B, the status quo ante. But the law, using market valuation, treats her loss as being at A−, giving her compensation of only $50,000. In fact, the $50,000 award moves Barbara from position A to position A*, at −$450,000. It is grossly undercompensatory.

If that's the case, it seems unfair to Barbara to use objective market valuation. But courts have gravitated to it in part because objective measures are much easier to administer. When a market is functioning well, it is easy to get figures for repair or replacement costs. Subjective measures exist only inside the head of the plaintiff and thus are harder to identify accurately. There is also the risk that plaintiffs will exaggerate subjective values after a loss. Thus, even if Barbara hated her house and valued it at less than the $50,000 cost of rebuilding, if the law allowed her to receive compensatory damages based on subjective valuation, she may be tempted (but for fear of committing perjury) to state her subjective value as $500,000.

One way that the law can allow subjective valuation in through the back door is to allow emotional distress damages as an element of damages in appropriate cases. Thus, a court in Barbara's negligence case against Alex might allow her to recover the $50,000 cost to repair the home plus some additional amount of damages to compensate for emotional distress. We return in Chapter 3.2 to a consideration of when emotional distress damages may be available as an element of damages.

Even with market-based valuation, issues of subjectivity can surface in cases involving damage to property that do not diminish the overall market value of the property. Consider these examples:

- Percy cuts down a tree on Quentin's land to use the lumber. The tree provided Quentin with shade near his home. The cost to replace the tree is $1,000, but the market value of the land without the tree is unchanged. (*See* Dobbs & Roberts at §3.3(5), pp. 233-236.)

- Ralph cuts down a tree from a forest of trees on Samir's land to use the lumber. Samir did not even notice that the tree was gone until Ralph told him about it. The cost to replace the tree is $1,000, but the market value of the land without the tree is unchanged.
- Tomas signs a contract with Ursula, a building contractor, to construct a building. The contract provides that Ursula will install plumbing using Alpha brand copper pipe. Ursula inadvertently uses Beta brand copper pipe instead, which is of identical quality to Alpha pipe. The error is discovered as the house is completed. The cost to replace the pipes in the building is $20,000, but the value of the home with Beta brand rather than Alpha brand remains unchanged. *See Jacob & Youngs, Inc. v. Kent*, 129 N.E. 889, 891 (N.Y. 1921).

In each of these examples, the costs to repair or replace are high, but the overall impact on market value of the loss is low. Plaintiffs have at times successfully argued for the repair or replace measure when they can show subjective value in the item that was lost or damaged, or at least when they can show they intended to actually make the repair or replacement. *See, e.g., McKinney v. Christiana Cmty. Builders*, 280 Cal. Rptr. 242, 246 (1991) (unpublished opn.); Dobbs & Roberts, *supra*. For example, Quentin may really want his shade tree replaced, and arguably the court should allow him to recover damages to do so. But one suspects that someone like Tomas might sue, claiming repair costs, and never make the repair, hoping to gain a windfall from the minor error of a contractor or the inadvertent tort of a defendant.

In cases where plaintiff cannot show any subjective reason to prefer the replacement cost, as in Samir's case against Ralph, it is tempting to say that there should be no damages. But an economist might bristle at the suggestion because it would create no deterrence for Ralph, who would pay no damages for the theft. Samir might then be forced to take expensive measures to prevent theft from people such as Ralph.

In response to these concerns, some courts will allow the more generous cost of repair measure when a defendant engages in a willful breach of contract. *See, e.g., Groves v. John Wunder Co.*, 286 N.W. 235, 236 (Minn. 1939). The same principle should apply to intentional torts as well, such as those committed by Percy and Ralph (but not the inadvertent breach by Ursula). The law also offers Quentin and Samir an alternative remedy, restitution (see Part III), which would allow them to recover the value of the *gain* to defendant, rather than damages tied to plaintiff's losses.

When measuring market value, courts usually measure damages *at the time of the loss*. In cases involving items that fluctuate in value, however, such as stocks or crops, courts sometimes show greater flexibility. As to stocks, courts are split on approaches, with many states "resolv[ing] doubts against defendant by awarding the highest value between the time of the wrong and the time of trial, the time of filing suit, or some similar date." *See* LAYCOCK & HASEN, p. 28. Similar kinds of issues arise when there is damage to a farmer's crops before those crops have matured. Assuming that a farmer may prove damages with reasonable certainty (see Chapter 6.1), a court might allow damages measured from the time the immature crops would have been harvested rather than at the time of the loss.

EXAMPLE

Example 4

Reconsider the fact pattern in Example 1: Heidi flattens Gary's 1966 Thunderbird convertible with a steamroller. The original purchase price of the car in 1966 was $3,000. Its current retail value as a collectible is $30,000. Gary recently turned down an offer to sell the car for $50,000. Putting aside possible emotional distress damages, how does the law measure Gary's loss of the car?

EXPLANATION

Explanation

Putting aside any emotional distress damages and assuming that the car has no scrap value that Gary can recover, a court will likely award Gary $30,000. The $3,000 original purchase price might ordinarily be evidence of a car's current market value; cars tend to lose value with age. But this is a collectible car, and it has gained value over time. We generally measure market value *at the time of the loss,* and therefore the $30,000 figure is appropriate. It appears that Gary valued the car at more than its market value; that is at least implicit in his failure to sell the car for above-market value. But courts generally will not allow Gary to recover this subjective measure of damages. Does the law's answer jibe with your own values as expressed in your answer to Example 1?

EXAMPLE

Example 5

Victor, while jogging, carelessly entered Wanda's garden and stepped on Wanda's prized tulips, which she had grown herself. The cost of tulip seeds is $50. The cost to buy fully grown replacement tulips is $500. Wanda had planned to cut these tulips and enter them in a flower contest, where the first prize was $1,000. She cannot enter purchased tulips into the contest. The value of Wanda's home is the same with and without the tulips. To what amount in compensatory damages is Wanda entitled if she can successfully sue Victor for negligence?

Explanation

A court is likely to award Wanda $500 for the tulips. Although it is true that the market value of her home has not decreased because of the loss of the tulips, the evidence shows that Wanda was growing these tulips for fun and potential profit; they were not like Samir's unnoticed lost tree in the earlier example. The fact that Victor acted negligently rather than deliberately, however, is an argument in favor of no damages (that is, damages as measured by the loss in value of the house). It seems least likely that Wanda will receive $1,000, or the amount she could have won if she could have entered her tulips in a flower contest. As we will see in Chapter 6.1, damages must be proven with reasonable certainty, and it is too speculative to say whether Wanda would have won the contest with her tulips. And again, we are ignoring the possibility that Wanda will ask for an additional amount of damages for her emotional distress.

Victor might try to argue he is liable to pay for only the cost of replacement seeds. But that appears undercompensatory, because it accounts neither for the value of whatever work Wanda put in to grow her tulips nor for the risk that the tulip seeds would not grow. It also does not follow the principle that we generally measure value at the time of the loss.

Example 6

Xavier puts in a "buy" order to his stockbroker Yolanda for 100 shares of Futurco stock, at $5.00 per share. Xavier sends $500 electronically to Yolanda. Yolanda bought the stock for Xavier (at a total cost of $500), but negligently sold it the same day (for the same $500 price). She failed to inform Xavier, putting the $500 into a general account for clients. One month later, Futurco stock is trading at $20.00 per share and Xavier puts in a "sell" order. Yolanda then tells Xavier of her error. Xavier sues, and at the time of trial Futurco stock is trading at $15.00 per share. To how much is Xavier entitled in damages?

Explanation

This problem raises an issue about property whose value fluctuates over time. If we measure the value at the time of the loss (which presumably occurred the same day as the purchase and sale of the stock), Xavier would be entitled only to $500. But we could choose a more generous measure, such as the highest value before Xavier discovered the loss (yielding damages of $2,000 (100 shares at the $20/share price)) or at the time of trial (yielding damages of $1,500 (100 shares at the $15/share price)). The rule to be applied will depend upon the jurisdiction.

2.3.2 Damages Without a Well-Functioning Market

When markets work well, the dispute is primarily an *evidentiary* one: what is the going price for mature tulips, or rebuilding a home, or emergency room visits? The parties may have pitched battles over this evidentiary question in particular cases, but the court's mission is clear: to figure out the market value to repair or replace the item damaged or lost. But not every loss has a potential repair or replacement value in a well-functioning market. For some losses, there is no market at all—most important, there is no good market for losses caused by emotional distress (or pain and suffering). We cannot refer to a market in pain to compute damages for Dan's broken arm. The next chapter will consider how courts value such losses (termed *noneconomic* losses or *special* damages by some courts, as compared to *economic* losses or *general* damages for losses that have a readier market measure).

Here we consider economic losses that occur in less than perfectly functioning markets. A good example is Barbara's refrigerator, destroyed in the fire set by Alex. Suppose Barbara bought the fridge five years ago for $600. A comparable fridge today costs $800. But if Barbara had tried to sell her five-year-old fridge just before it was destroyed, she would have been lucky to get $100 for it. Unfortunately for Barbara, the law generally uses market value at the time of loss, so she stands to get only $100 for the lost fridge.

Some courts will be more generous and allow a higher value based on replacement cost less depreciation for household goods and apparel. *See, e.g., Lane v. Oil Delivery Co.*, 524 A.2d 405 (N.J. Super. Ct. App. Div. 1987). But that more generous rule typically is not applied to other consumer goods, including cars.

Why is the fridge's value so low? Part of the reason is that there is not a robust market for certain used goods, and even where there is a market, prices tend to be depressed. Economist George Akerlof described a "lemon" effect that makes the market for such goods—he used the example of cars—poorly functioning. George Akerlof, *The Market for 'Lemons': Quality Uncertainty and the Market Mechanism*, 84 Q.J. ECON. 488 (1970). It is difficult to judge the quality of these goods, and uncertainty about whether the good is of high quality or is a poor-quality "lemon" pervades the market. Buyers offer lower prices for these goods to consider the uncertainty, and the lower price means *that fewer sellers with the high-quality goods would choose to sell.* In this way, higher-quality goods are driven from the market, leaving an abundance of "lemons."

Thus, when Barbara gets the $100 in damages for her fridge, she is taking a chance if she goes out to buy a used fridge at this price—it might be a lemon. If Barbara is lucky, she has purchased homeowners' insurance that provides for the cost of *replacing* lost items with new items of similar quality.[4] If she doesn't have insurance, she might look for another source of money to buy a new, comparable refrigerator. For these reasons, the $100 damage award likely will be undercompensatory.

Another circumstance in which markets don't function well is when there are few buyers or sellers. Consider a collection of family home movies, also destroyed in Barbara's fire. Before the fire, virtually no one would have been interested in buying those goods, but for Barbara they were very valuable. The movies are irreplaceable, and their only market value is sentimental value. In such cases, courts will sometimes allow recovery for their value—again, these are sometimes allowed not for the economic value of the destroyed goods, but as part of the noneconomic emotional distress damages. *See Williford v. Emerton*, 935 So. 2d 1150 (Ala. 2004); *see also Edmonds v. United States*, 563 F. Supp. 2d 196 (D.D.C. 2008) (trial court awarding $2,500 measured by plaintiff's "special value" but not by "sentimental value" for each of two irreplaceable photographs of plaintiff's father as a high school student that defendant destroyed).

Example 7

Zane owned an acre of land with his home in a rural part of the state. Alice bought land adjacent to Zane's land, with the intention of building a ranch to raise emus. Alice brought in a bulldozer to clear the part of her land with a dense collection of trees. Her workers accidentally cleared some of the dense trees growing on Zane's land as well. Zane sued Alice for trespass and sought damages. The uncontroverted evidence showed that the inadvertent clearing of Zane's land increased the market value of his land by $15,000. At trial, Zane testified as follows: "Well, I bought this land to build a retirement home on and I am 57 and my wife is 56, and she's not well, so she wants to get out in the country, too. And we bought that for that reason and now we are afraid to go out of our house. And the reason we're afraid is because of the exotic animals that will be put next to us. We hoped the trees would serve as a buffer." The jury awarded Zane $20,000. Can the award stand?

Explanation

There is no dispute that the market value of Zane's land has not decreased; it has increased. The only way that Zane can recover damages is if the court allows for the award of the subjective value of the land. Many courts would not allow Zane to recover such damages, but some would allow it when actual damages do not compensate the plaintiff for the loss. (These facts come from *Porras v. Craig*, 675 S.W.2d 503 (Tex. 1984). The Texas supreme court later overturned the case's holding. *Gilbert Wheeler, Inc. v. Enbridge Pipelines (East Texas), L.P.*, 449 S.W. 3d 474 (Tex. 2014)).

---

4. We put off until Chapter 6.4 the question whether Barbara would be allowed to keep *both* her insurance proceeds *and* damages from Alex.

2.4 NOMINAL DAMAGES

Suppose in Example 7 Zane did not claim any losses based upon his loss of his privacy. Instead, he is annoyed that Alice has sent her workers on his land—even though the workers' clearing of his land has increased its value. Is there any incentive for Zane to still sue for damages?

The answer may be "yes." In cases such as trespass, where there is no actual damage, a plaintiff might sue to obtain nominal damages, or a trivial sum of damages (such as $1) awarded by a court in lieu of actual damages. At first blush, it might appear irrational for Zane to sue for $1 in damages. Attorney's fees are likely to cost many times more than that expected recovery (and are usually not recoverable by the winning party (see Chapter 17.3)). But the $1 damage award can serve an important "declaratory" function: telling the world where the property line is between Zane and Alice, and declaring that it is a trespass for Alice to enter Zane's land.[5] (This can be especially useful if Zane and Alice have a bona fide dispute over the location of their property line.) Eventually, if Alice continues to trespass on Zane's land, Zane might go back to the court and point to the nominal damages award and Alice's continuing conduct as a reason to get an injunction ordering Alice to stay off Zane's land.

An award of nominal damages also serves the purpose of "vindicating" a plaintiff's rights. Musician Taylor Swift sued a radio personality for assault and battery for groping her, and she asked for only $1 in nominal damages. Even though the $1 is not compensatory, that lawsuit vindicated Swift's rights and provided valuable information to people about the actions of the defendant. *See* Sadie Blanchard, *Nominal Damages as Vindication*, 28 Geo. Mason L. Rev. 228 (2022).

In addition, an award of nominal damages might serve as a predicate to allow the jury to award punitive damages (Chapter 15.1). Many states require an award of compensatory damages before a jury can award additional punitive damages, and sometimes an award of nominal damages is enough to allow for the punitive award. *See* Richard C. Tinney, *Sufficiency of Showing of Actual Damages to Support Award of Punitive Damages—Modern Cases*, 40 A.L.R. 4th 11 §§6-9 (1985 & 2016 Supp.) (collecting cases on both sides of issue). *But see* N.J. Stat. Ann. 2A:15-5.13(c) (nominal damages cannot support the award of punitive damages).

Finally, an award of nominal damages can serve as a predicate to allow the jury to award attorney's fees in cases litigated under statutes that provide for the award of attorney's fees. But when the jury awards only nominal damages (and no other relief, such as a declaration or injunction), the

5. See Chapter 16 for a discussion of declaratory judgments, the quintessential declaratory remedy.

amount of attorney's fees allowed might be very small or none, as we shall see in Chapter 17.3.

Example 8

While Barry was sleeping in the grass on the quad, Charlene—who had never met Barry before but liked how he looked—came over and kissed him on the lips. Barry slept through the whole thing, but later heard about what happened from some friends. Barry wants to sue for the tort of battery, but tells you that he suffered no significant emotional distress. Would you advise Barry to sue for nominal damages?

Explanation

It depends upon what Barry would like to accomplish. If Barry wants to "send a message" to Charlene (or others like her), he might want to sue, assuming, as is likely, that he can make out the technical elements of an offensive battery. *See* Restatement (Third) of Torts—Intentional Torts to Persons §§ 1, 3 (Am. Law. Inst., Tent. Draft No. 4, 2019). Even without emotional distress damage, he should be able to obtain nominal damages. (He also might be able to recover damages for dignitary harm, discussed in the next chapter.) Because Barry would have to pay attorney's fees, it may cost him much more to sue than what he would recover in nominal damages. So he would have to feel pretty strongly about sending a message—unless the jurisdiction allows for the award of punitive damages to accompany nominal damages, and Barry hopes to recover a large amount in punitive damages.

2.5 TIME AND THE VALUE OF MONEY

2.5.1 Prejudgment and Postjudgment Interest

Recall Barbara, whose house Alex accidentally burned down. We said that if it would cost $100,000 for Barbara to rebuild the house, and if Alex paid Barbara the cost of the losses instantly, an award of $100,000 would restore Barbara to the rightful position. But payments do not come instantly in most cases. Alex may dispute liability or the amount of damages (or, worse for Barbara, Alex may not have enough money to pay for the damage he has caused).

Suppose that it takes one year from the time that Alex burns down the house until the time of judgment. Awarding Barbara $100,000 one year after the accident will not put her in the rightful position. To see why, imagine that the day after the fire, Barbara secured a loan to rebuild the property. The lender charged 10% interest per year (compounded annually, an assumption we'll continue to make throughout this chapter to keep things simple). She rebuilds the house as the lawsuit goes forward. One year after the fire, her loss is $110,000, not merely the $100,000 loss represented in Figure 2.1. See Figure 2.6.

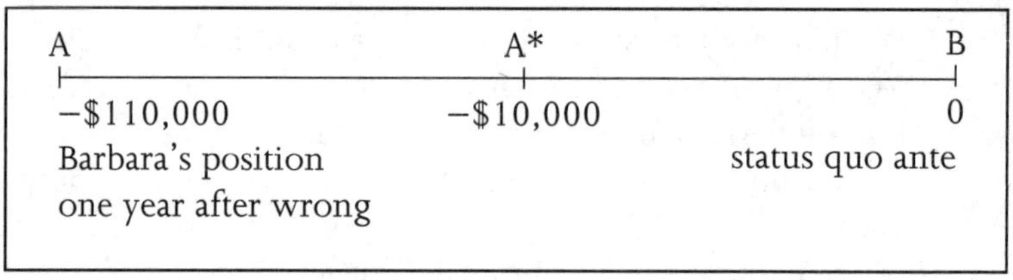

Figure 2.6

The jury measures the loss at the time of the wrong, or $100,000. But awarding Barbara $100,000 a year after the wrong does not restore her to the rightful position. Instead, it brings her only to A*, −$10,000. For this reason, courts sometimes allow the award of *prejudgment interest*, measured from the time of the wrong until the time of judgment. This award helps put plaintiff in the rightful position.

The availability of prejudgment interest depends upon the jurisdiction and sometimes on the type of case. Traditionally, prejudgment interest was unavailable when damages were not "liquidated" or "ascertainable." In practice, this meant that prejudgment interest was not available for personal injury actions. Some states have abandoned this rule and now allow for prejudgment interest even in personal injury cases.

When prejudgment interest is available, the rate of interest varies by jurisdiction. For example, Rhode Island sets the amount of prejudgment interest by statute at 12% per year. R.I. Gen. Laws §9-21-10. Other jurisdictions index the amount to some other measure. Iowa, for example, sets prejudgment interest "at a rate equal to the one-year treasury constant maturity index published by the federal reserve in the H15 report settled immediately prior to the date of the judgment plus two percent." Iowa Code §668.13.

In federal courts, prejudgment interest is routinely available, but there is no set rate of prejudgment interest. Accordingly, there is much room for creative arguments about which measure best puts the plaintiff back in the rightful position. *See* Michael S. Knoll & Jeffrey M. Colon, *The Calculation of Prejudgment Interest* (May 31, 2005), http://ssrn.com/abstract=732765.

There is much at stake in these federal cases. As Professors Knoll and Colon note: "When the injury occurred long before the judgment, prejudgment interest can greatly exceed the original judgment. . . . In 1992, the Seventh Circuit awarded plaintiffs $65 million in damages and $148 million in prejudgment interest in a suit arising out of the grounding of the supertanker, *Amoco Cadiz*, off the coast of Brittany on March 16, 1978." Because of the flexibility of the federal standard, the court's decision could be worth millions. The authors note that a 1% increase in the interest rate in the *Amoco Cadiz* case would have increased the award by $20 million, and that if the court had compounded interest quarterly rather than annually, the plaintiffs could have received an extra $11 million.

Postjudgment interest—for the period between the time of judgment and the time that the judgment debtor pays (or "satisfies") the judgment—is also necessary to put plaintiff in the rightful position. So suppose that a court awards Barbara $110,000 for the fire damages, with $10,000 of that money representing the prejudgment interest. Alex decides to appeal, and it is yet another year before Alex, upon losing the appeal, pays Barbara the damages. Barbara, who has borrowed money from the bank to pay for her repairs, is still accruing interest on her loan, so the award of $110,000 will not put her in the rightful position. Assuming she had to pay for another year of interest at $10,000, compounded annually (on her principal and interest), her total loan will now cost $121,000 to repay (in the second year, interest accrues at 10% on the $110,000 loan balance).

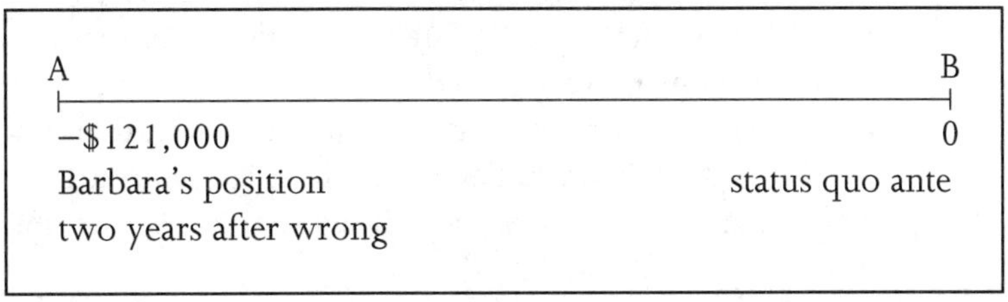

Figure 2.7

In the federal courts, postjudgment interest is awarded at the set rate of the 52-week Treasury bill, and many states set the rate by statute as well. At least some states allow postjudgment interest on the total amount of damages, including prejudgment interest. *See Quality Engineered Installation, Inc. v. Higley South, Inc.*, 670 So. 2d 929, 931 (Fla. 1996).

The new Restatement (Third) Torts: Remedies §14 (Am. Law Ins. Tent. Draft No. 2, 2023) allows for prejudgment interest "at a reasonable market rate, on the amount of damages found by the factfinder, from the date or dates the damage was incurred (or a reasonable approximation thereof) to the date of judgment" and postjudgment interest as allowed "by statute or rule of court."

Example 9

Enid alleges that Deirdre breached a contract to pay Enid $100,000 for a computer system that Deirdre has used in her business. The dispute takes place in Rhode Island and the issue is litigated in Rhode Island's court. If Deirdre is found liable for breach of contract, the court will order her to pay Enid $100,000 plus prejudgment interest. The current rate of interest that individuals can get on their money in a safe investment is 5%. Which party to the litigation will want to bring this case to trial quickly? How might that result differ if individuals can get 20% on their money in a safe investment?

Explanation

There may be reasons of liquidity (the fact that Enid needs the $100,000 now) that could lead Enid to push the case to trial as quickly as possible regardless of the interest rate. But putting aside such a concern, you can see that the rate of prejudgment interest can affect the parties' incentives to litigate quickly or slowly. When normal interest rates are low, defendants like Deirdre may want the case to be decided quickly, so that, if found liable, Deirdre won't have to pay a very high rate of interest. For Enid in such circumstances, prejudgment interest may look like a good "investment." Think of this: If Enid gets her $100,000 today from Deirdre and invests it in the bank at 5% (annual interest), after a year she will have $105,000. But if the case drags on for another year, Deirdre will owe her $112,000, because of Rhode Island's statutory 12% rate of prejudgment interest.

The incentives are reversed if general interest rates are high. If Enid can get 20% on her money, she'd rather have Deirdre pay now. Deirdre, on the other hand, would rather invest the $100,000 now in an investment yielding 20%, eventually paying off Enid under the statutory 12% rate and pocketing the difference.

2.5.2 Present Value

Prejudgment and postjudgment interest facilitate compensation for plaintiffs for harm that *has already occurred*. But sometimes a plaintiff receives compensation for injuries the jury believes plaintiff *will sustain in the future* because of the defendant's past conduct. Consider Frank, who caused serious injuries to Greta when he negligently ran her over with his Hummer. Suppose Greta, a 30-year-old woman who was healthy before the accident, is now paralyzed from the waist down. She can no longer work as a letter carrier, and she will need special medical care for the rest of her life.

By the time Greta's case against Frank goes to trial, Greta will have already incurred medical expenses and loss of wages from the time of the accident until the time of trial. The jury can decide the appropriate amount for these damages that have already occurred. Depending upon the state law, Greta may be entitled to prejudgment interest on at least some of these damages, and she should be able to obtain postjudgment interest as well for amounts reduced to judgment. Putting aside additional emotional distress damages, would compensation for these past losses put Greta in the rightful position?

No. Even if Frank compensates Greta for the harm that has *already occurred* as a result of Frank's actions, Greta still faces *future medical expenses and loss of wages*. Five years from now, Greta might still need weekly visits from a nurse and other medical care. She may also never be able to return to work. (If Greta could perhaps take a different job, a court might reduce her damages for failure to *mitigate* if she does not do so. See Chapter 6.2.)

These future damages present special valuation problems. Imagine that this year, Greta's medical bills as a result of the accident are $20,000, and the salary she would have earned (but for the injury) as a letter carrier is $35,000. The experts agree that she will suffer similar damages five years from now. Because we require the plaintiff to sue for all of her damages in a single trial (rather than come back to court periodically for an assessment of recent additional damages), a court will have to figure out how much to compensate Greta *now* for her future medical expenses and lost wages.

This is indeed a difficult undertaking that involves a host of educated guesses about the future. Will Greta need the same amount of medical care five years from now? How much will such medical care cost in five years? How much would Greta have earned five years from now had she not been injured? Would she have received promotions by then?

These problems are increased by the uncertain time frame for damages for serious injuries. Damages will have to be awarded to compensate Greta for the rest of her life in this single trial. Consider these questions: When would Greta have stopped working? How much longer will she live and need medical care? Even after the jury makes determinations of these amounts (in high-value cases, likely based upon the testimony of dueling experts), there is another complication: the time value of money.

Suppose the jury determines that five years from now, Greta will need the same level of medical care, which today costs $20,000, and that she would have been promoted two grades at the postal service, to a position where the current salary is $40,000. These figures do not consider the issue of inflation. Over time, prices rise. But predicting how much prices will rise is not easy. Indeed, knowing something about the general rate of inflation is not enough: the cost of medical care has in recent years exceeded the general inflation rate. Wages, too, might increase faster or slower than the general rate of inflation. It might be that postal workers' salaries in general have kept up with the general rate of inflation. And postal workers' salaries are easier to predict than salaries of those who have a more uncertain career path, such as that of a first-year associate at a large law firm. Can you predict with any certainty how much you will be earning ten years from now?

Imagine that the jury determines that the medical care today costing Greta $20,000 would cost $25,000 in five years, and that the salary for a postal worker who is two grades above Greta will be $45,000 five years from now. Five years from now, therefore, the jury's best guess is that Greta would need $70,000 for medical expenses and lost wages.[6]

But if the jury awards Greta $70,000 to compensate for expected losses five years from now, Greta would be *overcompensated* because she will have the use of that money five years early. If Greta received the $70,000 today, she could invest it for the next five years. At the end of five years, if she invested that $70,000 at 5% per year compounded annually, she would have over $89,000.

So we need a more sophisticated way to deal with this problem, one that considers two *countervailing tendencies*. On the one hand, the cost of things like medical care and wages will go up over time. On the other hand, Greta will have the money from the judgment before she needs it, and because she can invest the money, she will need less money now.

If these figures were exactly offsetting, we could ignore both the effects of medical and wage inflation and the benefits of getting the money early. And some courts have said it is permissible to do just that. *See Jones & Laughlin Steel Corp. v. Pfeifer*, 462 U.S. 523 (1983) (rejecting this "total offset" method as *mandatory* in the federal courts but noting that parties could stipulate to this method of computing damages). This means, to use the example above, that a jury might simply award Greta $20,000 per year for each year she is expected to need medical care, and $35,000 to replace her salary for each year she would have worked but for the accident. She can then take that money and invest it with the expectation that the principal from the judgment plus the interest income would give her just the right amount at the time she should need the funds.

But plaintiffs and defendants, at least in cases with large stakes, might battle over future cost and wage increases. They too might disagree over the proper rate of interest that Greta would be able to get for safe investments. Calculating *present value* allows jurors (or, more realistically, the expert witnesses upon whose testimony the jurors will rely) to consider these two countervailing forces at once.

To use a simple example, take Greta's medical care one year from now, which in today's dollars will cost $20,000. Suppose the evidence shows that medical care is expected to rise by 3% in the next year, and that Greta could invest her money in a safe investment for a year earning 4.5% interest. Rather than increase the $20,000 by 3% (to account for increased cost) and then decrease it by the 4.5% interest rate (to account for the amount Greta may earn on her money), we can simply "discount" the $20,000 by the difference in interest rates, or 1.5% (4.5% − 3%). Using a present value table or a present value calculator (easy to find on the Internet with a Google

6. Here, as elsewhere in this book, we are ignoring the issue of how taxation affects these calculations.

search), the value of that amount is $19,704.[7] The calculation must be done for each year of medical expenses and each year of wages.

This example shows how complicated the computation of future damages can be. We have dealt with only one year out of many years of Greta's expected future medical expenses. Small changes in assumptions can make a big difference over time. It is no wonder that in such cases, plaintiffs and defendants are going to bring in economic experts to present competing models of future damages. In a case with serious personal injuries, tens of thousands of dollars can be at stake depending upon the discount rate used.

Putting aside the technicalities and details, the RESTATEMENT (THIRD) TORTS: REMEDIES §15 (Am. Law Ins. Tent. Draft No. 2, 2023) provides that "For any damage that can be valued by prices in a market, and that the plaintiff will not incur until after the date of judgment, the plaintiff is entitled to recover only an amount that, if appropriately invested from the date of judgment to the date on which the damage will be incurred, would yield principal and interest that in total equals the amount of the damage. Principal categories of future damage subject to this rule are lost earnings or earning capacity, lost profits, and the cost of medical and rehabilitative services."

Example 10

You are Frank's lawyer. Do you want an economic expert who predicts that medical inflation and wage inflation will be high, or one who predicts it will be low? Do you want an expert who predicts a high rate of return on safe investments, or one who predicts a low rate? Is it ethical to shop for an expert on the basis of the expert's expected opinions?

Explanation

Generally speaking, it is better for defendants when the expert predicts that medical care inflation and wage inflation will be low, and that the general rate of return on investments will be high (plaintiffs will want the opposite assumptions to be made). Consider Greta's costs in ten years. A prediction that medical inflation and wage inflation will be low means that Greta won't need much more money ten years from now than she does today to make up for what she's lost. And the more money she can earn on her investments, the less principal she'll need today to yield the right amount tomorrow.

Ethically, one should not choose an expert who is going to commit perjury or sell her testimony to the highest bidder. But it is common practice to look at an expert's track record before retaining that expert and using that

7. For those using a present value table, one would look under the column for the 1.5% discount rate at period 1. The rate there is 0.98522157, which, when multiplied by $20,000, yields $19,704.

expert in a case. The most credible experts are those who sometimes testify for plaintiffs and sometimes testify for defendants.

EXAMPLE

Example 11

A jury awards Greta a sum of damages based upon the assumption that she will be able to earn 5% per year on her investments. Five years after judgment, Frank discovers that Greta invested her money in the stock market and earned an average of 18% on her money in the first five years. Can Frank go back to court and ask for a refund?

EXPLANATION

Explanation

No. The same is true if Greta was unable to earn as much on her money as the jury assumed, or if medical costs increased at a much faster rate than the jury predicted. Whatever damages are awarded at trial is usually the last word.

One way to deal with this uncertainty is to have defendants make periodic payments to plaintiffs every few years that are adjusted for inflation. Sometimes cases are settled to provide for such payments, with the defendant paying a lump sum to an insurer, who bears risks such as a change in the rate of inflation. Some states require the use of periodic payments in certain kinds of cases, such as medical malpractice cases.

CHAPTER 3

Tort Damages

3.1 INTRODUCTION TO TORT DAMAGES

This chapter considers special issues that arise in the context of tort damages, beginning with the general measure of tort damages. When we speak of the rightful position in torts cases, we are almost always comparing the position of plaintiff before the wrong committed by the defendant (the "status quo ante," which we set at 0) and the position of plaintiff after the wrong.[1] See Figure 3.1.

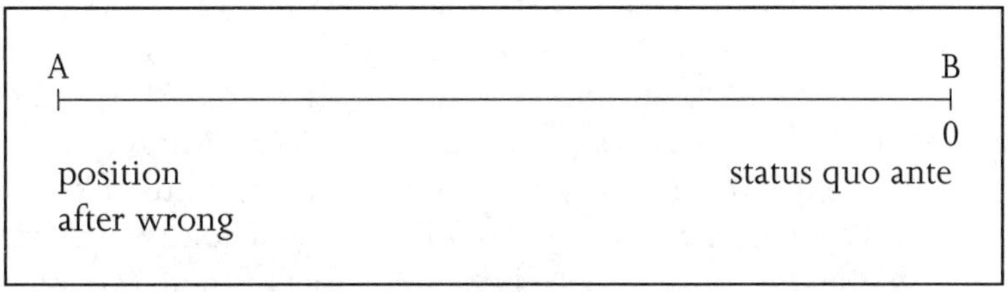

Figure 3.1

To use the final example of the last chapter, Greta was at B, or 0, before Frank ran her over. The accident moved her to some point below zero, at A. Tort damages are measured as (B − A), and at least theoretically, the award of

1. The notable exception is for fraud damages, discussed in Chapter 5. In addition, in certain torts cases, one may choose not to seek tort damages but instead to sue to recover in restitution. Part III of this book explores such restitutionary remedies.

damages equal to (B – A) should put Greta in the position she would have been in but for the wrong.

Greta's example presents many complications, especially because of the difficulty of measuring her damages for pain and suffering. Before we consider her case further, let's return to a simpler example from the last chapter, the case of Alex burning down Barbara's house:

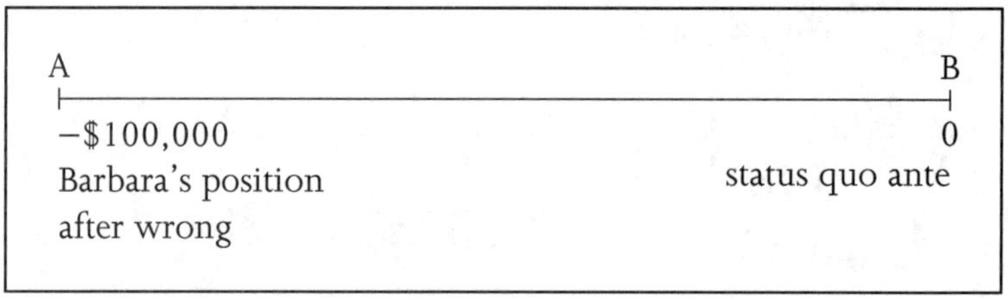

Figure 3.2

Mathematically, the court awards Barbara (B – A), or (0 – (–100,000)), or $100,000 (remember, convert the two minus signs into a plus sign). See Figure 3.2. Though the parties may vigorously dispute the correct value of A, the parties usually do not dispute that the court should award damages meant to put plaintiff in the position she would have been in but for the wrong, the goal of the (B – A) formula.

The use of this (B – A) formula for tort damages (which some call "reliance damages" for reasons that will become clear in the next chapter, dealing with contract damages) nicely illustrates cases where only nominal damages may be available. Recall Charlene, who committed a battery by kissing Barry in the quad while he was sleeping. Barry suffered no measurable damages (the facts told us he suffered no emotional distress), so in that case A = 0, and therefore (B – A) equals zero. Because Barry suffered no damages, he will lose his case for failure to prove damages, unless the court allows him to recover nominal damages or allows him to recover for loss of dignity apart from emotional distress. (On the potential to sue for loss of dignity aside from emotional distress, see Rest. (Third) Torts: Remedies §22 (Am. Law Inst. Tent. Draft No. 2, 2023).)

As we have already seen in earlier chapters, the idea that tort damages restore the plaintiff to the position she would have been in but for defendant's wrong can sometimes be little more than a fiction. The use of market valuation rather than subjective valuation, the inability of some plaintiffs to obtain prejudgment interest, and the lack of recovery (in most cases) of plaintiff's attorney's fees are all reasons we have already considered why a plaintiff's tort damages may be undercompensatory, thus putting plaintiff in a worse position than she would have been in had the defendant not injured her.

In tort damages, by far the largest gap in restoring plaintiff to the rightful position arises in serious personal injury cases such as Greta's. While in theory Barbara may be indifferent between her house being burned down by Alex and a sum of money compensating her for the loss of the house in the fire, it is hard to imagine that Greta, or anyone else, would agree to be permanently paralyzed or disabled in exchange for any sum of money, even if she were to be perfectly compensated for her medical expenses and future lost wages. Furthermore, if we are going to use money to compensate Greta for the emotional distress she has suffered, what is the proper measure of such damages? It is to this issue that we turn in the next section.

Example 1

Hillary steals Ira's digital camera and throws it into the river, destroying it. Ira bought the camera for $300 one year ago. Today, a camera with similar features is worth $200. The market value of Ira's camera at the time Hillary stole it was $75. Ira sues Hillary in tort. What is the value of B in Figure 3.1? What is the value of A? How much are Ira's total damages in his tort suit against Hillary?

Explanation

The value of B is the easy part of this question. It is always zero. From the preceding chapter, we know that courts typically use market value at the time of the loss to measure plaintiff's losses. This means that A would be $75. But Ira might be able to argue for the higher replacement cost measure of $200 less depreciation (the camera is a year old, and thus worth less than a new camera). Recall that some courts allow for the higher measure of damages based upon replacement costs for certain household and consumer goods. (Alternatively, Ira might argue for the higher measure of damages based upon Hillary's bad conduct.) The total compensatory damages would therefore likely be either $75 or some amount near $200, plus (potentially, depending on the jurisdiction) prejudgment interest and likely postjudgment interest. There are no future expected losses, so there is no need to reduce any amounts to present value. This may also be a case where additional punitive damages are available (see Chapter 15).

3.2 PAIN AND SUFFERING, EMOTIONAL DISTRESS, AND OTHER "NONECONOMIC" DAMAGES

Courts and lawyers use different terminology to describe types of compensatory damages; "general," "special," "actual," "pecuniary," and "consequential" are some of the common names.[2] The labels are sometimes

2. For discussion of terminology, see Dobbs & Roberts §3.3; Laycock & Hasen pp. 44-46; Rest. (Third) Torts: Remedies §4 (Am. Law Inst. Tent. Draft No. 1, 2022).

inconsistent and contradictory; to the extent possible, this book avoids such terminology and focuses instead on the principles that courts employ, regardless of the labels courts use. But terminology sometimes matters.

Here, it is important to introduce a relatively new and increasingly important damages term in tort cases: noneconomic damages. *Noneconomic damages* include damages plaintiffs may claim for items with no functioning economic market, such as pain, suffering, and emotional distress. Such damage claims are distinct from *economic damages*, which are damages for which there *is* an economic market, such as the lost wages, property damages, and medical expenses we considered in the last chapter. Of course, even though noneconomic damages involve losses for which there is no functioning market, the losses they compensate for still have great value to people; most people who suffer serious pain because of a defendant's tort likely would not have accepted the pain for any amount of money offered by the defendant before the tort.

The economic/noneconomic distinction is important, because in recent years some states have enacted statutes[3] that have limited the amount or availability of noneconomic damages as part of the "tort reform" movement in an effort to limit the ability of plaintiffs to recover large damages awards. In California, for example, plaintiffs who are injured by a health care provider may recover no more than $350,000 in noneconomic damages. *See* CAL. CIV. CODE §3333.2 (the amount will eventually rise to $750,000 under the newly revised statute and will be indexed to rise with inflation). The limit does not apply to other negligence suits.

Caps on noneconomic damages have been such a popular element of defendant-oriented tort reform in recent years because jurors sometimes award high noneconomic damages because there is no functioning market to serve as a baseline for jury determinations. The insurance industry in particular has claimed that caps on noneconomic damages are necessary to keep liability insurance rates—particularly medical malpractice insurance rates—in a reasonable range, pointing to a few cases of very high awards for noneconomic damages. On the other hand, plaintiffs' lawyers have argued that such caps are unnecessary, that the insurance "crisis" is a fiction, and that these limits tend to penalize the most severely injured people by undercompensating them. The empirical debate is rich, and is beyond what we can cover here.

In places where caps do not operate, and even in places where they do (for amounts below the cap), the question is how juries are to determine the value of noneconomic damages.[4] The problem begins with the lack of

3. Much of tort law is judicially created common law. Legislatures can modify or reverse particular aspects of the common law by passing a statute.

4. For a useful debate over this question and related questions, see Symposium, *Who Feels Their Pain? The Challenge of Noneconomic Damages in Civil Litigation*, 55 DEPAUL L. REV. 249 (2006). Perhaps

a working market. As in the case with subjective valuation, as discussed in Chapter 2, there is no objective baseline for jurors to use in picking a number to compensate for the pain and suffering that someone like Greta suffers as a result of the accident. Some economists want to look for market proxies such as the amount of insurance an individual would choose to buy covering her own health, but these measures generally are not introduced as evidence, and even among scholars debate rages over whether this insurance theory is appropriate for measuring noneconomic damages. For a critical analysis, see Ellen Smith Pryor, *The Tort Law Debate, Efficiency and the Kingdom of the Ill: A Critique of the Insurance Theory of Compensation*, 79 VA. L. REV. 91 (1993).

An experiment I like to run in my Torts and Remedies classes is to give a variety of fact patterns such as Greta's that involve both more and less severe personal injury cases in which plaintiffs suffer noneconomic damages. I ask the students to independently write down how much they, as jurors, would award in such cases for the noneconomic portion of the damages, and I then poll the class. The range of responses is astounding, with responses usually ranging anywhere from zero to millions of dollars.

How much would you award Greta? How did you decide on that number? What other information would you want to know before deciding on an amount?

As one of the party's lawyers, think about how you might argue on Greta's or Frank's behalf for the right amount of damages for Greta's pain and suffering. If you were Greta's lawyer, you might try to ask for a certain amount per day (the "per diem" argument), which, when carried out over a long period of time, can yield a significant amount of damages. Suppose you ask for $10 per hour, 16 hours a day, 7 days a week, 52 weeks per year, for 40 years. That amounts to over $2.3 million.[5] Some courts allow such per diem arguments so long as a jury is told that such arguments are not evidence, but others do not, on grounds that they may overly influence the jury. *See Botta v. Brunner*, 138 A.2d 713 (N.J. 1958) (partially overruled by statute). What could you, as Frank's lawyer, say in response to a per diem argument if plaintiff is allowed to make the argument?

Lack of adequate market valuation for noneconomic damages leads to other, bigger problems. We all recognize that in serious cases of noneconomic damages, any award of damages is likely to be undercompensatory because there is no amount of money that, say, a healthy 30-year-old woman would trade for a lifetime of paralysis and pain. On the other hand,

---

the title of Professor Abel's article sums up of the frustrations some scholars have shown with the award of noneconomic damages: Richard Abel, *General Damages Are Incoherent, Incalculable, Incommensurable, and Inegalitarian (but Otherwise a Great Idea)*, 55 DEPAUL L. REV. 253 (2006).

5. Should the amount of noneconomic damages be reduced to present value? Michigan by statute requires that damages be so reduced. *See* MICH. COMP. LAWS ANN. §600.6306(1)(e). But that is unusual.

courts (and society) won't tolerate infinitely large damage awards, while in cases of less severe noneconomic damages, some courts are suspicious that plaintiffs may overstate the extent of their noneconomic damages to reap a windfall from the defendant. Finally, the lack of any established market means that juries are likely to reach highly divergent decisions on the appropriate amount of noneconomic damages.

How do courts deal with these conflicting forces and the non-uniformity in those situations where the legislature has not imposed a cap or other limit on the amount of noneconomic damages?

Courts sometimes will lower the amount of such damages on a motion from the defendant on grounds that the amount of the award is so high as to "shock the conscience" (or some similar verbal formulation). The "shock the conscience" standard allows for more open-ended judicial review of verdicts; sometimes to achieve a level of uniformity across cases, judges will compare verdicts in similar cases and adjust outlier verdicts. But there is reason to worry that the cases for comparison are not fair (after all, these are cases that have gone to trial, not settled). The Restatement takes the position that a court should not overturn an award of damages that has gone to the jury unless the verdict is "grossly excessive" or "grossly inadequate" when compared to the evidence in the record. RESTATEMENT (THIRD) TORTS: REMEDIES §17(e) (Am. Law Inst. Tent. Draft No. 2, 2023).

Procedurally, the judge who wishes to lower the amount of damages awarded by a jury uses the device of *remittitur*, which gives the plaintiff the option of either taking the lower amount chosen by the judge or having a new trial on the issue of damages. In some jurisdictions, a judge may use the device of *additur*, which gives the defendant the option of taking a *higher* amount of damages chosen by the judge or a new trial on the issue of damages. But the *additur* procedure in some states, and on the federal level, has been held to violate the right to a jury trial and is therefore unavailable. (In a jurisdiction barring *additur*, a trial judge believing the amount of damages is too low can only order a new trial.) On the standards for remittitur or additur, *see id.*, §17(b) (remittitur standards); 17(c) (additur standards).

In addition, courts traditionally have put limits on plaintiffs' ability to recover damages for emotional distress that is unaccompanied by any physical injury to plaintiffs—in part out of the fear that plaintiffs could feign or exaggerate their emotional distress injuries. Some jurisdictions have relaxed the requirement of a "physical impact" to one requiring plaintiffs to be in the "zone of physical danger" (e.g., plaintiff suffers emotional distress when nearly hit by an automobile). Going further, in some jurisdictions, one can recover emotional distress damages for witnessing injury to another (e.g., witness sees victim run over by a car driven by defendant). But the courts often impose additional requirements on witness recoveries, such as a requirement that the witness suffer *severe* emotional distress and that the victim and witness be close relatives (or that the witness manifest some physical symptom from witnessing the injury). *See Dillon v. Legg*, 441 P.2d 912 (Cal. 1968); Restatement (Second) of Torts §46; Restatement (Third) of Torts: Liability for Physical and Emotional Harm §48. *See also* Restatement (Third) Torts: Remedies §22 (Am. Law Inst. Tent. Draft No. 2, 2023) (discussing types of tort cases in which damages may be available for emotional distress unaccompanied by physical harm).

Courts and the Restatement drafters also recognize special categories of cases in which emotional harm may be particularly foreseeable. Restatement (Third) of Torts: Liability for Physical and Emotional Harm §47 allows recovery for emotional harm that "occurs in the course of specified categories of activities, undertakings, or relationships in which negligent conduct is especially likely to cause serious emotional harm." The comments to the section mention cases such as those of mishandling human remains, or the presence of a "repulsive foreign object" in food, such as a condom or a rodent.

While many courts still would not allow recovery for emotional distress damages for the negligent or intentional killing of a pet (*see, e.g., Strickland v. Medlen*, 397 S.W.3d 184 (Tex. 2013)), and limit recovery to the often (negligible) market value of the pet, at least some courts have allowed plaintiffs to recover the medical costs to care for an injured pet. In *Kimes v. Grosser*, 195 Cal. App. 4th 1556 (2011), an appeals court held a jury could determine if a plaintiff whose cat the defendant shot with a pellet gun could recover up to $36,000 in medical costs to care for the cat. These damages are predicated on the emotional attachment of a person to his or her pet.

Finally, courts sometimes allow plaintiffs to recover for "dignitary" losses. A dignitary harm awards damages for an affront to the person, such as the offensive battery Charlene committed when she kissed Barry as he slept. As Dobbs and Roberts explain: "in a great many of the cases, the only harm is the affront to the plaintiff's dignity as a human being, the damage to his self-image, and the resulting mental distress." Dobbs & Roberts §7.1(1). Even without proof of emotional distress, courts sometimes allow the recovery of substantial damages "merely upon showing that the tort was committed at all." *Id.* The new Restatement (Third) Torts: Remedies §22(a)(1) (Am. Law Inst. Tent. Draft No. 2, 2023) sets forth the standards to recover for dignitary harm "if the factfinder infers significant dignitary harm and its value from the facts and circumstances of the tort itself."

EXAMPLE

Example 2

While undergoing a Caesarean section at the hospital, Emma suffered oxygen deprivation as a result of the negligence of Doctor G. The oxygen deprivation resulted in severe brain damage and left Emma in a permanent comatose condition. Can Emma recover noneconomic damages? If so, how much should she collect?

EXPLANATION

Explanation

The facts of this example are based on *McDougald v. Garber*, 536 N.E.2d 372 (N.Y. 1989). The problem is this: Suppose plaintiff is too injured to experience pain and suffering. Should compensation still be available? Plaintiff's lawyers argued that even if plaintiff could not experience emotional distress, loss of enjoyment of life was an objective loss (like the loss of a leg) that should be compensated for, even if plaintiff is not aware of the loss. Many courts accept such arguments (sometimes under the label "hedonic damages"). Some courts have accepted such arguments for an objective loss of enjoyment of life, as has the new Restatement. Restatement (Third) Torts: Remedies §20, cmt. i (Am. Law Inst. Tent. Draft No. 2, 2023). Other courts, like a majority of the *McDougald* court, rejected the argument. The majority noted the paradox under its rule that the greater the degree of brain injury inflicted by the negligent defendant, the smaller the award of damages. But the court said that this argument "has nothing to do with meaningful compensation for the victim" and is instead rooted in a temptation "to punish the defendant in proportion to the harm inflicted." The court did hold, however, that if there was evidence of *any* cognitive awareness on the part of the plaintiff, the plaintiff could recover damages for pain and suffering in an amount set by the jury.

As to the amount (assuming plaintiff has some cognitive awareness of pain), this is going to be a very difficult decision for the jury, with a very sympathetic and innocent plaintiff who suffered a terrible loss. It will be a delicate job on the part of defense lawyers to argue against a large damages award. Note that in California, the most that Emma could recover in noneconomic damages is $350,000, by statute. But if another plaintiff suffered an identical injury as the result of Doctor G.'s negligent driving, there would be no limit on the amount of noneconomic damages.

EXAMPLE

Example 3

Charlie donated blood at the local blood bank. Dave, the technician drawing the blood, accidentally drew Charlie's blood with a used needle. "Whoops," Dave said, explaining to Charlie that he should get tested for HIV (the virus which causes the disease AIDS) in six months because there was a small risk Charlie had been exposed to HIV by the used needle, and it took that long for HIV to show up in blood tests. Charlie suffered severe emotional distress for the next six months and saw a therapist regularly. Fortunately for Charlie, his blood test six months later was negative for any signs of HIV. Can Charlie recover damages? If so, for what?

Explanation

Charlie will have a strong argument for the costs of medical monitoring (including his HIV tests) to make sure that he does not have the potentially deadly disease. But those costs will be relatively low. Charlie will want to recover potentially larger damages for his emotional distress, which looks real and severe. On policy grounds, however, some courts have held that defendants cannot be liable for emotional distress damages for fear of getting a disease, unless the plaintiff can prove that she is more likely than not to actually get the disease. *Potter v. Firestone Tire & Rubber Co.*, 863 P.2d 795 (Cal. 1993). The courts are apparently concerned about a flood of suits arising from fear-of-cancer claims and similar claims related to toxic waste dumps.

Charlie could not meet the *Potter* standard with his negative HIV test result, and it looks like the damage rule, if applied in Charlie's jurisdiction, will ensure that Charlie's recovery will not restore him to the rightful position. Moreover, if Dave's conduct was only negligent, Charlie will not be able to recover punitive damages either (see Chapter 15).

Example 4

Jeff Spicoli was a student at Ridgemont High School. The school's principal saw Spicoli smoking what the principal believed, by shape and smell, to be a marijuana cigarette. Without recovering the cigarette or giving Spicoli a chance to explain himself, the principal suspended Spicoli for 20 days. Applicable constitutional precedent gives someone in Spicoli's position the right to a hearing before suspension. Spicoli suffered no emotional distress, and he did not contend he was innocent of the principal's allegations. He sued for the dignitary harm of losing his due process right to a hearing. Can Spicoli recover damages?

Explanation

This claim is somewhat distinct from the earlier claims in that here the intangible loss is not emotional distress but rather a dignitary harm—in this case, harm that occurs when a government body violated Spicoli's constitutional rights. In *Carey v. Piphus*, 435 U.S. 247 (1978), the Supreme Court held that proof of a constitutional violation entitled the student, Piphus, to nominal damages, but that he could not recover additional damages unless he could prove them (for example, prove that he suffered emotional distress). Piphus had argued the jury should be able to simply award him "presumed" damages (see section 3.4), but the Court rejected the argument. The Court distinguished cases where people have wrongly been deprived of a right to vote, approving of those cases. It makes for difficult line-drawing problems. *See* Restatement (Third) Torts: Remedies §22, cmt. i (Am. Law Inst. Tent. Draft No. 2, 2023).

3.3 SPECIAL RULES FOR WRONGFUL DEATH, SURVIVOR, AND LOSS OF CONSORTIUM ACTIONS

3.3.1 Wrongful Death

The ultimate mismatch between the rightful position standard and applicable damages rules occurs when the defendant's injury results in death. The mismatch occurs in two ways. First, there is no amount of money that most of us would ever exchange for our own lives; therefore any amount of money for wrongful death is going to be undercompensatory (especially considering that the person who has died as the result of the defendant's actions will not receive any of the money). Second, by an accident of history, wrongful death damages are statutorily limited to be less generous than the typical tort measures available to plaintiffs in cases that do not result in death. The upshot of this mismatch is that defendants often pay more damages when they seriously injure someone than when death results (hence the apocryphal morbid statement of the defense attorney, "Fortunately for my client, the plaintiff died").

I start with the history, because—as with much of the material that we will see in this book—the dead hand of history drives many of the current remedies rules that seem counterintuitive or outdated. To describe the history briefly,[6] in 1808 a judge in England rejected the husband's claim for damages when the defendant's wrongful conduct caused the death of the husband's wife, holding that the common law did not allow for such damages. *Baker v. Bolton*, (1808) 170 Eng. Rep. 1033 (K.B.). The English Parliament overruled *Baker* in 1846, but the statute doing so set forth limits on who could recover and the kind of damages allowed. The parliamentary decision precluded any further evolution of the common law, which meant that the

---

6. For more on the damages available for wrongful death, see Restatement (Third) Torts: Remedies §23 (Am. Law Inst. Tent. Draft No. 2, 2023):

> (a) Liability for wrongful death is created and governed by statute. The statutes and their interpretations vary widely, and each state's statute requires independent evaluation.
>
> (b) Except as otherwise provided by statute, a plaintiff who establishes a defendant's liability in tort for wrongful death is entitled to recover:
>
> (1) pecuniary damages, including compensation for lost financial support from the decedent, funeral and burial expenses, loss of services, and loss of inheritance, and
>
> (2) damages for loss of society, including affection, comfort, companionship, love, support, and, in the case of a marital relationship, sexual relations.

extent of plaintiffs' recovery in the case of wrongful death depended upon how the legislative body defined the scope of recovery.

Baker was accepted as precedent in many parts of the United States. Even today, the ability of a person to recover damages for the wrongful death of a family member depends upon, and is limited by, the particular state's wrongful death statute. Here is a portion of Kansas's wrongful death statute:

> (a) In any wrongful death action, the court or jury may award such damages as are found to be fair and just under all the facts and circumstances, but the damages, other than pecuniary loss sustained by an heir at law, cannot exceed in the aggregate the sum of $250,000 and costs.

KAN. STAT. ANN. §60-1903(a). Kansas has considered doubling the limit, but so far it has not done so. Note the key limiting feature here: heirs can recover for financial losses, but spouses face a cap of $250,000 on "non-pecuniary" damages, a term which the Kansas courts read as equivalent to noneconomic damages. *See Howell v. Calvert*, 1 P.3d 310, 316 (Kan. 2000). Children, as we shall see, cannot recover noneconomic damages for loss of a parent.

Kansas's wrongful death statute is generous compared to New Jersey's statute:

> In every action brought under the provisions of this chapter the jury may give such damages as they shall deem fair and just with reference to the pecuniary injuries resulting from such death, together with the hospital, medical and funeral expenses incurred for the deceased, to the persons entitled to any intestate personal property of the decedent. . . .

N.J. STAT. ANN. §2A:31-5. Note how the statute limits recovery for wrongful death only to pecuniary losses. The New Jersey Supreme Court defined pecuniary losses under this statute to include "the contributions, reduced to monetary terms, which the decedent might reasonably have been expected to make to his or her survivors," as well as "the hospital, medical and funeral expenses incurred for the deceased." *Smith v. Whitaker*, 734 A.2d 243, 248 (N.J. 1999). Moreover, punitive damages are not available under New Jersey's wrongful death statute. *Id.*

EXAMPLE

Example 5

Eric, driving home drunk from a party, runs over Ferdinand and his 8-year-old daughter Gina, killing them both. Ferdinand and Gina are survived by Henrietta (Ferdinand's wife and Gina's mother) and Isaac (Ferdinand's son and Gina's brother). Ferdinand worked as a schoolteacher, earning $60,000 per year. He was 40 years old. Henrietta and Isaac sue Eric for wrongful death, and both are emotionally devastated. Who can sue successfully? Explain.

EXPLANATION

Explanation

There is no way to confidently answer this question without knowing the state where the accident occurred and its applicable wrongful death statute. So let's consider things under the Kansas and New Jersey statutes I have provided. In Kansas, the "heirs at law" are able to recover, so you would need to consult Kansas law over who constitutes an heir. Assuming that Henrietta is an heir, she will be able to recover pecuniary damages (which will include funeral expenses for both her husband and child) and the present value of the expected support that Ferdinand would have provided to her had he not been killed by Eric. Recall from the last chapter that the jury, in computing this amount, would need to make predictions about the likely job and salary prospects for Ferdinand had he continued to work. The jury would likely start with the $60,000 per year salary and then, relying upon experts, would make certain assumptions about what Ferdinand would have earned for the rest of his working career and subtract out costs he would have incurred to support himself. The total amount of the award would then be reduced to present value.

Note that because Henrietta cannot prove with any reasonable certainty that she would have been financially supported at any time in her life by Gina had Gina not died, there would be no recovery for pecuniary damages for the death of Gina aside from funeral expenses. Henrietta would also be able to recover up to $250,000 each for non-pecuniary damages for emotional distress.

If Isaac does not count as an heir under Kansas law, he would not be able to recover anything (nor would any other relatives or close friends of Ferdinand or Gina who do not count as heirs). If he is an heir, as we'll see below in the discussion of loss of consortium claims, he can recover emotional distress damages for the death of a parent.

Things would be much the same for the surviving family members under New Jersey law, except that neither Henrietta nor Isaac could recover non-pecuniary damages in a cause of action for wrongful death. But, as we shall see, that does not exhaust the possible causes of action.

3.3.2 Survival of Personal Injury Actions

While Kansas may seem more generous than New Jersey when it comes to compensation for surviving family members of a tort victim, that's only because we have focused only on one possible cause of action, that for wrongful death. But there are other ways survivors may recover damages. Some states, like New Jersey for example, have reversed a common law rule that a personal injury action dies with the person. Consequently, surviving family members can recover damages for any pain and suffering that the tort victim suffered before his death. In New Jersey, even if a tort victim is killed instantly (and therefore suffered no pain before his death), the surviving family members can recover nominal damages for pain and suffering. Then, using those nominal damages as a hook, the surviving family members may recover punitive damages if the defendant's conduct was sufficiently bad. *Whitaker*, 734 A.2d at 253.

In Kansas, in contrast, there must be evidence of *conscious* pain and suffering before death for such damages to be recoverable in a survival action. *St. Clair v. Denny*, 781 P.2d 1043, 1049 (Kan. 1989). If there is such evidence, punitive damages may be awarded with the amount being based on the survival action only. *See Lake v. Res-Care Kansas, Inc.*, No. 98-1019-JTR, 2002 WL 32356436 (Kan. Feb. 4, 2002). This last limitation is significant because, as we shall see in Chapter 15.3, the amount of punitive damages generally must be within a single-digit ratio (that is, less than ten times) of the amount of compensatory damages. The Kansas rule would use the survival action damages as the baseline for judging the propriety of the ratio of punitive damages, which means that the punitive damage award would be much lower than an award that is pegged to damages that are recoverable in the wrongful death action as well.[7]

EXAMPLE

Example 6

Henrietta and Isaac (from Example 5) are New Jersey residents. Their lawyer, Jamie, sues Eric for wrongful death on the day before the statute of limitations runs on their claims. Jamie does not bring a survivor action, even though the evidence shows that before his death Ferdinand was in tremendous pain for a few hours after Eric ran him over. Eric, it turns out, is very wealthy. The jury awards wrongful death damages of $1 million, based upon the financial support that Ferdinand would have supplied to his surviving family members. May Henrietta and Isaac recover any other sums? From whom?

---

7. For more on the damages available in a survivor action, see Restatement (Third) Torts: Remedies §24 (Am. Law Inst. Tent. Draft No. 2, 2023):

> (a) Survival actions are created and governed by statute. The statutes and their interpretations vary widely, and each state's statute requires independent evaluation.
>
> (b) Except as otherwise provided by statute:
>
> (1) A plaintiff who establishes a defendant's liability in a survival action, for a tort that caused the decedent's death, is entitled to recover damages for the decedent's pre-death losses, including lost earnings or earning capacity (§18), medical expenses (§19), pain and suffering and emotional distress (§§20 and 21), and property damage (§30).
>
> (2) A plaintiff who establishes a defendant's liability in a survival action, for a tort that did not cause the decedent's death, is entitled to recover the damages that the decedent could have recovered if decedent had lived, but not including damages for any harm that is avoided by the decedent's death (such as pain and suffering after the date of death) or that would have resulted from the death even if no tort had been committed (such as lost earnings after the date of death). See §12(b).

Explanation

They should sue Jamie! Jamie has committed legal malpractice by failing to bring a survivor action. Not only would this have allowed Henrietta to recover for Ferdinand's conscious pain and suffering (which the jury could have valued highly), it would have given the jury a hook for the award of punitive damages against Eric, who engaged in bad conduct by driving drunk and causing the accident. As we will see in Chapter 15.3, the fact that Eric is wealthy may not be a constitutionally permissible reason to increase the amount of punitive damages, but it does suggest that Eric should be able to pay the damages. Because the statute of limitations has run, the chance to sue Eric has passed. This leaves a possible action against Jamie for failing to sue.

The broader lesson here is that lawyers bringing suit need to consider which causes of action allow for the remedies that are most advantageous for their clients. To the uninitiated looking at Henrietta and Isaac's case, it might appear that simply suing for "wrongful death" would be good enough. But, especially in this area of the law, where the dead hand of history controls so much, it is important to carefully research the right causes of action that allow for the most generous remedies for the clients.

3.3.3 Loss of Consortium Claims

One final claim that may be brought in connection with the death (and also in cases of serious injury) of a close relative is an action for "loss of consortium." Such claims compensate the surviving family member for the emotional distress that results from the death or injury of a loved one. In England, such claims are barred. In the United States, the rules on loss of consortium differ from state to state. Earlier cases tended to show a distinct gender bias, limiting recovery to husbands and fathers and disallowing recovery by wives, mothers, and children. Now, the gender bias has disappeared, and minor children are allowed to recover along with surviving spouses. *See* Restatement (Third) Torts: Remedies §25 (Am. Law Inst. Tent. Draft No. 2, 2023).[8]

8. Section 25 reads:

> (a) A plaintiff who establishes a defendant's liability in tort for loss of consortium is entitled to compensation for lost services and for loss of society, including affection, comfort, companionship, love, support, and, in the case of a marital relationship, sexual relations, resulting from the physical or emotional harm suffered by an injured family member.
>
> (b) In a case involving death, a plaintiff seeking damages for loss of consortium may obtain only one full compensation for the loss, whether in a wrongful-death action, a loss-of-consortium action, or partly in each, as the jurisdiction's rules specify.

Sometimes, a surviving spouse need not bring loss of consortium as a separate claim. Rather, the emotional distress damages (called non-pecuniary damages in this context) may be available in a statutory wrongful death action. Separate loss of consortium claims in those jurisdictions, however, might be needed in cases where a spouse is seriously injured but not killed.

In Kansas, a spouse may recover emotional distress damages (with a $250,000 cap) resulting from the injury or death of a spouse, whereas children (minor or adult) may not recover for the emotional loss resulting from injury to a parent. *Natalini v. Little*, 92 P.3d 567, 570 (Kan. 2004). Thus, children can recover loss of consortium damages for the death of a parent, but not for a parent's serious injury. (What is the logic behind that result?) *See Klaus v. Fox Valley Sys., Inc.*, 912 P.2d 703 (Kan. 1996).

In New Jersey, spouses may recover uncapped damages for loss of consortium, whereas children may not. *Russell v. Salem Transp. Co.*, 295 A.2d 862 (N.J. 1972). Moreover, parents may not recover for loss of consortium related to the death or injury of their children. *See Tynan v. Curzi*, 753 A.2d 187 (N.J. Super. Ct. App. Div. 2000).

Example 7

Jane and Kate are two women who live together as a married couple. The state they are living in did not recognize gay marriage until the Supreme Court recognized same sex marriage in *Obergefell v. Hodges*, 576 U.S. 644 (2015), but Jane and Kate never married. Jane is seriously injured in an automobile accident. May Kate recover for loss of consortium from the defendant, who caused the accident?

Explanation

The overwhelming weight of authority denies unmarried cohabitants the possibility of recovering damages for loss of consortium. Although a California court of appeal had at one point recognized the right of unmarried cohabitants to recover, the California Supreme Court rejected that precedent. *Elden v. Sheldon*, 758 P.2d 582, 589-590 (Cal. 1988). The fact that the U.S. Supreme Court has recognized that same-sex couples have a constitutional right to marry would be unlikely to help those couples who remain unmarried.

Why do the courts tend to be unwilling to extend loss of consortium claims? The *Elden* court explained why the cause of action must be "narrowly circumscribed": "We advanced as reasons for this policy the intangible nature of the loss, the difficulty of measuring damages, and the possibility of an unreasonable increase in the number of persons who would be entitled to sue for the loss of a loved one." Convincing?

Beyond fact patterns that involve non-married cohabitants, in the process of drawing lines there are always going to be examples of cases with unfair results. As explained earlier, Kansas allows children whose parents are killed by the tortious conduct of defendant to recover emotional distress damages. The state, however, allows no emotional distress damages for children whose parents are permanently disabled (even to the point of not being able to function at all as parents). In many cases, courts uphold distinctions that appear arbitrary, and they leave it to legislatures to pass statutes in this area to create more uniform rules of liability.

3.4 PRESUMED DAMAGES (DEFAMATION)

Defamation is a tort defined as "the act of harming the reputation of another by making a false statement to a third person." BLACK'S LAW DICTIONARY 448 (8th ed. 2004). Oral defamation is slander; written defamation is libel. *Id.* A plaintiff who is defamed may suffer a variety of damages, including business losses (due to a damaged reputation) and emotional distress.

As we will see in Chapter 6.1, plaintiffs ordinarily must prove that their damages are *reasonably certain* in order to be able to recover them. What is unusual about defamation is that the common law allowed plaintiffs who sued for defamation to recover damages *even if they could not prove with reasonable certainty that they suffered such damages.*[9] These "presumed damages" can be significant in particular cases. Alternatively, a plaintiff could seek proven actual damages, sometimes referred to as "special damages" in this context. These damages could include emotional distress and any proven losses due to a smeared reputation. Imagine someone falsely claiming that a mechanic is incompetent and caused an accident. It might be possible to prove damages from lost business opportunities, if it can be proven with sufficient certainty.

Why relax the certainty requirement in certain defamation actions? The idea is that damages from false statements that injure reputation are particularly hard to prove. It is not clear, however, that problems of proof in defamation actions are significantly different from problems of proof in other areas so as to justify the special rule of presumed damages in defamation cases.

Although defamation is a common law tort, the Supreme Court has ruled that the First Amendment places certain limits on the tort because

9. To be more precise, presumed damages were available only for cases of libel and for cases of "slander per se," involving. *See* DOBBS & ROBERTS, §7.2(3). The debate over the appropriateness of presumed damages in the defamation context continues today. A new Restatement project on Defamation and Invasion of Privacy may propose limiting presumed damages in defamation to nominal damages.

the threat of liability could inhibit speech that is protected by the First Amendment. This is not surprising, given the numerous defamation cases that are brought against the news media, which often raises freedom of speech and freedom of press exemptions as defenses.

The first Supreme Court case limiting the tort of defamation on First Amendment grounds held that public figures could not recover damages for defamation without proof that the defendant made a false statement with "actual malice," which means proof that the defendant made the statement either with knowledge of its falsity or with reckless disregard of the truth. *New York Times Co. v. Sullivan*, 376 U.S. 254 (1964).

These First Amendment concerns in defamation cases have come to limit certain defamation *remedies* as well. In *Gertz v. Robert Welch, Inc.*, 418 U.S. 323 (1974), the Supreme Court held that the First Amendment sometimes precluded the award of presumed damages, such as in cases where a private person sues for defamation involving a matter of public concern.[10] The Court explained the clash between defamation law and the First Amendment as follows:

> The common law of defamation is an oddity of tort law, for it allows recovery of purportedly compensatory damages without evidence of actual loss. Under the traditional rules pertaining to actions for libel, the existence of injury is presumed from the fact of publication. Juries may award substantial sums as compensation for supposed damage to reputation without any proof that such harm actually occurred. The largely uncontrolled discretion of juries to award damages where there is no loss unnecessarily compounds the potential of any system of liability for defamatory falsehood to inhibit the vigorous exercise of First Amendment freedoms. Additionally, the doctrine of presumed damages invites juries to punish unpopular opinion rather than to compensate individuals for injury sustained by the publication of a false fact. More to the point, the States have no substantial interest in securing for plaintiffs such as this petitioner gratuitous awards of money damages far in excess of any actual injury.

Id. at 349.

The Supreme Court then limited *Gertz* in *Dun & Bradstreet, Inc. v. Greenmoss Builders, Inc.*, 472 U.S. 749 (1985). There the Court upheld an award of $50,000 in presumed damages (and an additional $300,000 in punitive damages), and held that the First Amendment did not limit the award of presumed damages in defamation cases related to speech that "do not involve matters of public concern." *Id.* at 763.

10. The Supreme Court also limited the ability of plaintiffs to recover punitive damages in defamation cases involving issues of public concern.

EXAMPLE

Example 8

Helen Willing, who is mentally unstable, is protesting for several hours each day against her former attorneys, wearing a sign reading "Law-Firm of Quinn-Mazzocone Stole Money from me and sold me out to the insurance company." The statement is a false one and it constitutes defamation under state law. As the lawyer representing the law firm, are you better off trying to *prove* the firm's damages or simply seeking to get the jury to award presumed damages (if available in the jurisdiction)? Would an award of presumed damages against Willing violate the First Amendment?

EXPLANATION

Explanation

Assuming presumed damages are available, it is risky to rely solely on presumed damages because the jury will still have to be convinced that there is some damage. The more proof you can provide, the better. The problem for the law firm here is that it does not know who is going to see the sign or how the defamatory statement is going to affect the law firm's reputation. It may be possible to find potential clients who were deterred by the sign (or actual clients who fired the firm), but it seems unlikely you could find much proof that Helen Willing's tactics deterred clients from employing the firm. If you were a potential client on your way to the offices of Quinn-Mazzocone, wouldn't you think twice before going up the elevator to hire the firm?

In appropriate cases, it makes sense to provide proof of the emotional distress that the defamatory statement caused a plaintiff. In a business or legal context, however, it may be more difficult to obtain significant damages for emotional distress; lawyers might not make the most sympathetic plaintiffs, and emotional distress may not be available in a business dispute. A problem arises with non-sympathetic plaintiffs when serious emotional distress (which could be proven through direct testimony) and losses to reputation (which are difficult to prove) are both considerations. For example, suppose Willing falsely accused her lawyer of sexually harassing her and of embezzling money from her. That sort of claim could lead to serious emotional distress and difficult-to-measure reputational loss. Given the difficulty of measuring emotional loss, does it make sense that the plaintiff would have to prove his emotional distress with reasonable certainty but not his reputational loss?

Because of the difficulty of proving reputational loss in defamation cases, it might make more sense to get an injunction preventing the defendant from making defamatory statements in the future (this is especially true if the defendant would not be able to pay for the damage she may cause). Unfortunately for plaintiffs in this position, however, the First Amendment might bar that alternative remedy as well as a prior restraint on speech, a point we shall return to in Chapter 7.5. *See Willing v. Mazzocone*, 393 A.2d 1155 (Pa. 1978).

The First Amendment may limit the ability of the lawyers to get presumed damages in this case as well. It depends upon what the Supreme Court in *Dun & Bradstreet* considers to be speech that does "not involve matters of public concern." Is it of public concern whether a lawyer stole money from a client? Arguably, the answer is yes, but in the *Dun & Bradstreet* case itself, the Justices disagreed on whether a false statement in a credit report sent privately to five recipients was a statement of no public concern.

The bottom line in a case such as Willing's is that First Amendment concerns may limit the ability of defamed plaintiffs to get a remedy that will truly compensate them for losses attributable to the defamatory statement.

3.5 OTHER LIMITS ON TORT DAMAGES: PROXIMATE CAUSE AND THE ECONOMIC HARM RULE

Many first-year law students start their torts courses with *Vosburg v. Putney*, 50 N.W. 403 (Wis. 1891), a case in which an 11-year-old kicked a 14-year-old in the shin. Unfortunately for both plaintiff and defendant, plaintiff had a preexisting condition, and the kick led to a nasty bone infection that resulted in the permanent loss of the use of plaintiff's leg. Although *Vosburg* is an important case on the tort question of the intent necessary to commit the intentional tort of battery,[11] for our purposes *Vosburg* is most noteworthy for its damages rule: you take the plaintiff as you find him or her.

Also known as the thin-skulled or egg-shell plaintiff rule (think Humpty Dumpty falling off the wall), the principle is one where, when it comes to tort damages, a plaintiff can recover all of his damages, even if the *extent* of his harm was unforeseeable. As we shall see, this rule contrasts markedly with damages in contract law, where the foreseeability of the extent of the harm is usually a requirement for the recovery of damages.

The defendant in *Vosburg* certainly never intended to permanently disable the plaintiff, yet once the defendant tortiously injured the plaintiff, he became liable for the full extent of damages. Damages are likely to be substantial to compensate a child who will face pain, suffering, and disability for the rest of his life. The harshness of the thin-skulled plaintiff rule for defendants likely put pressure on tort law to limit damages in other ways, and it is to those other ways that we now turn.

---

11. The court held that intent to harm the plaintiff was not required for proof of battery, just an unconsented intentional touching.

First, we have already seen in section 3.2 that courts (and sometimes legislatures) have *limited the noneconomic damages* that some plaintiffs receive. Though in recent decades it certainly has become easier for plaintiffs to recover for such injuries, courts continue to impose—and even create—new limits on the ability of plaintiffs to recover for certain emotional distress and pain and suffering damages.

Proximate cause also functions like a limitation on damages even though it is, strictly speaking, part of plaintiff's prima facie case that she must prove in tort law. As anyone who has sat through a Torts class knows, the rules of proximate cause are confusing, contradictory, and complex. What is important for our purposes, however, is not to master the intricacies of the distinction between the directness test of the *Polemis* case[12] and the "foreseeability of type of harm" test in *Wagon Mound (No. 1)*.[13] Rather, it is to note that proximate cause holds certain acts as too "remote" or not a "substantial factor" in causing plaintiff's harm to act as a rule that limits damages, and one that does so on policy grounds. Recall Justice Andrews' famous words in his dissent in *Palsgraf v. Long Island R.R.*, 162 N.E. 99, 103 (N.Y. 1928) (Andrews, J., dissenting):

> A cause, but not the proximate cause. What we do mean by the word "proximate" is that, because of convenience, of public policy, of a rough sense of justice, the law arbitrarily declines to trace a series of events beyond a certain point. This is not logic. It is practical politics.

Indeed, Justice Andrews used this political explanation to justify a (now discredited) proximate cause rule for New York, which stated that if a defendant negligently started a fire and burned down a row of houses, the defendant would be liable to pay damages only for the first house burned. The destruction of the following houses, by contrast, was not "proximately caused" by the defendant's negligent conduct. *Id.*, discussing the rule in *Ryan v. New York Cent. R.R. Co.*, 35 N.Y. 210 (1866).

The policy behind the "one-house rule" of *Ryan* was a fear of "crushing liability": "To hold that the owner must not only meet his own loss by fire, but that he must guarantee the security of his neighbors on both sides, and

---

12. *In re Polemis & Furness, Withy & Co.*, 3 K.B. 560 (1921).

13. *Overseas Tankship (U.K.) Ltd. v. Morts Dock & Eng'g Co.*, [1961] A.C. 388 (P.C. 1961) (appeal taken from Austl.). Restatement (Third) Torts: Liability for Physical and Emotional Harm §29 may well add some much needed clarity to this area of the law by abandoning the Second Restatement's "substantial factor" test and replacing it with a rule that limits an actor's liability to harms "that result from the risks that made the actor's conduct tortious." This "harm within the risk" approach is roughly equivalent to the "foreseeability of type of harm" test adopted in the *Wagon Mound II* case.

to an unlimited extent, would be to create a liability which would be the destruction of all civilized society." *Id.* The court in *Ryan* thus placed the fear of crushing liability over the rights of the plaintiff to recovery. The court neither recognized bankruptcy law as a natural stopping point for the payment of damages, nor considered the inconsistency of this approach with the rationale behind the rule of *Vosburg* (which held defendants responsible for the full extent of damages caused to the plaintiff); rather, the *Vosburg* court held that between two parties, one of whom tortiously caused damage and the other of whom is innocent, it is fairer to put the burden of damages on the party who tortiously caused the damage.

Ryan is no longer good law even in New York, but the concern about crushing liability in tort law remains. In this regard, imagine that you are driving on one of the massive freeways that make Los Angeles famous, and because you are trying to text-message your friend while driving, you get into a fender-bender. You hit the car in front of you and get bashed from behind, and the three-car pileup you have created leads to a massive traffic jam. You cause literally hundreds of people behind you to be late for work, and they want to come after you because your negligence has led to their lost wages. (Indeed, in one of the cars behind you is a partner at the law firm where you worked as a summer associate, and you have caused her to miss a meeting that she would bill at $650 per hour.)

With this hypothetical, you may have gained a little more sympathy for the *Ryan* defendant who burned down the row of houses. Imagine if you could be liable for all the damages of everyone who was stuck in that traffic jam. It is no exaggeration to say that you might need to declare bankruptcy. Indeed, if it were the rule that those involved in an automobile accident would be liable to everyone who suffered economic harm as a result of the accident, the cost of obtaining automobile liability insurance might be prohibitive.

Fortunately for defendants who cause freeway accidents that tie up traffic, there is the *economic harm rule*. The rule provides that a plaintiff cannot recover for lost wages or other financial kinds of injury caused by a defendant's tortious conduct in the absence of physical impact resulting in personal injury or property damage.[14]

---

14. *See also* Restatement (Third) of Torts: Liability for Economic Harm §§1, 2 (Am. Law Inst. 2020), setting forth general principles for determining economic harm claims in tort. Note that these principles use the term "economic" in this case differently than the way I used it to contrast economic and noneconomic damages for purposes of limiting emotional distress and pain and suffering damage. Property damage does not count as "economic harm" for purposes of the economic harm rule, but it does count as economic damages under the rules differentiating between economic and noneconomic harm.

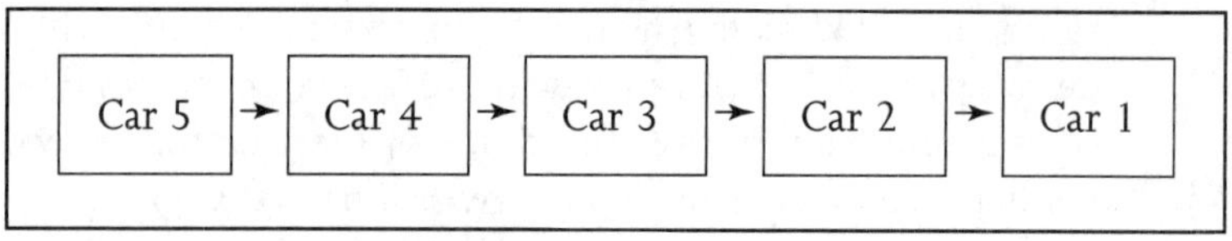

Figure 3.3 The Economic Harm Rule in Motion

To understand the application of this rule, reconsider the hypothetical using the diagram in Figure 3.3. You are the driver of Car 2. You rear-end Car 1 and then Car 3 crashes into you. Everyone agrees the accident is solely your fault. Cars 4 and 5 (not to mention cars 400 and 500) are then stuck for hours behind you on the freeway, but they were able to stop in time and were not involved in the collision. The driver of Car 3 and Car 4 work in the same office, and they are each paid $100 per hour for accounting services.

Under the economic harm rule, the drivers of Cars 1 and 3 can recover the full extent of the damages that you caused, from personal injury (whiplash anyone?) to property damage (dented bumper?) to lost wages on account of the accident. These lost wages are economic harm, but they can be *parasitic to* (that is, latch onto) the property damage and personal injury inflicted by the defendant. In contrast, the drivers of Cars 4 and 5 (and down the line), suffering neither property damage nor personal injury, cannot recover for their economic harm.

Note how this rule treats two similarly situated plaintiffs very differently. The drivers of Cars 3 and 4 both miss work because of your negligent driving. They work in the same place and get paid the same wages. But the driver of Car 3 gets to recover her economic losses because she was "lucky" enough to suffer personal injury or property damage from you as well.

What explains the economic harm rule? Again, the concern is crushing liability. The practical political concerns mentioned by Justice Andrews in his *Palsgraf* dissent animate the idea that sometimes the rightful position principle and the idea of full compensation for plaintiffs must give way for other social goods.

The economic harm rule is subject to an important exception: it does not apply when the only kind of harm a defendant can inflict upon the plaintiff is economic harm. Thus, if you go to your accountant and your accountant commits malpractice, causing you to pay a substantial tax penalty, the accountant cannot defend herself in a malpractice suit by claiming that you are only seeking compensation for economic harm. In this case, the only way that your accountant (as your accountant) can harm you is through this kind of economic harm, and if we applied the rule, accountants would virtually never be liable for accountant malpractice.

Example 9

Allied Chemical tortiously dumped a dangerous chemical into Chesapeake Bay, an area renowned for its commercial and sport fishing. The chemical caused a great deal of damage to the fish and wildlife, and as a result fishermen could not catch fish, owners of bait and tackle shops and restaurateurs lost business, and employees of the shops and restaurants were laid off. They all sue Allied. Must Allied pay for all the losses it caused?

Explanation

Although precisely how a court would sort through claims is open to question, it seems unlikely that all the people who suffered losses as a result of Allied's tortious chemical pollution would be able to collect damages. Some of the plaintiffs, such as the employees of the restaurants, would likely lose under the economic harm rule. Can you see why? They suffered no physical impact resulting in property damage or personal injury.

Other plaintiffs might lose on proximate cause grounds, on duty grounds (courts since *Palsgraf* have held that only *foreseeable plaintiffs* may recover in negligence actions), or, if they seek emotional distress damages, because of limits on those kinds of recovery.

In the actual case upon which this hypothetical is based, *Pruitt v. Allied Chem. Corp.*, 523 F. Supp. 975 (E.D. Va. 1981), Allied conceded that commercial fishermen who depended upon the sea could recover for their lost profits even though they suffered neither personal injury nor property damage (they did not own the fish in the sea). The court held that certain other classes of plaintiffs could recover (including the shop and marina owners) but that those who purchased and marketed seafood from commercial fishermen could not recover. Echoing Justice Andrews in *Palsgraf*, the court stated, "The Court thus finds itself with a perceived need to limit liability, without any articulable reason for excluding any particular set of plaintiffs."

If Allied had not conceded that it was liable to the commercial fishermen, the court could have held that Allied could escape liability to all plaintiffs under the economic harm rule. However, the court seemed concerned that strict application of the economic harm rule could create insufficient deterrence for potential defendants similarly situated to Allied. On the other hand, allowing everyone who suffered some indirect harm from Allied's spill to recover damages could indeed lead to the bankruptcy of Allied, and the inability of other companies like Allied to obtain reasonably priced insurance. It is these concerns of "practical politics" that sometimes lead courts to draw somewhat arbitrary lines in these cases.

EXAMPLE

Example 10

The negligence of the captains of two ships, the Shiras and the Tewksbury, led to a collision between them on the Buffalo River in January. After the ships collided, they drifted, with one of them barely nicking another ship, the Farr. The two damaged ships crashed into a bridge over the river, forming a dam that stopped all river traffic for the winter. Grain being hauled on the Farr spoiled and could not be unloaded, leading to a $1 million loss. Grain on another ship, the Gilles, also was lost, leading to $500,000 in spoiled cargo. The owners of both the Farr and the Gilles sue the owners of the Shiras and the Tewksbury for the value of their lost cargo. Should the court allow them to recover? Explain.

EXPLANATION

Explanation

These are the facts of a famous economic harm case, *Petitions of the Kinsman Transit Co.*, 388 F.2d 821 (2d Cir. 1968). The court there denied recovery under the economic harm rule, but it noted that the case related to the Farr was "more troublesome of the two because the Farr was struck by either the Shiras or the Tewksbury and where there is physical damage to a vessel the owner can recover for the loss of use until repairs are completed. . . . But apparently [the owners of the Farr have] not sought recovery for physical damage to the Farr." *Id.* at n.7. The footnote hints at a possible claim of legal malpractice against the lawyer for the owners of the Farr: had the lawyer sued for the relatively minor physical damage caused in the collision, it is likely that the much more substantial economic harm could have been recovered as parasitic to this property damage. For the owner of the Gilles, however, it does not appear that good lawyering could get around application of the economic harm rule. Again, the lesson is that understanding the details of the damages rules is crucial to maximizing your client's recovery or defense.

EXAMPLE

Example 11

Larry pulled into an office parking lot to visit his financial advisor, Moe. Unfortunately, as Larry was coming in, Moe negligently backed out of his parking space, crashing into Larry. Larry suffered back injuries, damage to his car, and lost wages for one month. Another of Moe's client's, Curly, who was also trying to exit the lot, was stuck behind the collision and could not exit the parking lot. Because of the collision, he missed two hours of work at his software firm, losing $200 in salary. Who can recover from Moe? In what amounts?

EXPLANATION

Explanation

Larry will be able to recover damages for his personal injury (including his pain and suffering damages, subject to state law rules), property damage, and lost wages. These lost wages are economic harm, but they are parasitic to the personal injury and property damage caused by physical impact.

As a review, make sure you understand how the court is going to value the back injury (past medical expenses plus expected future medical expenses, reduced to present value, plus noneconomic damages as allowed in the jurisdiction), the damage to the car (cost of repair or decline in market value; see Chapter 2), plus the lost wages and interest.

Curly does not get to recover for his lost wages, because he suffered no physical impact leading to personal injury or property damage. His case falls squarely into the economic harm rule exception. Curly could *not* successfully argue that the exception to the economic harm rule should apply in this case, even though he suffered economic harm caused by his financial advisor, Moe. In this case, Moe caused economic harm to Curly not *as his financial advisor* but *as a driver*. It is a mere coincidence here that Moe is Curly's financial advisor, and Moe could have just as easily caused personal injury or property damage to Curly through Moe's negligent driving.

CHAPTER 4

Contract Damages

4.1 INTRODUCTION TO CONTRACT DAMAGES: EXPECTANCY VERSUS RELIANCE

This chapter considers special issues that arise in the context of contract damages, beginning with the general measure of contract damages. As with tort damages, contract damages are concerned with restoring plaintiff to the *rightful position*, but as we shall see, courts usually measure the rightful position differently in torts and contracts cases.

Recall that when we speak of the rightful position in torts cases, we are almost always comparing the position of plaintiff before the wrong committed by the defendant (the "status quo ante," or Point B, which we set at 0) and the position of plaintiff after the wrong, Point A. See Figure 4.1.

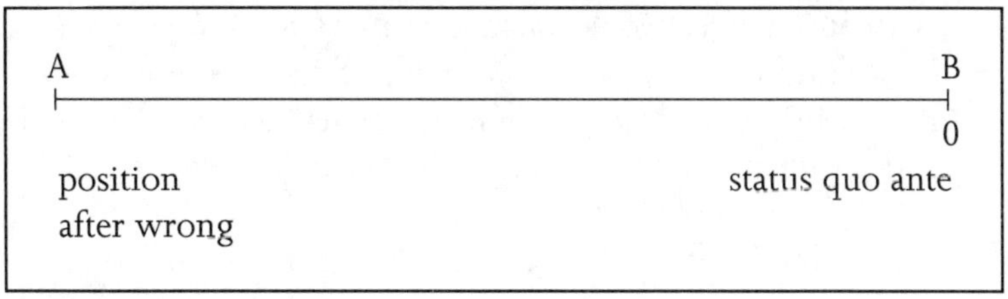

Figure 4.1

When it comes to damages in contracts, however, we are almost always comparing the position *that the plaintiff would have been in but for the wrong* ("breach") *committed by the defendant* and the position of the plaintiff after the wrong. Consider Figure 4.2.

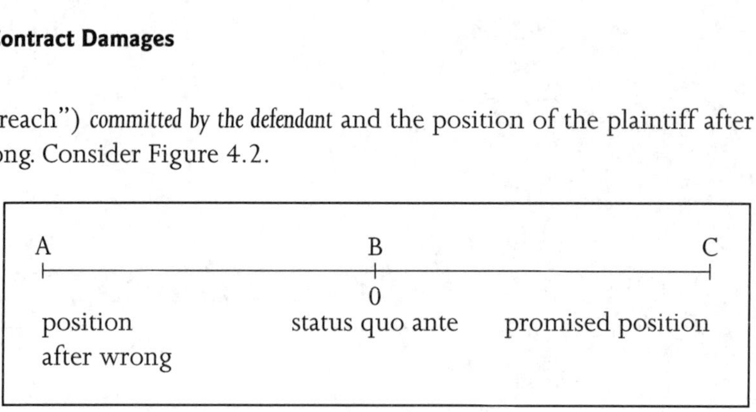

Figure 4.2

While the tort damage measure is typically (B – A), the contract damage measure is typically (C – A), or the *expectancy damages* (the difference between what was promised and what was received).

Why the difference? Consider this hypothetical. You own a window-washing business. You sign a contract with Gary's World of Glass to wash the 200 windows on the outside of Gary's showroom. Gary agrees to pay you $3,000 upon completion of the work. You pay your crew to wash the windows and buy some window-washing supplies. The total cost to you is $1,000. Your crew does a perfect job, but Gary refuses to pay, and you sue him for damages.

If we just used the regular tort measure of damages, your damages would be $1,000. You began at B, or 0, in relation to Gary. At the end of the transaction, you were out of pocket $1,000. Thus, A was –$1,000. It would take $1,000 to move you back to position B, making your damages under the tort measure $1,000.

In contract law, we would call those (B – A) damages your "reliance" damages. *In reliance on the contract with Gary*, you expended $1,000. In rare circumstances, as we will see in Chapter 5.3, courts will award plaintiffs in contracts suits only their reliance damages. But if you received merely reliance damages in this case, you likely would not feel as though you were put in the rightful position. Why not?

Imagine that Gary had not breached the contract. In that case, your account ledger would include costs of $1,000 (to perform the window-washing contract) and a payment of $3,000 from Gary's business. Thus, focusing only on this transaction, your business's net balance would have been up by $2,000—the profit you *expected* to make from the deal with Gary's World of Glass.

Contract law is about enforcing promises, and so the measure of damages *aims to put you in the same position as if the breaching party had performed the contract* (or what we might call the "rightful position" in contracts cases). This expectancy damages measure requires comparing your position after the wrong to the *promised position*—the position *you would have been in but for the defendant's breach*.

In the case with Gary, the promised position (position C in Figure 4.2) is $2,000. This represents the profit that you would have earned had Gary not breached the contract. Your total damages would be (C – A), or ($2,000 – (–$1,000)), or $3,000.

This makes sense if the law is aiming at the rightful position standard. If you received damages of $3,000 after you had spent $1,000 having Gary's windows washed, you would have a net profit of $2,000, or the same amount as if there had been no breach (putting aside issues of attorney's fees, court costs, and the time value of money, discussed in Chapter 2).

Although in this example the amount of damages is equal to the contract price, it is not always the case that expectancy damages equal the contract price. For example, as we'll see below and in Chapter 6.2, if Gary had breached the contract *before* you had performed, you would have been treated as though you had made reasonable efforts to find alternative work during that time. If you had failed to *mitigate* your damages when you had the opportunity to do so, your damages would have been below your contract price. We will see many other situations (including Examples 1 and 2) in which expectancy damages do not equal the contract price.

Supporters of expectancy damages have offered both moral and economic justifications for the practice. As a matter of morality, if people fail to keep the promises they *should* keep, then the law should require them to pay *as though* they kept their promises.[1] In contrast, "[c]ompensation based on the reliance interest would assume that it is equally acceptable to perform or withdraw the promise, and that the promisee's only right is not to be made worse off than if the promise had never been made." LAYCOCK & HASEN p. 35.

There are efficiency arguments in favor of the expectancy measure as well. Without expectancy damages, people would have less reason to count on others to keep their promises, and therefore they would not be able to plan as efficiently for the future. Imagine in your window-washing business that you did not know if your suppliers were going to show up with supplies as promised, or if your landlord was going to keep to his promises regarding maintenance of your leased space. Your employees might be wary of working for you if there were no laws backing up your promise to pay them wages for work completed. Future promises also have current value when they are backed up by expectancy damages.

Although the principle of expectancy damages is well ensconced in American law, it does have some academic critics. These critics argue that promisors should have the freedom to change their minds, or that promisees usually suffer little when a promise is broken, and therefore promisees

1. One of the leading moral arguments for contract law is found in CHARLES FRIED, CONTRACT AS PROMISE (1981).

should be able to recover no more than their reliance damages.[2] But this is by far a minority position among those who study American contract law.

Courts often give non-breaching parties the choice between reliance damages and expectation damages. This is useful for plaintiffs, especially in cases where expectation damages are hard to prove. They also could be useful in losing contracts. Many courts hold, however, that expectation damages should serve as a cap on the amount of damages one can recover. *See* RICHARD L. LORD, 24 WILLISTON ON CONTRACTS §64:5 (4th ed. 2018) ("Expectation damages usually set the upper limit of recovery because they are designed to give the plaintiff exactly what was bargained for, and no more or less."). In losing contracts, as we will see in Chapter 11.4, restitution may turn out to be the best remedy for plaintiffs when it is available.

Example 1

Assume the same facts as in the original window-washing example above except that Gary paid you half the money in advance. Upon completion of the contract, Gary refuses to pay the remaining balance. Putting aside attorney's fees, court costs, and the time value of money, what are your damages?

Explanation

This is a contract case, so we want to use our (C – A) expectancy damages measure rather than our (B – A) reliance damages measure. Thus, we need to compute the values of C and A. The value of C is the same as in the original hypothetical. You, as the owner of the window-washing company, expected a profit of $2,000 on this transaction. The value of A—the position you are in after Gary's breach—is a bit more complicated. It is sometimes useful to imagine a checkbook with money going in and out. In this variation on the window-washing hypothetical, you have costs of $1,000 and a payment from Gary of $1,500. This means that your position after the wrong is $500.

This is significant, and worth a pause. In all the examples we have seen up to this point, the plaintiff's position after the wrong, A, has been *below* B, the status quo of 0. In this case, A is above B. See Figure 4.3. Using the (C – A) formula, your damages would be $2,000 – $500, or $1,500.

---

2. One of the leading academic arguments against the expectancy measure of contract damages is found in P.S. ATIYAH, THE RISE AND FALL OF FREEDOM OF CONTRACT (1979).

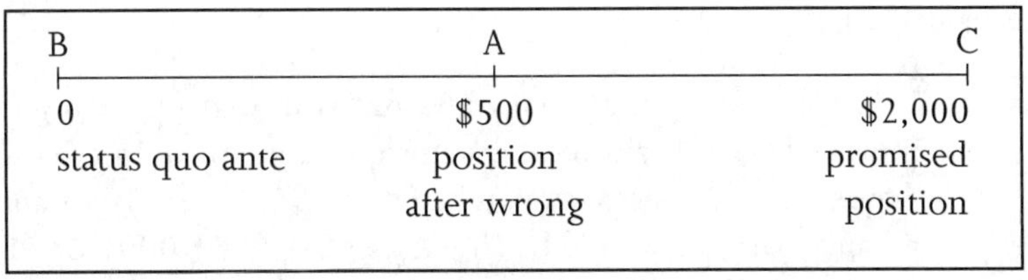

Figure 4.3

Example 2

Assume the same facts as in the original window-washing example above except that Gary breached the contract before you performed, so you incurred no costs. (To eliminate problems related to mitigation, assume that Gary did so just before you were supposed to perform, so there was no other work you could get for the appropriate time.) Gary paid you nothing in advance. Putting aside attorney's fees, court costs, and the time value of money, what are your damages?

Explanation

Because this is a contracts case, we want to use our expectancy measure of damages, (C – A). In this case, A is 0 because you have incurred no reliance costs: you have not paid for any workers to do the work, nor have you paid for any supplies. C remains at $2,000. Remember, C is *not* the contract price; it is the expected profit you stood to make had Gary kept his promise. Thus, your damages are (C – A), or $2,000.

Again, this makes sense. At the end of the day, had you performed the contract, you would have received $3,000 in payment and spent $1,000 to fulfill your end of the deal, leaving you with a profit of $2,000. The expectancy measure leaves you in exactly the same place as if there had been performance.

Example 3

If courts enforced only reliance damages and not expectancy damages, what would your damages be under the original hypothetical where you spent $1,000 to perform and Gary failed to pay you after you performed the contract? What would the reliance damages be in Example 2? What would they be in Example 1, and how does your answer in terms of Example 1 make any sense?

EXPLANATION

Explanation

Recall that reliance damages measure your damages using the (B – A) formula, where B is always the status quo ante, or 0. In the original example, A was –$1,000, because you had spent $1,000 on labor and supplies. Your reliance damages would be (B – A), or 0 – (–$1,000), or $1,000 (compare this to the $3,000 in expectancy damages from the original example).

In Example 2, (B – A) = 0. You had no reliance costs, and you therefore would recover nothing. (This compares to a recovery of $2,000 in expectancy damages.)

In Example 1, recall that you had received a $1,500 deposit, and that we computed the value of A as $500. Using the formula (B – A), the result would be something that looks like negative damages, –$500! (This compares to a recovery of $1,500 in expectancy damages.) When your damages total a negative number, it means that you are not entitled to damages.

When you think about it, this measure makes sense. Your reliance costs were $1,000, yet you received $1,500 as a deposit from Gary. So Gary's deposit more than covered your reliance losses. Indeed, if reliance were the proper measure of damages, Gary would likely be able to recover $500 from you through an action in **restitution**, covered in Part III of this book.

These three examples should have shown you how much less generous the reliance measure of damages is compared to the expectancy measure. Think about how Gary—or others in situations similar to Gary's—might be more willing to breach the contract if the usual measure of damages is reliance damages because the cost of breaching is lower.

Similarly, think about your own willingness to enter into contracts if the measure of damages was only the reliance measure. You might be less willing to enter into contracts because you will have to reduce (or "discount") the upside potential of the surplus you make from a contract by the chances that the other party is going to breach the contract. Also, though you may want to ask for payment in advance because of the chance the other party might breach, the other party knows you might breach as well, and therefore, that other party may also be less willing to make payments in advance.

EXAMPLE

Example 4

Assume the same facts as in the original window-washing example above except that Gary breached the contract after you had already spent $1,000 on the project. To complete the project, you would have had to spend an additional $2,500. What are your expectancy damages? What are your reliance damages?

Explanation

As soon as you start looking at the numbers, you will realize that this is a losing contract. Had Gary not breached the contract when he did, you would have spent $3,500 on a contract that would have yielded only a $3,000 payment. Thus, your expected position (had there been no breach) would have been a loss of $500. Your promised position in the expectancy formula is at −$500. Your position after the wrong is at −$1,000, or the amount you had spent in reliance on Gary's agreement to pay you.

Expectancy damages = (C − A) = −$500 − (−$1,000) = $500 Reliance damages = (B − A) = 0 − (−$1,000) = $1,000.

By now you should be able to see that expectancy damages put you in the same position that you would have been in had the contract been performed. Recall that if Gary had paid and you had performed, your bottom line would have been −$500 for this transaction. Similarly, if you had spent $1,000 in reliance costs and received $500 in damages, your bottom line upon recovering expectancy damages is −$500.

Because this is a losing contract, reliance damages look like a better deal for you than expectancy damages. There is, however, some authority stating that expectation damages should serve as a cap on the amount of damages one can recover. See Chapter 11.4. Under this rule, your reliance damages would be capped at the $500 expectancy damages measure.

There is another possible way for you to recover, however, depending on the rules of the jurisdiction. If you have given Gary a benefit by washing some of his windows, you might be able to recover in *restitution*. Indeed, as we will see in Chapter 11.4, non-breaching parties to losing contracts often choose restitution as a way of maximizing their recovery.

4.2 THE THEORY OF EFFICIENT BREACH

We have seen that both the moral theorists (who view contracts as binding obligations) and the economic theorists (who want the courts or legislatures to choose *efficient* legal rules) tend to favor the use of expectancy damages in contract disputes. But they take very different views on the propriety of certain breaches of contract.

Going back to our window-washing example, assume that you, rather than Gary of Gary's World of Glass, decided to breach the $3,000 window-washing contract. You did so because you have only one crew and you received a call from Wanda's World of Windows to wash the windows of their showroom on the same day, but Wanda was willing to pay you $6,000. It would cost you the same $1,000 to do the work for Wanda as it would cost for Gary.

Both the moral theorists and economic theorists agree that if you break the contract, you should have to pay expectancy damages. The difference is that the moral theorists would tell you not to break the contract because when you made the contract you undertook a moral obligation to fulfill it. The economist, on the other hand, would tell you to break the contract if it is efficient to do so.

To explain this efficiency point, let's suppose that you gave Gary a good price on the window-washing contract. When you breached the contract, Gary went out and hired a replacement window-washing company to do the job at the prevailing market rate of $3,500. (How do we know the going market rate? Look back at the discussion in Chapter 2 on market valuations.)

Gary's expectation damages are $500. Do you see why? He was promised window-washing services worth $3,500 for $3,000. Thus, his promised position (C) was $500, and he received nothing from you (though he had no reliance costs). His position after the wrong (A) is zero. Putting aside search costs to find a replacement window-washing company, his damages are $500 − 0, or $500. This puts Gary in the same position he would have been in had the contract been performed. He spent $3,500 to have his windows washed. Now his windows are washed, and after receiving the $500 in damages from you, his total cost is $3,000, exactly the position he would have been in but for your breach.

But now think about your ledger. Had you kept your end of the bargain with Gary, you would have made a profit of $2,000 (remember, you had $1,000 in expenses on a $3,000 contract). If you break the contract and wash Wanda's windows, your total profit will be $4,500, which is $2,500 better than if you had kept your promise. Why $4,500? Again, you have $1,000 in expenses, but this time you are working on a $6,000 contract. That gives you $5,000 profit. You then have to pay damages of $500 to Gary, which leaves you with an overall balance of $4,500.

You can now see why an economist would think that breach makes sense in this case. It is efficient. Note that Gary is no worse off (putting aside the aggravation that comes from the lawsuit), and you are much better off.[3] In the meantime, your services have gone to the highest-valued user, or Wanda in this case. An economist would call this an *efficient breach* and would encourage you to do it. (The moralist, as we have said, would discourage the breach because it requires you to break your word.)

Not all breaches are efficient—but when the market works well with enough competition we won't see many inefficient breaches. In our latest

---

3. Under the Kaldor-Hicks notion of efficiency (see Chapter 2), it is not required that Gary not be made worse off—it is only required that the gains to the winners exceed the losses to the losers. The fact that no party is made worse off means the transaction is also "Pareto efficient."

window-washing hypothetical, imagine that everything is the same except that you break the contract with Gary to do the job for Wanda at a cost of $3,100. When you break the contract, Gary is entitled to $500 for the breach. You take in $3,100 from Wanda, pay $1,000 in expenses, and then pay $500 to Gary, leaving you with $1,600. Remember, if you did not breach, you would have ended up with an overall profit $2,000.

Thus, if you understand these numbers, you would never choose to breach the contract with Gary *unless the additional amount you could make under the new contract exceeds the amount of damages you will need to pay to the non-breaching party.* In this case, Wanda would have to be offering more than $500 above Gary's contract price (and in the real world, probably considerably more than that if you care about your reputation) for it to be worthwhile for you to breach the contract.

Although the idea of efficient breach permeates current thinking about contract law, it is based on some unrealistic expectations. In Robert E. Scott, *Contract Design and the Shading Problem*, 99 Marquette L. Rev. 1, 10-11 (2015) (emphasis added), Professor Scott, one of the main thinkers behind the theories of efficient breach, in a major article with Professor Goetz, recognized that the theory may not work well in the real world:

> It was a nice try but, in fact, the theory does not fit the data very well. There are very few examples in the case law of an efficient breach in which one party has chosen not to perform and instead offered to pay the expectation damages that are subsequently assessed by a court. What commercial parties do who wish to reserve an option on the contract performance is to stipulate in the contract an exercise price for the option to terminate and walk away from the contemplated exchange. The option may take the form of "break up" fees, a stipulated damages clause, or a term that permits one party to terminate, cancel, return, or redeem goods. What parties do not do, however, is to leave the exercise price to be determined at the discretion of a court following a declaration of contract breach. In that sense, *efficient breach is both a null set as well as an oxymoron*. So, while we meant well, Goetz and I are probably primarily responsible for leading a generation of scholars down the wrong garden path.

Example 5

Use the same facts as in the original example in this section: you have a binding contract with Gary, and Wanda offers you $6,000 to do the same work for her instead of Gary. Gary, however, is one of your best repeat customers. Is it efficient for you to breach the contract with Gary? Even if it is efficient, what reasons would you have *not* to breach the contract with him?

EXPLANATION

Explanation

At first glance it appears efficient to breach the contract because the economic gains to the winners exceed any losses to the losers (and indeed, if damages are perfectly compensatory, Gary is made no worse off and you are made better off). But there are two reasons why you might choose not to breach the contract with Gary despite the efficiency of doing so. First, knowing Gary as you do, you might feel a moral obligation not to breach the contract. But even if you lack these moral scruples, it may not be in your economic interest to do so. Looking solely at the single transaction, it appears to make economic sense for you to breach. But if you have a long-term relationship with Gary, breaching now might harm your reputation with Gary as someone who keeps promises. Without that reputation, Gary might look to other businesses than yours next time he needs window-washing services. In other words, the economic theory posits that Gary is indifferent between your performance and substitute performance from another vendor so long as you pay damages to compensate him for the lost value of the contract. But in the real world, Gary would probably be far from indifferent, particularly if he knows that you breached the contract to take a better deal. The human factor in breaching a contract is relevant, whether one cares about the morality of breaking a contract or only about pure economic gain. If the reputational costs of breaching exceed the benefits of breaching, it would be inefficient to breach.

4.3 CONSEQUENTIAL DAMAGES

Recall the defendant in *Vosburg v. Putney* (the "thin-skulled plaintiff" case in Chapter 3.5) who was unlucky enough to kick another child who had a preexisting medical condition. The kick, which should have led to a small bruise and no lawsuit, led instead to the plaintiff's loss of use of that leg and the defendant's facing a huge damage judgment.

The tort rule is that a defendant is liable to the plaintiff for all damages proximately caused by defendant's conduct, whether or not those damages are foreseeable.[4] If this rule applied in contracts as well, it potentially could greatly increase the cost of contracting.

To understand why, consider the classic English case of *Hadley v. Baxendale* [1854] 9 Exch. 341, which you probably encountered in your Contracts class. The plaintiff operated a mill. The crankshaft at the mill broke, shutting

4. This is something of an oversimplification, of course. As we saw in the last chapter, sometimes proximate cause (scope of liability), the economic harm rule, or some other tort limitation allows defendants to escape liability for some damage that they cause.

down the mill. The plaintiff contracted with the defendant to bring the crankshaft to the engineers for repair. The defendant was late in delivering the crankshaft, breaching the contract. The mill was closed for a few extra days because of the late delivery, and the mill lost profits. Plaintiff tried to recover the lost profits caused by the defendant's breach. Just like the defendant in *Vosburg*, who was unlucky enough to kick the leg of the fragile plaintiff, the defendant in *Hadley* was unlucky enough to breach a contract with an economically fragile plaintiff.

The *Hadley* court, however, chose a different path from the one used by the *Vosburg* court. It set forth the following rule:

> Where two parties have made a contract which one of them has broken, the damages which the other party ought to receive in respect of such breach of contract should be such as may fairly and reasonably be considered either arising naturally, i.e., according to the usual course of things, from such breach of contract itself, or such as may reasonably be supposed to have been in the contemplation of both parties, at the time they made the contract, as the probable result of the breach of it.

The court then held that the plaintiff could not recover lost profits because they were not sufficiently foreseeable:

> Here it is true that the shaft was actually sent back to serve as a model for a new one, and that the want of a new one was the only cause of the stoppage of the mill, and that the loss of profits really arose from not sending down the new shaft in proper time, and that this arose from the delay in delivering the broken one to serve as a model. But it is obvious that, in the great multitude of cases of millers sending off broken shafts to third persons by a carrier under ordinary circumstances, such consequences would not, in all probability, have occurred; and these special circumstances were here never communicated by the plaintiffs to the defendants.[5]

The "rule" of *Hadley* thus divides the world of contract damages into those that are "natural," for which the plaintiff may recover, and those that are "consequential," for which plaintiff may recover only if the damages are sufficiently "foreseeable."

The dividing line between these "natural" damages (more commonly referred to as "general" damages) and consequential damages may at times

5. This portion of the opinion seems to contradict the beginning of the case, which reports, "The plaintiffs' servant told the [defendant's] clerk that the mill was stopped, and that the shaft must be sent immediately. . . ." *Hadley v. Baxendale*, [1854] 9 Exch. 341. *See also* Donald C. Langevoort, *Agency Law Inside the Corporation: Problems of Candor and Knowledge*, 71 U. Cinn. L. Rev. 1187, 1188 n.9 (2003): "*Hadley v. Baxendale* is confusing on its facts because of an inconsistency as to whether the railroad 'knew' of the factory's special needs. Its agent was apparently told, but it was unclear at that time whether that was sufficient notice to the principal."

not be crystal clear. Professors Dobbs and Roberts provide a good first cut at the distinction: "General damages measure the loss in the very thing to which the plaintiff is entitled. . . . Consequential damages measure something else; not the very thing the plaintiff was entitled to but income it can produce or losses it can avoid." DOBBS & ROBERTS §3.3(4).[6]

For example, if you break the contract with Gary to wash his windows, the loss of value on the contract constitutes his general damages. In the example above, those general damages are $500, or the difference between the price you were offering to do the job for ($3,000) and the going market rate for the transaction ($3,500). There are likely no consequential damages in this example. But suppose that Gary cannot get the replacement window washers to do the job for three days. In the interim, Gary loses sales from three customers, who come to his showroom and decide not to purchase windows because they are turned off by the dirty windows in Gary's store. These lost sales would be consequential damages—damages which Gary would not be able to recover from you unless they were foreseeable at the time of contracting, that is, unless you knew (or reasonably should have known) at the time of contracting that Gary would suffer these losses because of your breach.[7] If you knew about these potential losses at the time of contracting, you might have decided to charge Gary a higher premium to compensate for the increased risk you faced for breaching the contract.

Hadley sets forth *a default rule* that breaching parties are not liable for special losses plaintiff may suffer by virtue of the breach absent evidence the defendant knew (or perhaps should have known) of the danger of plaintiff suffering these special losses. This is a default rule because it is the rule that is in place unless the parties *bargain around it*. (The next section of this chapter discusses liquidated damages and other ways that parties may bargain around contractual remedies.) The default rule on consequential damages may lower the cost of contracting by picking the rule that most contracting parties would likely agree to if they actually bargained over it. Indeed, it has become common for parties to put a "no consequential damages" clause in their standard form contracts just to be sure that there won't be a claim later that the defendant actually knew of the special losses plaintiff would suffer in the event of defendant's breach. Here is language from a FedEx shipping contract:

> WE WILL NOT BE LIABLE FOR ANY DAMAGES, WHETHER DIRECT, INCIDENTAL, SPECIAL OR CONSEQUENTIAL, IN EXCESS OF THE DECLARED

6. Section 4.5 below discusses the Uniform Commercial Code's definition of consequential damages.

7. Even if the consequential damages in this circumstance were sufficiently foreseeable, Gary might have a problem proving the damages with reasonable certainty, a requirement we discuss in Chapter 6.1. Note also that special damages have to be specifically stated in a complaint in federal court. *See* FED. R. CIV. P. 9(g).

> VALUE [OF A SHIPMENT] . . . WHETHER OR NOT WE KNEW OR SHOULD HAVE KNOWN THAT SUCH DAMAGES MIGHT BE INCURRED, INCLUDING, BUT NOT LIMITED TO LOSS OF INCOME OR PROFITS.

If "no consequential damages" is the default rule for contracts claims, why is it not also the default rule for torts claims? The reason is that most torts do not involve a voluntary transaction entered into by two willing parties (think of the plaintiff in *Vosburg* who received the kick in the leg). In the world of torts, the costs of bargaining—what economists call transaction costs—are exceptionally high, so the parties will not bargain around any default rules. Thus, the choice of default rules matters a great deal in torts (much more than in contracts). The law chooses a rule allowing consequential damages in torts (the thin-skulled plaintiff rule) that arguably most of us would choose if transaction costs for torts were not so high.

The rule regarding consequential damages in contracts is subject to an important exception. Let's return for a moment to our original window-washing hypothetical where Gary breaches his promise to pay you $3,000 after you wash the windows perfectly.

We're going to add a few more facts to this fact pattern. Suppose that before you entered into the contract, you said to Gary: "It's a good thing for me that we've signed this contract. If I don't get this payment from you right after my crew washes your windows, I won't have enough money to pay my business rent and I'll be kicked out of my office." After Gary failed to pay for your services as promised, you are evicted from your office, thereby losing a great deal of other business.

In addition to suing Gary for general damages under the contract for the contract price that he owes you (the difference between what was promised and received, here $3,000), you may also consider suing him for the lost profits that resulted, arguing that they were consequential damages caused by Gary's nonpayment. It would be hard for Gary to claim that these damages were unforeseeable because *you specifically told him about the losses you would incur* if he failed to pay the contract on time. Thus, it looks like Gary could be on the hook to you for a lot more than the $3,000 contract price.

Fortunately for Gary (but unfortunately for you), the rule regarding consequential damages in contracts is subject to an important exception: when the only breach of contract is the nonpayment of money, the non-breaching party may not be able to recover for consequential damages. Instead, the non-breaching party may recover only the general damages (the unpaid money) plus interest at the prevailing legal rate of interest. *See Meinrath v. Singer Co.*, 87 F.R.D. 422 (S.D.N.Y. 1980).

The exception for nonpayment of money is itself subject to some exceptions, the most important being a suit by an insured against an insurer for a bad faith refusal to pay policy benefits. "The insured has no claim merely for failure to pay or delay in payment. But if the insurer refuses or delays in bad faith, knowing that it is liable, plaintiff can sue not only for interest but also for consequential damages, including emotional distress, and for punitive damages." *See* LAYCOCK & HASEN p. 50. The law treats these cases as torts, and not merely as breaches of contract, allowing for the recovery of consequential damages.

Do these distinctions make sense? If the true test for consequential damages in contracts cases is foreseeability, why shouldn't Gary have to pay you for those additional damages that were clearly foreseeable at the time of contracting—especially when you may well have to pay him for consequential damages you cause if you breach the contract? Perhaps the concern is that there would end up being many more disputes over what was "foreseeable" in cases involving the nonpayment of money than in other cases. Should a concern over the administrability of the rule allow the courts to treat you and Gary differently?

Perhaps the easiest way to deal with cases involving the nonpayment of money is to assume that non-breaching parties who are not paid will simply go out and borrow money from someone else to cover their expenses until the breaching party pays damages. One problem with this theory is that some of these non-breaching parties, who may be in dire financial straits, won't be able to borrow money or will have to borrow money at rates of interest higher than the prevailing rate (because they are bad credit risks). Note that non-breaching parties who must pay the higher rate of interest often cannot recover it. *See id.*

Why the exception to the exception in the bad faith insurance cases? This distinction may be easier to understand if one views insurance contracts as special: plaintiffs arguably are especially vulnerable, or plaintiffs are "buying peace of mind" rather than simply entering into business arrangements. Still, there's no denying that the rule, exception, and exception to the exception in the case of consequential damages will end up treating similarly situated non-breaching parties differently.

More generally, while the usual rule is that emotional distress damages are not available in contract, they may be available when the law treats the breach of contract like a tort (as in the insurance bad-faith cases). Some courts also allow them in other situations where emotional distress damage is particularly foreseeable. For example, in *Floyd v. Video Barn, Inc.*, 538 So. 2d 1322 (Fla. Dist. Ct. App. 1989), an appeals court held that a suit could go forward against a wedding videography company that recorded the wrong wedding and deprived the plaintiffs of wedding pictures. Although the court held that emotional-distress damages were not allowed for breach of contract, plaintiffs could also sue in tort for negligence and thereby recover such damages. But in *Sagnia-Blythe v. Gamblin*, 160 Misc. 2d 930 (Civ. Ct. N.Y. 1994), a court refused to allow emotional-distress damages where a custom dressmaker delivered bridesmaid dresses two hours late to a wedding and not in the promised condition. The court did allow damages for additional wedding costs associated by the delay, and it rejected a claim for intentional infliction of emotional distress, as it found the conduct not sufficiently outrageous under substantive tort law.

Example 6

Helena was moving to Chicago from Nashville. While in Chicago, she signed a contract with Ivan to rent an apartment at the rate of $1,500 per month for a year, beginning immediately. She told Ivan she would return to Nashville and transport her household items immediately. Helena returned to Nashville, packed up her things, and had a moving truck transport her stuff from Nashville to Chicago for $4,000. When Helena arrived in Chicago, she found that Ivan had rented the apartment to someone else for $2,200 per month for a year. Helena checked into a hotel for a week, at a rate of $125 per night. She put her stuff in storage for $300. After diligently searching for another apartment, she found one comparable to the one she had agreed to rent from Ivan for $2,000 a month. She signed a year lease at the new apartment. She sued Ivan for breach of contract. The court agreed that Ivan breached the contract and owed Helena damages. How much is Helena entitled to receive in damages? Explain.

Explanation

You can see here that there are going to be both general damages (for the loss of the apartment) and a host of consequential damages attributable to the breach. We begin with the general damages in an effort to figure out the promised position (C) of Helena.

Helena had a contract to rent an apartment for $1,500 per month that arguably had a market rate of $2,000 per month. (The $2,200 contract price for the apartment is some contrary evidence of the market rate, but it may be that the new renters are paying over the contract price. The facts tell you that $2,000 is the market rate for this type of apartment.) Helena thus was expecting $500 per month in gains ($2,000 market rate − $1,500 contract rate) for 12 months, or $6,000. Those are her general damages.

The next question is whether Helena may be able to recover *consequential damages*. Because this is a contracts case rather than a torts case, Helena may recover only consequential damages that were *reasonably foreseeable* to the contracting parties at the time of contract formation. Helena told Ivan that she was moving her stuff from Nashville, with the expectation that she could have moved in immediately. Arguably the jury will find that the additional damages that Helena suffered because of Ivan's breach were reasonably foreseeable to the parties.

In thinking about consequential damages, we are asking how Helena has been made worse off *because of the breach*. The best way to approach a problem like this is to look at all the potential damages items and ask separately whether each one is recoverable:

a. $4,000 *in moving expenses*. These are *not* recoverable. Helena would have paid this same amount whether or not Ivan breached, as it is the cost of moving from Nashville to Chicago. There's no indication that it cost her more for this transportation because of the breach.
b. *One week's hotel stay at $125 per night*. These damages likely *are* recoverable as compensatory damages. Because of Ivan's breach, Helena was out of pocket $875 in hotel bills, money she would not have had to pay but for Ivan's breach.
c. $300 *in storage expenses*. This item as well appears to be a consequential damages amount that Helena would not have incurred but for the breach. Had Ivan kept his promise, Helena would have moved into the first apartment immediately and avoided this extra expense.

Helena's position after the wrong (A) is −$1,175 ($875 in hotel expenses and $300 in storage costs). Her expectancy damages are (C − A), or $6,000 − (−$1,175), or $7,175.

Example 7

The Oregon Bank promised to loan Doyle and one of his businesses $1 million. At the time of the loan, the bank was aware that Doyle was in a distressed financial condition. The bank knew that at the time Doyle applied for the loan, Doyle had been unable to secure other financing. After the bank agreed to lend the money, bank officers reversed the decision. Doyle was unable to obtain a loan elsewhere, and as a result, he was unable to harvest timber on his property, losing profits of $10,000. Is Doyle entitled to recover for the lost profits?

Explanation

In this case, the lost profits would be a claim for consequential damages. One hurdle the plaintiff would face is that these consequential damages might not have been sufficiently foreseeable by the defendant. While it appears foreseeable that Doyle would have faced a business default if he did not receive the loan, it does not appear that the bank had specific information about this particular loss.

Even putting aside the question of foreseeability, there is the question whether a breach of a contract to *lend* money falls into the same category as the breach of a contract to *pay* money, for which the only kind of consequential damages available is the payment of interest at the prevailing legal rate. In *Doyle v. Oregon Bank*, 764 P.2d 1379 (Or. Ct. App. 1988), an Oregon appellate court refused to decide whether a plaintiff in Doyle's circumstances could recover damages for defendants' breach of a loan contract. Laycock and Hasen report that a majority of courts allow the recovery of consequential damages for breach of a loan agreement, provided the damages are sufficiently foreseeable. So here's another exception to the exception.

4.4 LIQUIDATED DAMAGES AND OTHER CONTRACTUAL LIMITATIONS ON REMEDIES

In the discussion of consequential damages above, I introduced the concept (which you likely already know from your Contracts course) of the *default rule*. This rule governs parties' contracts absent an express agreement otherwise. The excerpted FedEx provision above—which disclaims liability for consequential damages whether or not FedEx knew of a sender's specific needs to have a package delivered by a certain time—is an example of a contractual provision overriding a default rule.

Contractual provisions that alter default contractual remedies are fairly common. In addition to consequential damages disclaimers, contracts often contain attorney's fees provisions (providing that the winner must pay the loser for attorney's fees), and sometimes contracts contain other limitations on remedies besides consequential damages.

As with any provision of a contract, a clause changing the remedies available to the non-breaching party may be challenged in that particular case as unconscionable or as against public policy. You may recall from your Contracts class that parties can raise *procedural* unconscionability claims and, in some cases, *substantive* unconscionability claims. Procedural claims look at *how* the clause was presented to the party. A one-sided remedies provision buried in the fine print of an adhesion contract (a contract offered on a take-it-or-leave-it basis without the opportunity for negotiation, like the FedEx contract) could be struck down on procedural unconscionability grounds. To avoid such claims, contract drafters would do well to make sure that onerous remedies provisions are prominent in a contract and written in easy-to-explain language.

More difficult to make are arguments against limitations on remedies based on substantive unconscionability. These are claims based not upon *how* the parties bargained around a default remedies rule, but on the *fairness* of the bargain. For example, the California Supreme Court struck down, on substantive unconscionability grounds, a provision in an employment agreement that required employees to arbitrate their wrongful termination claims against the employer, but did not require the employer to arbitrate claims it may have had against the employees. *Armendariz v. Found. Health Psychcare Servs., Inc.*, 6 P.3d 669 (Cal. 2000). You can find more on unconscionability in Chapter 18.1.

Sometimes, limitations on the form of contract remedies are set by statute rather than by court decision. For example, Article II of the Uniform Commercial Code, which we will consider in more detail in the next section, provides that limitations on consequential damages for personal injury caused by consumer goods are prima facie unconscionable, while limitations for commercial losses are not. U.C.C. §2-719(3). To give another example, a California statute states that if a contract provides for only one side to receive attorney's fees if it prevails in a dispute arising from the contract, the contract is to be read so that it applies to *both* parties to the contract. CAL. CIV. CODE §1717.

Among the most important provisions parties use to contract around default remedies provisions are "liquidated damages provisions." These are provisions that, in the event of a breach by one of the parties, actually set the amount (or provide some formula or benchmark for setting the amount) of damages to the exclusion of jury-determined damages under the usual rules.

For example, Dana contracts with the state to build a highway. The contract provides that Dana will be paid $5 million for her work, and that the work is due January 1, 2012. It also provides that for every month Dana is late, she must pay the state $100,000 in damages. Dana is three months late. The state pays her only $4.7 million, deducting $300,000 under the contract's liquidated damages provision. Dana claims that the state suffered damages that were less than this $300,000 amount, and argues that the liquidated damages provision is unenforceable.

Before considering whether courts would hold the clause unenforceable, let's first ask *why* the state might have wanted this provision. Two reasons to include the clause are to *coerce Dana's performance, and to punish her for late performance.* If Dana knows she faces a sure $100,000 loss for each month that she is late, she's likely to want to do her best to get the contract completed on time.

This "coercion" is not necessarily unfair to Dana. Presumably, Dana and the state entered into this contract freely. Dana probably was able to demand something in exchange for her agreement to the provision. She may have received a promise of more money, which she could have used to pay extra workers to have made sure that the work was completed on time.

Another reason the state may have wanted the liquidated damages provision included in the contract is that computing actual damages in this case is likely to be difficult. *Liquidated damages clauses can remove uncertainty about how jurors are going to value the benefits of a contract.* How much does a state lose when one of its highways does not open on time? It is going to be hard to put a fixed figure on it, especially given the requirement that plaintiffs prove their damages with reasonable certainty (more on that in Chapter 6.1). Neither party can be sure about the extent of liability should Dave be late on the contract.

Given these benefits of liquidated damages provisions, it is puzzling why courts traditionally have been reluctant to enforce them. Courts may have viewed them as an encroachment on the power of the judiciary to set a remedy. RESTATEMENT (SECOND) OF CONTRACTS §356(1) sets forth the more modern view:

> Damages for breach by either party may be liquidated in the agreement but only at an amount that is reasonable in the light of the anticipated or actual loss caused by the breach and the difficulties of proof of loss. A term fixing unreasonably large liquidated damages is unenforceable on grounds of public policy as a penalty.

Thus, the modern law draws a distinction between enforceable and unenforceable liquidated damages provisions based upon the reasons the parties included the provision in the contract. If the reason is coercion or punishment (which might be evidenced by an "unreasonably large" liquidated damages provision), the clause is impermissible; if the clause is a good faith attempt to set the amount of compensatory damages, it is permissible. Of course, drawing the line between these two reasons is sometimes going to be difficult in practice, meaning that the parties are going to have to litigate over the enforceability of the liquidated damages clause. The irony is that under the Uniform Commercial Code, or U.C.C., the parties are going to have to introduce evidence of actual or anticipated damages, the very thing they were trying to avoid by including the provision in the contract in the first place.

Under this standard, a case like the highway construction case will be an easy one so long as the amount of damages is not extraordinarily large. *See Dave Gustafson & Co. v. State*, 156 N.W.2d 185 (S.D. 1968).

But note the paternalism of the rule: suppose the state agrees to pay Dana a generous amount for the contract in exchange for an exorbitant penalty provision in the contract to ensure Dana completes the work on time. Under the Restatement and *Dave Gustafson & Co.*, this limit is unenforceable, even if both parties went into the contract with their eyes open, and even if they explicitly bargained over the penalty provision in the contract. When a liquidated damages clause is unenforceable, non-breaching parties may recover remedies under default contract law rules.

Given this paternalism, some states are now more likely to treat liquidated damages provisions more like other contractual provisions, striking them down only if they are unconscionable or violate some other established contract law principle. *Commercial Real Estate Investment LLC v. Comcast of Utah II Inc.*, 285 P.3d 1193 (Utah 2012).

There is one other important damages limitation issue, one that arises most commonly under Article 2 of the U.C.C.: what happens when a limitation on a remedy "fails in its essential purpose"? We discuss that in the final section of this chapter.

EXAMPLE

Example 8

Assume the same facts as in our original Dana versus State hypothetical (involving the highway contract) except that the state wants to use a large amount of money to coerce Dana's compliance instead of running afoul of the standards for the enforceability of liquidated damages provisions. The state still wants the highway completed by January 1, 2024. The parties therefore include the following provision in their contract: "Dana shall finish all work by March 1, 2024, at a rate of $3 million. In the event Dana finishes early, she shall receive a bonus of $1 million per month that she completes the job before the deadline, with a maximum bonus of $2 million."

Is this clause enforceable? If so, does it accomplish the same purposes as the original liquidated damages provision?

EXPLANATION

Explanation

This clause would likely be held enforceable because it gives a *bonus* for early performance rather than a penalty for late performance. The prohibition on penalty clauses does not apply because there is no penalty for late performance. In some ways, the original penalty provision and the bonus provision are equivalent: Dana ends up with $5 million under either provision if she finishes building by January 1, 2024. But in other ways they are not equivalent. Under the original provision, Dana would be in breach of contract on January 2, 2024, but under the bonus provision there would be no breach until *March* 2, 2024. More generally, the bonus provision can provide only a carrot (an incentive) and not a stick (a penalty). If Dana is running *really* late, and doesn't have the highway completed on March 2, 2024, the contract's bonus provision does nothing to motivate her to finish on time. In contrast, the original penalty provision adds damages for each time period that Dana is late.

EXAMPLE

Example 9

James contracts with Kika, a contractor, to remodel James's kitchen. It is very important to James that the work be completed by June 1, because he is planning on having his boss and the firm's most important client over for a fancy dinner party on June 10. James tells Kika how urgent it is that the work be done on time. James says to Kika: "My job depends on it!" James and Kika draft up a contract for Kika to undertake the remodeling for $20,000, with the following provision: "Time is of the essence with this contract. If this contract is not completed by June 1, Kika will pay damages of $1,000, with the damages to double each day that Kika is late." Kika completes the kitchen on June 15. James, who was unable to have the dinner party at his house because Kika was late on the contract, is fired by his boss for this reason. A court finds that Kika has breached the contract by being late. To what damages is James entitled?

EXPLANATION

Explanation

The provision in the contract will undoubtedly be struck down as unenforceable in those states adhering to the traditional rule on penalty provisions in liquidated damages clauses because it will be seen as too harsh of a penalty. After 14 days, the penalty of $1,000, doubled every day, would have multiplied to $8,192,000! Obviously, the purpose of the clause was to coerce Kika's timely performance, but once the clause has failed to do so, the courts won't allow such a harsh result.

If the courts strike down the liquidated damages provision as unenforceable, James will be able to recover his regular contract damages. First, consider the promised position, C. The difference between what was promised and what was received was James's being able to get into his kitchen 14 days earlier. This will be hard to value. Perhaps James can point to the extra amounts of money he spent eating at restaurants during that period rather than eating at home.

But James is also going to want to recover for consequential damages (assuming the contract does not have a provision barring such consequential damages in the event the contractual, liquidated damages provision is struck down—a clause always worth considering for addition to a contract if you are drafting one). In this case, James is going to claim that the loss of his job was directly attributable to Kika's breach in being late with the kitchen remodel. Under the rule from *Hadley*, it appears that Kika could be on the hook for these extra damages because James specifically told Kika he could lose his job if his kitchen was not ready in time. Perhaps Kika took this as an exaggeration, or a jury, seeing the potential harshness of making Kika liable for James's loss of a job, may hold that such losses were not sufficiently foreseeable to allow James to recover for these damages.

4.5 CONTRACT DAMAGE ISSUES UNDER ARTICLE 2 OF THE UNIFORM COMMERCIAL CODE

[*Note:* This section goes into more detail than many instructors do in a Remedies course. You may want to skip it or just read the sections that pertain to issues covered in your course. But even if you are not responsible for these issues in your course, reading about the U.C.C.'s approach should help you understand the general issues in the course, as well as important material that could well be on your state's bar exam.]

Article 2 of the Uniform Commercial Code governs the sale of goods in all states in the United States.[8] It governs every domestic sales contract involving

8. Louisiana has adopted parallel provisions to the U.C.C. in its civil code. *See* Robert K. Rasmussen, *The Uneasy Case Against the Uniform Commercial Code*, 62 LA. L. REV. 1097, 1097 n.1 (2002). Though the U.C.C. Article 2 provisions are mostly uniform across the states, there

a moveable good, from a stick of bubble gum to a supercomputer. In this, the final section of this chapter, we consider the specific U.C.C. damage rules.

4.5.1 Buyers' Remedies

U.C.C. §2-711 sets forth the general rule on buyers' remedies. These remedies include the possibility (set forth in §2-716) that the buyer might obtain an injunction (order of specific performance) from a court requiring the seller to deliver the goods to the plaintiff, but we put off discussion of this equitable remedy until Part II of this book. At this point, we consider only U.C.C. Article 2 damages remedies.

Section 2-711 gives the buyer a choice of two damages remedies when the seller has failed to make delivery, repudiated the contract, or delivered goods that the buyer had rightfully rejected because they did not conform to the contract. Under either measure the buyer is *entitled to a refund of any funds paid to the seller* in addition to further damages.

(1) Cover. Under §2-712, a buyer can "cover" by making a good faith purchase of substitute goods without unreasonable delay. If the buyer makes such a good faith purchase, the buyer is entitled to the difference between the cover price and the contract price, together with incidental and consequential damages, less expenses saved as a consequence of seller's breach.

So the §2-712 formula is:

Amounts toward the purchase price paid to seller + (cover price − contract price) + incidental and consequential damages − expenses saved

For example, Lisa promises Mona in a valid written contract that she will deliver to Mona a 2013 red Lexus convertible for $25,000. The car is in excellent shape, except that it needs its air conditioning repaired at a cost of $1,000. Mona pays Lisa a $5,000 deposit. The next day, Lisa tells Mona she cannot deliver the car because it was damaged during delivery. Mona searches for a similar used car. She cannot find a 2013 red Lexus convertible in good condition, but she finds a 2014 silver Lexus convertible at a purchase price of $28,000. Lisa spends $50 in gas checking out cars before she purchases the silver Lexus. Assume the court finds that the purchase by Lisa of the silver Lexus convertible constitutes a reasonable "cover." If so, Lisa can recover:

are variations on interpretations of the Code across states, because some of the provisions are vague. *See id.* at 1105 & n.30.

\$5,000	(purchase price paid to seller)
+ \$3,000	(the difference between the cover price and contract price)
+ \$ 50	(the incidental cost of obtaining cover (see below for a definition of incidental damages)
− \$ 1000	(the expenses saved: the air conditioning repair no longer necessary)
= \$7,050	(Total damages)

The damages measure contained in §2-712 aims to do just what the (C − A) expectancy damages measure aims to do: to put the non-breaching party in the same position as if the seller had not breached the contract. The primary difference is that rather than using some indirect market measure of the loss (such as testimony from an expert as to the value of a 2013 red Lexus convertible in good condition) in valuing the difference between what was promised and what was received, §2-712 allows for the purchase of a substitute as a surrogate for determining that market value.

(2) Market Damages. Under §2-713, the buyer can recover the difference between the market price at the time when the buyer learned of the breach and the contract price, together with incidental and consequential damages less expenses saved. Market price is determined at the place of tender or, in the case of rejection after arrival or revocation of acceptance, at the place of arrival.

So the 2-713 market measure formula is:

> Amounts toward the purchase price paid to seller + (market price at the place of tender − contract price) + incidental and consequential damages − expenses saved

For example, suppose that the Mona-Lisa facts are exactly the same, but that after Lisa breached, Mona decided to buy a brand new red Lexus convertible for \$60,000. The court agreed that Lisa breached, but it decided that Mona's purchase did not constitute a good faith substitute purchase qualifying as "cover" under §2-712, because the new convertible was too different from the used car under the contract.

Without the ability to claim "cover," Mona would likely seek to recover damages under §2-713. In order to compute damages under this section, we need one more piece of information: the market price of the car at the time of the breach at the place of tender. Let us suppose the market price is $29,000.[9] Using these figures, Mona can recover:

$5,000	(her deposit)
+ $4,000	(the difference between the market price at the time the buyer learned of the breach and the contract price)
+ 0	(there do not appear to be any incidental or consequential damages in this example)
– $1,000	(the expenses saved: the air conditioning repair no longer necessary)
= $8,000	(Total damages)

Note again that this measure aims to give Mona her expectancy. The examples also show that sometimes a non-breaching party's cover might be lower (or higher in other cases) than the market measure of §2-713.

Remedy for Accepted Goods. In addition to these two measures, under §2-714, when the buyer has *accepted goods* that don't conform to the contract (how to determine when acceptance has happened is a subject more appropriate for a Contracts than a Remedies course) and the buyer has given notice of the non-conformity, the buyer can obtain damages resulting from the non-conformity "as determined in any manner that is reasonable," in addition to incidental and consequential damages. Moreover, when the buyer can prove a breach of warranty, the buyer can obtain from the seller "the difference at the time and place of acceptance between the value of the goods accepted and the value they would have had if they had been as warranted, unless special circumstances show proximate damages of a different amount."

For example, suppose that in the Mona-Lisa example, Lisa did not tell Mona that the car's air conditioning needed to be repaired. Instead, Lisa promised Mona that the air conditioning (along with the rest of the car) was in perfect working order. Mona took delivery of the car, and at some point under the U.C.C., the law treats Mona as having "accepted" the contract for the sale of the car. Once there has been an acceptance, Mona will be allowed to recover damages under §2-714. Her likely damages will be the $1,000 cost to repair the air conditioning, which seems to be the cheapest way to compensate Mona for "the difference at the time and place of

9. This figure supposes that Lisa was selling the car at a price below the market price. Why might Lisa do so? First, she might not know the going market price. Second, she might know the market price but be willing to cut the price in order to make a quick sale (perhaps she needs the money for something else).

acceptance between the value of the goods accepted and the value they would have had if they had been as warranted."

Incidental and Consequential Damages. For each of the three remedies above, the buyer may recover both *incidental* and *consequential* damages. The U.C.C. defines *incidental damages* as "expense reasonably incurred in inspection, receipt, transportation and care and custody of goods rightfully rejected, any commercially reasonable charges, expenses or commissions in connection with effecting cover and any other reasonable expenses incident to the delay or other breach." U.C.C. §2-715(1). It defines *consequential damages* to include "any loss resulting from general or particular requirements and needs of which the seller at the time of contracting had reason to know and which could not reasonably be prevented by cover or otherwise." Consequential damages also include personal injury or property damage that results from any breach of warranty. U.C.C. §2-715(2).

Significantly, the U.C.C. allows consequential damages to be excluded by contract, in which case they are not recoverable unless the exclusion is unconscionable. U.C.C. §2-719. As noted above, however, the Code treats exclusion of consequential damages for personal injury as prima facie unconscionable. U.C.C. §2-719(3).

Example 10

Ned agrees to buy a vintage pinball machine on eBay in excellent condition for $1,500, which includes shipping to his home. The price is to be paid upon delivery. Othello refuses to deliver the pinball machine. Ned finds an identical pinball machine at a local dealer for $1,400 and purchases it, but he pays an additional $50 for delivery. To what damages, if any, is Ned entitled?

Explanation

Ned is entitled to no damages. It appears that Ned has covered by buying the identical item from another dealer. Using the formula from earlier in the chapter, it appears that Ned has no damages:

Amounts toward the purchase price paid to seller + (cover price − contract price) + incidental and consequential damages − expenses saved

$$0 + (\$1{,}400 - \$1{,}500) + \$50 \text{ (delivery charge)} - 0 = -\$50$$

There are no damages.

EXAMPLE

Example 11

Same facts as in Example 10, but this time, Ned pays $1,500 in advance to Othello. To what damages, if any, is Ned entitled?

EXPLANATION

Explanation

It appears that Ned would be entitled to $1,500. Othello might argue that if we mechanically used the formula above, Othello would owe damages of only $1,450 ($1,500 − $100 + $50 − 0 = $1,450). However, that would award the benefit of Ned's covering to Othello, the breaching party. In such a case, Ned could simply argue for a refund of the purchase price under §2-711 and not seek cover. See *Allied Semi-Conductors Int'l, Ltd. v. Pulsar Components Int'l, Inc.*, 907 F. Supp. 618, 632 (E.D.N.Y. 1995) ("[The breaching party] cites no authority for the proposition that a breaching seller is entitled to retain a portion of the purchase price upon a buyer's proper rejection and return of defective goods in the event that the buyer covers its resale contract at a lower price than it paid to the breaching seller. In such a situation the aggrieved buyer sustains no cover damages as a consequence of the seller's breach and the seller's liability is limited to the purchase price paid as a matter of clear statutory mandate.").

EXAMPLE

Example 12

Same facts as in Example 10, but the fair market price of the pinball machine Othello promised to sell Ned is $1,800. What damages, if any, may Ned recover?

EXPLANATION

Explanation

This is a fairly unlikely real-world scenario because, in this case, there would be two sellers (Othello and the new seller) willing to sell the vintage pinball machine for significantly less than the market price. In any case, in this circumstance, Ned has a choice. First, because he did cover, he could use the formula of §2-712, which, as we know from Example 10, yields him no damages.

Alternatively, Ned could use the damages available under §2-713:

> Amounts toward the purchase price paid to seller + (market price at the place of tender − contract price) + incidental and consequential damages − expenses saved

0 + ($1,800 − $1,500) + 0 − 0 = $300

Note that we did *not* add in the $50 delivery charge that Ned sustained in making the substitute purchase. He is entitled to that only if he is claiming cover under §2-712. This is true even though costs of delivery generally count as incidental or consequential damages. The theory of §2-713 is about getting the difference in market costs, and costs of covering are not causally connected to this theory.

Othello may want to argue that Ned in fact did cover by making his substitute purchase, and therefore damages must be measured under the §2-712 measure, which is more advantageous to Othello. But the official comment to §2-712 explains that "cover is not a mandatory remedy for the buyer. The buyer is always free to choose between cover and damages for non-delivery under" §2-713. U.C.C. §2-712, official comment *b*.

EXAMPLE

Example 13

Pam, a farmer, agrees to buy six cows from Quincy for $700 per head. Quincy promises that these cows are suitable for breeding. Quincy delivers the cows, and Pam pays Quincy $4,200. The next day, Pam has a veterinarian examine the cows, and the veterinarian discovers that each of them is infertile. Pam calls Quincy and revokes her acceptance (which we will assume she can do under applicable contract law). She tells Quincy to pick the cows up. Quincy comes a week later to pick up the cows. Pam spent $200 caring for the cows during that week. The market value of a fertile cow is $700. The market value of an infertile cow is $300. Pam planned on using the six cows to breed other cows, and she expected to make a profit of $5,000 from selling their offspring. How much may Pam receive in damages? (Assume that under the U.C.C. she has rightfully rejected the cows.)

EXPLANATION

Explanation

Because Pam has revoked acceptance and there is no indication that she has covered, she is entitled to damages under §2-713. First, she is entitled to the *amounts toward purchase price paid to seller*, or $4,200. She receives nothing for the *difference between the market price and the contract price*, because they are identical. (Quincy was selling the goods at the market price, and Pam presumably can now go out and make a substitute purchase at the market price.) Note that the $300 value of the infertile cow is not relevant to the §2-713 formula.

Pam can also recover the $200 in incidental damages she incurred for the care of the goods she rightfully rejected. But she *cannot* recover the $5,000 in lost profits as consequential damages, because these damages cannot be considered to "include any loss resulting from general or particular requirements and needs of which the seller at the time of contracting had reason to know *and which could not reasonably be prevented by cover or otherwise*." This is the mitigation principle built into the Code. Pam cannot sit on her hands after the breach. If she still wanted to raise cows for their offspring, she should have gone out and bought replacement cows to breed. The facts tell us nothing about any *expenses saved*. Pam's total damages: $4,400.

EXAMPLE

Example 14

Same facts as in the last example, but assume that Pam does not have an inspection done, and she does not discover the cows are infertile for six months. She then notifies Quincy of the non-conformity, but he does nothing. Pam has spent $1,000 caring for the cows. She sends the cows to the slaughterhouse and receives $400 per head. How much may Pam receive in damages? (Assume that under the U.C.C. she has accepted the goods and cannot revoke her acceptance.)

EXPLANATION

Explanation

In this case, because Pam has accepted the goods, she must receive her remedy under U.C.C. §2-714. Pam may obtain damages resulting from the non-conformity "as determined in any manner that is reasonable" in addition to incidental and consequential damages. Moreover, by proving a breach of warranty, Pam may obtain from the seller "the difference at the time and place of acceptance between the value of the goods accepted and the value they would have had if they had been as warranted, unless special circumstances show proximate damages of a different amount."

In this case, Pam likely would be entitled to $2,400, representing the difference between the value of the six cows as they had been warranted ($700 each) and the value they actually had ($300 each) at the time and place of acceptance. Note that we do not use the value that the animals had six months later ($400), because §2-714 measures value at the time and place of acceptance.

Pam will also seek to recover the $1,000 that it cost her to care for the animals as incidental damages, and the $5,000 in lost profits as consequential damages. As to the $1,000, because Pam did not "rightfully reject" the goods, these damages likely do not qualify as incidental damages. To recover her lost profits, there will likely be a big question as to whether Pam reasonably could have prevented these damages from accruing. If, for example, she could have discovered the cows' infertility in a timelier manner, these damages would not be recoverable as consequential damages.

Note that if Pam could recover the additional $5,000 as consequential damages, Quincy could require that the jury *deduct expenses saved*. Thus, if it would have cost Pam an additional $800 to care for the cows had they been fertile, this amount would have figured into the actual profits she would have earned.

4.5.2 Sellers' Remedies, Including the "Lost Volume Seller"

Just as Article 2 of the U.C.C. gives buyers a choice of remedies, sellers dealing with breaching buyers have some choices as well. Under U.C.C. §2-703, sellers facing buyers who wrongfully reject goods, wrongfully revoke acceptance, or fail to pay as promised can cancel the contract, stop delivery of the goods, and then either resell and recover damages (§2-706), recover damages for non-acceptance (§2-708), or bring an action on the price (§2-709). We consider each of these in turn.

Resale (§2-706). The first option a non-breaching seller has is to resell the goods to another buyer. When the seller makes a resale "in good faith and in a commercially reasonable manner," "the seller may recover the difference between the resale price and the contract price together with any incidental damages allowed under the provisions of this Article (§2-710), but less expenses saved in consequence of the buyer's breach." (You should immediately see the parallel to the buyer's remedy of cover here.)

So the §2-706 formula is:

(contract price – resale price) + incidental damages – expenses saved

To use a variation on an earlier example, suppose Lisa promises Mona in a valid written contract that she will deliver to Mona a 2013 red Lexus convertible for $25,000. The car is in excellent shape except that it needs its air conditioning repaired at a cost of $1,000. Lisa promises to repair the air conditioning before delivering the car to Mona. Before Lisa has a chance to fix the air conditioning, Mona announces that she is not going to pay the contract price or take delivery of the car. This constitutes a breach of the contract. Lisa puts an ad in the local newspaper at a cost of $25 to sell the car. She gets a few offers, and sells it to the highest bidder, who pays $22,000 and does not require Lisa to repair the air conditioning.

Under U.C.C. §2-706, Lisa can recover the following:

$3,000	($25,000 – $22,000, the difference between the resale price and contract price)
+ $25	(incidental damages for the advertisement)
– $1,000	(expenses saved: the air conditioning that need not be repaired)
= $2,025	(Total damages)

Note that this is a way of measuring expectancy damages, assuming that the resale price is close to the contract price. Had the contract been fulfilled, Lisa would have sold a car worth $22,000 to Mona for $25,000 and yielded a $3,000 profit. Lisa then would have spent $1,000 on the air conditioning repair, which means that at the end of the day, her balance ledger would have shown a $2,000 gain. With Mona's breach, Lisa takes in $2,025 in damages and pays $25 for the ad, leaving her with that same $2,000 gain.

Damages for Non-Acceptance (§2-708). The seller need not make the immediate resale of the goods as contemplated by §2-706. Instead, the seller can recover under §2-708(1) "the difference between the market price at the time and place for tender and the unpaid contract price together with any incidental damages provided in this Article (§2-710), but less expenses saved in consequence of the buyer's breach." The section also provides an alternative measure of damages in §2-708(2) that we shall return to shortly.

So the §2-708(1) formula is:

(contract price – market price) + incidental damages – expenses saved

Thus, if Mona broke the contract to buy the red Lexus for $25,000, and Lisa did not resell it, Lisa could seek to recover damages under §2-708(1). Let's suppose that the market value of the car at the time and place of sale (and without the air conditioning repair) was $23,500. Under those circumstances, Lisa could recover under §2-708:

$1,500	($25,000 – $23,500, the difference between the resale price and contract price)
+ $0	(no incidental damages)
– 1,000	(expenses saved: the air conditioning that need not be repaired)
= $500	(Total damages)

Action on the Price (§2-709). When the buyer fails to pay for goods as they are due, and either the buyer keeps the goods or the goods are lost or damaged after the risk of loss has passed to the buyer, the seller can bring an action to recover the contract price plus incidental damages. The seller can also recover such damages for goods still in the seller's possession if the seller "is unable after reasonable effort to resell them at a reasonable price or the circumstances reasonably indicate that such effort will be unavailing."

Thus, the §2-709 formula is:

contract price + incidental damages

Thus, Lisa and Mona sign a valid contract for delivery of the red Lexus convertible for $25,000, provided Lisa repairs the air conditioning (at a cost of $1,000). Lisa repairs the air conditioning, and the car is delivered to Mona. The car is struck by lightning after it is delivered to Mona, and at this time, contract law says that "the risk of loss" has shifted to Mona. If Mona refuses to pay, Lisa may recover $25,000, the contract price. She has no incidental damages.

Incidental Damages (§2-710). Under the three damage formulas for sellers set forth above, the sellers are entitled to incidental damages (though not to consequential damages as buyers are). Section 2-710 defines seller's incidental damages to include "any commercially reasonable charges, expenses or commissions incurred in stopping delivery, in the transportation, care, and custody of goods after the buyer's breach, in connection with return or resale of the goods or otherwise resulting from the breach."

Suppose Lisa and Mona sign a valid contract for delivery of the red Lexus at a price of $25,000. Mona changes her mind after Lisa pays $300 to a delivery service to deliver the car. After the car is returned, Lisa spends $200 selling the car to another buyer. The $300 and $200 expenses are incidental damages that Lisa may recover in a claim for damages under §2-706.

The Lost Volume Seller. One issue that arises with some frequency (especially on Remedies exams) is the case of the lost volume seller. A leading case here is *Neri v. Retail Marine Corp.*, 285 N.E.2d 311 (N.Y. 1972). In *Neri*, buyer contracted to buy a new boat from a boat seller for $12,587.40. The buyer breached the contract, and the seller incurred $674 in costs for storing the boat until it could be sold to another buyer. The evidence indicated that the seller could have made the sale both to the original buyer and to the new buyer, and therefore the seller lost a profit of $2,579 on the first sale.

In considering the damages that the seller in *Neri* could receive,[10] note that damages under §§2-706 and 2-708(1) appear inadequate (damages under §2-709 would not be available because the buyer neither kept the goods nor were they lost or destroyed after risk of loss had passed to the buyer). Under §2-706, the difference between the contract price and the resale price is 0, leaving only the incidental damages of $674. But that amount of damages does not appear to put the seller in the rightful position because the seller *could have made both sales at a profit*. In essence, this awards only the seller's reliance damages (B – A, that amount below the status quo ante where the seller was left after the buyer's breach of contract).

Similarly, damages under §2-708(1) are inadequate, assuming that the contract price for the boat was equal to the market price. Again, the seller would be left with only the $674 in incidental (reliance) damages.

Most courts therefore invoke U.C.C. §2-708(2), which provides:

> If the measure of damages provided in subsection (1) is inadequate to put the seller in as good a position as performance would have done then the measure of damages is the profit (including reasonable overhead) which the seller would have made from full performance by the buyer, together with any incidental damages provided in this Article (§2-710), due allowance for costs reasonably incurred and due credit for payments or proceeds of resale.

So the §2-708(2) formula is:

profit + incidental damages – credit for junk value[11]

10. In the actual case, the buyer had given a deposit, which was then credited against the amount of damages the buyer owed the seller. (The buyer had the right to a return of the deposit after deducting damages, under principles of restitution.) But in this example, I ignore this aspect of the *Neri* facts to focus on the lost volume seller issue.

11. The reason I have used the term "credit for junk value" rather than "due credit for proceeds of resale" is that courts, including *Neri*, have read the section's language to apply only to junk value. *See Neri*, 285 N.E.2d at 314 n.2. Otherwise, if we really subtracted credits for resale, this would eliminate any profit and render the section nonsensical in this context.

Through §2-708(2), courts have allowed "lost volume sellers," such as the boat seller in *Neri*, to recover their *lost profits plus incidental damages*. In this case, that would be the $2,579 in lost profits plus the $674 in incidental damages, for a total of $3,253 in damages.

This measure puts the boat seller in the rightful position. Had the sale gone through, the boat seller would have realized a profit of $2,579. With the breach, the seller receives $3,253 in damages and, after paying for the costs of holding the boat, ends up with the same $2,579 profit.

Not every seller qualifies as a lost volume seller. According to one test, a non-breaching party claiming to be a lost volume seller "must establish the following factors: (1) that it possessed the capacity to make an additional sale, (2) that it would have been profitable for it to make an additional sale, and (3) that it probably would have made an additional sale absent the buyer's breach." *R.E. Davis Chem. Corp. v. Diasonics, Inc.*, 924 F.2d 709, 711 (7th Cir. 1991).

EXAMPLE

Example 15

Ian contracts to sell Courtney his private jet for $850,000 with delivery on June 1. On June 1, Courtney refuses to accept delivery. Ian immediately resells the jet to another buyer for $860,000. The reasonable market value of the jet is $800,000. What damages, if any, may Ian recover from Courtney?

EXPLANATION

Explanation

It appears that Ian may not recover any damages from Courtney. Because there has been a resale, §2-706 applies. Recall that the §2-706 formula is:

(contract price − resale price) + incidental damages − expenses saved

Because the contract price was lower than the resale price and there were no incidental damages, Ian has no damages.

Would Ian have been better off not selling? No. By selling to the new buyer, Ian received a profit of $60,000 (because the new contract price of $860,000 is $60,000 above the market price of $80,0000). If Ian had not sold, he would have been able to recover damages under §2-708(1) of:

(contract price − market price) + incidental damages − expenses saved

$$\$850,000 - 800,000 + 0 - 0 = \$50,000$$

Ian would have a $50,000 damages award plus a plane that he can presumably sell for $800,000, the going market rate. When he sells at the market rate, his ledger is up by only the $50,000, rather than the $60,000 that would apply if he had sold to the new buyer.

Notably, Ian cannot claim to be a lost volume seller. Unlike the boat seller in *Neri*, Ian has only one plane to sell.

Example 16

EXAMPLE

Pam, a farmer, agrees to buy six cows from Quincy for $700 per head. The current market price is $750 per head, but Quincy needs money quickly to pay off his farm debts. Quincy spends $250 transporting the cows to Pam's farm, but Pam breaches the contract, refusing to pay the $4,200 contract price. Quincy takes the cattle back to his farm. Two days later, and before Quincy has found another buyer, there is a scare over "mad cow disease," and the price of cattle plummets. The new market rate for the cows is $200. Rather than sell the cows at that price, Quincy decides to hold on to them. In the meantime, because Pam breached, Quincy does not have the money to make the loan payment for his tractor. The bank repossesses his tractor, and Quincy loses another $10,000 in income because he does not have a tractor to harvest his crops. What damages, if any, can Quincy recover from Pam?

Explanation

EXPLANATION

Quincy did not make a resale, so he cannot take advantage of §2-706. It looks like he would have to seek damages under §2-708(1) of:

(contract price − market price) + incidental damages − expenses saved

The contract price here is $4,200 (6 cows @ $700/head). The market price is $4,500 (6 cows @$750/head). Note that we use the market value *at the time of sale*, not later (when the market takes a nosedive to $200/head). The incidental damages are $250 (the cost of transporting the cows). There are no expenses saved. Thus:

$$(4200 - 4500) + 250 = -\$50$$

Quincy has no net damages under this formula and can recover nothing. At best, he could argue that §2-703 allows him to recover his incidental damages of $250.

Quincy cannot recover from Pam any consequential damages that he suffers from not being able to make his tractor loan payment as a result of

Pam's breach. Sellers under the U.C.C. are not permitted to recover consequential damages as buyers do. It thus appears that the U.C.C. follows the general exception for consequential damages that we saw earlier in this chapter (section 4.3); at most, some courts interpret the U.C.C. to allow sellers to receive interest on money unpaid under a contract as a form of "incidental" damages (*see Bulk Oil (U.S.A.), Inc. v. Sun Oil Trading Co.*, 697 F.2d 481 (2d Cir. 1983)).

EXAMPLE

Example 17

Same facts as above, except Quincy delivers the cows to Pam. It costs him $250 to deliver the cows. The next day, the government orders Pam to put the cows down to prevent the feared spread of a disease. Pam destroys the cattle and does not pay the $4,200 contract price. Quincy sues for damages. What result? Explain.

EXPLANATION

Explanation

In this case, Quincy will bring an action on the price under §2-709. Recall the §2-709 formula:

contract price + incidental damages

Quincy can recover the $4,200, assuming substantive contract law says the risk of loss of the goods passed to Pam at the time of delivery. Quincy *cannot* recover the $250 in transportation costs as incidental damages. These are expenses he would have incurred had Pam not breached. If we allowed Quincy to recover those additional damages, the damages measure would have left him better off than if Pam had performed the contract.

4.5.3 U.C.C. Article 2 Limitations on Remedies

As with non-U.C.C. contracts, default rules in contracts governed by Article 2 of the U.C.C. are subject, with some limits, to being overridden by express contractual provisions. Indeed, I have already noted that U.C.C. contracts can exclude consequential damages unless the exclusion is unconscionable. Exclusions for personal injuries resulting from defective products are prima facie unconscionable. *See* U.C.C. §2-719(3).

In addition, the Article 2 provision on liquidated damages mirrors the rules of the Restatement of Contracts. *See* U.C.C. §2-718(1) ("Damages for breach by either party may be liquidated in the agreement but only at an amount which is reasonable in the light of the anticipated or actual harm caused by the breach, the difficulties of proof of loss, and the inconvenience or nonfeasibility of otherwise obtaining an adequate remedy. A term fixing unreasonably large liquidated damages is void as a penalty.").

Perhaps the most interesting aspect of Article 2's approach to the parties' ability to change the default remedy rules appears in the official comment to section 2-719:

> Under this section parties are left free to shape their remedies to their particular requirements and reasonable agreements limiting or modifying remedies are to be given effect.
>
> However, it is of the very essence of a sales contract that at least minimum adequate remedies be available. If the parties intend to conclude a contract for sale within this Article they must accept the legal consequence that there be at least a fair quantum of remedy for breach of the obligations or duties outlined in the contract. Thus any clause purporting to modify or limit the remedial provisions of this Article in an unconscionable manner is subject to deletion and in that event the remedies made available by this Article are applicable as if the stricken clause had never existed. Similarly, under subsection (2), where an apparently fair and reasonable clause because of circumstances fails in its purpose or operates to deprive either party of the substantial value of the bargain, it must give way to the general remedy provisions of this Article.

The last reference in this excerpt refers to §2-719(2), providing that "[w]here circumstances cause an exclusive or limited remedy to fail of its essential purpose, remedy may be had as provided in this Act." In the typical case arising under this clause, a contract provides a strict limitation on remedy in the case of the seller's breach, such as limiting the buyer's remedy to repair or replacement of the product (at the seller's option). When the seller tries repeatedly to repair a faulty machine, the courts may declare that the remedy "has failed of its essential purpose" and resort to other contractual provisions or the default rules under the Act.

An interesting subsidiary question arises when the default rules and other contractual provisions conflict after a repair-or-replace remedy has failed its essential purpose. *Kearney & Trecker Corp. v. Master Engraving Co.*, 527 A.2d 429 (N.J. 1987), is a typical case. Buyer bought a computer-controlled machine tool from seller that repeatedly malfunctioned and could not be repaired. The contract provided *both* that the buyer's remedy was limited to repair or replacement at the seller's option *and* that the seller would under no circumstances be liable for any incidental or consequential damages. At first glance, it might appear that the limitation on incidental or consequential damages was lawyerly overkill given the repair-or-replace limitation, but the clause limiting consequential damages turned out to be quite prudent drafting.

The court ruled that the repair-or-replace remedy failed its essential purpose when the seller could not successfully get the machine to work. The question the court faced then was whether the buyer could recover consequential damages under §2-714 or whether the limitation on consequential damages clause in the contract remained valid. The New Jersey Supreme Court in *Kearney & Trecker Corp.* noted the conflict among the courts on the issue, and sided with the seller, holding the consequential damage limitation enforceable so long as the clause was not unconscionable. Other courts have held the consequential damages limitation unenforceable, thereby allowing the buyer to recover consequential damages.

Note that the holding of *Kearney & Trecker Corp.* did not deprive the buyer of all remedies. Under §2-714(2), the buyer can obtain the difference between the value of the machine as warranted and the value of the machine as delivered. Thus, if the seller promised a machine tool that could do x, and such a machine tool has a value of $1 million if working and zero if constantly broken, §2-714(2) could allow the buyer to recover a significant amount of damages (perhaps $1,000,000 – 0).

EXAMPLE

Example 18

Rex promises to deliver a fancy CT scanner to Samantha for use in her high-tech medical lab in exchange for a payment of $2 million. They sign a form contract provided by Rex. The contract provides that the only remedy Samantha has in case the machine fails to work as promised is repair or replacement at Rex's option. It further provides that "in the event the repair or replacement remedy is found to fail of its essential purpose, the buyer shall be entitled to liquidated damages of $10,000." Samantha pays in full for the machine, but for six months the machine is broken more than it works. A court determines that Rex's failure to deliver a working machine constitutes a breach of contract. To what damages, if any, is Samantha entitled?

EXPLANATION

Explanation

Samantha will want to recover damages under §2-714 for the difference between the value of the CT scanner as warranted (a working scanner) and as delivered (very little), plus any incidental and consequential damages (such as lost business because of the broken scanner). Rex will argue that the remedy is limited to repair and replacement, but a court, following *Kearney & Trecker Corp.*, will likely hold that the repair-or-replace remedy failed in its essential purpose.

Rex would likely then argue that Samantha's damages should be limited under the liquidated damages provision. But under U.C.C. §2-718, a court could well hold that the liquidated damages provision does not appear to be a reasonable amount in light of actual or anticipated harm (Samantha would be receiving only $10,000 for a nonworking machine that she paid $2 million to buy). Alternatively, a court might declare the liquidated damages provision substantively unconscionable. If that is the case, as in the case in which the court strikes down the liquidated damages provision, Samantha will be able to recover her damages under §2-714, damages that could be substantial.

CHAPTER 5

The Unusual: Expectancy Damages in Tort and Reliance Damages in Contract

5.1 REVIEW OF THE USUAL TORT AND CONTRACT DAMAGE MEASURES

As we have seen in the last two chapters, the usual measure of tort damages is the reliance measure (B – A), and the usual measure of contract damages is the expectancy measure (C – A). See Figure 5.1.

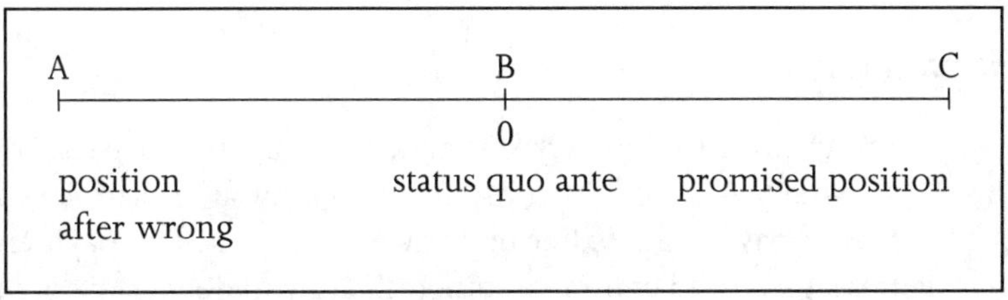

Figure 5.1

In this chapter, we consider the relatively rare situations in which (1) a plaintiff seeks to recover expectancy damages in tort or (2) a non-breaching party is permitted to recover only reliance damages in contract. Before turning to those exceptions, however, here are some brief review examples so that you can consider the usual rules in tort and contract cases.

Example 1

Tina, driving negligently, runs over Ursula's foot. Ursula pays $10,000 in medical bills, misses work for six weeks (she is paid $1,000 per week as a secretary), and still experiences a great deal of pain (the accident itself was excruciating for Ursula). Ursula is an avid tennis player, and the doctors believe she won't be able to play tennis again for at least two years. To what damages is Ursula entitled?

Explanation

This is a standard torts case, so we want to use our (B – A) reliance damages rather than the (C – A) expectancy damages formula. As you should see, we would never consider using expectancy damages here because, between Tina and Ursula, *there is no promised position*. So we are concerned only with figuring out position A, Ursula's position after the wrong. Ursula will be able to recover her reasonable medical expenses ($10,000) and lost wages ($1,000 for six weeks, or $6,000). There do not appear to be any future medical expenses or future lost wages, which saves us from having to worry about reducing future payments to present value. Ursula will also be able to recover something for her pain and suffering/emotional distress, including any emotional distress she is likely to suffer in the future from pain and the inability to play tennis (this amount perhaps should be reduced to present value). As for economic damages, she likely would be able to obtain prejudgment interest.

Example 2

Vinny promises to sell Walter a painting by Picasso. The painting has a market value of $1 million, but Vinny agrees to accept $900,000 if Walter pays cash. Walter makes a $100,000 down payment, and the parties sign a valid contract requiring Vinny to deliver the picture by the next day. Unfortunately, the painting is destroyed in a fire in Vinny's home. (Assume that substantive contract law says this risk of loss remained on Vinny, and that by failing to deliver the painting Vinny breached his contract with Walter.) Walter is very disappointed. He goes out and purchases a painting by Cezanne for $2 million. To what damages is Walter entitled?

Explanation

Because this is a contracts case, we will use the expectancy measure of damages. But rather than the generic (C – A) formula, we will use the U.C.C. Article 2 damage provisions for buyers. (U.C.C. Article 2 applies because this contract is for the sale of a painting, which qualifies as a good.) Walter is entitled to a refund of his purchase price ($100,000). He would not be successful in arguing that he "covered" (U.C.C. §2-712) when he purchased the Cezanne—though they are both paintings, the Cezanne and Picasso differ significantly in value, so a court would be unlikely to view the Cezanne painting as a substitute purchase.

Accordingly, Walter will seek damages under the U.C.C. §2-713 formula:

> Amounts toward the purchase price paid to seller + (market price at the place of tender – contract price) + incidental and consequential damages – expenses saved

$100,000	(amount toward purchase price)
+ $100,000	($1 million market price at the place of tender – $900,000 contract price)
+ 0	(there is no evidence of any incidental or consequential damages)
– 0	(there is no evidence of expenses saved)
= $200,000	(Total damages)

Note that the C – A formula would yield exactly the same result. (Make sure you understand why by computing the values of C and A.) If Walter is limited to recovering his reliance damages, he will get only his $100,000 deposit back and no compensation for the lost "benefit of the bargain."

5.2 EXPECTANCY DAMAGES IN TORT? THE SPECIAL CASE OF FRAUD

The question of expectancy damages in tort usually does not come up. When Tina hits Ursula with her car, there is no "promised position," making the possibility of locating C in Figure 5.1 an impossibility. Instead, courts award reliance damages to restore Ursula to a point as close as possible to the status quo ante with an award of money.

In tort cases involving fraud, however, there *is* a promised position. Here is how the RESTATEMENT (SECOND) OF TORTS §525 defines the tort of fraudulent misrepresentation:

> One who fraudulently makes a misrepresentation of fact, opinion, intention or law for the purpose of inducing another to act or to refrain from action in reliance upon it, is subject to liability to the other in deceit for pecuniary loss caused to him by his justifiable reliance upon the misrepresentation.

Fraudulent misrepresentations involve false statements, which can be promises just like a contractual promise. Therefore, in fraud cases, there is at least the possibility of a recovery based upon the expectancy measure even though the case is a torts case. To use an example from the last chapter, suppose that Ivan had intentionally lied to Helena, who had come from Nashville to Chicago looking for an apartment to rent. Ivan lied when he told Helena that he had an apartment available to rent for a year at $1,500 a month, in order to obtain the deposit from Helena. Regardless of whether Ivan's conduct counts as a breach of contract, it appears his conduct would satisfy the elements of fraudulent misrepresentation under the Restatement of Torts.

Recall some additional facts about the Helena-Ivan hypothetical. Helena returned to Nashville, packed up her things, and had a moving truck transport her belongings from Nashville to Chicago for $4,000. When Helena arrived in Chicago, she discovered that Ivan had rented the apartment to someone else for $2,200 per month for a year. Helena checked into a hotel for a week at $125 per night. She put her belongings in storage for $300. After diligently searching for another apartment, she found one comparable to the one she had agreed to rent from Ivan for $2,000 a month. She signed a year lease at the new apartment.

If Helena were able to recover only her reliance damages from Ivan, her recovery would be limited to the week's hotel stay ($875) and the storage expenses ($300). These are damages for which she is "out of pocket," a term frequently used in tort fraud cases. Giving her those damages puts her in the same position as if there had been no fraudulent promise. Under the reliance measure, she would *not* be eligible for the $6,000 annual differential in rent payment between the contract price she was promised and the going market rate.

Some courts have taken the position that when a plaintiff like Helena pleads her cause of action in tort rather than contract, she is limited to these reliance (or out-of-pocket) damages. *See Smith v. Bolles*, 132 U.S. 125 (1889); LAYCOCK & HASEN pp. 40-41. In jurisdictions still following this rule, why would anyone ever plead a cause of action in tort rather than allege breach of warranty in contract? There are a number of possible reasons to do so (apart from attorney malpractice!):

- The tort cause of action might allow for punitive damages, which are generally not allowed in contract.
- The tort cause of action might make it easier to recover for certain consequential damages even if not foreseeable by the breaching party at the time of the contracting/misrepresentation.
- The contract cause of action might prove problematic (for example, if there was not a valid contract because the contract was not in writing as required by the statute of frauds).
- The tort cause of action might be subject to a longer statute of limitations than the contract cause of action (though in practice it is often the other way around).

In many jurisdictions today, however, the rule against allowing plaintiffs to recover expectancy damages in tort suits has been relaxed. Courts sometimes refer to such expectancy damages in fraud suits as "benefit of the bargain" damages.

The RESTATEMENT (SECOND) OF TORTS §549 provides the following remedies in the case of a fraudulent misrepresentation:

> (1) The recipient of a fraudulent misrepresentation is entitled to recover as damages in an action of deceit against the maker the pecuniary loss to him of which the misrepresentation is a legal cause, including
>
> (a) the difference between the value of what he has received in the transaction and its purchase price or other value given for it; and
>
> (b) pecuniary loss suffered otherwise as a consequence of the recipient's reliance upon the misrepresentation.
>
> (2) The recipient of a fraudulent misrepresentation in a business transaction is also entitled to recover additional damages sufficient to give him the benefit of his contract with the maker, if these damages are proved with reasonable certainty.

Thus, under the Restatement and in a majority of states (32, according to the 1977 Reporter's Note to §549), Helena will likely be able to recover not only her reliance damages, but also the additional $6,000 lost rent expectancy differential under §549(2), which allows for expectancy damages in fraudulent business transactions when proven with reasonable certainty. Depending on the jurisdiction, Helena might be able to sue for punitive damages as well.

The law regarding when expectancy damages are available in tort suits alleging fraudulent misrepresentation remains unclear in a significant minority of jurisdictions. While some states still generally allow for recovery of reliance damages only (for example, New York—*see Lama Holding Co. v. Smith Barney, Inc.*, 668 N.E.2d 1370, 1373-1374 (N.Y. 1996)), others, following the lead of *Selman v. Shirley*, 85 P.2d 384 (Or. 1938), have developed a "flexible" test depending upon the circumstances of each case. *See also* Charles T. McCormick, Handbook on the Law of Damages §121 (1935) (suggesting that the trial judge should use discretion in deciding which measure of damages should apply in fraud cases, "in view of the probable moral culpability of the defendant and of the definiteness of the representations and the ascertainability of the represented value"). For a strong critique of the *Selman* "flexible" test, see *Goldstein v. Miles*, 859 A.2d 313 (Md. Ct. Spec. App. 2004). In *Goldstein*, the court held that a plaintiff suing for fraud could not recover expectancy damages absent proof that there was an otherwise *enforceable contract* between the parties.

Note also that the Restatement §549 standard allows recovery only for "pecuniary loss"; it mentions nothing about whether a plaintiff may recover *emotional distress* damages in a case involving fraudulent misrepresentation, and a fair reading is that it does not. Obviously, it is much more attractive for lawyers to bring suit in tort (rather than contract) for fraudulent misrepresentation if emotional distress damages will be available to plaintiffs in particular cases.

Professors Dobbs and Roberts report that emotional distress damages generally are unavailable in misrepresentation cases, because those are primarily economic torts. Dobbs & Roberts §9.1(4). They note that when such damages are allowed, it is often damages for another tort that allows for emotional distress damages. *Id.*

See McConkey v. AON Corp., 804 A.2d 572, 593 (N.J. Super. Ct. App. Div. 2002) (summarizing Dobbs). The court in *McConkey* noted that "[n]o judicial consensus exists on the propriety of awarding damages for emotional distress in fraud cases." *Id.*

EXAMPLE

Example 3

Xavier sells an exercise machine, the "Fat-eraser," on television, promising that it is "guaranteed to take inches off your waistline in 30 days." Yoko buys the Fat-eraser for three easy payments of $39.99 and uses it as directed. Yoko uses it for 30 days, but it has no effect on her waistline. Indeed, the product is designed poorly, and Yoko injures her back using it, incurring doctor's bills of $1,000. Xavier sold the Fat-eraser with a contract limiting liability to repair or replacement at the seller's option. A similar exercise machine that would have taken inches off Yoko's waistline in 30 days using a similar effort from Yoko would have cost Yoko $500. What damages may Yoko receive?

EXPLANATION

Explanation

This is a contract for the sale of goods, governed by Article 2. U.C.C. §2-721 allows victims of fraudulent misrepresentation to get all remedies available for non-fraudulent breaches. Therefore, even though the contract contains a clause limiting Xavier's liability to repair or replacement, this likely won't limit damages in this case. In the first place, any tort suit for injuries Yoko received from the defective product may be recovered in tort despite the provision. *See* U.C.C. §2-719(3). Thus, the $1,000 should be recoverable.

Additionally, Xavier has made an express warranty that the product would take inches off a user's waistline in 30 days—which the product failed to do. Yoko will therefore argue that she should be entitled to damages for the difference between the product as warranted ($500) and the value of what she received (arguably 0). Neither repair nor replacement will remedy the product's failing to live up to the warranty; the provision therefore likely failed in its essential purpose.

Yoko might want to sue instead in tort even if she would be limited to her reliance damages and medical expenses. The reliance damages here are $119.97 (the three easy payments of $39.99) plus the $1,000 in medical expenses. But if she is able to sue in tort, she might also be able to get emotional distress/pain and suffering damages along with punitive damages.

EXAMPLE

Example 4

Phillip works as the manager of insurance services at Ross and Company. He is approached by A & A to leave that position and to come work for A & A as the director of insurance services for a $20,000/year raise. Phillip asks Frank, the CEO of A & A, about whether Frank is contemplating selling A & A in the near future to a larger insurance company. Frank tells Phillip that there are no such plans, but this is a lie. Frank wants Phillip to come in and get the business into shape so that it will be more attractive to a buyer (that is, he wants to fatten up the turkey before Thanksgiving). Phillip takes the job as an at-will employee and, based on Frank's statements, assures all of the employees at the firm that it is not going to be offered for sale. Six months later, Frank tells Phillip that he has sold A & A to a larger insurance company, and that Phillip has one day to move out of his office. Phillip feels sick to his stomach. Phillip, having repeated Frank's lies to so many people, is not able to find a job in the insurance industry. He is now working as a data entry consultant for half of what he was paid at A & A. Assuming Phillip can prove that Frank and A & A committed the tort of fraudulent misrepresentation, to what damages is Phillip entitled?

EXPLANATION

Explanation

This fact pattern is based on the *McConkey* case cited above. Phillip was hired as an at-will employee (meaning he could be fired any time without the firm incurring liability). Therefore, under substantive contract law, he likely does not have a cause of action for breach of contract. The fraud committed by Frank might allow Phillip to rescind (or cancel) the contract, as we will see in Chapter 14, but that likely is not a helpful remedy here.

Assuming that Phillip can make out the elements for the tort of fraudulent concealment, the courts would differ on whether he could get expectation (or benefit of the bargain) damages. Some courts would hold that because there was no enforceable promise (such as a promise of employment), plaintiff could recover only reliance damages.

Phillip is going to claim the loss of past and future salary, which he suffered from giving up his original job in reliance on Frank's promise that the business would not be sold. The jury would have to determine that loss in salary, which arguably would restore Phillip to the position he would have been in had there been no wrong. It is here that the difference in reliance and expectancy damages might matter.

Suppose Phillip's salary at Ross and Company was \$100,000 per year, his salary at A & A was \$120,000 per year, and his salary working in data entry is \$60,000 per year. In terms of reduced wages, reliance damages would measure how much better off Phillip would have been if he had never taken the A & A job. Thus, for reliance damages, we would be looking at the difference in salaries between a continued career at Ross and Company and Phillip's new career path in data entry. It appears we would not compare the difference between *his wages at A & A* and those at his data entry job. That comparison appears to be the appropriate measure for expectancy damages. What would his salary path have looked like had he continued to work in the field at his new position at A & A, and how does that position differ from where he ended up in data entry?

If Phillip sues in tort, he would also want to recover emotional distress damages for this fraud, but many courts would deny Phillip damages for this distress. This looks like an economic transaction and not like a contract where fraud or breach would likely give rise to serious emotional distress damages (such as a contract for funeral services).

In the actual *McConkey* case, the court allowed the plaintiff to recover damages for lost past earnings, lost future earnings (which need to be properly discounted to present value), and punitive damages (the court upheld the \$5 million punitive damages award). It reversed the jury's award of \$2 million in emotional distress damages, finding that even if New Jersey would allow plaintiffs to recover such damages as part of the tort of misrepresentation, there was not enough evidence in this case to sustain them: "There is no evidence that plaintiff's purported suffering was of long duration, or that his daily routine or functions were interrupted."

5.3 RELIANCE DAMAGES IN CONTRACT?

Just as it is unusual to have plaintiffs in torts cases asking for expectancy damages, it is unusual for plaintiffs in contracts cases to receive only reliance damages. Because reliance damages are going to be less than expectancy damages, it won't be the plaintiff who asks for them—except as a fallback when expectancy damages are not available. Rather, the defendant will be the party arguing that plaintiff should recover no more than reliance damages.

There are three recognized situations in which courts may award reliance damages rather than expectancy damages in contract:

- The non-breaching party has a problem with the substantive contract claim, such as a lack of consideration or lack of a writing as required by the statute of frauds.
- There are compelling public policy reasons to limit damages to a lesser amount.
- The non-breaching party has trouble proving expectancy damages with reasonable certainty.

We consider each of these scenarios in turn.

Problems with the Substantive Contract Claim. In the classic contracts case of *Ricketts v. Scothorn*, 77 N.W. 365 (Neb. 1898), a grandfather saw his granddaughter working in a store. He told her, "None of my grandchildren work and you don't have to." He then gave her a promissory note for $2,000 plus 6% annual interest (a substantial sum at the time). He had not paid off that note by the time he died, and the granddaughter brought an action against the grandfather's estate. The estate defended by raising a substantive contracts objection: the promise from the grandfather lacked consideration; it looked like a gift.

The court held that the granddaughter's reliance on the promise from the grandfather created an "estoppel" that prevented the estate from raising lack of consideration as a defense.

Allowing the granddaughter in *Ricketts* to recover the full $2,000 payment plus interest gave her the expectancy damages in the contract. That is, the court let the granddaughter recover the same damages she would have received had the contract been supported by consideration.

Reliance represents a middle path between non-enforcement of the promise and treating the contract as valid—as the product of a bargained-for exchange. For example, suppose that after the granddaughter received the promissory note, she quit working and borrowed $200 from the bank for her living expenses until the grandfather paid (remember that these 1890s dollars went a lot farther!). The $200 would be her reliance damages.

When should a court decide in such circumstances whether to award the usual expectancy damages or the less generous reliance measure? On this question, the RESTATEMENT (SECOND) OF CONTRACTS has been influential. Section 90(1) provides:

> A promise which the promisor should reasonably expect to induce action or forbearance on the part of the promisee or a third person and which does induce such action or forbearance is binding if injustice can be avoided only by enforcement of the promise. The remedy granted for breach may be limited as justice requires.

Comment *d* to the section further states:

> A promise binding under this section is a contract, and full-scale enforcement by normal remedies is often appropriate. But the same factors which bear on whether any relief should be granted also bear on the character and extent of the remedy. In particular, relief may sometimes be limited to restitution or to damages or specific relief measured by the extent of the promisee's reliance rather than by the terms of the promise. See §§84, 89; compare Restatement, Second, Torts §549 on damages for fraud. Unless there is unjust enrichment of the promisor, damages should not put the promisee in a better position than performance of the promise would have put him. See §§344, 349. In the case of a promise to make a gift it would rarely be proper to award consequential damages which would place a greater burden on the promisor than performance would have imposed.

The Restatement's approach, therefore, gives discretion to courts to limit a plaintiff's recovery of reliance damages "as justice requires," such as when reliance serves as a substitute for consideration.

The Restatement takes a similar position on the availability of reliance damages when parties to a contract fail to satisfy the statute of frauds. Under §139, reliance can substitute for a writing to satisfy the statute of frauds, but the courts must limit remedies as justice requires. Although this Restatement section has been influential, not all courts have adopted it or adopted it fully. In Alaska, for example, plaintiffs can recover reliance damages for breach of an employment contract that fails to comply with the statute of frauds, but plaintiffs cannot recover reliance damages for breach of a contract for the sale or lease of real estate that fails to comply with the statute of frauds. *Valdez Fisheries Dev. Ass'n v. Alyeska Pipeline Serv. Co.*, 45 P.3d 657, 669 (Alaska 2002).

Policy Reasons to Limit Damages to Reliance Damages. *Sullivan v. O'Connor*, 296 N.E.2d 183 (Mass. 1973), is the leading case on the use of reliance damages rather than expectancy damages for reasons of policy in a contracts case. Plaintiff was an entertainer who contracted with defendant, a plastic surgeon, for a nose job. The surgeon promised the plaintiff a more beautiful nose, but plaintiff was left in worse condition than she was in before the operation.[1] She endured pain, suffering, and emotional distress as a result of the operations. She sued the doctor in tort (for malpractice) and for breach of contract—in particular, for breach of the promise of a better nose.[2] The jury found for the doctor on the malpractice claim but for the plaintiff on the breach of contract claim. (These verdicts are not inconsistent; the doctor could have complied with the customary standard of care in performing the surgeries but still have broken his promise to provide a better nose.) Thinking only about the status of plaintiff's nose for a moment (and putting aside the emotional distress damages), we can see a nice contrast between the expectation and reliance measures (see Figure 5.2).

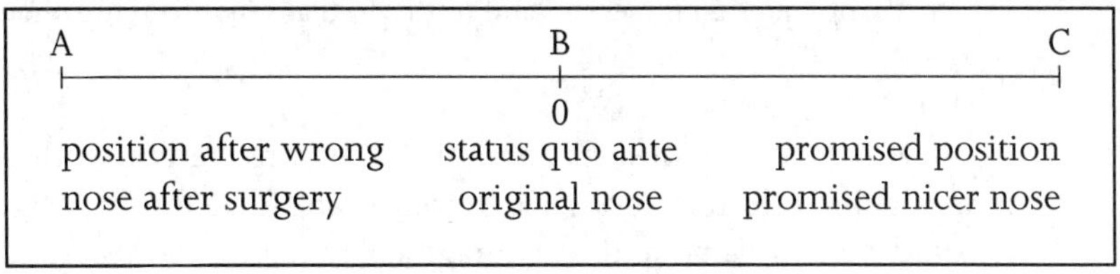

Figure 5.2 *Sullivan v. O'Connor*

To award plaintiff reliance damages (B – A) is to compensate her enough to bring her from her bad nose after the surgery back to the status quo ante. To award plaintiff expectation damages (C – A) is to award her between what she was promised (the nicer nose) and what she ended up receiving (the worse nose after surgery), putting her in the same position as if the contract had been performed as promised.

The trial judge allowed plaintiff to recover her reliance damages, and both sides objected. The doctor wished to repay only his charges for her original surgery (his gain using a restitution measure) and not any pain

1. According to the court, "the plaintiff's nose had been straight, but long and prominent; the defendant undertook by two operations to reduce its prominence and somewhat to shorten it, thus making it more pleasing in relation to the plaintiff's other features. Actually the plaintiff was obliged to undergo three operations, and her appearance was worsened. Her nose now had a concave line to about the midpoint, at which it became bulbous; viewed frontally, the nose from bridge to midpoint was flattened and broadened, and the two sides of the tip had lost symmetry." *Sullivan*, 296 N.E. 2d at 185.

2. Upon reading the facts of this case, you might recall a similar, earlier contracts case, *Hawkins v. McGee*, 146 A. 641 (N.H. 1929). In the so-called "Hairy Hand case," the defendant doctor promised the plaintiff with a deformed hand a perfect hand. In *Hawkins*, the court allowed the plaintiff to recover expectancy damages: the difference between what was promised and what was received.

and suffering damages. The plaintiff wanted expectation damages, but abandoned that claim on appeal.

The court held that reliance damages were the appropriate measure in this case. Note that this is not a case, like the earlier cases we discussed, where the underlying contract was unenforceable. The parties had a valid contract for surgery. Instead, the court pointed to a *policy reason* for limiting the damages to reliance damages in such cases:

> Considering the uncertainties of medical science and the variations in the physical and psychological conditions of individual patients, doctors can seldom in good faith promise specific results. Therefore it is unlikely that physicians of even average integrity will in fact make such promises. Statements of opinion by the physician with some optimistic coloring are a different thing, and may indeed have therapeutic value. But patients may transform such statements into firm promises in their own minds, especially when they have been disappointed in the event, and testify in that sense to sympathetic juries.

Id. at 186.

Fearing that a meager restitution measure (return of the doctor's fee) would provide not enough deterrence and that the expectation measure could be too harsh and discourage encouraging words from doctors, the court settled on the middle ground of reliance damages.

The court also rejected the defendant's argument that pain and suffering damages should be non-compensable, finding the question turned on the intent of the parties to the particular contract: "Suffering or distress resulting from the breach going beyond that which was envisaged by the treatment as agreed, should be compensable on the same ground as the worsening of the patient's conditions because of the breach." *Id.* at 189.

Let's explore further the choice between expectancy and reliance damages. To make things concrete, albeit a bit artificial, let's assume that had the nose surgery been successful, plaintiff would have had to undergo two operations and the pain of each of these operations would have been worth $10,000. Because the first two surgeries were unsuccessful, however, she had to undergo a third operation. Assume the jury would have valued the pain associated with the third operation at $15,000. The emotional distress resulting from having a worse nose was valued at $50,000. Plaintiff valued the promised nose at $100,000 (less the $20,000 in pain from undergoing the two operations to achieve it, and the $5,000 contract price for the surgeries, for a $75,000 expected gain). How would we compute the damages plaintiff should receive under (a) the expectancy measure and (b) the reliance measure?

Let's begin with the expectancy measure by considering the plaintiff's promised position. Had the surgery been successful, plaintiff would have received the promised nose valued at $100,000 – $20,000 (pain from the first two operations) – $5,000 (contract price) = $75,000. So C = $75,000.

The value of A (the position she is in after the wrong) is comprised of the following losses:

- $20,000 (pain of the first two operations)
- $5,000 (contract price)
- $15,000 (the pain of the third operation)
- $50,000 (the emotional distress from having the worse nose)

for a total position below zero, of −$90,000. Total damages: $75,000 − (−$90,000) = $165,000. See Figure 5.3.

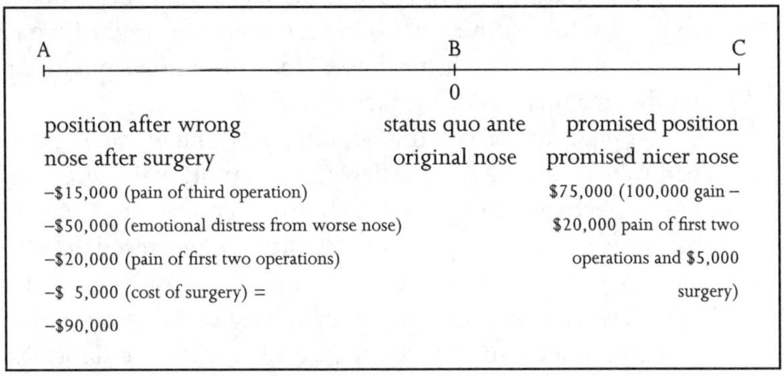

Figure 5.3 *Sullivan*—Detailed Look at Damages

Note how this $165,000 damage measure puts the plaintiff in the same position as she would have been in had the doctor performed the contract as promised. If the contract had been performed as promised, plaintiff would have had a gain of $100,000 and "expenses" of $25,000 (the hard cost of the operation and the soft costs of the pain of the first two surgeries). She would have been ahead by $75,000, the value embodied by plaintiff's new and improved nose.

Now consider the $165,000 damage award. Plaintiff uses the first $25,000 to pay herself back for her originally anticipated "expenses," bringing the figure down to $140,000. The next $65,000 compensates the plaintiff for the pain of the third operation and the emotional distress from having the worse nose—both expenses she incurred because of the defendant's breach. This leaves her with $75,000, exactly where she would have been had the defendant kept his promise. The difference is that plaintiff has this $75,000 value in cash, rather than in an improved appearance.

Consider now the alternative reliance measure. Remember, the goal of reliance damages is to put the plaintiff in the position she would have been in had there been no contract. The measure of damages here is (B − A), or 0 − (−$90,000), or $90,000. Had the contract never been entered into, the plaintiff never would have paid the $5,000 fee, suffered the pain from the first two operations ($20,000),[3] suffered the pain from the third operation ($15,000), or suffered the emotional distress from having the worse nose ($50,000). These losses total $90,000. Under the reliance measure, the plaintiff does *not* receive any damages compensating for the $75,000 promised gain under the contract.

Problems with Certainty. The final type of case in which courts sometimes award a non-breaching party reliance damages rather than expectancy damages occurs when the plaintiff has difficulty proving the value of the expectancy. The court in *Sullivan v. O'Connor* raised this point as a further rationale for awarding only reliance damages, noting: "To attempt, moreover, to put a value on the condition that would or might have resulted, had the treatment succeeded as promised, may sometimes put an exceptional strain on the imagination of the fact finder."

Applied to *Sullivan*, this argument is unconvincing. If the jury already had valued the pain and suffering and emotional distress related to the difference between the post-breach nose and the status quo nose, how much harder is it to come up with a value for the promised nose as well? But there are other cases where certainty is a greater problem, and thus the resort to reliance damages over expectancy damages makes more sense.

Consider in this regard the facts of *Copeland v. Baskin Robbins U.S.A.*, 117 Cal. Rptr. 2d 875 (Cal. Ct. App. 2002). Baskin Robbins was looking to sell one of its ice cream plants, and Kevin Copeland was interested in buying it. They entered into negotiations, signing an agreement to negotiate in good faith. Copeland made it clear to Baskin Robbins that a key part of the deal was that Baskin Robbins would purchase a large amount of ice cream manufactured by him at the plant (about 7 million gallons over a three-year period). Eventually, Baskin Robbins would not agree on a side deal for purchasing ice cream from Copeland, and the purchase fell through. As the court put it, "'[m]any millions of dollars' in anticipated profits had melted away like so much banana ripple ice cream on a hot summer day." *Id.* at 879. Realizing that he could not take the risk in buying the plant without the deal to sell the ice cream, Copeland sued for breach of contract.

While the court rejected the idea that a contract to negotiate in good faith was unenforceable (thus, as in *Sullivan*, the parties had a valid binding contract), it held that Copeland could not recover his expectancy damages from breach of such an agreement. "The plaintiff cannot recover for lost expectations (profits) because there is no way of knowing what the ultimate terms of

---

3. As the *Sullivan* court noted: "Indeed it can be argued that the very suffering or distress 'contracted for'—that which would have been incurred if the treatment achieved the promised result—should also be compensable on the [reliance] theory. . . .For that suffering is 'wasted' if the treatment fails. Otherwise stated, compensation for this waste is arguably required in order to complete the restoration of the status quo ante." *Sullivan*, 296 N.E.2d at 189.

the agreement would have been or even if there would have been an ultimate agreement." *See Copeland*, 117 Cal. Rptr. 2d at 885. Instead, damages "are measured by the injury the plaintiff suffered in relying on the defendant to negotiate in good faith. This measure encompasses the plaintiff's out-of-pocket costs in conducting the negotiations and may or may not include lost opportunity costs." *Id.* In the actual case, plaintiff did not try to prove he had any reliance costs, and therefore the court concluded he could recover nothing.

EXAMPLE

Example 5

Same facts as in *Ricketts* but assume that after the grandfather makes the promise, the granddaughter goes to the bank and gets a $2,000 loan to buy a house. When the grandfather fails to pay, the bank evicts the granddaughter, and she becomes homeless. Living on the street, she develops a number of diseases and incurs $4,000 in medical bills. To what damages, if any, is the granddaughter entitled to in a jurisdiction that has adopted the RESTATEMENT (SECOND) OF CONTRACTS §90?

EXPLANATION

Explanation

Recall that under the RESTATEMENT (SECOND) OF CONTRACTS §90, the remedy may be limited as justice requires. In this case, a court could decide that justice requires enforcing the entire contract ("full-scale enforcement by normal remedies is often appropriate," *id.* cmt. *d*). The contract here is a promise to pay money, however, and normal expectation damages would limit the recovery to the promised amount of money plus interest at the prevailing rate—$2,000 plus interest in this case.

The granddaughter could argue that she should get her reliance damages—which should include her medical expenses that are a consequence of the grandfather's breach. A court would be quite reluctant to grant such damages for two reasons. First, under *Hadley*, it does not appear that such damages are a foreseeable consequence of the grandfather's breach. Second, comment *d* to the Restatement section provides that "[i]n the case of a promise to make a gift it would rarely be proper to award consequential damages which would place a greater burden on the promisor than performance would have imposed."

EXAMPLE

Example 6

Same facts as in *Sullivan v. O'Connor*, except assume that before the surgeon promises the plaintiff a beautiful nose, plaintiff tells the surgeon: "I must have a more beautiful nose. I have been promised the lead in a new movie, contingent on my obtaining plastic surgery to fix my nose's appearance. They are going to pay me $200,000 for the role, and if the movie is successful it will launch my career as a movie star, which could earn me millions of dollars in the future." Unfortunately, after the unsuccessful surgery, plaintiff loses her movie role. How, if at all, does this change the calculation of damages in this case?

EXPLANATION

Explanation

To the extent that the court is compensating only for reliance damages (for the policy reasons set forth in *Sullivan*), these additional facts do not affect the amount of damages. We do not treat forgone opportunities as reliance costs; rather, they are part of the expectancy. To put plaintiff back to the status quo ante would require only payments for the pain of the three surgeries, the cost of the surgery, and the emotional distress that comes from having the worse-looking nose.

If plaintiff could recover expectation damages, it is possible that these additional facts could affect the amount of recovery. In essence, the plaintiff would be arguing that her promised position was high because of the promise of the contract. These appear to be consequential damages (coming after the initial breach, which is the failure of the surgery to produce a more beautiful nose). The $200,000 lost salary could be recoverable as consequential damages because the statement by the plaintiff to the surgeon shows that the lost, potential profit was reasonably foreseeable. Some courts have held, however, that when the breach of a contract would cause disproportionate damages given the risks taken, these damages would not be recoverable. *See Postal Instant Press, Inc. v. Sealy*, 51 Cal. Rptr. 2d 365, 373 (Cal. Ct. App. 1996); *see also* Restatement (Second) of Contracts §351(3) ("A court may limit damages for foreseeable loss by excluding recovery for loss of profits, by allowing recovery only for loss incurred in reliance, or otherwise if it concludes that in the circumstances justice so requires in order to avoid disproportionate compensation."). The damages related to future career prospects seem too uncertain to be recoverable, for reasons we will consider in the next chapter.

EXAMPLE

Example 7

Same facts as in the *Copeland* case but assume the following: Baskin Robbins and Copeland sign a valid contract for Copeland to buy the ice cream factory for $2 million. Baskin Robbins promises to buy at least 7 million gallons of ice cream over three years at the price of $1 over Copeland's cost, with "cost" determined by a complex formula in the contract. After Copeland takes possession of the factory, but before he invests anything to gear up the factory, Baskin Robbins announces it will buy no ice cream from him. (This anticipatory repudiation constitutes a breach of contract under substantive contract law.) Over the next three years, Copeland does his best to sell ice cream, and he sells 3 million gallons of ice cream to other sellers, earning a profit of $1 per gallon. To what damages is Copeland entitled?

EXPLANATION

Explanation

The parties have a valid written contract, and there are no policy reasons for limiting Copeland to recovering only his reliance damages. Accordingly, if he can prove his damages with reasonable certainty, he is going to be able to recover expectancy damages. Also, since this is a contract for the sale of goods, Article 2 of the U.C.C. governs. The buyer has breached, so the seller can resort to his remedies for breach.

One possibility is that Copeland will claim damages under U.C.C. §2-706, which gives the seller the difference between the contract price and the retail price plus incidental damages less expenses saved. Copeland stood to make $7 million on the contract. After the breach, he sold enough ice cream to make only $3 million on the contract. Copeland is left with $4 million plus any incidental costs associated with making the new $3 million sales, less any expenses he saved from having to produce only 3 million rather than 7 million gallons of ice cream. (Some of these costs are going to be reflected in the "cost" element of the contract price formula, and an economist will have to look carefully to figure out how to measure the costs correctly.)

Alternatively, Copeland might argue that he was a lost volume seller. Specifically, he might try to prove that he had the capacity to produce both the ice cream under the original contract with Baskin Robbins and the new ice cream he sold after Baskin Robbins breached. If he can meet the requirements of a lost volume seller, he would be able to recover his "profit (including reasonable overhead) which the seller would have made from full performance by the buyer, together with any incidental damages" less the junk value of any salvage value of goods rejected by the buyer. U.C.C. §2-708(2). Copeland would recover $7 million under this measure. There do not appear to be any incidental damages associated with not producing the 7 million gallons (he cannot look at his costs of producing the 3 million other gallons of ice cream), nor is there any salvage value to any goods rejected by the buyer.

CHAPTER 6

Ensuring the Rightful Position: A Look at Certainty, Mitigation, Offsetting Benefits, and the Collateral Source Rule

So far, we have established that damages are meant to put the plaintiff in the rightful position, and much of the discussion in the last four chapters dealt with how damage rules are an attempt to do so. In this chapter, we deal with four more issues to round out our discussion of damages and the rightful position standard:

1. How certain does the jury have to be about the amount of damages suffered by plaintiff?
2. What steps must the plaintiff take to minimize loss?
3. How should we treat expenses and losses that plaintiff avoids because of the defendant's wrong?
4. How should we treat collateral sources—that is, insurance and government payments that plaintiff receives on account of injuries caused by the defendant?

6.1 THE CERTAINTY REQUIREMENT

It is often said that the plaintiff must prove damages with "reasonable certainty." This statement needs to be taken with a grain of salt in the context of civil litigation, where the dominant standard is that plaintiff must prove her prima facie case by a preponderance of the evidence—a "more likely than not" standard that is much lower than the "beyond a reasonable doubt" standard applicable in criminal cases. Just as plaintiff must prove the other elements of the case (for example, that defendant breached either a duty in a negligence case or a contract in a contracts case) under this preponderance standard, plaintiff must prove damages as an essential element of the prima facie case by the same standard.[1]

Here, we need to distinguish between proof of whether plaintiff suffered damages *at all* (an issue that does need to be proven by a preponderance of the evidence) and whether there is enough evidence to go to the jury so that the jury can set an amount of damages consistent with the evidence.

Here is how the standards are set out in the new Restatement (Torts) Third: Remedies §5 (Am. Law. Inst. Tent. Draft No. 2, 2023):

> **(a) Fact of Damage (Preponderance of the Evidence).**
> The plaintiff must prove by a preponderance of the evidence that defendant's tort was a cause of the harm or harms for which the plaintiff seeks compensation. This requirement is often referred to as proving the "fact of damage." Whether the plaintiff has done so is an issue for the factfinder.
>
> **(b) Amount of Damages (Reasonable Certainty).**
> (1) Except as provided in Subsection (b)(3), a plaintiff must offer sufficient evidence to establish the amount of damages with reasonable certainty. Whether the plaintiff has done so is an issue for the court.
>
> (2) The reasonable-certainty standard requires the plaintiff to offer evidence sufficient to satisfy the court that the factfinder has a reasonable evidentiary basis from which to estimate an approximate amount of damages. In applying this standard, a court must take into account the nature of the tort, the nature of the harm, and the evidence that is or should be reasonably available. Proving the fact of damage and offering the reasonably available evidence on the amount of damages is generally sufficient to satisfy this standard, but in exceptional cases, no available evidence is sufficient to support an estimate based on evidence rather than a guess. The reasonable-certainty standard does not require plaintiff to prove any specific dollar amount of damages by a preponderance of the evidence.
>
> (3) "Noneconomic" damages that cannot be measured by any value in a market, such as pain and suffering, emotional distress,

1. We have seen two exceptions to this principle. Chapter 2 first noted that plaintiffs sometimes may recover nominal damages (such as $1) when plaintiff cannot prove that she suffered actual (compensatory) damages. These nominal damages often serve as a "declaration" to the world of the rights of plaintiff and defendant or provide a hook for the award of punitive damages or attorney's fees. Second, Chapter 3 noted that plaintiffs alleging defamation sometimes may be able to recover "presumed damages" when they cannot (or do not wish to) prove actual damages.

> dignitary harms, and the like, are so inherently imprecise that the reasonable-certainty standard cannot meaningfully be applied. Courts may review the amount of such damages only after the factfinder has awarded them and only under the standards for judicial review of allegedly excessive or inadequate damages in §17.

Note the last part of this Restatement section discussing setting damages for emotional distress, dignitary harm, and similar "noneconomic" damages: the rules of reasonable certainty do not apply. Instead, those amounts are reviewed for being "grossly excessive" or "grossly inadequate" under §17. (See the discussion of this issue in Chapter 3.2.)

In contracts cases, and in torts cases when it comes to economic damages like lost profits or earnings and medical expenses, courts are a bit more demanding in terms of the proof of certainty of damages. Restatement (Second) of Contracts §352 provides: "Damages are not recoverable for loss beyond an amount that the evidence permits to be established with reasonable certainty." The comments to the section emphasize that more certainty is required in contracts cases compared to torts cases.

The certainty principle frequently arises in contracts cases involving a non-breaching party's claim for lost business profits as damages. An illustrative case is *RSB Lab. Servs., Inc. v. BSI, Corp.*, 847 A.2d 599 (N.J. Super. Ct. App. Div. 2004). In *RSB*, plaintiff ran a "bleeding station," an office to which doctors refer patients to have blood or other bodily fluids drawn for analysis in a laboratory. (Patients would probably rather not hear the term doctors use to refer to such a facility!) The business was a successful one, and the plaintiff decided to convert the business into a full-service medical laboratory. Plaintiff secured the necessary license and had a strong potential client base for the full lab from its existing bleeding station business.

Plaintiff contracted with the defendant to buy laboratory equipment, most importantly a refurbished "Hitachi 704" machine used to detect chemical imbalances in the blood. Ultimately, the defendant could not get the supplied Hitachi 704 to work properly, thereby breaching the contract. Plaintiff abandoned the plans for the full-service laboratory and sued for breach of contract. The jury agreed that the defendant breached, and the question on appeal concerned the damages.

An accountant testified at trial as an expert witness for plaintiff on the amount of damages. The expert reviewed paperwork from the existing bleeding station business, obtained data about the profitability of competitors, and performed other work to estimate the amount of profits plaintiffs would have made in running a full-service medical laboratory. The jury awarded approximately $255,000 in damages for lost profits, attorney's fees (allowed under the contract), costs, and prejudgment interest.

On appeal, the main issue was whether the full-service laboratory was a continuation of the bleeding station business or a new business. To someone unfamiliar with the legal issues surrounding the certainty principle, that question probably seems a bit bizarre. Why should plaintiff's recovery of damages for lost profits turn on whether the plaintiff's losses came from a new or existing business?

The answer is that New Jersey is among a minority of jurisdictions that has a per se rule that new businesses cannot recover damages for lost profits. These minority jurisdictions view such damages as too speculative, violating the certainty requirement. This is an older view of the certainty requirement that most jurisdictions and the Restatement have rejected.[2] Restatement (Second) of Contracts §352. Fortunately for the plaintiff in *RSB*, the New Jersey appellate court concluded that the full-service laboratory was a continuation of the bleeding station business, and therefore the plaintiff could recover the lost profits. Unfortunately for other plaintiffs in New Jersey, however, the court reaffirmed the so-called "new business rule" in New Jersey, rejecting cases from the Third Circuit, predicting that the New Jersey Supreme Court would overturn the rule. Thus, until the New Jersey Supreme Court rules otherwise, it appears that plaintiffs starting new businesses won't be able to prove their claims for lost profits in courts applying New Jersey law.

In the majority of jurisdictions that have rejected the new business rule, plaintiffs who claim lost profits from new businesses don't get a free ride on proving damages. Defense lawyers can hammer home the certainty requirement to the jury, arguing about all kinds of reasons why the plaintiff's claim for lost profits from a new business is too speculative. Thus, in a majority of jurisdictions, whether a claim is too speculative is decided on a *case-by-case basis by the jury* rather than rejected on a per se basis as in jurisdictions like New Jersey.

Example 1

Yoni owns a business selling the latest trendy fashions. Sometimes he makes great profits, but at other times his business does quite poorly if he fails to predict the latest fashion trends. Yoni hires Zena, a contractor, to remodel his business. Zena promises to complete construction in three months. Zena is late, however, and it takes her seven months to

2. Similarly, comment 4 to U.C.C. §2-715 (on incidental and consequential damages) provides: "The burden of proving the extent of loss incurred by way of consequential damage is on the buyer, but the section on liberal administration of remedies rejects any doctrine of certainty which requires almost mathematical precision in the proof of loss. Loss may be determined in any manner which is reasonable under the circumstances." Article 2 applies to the *RSB* contract because it is a contract for the sale of goods. New Jersey has adopted §2-715. *See* N.J. Stat. Ann. §12A:2-715. But the comments are not part of the statute, and §2-715 itself does not necessarily preclude New Jersey's new business rule.

complete the remodeling work. Zena's failure to finish on time constitutes a breach of contract. May Yoni recover his lost profits? If so, how will he prove them?

EXPLANATION

Explanation

Yoni has an existing business, so the per se new business rule won't bar his recovery of lost profits even in the minority of jurisdictions (such as New Jersey). Even though the new business rule does not apply, it is uncertain whether Yoni would be able to prove his damages with reasonable certainty. Yoni's past performance is the best predictor of profits. Because he is in a business in which sometimes he makes a profit and sometimes he does not, Zena's lawyer will have an opening to argue to the jury that the award of damages in this case would be too speculative. Yoni's lawyers would have to make some argument as to why his business would have been profitable during the four-month period in which the store remained closed due to Zena's breach.

EXAMPLE

Example 2

Marcia Miller was driving. She and her passenger are severely injured when Miller's new car crashes into a wall. According to Miller, the car's accelerator got stuck, thereby causing an unavoidable collision with a retaining wall. The automobile is a total loss. While Miller is recuperating in the hospital, her father, who is an attorney, contacts Malkin, an agent of Insurer, her automobile insurer. Miller's father informs Malkin that Marcia wants to retain possession of the automobile in order to have it examined by an expert for defects. Her father is of the opinion that his daughter has a products liability claim against the manufacturer. Malkin tells Miller and her father that Insurer wants temporary possession of the car because they plan to have an expert examine it for defects as they anticipate that the passenger injured in the accident will file a claim against Allstate. Eventually the parties reach an agreement whereby Miller relinquishes possession of the car to Insurer so it may prepare for its defense against the claim by the passenger. In exchange, Insurer promises to preserve the car and to make it available for inspection by Miller's experts. The existence of the oral agreement is not disputed. Before any expert examination is performed, however, Insurer, in breach of the agreement, sells the car to a salvage yard, where it is disassembled and disposed of. Miller sues Insurer, alleging that, as a result of Insurer's breach of the agreement to preserve the wrecked automobile for expert inspection, she is denied the opportunity to maintain a products liability action against the manufacturer. To what damages, if any, is Miller entitled for Insurer's breach of contract?

EXPLANATION

Explanation

The statement of facts in this example is taken from a Florida appellate court opinion, *Miller v. Allstate Ins. Co.*, 573 So. 2d 24 (Fla. Dist. Ct. App. 1990). This case presents a very difficult question under the certainty principle. It is well established, as the *Miller* court noted, that "although damages usually must be established within a reasonable degree of certainty, . . . when the difficulty in establishing damages is caused by the defendant, he should bear the risk of uncertainty that his own wrong created." *Id.* at 28. So if an arsonist burns down plaintiff's house and destroys all of plaintiff's belongings, the arsonist cannot defend a tort suit on grounds that plaintiff cannot prove the value of his possessions with reasonable certainty.

This case is harder, however, because the destruction of plaintiff's car did not deprive her of her property but only of a *chance* to prove her products liability case against a manufacturer. We don't know whether the destroyed car was defective. In the case of the arsonist, in contrast, there is no question that the fire caused plaintiff's losses; the only question is the *market value* of those losses.

In the *Miller* case, the court allowed plaintiff to recover damages for the loss of the *opportunity* to prove her products liability case. It is not clear, however, exactly how the jury is supposed to value this lost opportunity. To award the full value of a products liability suit that only had a chance of success seems to put the plaintiff in a position better than the rightful position (she was deprived of a *chance*, not of a sure claim).

One possible way to award damages consistent with the rightful position standard would be to assess the damages that plaintiff would have been able to recover in the products liability suit had it been successful, discounted by the probability that plaintiff would have successfully proven her products liability case. For example, if plaintiff could have recovered damages of $100,000 from the products liability suit, and the jury believed she had a 30% chance of winning her products liability suit, her damages would be $100,000 × 0.30, or $30,000. But defendants could reasonably question whether such a standard is consistent with the usual preponderance of the evidence standard applicable in civil cases: looking at the 30% figure, we cannot say she was more likely than not to have sustained these losses. All in all, a very difficult question.

6.2 THE MITIGATION REQUIREMENT

6.2.1 Avoidable Losses: Rules and Economic Rationale

In assessing damages, the law treats plaintiffs as though they took reasonable steps to avoid further loss whether or not they actually did so. This "avoidable consequences" or "mitigation" rule helps defendants minimize the amount of damages they must pay, and when it is misunderstood or misapplied by plaintiffs, it can lead to damages awards that leave plaintiffs in a position below the rightful position.

To take a simple example, suppose Alice negligently knocks Bea over on the street. Bea gets some cuts and scrapes on her right leg. Rather than take care of the cuts and scrapes by applying an antibiotic ointment, Bea does nothing. Bea develops a stubborn infection, and her leg eventually is amputated to prevent the infection from killing her.

At first glance, Bea might look no different from the plaintiff in *Vosburg* (see Chapter 3) who lost a leg as the result of the defendant's kick. There we said the defendant had to pay for all the damages he caused under the "thin-skulled" or "egg shell" plaintiff rule: you take the plaintiff as you find him or her. Though plaintiff sought medical attention, he still lost the use of his leg. Plaintiff in *Vosburg* recovered damages covering the entire loss he suffered.

In the Alice-Bea hypothetical, however, the additional harm could have been prevented by Bea, but it wasn't. In that situation, a court would say—if Alice's lawyer raised the issue—that Bea could recover only for losses that were *unavoidable*. This failure to mitigate, therefore, could prevent Bea from getting damages to restore her to the rightful position. To give a numerical example, suppose that a jury would value Bea's loss of a leg (and accompanying noneconomic damages) at $500,000. If we consider Bea's position after the wrong, she is at −$500,000. If the jury believes, however, that it is more likely than not that Bea could have avoided the loss of the leg through reasonable mitigation, and that if she had mitigated her injury she would have suffered $1,000 in damages, Bea recovers only the $1,000. This leaves her at −$499,000 (Point A-)—far from B, the status quo ante. See Figure 6.1.

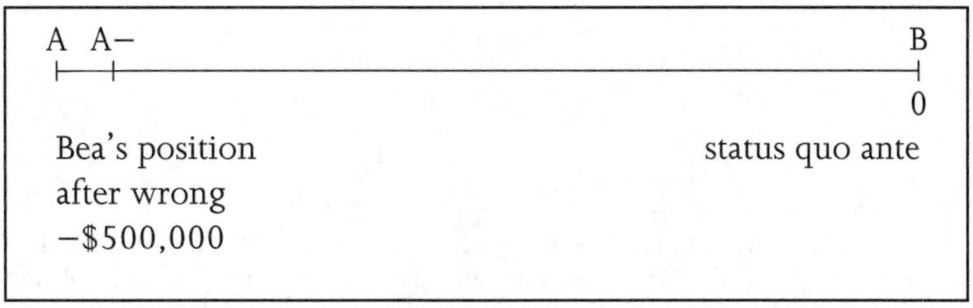

Figure 6.1

Though it is sometimes said that plaintiffs have a "duty to mitigate," this terminology is confusing. Alice cannot be sued by Bea if Bea fails to take reasonable steps to mitigate her injuries. But because the law of damages requires the jury to treat Bea as though she mitigated when the defendant raises the issue, Bea has every incentive to mitigate. (Besides the possibility of tort recovery, Bea has every incentive to take reasonable steps to mitigate because damages cannot adequately substitute for the loss of a leg; thus, we would expect Bea would still take care of the health of her leg.)[3]

We can easily see the potential unfairness to defendants in allowing plaintiffs to "pile on damages" that reasonably could be avoided. But there is an efficiency rationale for the rule as well: so long as plaintiffs understand the rule in advance, it makes plaintiffs no worse off and makes defendants better off.[4] To illustrate it, consider the classic mitigation case, *Rockingham County v. Luten Bridge Co.*, 35 F.2d 301 (4th Cir. 1929). Rockingham County contracted with Luten Bridge Company to build a bridge. After the bridge company had spent about $1,900 on labor and materials, the county said it was breaching the contract. The county no longer wanted the bridge, because it had changed its development plans, and therefore it did not want to pay any more for a "bridge to nowhere."

Even after the county told the bridge company about the breach, however, Luten continued to build the bridge. Luten then sued for $18,000, the amount plaintiff claimed it was due for the work done.

Let's suppose that the total cost of the bridge for the bridge company was $10,000. Had there been no breach, the bridge company stood to make a profit of $8,000 ($18,000 – $10,000), or Luten's promised position.

Now, suppose we did *not* have the mitigation rule and the bridge company had completed its work. In assessing the bridge company's total damages, its promised position, C in Figure 6.2, was $8,000, or the profit it was anticipating before the breach. Its position after the wrong, A, was –$10,000, or the amount the company spent building the bridge. Its total damages would be (C – A), or $8,000 – (–$10,000), or $18,000. After paying itself back for its expenses ($10,000), the bridge company's ledger would show a profit of $8,000. The county, on the other hand, is out $18,000 with a bridge to nowhere.

3. Here is how the RESTATEMENT (THIRD) TORTS: REMEDIES §8(a) (Am. Law Inst. Tent. Draft No. 1, 2022) puts the avoidable consequences principle in the context of negligence or a strict liability tort: "A plaintiff cannot recover damages for any item or increment of harm caused by defendant's negligent or strict-liability tort if defendant proves that, after the commission of the tort and after the plaintiff became aware of that item or increment of harm (incurred or impending), the plaintiff could have avoided that item or increment of harm by reasonable effort or expenditure and without undue risk, difficulty, or embarrassment, and failed to do so."

4. Not only is the rule Kaldor-Hicks efficient (see Chapter 2, footnote 2) because the gains to the winners exceed the losses to the losers, but it is also Pareto efficient because no party is made worse off and at least one party is made better off.

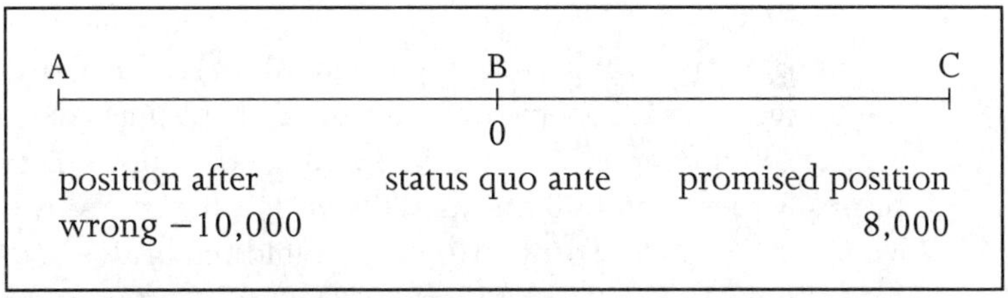

Bridge company profit: $8,000
County's cost: $18,000

Figure 6.2 Bridge Company Damages Under No Mitigation Rule

Now consider the same county-bridge scenario except that this time, there is a mitigation rule, and the bridge company stops working immediately when it hears of the breach (after it has spent $1,900—its reliance costs). The bridge company then promptly sues for damages.

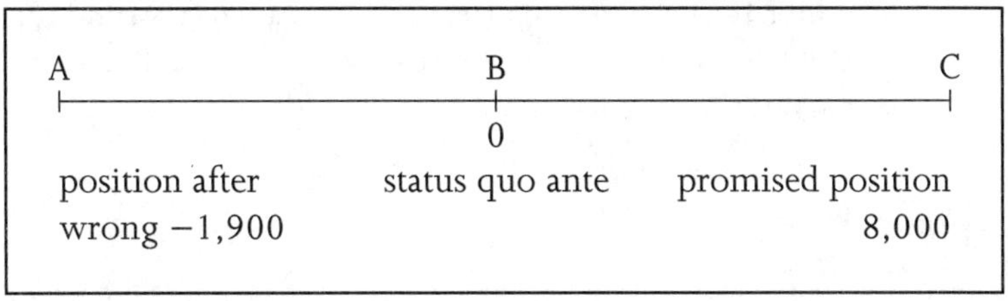

Bridge company profit: $8,000
County's cost: $9,900

Figure 6.3 Bridge Company Damages Under a Mitigation Rule Where Bridge Company Mitigates

As in the last example, the bridge company's promised position, C, was $8,000, or the profit it was anticipating before the breach. Its position after the wrong, A, was −$1,900, or the amount the company had spent in building the bridge until it heard about the breach. (See Figure 6.3.) Its total damages would be (C – A), or $8,000 – (−$1,900), or $9,900. After paying itself back for its expenses, the bridge company's ledger would show a profit of $8,000. The county, on the other hand, is out $9,900, with only a partially built bridge to nowhere.

The example demonstrates the economic efficiency of the mitigation rule. Whether or not there is a mitigation rule, the bridge company ends up with $8,000 in profit. A mitigation rule, however, saves the county $8,100, which represents the cost of completing the bridge to nowhere after the county had told the bridge company of the county's breach. The rule is thus efficient because it leaves a non-breaching party (who understands the rule) in the same position, but also can greatly aid the defendant.

The result in the *Rockingham County* case demonstrates that a plaintiff fails to mitigate at its own peril. Using the numbers set out above, the law allows the bridge company to recover damages *as though it mitigated*, meaning damages of $9,900 rather than the $18,000 contract price. Because the bridge company spent $10,000 finishing the bridge, the company ends up with its ledger at −$100 (it spent $10,000 to build the bridge and received damages of only $9,900) rather than at +$8,000, a costly mistake.

EXAMPLE

Example 3

Charlie is driving down Main Street very carefully, but he is not wearing a seat belt. Daniella is driving drunk the wrong way down Main Street, and slams headfirst into Charlie's car. Charlie is paralyzed from the waist down because of the accident, and he won't be able to work again. A jury considering the extent of his damages would value them at $1 million. The experts agree that if Charlie had been wearing a seat belt, he would only have sustained relatively minor injuries, and his damages would not have exceeded $50,000. Should Charlie's failure to wear a seat belt be considered a failure to mitigate? If so, what should Charlie's damages be?

EXPLANATION

Explanation

The question of how to deal with an injured party's failure to wear a seat belt has been a contentious issue in the states. The failure to wear a seat belt might be relevant to the question of mitigation, the tort affirmative defense of comparative negligence (which in many states would reduce the plaintiff's recovery based upon the jury's determination of the percentage of plaintiff's fault or responsibility in not wearing the seat belt), or neither. *See Derheim v. N. Fiorito Co.*, 492 P.2d 1030 (Wash. 1972). Other courts (and in some cases legislatures via statute) have allowed evidence of plaintiff's failure to wear a seat belt as relevant to the mitigation question. *See Spier v. Barker*, 323 N.E.2d 164 (N.Y. 1974); N.Y. VEH. & TRAF. §1229-c(8).

The *Spier* court noted the chronological oddity, however, of treating the failure to wear a seat belt as a mitigation issue:

> We concede that the opportunity to mitigate damages prior to the occurrence of an accident does not ordinarily arise, and that the chronological distinction, on which the concept of mitigation damages rests, is justified in most cases. However, in our opinion, the seat belt affords the automobile occupant an unusual and ordinarily unavailable means by which he or she may minimize his or her damages *[p]rior* to the accident.

Spier, 323 N.E.2d at 168 (emphasis added).

The issue would matter a great deal to Charlie. Under a rule treating the failure to wear a seat belt as a failure to mitigate, if the jury finds that had Charlie mitigated, he would have suffered only $50,000 in damages (rather than the $1 million he actually suffered), Charlie's recovery would be $50,000.

6.2.2 Mitigation Under Article 2 of the U.C.C.

Note how the U.C.C. provisions build in mitigation principles. When a seller breaches and a buyer does not cover (we'll be talking about when the buyer *does* cover in the next section, on offsetting benefits), the buyer is entitled to market damages under §2-713 (see Chapter 4.5.1). Recall the formula:

> Amounts toward the purchase price paid to seller + (market price at the place of tender − contract price) + incidental and consequential damages − expenses saved

Recall the hypothetical from Chapter 4 in which Mona agrees to buy an automobile worth $29,000 for $25,000. Putting aside amounts already paid to the seller (Lisa), incidental and consequential damages, and expenses saved, Mona is entitled to $4,000, the difference between the market price at the time of tender and the contract price. This formula *builds in the idea of mitigation*. It treats Mona as if she went out and made the substitute purchase of the automobile for $29,000. By giving her $4,000 in damages (again, ignoring the further complications in the §2-713 formula), she gets the same benefit of the bargain: she gets to have her red Lexus convertible for a total cost of $25,000, $4,000 below the going market price.

The same principle is at work when a buyer breaches a contract governed by Article 2 of the U.C.C. When the buyer breaches and the seller does not resell immediately (we'll be talking about when the seller does resell in the next section, on offsetting benefits), the seller is entitled to damages for non-acceptance under §2-708(1):[5]

> (contract price − market price) + incidental damages − expenses saved

5. We are ignoring cases governed by §2-709, when the goods have been accepted but not paid for. See Example 4 in this chapter, discussing mitigation issues under §2-709. The next section, on offsetting benefits, discusses lost volume seller issues.

Again, recall the hypothetical from Chapter 4 where Mona broke the promise to buy the automobile from Lisa. If Mona agreed to buy it for $1,500 above the market price, then Lisa is entitled to that difference (putting aside incidental damages and expenses saved). The formula treats Lisa *as though she resold the car* at the (lower) market price, even if she doesn't sell the automobile. When Lisa doesn't sell and gets damages from Mona, she is left in the same position as if the contract had gone through. She has the value of the automobile plus the $1,500 profit she expected to make on the sale to Mona.

Example 4

Ernesto manufactured a custom piece of glass to be installed in Fred and Gertrude's dream home. Fred and Gertrude promised to pay $10,000 for the glass. Ernesto received a $5,000 deposit. After Ernesto finished manufacturing the glass but before he delivered it, Fred and Gertrude decided to get a divorce, and a court determined they breached the contract by not paying. Ernesto cannot resell the glass to anyone else because it is a custom size and shape. Its value as scrap is $100. How much may Ernesto recover in damages from Fred and Gertrude?

Explanation

This is a contract for the sale of a moveable good governed by Article 2 of the U.C.C. Recall that sellers can bring an "action for the price" under §2-709 for goods still in the seller's possession if the seller "is unable after reasonable effort to resell them at a reasonable price or the circumstances reasonably indicate that such effort will be unavailing." A custom piece of glass cannot be resold. The §2-709 formula is:

contract price + incidental damages

Ernesto has already received $5,000 in payment. He should be able to recover an additional $5,000 toward the contract price, plus any incidental damages he had in having to store the good. Ernesto's recovery should be reduced by $100, the scrap value of the window.

Example 5

Same facts as in Example 4, but Fred and Gertrude don't get a divorce. Instead, Ernesto, who is busy with other jobs, fails to deliver the glass window as promised to Fred and Gertrude's house on July 1. The market price of a replacement window is $10,000, but it will take two weeks to manufacture and deliver. July 1 was the day that Fred and Gertrude had all of their possessions delivered to the house. Because the house was missing the large glass window, thieves were able to enter the house and steal $50,000 worth of Fred and Gertrude's goods. How much may the couple recover from Ernesto?

EXPLANATION

Explanation

Again, this contract is governed by Article 2 of the U.C.C. Fred and Gertrude did not go out and cover, so they should be able to recover damages under the §2-713 market measure:

> Amounts toward the purchase price paid to seller + (market price at the place of tender − contract price) + incidental and consequential damages − expenses saved

They certainly can recover the $5,000 purchase price paid to the seller. The difference between the market price and the contract price is 0 (both Ernesto and the market would charge $10,000 for the window). The real battle here is going to be over the consequential damages. Ernesto has two arguments as to why he should not have to pay consequential damages for the stolen property. First, it may not have been reasonably foreseeable that Fred and Gertrude would suffer these losses. Sure, a missing window can be an opportunity for crime. But most people would have taken steps (such as having the area boarded up with plywood) until a replacement window could be made available. Unforeseeable consequential damages are not recoverable. The second point is related to the first: Fred and Gertrude failed to take reasonable steps in mitigation to provide a temporary barrier to prevent entry into their home. They therefore might not be able to recover anything beyond the $5,000 deposit from Ernesto.

If Fred and Gertrude had been smart and had the area boarded up with plywood, the expenses of doing so arguably would count as incidental damages that they could recover under U.C.C. §2-715(1) as "reasonable expense incident to the delay or other breach."

6.2.3 What Are "Reasonable" Steps in Mitigation?

While the law treats plaintiffs as though they took reasonable steps to mitigate losses, it is not required that they take unreasonable steps to avoid loss to help the defendant. Recall the new Restatement (Third) Torts: Remedies §8(a) standard of a step that could be taken "without undue risk, difficulty, or embarrassment" to the plaintiff.

A good example of this principle is found in *McGinley v. United States*, 329 F. Supp. 62 (E.D. Pa. 1971). There the court held that plaintiff, who had already undergone surgical procedures to alleviate pain from a herniated disc in his back, could collect future lost wages damages for his back injury. The court rejected the defendant's argument that the damages should have been reduced because plaintiff refused to undergo additional surgery to help his back problem, which could have allowed him to work.

The court held that plaintiff need not have mitigated by having further surgery, which had only a 60% to 70% chance of being successful and could in fact have worsened his condition. The court wrote:

> It is, of course, settled law that if injuries may be cured or alleviated by a simple and safe surgical operation, then refusal to submit thereto should be considered in mitigation of damages. . . . This is not true, however, where the operation is a serious one, or one attended by grave risk of death or failure. . . . A plaintiff has a duty to submit to reasonable medical treatment and the test of reasonableness is to be determined by the triers of fact.

Id. at 66 (citations omitted).

Often, steps to mitigate are straightforward. For example, if the lab owner in the *RSB* case easily could have purchased a different "Hitachi 704" machine for use in the lab, the failure to do so would preclude the recovery of any damages (such as lost profits) that could have been avoided by the substitute purchase. In other words, rather than sit around thinking about one's losses caused by a defendant, a plaintiff needs to go out and proactively take reasonable steps to minimize the loss.

One area where the mitigation issue is often litigated concerns claims for lost wages when the plaintiff fails to obtain substitute employment. A famous case in this regard is *Parker v. Twentieth Century–Fox Film Corp.*, 474 P.2d 689 (Cal. 1970), involving the actress Shirley MacLaine. MacLaine had a contract with the Twentieth Century Fox movie studio to star in a movie musical called "Bloomer Girl." Her contract provided for filming in California and for MacLaine's approval of the director. Fox breached the contract. Right after the breach, Fox offered her a part in a Western movie, "Big Country, Big Man," to be filmed in Australia (without MacLaine's choice of director).

When MacLaine sued for breach, Fox argued that MacLaine failed to mitigate her damages because she did not accept the substitute employment. The California Supreme Court rejected the argument, holding that an employee must take alternative employment to mitigate only when the employment is not different or inferior from the promised employment. Here, the court said that the new employment was different: it involved no singing or dancing; it was a Western, not a musical; MacLaine had no choice of director; and it had been filmed in Australia, not California.

The rule in *Parker* is one that primarily protects the social position of a professional. A court is not going to hold that an attorney who has been wrongfully terminated from his job at a law firm must mitigate damages by taking a job flipping hamburgers at McDonald's, but it might hold that an unskilled garment worker who has been wrongfully terminated from a job in a clothing factory has to take that McDonald's job. In part, this rule might be justified, because it is going to be much harder for the fired attorney to get another attorney's job after working some time at McDonald's than for the garment worker to get a similar job after working some time at McDonald's. Still, there's a certain elitism to the rules regarding mitigation and employment.

Example 6

Hila runs over Ivan with her Hummer, causing serious internal injuries. Because of Ivan's religious convictions, he refuses to have a blood transfusion, and dies. Ivan's family brings a wrongful death case against Hila. The undisputed medical evidence establishes that had Ivan taken the blood transfusion, he would have recovered completely, suffering only $15,000 in damages. Should the court allow Ivan's family to recover no more than the $15,000, on grounds that Ivan failed to mitigate?

Explanation

This hypothetical puts the rule on mitigation directly in conflict with First Amendment principles of religious freedom. Putting aside the religion issue, failure to undergo a life-saving blood transfusion is going to be viewed by most juries as an unreasonable choice, and the jury would likely find that the injured party should have mitigated. But the freedom of religion issue complicates matters a great deal. If a jury would hold that the failure to mitigate was unreasonable, it might be making a decision that the injured party's religious convictions were unreasonable.

Perhaps unsurprisingly, courts have split over how to deal with the mitigation question in these circumstances. *Compare Munn v. Algee*, 924 F.2d 568 (5th Cir. 1991) (religious views irrelevant to mitigation question), *with Rozewicz v. New York City Health and Hosps. Corp.*, 656 N.Y.S.2d 593 (N.Y. Sup. Ct. 1997) (no issue of mitigation and no assumption of risk defense if refusal was based on sincere religious belief), *and Williams v. Bright*, 658 N.Y.S.2d 910 (N.Y. App. Div. 1997) (no mitigation problem if injured party acted as a "reasonable believer"). Consider whether or not Ivan looks like the "thin-skulled" plaintiff we've seen in earlier chapters. Is it true, when you injure someone with these religious convictions, that you "take the plaintiff as you find him"?

6.3 OFFSETTING BENEFITS

Mitigation claims arise when a plaintiff can take steps to avoid further loss but fails to do so. The issue of *offsetting benefits* arises when a plaintiff actually takes steps to avoid loss. In such a case, those steps taken to avoid loss must be taken into account in computing plaintiff's damages so as to prevent the plaintiff from obtaining a double recovery.[6]

Recall the window washing hypothetical from Chapter 4. You own a window washing business. You sign a contract with Gary's World of Glass to wash the 200 windows on the outside of Gary's showroom. Gary agrees to pay you $3,000 to wash the windows upon completion of the work.

Suppose that two weeks before you are supposed to begin washing Gary's windows, Gary breaches. You then receive a call from John offering you $3,000 to do the same work at his business on the same day. To do either Gary's original job or John's job would cost you $1,000. You do not have multiple crews, and there is no way you would have been able to complete both Gary's job and John's job. You accept the deal with John and then sue Gary for damages.

In this hypothetical, there is no question that although Gary has breached the contract, you will not be entitled to damages. To see why, recall that if Gary had kept his promise, your ledger would have been up $2,000 (the profit on the job: the $3,000 contract price less your $1,000 cost). If you sued Gary for breach of contract, at first glance it would appear that you would be entitled to $2,000: the difference between the promised position (C) of $2,000 and the position after the wrong (A), when you were paid nothing by Gary, or 0.

This analysis is incomplete, however, because it fails to take into account the offsetting benefits issue. Gary's breach *has freed up resources* that you may use for other jobs. When you took the job with John, you used resources you could not have used had Gary kept his promise. We must take this into account in the calculation. Because the job with John yielded the same $2,000 profit, and because there were no incidental costs (such as searching for a new job) or consequential damages, your damages would be zero.

It might be tempting for you then to say that there's no point in taking that additional job from John, in the hopes that a jury would award you the $2,000 profit from the original job (better to get the $2,000 from

---

6. The RESTATEMENT (THIRD) TORTS: REMEDIES §9 (Am Law Inst. Tent. Draft No. 2, 2023) states the general principle in the torts context: "If a defendant's tort harms the plaintiff and also causes or enables the plaintiff to receive a benefit that the plaintiff could not have received but for the tort, the plaintiff's damages generally should be reduced by the amount of the benefit. But the court may refuse to set off such a benefit if it would be inequitable or inappropriate to do so. The court must not set off any benefit that plaintiff is entitled to retain under §10 on compensation from collateral sources."

not working than from working, perhaps). But that would be a mistake, because, as we just saw in section 6.2, the failure to take reasonable steps in mitigation reduces the plaintiff's recovery. The law is going to treat you as if you took reasonable steps in mitigation whether you did so or not.

Now suppose that John called and offered to hire you for the same $3,000 contract price, but because John has more windows, it is going to cost you $1,300 rather than $1,000 to complete the job. It is reasonable for you to take the job with John, because if you don't, there is a good chance you won't find other work to do that day. In that case, you would be able to recover damages based on the difference between the promised position (C) and the position you ended up in after the wrong (A). See Figure 6.4.

In this case, the promised position (C) is the $2,000 profit you would have made had Gary not breached. The tricky part here is the position after the wrong (A). By taking the substitute job with John, your ledger is up by $1,700 (the difference between the substitute contract price of $3,000 and your $1,300 costs). The total damages are $300 (C – A).

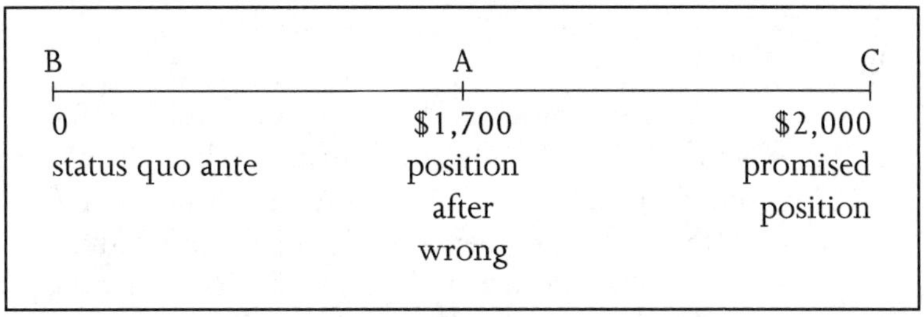

Figure 6.4 Profits After Offsetting Benefits Taken into Account in Window Washing Hypothetical

You should see how this calculation of damages makes sense. You take on the substitute work, ending up with $1,700 in profits on your ledger. The $300 in damages moves you to $2,000, the position you would have been in but for Gary's breach of contract.

Offsetting benefits arise not only when resources are freed up on account of defendant's wrong. They also occur when there are *expenses saved* on account of the breach. Indeed, we have already seen this principle at work in one of the Lisa-Mona hypotheticals from Chapter 4 under U.C.C. §2-712.

Lisa promises Mona in a valid written contract that she will deliver to Mona a 2013 red Lexus convertible for $25,000. The car was in excellent shape, except that it needed its air conditioning repaired at a cost of $1,000. Mona pays Lisa a $5,000 deposit. The next day, Lisa tells Mona she cannot deliver the car, because it was damaged during delivery. Mona searches for a similar used car. She cannot find a 2013 red Lexus convertible in good condition, but she finds a 2014 silver Lexus convertible at a purchase price of $28,000. Lisa spends $50 in gas checking out cars before she purchases the silver Lexus. Assume the court finds that the purchase by Lisa of the silver Lexus convertible constitutes a reasonable cover.

The purchasing of a substitute car takes care of any issues related to mitigation. Here, consider the $1,000 air conditioning repair expense that Lisa was able to avoid in making her substitute purchase. This is an expense saved, and it counts as an offsetting benefit *that must be subtracted from the total recovery under* the §2-712 formula.[7]

Lisa can recover:

$5,000	(purchase price paid to seller)
+ $3,000	(the difference between the cover price and contract price)
+ $50	(the incidental cost of obtaining cover (see above for a definition of incidental damages))
− $1,000	(the expenses saved: the air conditioning repair no longer necessary)
= $7,050	(Total damages)

U.C.C. seller's remedies also account for mitigation and offsetting benefits issues. U.C.C. §2-706 provides that when the seller makes a resale "in good faith and in a commercially reasonable manner," "the seller may recover the difference between the resale price and the contract price together with any incidental damages allowed under the provisions of this Article (§2-710), but less expenses saved in consequence of the buyer's breach."

The one instance where proceeds of resale are not subtracted as an offsetting benefit arises in the case of the lost volume seller, described in more detail in Chapter 4.5.2. Resale proceeds do not count as an offsetting benefit for the lost volume seller, because the whole idea behind the lost volume seller concept is that the seller could make both sales at a profit. To use an example not governed by Article 2 of the U.C.C., if you had enough staff at your window washing business to wash *both* Gary's windows *and* John's windows and earn your profits, you might be able to recover the $2,000 profit you expected to make on the contract with Gary. In that circumstance it would not be a double recovery for you to collect

7. Recall that the §2-712 formula is:

> Amounts toward the purchase price paid to seller + (cover price − contract price) + incidental and consequential damages − expenses saved

both damages from Gary and contract proceeds from John. In contrast, in the original hypothetical, where you could do only one of the two jobs, allowing you to recover both sums *would* be a double recovery, giving you $2,000 from Gary and $2,000 in profits from the job with John, putting you in a position $2,000 better than you would have been in had there been no breach.

Example 7

Rudolph was a successful ballet dancer until Jesse robbed him one day. In the course of the robbery, Jesse shot Rudolph in the leg. Rudolph suffered serious personal injuries and will never be able to dance again. His salary at the Big City Ballet was $100,000 per year, for working 80-hour weeks when the ballet was in season. He likely would have worked for 10 more years as a ballet dancer. His past medical bills for the shooting were $50,000, and he will need physical therapy for the next five years. He has suffered serious emotional distress. While recuperating, Rudolph wrote a novel that has turned out to be a blockbuster, earning him $2 million in royalties. He never would have had the time to write the novel while dancing. He has signed an advance of $3 million for his next novel. A jury finds Jesse liable for the tort of battery. What damages may Rudolph recover from Jesse?

Explanation

Putting aside the offsetting benefits issue for a moment, Rudolph is going to be entitled to his past and expected future wages and medical expenses, discounted to present value. There could be testimony as to what Rudolph's salary would be over his expected 10-year career as a ballet dancer, as well as his future earning potential losses as a result of the shooting. He will also be able to get $50,000 in medical expenses, plus the expected future costs of physical therapy as discounted to present value. He will also be able to recover his emotional distress damages, which could be substantial.

The interesting offsetting benefits issue in this case arises from Rudolph's writing of the novel. It appears that the shooting freed up resources (namely, Rudolph's free time) that allowed for the writing of the novel. Just as you could not wash both Gary's windows and John's windows, Rudolph could not both dance ballet and write the novel. One could argue that that Rudolph's damages should be reduced by the significant benefits he has received (and will receive, discounted to present value) for his future career as a novelist. Perhaps Rudolph's lawyer can convince a court that these damages should be used to offset only the future lost wages, rather than the entirety of the damages (including medical expenses and emotional distress damages).

6.4 THE COLLATERAL SOURCE RULE

Suppose Ken drove his car down the street, crashing into Lola's fence. The crash causes $1,000 in property damage. Lola makes a claim with her insurance company. The company applies Lola's $250 deductible to her claim, sending her a check for $750 to pay for repairing the fence. Lola then sues Ken for negligence, and the jury agrees that Ken was negligent.

If we apply the principles from the previous section of this chapter, on offsetting benefits, Lola should be entitled to only $250 in damages. She received the $750 check from her insurance company *as a benefit* that she would not have received but for Ken's wrong. In this way, the insurance check is like John's payment for washing your windows, which you received *as a benefit* after Gary breached the window-washing contract. Recall that we must deduct those payments from John under offsetting benefit principles.

But we do not treat the two kinds of benefits the same. Under the *collateral source rule, insurance and certain government benefit payments that are wholly independent of the tortfeasor do not get deducted from the plaintiff's award of tort damages*. Lola therefore would get to keep her $750 insurance payment *and* collect $1,000 in damages, bringing her to a *better position* than had Ken not crashed into her fence. As illustrated in Figure 6.5, after the wrong, Lola moves to position A, which is at −$1,000. The award of $1,000 in damages from Ken moves Lola back to 0 (B), the status quo ante. The additional check from Lola's insurance company, however, moves her to a position better than 0, to B+, which is at +$750. Thus, after the accident, recovery of damages, and receipt of money from the collateral source, Lola is in a better position than she would have been in (position B, or 0) had Ken never crashed his car into Lola's fence.

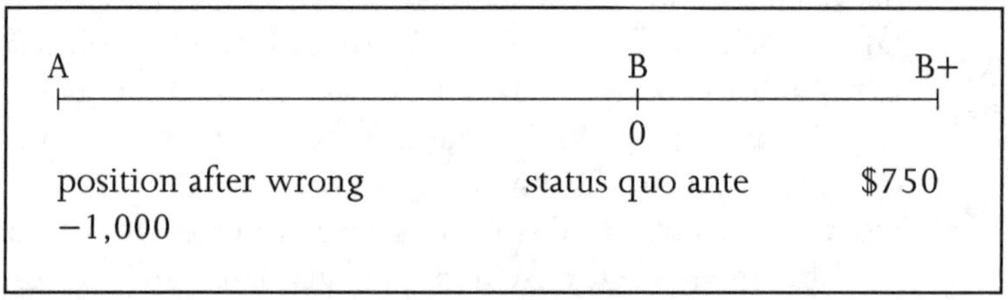

Figure 6.5 Plaintiff's Position Under the Collateral Source Rule

What counts as a collateral source? According to the Restatement (Third) Torts: Remedies §10 (Am. Law Inst. Tent. Draft No. 2, 2023),

> (a) Except as otherwise provided by statute, the plaintiff's damages must not be reduced on account of any payment or benefit, in cash or otherwise, that a collateral source pays or provides to or on behalf of the plaintiff either:
>
> (1) gratuitously,

(2) in performance of an obligation undertaken for consideration paid before plaintiff discovered the injuries or losses,

(3) under the terms of an insurance policy, whenever purchased, or

(4) under the terms of a social-welfare program sponsored by a government or nonprofit entity.

(b) A collateral source is a person or entity that is either:

(1) independent of any defendant, or

(2) a defendant or affiliated entity acting in a different capacity from the one in which defendant committed the tort and paying from a fund to which plaintiff contributed, or to which another person contributed on plaintiff's behalf.

In the Lola example, the insurance company payments fall under §10(a)(3) and are therefore not considered in computing offsetting benefits because it is a collateral source.

Why does the collateral source rule allow plaintiffs such as Lola to get what appears to be a double recovery? The most persuasive answer is that the rule encourages people to purchase insurance. There are going to be a number of cases where an injured person won't have a defendant to sue, or the defendant will have no assets to pay for damages. The collateral source rule encourages potential tort victims to purchase insurance.

There is also a potential fairness argument. If we limited Lola to recovering only $250, it means that *Ken*, rather than *Lola*, would get the benefit of the insurance Lola purchased. On the other hand, it is Gary, rather than you, who gets the benefit of the payments you receive from John after Gary breached the contract with you.

The California Supreme Court also has justified the rule "to compensate for the attorney's share" of the damages award that personal injury plaintiffs receive under a contingency fee agreement. *See Helfend v. Southern Cal. Rapid Transit Dist.*, 465 P.2d 61 (Cal. 1970). But the collateral source rule seems to be a blunt tool with which to deal with problems of attorney's fees.

The collateral source rule also does not *inevitably* lead to a double recovery. For example, if Ken ran over Lola rather than Lola's fence, and Lola sought damages for the personal injuries she sustained, she might be able to recover damages for her medical expenses as well as have her medical expenses paid by her private insurer (a collateral source). But her contract with the medical insurance company could contain a *subrogation clause*, requiring that any payments Lola receives to compensate her for medical expenses must first go to pay back the insurer for its costs in taking care of Lola.[8]

8. This subrogation clause can create some interesting incentives when it comes to settling cases. Plaintiff and defendant might collude to classify very little of a settlement payment as reimbursement for medical expenses, thereby attempting to avoid the subrogation rule.

Because plaintiffs may in some cases receive a double recovery, some states have abolished or changed the rule, often by statute (though the restrictions have sometimes been challenged as violating applicable state constitutional provisions). In California, for example, Civil Code §3333.1 abolishes the collateral source rule as to medical malpractice claims against health care providers. That section provides, however, that plaintiff may recover the value of the premium payments paid to become entitled to the insurance benefits.

Notably, when Congress established the fund to compensate victims of the terrorist attacks on September 11, 2001, it expressly provided that the special master administering the fund deduct the amount of compensation "by the amount of the collateral source compensation the claimant has received or is entitled to receive as a result of the terrorist-related aircraft crashes of September 11, 2001." Air Transportation Safety and System Stabilization Act, Pub. L. No. 107-42, §(405)(b)(6). It included among collateral benefits "all collateral sources, including life insurance, pension funds, death benefit programs, and payments by Federal, state, or local governments" related to the September 11 attacks. *Id.*, §402(4).

In his final report, the special master stated that the issue of collateral source reductions "proved to be one of the fund's most contentious issues," with some opponents "vociferously argu[ing]" that the rule "unfairly penalized families of victims who planned ahead by purchasing life insurance or other means of securing financial security for their families and that collateral sources are typically not offset in wrongful death suits." Final Report of the Special Master of the September 11 Victim Compensation Fund of 2001 at 44. https://securitypolicylaw.syr.edu/wp-content/uploads/2012/09/Special-Masters-Final-Report.pdf. The special master created detailed rules "to reconcile the unequivocal language of the Act on collateral offsets with the Fund's purpose of providing financial support to victims' families based upon their individual needs and circumstances." *Id.* If you were in Congress, would you have included a rule on deducting collateral sources? Why, or why not?

Example 8

Miguel is injured in an automobile accident caused by Nancy. He receives $10,000 worth of medical care, paid for by his health insurer. Miguel paid a $500 premium for the medical coverage during the relevant time period. Miguel misses six weeks of work, thereby failing to earn $15,000 in salary. The jury awards plaintiff $25,000 in economic damages and $6,000 in noneconomic damages for his pain and suffering. Should the judge deduct the value of the medical care paid for by Miguel's insurance company from Miguel's award? If so, how much should the judge deduct?

(Defendant might agree to do this in order to pay a lower overall amount to the plaintiff.) Such practices, at the very least, raise serious ethical concerns.

Explanation

If the jurisdiction applies the collateral source rule, the value of the medical care paid for by the insurer should *not* be deducted; that is the point of the collateral source rule. Miguel therefore can get a double recovery for the medical portion of the cost of his injuries (that is, his medical care has been paid for by his insurer, and he receives additional amounts to compensate him for this medical care from the jury's award of damages paid by Nancy). Miguel won't get the double recovery, however, if the contract with his medical insurer contains a subrogation clause, and the insurer actually goes after Miguel for the payment (not all insurers will do so).

If the jurisdiction has repealed the collateral source rule, then those costs must be deducted from Miguel's recovery, less the payment of premiums. Thus, if the jury awarded $25,000 in economic damages, the judge would have to deduct $9,500 ($10,000 in benefits less the $500 premium) from the award, leaving Miguel with a total of $15,500 in economic damages (the award for noneconomic damages is not affected).

Example 9

Robert is a veteran entitled to free medical care from the Department of Veterans Affairs of the U.S. government. While recovering from surgery at a government-run Veterans Hospital, the staff negligently disconnects the alarm system on the ventilator to which he was attached. While the alarm was disconnected, the tube supplying oxygen to Robert became disengaged. When these disconnections were discovered, approximately eight minutes later, Robert was in complete cardiac arrest. He was not resuscitated for approximately a half hour. The oxygen deprivation left Robert with irreversible brain damage, requiring a ventilator for breathing and a nasogastric tube for nutrition and hydration. He sued the government hospital for negligence and won the suit. Experts project he is going to need $1 million worth of future medical care, which he receives free as a veteran. The court awards Robert $1 million in future medical costs. May Robert receive these damages?

Explanation

This question implicates §10(b)(2) of the new Torts: Remedies Restatement. The facts of this hypothetical come from *Molzof v. United States*, 6 F.3d 461 (7th Cir. 1993). If the jurisdiction has repealed the collateral source rule, Robert would not be able to recover that $1 million, because he is going to receive that future medical care for free. The more difficult question occurs in states that continue to apply the collateral source rule. Recall that the rule requires that the collateral sources be wholly independent of the tortfeasor. In this case, the U.S. government Veterans Administration is both paying for the medical care *and* paying the tort damages.

In the actual *Molzof* case, the court ruled that plaintiff could recover the damages without an offset:

> Just because both recoveries come from the *defendant*, however, does not necessarily mean that they are coming from the same *source*. "The source of the funds may be determined to be collateral or independent, even though the [tortfeasor] supplies such funds . . . . Application of the collateral source rule depends less upon the source of funds than upon the character of the benefits received." Thus, in order to determine whether the collateral source rule is applicable, courts have looked to the nature of the payment and the reason the payment is being made rather than simply looking at whether the defendant is paying twice.

(Citation omitted.)

The court held that as to future medical payments, the collateral source rule would not apply:

> The plaintiff may not be satisfied with the public facilities; he may feel that a particular private physician is superior; in the future because of over-crowded conditions he may not even be able to receive timely care. These are only a few of many considerations with which an individual may be faced in selecting treatment. The plaintiff's past use of the government facilities does not ensure his future use of them. He will now have the funds available to him to enable him to seek private care. He should not be denied this opportunity.

PART II

Equitable Remedies

CHAPTER 7

Injunctions and Other Equitable Remedies: Stop Me Before I Harm (Again)!

7.1 INTRODUCTION: INJUNCTIONS AS SPECIFIC RELIEF

We first saw in Chapter 1 the concept of the "rightful position": the position in which plaintiff would be but for the defendant's wrong. Part I of this book focused on how courts (sometimes unsuccessfully) use compensatory damages to restore plaintiff to the rightful position after the defendant's wrong. In this part, we focus on how *injunctions*—court orders to defendants (or others) to do or not do something—can keep the plaintiff in the rightful position by preventing the plaintiff from being harmed or minimizing the extent of such harm.

Recall one of Chapter 1's early hypotheticals that contrasted damage awards with restitution: Alice steals $100 from Bob's wallet, runs to the casino, gambles, and walks away from the table with $1,000. The court could award Bob compensatory damages of $100, bringing Bob back to the rightful position, or the court could give him a restitutionary award of $1,000, which would force Alice to give up her ill-gotten gains. See 7.1.

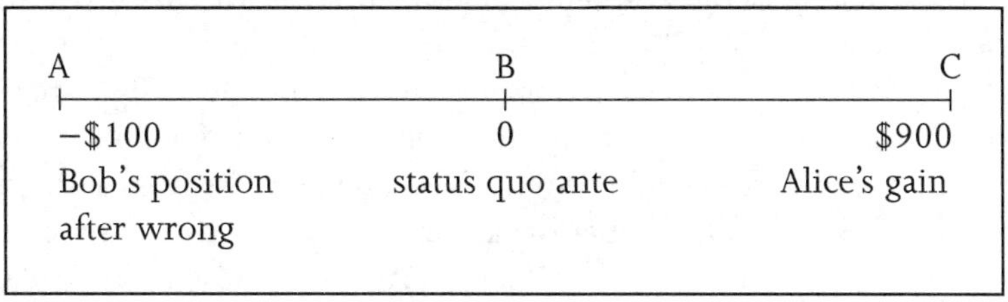

Figure 7.1

In the Alice-Bob example, an injunction is no help. The harm is complete and there is nothing a court order can do (short of ordering Alice to return the money, something we'll consider a little farther down the line).

Suppose, however, that before Alice stole the money, she warned Bob of the theft (far-fetched to be sure, but we'll encounter some real-world examples soon enough). A court order—or injunction—that would have prevented Alice from stealing Bob's money serves to prevent the harm from ever occurring. Thinking about Bob's status in terms of Figure 7.1, *an injunction would have kept Bob in position B*, the status quo ante, obviating the need for him to recover his losses from Alice. In other words, like damages, an injunction can aim at the rightful position. Unlike damages, an injunction can potentially *keep* plaintiff in that position rather than having to restore plaintiff to that position. What's more, when injunctions work, they eliminate the risks that plaintiffs face when seeking damages. Damages, for example, might be too hard to measure, or the defendant may be difficult to find, poor, or judgment-proof. A plaintiff might decide it is simply better to prevent harm, rather than allow the harm and then seek an after-the-fact remedy.

Why would Alice obey a court order? Perhaps she would not, but most litigants do obey court orders, such as injunctions, which can be backed up with the court's *contempt* power (discussed in Chapter 10). Contempt can help motivate reluctant defendants to act when they otherwise would not or refrain from acting when they otherwise would. (Why not issue a court order *requiring* Alice to pay money in the case of damages? Generally speaking, outside cases involving family law issues—such as child support—a damages judgment is *not* backed up by the court's contempt power. We discuss ways that successful plaintiffs may recover damages in Chapter 17.1.)

Injunctions are a neat tool to have in the lawyer's toolbox. Indeed, you already came across injunctions in your first year of law school in contracts class under the label "specific performance." Consider this example: Oscar contracts with Pnina for Pnina to manufacture a custom-made widget for use in Oscar's broom factory. Without the widget, which takes weeks to manufacture, the factory cannot operate. There are no spare widgets available for sale. About halfway into the job, Pnina announces she is going to breach the contract because a better opportunity has arisen for her (think: "efficient breach" from Chapter 4.2).

Oscar could sue Pnina for damages, but he really wants the widget. You can see that a court order, or injunction, requiring Pnina to deliver the completed widget could be Oscar's best remedy. We call that the remedy of *specific performance*. Specific performance is simply an injunction ordering a breaching party to a contract to perform as promised (the order is sometimes accompanied by a judgment that the breaching party pay damages for the delay in performance).

Note the use of the term "specific." Specific performance and other types of injunctions are forms of *specific relief* that give the plaintiff the very thing he or she lost (or stands to lose). Oscar, for example, gets his promised widget. Specific performance contrasts with damages, which is a kind of *substitutionary relief*: money substitutes for the thing that plaintiff has lost. If Oscar gets only damages (cover damages under U.C.C. §2-712 or market damages under U.C.C. §2-713—see Chapter 4.5), he is not in as good a position as he would be if he gets the widget. With damages, he will have to go out and purchase a *substitute* for the custom-made widget or make a new plan for allocating his resources at the broom factory. Also, with a damages remedy, he bears the risk of the court's errors in valuing the widget.

Over the next four chapters, this book explores injunctions and related remedies, answering the following kinds of questions:

- What must a plaintiff show to obtain an injunction?
- What factors should courts consider in choosing between specific relief, such as an injunction, and substitutionary relief, such as damages?
- Can injunctions be used to restructure government institutions such as prisons and school systems?
- How and under what circumstances may injunctions be modified?
- To what extent may injunctions bind or burden third parties?
- Under what circumstances may a plaintiff obtain preliminary relief, such as a preliminary injunction, to prevent harm from occurring before a case goes to final judgment?
- What kinds of contempt power do courts have, and under what circumstances may parties ignore injunctions without facing a court finding of contempt?

EXAMPLE

Example 1

Quincy and Rudolfo are neighbors. As a courtesy, Quincy lets Rudolfo know that he is planning on cutting down a large oak tree near the property line between their two houses to put in a swimming pool. Rudolfo believes the tree is on his side of the property line (meaning Quincy does not have the legal right to cut it down), and Rudolfo does not want it cut down: it provides shade for his backyard, which he enjoys during the summer months. Quincy insists that the tree is on his side of the property line, and that he has the right to cut it down.

Assume that Rudolfo is right: the tree is in fact on his property. Before reading the rest of this chapter and learning the rules related to injunctions, ask yourself the following questions:

a. Should Rudolfo have the choice between damages for the lost tree and an injunction preventing Quincy from cutting it down, or should the law prefer one remedy over the other?
b. Which remedy places a greater burden on the courts?
c. Which remedy is more likely to put (or keep) Rudolfo in the rightful position?

Does your answer to any of these questions change if Rudolfo does not depend on the tree for shade or otherwise care if it is cut down?

Explanation

EXPLANATION

(a) There are of course no "right answers" to these normative questions. But it is useful to begin this material by testing your own values before learning the rules applicable to injunctive relief. Many students would leave the choice to Rudolfo, and most students in Rudolfo's position would prefer the injunction in part because of the difficulty of replacing a mature tree providing shade in someone's backyard, and in part because of the difficulty of computing damages for the loss of the tree.

(b) Both remedies impose some burdens on the courts. With damages, the court is going to have to compute the amount of damages. With an injunction, the court may need to determine whether Quincy violated the injunction and, for this reason, whether to punish Quincy for contempt. In the abstract, it is difficult to say which is more burdensome.

(c) Injunctive relief is more likely to keep Rudolfo closer to the rightful position for the aforementioned reasons: the difficulty of using money to buy a replacement for what would be lost and the difficulty of measuring the value of the lost tree to Rudolfo.

Notice, however, that the answers to these questions may depend at least in part on the specifics about the losses. Thus, for example, suppose the tree provided no shade or aesthetic value to Rudolfo. If that were the case, the computation of damages might be easier (we would not need to worry about the value of a mature, shady tree on the property), and we might be less interested in backing up a judicial remedy with the contempt power. Giving Rudolfo the right to an injunction can also have important distributional consequences (that is, consequences for how much money Quincy is going to have to transfer to Rudolfo for the removal of the tree). With a damages remedy, the court sets the price for removal. With an injunction, Rudolfo can hold out for a higher price, especially if Quincy really needs that tree removed in order to put in his swimming pool. This means that Rudolfo may get a windfall for the removal of the tree if the parties must bargain around Rudolfo's right to an injunction. You should be able to see the potential bargaining power that the right to an injunction could give to Rudolfo.

It is not even clear that the parties would reach a bargain in such circumstances. In a situation of "bilateral monopoly," where there is only one buyer and one seller (Rudolfo is the only one selling the right to remove a tree, and Quincy is the only one who wants to buy the right to remove the tree), the parties might not bargain efficiently for the removal of the tree. Rudolfo, for example, might drive too hard a bargain even if it is in both of their interests for the tree to be removed.

If the concepts in the last two paragraphs sound familiar, it is because they are related to the debate in the economic analysis of law over the choice between "property rules" (such as injunctions) and "liability rules" (such as damages) when transaction costs (the costs of bargaining) are high. For the classic articles in this area, see Guido Calabresi & A. Douglas Melamed, *Property Rules, Liability Rules, and Inalienability: One View of the Cathedral*, 85 HARV. L. REV. 1089 (1972); and Ronald H. Coase, *The Problem of Social Cost*, 3 J.L. & ECON. 1 (1960). A wide-ranging and fascinating debate beyond the scope of this book is taking place in the "law and economics" arena over the efficiency of the choice between damages and injunctions. In brief, the conventional economic wisdom appears to be that courts should prefer injunctions when transaction costs (the costs of bargaining) are low and damages when transaction costs are high. When transaction costs are low, the parties will be expected to bargain to an efficient allocation of resources (this market transaction, then, would determine whether the tree should be removed). Injunctions let the market, rather than the courts, set the price for violation of a legal right, and the parties are more likely than the court to set an accurate price. In contrast, when there are high transaction costs (as with the bilateral monopoly situation described between Quincy and Rudolfo), the parties may not bargain to an efficient result. In such circumstances, it is more efficient to allow Quincy to cut the tree and the court to set the efficient price.

The economic analysis suggests that courts should decide on the propriety of injunctions rather than damages based upon the extent of transaction costs in bargaining. Regardless of whether that is a practical endeavor for the courts, it does not appear that courts do so in deciding on the propriety of granting an injunction. Moreover, it does not appear that much bargaining takes place typically after courts issue injunctions. *See* Ward Farnsworth, *Do Parties to Nuisance Cases Bargain after Judgment? A Glimpse Inside the Cathedral*, 66 U. CHI. L. REV. 373 (1999).

7.2 REQUIREMENTS FOR INJUNCTIONS, THE ORIGINS OF EQUITABLE RELIEF, AND A NOTE ON REPLEVIN

Regardless of your answers to the questions posed in Example 1, the fact of the matter is that injunctions are not available as a matter of course. As we shall see, in order to obtain an injunction (rather than settling for another remedy, such as compensatory damages), a plaintiff is typically going to have to prove two things (though the standards may be changing, as we shall see in section 7.5 below):

1. *Propensity:* The defendant is likely to engage in the conduct that plaintiff seeks to enjoin; and
2. *Irreparable injury:* A "legal" remedy, such as damages, is not as good a remedy for plaintiff as an injunction.

Even when plaintiff makes such a finding, however, a court may decline to grant an injunction where

3. Other strong policy reasons exist for denying the injunction.

Article 2 of the U.C.C. (applicable to the sale of moveable goods—see Chapter 4.5) similarly limits the availability of the injunctive remedy of specific performance, though in a more open-ended way than the classic common law formulation above. U.C.C. §2-716(1) provides that for non-breaching buyers, "Specific performance may be decreed where the goods are unique or in other proper circumstances."[1]

What explains why injunctive relief is not available as a matter of course? The answer is in large part a vestige of a centuries-old turf war among English courts. This is not the place to detail the story,[2] but briefly: Different courts began to emerge in England in the thirteenth century. The Chancery branch of the Court of the Exchequer began as a court designed to handle, among other things, requests to the king for justice or mercy from complainants who claimed they could not get justice in other courts. Eventually, "the Chancellor," or the head of this court branch, was given the power to grant such relief in appropriate cases backed by what we would now call contempt power.

---

1. The comments to the section explain that it is an attempt to "further a more liberal attitude than some courts have shown" in the grant of specific performance. It also notes that "inability to cover is strong evidence of 'other proper circumstances'" justifying the remedy of specific performance. In recent years, U.C.C. drafters have considered, but not adopted, a proposal to make specific performance more easily available for *non*-consumer contracts. As a consumer, wouldn't you want specific performance made available more easily?
2. For details, see F.W. MAITLAND, EQUITY 1-7 (1969).

From this origin sprang the "chancery," or "equity," courts, which granted "equitable relief," including injunctions. The equitable relief issued by the chancery courts encroached on the power of other courts, however, and eventually, the English crown prohibited the equity courts from granting relief unless the complaining party could demonstrate that he had no adequate remedy in the law courts (our "courts of law" that grant remedies such as "legal relief").

One would think this debate would have little relevance to contemporary law, especially given that today, centuries after this turf war, the courts of law and courts of equity have merged into a single court in most places. In California, for example, one can go into a superior court and ask for legal relief such as damages or equitable relief such as injunctions. The same is true of federal district courts, which grant equitable relief such as injunctions all the time.

Nonetheless, in order to get equitable relief even today, a plaintiff must demonstrate that *she has no adequate remedy at law* (otherwise known as the "irreparable injury" rule).[3] Section 7.4 discusses what it means for a legal remedy to be "inadequate," but before we get to that, there are a few other matters to consider.

How does one know, for example, what qualifies as a legal or equitable remedy? The answer largely comes from history. At least for remedies that existed before the merger of the courts, the question is whether the remedy would have been granted by the law courts or the equity courts. Those granted by the law courts are legal remedies and those granted by the equity courts are equitable remedies. *See* DOBBS & ROBERTS §1.2 (contrasting remedies "at law" and remedies "in equity").

A claim for compensatory damages, as mentioned, is a classic legal remedy, and a claim for an injunction is a classic equitable remedy. Other important equitable remedies include rescission and constructive trusts—discussed in Part III. Remedies for breach of trust are equitable as well, and equity courts historically played a key role in the development of the law of trusts.

For remedies that did not exist before the merger of the courts, the question whether to classify a remedy as "legal" or "equitable" is more difficult and has important consequences. For example, plaintiffs seeking equitable relief must satisfy the burden of showing irreparable injury. Also, the Seventh Amendment to the U.S. Constitution grants the right to a jury trial for actions at common law, but not for suits in equity. (Many states have parallel provisions in their constitutions.) The issue of whether a modern statutory remedy is legal or equitable has vexed the U.S. Supreme Court in several

3. The notion of having no adequate remedy at law and the irreparable injury rule are just different formulations of the same concept. *See* DOBBS AND ROBERTS §1.1; LAYCOCK & HASEN p. 308 ("Despite occasional attempts to distinguish these statements, they are simply two formulations of the same rule. 'Irreparable harm occurs when a party has no adequate remedy at law, typically because its injuries cannot be fully compensated through an award of damages.' General Motors Corp. v. Harry Brown's, LLC, 563 F.3d 312, 319 (8th Cir. 2009). Both formulations are in common use.").

contexts, including decisions on the right to a jury trial. *See, e.g., Chauffeurs, Teamsters and Helpers, Local No. 391 v. Terry*, 494 U.S. 558 (1990) (applying a two-part test to determine whether plaintiff's action against labor union for alleged breach of duty of fair representation was legal or equitable—and therefore whether plaintiff was entitled to a jury trial); *Mertens v. Hewitt Assocs.*, 508 U.S. 248 (1993) (deciding what "equitable relief" meant in the context of plaintiff's claim for a remedy under a provision of federal ERISA statute); *Dairy Queen, Inc. v. Wood*, 369 U.S. 469 (1962) (in an action presenting both legal claims and equitable claims, courts should resolve the legal questions first through a jury trial). If you are a plaintiff who wants equitable relief such as an injunction, you likely won't have the right to a jury trial.

Furthermore, there is also a class of equitable defenses that defendants may raise only in connection with plaintiff's request for equitable relief (explored in Chapter 18).

The dead hand of history seems like a pretty weak reason to require plaintiffs to jump through the "irreparable injury" hoop, given that today the same courts can give both legal and equitable relief. Indeed, some have argued that in modern law, the irreparable injury rule is dead—that courts do not take the rule seriously. *See* DOUGLAS LAYCOCK, THE DEATH OF THE IRREPARABLE INJURY RULE (Oxford University Press 1991). As you work through the material, ask yourself what role the irreparable injury rule does, and should, play in the law of remedies.

One possible answer to the continued apparent discrimination against injunctions and equitable relief is that there should be extraordinary reasons to grant specific relief because specific relief is more onerous. Do we really want to *require* Pnina, under the threat of a contempt holding, to supply the custom-made widget for Oscar's broom factory if she does not want to? Maybe the law should instead prefer that Oscar receive money to cover his losses when it is feasible.

We'll explore this explanation further in this chapter, but it is worth noting that some legal relief can be *specific* as opposed to the usual substitutionary remedy of compensatory damages. For example, *replevin* is a legal remedy that allows for specific relief: in some circumstances, a plaintiff can use replevin to recover personal property wrongfully taken by the defendant. (Chapter 13 further explores replevin.) Because replevin is a legal remedy, a plaintiff need *not* prove irreparable injury to get it.[4]

4. For its part, Article 2 of the U.C.C. does not give non-breaching buyers a right to replevin as a matter of course. Under §2-716(3), "The buyer has a right of replevin for goods identified to the contract if after reasonable effort he is unable to effect cover for such goods or the circumstances reasonably indicate that such effort will be unavailing or if the goods have been shipped under reservation and satisfaction of the security interest in them has been made or tendered." This right does not appear to be broader than the right to specific performance set forth in U.C.C. §2-716(1).

As Laycock argues, any defense of the irreparable injury rule for equitable relief based upon *specific* relief will have to deal with the availability of replevin (a specific *legal* remedy) as a matter of course in appropriate cases.

EXAMPLE

Example 2

Susan has stolen your family's prized chalice. Its market value is $10,000, and its sentimental value to you is greater than $10,000. In your suit against Susan for the tort of conversion (the correct tort cause of action to recover damages for Susan's theft), would you prefer damages, an injunction ordering return of the chalice, or replevin? Could you ask the court to give you *both* compensatory damages *and* an injunction?

EXPLANATION

Explanation

Each of these remedies has costs and benefits. The main cost of a damages remedy in this example is that it is likely to be undercompensatory. As we saw in the chapters on damages, courts usually base their award of compensatory damages on market measures, and a $10,000 market measure is not going to compensate for the full value of the chalice to you. On the other hand, some courts say that in order to recover punitive damages (see Chapter 15) aimed at punishing and deterring bad conduct, a court must first award compensatory damages. Thus, damages might be a good way to get a large recovery. This assumes, of course, that Susan would have the resources to pay (compensatory and possibly punitive) damages. If Susan does not have the resources, a damages award will be worthless.

The main benefit of both injunctive relief and replevin is that each entitles you to *specific* relief: you get back the very item that has been taken from you. You likely won't be able to recover punitive damages. The preference between replevin and an injunction might depend upon whether you know where Susan has put the chalice. If you know the location of the chalice, and it is easily accessible, then replevin may be a better remedy because as a legal remedy, you need not demonstrate irreparable injury. After the court agrees that you are entitled to replevin, you can get an order from the court directing the sheriff to seize the property. (More on ancillary remedies such as seizure can be found in Chapter 17.1.)

Alternatively, if you don't know where the chalice is, then replevin would be of little use to you. In such circumstances, you likely will want an injunction that would order Susan to turn over the chalice or be held in contempt of court. If it turns out that the chalice is not available (perhaps Susan has sold it and it cannot be found), then damages would be best. If and when Susan has assets, they can be seized by the sheriff and sold to pay you back for your losses.

A court will not allow you to recover both damages (for the full amount of the chalice) and an injunction (ordering a return of the chalice). That would allow you a double recovery. To see why, consider Figure 7.2.

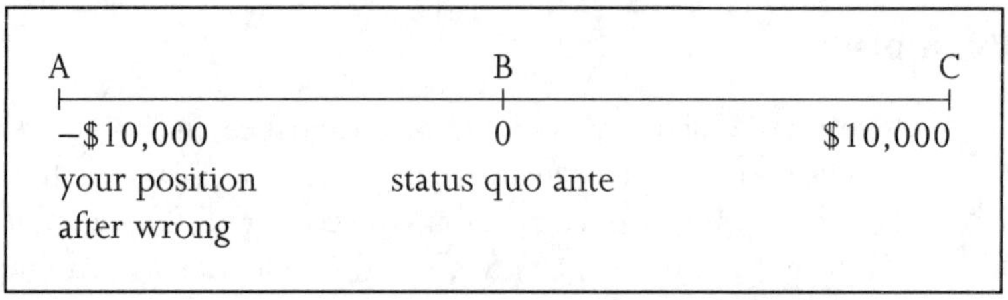

Figure 7.2

Putting aside the sentimental value (and other complications of damages discussed in Part I), your position after the wrong is A, −$10,000. When you receive the chalice back through the injunction, it brings you back to B, the status quo ante (0). If the court also awards damages for the loss, $10,000, it brings you to position C, +$10,000. Thus, you end up in a position *better than* if there had been no theft.

Now you might take the position that this is perfectly appropriate. Susan engaged in theft and should be punished. But that's not supposed to be the purpose of either compensatory damages or injunctions, which are based on the rightful position standard. We could use punitive damages to punish Susan (and sometimes restitution as well, as we will see in Part III). But courts ordinarily will make you *elect a remedy* at some point to *preclude double recovery*.

That's not to say that one can never receive damages along with an injunction. In this case, if you obtain an injunction and get the return of the chalice, you are also entitled to damages for the temporary loss of use of the chalice. Thus, if Susan steals the chalice on January 1 and you don't get it back until March 1, you suffered two months without the chalice that you own. That loss may be hard to value, but it is not a double recovery to both give you back the chalice and award you damages for the loss in the interim.

A similar concept applies in the case of specific performance. Suppose Pnina promised to deliver to Oscar the widget that he needs to run his factory by January 1. Pnina breaches, and the court orders specific performance. By the time Pnina finishes making the widget, it is March 1, and the factory has been closed for two months. Courts will often allow a grant of specific performance to be accompanied by *delay damages*—the equivalent of damages for the temporary loss of use in the chalice example to compensate for the delay in promised performance. This does not give a double recovery: had Pnina performed as promised, Oscar would have had the widget on January 1, and he would not have suffered losses in his closed factory from January 1 to March 1. By granting specific performance in a situation where Pnina cannot perform until March 1, the court is not fully restoring Oscar to the rightful position. He is still out the losses for two months. Only the injunction *plus* delay damages will put Oscar into the rightful position.

7.3 THE PROPENSITY REQUIREMENT AND THE SCOPE OF INJUNCTIONS

7.3.1 Propensity, Ripeness, and Mootness

Before turning in depth to the irreparable injury requirement, we first consider the propensity requirement for injunctions along with the proper scope of injunctions (an issue Chapter 8.1 returns to in considering "structural injunctions").

The *propensity* rule requires that plaintiffs demonstrate there is a *realistic threat from the defendant of future harm (or future injury from past harm)* before a court will issue an injunction. Demonstrating propensity sometimes is a no-brainer because the defendant has already committed wrongful conduct, and it is a question of preventing future harm. For example, after Pnina announced she was breaching the contract to produce the custom-made widget, there is no question that Oscar is about to suffer harm. The same is true when Quincy announces to Rudolfo that he plans to cut down the tree on their property line. Thus, propensity sometimes is easily found whether the injunction is *reparative* (preventing the future bad effects of past harm, as in the Oscar-Pnina hypothetical) or *preventive* (preventing future harm, as in the Quincy-Rudolfo hypothetical).

But sometimes the matter of propensity is not quite as clear. Suppose Rudolfo and Quincy are neighbors who do not get along. Rudolfo sees Quincy out in Quincy's yard with some contractors, and he *suspects* Quincy is going to remove the tree (which is on Rudolfo's property) to build a swimming pool. If Rudolfo goes to court to seek an injunction preventing the removal of the tree, the court is going to require some proof of *propensity*, which in this case means proof that Quincy is really going to remove the tree. It might be, however, that Quincy is not considering removing the tree, or it might be that Quincy did not plan to remove the tree without first obtaining Rudolfo's permission.[5]

Why shouldn't a court simply issue the injunction so that Rudolfo can be sure that Quincy would think twice before removing the tree? (Quincy, remember, would be thinking twice because of the possibility that he would be held in contempt for violating a court order.) The power of a court order is not used lightly, and there is a danger that if injunctions were easily obtained, Rudolfo would be coming to court all the time seeking them. This could both put an administrative burden on the courts (and an

5. Occasionally, courts will mislabel this propensity concern as one about irreparable injury.

unnecessary one at that if there is no danger that Quincy or one of Rudolfo's other neighbors is going to do anything to harm him) and potentially give Rudolfo an unfair advantage in disputes with his neighbors. The fear of mistakenly being held in contempt by the courts might chill Quincy and others from exercising their legitimate property rights.

Propensity problems generally come in two varieties before the court: *ripeness* and *mootness*.[6] The revised Quincy-Rudolfo hypothetical is a good example of a ripeness problem: there is insufficient evidence that defendant will engage in the prohibited conduct to justify issuing an injunction. That's not to say it makes bad litigation sense for Rudolfo to *seek* such an injunction. To support Quincy's ripeness argument, if Quincy's lawyer provides an affidavit from Quincy swearing under oath that he's not going to touch Rudolfo's tree without permission, this will serve Rudolfo's interests. Even though that promise is not as good as a court order backed by the power of contempt, if Quincy later removes the tree after signing such an affidavit, a court will likely be unsympathetic to Quincy when Rudolfo later sues for damages (and possibly punitive damages, too).

The new Restatement (Torts) Third: Remedies §46 (Am. Law. Inst. Tent. Draft No. 2, 2023) on "Ripeness and Mootness" succinctly sets forth the propensity requirement in the torts context:

> A court should deny an injunction if:
>
> (1) there is not a sufficient likelihood that defendant will commit a tortious act (or a tortious failure to act) that causes future harm to plaintiff, and
> (2) an injunction could not provide an effective remedy for any harm to plaintiff that defendant's tort is already causing or has already caused.

How much certainty must there be that defendant will engage in the prohibited conduct? There must be at least a "credible threat" of injury,

---

6. You may already be familiar with the concepts of mootness and ripeness from either a constitutional law or federal courts course. Federal courts, under Article III of the United States Constitution, are empowered to hear only "cases or controversies." Thus, if a case is not ripe or is moot, a federal court is without the power to hear it. Do not, however, equate the concepts of ripeness and mootness for *constitutional purposes* with ripeness and mootness for purposes of meeting the *propensity test* for the granting of an injunction. A case can be ripe enough to meet the constitutional requirement, yet a court could still deny an injunction for lack of propensity. *See, e.g., United States v. W.T. Grant Co.*, 345 U.S. 629, 635 (1953). In that case, the Supreme Court held that the plaintiffs met the constitutional standard because a controversy continued to exist in that the defendant could return to his old ways. But it upheld a district court decision to deny an injunction on mootness grounds. "The necessary determination is that there exists some cognizable danger of recurrent violation, something more than the mere possibility which serves to keep the case alive." *Id.* at 633. That standard may be hard to apply in practice, but it does demonstrate the difference between the constitutional and non-constitutional mootness and ripeness questions.

Susan B. Anthony List v. Driehaus, 573 U.S. 149 (2014). In some cases, such as one against the federal government involving national security, the Supreme Court has suggested a stronger showing. *Clapper v. Amnesty Int'l*, USA, 568 U.S. 398, 409 (2013) (threatened injury "must be certainly impending").

Mootness claims arise when a defendant has engaged in certain injurious conduct in the past but has since ceased and stated that she won't engage in the conduct anymore. Courts in such circumstances will need to make a *credibility determination* as to whether the defendant is likely to engage in the prohibited conduct again. If the defendant is likely to do so, the propensity requirement is met because there is a realistic threat of further violation.

But if the defendant has already engaged in harmful conduct, why not issue an injunction related to the prior conduct? The answer is that an injunction must be geared toward *future conduct* or toward the *future bad effects* of past conduct. As for past conduct that has already caused harm, the courts will have to deal with this using damages or some other backward-looking remedy, not through an injunction.

Suppose, for example, that Quincy was in the process of removing *four trees* from Rudolfo's property in order to put in a swimming pool. Rudolfo goes to court after three of the four trees have been removed. Suppose further that the removal of one of those trees has caused Rudolfo's garage to collapse, and the foundation of his house is threatened as well unless the ground on Quincy's property is shored up.

Rudolfo should be able to:

- Get damages for the loss of the three trees and the collapse of his garage (and potentially punitive damages, depending upon the state's law related to punitive damages).
- Obtain a preventive injunction barring the removal of the fourth tree (this is an injunction *preventing future harm*).
- Possibly obtain a reparative injunction requiring Quincy to shore up the area near the removed tree that is threatening the foundation of Rudolfo's house (this is an injunction preventing *future bad effects* of past harm).

Note that in this list of remedies, there is nothing that an injunction can do to deal with the loss of the three trees or the collapse of the garage. Remember, injunctions are aimed at the future, *not* the past.

EXAMPLE

Example 3

The city of Pacificana has a long history of official and unofficial discrimination against African Americans. It conducts a local election in which the city does nothing to prevent the Ku Klux Klan from intimidating African American voters and keeping them from the polls. The undisputed evidence shows that because there are more white than black voters and because blacks and whites vote for different candidates in the election, the election results would not have changed even if there had been no intimidation. The court determines that the city violated the Fourteenth and Fifteenth Amendment rights of African American voters in the city.

Should African American voters be entitled to an injunction ordering the holding of a new election? To what other relief, if any, should they be entitled?

Explanation

This example is loosely based on *Bell v. Southwell*, 376 F.2d 659 (5th Cir. 1967). At first glance, it might appear that an injunction would be useless to the plaintiffs. The harm has already occurred (like the removed trees in the revised Quincy-Rudolfo hypothetical), and rerunning the election would not make any difference to the outcome. Given what social scientists call "racially polarized voting" where white voters and minority voters tend to support different candidates for office, we can predict the same candidate is likely to have won even if there had been no voter intimidation.

But that misses the larger symbolic value of voting. African American voters, and all other voters in the district, would be living in a city where the officials serving out their terms were elected in unconstitutional, racially discriminatory elections. That is the future negative effect of the past harm, and a reparative injunction can prevent this future bad effect through a new election (even if that means that the election *results* are the same).

Those plaintiffs who were denied the right to vote on account of race might also seek an action for damages to compensate them for this past dignitary harm. A new election minimizes *additional harm*, but it does not eliminate the dignitary harm that has *already taken place* on Election Day. As for how such harm should be calculated, consider the material in Part I of this book.

Example 4

Building on the facts of Example 3, before the next election, African American plaintiffs seek a court order requiring the city of Pacificana to take steps to ensure that no voters are intimidated when they seek to exercise their constitutional right to vote free of racial discrimination. The city argues that no injunction is necessary because the question is now moot. How should the court rule?

EXPLANATION

Explanation

While it is true that the issue of voter intimidation is now moot for purposes of the *last* election, the question before the court now is whether the city is currently taking adequate steps to prevent a recurrence of the unconstitutional failure of the city to protect African American voters from voter intimidation in *the next election*. In ruling on the request, the court is going to have to consider the likelihood that private actors would attempt to intimidate black voters again and the extent of the plans the city has undertaken to prevent such action from taking place in the future. The court's decision on whether to issue an injunction may turn at least in part on a *credibility determination* by the court on the intent of city officials. Are city officials vigilantly protecting voters' constitutional rights? If the court has doubts about the city's credibility, it would likely issue the injunction to prevent future harm that would come from *new* intimidation at the *next* election.

7.3.2 The Proper Scope of Injunctive Relief

Suppose Quincy makes it crystal clear to Rudolfo that he is going to remove the tree on Rudolfo's property to build a swimming pool on his own property. In such circumstances, Rudolfo will not have a problem-proving propensity. Assuming he can meet the other requirements for an injunction (discussed below), the battle between the parties may shift from *whether* the court should grant an injunction to *the scope* of the injunction.

Consider these two alternative injunctions, both of which would prevent Quincy from removing the tree (and subject him to contempt for failing to do so):

Injunction A

The court hereby orders and decrees that Quincy shall not remove the old oak tree currently on the property line between Quincy's house, located at 123 Main Street, and Rudolfo's house, located at 125 Main Street.

Injunction B

The court hereby orders and decrees that Quincy shall not remove any tree currently on the property of Quincy or property line between Quincy's house, located at 123 Main Street, and Rudolfo's house, located at 125 Main Street. Furthermore, Quincy shall not construct a swimming pool on his property or make any other improvements on his property without obtaining the consent of Rudolfo or an order of this court. Furthermore, Quincy will take no steps to harm any trees located on the property of Quincy or on the property line between Quincy's house and Rudolfo's house, and will actively take steps to maintain the health of all trees on the property and the property line at all times.

Quincy, of course, would prefer Injunction A, and Rudolfo would prefer Injunction B. To decide which the court should choose, we first have to ask what the court is trying to accomplish when it issues the injunction. If the court is aiming for the rightful position standard, arguably Injunction A is better than Injunction B, which appears to put Rudolfo in a *better* position than he would have been in had Quincy not threatened to take down the tree. (Do you see why? For one thing, Rudolfo would have the benefit of a court order preventing Quincy from making *any* improvements on his property without Rudolfo's permission or a court order.)

On the other hand, some of the measures contained in Injunction B could be defended on rightful position grounds. One could say that the requirement that Quincy take no steps to harm trees on his property could protect Rudolfo's rightful position (i.e., the right to be on his property without any interference with his trees by Quincy). Some people refer to such measures as *prophylactic* injunctions because they *protect* the rightful position but are not keeping plaintiff in the rightful position itself.

The choice between Injunction A and Injunction B is in some sense a choice between who should bear the risk of problems with the court's order. Injunction A puts that risk on Rudolfo because it offers very little by way of prophylaxis; there may be ways that Quincy could get what he wants without violating the court's order, such as by not watering the tree until it dies. Injunction B puts the risk on Quincy by barring him from engaging in a whole host of otherwise legal activities such as cutting down trees wholly on his property or making improvements unrelated to the disputed swimming pool project.

Some courts might choose Injunction B not to protect Rudolfo's place in the rightful position, but to serve an ill-defined desire to "do justice." Recall the origin of the equity courts: these began to give pleas to the king for a just result unattainable in the law courts. Some judges today still probably view their equity power more broadly than simply as a power to ensure that plaintiff stays in the rightful position. *See* LAYCOCK & HASEN p. 254 ("At its extremes, [this] tradition says that once there is a violation that brings a case into the equity court, the chancellor has a roving commission to do good."). Furthermore, "[s]uch talk [about the flexibility of equity and the discretion of trial judges in equity cases] led to the famous complaint that relying on the chancellor's conscience as a measure of justice is like relying on the chancellor's foot as the measure of length." *Id.* at 308.

As we will see in the next chapter, as a matter of *constitutional law*, the Supreme Court has signaled that in institutional reform litigation (so-called "structural injunctions"), courts must aim for the rightful position standard and not give remedies less well connected (or completely unconnected) to the harm that could occur to the plaintiff. In certain circumstances, however, it may be hard to tell the difference between an Injunction B that is aiming at the rightful position (but providing a bit of extra protection for the plaintiff—the prophylactic injunction) and a broader injunction dressed up to look like a prophylactic injunction.

The new RESTATEMENT (TORTS) THIRD: REMEDIES §44 (Am. Law. Inst. Tent. Draft No. 2, 2023) on the scope of injunctions endorses the rightful position standard with a recognition of the need in some circumstances to provide prophylactic protection for tort plaintiffs:

> (a) A permanent injunction intended to provide a complete remedy should place the plaintiff, as nearly as possible, in the position that the plaintiff would occupy if no tort were committed, or keep the plaintiff in that position, by preventing the commission of the tort, by preventing the harm that the tort would have caused, or by repairing the harm that the tort has already caused.
>
> (b) A permanent injunction should prohibit the particular tortious conduct or prevent or repair the particular harms, threatened or actual, that make the injunction necessary. The injunction should not restrict defendant's conduct more than necessary to achieve these purposes. To prevent the threatened or actual harms, it is sometimes necessary to restrict the defendant's conduct more than the law would otherwise require.

Example 5

Consider again the example of the voting discrimination in Pacificana (Examples 3 and 4). How would you draft a preventive injunction applicable to the next election? What prophylactic measures might you consider to keep the plaintiffs in the rightful position?

Explanation

This is a really difficult one to answer. It is not an easy exercise to actually draft an injunction. You want an order that would require the police department, with a history of discrimination, to protect its African American residents from discrimination by third parties. You'll need to ask yourself the question about how specific the injunction should be. If you make it too general, it will be useless to coerce compliance through the contempt power. Imagine, for example, an injunction that says: "The police department of the City of Pacificana shall take all reasonable steps to prevent intimidation of voters on election day." If voters are still intimidated, how would these voters prove that the police department failed to take "all reasonable steps"?

On the other hand, getting into specifics could require some micromanaging of the police department beyond the expertise of the court. Imagine, for example, an injunction that provides in relevant part: "The police department of the City of Pacificana shall take all reasonable steps to prevent intimidation of voters on election day, including but not limited to the stationing of two police officers at every polling place for the duration of Election Day." The city may not have enough police officers to do so, and it is not clear that this is the best use of resources. (For example, if there is racial segregation in the city as well, it might make more sense to post the police officers in African American neighborhoods only.)

The court also may be tempted to go beyond the rightful position standard in the name of a prophylactic measure. Consider, for example, part of an injunction requiring the city to "require all poll workers to attend racial sensitivity training before Election Day." Such training may be a very good thing, but it is not necessarily well connected to a problem of outside agitators (the KKK) disrupting polling place activities. That kind of problem requires a response by law enforcement, not sensitivity training. Yet there is going to be a temptation for some judges, while they are already writing an injunction, to put some other provisions into the injunction as well (just as judges or juries might be tempted to give plaintiffs more damages than they have proven for various reasons).

Example 6

How would you draft an injunction to ensure Pnina's performance of the Oscar-Pnina widget contract?

Explanation

The order might be as simple as requiring Pnina to deliver the widget by a set date. But depending upon the complexity of the project and the willingness (and need) of the court to remain involved to ensure Pnina's performance, a court might order Pnina to make certain amounts of progress by set dates, and to file reports with the court informing the court of such progress. Alternatively, the court might approve of some mechanism that would allow Oscar to check on Pnina's progress and bring matters to the court's attention as necessary.

7.4 THE IRREPARABLE INJURY REQUIREMENT

In most of the examples in this chapter so far, plaintiffs seeking injunctions should have little trouble with the irreparable injury requirement. Consider Oscar, who cannot get the custom-made widget that Pnina has begun manufacturing but has not completed. Or consider Rudolfo, who is going to lose the shade provided by a mature tree that Quincy is about to cut down. Or consider the African American voters of the City of Pacificana, who stand to lose the constitutional right to vote because the city won't protect them against threats of violence and intimidation by the KKK.

These are *easy* cases under the irreparable injury rule. *In each case, damages are not going to be as good a remedy as injunctive relief.* Money is a poor substitute for the widget that runs the factory, the irreplaceable shade tree, or the precious right to vote. Money provides *some* compensation, as it is obviously better than nothing, but money is not as good as getting the specific relief requested in the injunction.

For this reason, courts traditionally have found the irreparable injury rule met when the loss is something not easily replaceable. This instinct, along with the overstated idea that each parcel of land is unique (and not replaceable by another[7]), explains the common law's allowance of specific performance for contracts involving the sale of land. The concept of irreplaceability appears as well in Article 2 of the U.C.C.'s insistence that specific performance be available when the goods are unique, and in §2-716's comment noting that specific performance is also appropriate when the non-breaching buyer cannot easily go out and cover through a substitute purchase. The more difficult it is to find a substitute product, the clearer it is that the contract is one that involves a unique good (which may make us question whether the U.C.C.'s test for specific performance really applies outside the concept of unique goods).

But suppose cover *was* easy for Oscar. The widget is not custom-made, and he could easily get the widget elsewhere. The U.C.C. standard suggests that Oscar *cannot* get an order of specific performance. Instead, he is expected to cover and then sue Pnina for *damages* (or, if he fails to cover, then as we saw in Chapter 6, principles of mitigation treat him as though he covered). The common law standard appears to be the same, though Oscar could perhaps argue that damages are inadequate because he has to go through the hassle of making another purchase that might not be as good.

But think about this rule for a moment. Oscar and Pnina have entered into a contract, and midway through performance Pnina has announced that she plans to breach the contract. In most cases, Oscar is not going to *want* Pnina's performance and he would be happy to get damages; he may never want to conduct business with (or even see) Pnina again. By the time contract disputes end up in litigation, there is usually a great deal of acrimony between the two parties. If Oscar is nonetheless *asking* for specific performance, it must be because there is something particularly valuable to him about Pnina's performance such that he is willing to continue doing

7. The idea might apply when one thinks of a family home or estate, but it is not true of fungible real estate, especially real estate that is purchased for its investment value. For an investor, Lot 233 may be no more or less desirable than Lot 422.

business with her (after all, if she fails to make the widget well, there is the risk of further litigation between two parties already angry with one another, and why risk that?).

What this analysis suggests is that when a non-breaching party to a contract *asks* a court to grant specific performance, that action itself is usually good evidence that the irreparable injury rule has been met; that is, if the non-breaching party is trying to force the breaching party to continue the contractual relationship, it is because damages are not as good a remedy as injunctive relief.

Speaking more generally, outside the context of specific performance, it will also often be the case that when faced with a defendant's propensity to commit a violation, a plaintiff seeking injunctive relief can quite easily show that a legal remedy would be inadequate. Consider even the extreme case in which Rudolfo couldn't care less about the tree on his property. It is difficult to imagine a court today holding that Quincy has the right to go onto Rudolfo's property, cut down one of Rudolfo's trees against his will, and simply pay Rudolfo for damages later. Such a rule seems to be an affront to our current notions about property rights and the ability to exclude outsiders from protected areas. A damages award intrinsically, then, is not as good as an injunction even when the party seeking the injunction has no reason to seek it other than as a vindication of his rights.

The new Restatement (Torts) Third: Remedies §43(c) (Am. Law. Inst. Tent. Draft No. 2, 2023), following the tradition of the earlier Restatements, does not phrase the choice of damages or injunction (more generally, the choice of legal versus equitable relief) as a matter of meeting the irreparable injury rule. Instead it posits that "the court should grant the better of the two remedies after considering all the costs and benefits of each, giving substantial weight to plaintiff's need for a complete and effective remedy."

In some circumstances, however, courts may use the irreparable injury rule as a reason for denying an injunction even when damages would not be as good a remedy. The next section offers a number of policy reasons why courts might decide to bar an injunction even when plaintiff can prove propensity and irreparable injury.

Example 7

EXAMPLE

Toyota of Pacificana enters into a contract with Ursula to sell Ursula a ruby red Toyota Camry. It is a limited-edition color, but otherwise, it is the same as other Camrys. The contract price is $30,000, which is the going market price. After the parties enter into a binding contract, but before the car is delivered, Victor offers to buy the car from the dealership for $38,000. Toyota of Pacificana tells Ursula it is going to breach the contract and sell the car to Victor. Toyota of Pacificana checks its computer database and finds that there are no other ruby red Camrys available in the area. They offer to sell her a blue, white, or black Camry for $29,000, which is $1,000 below the market price. If Ursula goes to court seeking an order of specific performance, will the court grant it to her? What if the evidence shows that if the court grants her specific performance, she is going to turn around and sell the car to Victor for a quick $8,000 profit?

Explanation

This is a contract for the sale of a moveable good, meaning it is governed by Article 2 of the U.C.C. Recall that under §2-716, a court will grant specific performance when a good is unique or in other proper circumstances, such as when a plaintiff cannot cover. The application of this rule to these facts depends on whether the "limited edition ruby red" color makes this good unique. Arguably it does, or Victor would not have come in to pay such a premium for the car, and Ursula would have settled for a Camry in another color at a discount. The court should grant specific performance.

It should not matter that Ursula might turn around and sell the car to Victor for an $8,000 profit. After all, a buyer's right to specific performance does not require that the buyer demonstrate some *sentimental* or *personal* value in the unique property. It might be unique *because* it yields a higher market price. Because the parties entered into a binding contract for a unique good, it looks like the U.C.C. will let Ursula get the car and capture any profits from Victor should she choose to sell it.

7.5 DOES *eBAY* SET A NEW STANDARD FOR GRANTING INJUNCTIONS IN FEDERAL COURT?

As noted in section 7.2 above, plaintiffs seeking injunctions typically must show irreparable injury and propensity in order to obtain an injunction, subject to certain policy concerns (discussed below in section 7.6). However, in a 2006 case, *eBay Inc. v. MercExchange, L.L.C.*, 547 U.S. 388 (2006), the Supreme Court added confusion to the standard for the issuance of injunctions, at least in federal courts.

In *eBay*, the Court rejected a rule adopted by the United States Court of Appeals for the Federal Circuit holding that a patent holder whose patent had been infringed in most cases had the right to an injunction against the infringer. Uncontroversially, the Supreme Court rejected such a *per se* rule. But controversially, the Court set out the standard for determining whether an injunction should issue:

> According to well-established principles of equity, a plaintiff seeking a permanent injunction must satisfy a four-factor test before a court may grant

> such relief. A plaintiff must demonstrate: (1) that it has suffered an irreparable injury; (2) that remedies available at law, such as monetary damages, are inadequate to compensate for that injury; (3) that, considering the balance of hardships between the plaintiff and defendant, a remedy in equity is warranted; and (4) that the public interest would not be disserved by a permanent injunction.

Although the Supreme Court referred to these as "well-established principles of equity," in fact, "Remedies specialists had never heard of the four-point test. . . . [T]he Court appears to vindicate a 'traditional' standard for a *final* injunction that never existed, except perhaps for a *preliminary* injunction." Doug Rendleman, *The Trial Judge's Equitable Discretion Following* eBay v. MercExchange, 27 Rev. Litig. 63, 76 n.71 (2007).

Despite these academic criticisms, the Supreme Court reaffirmed this *eBay* standard in *Monsanto Co. v. Geertson Seed Farms*, 561 U.S. 139, 158 (2010). A law review article on the subject by Professors Gergen, Golden, and Smith in the *Columbia Law Review* criticizing the Court for its perhaps unwitting *eBay* standard so far has not gotten the Court's attention. Mark P. Gergen, John M. Golden & Henry E. Smith, *The Supreme Court's Accidental Revolution? The Test for Permanent Injunctions*, 112 Colum. L. Rev. 203 (2012). Federal courts now increasingly rely on the standard.

One specific problem with the "*eBay*" test is that there does not appear to be a difference between the first and second prongs, a point that should be clear if you've read section 7.2 above. Indeed, on remand from the Supreme Court, the trial court said as much: "The irreparable harm inquiry and remedy at law inquiry are essentially two sides of the same coin; however, the court will address them separately in order to conform with the four-factor test as outlined by the Supreme Court." *MercExchange, L.L.C. v. eBay Inc.*, 500 F. Supp. 2d 556, 569 n.11 (E.D. Va. 2007).

Another problem with the *eBay* standard is the treatment of the balance of hardships and the public interest standard. Balance of hardships is a standard usually applied in *preliminary injunction* cases, as we shall see in Chapter 9. To the extent that the defendant argues that hardship on defendant or the public interest weighs against granting the injunction, these have typically been *affirmative defenses* raised by the defendant (see Rendleman, *supra*, at 82-88), and not factors to be *disproved* by the plaintiff.

Although *eBay* has been influential in the federal courts, most state courts have simply ignored *eBay*. "The most important fact about *eBay* and *Monsanto* for this Restatement is that the state courts have largely ignored them. As of March 1, 2023, *eBay* has been cited in 4969 federal cases and only 34 state cases. *Monsanto* has been cited by 1171 federal cases and nine state cases. A significant fraction of the state citations to these cases were to incidental points separate from the four-part test, or they appeared in cases of federal claims asserted in state court, or they contrasted the state rule with the federal rule. The bottom line is that *eBay* and *Monsanto* have had no significant effect on the state law of injunctions against tort." RESTATEMENT THIRD, TORTS: REMEDIES §43, Reps. note h (Am. Law. Inst. Tent. Draft No. 2, 2023); *see also In re COVID-Related Restrictions on Religious Services*, 285 A.3d 1205, 1230 (Del. Ch. 2022) (rejecting *eBay* for Delaware chancery cases).

Example 8

The Pacifica Preservation Society (PPS) seeks a permanent injunction barring Big Developer Co. (BDC) from removing a historic oak tree from property that BDC recently bought. BDC wants to remove the tree to make way for a $10 million development project. PPS argues that the tree is protected by a state law preserving old trees. Assume that PPS can prove that the tree is protected by the statute. Neither PPS nor BDC puts on any evidence as to the hardship an injunction barring the removal of the tree would cause to BDC. Nor does either side put on any evidence of whether removing or preserving the tree would be in the public interest. How should a court rule on PPS's request for an injunction, assuming the court applies the *eBay* standard for the granting of permanent injunctions?

Explanation

Though it is not clear how the court should rule in this case, PPS has done itself no favors by failing to put in evidence regarding the balance of the hardships to the parties and the public interest. Under the *eBay* standard, the *plaintiff* bears the burden of bringing in evidence on these questions (though traditionally these were generally considered affirmative defenses to be raised and proved by defendants). There's still a chance that the court will grant the injunction, if there is enough evidence of irreparable injury/ no adequate remedy at law (a single factor, but one that the Supreme Court lists as two factors in *eBay*). Even though irreparable injury should be easy to prove (after all, how can damages replace an historic tree?), proof of such injury might not be enough for the granting of an injunction in this case under the *eBay* standard.

7.6 OTHER POLICY REASONS FOR COURTS TO DENY INJUNCTIONS

The preceding section demonstrated that when a plaintiff who faces a defendant likely to violate plaintiff's rights asks for an injunction rather than settling for damages, it is usually for a good reason: damages just won't be as good as the specific relief offered by equity and backed by the power of contempt.

But courts sometimes hide behind the language of the irreparable injury rule to deny an injunction on policy grounds. More forthrightly, courts sometimes will deny an injunction expressly on policy grounds, even acknowledging that plaintiffs have proven irreparable injury and propensity.

Professor Laycock, in his book *The Death of the Irreparable Injury Rule*, offers some wonderful examples of courts misusing the irreparable injury rule to reach a result that many of us would agree with on policy grounds. *See* LAYCOCK, THE DEATH OF THE IRREPARABLE INJURY RULE, at 60-192. Most notable is his discussion of *Van Wagner Advertising Corp. v. S & M Enterprises*, 492 N.E.2d 756 (N.Y. 1986).[8]

In *Van Wagner*, the owner of a building near Manhattan's midtown tunnel leased to Van Wagner Advertising space to erect a billboard on the building's eastern wall. The space faced an exit to the tunnel (a prime billboard spot, no doubt). The lease period was three years with an option to renew for seven additional years. Van Wagner erected a billboard and subleased it to another party for three years. Near the beginning of the lease period, the building's owner sold to a new owner and purported to cancel the lease with Van Wagner. The new owner wanted to tear down the building (including the billboard) and some adjacent property it had purchased in order to build a new major residential-commercial development on the block, a major construction project.

By the time the case got to New York's highest court, the Court of Appeals, the main question was not about whether the building's owner had breached the contract (it did), but whether Van Wagner was entitled to specific performance. Under the rules we have already seen, this appears to be an easy case for the court to grant the injunction:

1. *Propensity:* The building's owner had already breached the contract and was going to tear down the building. There was no question that the owner posed more than a mere threat to violate Van Wagner's rights.
2. *Irreparable injury:* It does not look like damages would be as good a remedy for Van Wagner as the injunction. Remember that some courts treated contracts involving real estate as prime candidates for specific performance under the idea that each piece of land is unique. While that notion might not be true uniformly, this seems to be a particularly strong case: how much is the advertising seen by thousands of people each day stuck in traffic while trying to emerge from Manhattan's midtown tunnel worth? On top of that, remember that Van Wagner had subleased to another party, who is now going to be able to sue Van Wagner for breaching *that* lease. On top of that,

8. Even though this is an interesting example for students of Remedies, it is not as interesting as the party name *S & M Enterprises* might lead you to think.

> what is the value of the seven-year option on the property? All of these factors are reasons for concluding that Van Wagner could meet the irreparable injury requirement.
>
> But that's *not* what the New York court held. It first stated that the rule about specific performance being available as a matter of course in real estate contracts did not apply to the *leasing* but to the *sale* of property. It also noted that "at some level all property may be interchangeable with money"—a view the court conceded undermined the basis for ever finding irreparable injury. It then concluded that there was no irreparable injury because the trial court correctly determined "that the value of the 'unique qualities' of the demised space could be fixed with reasonable certainty and without imposing an unacceptably high risk of undercompensating the injured tenant."

Laycock (Death of the Irreparable Injury Rule, at 162) points out the inconsistency of this analysis with the usual understanding of the irreparable injury rule:

> These damages are imperfect at best, and may be seriously defective. Van Wagner lost any chance to charge a higher rent for years four through ten, and the court made no effort to compensate that loss. More important is the sublessee, the advertiser who bargained for three years of exposure to the tunnel exit. His damages seem entirely unmeasurable. Either he loses his expectancy entirely, receiving no compensation other than release of his obligation to pay rent, or Van Wagner is liable for the speculative value of the advertiser's lost expectancy. Van Wagner got no compensation for that liability, and the court did not venture an opinion on how to measure the advertiser's damages.

That's not to say that the court got the *result* wrong in this case. Indeed, the court's result was likely correct on an alternative ground cited by the trial court: there was so much *hardship on the defendant* that Van Wagner should be denied the right to an injunction. The court wrote: "It is well settled that the imposition of an equitable remedy must not itself work an inequity, and that specific performance should not be an undue hardship." What hardship? If Van Wagner gets its injunction, it can hold up a major redevelopment of a block of midtown Manhattan.[9] So the court likely reached the right result, but it (unnecessarily, given the alternative ground for decision) mangled the irreparable injury rule along the way.

---

9. An economist might respond that it is very unlikely that Van Wagner, if given the right to specific performance, would actually hold up such a major development. Instead, the building's owner would likely pay Van Wagner some generous amount (more than the amount a court would award in damages to Van Wagner) to give up the property right to keep the billboard up. For a discussion of the economic analysis, and the likelihood of such bargaining, see this chapter's Example 1 and its explanation.

Hardship to the defendant is one policy reason for denying an injunction to a plaintiff who can prove irreparable injury and propensity. It is not, however, necessarily an easy argument to make. Courts do *not* simply balance the hardship to the plaintiff and the hardship to the defendant in deciding whether or not the plaintiff is entitled to an injunction.[10]

Even in cases when the defendant is an intentional wrongdoer, courts will often refuse "in equity" to consider such a hardship argument. (Ask yourself if the building owner is a wrongdoer here. As discussed in Chapter 4, at least some courts do not consider breaching parties to a contract to be wrongdoers, at least in most circumstances.) In some cases in which there is disproportionate harm to the defendant compared to the gain to the plaintiff in granting an injunction, however, a court may deny the grant of an injunction on grounds of preventing hardship.

There are other policy reasons as well why courts might deny injunctions to plaintiffs who otherwise meet the requirements for an injunction. Consider the right to a jury trial, which, as noted above, is guaranteed in federal courts by the Seventh Amendment and in many state constitutions. Considering our Oscar-Pnina widget breach of contract example again, if Oscar asks for a suit for damages, most state constitutions would grant Oscar the right to a jury trial. But if Oscar asks for specific performance, in many states he would have no right to a jury trial because he is seeking an equitable remedy.[11]

Oscar is in a good position: he can choose damages over specific performance if the right to a jury trial is important enough to him. But note that if Oscar chooses specific performance, that also deprives *the defendant*, Pnina, of the right to a jury trial. A court therefore might deny Oscar's claim for specific performance *because it deprives the defendant of the right to trial by jury*.

Many defendants may be just as happy with a bench trial (that is, a trial before a judge and not a jury). In my review of the cases involving equitable relief with requests by *defendants* for a jury trial, I found a number of cases in which a large corporate lender sought to foreclose on the property of a poor defendant or failing small business. You can see why in such circumstances *defendants* might want the right to a jury trial.

In many jurisdictions, a complaint like Pnina's for a jury trial would fall on deaf ears. *See Nat'l City Bank v. Abdalla*, 722 N.E.2d 130, 134 (Ohio App. 1999) (rejecting argument of defendant in foreclosure action to a jury trial: "Neither party may assert the right to a jury trial in an equitable action").

---

10. Under the *eBay* standard, as discussed in section 7.5 above, the plaintiff may bear the burden of coming forward with evidence as to the balance of the hardships.

11. In some states, statutes provide for the right to a jury trial for at least some equitable claims. *See Smith County Educ. Ass'n v. Anderson*, 676 S.W.2d 328, 337 (Tenn. 1984).

The rule from the Ohio case makes some sense; it would be a pretty harsh result for plaintiffs seeking injunctions if their rights to equitable relief could be quashed by a defendant's simple demand for a jury trial. Concerned with defendants' right to a jury trial, however, some jurisdictions have reached a compromise position. In North Dakota, for example, "one against whom an action is brought may not be deprived of the right to a jury trial unless the party seeking to avoid a jury trial clearly and unambiguously shows that he is seeking an equitable remedy and that he is clearly entitled to it if he proves the facts as alleged in his complaint." *Gen. Elec. Credit Corp. v. Richman*, 338 N.W.2d 814, 818 (N.D. 1983).[12]

Freedom of speech as guaranteed by the First Amendment can also be the basis for denying an injunction to plaintiffs otherwise entitled to them. Consider the facts of *Animal Rights Foundation of Florida, Inc. v. Siegel*, 867 So. 2d 451 (Fla. App. 2004). David Siegel sold timeshare condominiums in Florida. To draw customers, he hired "Tiger's Eye Productions" for twice-weekly animal shows. The Animal Rights Foundation of Florida began a letter writing campaign and picketing in front of Siegel's residence and business location, claiming he was promoting cruelty to animals through the shows. He sued for libel and slander.

The trial court initially denied a request for a preliminary injunction, but when the protests continued, the court granted it. (The fact that it was a preliminary injunction rather than a permanent injunction is irrelevant for our purposes. Assume that a court has determined that the animal rights group in fact engaged in libel and slander.) The injunction in pertinent part provided:

> That defendants Heather Lischin and the Animal Rights Foundation of Florida, and their servants, employees, agents and any person or entity acting on their own behalf or at their request, and any person in active concert or participation with them (hereinafter "Defendants") are forthwith and immediately enjoined from tortiously interfering with Plaintiffs' advantageous business relationships by directly or indirectly publishing verbally, or in writing the following statements:
>
> "David Siegel abuses animals"
> "David Siegel condones animal abuse"
> "Now featuring at Westgate Animal abuse"
> "David Siegel supports animal abuse"
> "Westgate supports animal abuse"
> "Westgate supports cat beater"
> "David Siegel supports cruelty to animals"
> "Westgate supports cruelty to animals"

---

12. For additional complications since *Richman* involving the North Dakota right to a jury trial in equitable cases, see Edward E. Erickson, *The Right to a Jury Trial in Equitable Cases*, 69 N.D. L. Rev. 559 (1993).

> "Now featuring at Westgate animal abuse" and
> "Westgate refuses to stop sponsoring animal cruelty," to:
>
> (1) Plaintiffs' actual or prospective customers and their guests at the entrance to, or within any of Plaintiffs' timeshare in Florida. "Customers" shall mean all persons who have been invited by Plaintiffs, either directly or indirectly, to purchase or lease a timeshare unit at any of Westgate Resorts, Ltd's resorts. "Guests" shall mean all persons who have been invited by customers of Westgate Resorts, Ltd. "Invited" means those persons who have come to any of Westgate Resorts, Ltd's resorts as a result of any advertising, marketing or promotional activities by Westgate Resorts, Ltd.
> (2) David Siegel's neighbors at the entrance to, or within, the subdivision wherein the Home is located.[13]

By a 2-1 vote, the Florida appellate court held that the injunction was an unconstitutional prior restraint on speech and therefore had to be reversed. The court also reversed other parts of the injunction limiting the number of protesters and the protesters' use of megaphones. The dissenting judge held that part of the injunction was constitutional because there was good evidence that some of the statements were libelous (defendants admitted that there was no evidence Siegel himself or his company Westgate were "abusing animals") and the defendants' conduct was harassing Siegel.

A First Amendment defense to injunctive relief did not leave Siegel without a remedy. If he could prove defamation, he would be allowed to recover damages. But damages in a defamation case, even "presumed damages" for loss to reputation (see Chapter 3.4), are rarely going to be as good for a defendant as an injunction: there is no way to know how many of Siegel's potential customers were scared away by the claims of the animal rights activists, or how many of those customers otherwise would have made a sale had they not been deterred by the statements. Plaintiff is left with a remedy, but likely a remedy that is not nearly as good as an injunction.

Personal service contracts are another policy area where courts sometimes refuse to issue injunctions. Consider *Beverly Glen Music, Inc. v. Warner Communications, Inc.*, 224 Cal. Rptr. 260, 260 (App. 1986):

---

13. As a matter of drafting and the scope of the injunction, how would you grade this injunction? Consider whether it would be a violation of the injunction for defendants to hire an airplane to fly over Siegel's business location and residence with a large photograph of a tortured animal accompanied by a brightly colored sign reading: "David Siegel and Westgate want animals to DIE, DIE, DIE!!!!" If it would not be a violation, how could you rewrite the injunction to more effectively cover such conduct? You should see the trade-off between being specific and being general. By being specific, the defendant is less able to claim that his conduct did not violate the injunction. But by being specific, the plaintiff opens up "loopholes" that violate the spirit but not the letter of the injunction. Courts generally won't hold a person in contempt for violating the spirit of the injunction. The best way to deal with this problem (though it is an imperfect way) is to provide examples and add some general language such as "or similar language disparaging Siegel's treatment of animals."

> In 1982, plaintiff Beverly Glen Music, Inc. signed to a contract a then-unknown singer, Anita Baker. Ms. Baker recorded an album for Beverly Glen which was moderately successful, grossing over one million dollars. In 1984, however, Ms. Baker was offered a considerably better deal by defendant Warner Communications. As she was having some difficulties with Beverly Glen, she accepted Warner's offer and notified plaintiff that she was no longer willing to perform under the contract. Beverly Glen then sued Ms. Baker. . . .

The California appellate court noted that the universal rule that contracts to render personal services cannot be specifically enforced. "To do so runs afoul of the Thirteenth Amendment's prohibition against involuntary servitude." Thus, Beverly Glen could not get an injunction ordering Anita Baker to record the album for them.

A common way around the prohibition, however, is for the non-breaching party to seek an injunction barring the defendant from rendering personal services for someone else. "The net effect is to pressure the defendant to return voluntarily to his employer by denying him the means of earning a living. Indeed, this is its only purpose, for, unless the defendant relents and honors the contract, the plaintiff gains nothing from having brought the injunction."[14]

The court in *Beverly Glen* held that a California statute prohibited enforcing the "negative" contract against Baker,[15] but other courts have upheld such contracts. *See Nassau Sports v. Peters*, 352 F. Supp. 870 (E.D.N.Y. 1972) (upholding an injunction barring a professional hockey player signed with National Hockey League team from playing for a team in the rival World Hockey Association league). Still, it is difficult to find many modern cases analyzing the use of these negative injunctions, which suggests that plaintiffs may not be seeking them all that often. One reason is that such negative injunctions are unnecessary given that prohibitions on working for competitors are now commonly contained in covenants not to compete, and litigation today centers on whether such covenants are enforceable or against public policy.

Burden on the court is a final policy reason why courts may decline injunctive relief. In this regard, consider *Diaz v. Kay-Dix Ranch*, 88 Cal. Rptr. 443

---

14. The leading case supporting the use of "negative" injunctions in personal service contracts is *Lumley v. Wagner*, 42 Eng. Rep. 687 (1852), involving breach of an opera singer's contract to sing at an opera house.

15. For a similar case on statutory grounds out of Montana, see *Reier Broadcasting Co. v. Kramer*, 72 P.3d 944 (Mont. 2003). The California statute, Cal. Civ. Code §3423(e), has since been amended to allow courts to grant such negative injunctions only for "a contract in writing for the rendition of personal services from one to another where the promised service is of a special, unique, unusual, extraordinary, or intellectual character, which gives it peculiar value, the loss of which cannot be reasonably or adequately compensated in damages in an action at law, and where the compensation for the personal services" meets one of two complex formulas for the amount of compensation in the statute. It is unclear from the face of the statute why the California legislature wrote in these complex formulas. Perhaps there was pressure from some industry to include or exclude certain classes of contracting parties.

(App. 1970). A group of legal California farm workers concerned about competition from undocumented workers from Mexico sought an injunction against three private ranches "requiring defendants to make some reasonable inquiry into the citizenship or immigration status of employment applicants as a preliminary to hiring." Among the reasons the appellate court had for sustaining the trial court's denial of an injunction was the burden on the courts:

> If defendants are to be enjoined, other California farm operators may be similarly enjoined. A network of these injunctions may cover growers in rural counties. A single superior court may be called upon to issue dozens of these injunctions. As this court envisions these injunctions in practical operation, farm operators or their foremen will put each new worker through a relatively simple interrogation and request for documentation. . . . The farm operator or foreman will be called upon to determine the status, legal or illegal, of each new worker. . . . Injunction violations would subject employers to judgments of contempt, punishable by fine or jail. . . . Eligible workers or other observers would report seeming violations, contempt citations would issue and judicial hearings held. At peak employment seasons the superior courts in rural counties would sit in judgment over charges of contempt and over the form and adequacy of investigations. Multiple injunctions covering a wide segment of California agriculture would have the cumulative effect of a statutory regulation, administered by the superior courts through the medium of contempt hearings. The injunctive relief sought by plaintiffs would subject farm operators to burdensome, if bearable, regulation, and the courts to burdensome, if bearable, enforcement responsibilities.

The court concluded that "[w]eighed alone on any scale of human values, the farmworkers' need is vastly more acute than the prospective predicament of injunction-saddled employers. [In addition], the comparative efficacy of federal action, tips the scales against injunctive relief."

Note the judgment the court made about the system of injunctions that give courts "burdensome, if bearable, enforcement responsibilities." Just how burdensome does an injunction have to be before it is *too* burdensome? There is likely no single answer to that question. The answer, however, turns not only on how *burdensome* an injunction might be on the courts, but also on how *important* the social policy is that the injunction seeks to further. On this point, think of injunctions aimed at desegregating public schools in the South. As we will see in the next chapter, these injunctions were terribly burdensome on the courts, with some lasting for decades and requiring that courts get into the micromanagement of school policy. Yet many would claim that the heavy burden of the injunctions on the courts was but a small price to pay given the value of desegregation.

In sum, courts sometimes deny injunctions to plaintiffs who can prove irreparable injury and propensity for policy reasons. Here is a non-exhaustive list of policy reasons discussed in this section:

- Undue hardship to the defendant
- Preserving defendant's right to a jury trial
- First Amendment concerns
- Concerns about restraining labor/involuntary servitude
- Burden on the court

As in *Van Wagner*, be wary of courts that find that a plaintiff cannot meet the irreparable injury requirement for the issuance of injunctions. Courts sometimes care more about an unstated policy reason for denying the injunction than the now-dead hand of the Chancellor that seems to be denying the plaintiff the specific relief that aims most directly—or at least more directly than damages—at the rightful position. Litigants should not be afraid to confront *both* irreparable injury and policy arguments directly.

EXAMPLE

Example 9

Same facts as in the Siegel animal rights case, but assume that the evidence conclusively shows that the animal rights activists have no assets. This means that if a jury awards Siegel damages, he would not be able to collect them. How, if at all, does this change the analysis of whether the court should grant the injunction prohibiting the activists' speech?

EXPLANATION

Explanation

The fact that the defendants have no assets is another factor (on top of others) showing that Siegel faces irreparable injury: damages are not going to be adequate to put the plaintiff in the rightful position. Whether that should trump the First Amendment right to speak is a difficult question. On the one hand, if the defendants have no assets, Siegel is going to be left with no remedy at all: the First Amendment precludes an injunction that keeps him in the rightful position and any damages awarded cannot be collected. On the other hand, making the inability to collect damages the dispositive factor in deciding this case has uncomfortable ramifications. Discussing a similar claim arising in *Willing v. Mazzocone*, 393 A.2d 1155 (1978), Laycock (The Death of the Irreparable Injury Rule, at 164) writes: "The court correctly saw that it could not enjoin indigent speakers if it would not enjoin wealthy speakers: 'conditioning the right of free speech upon the monetary wealth of an individual' would be intolerable."

EXAMPLE

Example 10

A client comes to you complaining about the conditions in which client's brother lives in state prison (the brother is in prison for life, without the possibility of parole). The client believes, and you agree upon diligent investigation, that the conditions violate numerous provisions of the U.S. Constitution, including the Eighth Amendment prohibition against "cruel and unusual punishment." Should you sue for damages, an injunction, both, or neither?

EXPLANATION

Explanation

As a first thought, you might consider damages for past harm and injunctive relief aimed at improving conditions in the future. But bringing either kind of claim carries serious complications. First, the Supreme Court has read the Eleventh Amendment of the U.S. Constitution to bar suits for damages against the state, allowing only injunctive relief (a sort of reverse "irreparable injury" rule). *Edelman v. Jordan*, 415 U.S. 651, 677 (1974). Individual state officers who have violated the brother's constitutional rights might be subject to damages claims under 42 U.S.C. §1983 (most commonly known as a "section 1983" lawsuit).

Injunctive relief against the prison system is possible, and, as we will see in the next chapter, prisoners in the past have brought significant class actions in federal court to reform prisons. Such suits, however, are now limited by the Prison Litigation Reform Act (PLRA), which narrowly sets forth the kind of prospective relief that may be available. *See* 18 U.S.C. §3626. The PLRA also requires that a complaining prisoner exhaust administrative remedies before suing in court, 42 U.S.C. §1997e(a), a provision the Supreme Court recently construed against prisoners in *Woodford v. Ngo*, 548 U.S. 81 (2006). The next chapter considers in more depth how the PLRA limits prospective relief.

The more general point: if you are going to sue a government defendant for either damages or an injunction, you had better carefully check both the constitutional and statutory limits on such suits.

EXAMPLE

Example 11

The Wilkinsons lived in the Vista subdivision, where all the homes had to abide by the covenants contained in the deed of sale. Among the covenants was a prohibition on placing "manufactured homes" on the land, except for homes that (1) complied with federal and state requirements for safe homes and that (2) met all the regulations and standards of the New Mexico Construction Industries Division (CID). The Wilkinsons gave their property to their daughter, Jane Brown, who wanted to put a manufactured home on the land. Brown knew about the covenant. She contacted one company, Preferred, whose products complied with the covenant's requirements, but that company had a nine-month waiting list for a home. She then bought her home from another manufacturer that complied with federal and state requirements, but that failed to meet a few relatively minor standards of the New Mexico CID. The homeowners association immediately objected. Smith did not remove the home, and the association sued. The trial court found that the differences between a Preferred home and the one purchased by Brown to be inconsequential. It would cost $25,000 to $30,000 to remove the home. The entire home's purchase price was $60,000.

Assume there is no question that Brown's home violated the covenant and the only question is one of remedy. Should the court grant the association's request for an injunction to remove the home or should the association receive only damages?

EXPLANATION

Explanation

There is no question about *propensity* here. Brown had already brought the home onto the land in violation of the subdivision's restrictive covenant. Nor does there seem to be much of a question about irreparable injury. Presumably, these restrictions are in the covenant for either aesthetic or safety reasons. Either way, it will be hard to measure the losses to the association and other owners stemming from Brown's failure to abide by the restrictive covenant.

There are three policy reasons, however, why a court might wish to deny the injunction. The first is the burden to the defendant. The cost to remove the home is very high, especially when considered in relation to the cost of the unit itself. Hardship to the defendant is a tough claim to make here, even to a court acting in equity that has some discretion in granting a remedy. Brown knew of the restrictive covenant, and she even took steps to comply. Because she did not want to wait, however, she willfully violated the covenant. A court probably would be unsympathetic to her plight. (However, compare her plight to that of the defendant in *Van Wagner*. Is her behavior any worse than that of the seller who breached the lease for the billboard?)

Second, a court may think that the covenant itself is unfair, at least as applied to an owner who wishes to bring onto the land a manufactured home that comes close to complying with the standards of the association. To the extent that a court that sits in equity wishes to "do equity" (that is, to do what is fair), there is an argument to deny the injunction.

Finally, this might be a case in which the *defendant*, rather than the *plaintiffs*, wants the right to a jury trial. The defendant might reason that jurors are likely to be sympathetic with a homeowner fighting an association that appears to be enforcing its rules in a very strict manner. Sometimes those on such an association go on power trips, enforcing rules for their own sake rather than out of any logic.

The facts of this hypothetical are based on *Aragon v. Brown*, 78 P.3d 913 (N.M. Ct. App. 2003). In the actual case, the trial court denied the injunction on grounds that the covenant was "not reasonable, and should not, in equity, be enforced." A divided New Mexico appellate court reversed, finding that the provision was not against public policy, and that "a general inquiry into whether restrictive covenants running with the land are reasonable is not a proper inquiry in considering whether to grant an injunction to enforce such covenants."

The dissent thought the trial court was right to deny the injunction: "The Association failed to demonstrate to the trial court any real, much less legitimate, purpose served by excluding homes that are the functional equivalent of homes that are allowed."

The majority opinion did not discuss the right to a jury trial, nor was it moved by the amount that it would cost Brown to comply with the injunction.

CHAPTER 8

Advanced Topics in Injunctions

Chapter 7 set forth the basic rules for the issuance of injunctions: injunctions are forward-looking court orders aimed either at preventing future harm (the *preventive* injunction) or at preventing the future bad effects of past harm (the *reparative* injunction). A plaintiff requesting an injunction must prove both that the defendant has engaged in—or at least made a realistic threat of engaging in—prohibited conduct (*propensity*), and that a legal remedy such as damages is not as good for the plaintiff as an injunction (*irreparable injury*). Even then, courts sometimes deny injunctions on various *policy grounds*. Courts typically tailor an injunction toward the goal of keeping the plaintiff in the rightful position (*the rightful position standard*), but courts sometimes go further and issue injunctions that protect the rightful position through broader steps (the *prophylactic* injunction). In some circumstances, courts granting injunctions view their role more broadly, and grant broad injunctions in the name of equity (evoking the image of the original Chancellor's discretion).

In this chapter, we consider four advanced topics in the law of remedies: (1) the proper scope of injunctive relief in public institutional litigation (structural injunctions) and the related question of consent decrees, (2) the standards for modifying already existing injunctions, (3) the rights and obligations of third parties in relation to injunctive relief, and (4) the propriety of injunctions which apply nationwide. Chapter 9 looks at *preliminary* injunctive relief, including preliminary injunctions, temporary restraining orders, and injunction bonds. Chapter 10 examines the *contempt power*, which courts use to enforce injunctions.

8.1 STRUCTURAL INJUNCTIONS (OR INSTITUTIONAL REFORM LITIGATION)

8.1.1 Structural Injunctions, the Rightful Position, and the Roving Commission to Do Good

As we saw in the preceding chapter, plaintiffs may seek injunctions in both private law and public law litigation. When Oscar asks a court to order Pnina to specifically perform the contract by requiring her to produce the promised widget, Oscar seeks an injunction that serves only his *private* aims. But when the voters of the City of Pacificana seek an injunction requiring the police to provide protection against KKK intimidation when they go to vote at the polls, the injunction is a form of *public law* litigation that benefits more than a private party.

Beginning with *Brown v. Board of Education* (*Brown II*), 349 U.S. 294 (1955), civil rights activists used injunctive relief as a major public law tool for facilitating social change on a large scale. *Brown II* required courts to desegregate Southern schools using injunctive relief: "[T]he *Brown II* Court granted district courts the authority not only to overhaul every aspect of educational administration, but also to revise 'local laws and regulations which may be necessary in solving the foregoing problems.'" Marshall Miller, Note, *Police Brutality*, 17 Yale L. & Pol'y Rev. 149, 194 (1998) (quoting *Brown II*).

Desegregating a school system takes time, and it requires a more complicated series of injunctions than a simple order such as that requiring Pnina to deliver the widget to Oscar by June 1. Professor Owen Fiss coined the term "structural injunction" to connote the series of injunctions necessary to restructure government institutions in civil rights litigation. As Fiss explains:

> The civil rights injunction takes many forms, but none as significant as the structural injunction: the formal medium through which the judiciary seeks to reorganize ongoing bureaucratic organizations so as to bring them into conformity with the Constitution. The structural injunction represents the most distinctive contribution to our remedial jurisprudence drawn from the civil rights experience, and though the structural injunction has been used in all manner of cases—housing, mental health, and prisons—its origins in civil rights litigation are never forgotten. The structural injunction received its most authoritative formulation in civil rights cases, specifically those involving school desegregation, and has been legitimated in terms of those cases.

Owen Fiss, *The Allure of Individualism*, 78 Iowa L. Rev. 965 (1993).

Structural injunctions blossomed in the Warren Court era as scholars looked to courts to solve social problems, particularly problems of racial discrimination.[1] There were many success stories from such litigation, but the litigation also enmeshed federal courts in the micromanagement of government institutions—sometimes with mixed results. Many now refer to this set of injunctions by a different name, "institutional reform litigation."

Federal district courts held on to some of these cases for years, with many litigants graduating (or even dying) before the cases reached a conclusion. Especially in the earlier years, some of these injunctions restructured government institutions in ways not tied to the rightful position standard (closer to the Chancellor's "roving commission to do good," discussed in Chapter 7), a role defended by some scholars and, in more recent years, rejected by the Supreme Court. As Fiss explains, "[t]he fate of the structural injunction has . . . been tied to that of the civil rights movement. The remedy grew in power and scope over a twenty-year period, beginning in 1954 and continuing until 1974. Ever since, it has been under attack." *Id.* at 965.

Swann v. Charlotte-Mecklenberg Board of Education, 402 U.S. 1 (1971), is a good example of the Supreme Court's treatment of structural injunctions in the pre-1974 period. In that case, the district court enacted a far-reaching mandatory busing plan to end school desegregation that was upheld by the Supreme Court. Arguably, the plan went much further than the rightful position because the plan integrated schools much more than they would have been had there been state-mandated school desegregation: even without *de jure* (formal, government-mandated) segregation, many Southern schools would have remained segregated because of *de facto* voluntary segregation in housing. The remedy of forced busing upheld by the Supreme Court in *Swann* put the plaintiffs in a *better* position than if there had been no state discrimination. This is not to say the structural injunction remedy was unjustified (a judgment call you can make yourself); it is to say only that the structural injunction was not tightly tied to the rightful position standard.

Milliken v. Bradley, 418 U.S. 717 (1974), marked the beginning of the change in the Supreme Court's attitude toward structural injunction remedies. There, the Court rejected a remedy to end school segregation in Detroit—which would have included busing children from Detroit and neighboring suburbs—that had not been found to violate the Constitution. The Court held that an *interdistrict* (i.e., between districts) remedy was not appropriate when there was proof only of an *intradistrict* (i.e., within one district) violation.

---

1. In addition to Fiss's work, *see especially* Owen Fiss, Injunctions (1972); and Owen Fiss, The Civil Rights Injunction (1978). Abram Chayes wrote a leading defense of the courts' role in promoting social change through structural injunctions. *See* Abram Chayes, *The Role of the Judge in Public Law Litigation*, 89 Harv. L. Rev. 1281 (1976). I focus on the desegregation cases in this chapter, even though they are dated, because they were formative in judicial and scholarly thinking about "structural injunctions" and critiques of those injunctions.

In more recent years, the *Milliken* line of cases has won out at the Supreme Court. Consider litigation over desegregation of the Kansas City, Missouri, public schools. Eighteen years (!) after the litigation began, the Supreme Court for the third (!) time considered a remedial aspect of the trial court's decision. This trip to the Court resulted in the Supreme Court's rejecting the district court's most recent remedial order, which, among other things, required a tax increase to fund massive spending to improve the school system. *Missouri v. Jenkins (Jenkins III)*, 515 U.S. 70 (1995).[2]

The district court ordered major improvements to the school system to make the system more attractive to white students who had left the district for private schools (the goal of "desegregative attractiveness"). One of the court orders required spending at an annual cost of over $200 million, including financing for

> high schools in which every classroom will have air conditioning, an alarm system, and 15 microcomputers; a 2,000-square-foot planetarium; green houses and vivariums; a 25-acre farm with an air-conditioned meeting room for 104 people; a Model United Nations wired for language translation; broadcast capable radio and television studios with an editing and animation lab; a temperature controlled art gallery; movie editing and screening rooms; a 3,500- square-foot dust-free diesel mechanics room; 1,875-square-foot elementary school animal rooms for use in a zoo project; swimming pools; and numerous other facilities.

By a 5-4 vote, the Supreme Court rejected the remedy adopted by the district court. The majority saw the remedy as not appropriately tied to the scope of the constitutional violation and therefore not tied to the rightful position. ("[T]he nature of the remedy . . . is to be determined by the nature and scope of the constitutional violation.") The constitutional violation was *state-mandated segregation* in the public schools, not the *private* decisions of white students (and their families) to leave the public school system once the courts ordered the schools' desegregation.[3]

The relevant question for the majority appeared to be: what position would students in the Kansas City school system have been in had the government not intentionally segregated students on the basis of race? The majority believed that these students likely would *not* have been in a racially integrated and well-funded public school system, and therefore the district court could not order such a remedy. In other words, for the majority, it was

2. *Missouri v. Jenkins (Jenkins I)*, 491 U.S. 274 (1989), considered attorney's fees. *Missouri v. Jenkins (Jenkins II)*, 495 U.S. 33 (1990), considered whether court-ordered tax increases could be used to pay for the desegregation remedy.

3. The majority also held that to the extent to which the district court was seeking to attract students from *outside* the boundaries of the school system, it was improperly imposing an *interdistrict* remedy for an *intradistrict* problem, in violation of *Milliken v. Bradley*. We return to this issue in section 8.3 below.

court-ordered desegregation rather than segregation that led to the white flight, and therefore the court could not impose a magnet-like remedy (i.e., very attractive public school programs) to attract back the white students.

The dissenters disagreed on this point, believing that it was ultimately the costs of *paying for desegregation* that led to the white flight:

> Property tax-paying parents of white children, seeing the handwriting on the wall in 1985, could well have decided that the inevitable cost of cleanup would produce an intolerable tax rate and could have moved to escape it. The District Court's remedial orders had not yet been put in place. Was the white flight caused by segregation or desegregation? The distinction has no significance.

Jenkins III (Souter, J., dissenting).

Regardless of whether the majority or the dissent had the better argument in *Jenkins* III, Supreme Court majorities in recent years have made it abundantly clear that courts should target remedies toward the rightful position. For example, in *Lewis v. Casey*, 518 U.S. 343 (1996), a prison reform case, the district court found that one prisoner had been injured by the failure of the prison library "to provide the special services [the prisoner] would have needed, in light of his particular disability (illiteracy), to avoid dismissal of his case." Yet the district court ordered a variety of systemwide changes to the state's prison libraries, including the addition of "special services or facilities required by non-English speakers, by prisoners in lockdown, and by the inmate population at large." The Supreme Court held that proof of two instances of inadequate library assistance "were a patently inadequate basis for a conclusion of systemwide violation and imposition of systemwide relief."

While most of these recent Supreme Court structural injunction cases arose when lower courts gave plaintiffs *more* than the rightful position, the Supreme Court has affirmed that the same principle applies when courts give *less* than the rightful position. In *United States v. Virginia*, 518 U.S. 515 (1996), for example, the United States Court of Appeals for the Fourth Circuit had determined that the state-run Virginia Military Institute (VMI) unconstitutionally discriminated against women through its male-only admissions policy. But the lower court also had suggested that Virginia could solve the constitutional problem by opening a "parallel" "Virginia Women's Institute for Leadership" (VWIL).

The Supreme Court rejected this proposed solution, because the lower court "did not inquire whether the proposed remedy . . . placed women denied the VMI advantage in the position they would have occupied in the absence of discrimination." The Supreme Court rejected the remedy on grounds that the proposed women's program was "different in kind from VMI and unequal in tangible and intangible facilities." There was no way that the new VWIL, for example, could replicate the advantages that came from being a VMI alumnus—part of the "old boy" network.

In his dissenting opinion, Chief Justice Rehnquist agreed that VMI's gender admission policy was unconstitutional, but he argued that the remedy could include the creation of a separate women's school. He further wrote that the state need not create a "VMI clone for women"; it would be enough for the schools to be of the "same overall caliber." He concluded: "[One institution] could be strong in computer science, the other could be strong in liberal arts."

Despite these signals from the Supreme Court, the tradition of broad structural injunctions continues to have support among legal scholars,[4] and lower court judges involved in institutional litigation sometimes continue to "do equity" in structural injunction cases, going beyond the rightful position standard. Today, however, a judge doing that runs a higher risk of reversal by the Supreme Court, and may be more likely to write a broad remedy in the language of the "rightful position," defending broader remedies as "prophylactic measures" aimed at achieving that rightful position.

The Supreme Court's most recent word on the scope of structural injunctions was more forgiving of a strict "rightful position" standard. In *Brown v. Plata*, 563 U.S. 493 (2011), the Court in a 5-4 vote upheld a three-judge court order in long-running California prison litigation to release California prisoners to alleviate prison overcrowding. The constitutional violations stemmed from serious deficiencies in the prison health care system. Justice Kennedy wrote the opinion joined by the Court's four liberal Justices. The dissenters did not believe that the remedy matched the wrong and argued that releasing prisoners early would harm the public interest.[5] As we will see in section 8.2, the conservative justices on the Supreme Court have more recently made it easier to end structural injunctions by easing the standards for modification.

Example 1

EXAMPLE

You are a federal district judge and you have just determined that a state-run mental hospital has been violating the constitutional rights of its patients through inadequate care. How would you begin the process of using a structural injunction to remedy the constitutional violation? Once the injunction

4. Some legal scholars agree with Owen Fiss's 1979 argument against the rightful position standard in structural injunction cases: "The object of the structural remedy is not to eliminate a 'violation' in the sense implied by the tailoring principle, but rather to remove the threat posed by the organization to the constitutional values. The concept 'violation' can be used to describe the object of the remedy only if it is understood in a prospective, dynamic, and systemic sense." Owen Fiss, *Foreword—The Forms of Justice*, 93 HARV. L. REV. 1, 47-48 (1979). Legal scholars who oppose Fiss's view fear giving judges such open-ended powers to craft remedies not tailored to the extent of the wrong committed by the defendant.

5. Justice Scalia, in his typical bombastic fashion, began his dissent by stating, "Today the Court affirms what is perhaps the most radical injunction issued by a court in our Nation's history."

is put in place, how would you monitor whether or not there has been compliance with your orders?

EXPLANATION

Explanation

As a federal district judge, you likely would come in knowing very little about the running of a hospital. Courts sometimes appoint "special masters" to assist in evaluating problems and crafting solutions. In extreme cases, courts have appointed experts to temporarily run a hospital. Much of how well the remedy works to cure constitutional violations is going to depend upon the lawyers in the case. Competent plaintiffs' lawyers are usually essential to effective implementation of a structural injunction. In addition, the cooperation or recalcitrance of defendants may dictate the speed with which structural injunctions are implemented. Government lawyers can take steps that can slow down or sabotage the process of reform.

Monitoring compliance with ongoing structural injunctions is also a challenge for courts. At a minimum, courts in such cases often require the parties to file periodic reports and hold hearings to evaluate progress that is made. When there are problems with implementing the orders of the court, the court will often modify its order to better effectuate its remedies. Again, competent plaintiffs' counsel plays a key role in the successful implementation of a structural injunction.

EXAMPLE

Example 2

If you were a Justice of the U.S. Supreme Court reviewing the remedy imposed by the district court in *Jenkins* III, would you support it, or oppose it? Explain the reasons for your answer.

EXPLANATION

Explanation

Obviously, there is no right or wrong answer to this thought question. Rather, the question is aimed at getting you to think about whether you believe courts deciding public law litigation that restructures government institutions should aim their remedies at the rightful position standard or should have broader "equitable" power to improve the institutions and society. The risk of sticking with the rightful position is that courts may end up giving plaintiffs an incomplete remedy—one that, because of the limited power of the courts to enact social change and fully prevent the future bad effects of past harm, gives plaintiffs less than the rightful position. We call this a problem of "underremediation." The risk of going beyond the rightful position is that the courts give remedies completely untethered to the wrong committed by the defendants, thereby burdening the defendants (and, potentially, third parties, as we shall see) with obligations to solve problems not directly traceable to defendants' wrongs. We call this a problem of "overremediation."

Unsurprisingly, the willingness to bear these risks has some correlation to political preferences. Liberals are willing to give more than the rightful position to avoid underremediation, and conservatives are willing to risk underremediation so as not to place unfair burden on state defendants to solve social wrongs. Federalism weighs heavily in these cases. Consider that the liberals on the Supreme Court were the dissenters in *Jenkins III* and that some of the conservatives on the Court dissented in the *VMI* case. (Justice Thomas, whose son was attending VMI, did not participate in the case.) *Brown v. Plata* depended upon the vote of perennial "swing" justice Anthony Kennedy, who has since retired. Will a more conservative Court move further toward underremediation?

8.1.2 Consent Decrees

Some public law litigation over restructuring government institutions ends not with an adversarial trial and judgment, but with settlement of the case. In public law litigation, settlements tend to be embodied in *consent decrees*, which are court orders crafted by the parties that, like regular injunctions, are backed up by the power of contempt.

Why a consent decree rather than a simple private settlement agreement? A settlement agreement is a contract and is not backed up by the power of contempt. Breach of a settlement agreement will ordinarily require a new lawsuit. In contrast, entry of a consent decree keeps the federal court's involvement in the case and ensures that the court monitors the progress of the parties.

A good example is the consent decree that the Los Angeles Police Department entered into in 2000 following a U.S. Department of Justice investigation alleging that the LAPD violated the constitutional rights of L.A. residents. The decree was to last for five years, but at the end of the five-year period some of its central requirements (including the creation of a computer database to track police officers' disciplinary records) had not yet been implemented, leading to calls for the consent decree to be extended for at least another two years.[6] The fact that the requirements of the consent decree had not all been implemented in a five-year period demonstrates how difficult it is to get institutional change.

Consent decrees can be valuable tools for settling (and enforcing) government institutional litigation, but they raise two sets of concerns.

6. Erwin Chemerinsky, et al., *The LAPD Still Needs Policing*, L.A. Times, May 3, 2006.

First, consent decrees can be used to bind successive government administrations to policies they may not agree with. *See* Michael W. McConnell, *Why Hold Elections? - Using Consent Decrees to Insulate Policies from Political Change*, 1987 U. Chi. Legal F. 295. In the LAPD case, for example, the United States Department of Justice, which agreed to the consent decree, was headed by Democrats under Bill Clinton, who wanted a strong remedy. In 2006, however, when the consent decree was due to expire, the Department of Justice, this time headed by Republicans under George W. Bush, did not want the decree extended. The court did so anyway.[7]

Second, a consent decree can be the product of collusion from the start, because (outside of the prison context, as we will soon see), there is no requirement that a consent decree be limited to a remedy that keeps the plaintiffs in the rightful position. Imagine you are the head of the Kansas City Municipal School District involved in the *Missouri v. Jenkins* litigation. How hard would you fight against a court order that would raise property taxes in order to fund vast new programs for your district and to raise salaries for your teachers? The trial court orders in effect achieved for the poor and overextended public school system in Kansas City something that was likely impossible to achieve politically: a massive infusion of public funds to build up the school system.

Because of this danger of collusion, it is often left to other parts of the government (the state government in the *Jenkins* litigation) or other private parties to argue against the entry of consent decrees that can serve to benefit both plaintiffs and the (nominal) defendants.

When parties agree to a consent decree and no one objects, courts are not called upon to ensure that the agreements do more than keep the plaintiffs in the rightful position. After all, a defendant can settle an automobile accident by offering plaintiff more money than the plaintiff demands. But the public interest is at stake in structural injunction litigation, so overremediation can have consequences for others (such as the taxpayers who would foot the bill for the school system fix in Kansas City).

EXAMPLE

Example 3

You are a lawyer for the Pacifica Police Department, which has been sued for violating the constitutional rights of the citizens of Pacifica by using excessive force and making many false arrests. Your case has been set before a very liberal federal district court judge, who has made it clear that the court is very likely to find that the department indeed has violated the rights of Pacifica residents. Your client wants the court to impose as little reform as possible. Do you favor (1) taking the case to trial, (2) consenting to the

7. Jim Newton, *Shaking the "Warrior Cop" Mentality a Test of City's Will*, L.A. Times, July 16, 2006.

entry of a consent decree settling the case, or (3) entering into a settlement agreement with the plaintiffs?

Explanation

EXPLANATION

This is a difficult question to answer in the abstract because it requires you to compare the deal you could likely get from the plaintiffs with the likely remedies that the court would impose on you if the case goes to trial. What the plaintiffs might be willing to settle for will be influenced by plaintiffs' lawyer's own view of what the trial court is likely to impose as a remedy.

The one easy part of the question is the choice between a settlement agreement and a consent decree. Your client would much prefer a settlement agreement over the consent decree. If the plaintiff later believes your client violated a settlement agreement, the plaintiff would likely have to bring a new suit (alleging a breach of that contract) and could not rely on the power of contempt. The federal district court judge's hands will be kept in the matter for the duration of the consent decree.

8.1.3 How Congress May Limit Remedies: The Prison Litigation Reform Act Example

Though structural injunction litigation began in the school desegregation context, many suits through the years have involved prisoners protesting prison conditions. *Lewis v. Casey*, the library assistance case described above, represents one of the less consequential of these claims. A case of much more consequence was *Hutto v. Finney*, 437 U.S. 678 (1978), involving the deplorable conditions in Arkansas prisons. To give but one of the disturbing examples mentioned in the case, prisoners in "punitive isolation" at one of the state's prisons faced the following conditions:

> An average of 4, and sometimes as many as 10 or 11, prisoners were crowded into windowless 8' × 10' cells containing no furniture other than a source of water and a toilet that could only be flushed from outside the cell. At night the prisoners were given mattresses to spread on the floor. Although some prisoners suffered from infectious diseases such as hepatitis and venereal disease, mattresses were removed and jumbled together each morning, then returned to the cells at random in the evening. Prisoners in isolation received fewer than 1,000 calories a day; their meals consisted primarily of 4-inch squares of "grue," a substance created by mashing meat, potatoes, oleo, syrup, vegetables, eggs and seasoning into a paste and baking the mixture in a pan.

The Supreme Court upheld a part of the district court's order limiting prisoners to no more than 30 days' punishment in punitive isolation. The majority held that "[t]he vandalized cells and the atmosphere of violence were attributable, in part, to overcrowding and to deep-seated enmities growing out of months of constant daily friction. The 30-day limit will help to correct these conditions."

Then-Justice (later Chief Justice) Rehnquist, in dissent, stated that "[n]o person of ordinary feeling could fail to be moved by the Court's recitation of the conditions formerly prevailing in the Arkansas prison system," but he disagreed with the remedy: "[T]he district Court's order limiting the maximum period of punitive isolation to 30 days in no way relates to any condition found offensive to the Constitution."

In *Hutto*, the Supreme Court majority viewed the limit on time in punitive isolation as a prophylactic one to guard the rightful position; the dissent saw the link between wrong and remedy as too attenuated to justify the remedy—it saw the majority as simply imposing its vision of justice. Was Justice Rehnquist right? And if he was, does that mean that the majority reached the wrong result? The latter question is one each of us has to decide for himself or herself.

Prison litigation, both major and minor, continued to be a major factor in the late twentieth century,[8] and it provides a very good case study of the kinds of limits Congress might impose on court remedies in the institutional litigation context.

In 1996, Congress eventually stepped in with the Prison Litigation Reform Act[9] (PLRA) to limit prison-related litigation. The act imposes many barriers to prison litigation, including a requirement that a complaining prisoner exhaust administrative remedies before suing in court, 42 U.S.C. §1997e(a), a provision the Supreme Court recently construed against prisoners in *Woodford v. Ngo*, 548 U.S. 81 (2006).

The most important limit on remedies appear in 18 U.S.C. §3626, entitled "Appropriate Remedies with Respect to Prison Conditions." Part (a)(1)(A) appears to enshrine a narrow rightful position standard to be applied to prison condition litigation:

> Prospective relief in any civil action with respect to prison conditions shall extend no further than necessary to correct the violation of the Federal right of

8. "By 1984 (the first year for which data are accessible), 24% of the nation's 903 state prisons (including at least one in each of forty-three states and the District of Columbia) reported to the federal Bureau of Justice Statistics that they were operating under a court order. In 1983 (the first year these data exist for jails), 15% of the nation's 3,338 jails (including at least one in all but two of the forty-five states that had jails, and the District of Columbia) reported court orders. Litigants had been particularly active—or particularly successful—in large facilities: the prisons under court order housed 42% of the nation's state prisoners, and the jails under court order housed 44% of the nation's jail inmates, and for both jails and state prisons, about half of the nation's largest facilities were under court order." Margo Schlanger, *Beyond the Hero Judge: Institutional Reform Litigation as Litigation*, 97 Mich. L. Rev. 1994, 2004 (1999) (book review).

9. Prison Litigation Reform Act, Pub. L. No. 104-134, 110 Stat. 1321 (1995).

> a particular plaintiff or plaintiffs. The court shall not grant or approve any prospective relief unless the court finds that such relief is narrowly drawn, extends no further than necessary to correct the violation of the Federal right, and is the least intrusive means necessary to correct the violation of the Federal right. The court shall give substantial weight to any adverse impact on public safety or the operation of a criminal justice system caused by the relief.

This provision would appear to make it more desirable for lawyers representing prisoners to enter into consent decrees, which could give more than the constitutional floor allowed under §3626(a)(1)(A). But §3626(c)(1) appears to foreclose that option: "In any civil action with respect to prison conditions, the court shall not enter or approve a consent decree unless it complies with the limitations on relief set forth in subsection (a)." In other words, just like court orders issued at the end of a trial, consent decrees may not offer more than the constitutional floor. The PLRA, however, allows the parties to enter into settlement agreements that are not consent decrees (and therefore lack the court supervision and court's power of contempt). The Act also changes the rules for the modifications of injunctions, the topic of the next part of this chapter.

The PLRA appears aimed at limiting both the amount of prison condition litigation and the extent of the remedies ordered or approved by the federal courts. But has it had that effect? Professor Schlanger concludes:

> By drastically widening the escape route for correctional jurisdictions seeking to terminate court orders, interposing a difficult administrative exhaustion hurdle for maintenance of a court-order lawsuit, and squeezing the funding for the advocates who seek court orders, the PLRA has contributed to a major decline in the regulation of prisons and jails by court order. Nonetheless, even after the PLRA, court-order incidence remains quite high in the final correctional censuses. There is increasing variation among states, and in a few states, jails and prisons continue to experience a great deal of injunctive regulation.

Margo Schlanger, *Civil Rights Injunctions over Time: A Case Study of Jail and Prison Court Orders*, 81 N.Y.U. L. Rev. 550, 602 (2006).

The effect of the PLRA is important beyond the prison context. During the Bush administration, Congress considered "the Federal Consent Decree Fairness Act proposed to implement restrictions similar to the PLRA's in other topical areas of governmental injunctive litigation." *Id.* at 557. A future conservative administration could revive such a proposal.

Example 4

EXAMPLE

If you were a member of Congress, would you support the Federal Consent Decree Fairness Act or similar legislation that would bar federal courts from, among other things, enforcing consent decrees that do more than give plaintiffs the constitutional floor? Why, or why not?

EXPLANATION

Explanation

Your answer to this question will likely mirror your response to Example 2. Both questions are aimed at making you consider to what extent federal court judges should be trusted with institutional reform litigation in the face of proven constitutional violations by state actors. Limits such as the PLRA and the proposed new federal legislation show a Congress that is skeptical that courts are going to be willing to stick with a narrow reading of the rightful position standard in crafting injunctions or in approving consent decrees. Professor Schlanger's research suggests that legislation like this could have the effect of limiting the amount of successful litigation. Are you willing to risk underremediation in the name of preventing overremediation? Again, this question likely correlates with your political views about how much the government can be trusted to solve social problems.

EXAMPLE

Example 5

Returning to the situation in Example 1, you are a federal judge overseeing litigation regarding constitutional violations at a state-run mental health facility. The parties have reached an agreement that would vastly improve the conditions of the hospital, including the building of private rooms for most of the facility's patients. You do not believe that this remedy is constitutionally required to cure the constitutional violations by the health facility. Are you permitted to approve the consent decree? Should you do so?

EXPLANATION

Explanation

The Prison Litigation Reform Act does not apply outside the context of prison condition litigation—thus it does not pose any barrier to your approval of the consent decree. Normally, if both parties agree to a remedy (and there are no intervening parties who object), the court is bound to approve the consent decree. Judges tend to like settlement of litigation (if for no other reason than that it clears the docket for other cases), and in the absence of any indication that the settlement is against the public interest, most courts would likely sign the consent decree even if it gave a better remedy than the judge would have given at the end of the litigation. But the Supreme Court has recently said that there must be a connection between the consent decree and the "federal interests" plaintiffs sought to protect by bringing suit in the first place. Moreover, the consent decree must "further the objectives of the law upon which the complaint was based." *Frew v. Hawkins*, 540 U.S. 431, 437 (2004). An appellate court could well reverse a consent decree that is completely untethered to the federal wrong alleged in the case.

8.2 MODIFYING EXISTING INJUNCTIONS

Not only in cases involving structural injunctions, but especially in those cases, because they can go on for many years, courts often are asked to modify or extend injunctions in the face of new or changed circumstances. Courts also may do so, as in the case of the LAPD consent decree described above, because the defendant has failed to comply with the court's original order. Oftentimes, a defendant's failure to comply won't lead to a finding of contempt (because the plaintiffs won't be able to prove a willful disobedience of the court's order); instead, the court will issue a new set of orders with which the defendant will need to comply.

The leading case on modifying injunctions (and consent decrees) in federal court is a pre-PLRA prison conditions case, *Rufo v. Inmates of Suffolk County Jail*, 502 U.S. 367 (1992). *Rufo* changed prior law by making it easier for parties to seek modification, such as when a party wishes to reopen a case that had gone to final judgment. (The proper procedure is for the party to make a motion for modification under Federal Rule of Civil Procedure 60(b).)

Rufo provides a non-exhaustive list of grounds for modifying an injunction or consent decree:

- "When changed factual conditions make compliance with the decree substantially more onerous."
- "When a decree proves to be unworkable because of unforeseen obstacles."
- "When enforcement of the decree without modification would be detrimental to the public interest."
- "When the statutory or decisional law has changed to make legal what the decree was designed to prevent."
- "If the parties had based their agreement on a misunderstanding of the governing law."

The Supreme Court reaffirmed the "flexible standard" of *Rufo* in *Frew v. Hawkins*, 540 U.S. 431 (2004), explaining that when state defendants are involved, "principles of federalism require that state officials with front-line responsibility for administering the program be given latitude and substantial discretion." Moreover, "[t]he federal court must exercise its equitable powers to ensure that when the objects of the decree have been attained, responsibility for discharging the State's obligations is returned promptly to the State and its officials. . . .If the State establishes reason to modify the decree, the court should make the necessary changes; where it has not done so, however, the decree should be enforced according to its terms."

The Court made that point even more emphatically in *Horne v. Flores*, 557 U.S. 433 (2009). At issue was a federal district court's refusal to modify an injunction in a class action case involving Arizona's noncompliance with a federal statute requiring the state to take "appropriate actions to overcome language barriers" in schools. The five conservative Justices on the Court criticized both the district court and the Ninth Circuit for their failure to apply the flexibility of *Rufo* when the state asked for an injunction against it to be modified. The *Horne* opinion includes a lengthy discussion of the propriety of modifying injunctions in what it termed "institutional reform litigation," stressing a point raised earlier in this chapter—the danger of collusion and of locking in reforms that bind successor elected officials: "Injunctions of this sort bind state and local officials to the policy preferences of their predecessors and may thereby 'improperly deprive future officials of their designated legislative and executive powers.'" *Id.* at 449 (quoting *Frew*).

According to the dissenting Justices in *Horne*, the majority opinion changes the *Rufo* standard for "institutional reform litigation" (though the majority and dissent cannot agree on what the term actually means): "The Court adds that in an 'institutional reform litigation' case, a court must also take account of the need not to maintain decrees in effect for too long a time, the need to take account of 'sensitive federalism concerns,' and the need to take care lest 'consent decrees' reflect collusion between private plaintiffs and state defendants at the expense of the legislative process." *Id.* at 488 (Breyer, J., dissenting) (citations omitted). Justice Breyer questioned "whether the Court has set forth a correct and workable method for analyzing a Rule 60(b)(5) motion." *Id.* at 490. "[T]he tone is very different from *Rufo*; the Court seems to be pressing for easy and early modification in institutional reform cases." Laycock & Hasen p. 286.

The PLRA has its own provision on consent decrees in prison condition litigation, allowing the state to reopen any existing prison condition injunction or consent decree where the injunction or decree gave prison plaintiffs more than the constitutional minimum requirements. Under the PLRA, the defendant or intervenor "shall be entitled to the immediate termination of any prospective relief if the relief was approved or granted in the absence of a finding by the court that the relief is narrowly drawn, extends no further than necessary to correct the violation of the Federal right, and is the least intrusive means necessary to correct the violation of the federal right." 18 U.S.C. §3626(b)(2). But the injunction does not terminate if the court finds that it now meets these requirements.

EXAMPLE

Example 6

While a United States Supreme Court case is pending over whether the double bunking of inmates violates the Eighth Amendment's prohibition on cruel and unusual punishment, the state of Pacifica and inmates at the Pacifica state prison enter into a consent decree to settle the inmates' suit over prison conditions. Among the terms of the decree is a prohibition on double bunking.

a. Before the PLRA, could a trial court approve such a consent decree?

b. After the PLRA, could a trial court approve such a consent decree?

EXPLANATION

Explanation

(a) The court may approve the consent decree. Before the PLRA, there was no requirement that consent decrees provide no more than the constitutional floor. The applicable federal right is uncertain, so even under the *Frew* standard there seems little question that a district court could justify its order as protecting the federal rights at issue in the lawsuit.

(b) The PLRA would not necessarily bar a district court's agreeing to this aspect of the consent decree. If the question is uncertain and before the Supreme Court, then arguably a consent decree prohibiting double bunking goes no further than what federal law requires.

EXAMPLE

Example 7

Same facts as Example 6. Assume the trial court signs off on the consent decree, which is entered into before Congress passes the PLRA. After final judgment, the Supreme Court determines that double bunking does not violate the Eighth Amendment. The state moves to modify the consent decree to allow it to double-bunk prisoners.

a. Before the PLRA, how should the district court rule?

b. After the PLRA, how should the district court rule?

EXPLANATION

Explanation

(a) These are the facts of the *Rufo* case, and in the actual case the Supreme Court allowed modification. The Supreme Court in *Rufo* said that the change in law alone could not provide the basis for reopening the consent decree, and there was no requirement that the consent decree meet the constitutional minimum. However, the Court said that if the sheriff could establish "that the parties to the consent decree believed that single celling of pretrial detainees was mandated by the Constitution, this misunderstanding of the law could form a basis for modification." It appears that there was no "misunderstanding," only uncertainty over what the Supreme Court ultimately would hold.

Should the resolution of that uncertainty allow the parties to undo a bargain they struck when things were uncertain? If so, the incentive to settle cases will be lowered. To see why, consider this: Plaintiffs want a settlement package that includes X, Y, and Z. Defendants are willing to offer X and Y, but not Z. Plaintiffs agree to the bargain rather than litigating; plaintiffs' expectation is that the court will award X + Z, but not Y, and plaintiffs prefer X + Y over X + Z. The parties settle for X + Y. The Supreme Court later decides that Y is not required by federal law. The district court then modifies the injunction, removing the Y requirement, leaving plaintiff with only X. Plaintiffs would have been better off litigating, which would have left them with X + Z rather than now being left with only X.

(b) Under the PLRA, even if the parties entered into a binding settlement agreement enforced by the court through the consent decree, the state may move for immediate termination on grounds that the constitutional minimum has changed, and the consent decree gives more than the constitutional minimum. Defendants from *Rufo* took just such an approach to modify the consent decree after Congress passed the PLRA. *See Inmates of Suffolk County Jail v. Rouse*, 129 F.3d 649 (1st Cir. 1997). As this example shows, there is less and less incentive for plaintiffs to settle these cases, because defendants can reopen them if and when courts further constrict the rights of prisoners to certain minimal prison conditions.

EXAMPLE

Example 8

As part of a final judgment brought by residents of a state-run mental health facility, the trial court orders the construction of a new hospital within five years, at an expected cost of $20 million. Two years later, before construction is to begin, the state seeks to modify the injunction on grounds that current construction costs would double the cost of the project to $40 million. The ballooning cost is partly the result of inflation, and partly the result of an unexpected housing boom that has raised the labor costs for construction. Should the court modify its order?

EXPLANATION

Explanation

The state will argue that factual conditions have changed to make compliance with the court's order substantially more onerous (double the price) because of a rise in construction costs that was not actually foreseen by the parties. The plaintiffs will likely argue that some inflation costs could have been foreseen, and mere additional expense should not be a basis for modifying the court's judgment. Under *Frew* and *Horne*, the court is going to have to give considerable deference to the state's call for modification.

To a great extent, the question will likely turn on the alternatives posed by the state. The court is not going to order modification if the state cannot come up with another plan that remedies the constitutional problems. In other words, it is not enough to show that a remedy is more expensive if in fact that remedy is still needed to vindicate a constitutional right. If, for example, the state can demonstrate that it could solve the constitutional problems much more cheaply through remodeling the existing facility rather than building a new facility, the court is likely to take very seriously a request for modification.

8.3 INJUNCTIONS AND THIRD PARTIES

In a typical private law adjudication, an injunction does not have much effect on third parties. For example, when the court orders specific performance against Pnina requiring her to produce the widget for Oscar, the order likely will have little to no impact on third parties (by third parties I mean individuals who are not parties to the lawsuit). In public interest litigation, by contrast, thousands of non-parties may be affected.

In the *Swann* case, for example, the court ordered a busing remedy that affected many students who were not parties to the litigation but who were made part of the remedy. Since *Swann*, the Supreme Court has grappled with the extent to which an injunction may *burden* third parties. In the *Milliken* case, for example, as noted above, the Court rejected an *interdistrict* remedy to solve school segregation problems in the single district of Detroit.

Somewhat contrary to *Milliken*, in *Hills v. Gautreaux*, 425 U.S. 284 (1976), the Supreme Court held that third parties could be *substantially burdened* in the pursuit of federal remedies. There, the Court upheld the ability of the United States Department of Housing and Urban Development to take remedial action outside the city limits of Chicago to remedy problems with race discrimination in a Chicago Housing Authority program. The remedy consisted in part of providing vouchers to poor Chicago residents to pay for housing in Chicago suburbs. "An order directed solely to HUD would not force unwilling localities to apply for assistance under these programs but would merely reinforce the regulations guiding HUD's determination of which of the locally authorized projects to assist with federal funds." The localities faced a large burden because as a result of the court's order to HUD, they were going to be faced with an influx of new poor residents who were likely going to need significant social services.

It is unclear whether *Gautreaux* remains good law following *Jenkins* III. Recall that one of the reasons the Supreme Court in *Jenkins* III rejected the proposed remedy for the Kansas City school district was its effect on neighboring school districts. But, as in *Gautreaux*, the effect was only indirect: the magnet programs of the Kansas City school districts were meant to attract "white flight" students from the suburbs.

The *Jenkins* III majority held that this remedy aimed at "desegregative attractiveness" placed too high a burden on the suburban school districts, which would lose students. The dissenters accused the majority of silently overruling *Gautreaux*. At this point, the extent to which third parties may be burdened in structural injunction litigation is somewhat unclear, but the

Court today is obviously more concerned about protecting values of federalism (states' rights) than it has been in the past. If *Gautreaux* arose today, it is not clear that a Supreme Court majority would decide it the same way.

Though the precise extent to which injunctions may burden third parties remains unclear, clearer are the rules relating to *direct orders* to third parties. Those orders must be "minor and ancillary." Thus, even the filing of quarterly reports by a non-wrongdoing party might be too excessive. *See General Building Contractors Ass'n v. Pennsylvania*, 458 U.S. 375 (1982); *see also Baltimore Neighborhoods, Inc. v. LOB, Inc.*, 92 F. Supp. 2d 456, 472 (D. Md. 2000) (condominium association could be ordered to provide access to buildings to allow for retrofitting to comply with Americans with Disabilities Act and Fair Housing Act; court characterizes order as "minor" and "ancillary").

Although direct orders sound more onerous than indirect burdens, the distinction would probably be lost on most third parties. Consider a student who wants to remain at a nearby school: that student would find it much less burdensome to fill out occasional paperwork than to attend a different school under a busing plan.

Example 9

A federal district court issues an order requiring the forced integration of schools in the city of Pacificana, against the objections of the white residents of the city, including the police chief. Can the district court order the Pacificana police department to assist in integrating the schools?

Explanation

Certainly if the police department is part of the city, and the city has been adjudicated a constitutional wrongdoer, then a court may order the police department to carry out the mandates to effectuate the trial court's order.

The more difficult question arises when the police department is not an adjudicated wrongdoer, but is instead, like the suburban school districts in *Jenkins III*, a burdened innocent third party. Some take the position that the police could not be ordered to aid the court absent some adjudication of wrongdoing. But see *Matter of Boung Jae Jang v. Brown*, 560 N.Y.S.2d 307 (App. 1990), holding that the trial court had inherent authority to enforce its order and that the police had a duty to enforce the law when ordered to do so by the court.

The court suggested that its rule might not extend to parties besides the police department, especially parties over whom the court had not exercised its jurisdiction: "We decline to hold that the Police Department's duty to enforce the law is contingent upon its being formally joined as a party to each and every proceeding in which it may ultimately be required to engage in some type of law enforcement activity."

What is interesting about the case is that it is not just one about burdens: the court actually *ordered* the police to keep demonstrators at least 50 feet from the entrance to a store. Why is this not more than a minor and ancillary order barred by the *General Building Contractors Association* case? Perhaps the answer is that the police are going to be treated differently in terms of direct orders as well.

8.4 NATIONWIDE (OR UNIVERSAL) INJUNCTIONS: POLITICAL WARFARE IN FEDERAL COURTS

In a typical lawsuit, even institutional reform litigation against government entities, the injunction applies to a limited number of people and to a limited place, such as a school system in a particular city or area. But what of challenges to a *federal* government policy? Does a single district court have the power to issue a nationwide injunction, binding on the federal government throughout the country? If such power is available, is it wise for district courts to exercise the power nationwide?

This issue gained increased salience in the last decade as Republican states started challenging Obama administration laws and policies in favorable federal district courts, seeking nationwide relief. The trend continued when President Trump took over, only this time it was Democratic states challenging Trump administration laws and policies in different favorable federal courts. With President Biden in office, the action shifted to Texas, where judges skeptical of the Administration's powers issued nationwide injunctions limiting the scope of administration rules.

A prominent example was *Texas v. United States*, 86 F. Supp. 3d 591 (S.D. Tex. 2015), aff'd, 809 F.3d 134 (5th Cir. 2015), *aff'd by an equally divided Court*, 579 U.S. 547 (2016). The state of Texas, along with 25 other states, challenged an Obama administration rule, the Deferred Action for Parents of Americans and Lawful Permanent Residents (DAPA), which essentially stopped the federal government from enforcing federal immigration laws against the parents of children born in the United States who were in the United States illegally. A federal district court in the Southern District of Texas ruled that DAPA likely violated the Administrative Procedure Act, and it issued a preliminary injunction barring enforcement of DAPA nationwide. The Fifth Circuit affirmed. The Supreme Court, at that point down one Justice after the death of Justice Scalia, divided 4-4 in the case along liberal and conservative lines, and a tie counted as an affirmance leaving the ruling standing and the nationwide injunction in place.

It was not the only nationwide injunction sought by conservative states and issued against Obama administration policies. Once Donald Trump came into office, liberal states began suing. A federal court in Washington State issued a nationwide injunction against a Trump executive order temporarily barring entry into the United States of most persons from six predominantly Muslim countries. *Washington v. Trump*, 2017 WL 462040 (W.D. Wash. Feb. 3, 2017). The Ninth Circuit denied the request for a stay, *Washington v. Trump*, 847 F.3d 1151 (9th Cir. 2017), and the Trump administration abandoned further appeal, withdrawing the order and writing a new one, which was then quickly subjected to nationwide injunctions issued by federal courts in Hawaii and Maryland.

The nationwide injunction therefore has become a potent tool in political and partisan warfare between the federal government and states representing the opposite political party. There is much to be said for a nationwide injunction: it assures uniformity and raises an issue that could be resolved definitively for the entire country, potentially by the Supreme Court. It would be odd, for example, to have federal immigration law be different in Texas and California.

The use of nationwide injunctions raises problems, too, most notably the forum shopping that happens with the practice, and the lack of percolation of issues in lower courts before being resolved by the Supreme Court. As Professor Samuel Bray notes, "If the national injunction issued by the district court is a preliminary one, the Supreme Court might even decide a major constitutional question on a motion for a stay. That very nearly occurred with the Take Care Clause claim in *Texas v. United States*, and with important questions about executive power and religious freedom challenges to the immigration order of President Trump." Samuel Bray, *Multiple Chancellors: Reforming the National Injunction*, 131 HARV. L. REV. 417 (2017).

Professor Bray notes that the nationwide injunction is a relatively new phenomenon and has no historical English analogue. There was just one chancellor, who sat nationally in England, resolving these disputes. Our current system, where every federal judge is a chancellor, may put too much power into the hands of a single judge, especially when that judge has the power of contempt and can essentially be chosen by the parties. Professor Bray defends a rule limiting court orders to the parties before the court:

> A federal court should give a plaintiff-protective injunction, enjoining the defendant's conduct only with respect to the plaintiff. No matter how important the question and no matter how important the value of uniformity, a federal court should not award a national injunction. This rule, if adopted by the courts or by Congress, would alleviate the forum-shopping problem. It would restore the percolation of legal questions through the different courts of appeals, allowing each circuit to reach its own conclusion pending resolution by the Supreme Court. And it would nearly eliminate the risk of directly conflicting injunctions.

Both conservative and liberal Supreme Court Justices have recently expressed concerns about nationwide injunctions: Justice Neil Gorsuch, joined by Justice Clarence Thomas, expressed serious doubts about the power of courts to issue universal injunctions:

> Equitable remedies, like remedies in general, are meant to redress the injuries sustained by a particular plaintiff in a particular lawsuit. When a district court orders the government not to enforce a rule against the plaintiffs in the case before it, the court redresses the injury that gives rise to its jurisdiction in the first place. But when a court goes further than that, ordering the government to take (or not take) some action with respect to those who are strangers to the suit, it is hard to see how the court could still be acting in the judicial role of resolving cases and controversies. Injunctions like these thus raise serious questions about the scope of courts' equitable powers under Article III.
>
> It has become increasingly apparent that this Court must, at some point, confront these important objections to this increasingly widespread practice. As the brief and furious history of the regulation before us illustrates, the routine issuance of universal injunctions is patently unworkable, sowing chaos for litigants, the government, courts, and all those affected by these conflicting decisions. Rather than spending their time methodically developing arguments and evidence in cases limited to the parties at hand, both sides have been forced to rush from one preliminary injunction hearing to another, leaping from one emergency stay application to the next, each with potentially nationwide stakes, and all based on expedited briefing and little opportunity for the adversarial testing of evidence.
>
> This is not normal. Universal injunctions have little basis in traditional equitable practice. Their use has proliferated only in very recent years. And they hardly seem an innovation we should rush to embrace. By their nature, universal injunctions tend to force judges into making rushed, high-stakes, low-information decisions. The traditional system of lower courts issuing interlocutory relief limited to the parties at hand may require litigants and courts to tolerate interim uncertainty about a rule's final fate and proceed more slowly until this Court speaks in a case of its own. But that system encourages multiple judges and multiple circuits to weigh in only after careful deliberation, a process that permits the airing of competing views that aids this Court's own decisionmaking process. The rise of nationwide injunctions may just be a sign of our impatient times. But good judicial decisions are usually tempered by older virtues.
>
> Nor do the costs of nationwide injunctions end there. There are currently more than 1,000 active and senior district court judges, sitting across 94 judicial districts, and subject to review in 12 regional courts of appeal. Because plaintiffs generally are not bound by adverse decisions in cases to which they were not a party, there is a nearly boundless opportunity to shop for a friendly forum to secure a win nationwide. The risk of winning conflicting nationwide injunctions is real too. And the stakes are asymmetric. If a single successful challenge is enough to stay the challenged rule across the country, the government's hope of implementing any new policy could face the long

> odds of a straight sweep, parlaying a 94-to-0 win in the district courts into a 12-to-0 victory in the courts of appeal. A single loss and the policy goes on ice—possibly for good, or just as possibly for some indeterminate period of time until another court jumps in to grant a stay. And all that can repeat, *ad infinitum*, until either one side gives up or this Court grants certiorari. What in this gamesmanship and chaos can we be proud of?

Department of Homeland Security v. New York, 140 S. Ct. 599, 600-601 (2020) (Gorsuch, J., concurring in the grant of a stay).

Justice Kagan, speaking at an event at Northwestern Law, expressed similar sentiments:

> This has no political tilt to it . . . You look at something like that and you think, that can't be right . . . In the Trump years, people used to go to the Northern District of California, and in the Biden years, they go to Texas. It just can't be right that one district judge can stop a nationwide policy in its tracks and leave it stopped for the years that it takes to go through the normal process.

Josh Gerstein, *Kagan Repeats Warning That Supreme Court Is Damaging Its Legitimacy*, Politico (Sept. 14, 2022).

Example 10

Do you favor or oppose the power of federal courts to issue nationwide injunctions? Does your answer depend on who is president or whom you expect to be president?

Explanation

There is no right answer to this question. It is meant to get you to see the situational ethics of the question. If you did not know who would be president for the next 10 years, which would you favor and why?

CHAPTER 9

Preliminary Injunctions and Other Preliminary Relief

9.1 INTRODUCTION TO PRELIMINARY RELIEF

All of the remedies considered so far in this book are those that come at *final judgment*, after a trial or dispositive motion (such as a summary judgment motion) leads the court to enter a judgment in favor of one of the parties.[1] Sometimes, however, a party wants relief before final judgment. Consider the following three scenarios:

- You represent the Pacifica Preservation Society, and you've just received a tip that tomorrow morning at 8 a.m. a wrecking ball is going to knock down the Oldtime Hotel, which you believe is a historic landmark protected against destruction by state law. You want to get an injunction barring the destruction of the hotel.
- William is severely injured in an automobile accident with Xandra. He can no longer work and has used up his savings. He sues Xandra for negligence, but in the meantime he has no money to live on.
- Yvette and Zane are business partners. Yvette believes that Zane, because of a recent severe psychological disorder, is causing the business to suffer serious financial losses. Yvette wants to dissolve the partnership and salvage at least her share of the partnership's assets.

---

1. The last chapter considered "consent decrees," which are settlement agreements by the parties signed by the district court and enforceable through the court's contempt power. These consent decrees are embodied in a final judgment.

In each of these cases, waiting for final judgment (which could literally be *years after* the time of the filing of the complaint) may cause the decision to come too late: the Oldtime Hotel might be destroyed, William may have to declare bankruptcy or even end up being homeless, and Zane could squander the partnership's assets.

What the plaintiffs in these cases really want is *preliminary relief*: some court order *before* final judgment that can aid the plaintiff. The problem is, however, that before final judgment the court does not know if, in fact, plaintiff is entitled to the relief sought. What if Pacifica law does not really protect the hotel as a historical landmark, or if a jury finds the accident was William's fault rather than Xandra's, or if Zane is sane? At the very least, any court granting preliminary relief is going to have to consider *the risk of error* that accompanies the granting of preliminary relief.

In this chapter, we consider the rules related to the most common type of preliminary relief sought, the preliminary injunction, and how the courts deal with the risk of error. In Chapter 17.2, we consider receiverships and freeze devices that can save Yvette from insane Zane. But before we go on, it is worth noting that in most jurisdictions the law generally will not allow William to seek "preliminary damages" in his suit against Xandra. That is, the law has no form of preliminary relief for the payment of damages.

Why is William treated worse than the historical society or Yvette? The answer again appears to be historical:

> The rule against preliminary damage awards is usually said to be absolute or nearly so. This rule is sometimes explained as a corollary of the irreparable injury rule: if plaintiff seeks only money, damages after final judgment will be an adequate remedy. That will sometimes be true, but not if plaintiff suffers severe financial hardships in the meantime. In fact, the rule seems to be an unjustified artifact of the law-equity distinction.

LAYCOCK, THE DEATH OF THE IRREPARABLE INJURY RULE 112 (1991).[2]

Besides history, there are two practical reasons why courts may not have developed the practice of allowing the preliminary recovery of damages. First, preliminary relief requests burden the courts by requiring that cases go through at least two iterations (first for preliminary relief and then for final judgment), running the risk of error during the preliminary stage or stages. It may be worth the double gearing up of the court machinery in cases of truly irreplaceable losses (we cannot "un-demolish" the historic building), but it is not worth the effort for a fungible good such as money.[3]

---

2. Professor Laycock notes an exception to this rule for "cases enjoining termination of a series of periodic payments." *Id.*

3. Fungible goods are those that are easily exchangeable and identical in quality. Thus, if you have a $100 bill and I have two $50 bills, they are fungible. I am indifferent between possessing my $100 worth of currency and yours.

Perhaps too the "financial hardship" cases such as William's are likely to be rare. Even in tort cases involving serious injury, plaintiffs often can obtain medical care either through their health insurance company or through the state. The plaintiff awaiting final judgment often can borrow money in the interim, sometimes against his future recovery if he has a good case, albeit at a high rate of interest if the plaintiff presents a financial risk to the lender.[4]

Second, it would be harder for courts to correct errors in the granting of "preliminary damages" compared to correcting erroneously issued injunctions or receivership orders. If the court gives William money from Xandra preliminarily pending final judgment, and it ultimately determines that Xandra is not liable, William may have used up (or hidden) the money he now needs to pay back to Xandra. In contrast, there are steps such as injunction bonds (see section 9.3 below) that courts can use to protect defendants against erroneously issued preliminary injunctions. Perhaps courts should consider allowing preliminary damages in cases in which a plaintiff could post a bond (similar to appeal bonds posted by defendants to avoid paying judgments during an appeal). But if a plaintiff could afford such a bond, she likely would not need the preliminary relief!

In sum, in most cases, the social costs of awarding preliminary damages appear to exceed the benefits of doing so, except perhaps in the case where the failure to do so causes financial hardship. In the latter class of cases, a plaintiff is most likely to spend the money from the defendant and will be unable to repay it in the event the court determines at final judgment that the defendant in fact does not owe plaintiff any damages.

The remainder of this chapter considers three issues related to *preliminary injunctive relief.* We begin with the standards courts use when issuing preliminary injunctions. Next, we turn to injunction bonds. We conclude with a look at temporary restraining orders, including issues related to notice.

EXAMPLE

Example 1

Before reading the rest of this chapter, test your intuition. Considering the case of *Pacifica Preservation Society v. Oldtime Hotel, Inc.*, what factors should the court consider in deciding whether or not to grant preliminary relief preventing the Oldtime Hotel from being wrecked pending final judgment?

---

4. As noted in Chapter 4.3, when a defendant fails to pay money when due, the nonbreaching party cannot recover consequential damages other than interest on the money owed. So if William becomes homeless while waiting for final judgment and has his teeth knocked out in a street fight, Xandra won't have to pay for William's teeth repair. Instead, if William wins, at final judgment William may recover only the general damages he is owed (the unpaid money) plus interest at the prevailing legal rate. If William is a high credit risk and can borrow money only at a very high rate of interest, he will *not* be able to recover at that higher rate.

Explanation

Chapter 7 explained that when a court considers granting a *permanent* injunction, it must consider matters related to *propensity* (the likelihood that the defendant will engage in prohibited conduct), *irreparable injury* (the inability of the court to fully remedy plaintiff's injury through damages or another legal remedy), and *policy considerations* (such as the burden on the court).

These factors are important in the preliminary injunction phase as well, but they must be considered in the context of the *preliminary* nature of the relief sought. As you think about the criteria that courts should use in evaluating a request for *preliminary* relief, they probably fall into these three categories:

a. Likelihood of plaintiff's success on the merits (which will include an evaluation of the propensity, irreparable injury, and policy considerations to be decided more fully in considering the case on the merits)
b. Risk of error (what would happen to the defendant or plaintiff if the court should err in its preliminary evaluation)
c. The public interest

If you came up with these criteria on your own, congratulations! These are the three basic criteria the courts consider in deciding whether to grant preliminary relief. If you did not come up with these factors, don't worry. The next section discusses these criteria in detail.

Example 2

Considering again *Pacifica Preservation Society v. Oldtime Hotel, Inc.* (from Example 1), suppose you find out that the Acme Wrecking Company is the company that will be using the wrecking ball to bring down the hotel tomorrow morning. Can the court order Acme not to bring down the building? (Note: this problem requires familiarity with the material in the previous chapter.)

Explanation

This question is meant to make you consider the material covered at the end of the last chapter, on injunctions and third parties. If Acme is a non-party, the rule from *General Building Contractors* says that Acme cannot be asked to do more than comply with a "minor and ancillary" order. Whatever else that means, it is probably not too much of a burden on Acme to refrain from knocking down the hotel pending a further order of the court. But there may be a way to avoid litigating this "third party" issue. If it is possible to join Acme as a wrongdoer, then it will be no problem having the court issue an order enjoining Acme from demolishing the hotel pending further proceedings in the court.

9.2 PRELIMINARY INJUNCTIONS (AND STAYS)

Back on the record in the case of *Pacifica Preservation Society v. Oldtime Hotel, Inc.*, you are now before Judge Unfriendly trying to get a preliminary injunction preventing the destruction of the Oldtime Hotel pending a final judgment. What are you going to have to show?

Before we turn to what you will need to show to get *preliminary* relief, it is useful to begin by thinking about what you would need to show if you were seeking a *permanent* injunction enjoining the destruction of the hotel on grounds that Pacifica's historic preservation law prevents its destruction. In seeking permanent relief, you would have to show:

1. *Propensity.* You need to show that there is a realistic threat of harm. This factor really breaks down into two parts. First, you have to show that the Oldtime Hotel is protected from destruction by the state law. Second, if it is protected, you have to show that the defendant is likely to destroy the hotel.

   Note that the kinds of proof you would need for these two issues are very different. For example, it might be that there is no dispute that the defendant intends to tear down the hotel. The only question is one of statutory interpretation: does the state law protect the Oldtime Hotel?[5] On the other hand, if the dispute turns on credibility, the judge might need to hear from witnesses before determining whether or not the defendant intends to tear down the building.
2. *Irreparable injury.* Thinking about this issue for purposes of a final judgment, there seems little question that the historic society (assuming it has standing—a question for a Federal Courts course) faces irreparable injury. Damages would not be as good as a preserved building: one cannot use money to build a "new" building of historic significance. As we shall see, the irreparable injury question is somewhat more complicated when it comes to requests for *preliminary* relief.
3. *Other policy considerations.* Issues such as the burden on the court or First Amendment concerns may arise in some cases.

5. If that's the heart of the case, and it presents a purely legal question, it is not uncommon for a court to combine a hearing on the preliminary injunction with a hearing on the merits and simply issue a final judgment. *See* Fed. R. Civ. P. 65(a)(2).

How do things differ when a plaintiff is seeking a preliminary injunction rather than a permanent injunction? First, because the request is preliminary, plaintiff need not prove his case with as much evidence as will be needed for a final judgment: "The purpose of a preliminary injunction is merely to preserve the relative positions of the parties until a trial on the merits can be held. Given this limited purpose, and given the haste that is often necessary if those positions are to be preserved, a preliminary injunction is customarily granted on the basis of procedures that are less formal and evidence that is less complete than in a trial on the merits. A party thus is not required to prove his case in full at a preliminary-injunction hearing." *University of Texas v. Camenisch*, 451 U.S. 390, 395 (1981).

As with the case of permanent injunctions issued after final judgment, the court considering a request for a preliminary injunction is going to be concerned about propensity, irreparable injury, and other policy considerations.[6] But the test is somewhat different in the case of a preliminary injunction because the court has not yet adjudicated the defendant a wrongdoer, and there is a risk that the court could err in granting or denying a request for a preliminary injunction.

In general, the court is going to be most concerned about the plaintiff's likelihood of success on the merits (which takes a preliminary look at the issues of propensity, irreparable injury, and policy considerations at issue in the permanent injunction stage), the risk of error, and the public interest. Although there are many verbal formulations, the Supreme Court set forth the standard in this way: "A plaintiff seeking a preliminary injunction must establish that he is likely to succeed on the merits, that he is likely to suffer irreparable harm in the absence of preliminary relief, that the balance of equities tips in his favor, and that an injunction is in the public interest." *Winter v. National Resources Defense Council, Inc.*, 555 U.S. 7, 20 (2008).[7] Also, as we shall see, in many courts, plaintiffs will have a much easier time seeking a preliminary injunction that *preserves (or at least appears to preserve) the status quo* than one that seeks to *change* the status quo.

---

6. You may recall that in the *Animal Rights Foundation of Florida v. Siegel* case, discussed in Chapter 7, the court held that an injunction barring animal rights protesters from carrying signs in front of defendant's business and residence violated the First Amendment. That case involved a preliminary, not a final, injunction. The court there barred the preliminary injunction on policy grounds.

7. There remains controversy over whether the plaintiff must prove *all* the elements in each case seeking a preliminary injunction, or whether a "sliding scale" approach applies. Justice Ginsburg, in her dissent in the *Winter* case, wrote that historically, "courts have evaluated claims for equitable relief on a 'sliding scale,' sometimes awarding relief based on a lower likelihood of harm when the likelihood of success is very high. This Court has never rejected that formulation, and I do not believe it does so today." *Id.* at 51 (citation omitted). Some lower courts have retained a sliding scale on the understanding that under *Winter* the party seeking the preliminary injunction must make at least some showing on each of the elements. *See Alliance for the Wild Rockies v. Cottrell*, 632 F.3d 1127 (9th Cir. 2011).

Courts and others sometimes refer to the balancing process that the court undergoes in deciding on a motion for a preliminary injunction as a *balancing of the hardships*. This balancing is different from the balancing that courts sometimes undertake at final injunction. Recall from Chapter 7 that when the defendant who has been found liable faces a very serious hardship from an injunction, and that hardship greatly outweighs the benefits of the injunction to the plaintiff, courts will sometimes deny an injunction (think of *Van Wagner* and the billboard). Typically, however, proof that an adjudicated wrongdoer will endure some hardship will *not* be enough to defeat a successful plaintiff's request for a *permanent injunction*.[8]

But because of the risk of error in the *preliminary injunction* stage—the defendant has not yet been adjudicated a wrongdoer—courts must more carefully balance hardships to *each side*. Importantly, in thinking about the hardships to each side for purposes of the risk of error analysis, we are concerned *only* with the irreparable harm that can occur between the time the plaintiff seeks the preliminary injunction and final judgment—we are not concerned with irreparable harm that would occur only *after* final judgment.

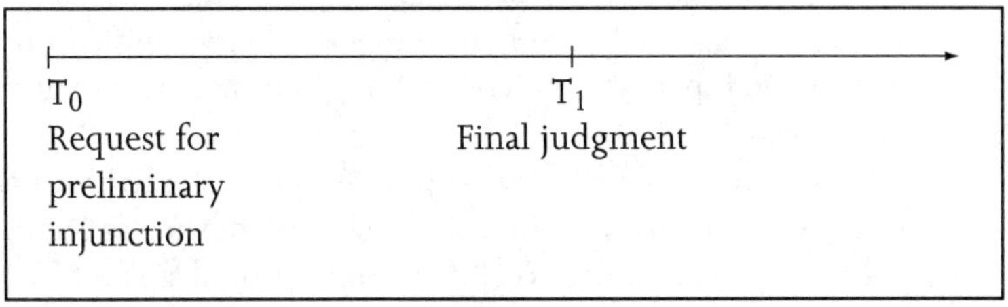

Figure 9.1

Thus, looking at Figure 9.1, plaintiff makes a request for a preliminary injunction at time T_0, and a final judgment will be issued at time T_1. For a preliminary injunction, we are concerned only about irreparable harm faced by plaintiff or defendant in the T_0-T_1 time period. At the preliminary injunction stage, courts should not consider irreparable harm occurring at or after time T_1. For a permanent injunction issued at final judgment, courts are concerned about irreparable injury from time T_1 into the future.

Consider these rules for granting preliminary injunctions in the context of *Pacifica Preservation Society v. Oldtime Hotel, Inc.* If the court fails to issue the preliminary injunction and it erred in doing so (because at final judgment the court decides that the Oldtime Hotel is protected by the state's historic preservation laws), the plaintiff is going to suffer a great deal of irreparable harm. The building will be destroyed, and there will be no way to resurrect it as a historic building.

8. As noted in Chapter 7.5, the *eBay* case imposes a new test in federal courts for *permanent* injunctions, including new requirements for plaintiffs to come forward with evidence regarding the "balance of the hardships."

On the other hand, if the court grants the preliminary injunction and it erred in doing so (because at final judgment the court decides that the Oldtime Hotel is *not* protected by the state's historic preservation laws), the defendant is going to suffer some harm (perhaps irreparable harm). Imagine, for example, that the defendant planned on building a new development on the property, and this delay will cost the defendant a great deal of money (perhaps even exposing the defendant to liability to Acme Wrecking Company and other contractors for breach of contract) as well as inconvenience. It is possible the whole project could fall apart.

In thinking about the harm faced by each party, we might agree that the harm facing the plaintiffs is greater than the harm facing the defendant because the building is irreplaceable but money is not. But that's too simplistic an analysis. First, your answer might change if the defendant faces *millions of dollars* in losses if the project is delayed. It is going to be very hard to *value* the loss of a historic building, but at some point a court may decide that the harm to the defendant for delaying the project is just too high (though if the society could pay for the million dollars of harm should it turn out on final judgment the preliminary injunction should not have been issued, perhaps the court should not take it into account in looking at *irreparable* loss).

Moreover, an analysis that just compares the harm to each party if the court guesses wrong ignores the likelihood of success on the merits. A court should be more willing to grant an injunction if a plaintiff has a 95% chance of ultimately winning the case than if she has only a 5% chance.

So let's say that if the preliminary injunction is erroneously denied, plaintiff would suffer the loss of the building, which we will value at $1 million, and defendant would suffer $50,000 in delay costs if the preliminary injunction is erroneously granted. Suppose further that if the court took a peek at the merits, it would estimate that plaintiff's chances of succeeding on the merits—in this case, proving that the state law in fact prevents the destruction of the hotel—is 10%. The fact that the chances of plaintiff's success are relatively low must be factored into the court's balancing.

Judge Posner has presented an algebraic way to factor in both likelihood of success on the merits and the harm to each party that comes from an erroneously granted injunction:

Grant [the preliminary injunction] but only if $P(H_p) > (1 - P)H_d$, where P is the probability that the plaintiff will prevail in the full trial on the merits (and therefore $1 - P$ is the probability that the defendant will prevail), H_p is the irreparable harm that the plaintiff will suffer unless a preliminary injunction is granted to maintain the status quo pending the trial, and H_d the irreparable harm the defendant will suffer if the preliminary injunction is granted.

Richard A. Posner, Economic Analysis of Law 776 (9th ed. 2014).[9] In other words, under the Posner formula a court calculates the *expected loss* each side would face if the court erred, by multiplying likelihood of each party's success by the extent of loss the party would face if the court guessed wrong at the preliminary injunction stage.

Applying this formula to the *Oldtime Hotel* example above yields the conclusion that the court should grant the preliminary injunction:

> P, the probability of plaintiff's success on the merits, is .10 (10%).
> H_p, the irreparable harm that plaintiff will suffer if the preliminary injunction is denied, is \$1 million.
> 1 – P, the probability of defendant's success on the merits, is .90 (90%).
> H_d, the irreparable harm that the defendant will suffer, is at most[10] \$50,000.

Multiplying, $P(H_p) = .10 \times \$1{,}000{,}000$, or \$100,000, which is greater than $(1 - P)H_d = .90 \times \$50{,}000$, or \$45,000. Because \$100,000 > \$45,000, the preliminary injunction should be granted.

As you can see, this formula is very sensitive to the numbers that are put into it. For example, if the court valued the harm to the plaintiff at \$400,000 (rather than \$1 million), or the harm to the defendant at \$150,000 (rather than \$50,000), the court would conclude that the injunction should not be issued.

This formula is helpful in getting courts and parties focused on the right factors, but its importance could be exaggerated. Indeed, the formula gives a false aura of scientific exactness to the process of a court's balancing the hardships, which often will be more of a gestalt, seat-of-the-pants analysis than a hard calculation. (*See American Hosp. Supply Corp. v. Hospital Products Ltd.*, 780 F.2d 589, 609 (7th Cir. 1986) (dissenting opinion stating, in a case where Judge Posner set forth the mathematical test in a majority opinion, that the traditional test for preliminary injunctive relief "may not exhibit the 'precision' the majority seems to demand, but such 'precision' is antithetical to the underlying principles of injunctive relief. Equity, as the majority concedes, involves the assessment of factors that cannot be quantified.").)

In the real world, courts will often find it impossible to come up with numbers to plug into the formula, especially because in many cases we are dealing with harm that is "irreparable" *because* it is so hard to value. Think of

---

9. To consider the public interest, its value (represented by some dollar amount) could be added to either side of the equation as appropriate.

10. I say "at most" because arguably this \$50,000 is not *irreparable* harm and there is no irreparable harm at all. If there is no irreparable harm at all, then under Judge Posner's formula the injunction should be granted because defendant's side of the equation equals zero: $.90 \times 0 = 0$.

the loss of a historic landmark like the Oldtime Hotel. How is a court to put a price on the value of its preservation to the society or to the public? Or suppose a delay would cost the defendant a partner in a new development project. How is the court to value that lost benefit? Finally, how is the court to assess the likelihood of success on the merits other than by reaching a preliminary decision on the merits and self-assessing the likelihood the judge will change his or her mind after a fuller exploration of the merits?

On this last point, it is worth considering Judge Posner's analysis of the stay order issued by the Supreme Court in *Bush v. Gore*. A *stay* is an order by an appellate court suspending the implementation of a lower court order or judgment. The standards for granting a stay are very much like those governing the issuance of a preliminary injunction because a stay too is a preliminary order in effect only until the higher court decides the merits of the appeal. *See Rostker v. Goldberg*, 448 U.S. 1306, 1308 (1980) (Brennan, J., in chambers).[11]

Arguably the most famous stay order in American history was issued in the midst of the dispute over the 2000 presidential election in Florida. The winner of the electoral votes in Florida would become the next president (thanks to the workings of the Electoral College), and Democrat Al Gore and Republican George W. Bush were battling in court over the recounting of ballots, with Bush leading by 537 votes out of about 6 million cast.[12] On Friday, September 8, 2000, the Florida Supreme Court ordered a counting of all "undervoted" ballots across the state of Florida. *Gore v. Harris*, 772 So. 2d 1243 (Fla. 2000). The next day, the U.S. Supreme Court stayed that order, *Bush v. Gore*, 531 U.S. 1046 (2000), and the Court, after briefing and oral argument in the course of two days, reversed the Florida Supreme Court, ending the recount and leading to the election of George W. Bush. *Bush v. Gore*, 531 U.S. 98 (2000).

In a later-published analysis, Judge Posner (who was not a judge in any of the proceedings) agreed that the harm to Al Gore in granting the stay of the recount was much greater than the harm to George W. Bush in rejecting the stay. The period within which to certify the presidential electors for Florida was fast approaching, and the decision to stay the counting meant that the counting likely could never be completed, and Gore never would have the possibility of taking the lead in the recount. Bush, in contrast, risked a hard-to-value "cloud" over the legitimacy of his election should the Florida courts declare Gore the winner, and be reversed later by the U.S. Supreme Court.

---

11. When a party seeks to stay enforcement of a money judgment (such as a judgment for damages) pending appeal, it is often necessary to obtain an *appeal bond* guaranteeing payment to the plaintiff. *See, e.g.*, CAL. CODE CIV. PROC. §917.1 (setting forth rules and amounts of appellate "undertakings" to stay money judgment on appeal). The text refers to stay orders not involving money judgments.

12. For more detail about the Florida controversy, *see* RICHARD L. HASEN, THE SUPREME COURT AND ELECTION LAW: JUDGING EQUALITY FROM BAKER *V.* CARR TO BUSH *V.* GORE 41-46 (2003).

Despite the much greater harm facing Gore (let's value it at $1 million, compared to $100 for Bush[13]), Judge Posner concluded that the court was right to grant the stay, because Gore's chances of success were zero. *See* RICHARD A. POSNER, BREAKING THE DEADLOCK: THE 2000 ELECTION, THE CONSTITUTION, AND THE COURTS 164-165 (2001). In other words, Judge Posner concluded that *by the time the Supreme Court agreed to grant the stay*, a majority of Justices had made a conclusive determination that Gore was going to lose on the merits: $1 million times zero is still zero, and Bush's expected losses, while low—in this case $100 (1 × $100)—exceeded zero.

We might think of Judge Posner's position as a hyperlegal realist position, but look at how sensitive it is to his estimation. If, at the time the Court decided on the stay, Gore had just a 1% chance of changing one Justice's mind following briefing and oral argument (the Supreme Court was 5-4 on the stay and in the final case on the remedy), Posner's formula tells us that the Supreme Court should have denied the stay.[14]

Finally, an important note about the status quo and about mandatory and prohibitory injunctions. In the *University of Texas* case, the Supreme Court wrote about the purpose of the preliminary injunction as being "merely to preserve the relative positions of the parties until a trial on the merits can be held." The idea that preliminary injunctions should generally preserve the status quo is one that many courts and lawyers adhere to. But in some cases, plaintiffs want affirmative relief (a court order to defendant to do something) rather than just preservation of the status quo.

Judge McConnell offered a defense of preserving the status quo in *O Centro Espirita Beneficiente Uniao Do Vegetal v. Ashcroft*, 389 F.3d 973, 1015 (10th Cir. 2004) (McConnell, J., concurring): "It is one thing for a court to preserve its power to grant effectual relief by preventing parties from making unilateral and irremediable changes during the course of litigation, and quite another for a court to force the parties to make significant alterations in their practices before there has been time for a trial on the merits."[15]

---

13. These numbers are, of course, arbitrary, but they are useful in the sense that it demonstrates that the harm to Gore in halting the recount (losing the presidency) was arguably much higher (in this numerical example, 10,000 times greater) than the harm to Bush in allowing the recount to go forward.

14. One percent of $1,000,000 is $10,000 ($H_d$), which greatly exceeds the expected loss for Bush of $99 (.99 × $100) ($H_p$).

15. What is the "status quo"? It is "the last uncontested status that preceded the parties' controversy." *Department of Parks and Recreation v. Bazaar Del Mundo, Inc.*, 448 F.3d 1118, 1124 (9th Cir. 2006). But it may not always be easy to recognize the status quo. Commenting on Judge McConnell's opinion in *O Centro*, Judge Posner wrote: "Now it may be that [the considerations raised by Judge McConnell] are better invoked on a case-by-case basis than made the basis of a rule that depends on a judge's ability to determine what state of affairs should be viewed as the status quo." *Chicago United Industries, Ltd. v. City of Chicago*, 445 F.3d 940, 946 (7th Cir. 2006).

Some courts also hold that plaintiffs must meet a higher standard when seeking a *mandatory injunction*, or ordering a defendant to do something and thereby changing the status quo, as opposed to a *prohibitory injunction*, or ordering a defendant to refrain from doing something. In addition, there's a connection between this point and the status quo point: in most cases, a prohibitory injunction is most likely to preserve the status quo and a mandatory injunction is most likely to change the status quo.[16]

Cases indeed say that plaintiffs face a higher burden when requesting a mandatory preliminary injunction, *see, e.g., Louis Vuitton Malletier v. Dooney & Bourke, Inc.*, 454 F.3d 108 (2d Cir. 2006), but courts do grant mandatory preliminary injunctions in appropriate cases, even if it means making a change in the status quo. Even Judge McConnell noted: "In recent decades, most courts—and all federal courts of appeal—have come to recognize that there are cases in which preservation of the status quo may so clearly inflict irreparable harm on the movant, with so little probability of being upheld on the merits, that a preliminary injunction may be appropriate even though it requires a departure from the status quo." *O Centro*, 389 F.3d at 1013 (McConnell, J., concurring).

To avoid issuing a "disfavored" mandatory injunction, a court will sometimes use language to cast a mandatory injunction in a prohibitory way. For example, in *Bingham v. Oregon School Activities Association*, 24 F. Supp. 2d 1110 (D. Or. 1998), a trial court held that, under the Americans with Disabilities Act, a high school had to let a student play on a sports team despite state eligibility rules that appeared to exclude him. But rather than order the school in a preliminary injunction to allow the student to play, the court characterized its order as prohibitory: "Relief can be afforded by an order prohibiting defendant from imposing any sanctions against [plaintiff], plaintiff's coach, or the athletic programs in which plaintiff participates pursuant to this court's ruling."[17] *Id.* at 1115. Semantics aside, it seems clear that this was an affirmative order to include plaintiff in the sports program.

---

16. This is not inevitably so, however, when the status quo is one of action. For example, a city clerk routinely considers parade permit requests promptly and issues the permits when the group requesting one meets all of the city's requirements. However, the clerk refuses to promptly consider a parade permit request submitted by a politically unpopular group. The group might seek a preliminary injunction that would require the clerk to consider the permit request promptly. That would be a mandatory injunction (it requires the clerk to do something), but arguably it *preserves* the status quo of the clerk routinely considering parade permit requests promptly.

17. To its credit, the court added: "At any rate, even pursuant to the higher standards advanced by the OSAA [for mandatory injunctive relief], I find that plaintiff is entitled to preliminary injunctive relief." *Id.* at 1115.

EXAMPLE

Example 3

Another election law example: In 2003, enough California voters signed petitions to trigger the recall election of Governor Gray Davis, the first such election in California history. Many lawsuits were filed challenging different aspects of the recall election. One of the suits argued that, following *Bush v. Gore*, it would violate the Equal Protection Clause of the U.S. Constitution to conduct a statewide recall election under which voters in some counties used antiquated punch card voting machines (the same machines that became so notorious in the 2000 Florida controversy) while other voters used much more reliable voting machinery. With the recall scheduled for October 2003, the ACLU moved for a preliminary injunction in August, two months before the election, asking for the election to be delayed until California election officials could replace the punch cards (which would have been in March 2004, when the state, pursuant to an earlier consent decree, was scheduled to discontinue using punch card voting machines). The trial judge denied the request for a preliminary injunction, holding, among other things, that plaintiffs were not likely to succeed on the merits because they misread the requirements of the Supreme Court's holding in *Bush v. Gore*. There was also a dispute over how many votes would be lost by using punch card voting machines. The district court took two weeks to deny the motion, and the ACLU appealed to the Ninth Circuit. A Ninth Circuit panel heard argument at the beginning of September, about a month before the election. By that time, the campaigns (both for and against the recall, and for replacement candidates, should the recall succeed) were well underway.

What factors should the Ninth Circuit consider in deciding whether or not to grant the injunction? How should it decide the case?

EXPLANATION

Explanation

It is very common for election-related disputes, because of their time sensitivity, to be decided on a motion for a preliminary injunction followed by interlocutory appeal on an expedited basis to an appellate court. The first question faced by any appellate court is the standard for review. It is often said that an appellate court reviews a trial court's decision on a preliminary injunction under a rather deferential "abuse of discretion" standard. But that is a bit misleading in the election context, because many of these cases are decided on pure issues of law, and appellate courts have held that a trial court abuses its discretion when it decides an issue on an improper legal basis: appellate courts generally *do not* defer to trial courts' interpretation of applicable law, and therefore in many of these cases the review can be broad and not deferential to the lower court.

In considering whether to grant the preliminary injunction, the first question was the likelihood of success on the merits. When the Ninth Circuit first heard the case, a three-judge panel concluded plaintiffs were likely to succeed on the merits: the use of these unreliable punch card machines in only some California counties violated voters' equal protection rights under *Bush v. Gore*. *Southwest Voter Registration Education Project v. Shelley*, 344 F.3d 882 (9th Cir. 2003). In doing so, the Ninth Circuit reversed a federal district court judge who denied the injunction.

The case was immediately taken en banc, and an 11-judge panel disagreed with the original appellate court's reading of *Bush v. Gore*, though it did not officially reject that reading. *Southwest Voter Registration Education Project v. Shelley*, 344 F.3d 914, 918 (9th Cir. 2003) (en banc) ("We have not previously had occasion to consider the precise equal protection claim raised here. That a panel of this court unanimously concluded the claim had merit provides evidence that the argument is one over which reasonable jurists may differ.").[18]

The court, however, held the first Ninth Circuit panel erred in granting the injunction because it did not sufficiently consider the public interest:

> If the recall election scheduled for October 7, 2003, is enjoined, it is certain that the state of California and its citizens will suffer material hardship by virtue of the enormous resources already invested in reliance on the election's proceeding on the announced date. Time and money have been spent to prepare voter information pamphlets and sample ballots, mail absentee ballots, and hire and train poll workers. Public officials have been forced to divert their attention from their official duties in order to campaign. Candidates have crafted their message to the voters in light of the originally-announced schedule and calibrated their message to the political and social environment of the time. They have raised funds under current campaign contribution laws and expended them in reliance on the election's taking place on October 7. Potential voters have given their attention to the candidates' messages and prepared themselves to vote. Hundreds of thousands of absentee voters have already cast their votes in similar reliance upon the election going forward on the timetable announced by the state. These investments of time, money, and the exercise of citizenship rights cannot be returned. If the election is postponed, citizens who have already cast a vote will effectively be told that the vote does not count and that they must vote again. In short, the status quo that existed at the time the election was set cannot be restored because this election has already begun.

Id. at 919. The public's interest was a weighty one to be sure, but the public's interest cut both ways in this case. What about the harm to voters who

18. The court then said the district court judge did not abuse his discretion in finding no *Bush v. Gore* violation (an odd ruling, because this was a legal question and the district court's legal opinion was not entitled to any deference), but that plaintiffs had a stronger case on the merits on a claim under the federal Voting Rights Act.

would be voting on voting machines that (the ACLU alleged) were much less likely to count a valid vote? The Ninth Circuit en banc court held: "We must of course also look to the interests represented by the plaintiffs, who are legitimately concerned that use of the punch-card system will deny the right to vote to some voters who must use that system. At this time, it is merely a speculative possibility, however, that any such denial will influence the result of the election." *Id.* at 919-920.

That analysis had it wrong because there was no easy post-election remedy. The harm was really irreparable. Indeed, statistics after the election showed that more than 5% of ballots cast in Los Angeles County (a punch card county) did not include a valid vote on the recall, compared to only 0.74% of ballots in Alameda County (using electronic voting machines). Had the election been close, there would have been no way to figure out how to count votes that were not properly recorded on the punch cards. Would the Ninth Circuit have voided the election and ordered a new one, an even more intrusive remedy than the delay ordered by the first, three-judge panel? Fortunately for the people of California, the recall election was not close, so the Ninth Circuit did not have to consider a possible post-election remedy for punch card problems.

This real-world example should show you how limited the Posner formula is in answering the question whether a court should issue a preliminary injunction, and how fluid the balancing must be. Indeed, the balancing equation changed over time. The public's investment in the recall election was relatively minimal on August 7, when the ACLU filed its initial case in the federal district court, but by mid-September, when the Ninth Circuit heard the recall case (for the second time), those public interests were great. Not only were there public interest concerns on both sides; there was considerable uncertainty as to both the facts (how unreliable *are* punch card machines compared to other voting devices?) and the law (what does the Equal Protection Clause require when it comes to voting?). Moreover, all of this occurred in a highly charged political atmosphere, where the political leanings of the judges at least appeared to have some correlation with their views on the propriety of preliminary injunctive relief.

EXAMPLE

Example 4

You represent Oscar in his long-running dispute (after all, it has been going on since Chapter 7) with Pnina over Pnina's failure to produce the widget she promised that is needed to run Oscar's factory. Pnina argues that Oscar breached the contract first by failing to pay the promised price and by failing to give Pnina the specifications to make the widget. Oscar's factory is closed, and he wants you to obtain a preliminary injunction requiring Pnina to continue working on the widget. What kind of evidence will you need to bring in to support your client's motion for preliminary relief?

EXPLANATION

Explanation

This is a nuts-and-bolts type of question involving a dispute—unlike the dispute in Example 3—that has little or nothing to do with the public interest (unless Oscar's factory is producing something that the public needs and cannot obtain elsewhere). You want to marshal evidence showing that Oscar is likely to succeed on the merits and that the irreparable harm he faces in the T_0-T_1 period will greatly exceed Pnina's harm.

In terms of likelihood on the merits, of course, you will want to have a copy of the contract itself, plus any other documentary evidence such as receipts, bank statements, letters, and e-mails. It also would be useful to have an affidavit from Oscar and any other material that can prove that Oscar is likely to succeed in proving that Pnina, rather than Oscar, breached the contract.

It will also be necessary to get evidence supporting the irreparable harm claim; perhaps you can find a factory engineer or other employee who can sign an affidavit about how crucial the widget is for the operation of the factory. Someone else might need to write an affidavit about the lack of availability of the widget elsewhere on the market. Finally, any evidence showing that continued work on the widget pending final judgment will not create any irreparable harm for Pnina would be useful (though you may not be in possession of any such information).

One argument that Pnina might make against Oscar is that the court should impose a higher standard because he is seeking a *mandatory injunction*, ordering Pnina to produce the widget, rather than a *prohibitory injunction*, ordering Pnina to refrain from doing something. (It seems a stretch for Oscar to argue for a prohibitory injunction on grounds that the court would be preventing Pnina from not continuing work on the widget.) Still, if Oscar has a strong showing of success in his favor and a balance of the hardship strongly favoring him, why should the court deny preliminary relief simply because the relief he requests is affirmative relief?

Finally, in thinking about how to present Oscar's case to the court, it is useful to draft a proposed order for the court to sign. It should be carefully drafted and tailored to the rightful position standard. It should be an order that is easy to enforce through the power of contempt if necessary, and not full of unclear language. If you are in federal court, the order must comply with Fed. R. Civ. P. 65(d):

> (d) **Contents and Scope of Every Injunction and Restraining Order**.
>
> (1) *Contents*. Every order granting an injunction and every restraining order must:
>
> (A) state the reasons why it issued;
>
> (B) state its terms specifically; and

(C) describe in reasonable detail—and not by referring to the complaint or other document—the act or acts restrained or required.

(2) *Persons Bound.* The order binds only the following who receive actual notice of it by personal service or otherwise:

(A) the parties;

(B) the parties' officers, agents, servants, employees, and attorneys; and

(C) other persons who are in active concert or participation with anyone described in Rule 65(d)(2)(A) or (B).

Take a few minutes and try to write out the court order. It is not as easy as you might think.

9.3 INJUNCTION BONDS (OR "SECURITY"), WITH A NOTE ON *NE EXEAT*

As we saw in section 9.2, much of what drives preliminary injunction analysis is uncertainty and the risk of error. The balancing test for preliminary injunctions is one way that courts deal with the risk. The injunction bond (or the providing of "security") is another means of doing so. Under Federal Rule of Civil Procedure 65(c), "The court may issue a preliminary injunction or a temporary restraining order only if the movant gives security in an amount that the court considers proper to pay the costs and damages sustained by any party found to have been wrongfully enjoined or restrained. The United States, its officers, and its agencies are not required to give security."

The injunction bond works to reduce the risk of uncertainty by shifting some of that risk to the plaintiff. The bond requires the plaintiff to pay the defendant for damages that accrue during the period between the granting of the preliminary injunction and final judgment if the court determines at final judgment that injunctive relief is not warranted.

To see how the injunction bond changes plaintiffs' incentives and thereby reduces the risks of uncertainty, let's return to the case of *Pacifica Preservation Society v. Oldtime Hotel*. Suppose that the Society values the preservation of the hotel at $100,000. Stopping the hotel demolition project from the point of preliminary injunction to final judgment is going to cost the defendant $400,000 in costs for delay.

Without the injunction bond, the plaintiff would not take the defendant's costs into account in deciding whether to seek a preliminary injunction. (The court presumably would do so in balancing the equities.) Suppose, however, that the court requires the Society to purchase an injunction bond worth $400,000. The Society will go to a bonding company that likely will require the Society to sign over property worth $400,000 to the bonding company, plus pay some additional premium for the service in writing the bond (we'll set the premium amount here at $20,000), an amount which will *not* be refunded whether or not the Society succeeds at final judgment.

Would the Society agree to purchase the injunction bond, or would it forgo the preliminary injunction? The answer may well depend upon the Society's assessment of its likelihood of succeeding on the merits. If the Society believes it has a 10% chance of succeeding at final judgment, its expected loss on the bond is .90 (the defendant's chance of success) multiplied by the $400,000 value of the bond, or $360,000, plus the $20,000 premium, for a total of $380,000. The Society would not seek the preliminary injunction, because the $380,000 cost greatly exceeds the $100,000 value of preserving the hotel.

In contrast, if the Society believes it has a 95% chance of success on the merits, it could well decide to go forward in seeking the injunction even if it has to purchase the bond. Under these circumstances, its expected loss is .05 (the defendant's chance of success) multiplied by the $400,000 value of the bond, or $20,000, plus the $20,000 premium, for a total cost of $40,000. The Society could decide to seek the preliminary injunction, because the $40,000 cost is less than the $100,000 value of preserving the hotel.[19]

Injunction bonds benefit defendants, and smart defense counsels will do what they can to get bonds to fully cover the losses their clients would suffer if the court erroneously grants the plaintiff's request for a preliminary injunction. Injunction bonds also are likely to discourage plaintiffs from seeking preliminary injunctions, especially in cases where the plaintiff's case appears weak or where the defendant's damages during the T_0-T_1 period (see Figure 9.1) are expected to be large.

The main social problem with injunction bonds is that they can discourage public interest litigation, or even private litigation where poor plaintiffs face defendants who would suffer substantial losses upon the granting of a preliminary injunction.

For example, suppose that the Society has very few assets, but it values the Oldtime Hotel at $1 million. Under these circumstances, it could well want to seek an injunction even under the conditions described above, where the society has only a 10% chance of success. But the society may not have the money to pay for the bond. Indeed, even if the Society is confident (95%) that it is going to win, it still may have trouble pledging adequate security for the bond.

19. This example assumes that the Society is neutral about risk. If the society is risk-averse, it might be less willing to seek an injunction if required to post an injunction bond.

For this reason, courts sometimes waive the requirement of a bond.[20] The First Circuit, for example, set forth a two-part test:

> First, at least in noncommercial cases, the court should consider the possible loss to the enjoined party together with the hardship that a bond requirement would impose on the applicant. Applicants in commercial cases—merchants, manufacturers, and others—can be assumed capable of bearing most bond requirements, so hardship to them is less of a factor. Second, in order not to restrict a federal right unduly, the impact that a bond requirement would have on enforcement of the right should also be considered. One measure of the impact lies in a comparison of the positions of the applicant and the enjoined party. A bond requirement would have a greater adverse effect where the applicant is an individual and the enjoined party an institution that otherwise has some control over the applicant than where both parties are individuals or institutions.

Crowley v. Local No. 82, Furniture & Piano Moving, 679 F.2d 978, 1000 (1st Cir. 1982), *rev'd on other grounds*, 467 U.S. 526 (1984). Is it fair to cut more slack for a plaintiff in a noncommercial case than in a case involving a small business seeking an injunction against a much larger corporation?

Once the bond is in place, most courts take the view that trial courts do not have the discretion to decide whether or not to allow successful defendants to recover damages up to the amount of the bond. *See Coyne-Delany Co. v. Capital Development Board*, 717 F.2d 385 (7th Cir. 1983). But in such circumstances, the plaintiff cannot be liable to the defendant for damages in excess of the bond, even if the defendant proves damages exceeding that amount. At some state courts, however, damages for a wrongfully issued preliminary injunction can exceed the amount of the bond when the plaintiff sought the preliminary injunction *in bad faith. See Ex parte Waterjet Systems, Inc.*, 758 So. 2d 505, 513 (Ala. 1999).

Note that to the extent defendant's harm can be protected with an injunction bond, it looks less "irreparable" in the balancing of the hardships that courts undertake in deciding whether or not to issue the preliminary injunction.

A final note on preliminary relief and bonds: In rare circumstances, courts will issue a preliminary injunction *barring a person from leaving a jurisdiction* pending some further action. Such injunctions traditionally required the plaintiff to seek a writ called *ne exeat* (Latin for "let him not go out"). One way of helping to enforce such an order is requiring the defendant to post a *ne exeat* bond, which is forfeited if the defendant leaves the jurisdiction.

The federal government sometimes seeks *ne exeat* writs and bonds when a defendant owes taxes and appears to be preparing to leave the country. More commonly today, *ne exeat* orders relate to custody proceedings. Consider the case of *Faris v. Jernigan*, 939 So. 2d 835 (Miss. App. 2006). Husband and Wife

---

20. Consider whether such discretion is consistent with the language of Fed. R. Civ. P. 65(c), requiring a bond "in an amount that the court considers proper to pay." To argue that it is consistent, one would have to take the position that zero could be a proper sum.

got a divorce and had a bitter custody dispute, which included allegations of sexual abuse of the couple's child that were raised by the mother but rejected by the court. The court had originally awarded custody of Child to Wife, but the court awarded custody to Husband after finding that Wife had made material misrepresentations to the court about Husband's treatment of Child.

Wife moved out of state, and the court required Wife to post a $5,000 *ne exeat* bond to be able to have Child visit Wife overnight out of state. Wife posted the bond and then failed to return the child. The court held Wife in criminal contempt and ordered the bond forfeited. Wife returned Child, surrendered to authorities, and spent 13 months in jail for her willful contempt of court. After release, the court allowed Wife increasingly less restrictive and more frequent visits. Wife again requested that Child visit her out of state, and the court agreed to allow such visits, but only upon the posting of a new *ne exeat* bond in the amount of $40,000 (plus the payment of Husband's $40,000 in attorney's fees in the contempt and custody actions).

The appellate court upheld the $40,000 *ne exeat* bond requirement against Wife's claim that the amount was too high: "the amount of the bond was proper in light of [Wife's] past willingness to forfeit a $5,000 *ne exeat* bond, and related actions which resulted in [Husband] incurring more than $75,000 in attorneys' fees and other associated expenses."

EXAMPLE

Example 5

Alice, on behalf of a nonprofit neighborhood association, obtained a preliminary injunction in federal court barring the construction of Betty's new commercial development on grounds that the development would constitute a nuisance. Betty maintains that the property is not a nuisance. The nuisance question is a factual one that ultimately will require the court to consider the testimony of witnesses.

a. Is the court required to make Alice post an injunction bond?

b. If the court fails to require the bond, may Betty obtain damages caused by the delay, if the federal court on final judgment determines that Betty's project is not a nuisance?

EXPLANATION

Explanation

(a) Some courts reading Rule 65(c) would say that an injunction bond in some amount is required. Other courts, following the *Crowley* test or a similar test, could decide that the hardship on Alice is too great, and the public interest is served by no bond, or a bond in a very small amount. Likely a court will want to know more about the financial positions of the parties before deciding whether or not to waive a bond requirement. Ask yourself whether you would waive the bond requirement if you were the judge and you had the power to do so. If your answer is yes, should it matter if Alice's chances of success on the merits are only 10%? If your answer is no, should it matter if Alice's chances of success on the merits are as high as 90%?

(b) If there is no bond, there will be no liability for the costs of delay. *See Manta Management Corp. v. City of San Bernardino*, 44 Cal. Rptr. 3d 35, 41 (App. 2006) (nonpublished and remanded on other grounds, 43 Cal. 4th 400 (2008)) ("Under most circumstances, if a preliminary injunction is dissolved as having been improperly granted, the formerly enjoined party may recover damages only by proceeding against the injunction bond or surety. If no bond was required as a condition of issuance of the preliminary injunction, or if the amount of the bond was insufficient to compensate the enjoined party, the party may recover his damages only if he can prevail in an independent action for malicious prosecution, i.e., by showing that the injunction was obtained maliciously and without probable cause. This is true both under California's statutory scheme relating to injunctions and under federal law.").

The *Manta* case presents an interesting variation on these facts. Defendant operated a business and converted that business into an "adult cabaret" featuring nude dancing. The City of San Bernardino claimed that the adult cabaret violated applicable zoning laws, and it sought an injunction preventing the business from operating. The defendant claimed the zoning law violated the First Amendment and could not be enforced.

The court granted the preliminary injunction, and the city was not required to post an injunction bond because state law provided that preliminary injunctions obtained by municipalities were exempt from the bond requirement. The appellate court later held that the preliminary injunction was improperly granted because the zoning law violated the First Amendment.

The defendant then sued the city for lost profits during the time his business was closed. The appellate court held that the defendant could in fact obtain damages even though there was no injunction bond, despite the usual rule limiting defendants to recovery under the bond. It analogized the "malicious prosecution" exception described above to the city's violation of the defendant's constitutional rights. In both cases, the court said, the tortious action justified allowing the wrongfully enjoined defendant to recover damages that exceeded the amount (if any) of the injunction bond.

Example 6

Same facts as in Example 5, but assume that the court requires Alice and her association to post a $50,000 bond. The court later rules for Betty at final judgment and she seeks to recover damages for delay of the project. How much can Betty recover if she can prove that she suffered (a) $20,000 in damages? (b) $60,000 in damages?

To what extent can Alice defend against Betty's claim for payment on the bond on the basis that she honestly and reasonably believed she had a good case against Betty?

Explanation

(a) Betty can recover the full $20,000 under the bond, provided she can prove her damages with reasonable certainty. *Nintendo of America, Inc. v. Lewis Galoob Toys, Inc.*, 16 F.3d 1032, 1038 (9th Cir. 1994).[21]

(b) Betty can recover only up to the $50,000 amount of the bond, unless perhaps she can prove in a separate malicious prosecution action that Alice had no reasonable basis for bringing her suit or that Alice sought the injunction in bad faith. See the explanation to Example 5(b).

Whether Betty seeks $20,000 or the full $50,000 amount of the bond, it is no defense to payment on the bond that Alice prosecuted the case in good faith. Betty is entitled to recover the damages she can prove with reasonable certainty up to the amount of the bond.

9.4 TEMPORARY RESTRAINING ORDERS

9.4.1 Why Seek a Temporary Restraining Order?

If you were really the lawyer representing the Pacifica Preservation Society seeking to prevent the wrecking ball from knocking down the Oldtime Hotel tomorrow morning, you would need to move faster than the wheels of justice usually turn to obtain a preliminary injunction. In some places, it might take months to get a preliminary injunction motion heard and an injunction issued by a court.

The fastest type of relief available is a *temporary restraining order*, or TRO. The standard for issuing a TRO is basically the same as the standard for issuing a preliminary injunction, *Bieros v. Nicola*, 857 F. Supp. 445, 446 (E.D. Pa. 1994), but because of exigent circumstances and the usual short duration of the TRO, the court will issue one on less of a showing than is required for a preliminary injunction. In other words, if you are waking up a judge in the middle of the night for an emergency order, you are typically asking the judge to issue a TRO, not a preliminary injunction.

If you are going to wake up a judge in the middle of the night to get a TRO, it had better be important. Most matters can wait until the next business day, and a lawyer who uses extraordinary procedures to obtain relief that could be

21. For more on the reasonable certainty requirement, see Chapter 6.1.

obtained in the normal course of business runs the risk of alienating the judges who are going to be deciding that case and others the lawyer might bring later.

What should the TRO request look like, whether on an examination or in real life? Be organized and comply with local court rules. Especially when courts must make decisions on an expedited basis, the clearer you can make the issues for the court, the better. Make it clear:

- Who are the parties in the lawsuit?
- What is the legal issue?
- Why is immediate preliminary relief required? (Include a discussion of immediate and irreparable harm facing the party seeking the relief.)
- Why is plaintiff likely to prevail on the merits?

A court cannot issue a TRO without notice unless "specific facts in an affidavit or a verified complaint clearly show that immediate and irreparable injury, loss, or damage will result to the movant before the adverse party can be heard in opposition." FED. R. CIV. P. 65(b). Include necessary affidavits, copies of relevant statutes, regulations, contracts, or other relevant documents. You will also want to carefully prepare a proposed court order for the judge to sign.

Example 7

Your client, who owns a factory, has been involved in a bitter fight with a supplier over whether the supplier breached the contract between them by supplying inferior materials for use in the factory. Your client has refused delivery of the supplier's materials, claiming the supplier breached the contract by not sending conforming goods. The supplier, in contrast, believes your client breached the contract and the supplied goods do meet the specifications in the contract. Your client has gone ahead and made a substitute purchase of goods from another supplier at double the price, the best price your client could find on short notice. That has created a cash-flow problem for your client, who needs money now for the cost of cover. Your client wants you to go into court seeking a TRO to get the money paid now. Can and should you do so?

Explanation

A temporary restraining order would be inappropriate in this context for at least two reasons. To begin with, a TRO is a form of equitable relief, and the client wants damages, a form of legal relief not available through any kind of injunction (including a TRO). It would potentially be a different situation if your client had an emergency need for specific performance (the supplier actually delivering conforming goods). That would be a form of equitable relief. Another problem is that your client's injury is not irreparable—indeed, he is seeking money damages after going out and covering. While the loss of money may impose a hardship on your client, courts will not order damages until a full resolution of the case on the merits. Your client's option is to borrow money from someone else, perhaps at a high rate of interest, while the case is pending.

9.4.2 Important Procedural Differences Between a Preliminary Injunction and a Temporary Restraining Order

There are a few salient procedural differences between a preliminary injunction and a TRO. These differences are important and could affect the overall nature of the case. The TRO practice introduces the case to the judge and will color much of what comes after.

Notice. Fed. R. Civ. P. 65(a)(1) provides that a court cannot issue a preliminary injunction without first giving notice to the adverse party. In contrast, Fed. R. Civ. P. 65(b) provides:

> The court may issue a temporary restraining order without written or oral notice to the adverse party or its attorney only if:
>
> (A) specific facts in an affidavit or a verified complaint clearly show that immediate and irreparable injury, loss, or damage will result to the movant before the adverse party can be heard in opposition; and
>
> (B) the movant's attorney certifies in writing any efforts made to give notice and the reasons why it should not be required.

Courts generally require the party seeking the TRO to provide some kind of informal notice to the adverse party as a matter of constitutional imperative, at least when it is possible to do so, absent some compelling justification for not giving notice. Rule 65 governs in federal court, and in state court such notice is usually going to be required by the Due Process Clause of the U.S. Constitution.[22]

It is usually possible to give notice of a hearing, and in any case notice of a court order will later be necessary to make the TRO enforceable. What might be a compelling justification for not giving notice when a plaintiff can locate a defendant? The only one that seems likely to work is that providing notice of the hearing will give defendant a chance to engage in prohibited conduct before the court has a chance to order the defendant not to do so.

---

22. On this point, see *Carroll v. President and Commissioners of Princess Anne*, 393 U.S. 175 (1968). *Carroll* discussed the issue in the context of a First Amendment case, but such notice (in normal circumstances and where possible) seems required by the Due Process Clause, and the rule requiring notice is not limited to First Amendment cases.

Appealability Preliminary injunction orders are appealable in federal courts under 28 U.S.C. §1292(a)(1). In contrast, orders granting or denying TROs are typically not appealable. *See* 11 Wright, Miller & Kane, Federal Practice and Procedure §2947 (2006). This rule, however, is subject to some exceptions.

First, as explained below, some courts treat TROs issued *with* notice that last for more than 14 or 28 days as having morphed into preliminary injunctions, which are appealable. *See Sampson v Murray*, 415 U.S. 61 (1974); *but see Granny Goose Foods, Inc. v. Brotherhood of Teamsters and Auto Truck Drivers Local No.* 70, 415 U.S. 423 (1974).

Second, some courts treat TROs as appealable when the order "threatened to inflict irretrievable harms before the TRO expired." *Ohio Republican Party v. Brunner*, 543 F.3d 357, 360 (6th Cir. 2008). This can occur, for example, when a court issues a TRO changing a rule for voting in the period just before the election.

Third, some courts treat TROs as appealable when the TRO "possesses the qualities of a preliminary injunction," meaning that the court held an "adversary hearing" and the "basis for the court's order was strongly challenged." *Serv. Emps. Int'l Union v. Nat'l Union of Healthcare Workers*, 598 F.3d 1061, 1067 (9th Cir. 2010) (SEIU). Courts may be beginning to stretch this rule to allow more TROs to be appealed. In the *SEIU* case, the parties filed detailed written memoranda in the case and the court held a two-day hearing.

But the Ninth Circuit relied on *SEIU* in a high-profile challenge to President Trump's first executive order barring entry into the United States of persons from six predominantly Muslim countries. Following a short hearing, a federal district court issued a TRO blocking implementation of the policy temporarily and scheduled a preliminary injunction hearing. The trial court order granting the TRO included virtually no reasoning. The federal government appealed the TRO to the Ninth Circuit, and the state of Washington resisted, arguing the TRO was not appealable. The Ninth Circuit agreed the TRO was appealable:

> We are satisfied that in the extraordinary circumstances of this case, the district court's order possesses the qualities of an appealable preliminary injunction. The parties vigorously contested the legal basis for the TRO in written briefs and oral arguments before the district court. The district court's order has no expiration date, and no hearing has been scheduled. Although the district court has recently scheduled briefing on the States' motion for a preliminary injunction, it is apparent from the district court's scheduling order that the TRO will remain in effect for longer than fourteen days. In light of the unusual circumstances of this case, in which the Government has argued that emergency relief is necessary to support its efforts to prevent terrorism, we believe that this period is long enough that the TRO should be considered to have the qualities of a reviewable preliminary injunction.

Washington v. Trump, 847 F.3d 1151, 1158 (9th Cir. 2017).

Finally, it is also possible that a court's refusal to modify a temporary restraining order might be appealable as an interlocutory order under 28 U.S.C. §1292(b), which grants discretion to courts of appeal to review otherwise non-appealable orders when the district court is "of the opinion that such order involves a controlling question of law as to which there is substantial ground for difference of opinion and that an immediate appeal from the order may materially advance the ultimate termination of the litigation."

Duration A preliminary injunction may remain in effect pending a final judgment in the case. In contrast, a TRO issued without notice "expires at the time after entry—not to exceed 14 days—that the court sets, unless before that time the court, for good cause, extends it for a like period or the adverse party consents to a longer extension. The reasons for an extension must be entered in the record." Fed. R. Civ. P. 65(b). Thus, TROs *without notice* can last no more than 28 days total. (The older rule had a 10-day period, with a similar 10-day renewal period, which is important to know when reading older cases concerning TROs.)

The rules do not provide how long a TRO *with notice* may last. What becomes of a TRO issued with notice that lasts for more than 28 days? Does it dissolve on its own, or morph into a preliminary injunction?[23] The text of Rule 65 is not clear, and the precedents are somewhat unclear as well, though courts seem to be following the morphing rationale. Judge Posner, writing for a Seventh Circuit panel, held that if a TRO is "kept in force by the district court for more than 20 days [now presumably 28 days] without the consent of the parties, the order is deemed a preliminary injunction and so is appealable, since otherwise a district court could by the simple expedient of extending the TRO circumvent . . . the right of appeal." *Chicago United Industries Ltd. v. City of Chicago*, 445 F.3d 940, 943 (7th Cir. 2006).[24] It would probably make sense for the drafters of the Federal Rules of Civil Procedure to clarify this rather fundamental question.

---

23. As we will see in Chapter 10, the decision has real consequences for a litigant who decides to violate a temporary restraining order that has been in effect for more than 28 days (or 14 days if not renewed). If the TRO remains in effect, violating it can result in a finding of *contempt*. But if the order is not in effect, there is no possibility of a contempt holding.

24. The court ruled that this treatment of TROs lasting more than 20 (now 28) days applied to TROs issued with or without notice. Applying the rule *only* to TROs issued without notice "would enable a district court to issue a preliminary injunction of indefinite duration without any possibility of the defendant's appealing, simply by calling the injunction a temporary restraining order and being careful to notify the defendant in advance of issuing it. Moreover, a TRO issued after notice, especially if there is a hearing, is procedurally as well as functionally even more like a preliminary injunction than a TRO issued without notice and hearing, so it would be a considerable paradox if only the latter type of TRO were appealable after 20 [now 28] days." *Id.* at 946.

EXAMPLE

Example 8

You are the lawyer for the Pacifica Preservation Society, and you are earnestly preparing your motion for a TRO to prevent the destruction of the Oldtime Hotel tomorrow morning at 8 a.m. You honestly believe that if you give notice to the lawyers for the Oldtime Hotel, their clients will bring in the wrecking ball earlier than the hearing on the TRO, thereby avoiding violating any court order but altering the status quo. Can you seek a TRO without notice? What should be in the papers supporting your request for a TRO?

EXPLANATION

Explanation

The rule itself does not require notice in all cases, only an explanation for why notice may not have been given. An affidavit from you stating your belief that actions would be taken before the TRO could be issued if you gave notice would likely be sufficient under these facts. (Without such an exigency, failure to give notice to the other party would likely violate due process guarantees in the U.S. Constitution.) If you are not giving notice to the other side, you should ask the court to issue an order of short duration, to be followed up by a second hearing, with notice, that would allow the court to hear from both sides of the controversy (without the risk of the wrecking ball mooting a later court order) before extending or modifying the TRO.[25]

There are probably not many real-world situations where an adverse party would go ahead and change the status quo after receiving notice of a hearing aimed at preserving that status quo. (The most common such case is a temporary restraining order in a domestic violence situation, where it might put the plaintiff's life or well-being at risk to give notice in advance of a hearing that the plaintiff is seeking a "stay away" order.) Even though a party changing the status quo before the court issues the TRO technically would not be in contempt (see the next chapter), doing so is not likely to endear the party to the judge who will be handling any future litigation arising out of the controversy.

---

25. Rule 65(b) provides in pertinent part: "If the order is issued without notice, the motion for a preliminary injunction must be set for hearing at the earliest possible time, taking precedence over all other matters except hearings on older matters of the same character. At the hearing, the party who obtained the order must proceed with the motion; if the party does not, the court must dissolve the order . . . on 2 days' notice to the party who obtained the order without notice—or on shorter notice set by the court—the adverse party may appear and move to dissolve or modify the order. The court must then hear and decide the motion as promptly as justice requires."

CHAPTER 10

Enforcing the Injunction: The Power of Contempt

10.1 INTRODUCTION TO THE CONTEMPT POWER

One of the great benefits plaintiffs get from injunctions (including preliminary injunctions and temporary restraining orders—and this same benefit applies to other equitable relief) is that the court's order is backed up by the *contempt power*. When we speak of the power of contempt, however, we are really talking about three separate powers used by courts (though courts in some jurisdictions do not possess the third power):

1. *Civil coercive contempt*. This is the power of the court to impose fines payable to the state, or jail time, *to coerce the defendant's compliance* with the court's order.

Example: In Oscar's suit against Pnina for specific performance of their contract for the widget, the court (in a final judgment) orders Pnina to turn over the widget to Oscar by January 1. Pnina fails to do so. The judge threatens Pnina with fines of $1,000 per day until she does so. Pnina turns over the widget after five days and must pay a $5,000 contempt fine for disobedience of the court's order.

2. *Criminal contempt*. This is the power of the court to *punish a defendant's willful failure to comply* with the court's order.

Example: In the same Oscar-Pnina suit, the judge orders Pnina to turn over the widget by January 1. Pnina deliberately refuses to do so, though she has the widget hidden at her factory. The judge finds beyond a reasonable doubt that Pnina willfully disobeyed the court's order and fines her $20,000.

3. *Civil compensatory contempt*. This is the power of the court to *award damages to the plaintiff* for defendant's failure to comply with the court's order.

Example: In the same Oscar-Pnina suit, the judge orders Pnina to deliver the widget to Oscar by January 1. Pnina does not do so until January 10. Oscar proves that he has suffered $40,000 in damages because of the delay in complying with the court's order. The court will order Pnina to pay Oscar $40,000.

We will consider each of these contempt powers in turn, and then examine two additional issues. First, we consider the "collateral bar rule," which prevents defendants from defending themselves against a *criminal* contempt charge on grounds that the court's injunction was unlawful or incorrect. Second, we consider whether third parties may be held in contempt for violating court orders.

Although the three contempt powers appear to be distinct from one another, sometimes courts have trouble identifying which category a type of contempt citation fits into, or label an order as "contempt" when it doesn't squarely fit into any of the three categories. In addition, as we shall see, when civil coercive contempt payments are high enough, courts sometimes require the additional criminal procedure protections required for criminal contempt.

EXAMPLE

Example 1

While driving a Ford pickup truck, Mark was involved in a rollover accident. Mark then brought a products liability damages action against Ford Motor Company. A federal district court imposed sanctions after determining that Ford's lawyer, Lawrence, violated two pretrial orders prohibiting Ford from introducing evidence that Mark had been drinking before the accident and had not been wearing his seat belt at the time of the accident. The district court ordered Ford and Lawrence to pay sanctions to Mark and to the district court, intended to reimburse Mark for unnecessary expenses and attorney's fees, and to reimburse the district court for the costs of empaneling the jury. The court also found Lawrence in contempt of court for deliberately violating the pretrial order relating to alcohol use and revoked his *pro hac vice* status (which allowed him to appear in court in a state in which he was not a member of the bar) and permanently barred Lawrence from appearing *pro hac vice* in the Missoula Division of the United States District Court for the District of Montana.

What kind of contempt order did the court impose?

Explanation

This example is based upon *Lasar v. Ford Motor Co.*, 399 F.3d 1101 (9th Cir. 2005), and it is a useful example for you to test your own instincts before we get into more of the details about the rules courts use to differentiate among the different types of contempt. To analyze this case, note that the order can be broken down into three parts:

a. *Money to compensate Mark for his attorney's fees and costs.* This looks like civil compensatory contempt, because it is intended to compensate Mark for Lawrence's (and therefore Ford's) violation of a court order.
b. *Money to compensate the court for its time.* It is hard to see that this is compensatory contempt because it is aimed at compensating the *court*, not the plaintiff, and the money will be going to the government. However, the court stated a purpose to compensate, not punish, so it does not look like the court was requiring proof of deliberate intent. Nor is there any way defendants could have avoided the fine, meaning it does not look like civil coercive contempt. In the actual case, the Ninth Circuit concluded that this was a kind of *civil* contempt, and the greater protections of criminal procedure did not apply. The money was going to the government, true, but it was going there to compensate the court for its wasted time. The court's result makes some sense, but that result is not an obvious one given the various definitions of contempt.
c. *Revocation of* pro hac vice *status.* This looks punitive: the court is punishing the defendant for disobeying the court's orders. In the actual case, the Ninth Circuit agreed this was criminal contempt, but the court said that the punishment was relatively minor and therefore the defendants did not get the full panoply of criminal procedure protections: "So long as the [trial] court did not impose serious criminal penalties, due process did not require the district court to conduct a full-blown trial." *Id.* at 1112. The court did hold that the sanction of a *lifetime ban* was improper in this case because the court did not give notice before imposing the penalty that it was considering such a ban. It therefore did not reach the question whether a full-blown trial would have been required to impose a lifetime ban—assuming adequate notice of the potential punishment was made in advance.

The lesson here: though we will examine the "three" categories of contempt orders, it is sometimes difficult to tell which kind of contempt a court was imposing on a defendant. Because the protections for the defendant differ depending upon the type of contempt found by the court, it is necessary to impose some rules for categorization. The material in the rest of the chapter helps in that process, but difficult cases remain.

10.2 CIVIL COERCIVE CONTEMPT

Civil coercive contempt is the type of contempt often presented in the movies, usually featuring the obstinate journalist who goes to jail rather than reveal the name of a protected source. In recent years, there have been a number of real-world examples along these lines.

Journalists, of course, are only the most prominent among those who might be fined or imprisoned by a court using *civil coercive contempt*. But they are not the only examples.

Former U.S. Army intelligence analyst Chelsea Manning was sentenced to 35 years in prison in 2013 for disclosing classified materials to WikiLeaks without authorization. President Obama commuted her sentence in 2017. The release did not end her legal troubles. Manning was jailed in coercive civil contempt for 62 days in 2019 for failing to disclose information about WikiLeaks to a federal grand jury. Authorities released her after the grand jury's term expired, but just days later she headed back to jail after she refused to speak with another grand jury. Jacey Fortin, *Chelsea Manning Ordered Back to Jail for Refusal to Testify in WikiLeaks Inquiry*, N.Y. Times (May 16, 2019). Manning was released in March 2020 but is still being required to pay $256,000 in fines because of her refusal to speak to the second grand jury. Charlie Savage, *Chelsea Manning Is Ordered Released From Jail*, N.Y. Times (Mar. 12, 2020). If she is unable to pay, which seems likely, she cannot be imprisoned for failure to do so.

Other common examples include organized crime members who won't testify against co-conspirators upon a grant of immunity, or a parent in a custody dispute who has illegally kidnapped a child and taken that child to an undisclosed location. In such circumstances, many of us would be sympathetic to court efforts to use the contempt power to coerce the release of important information.

Here are a few notable features about coercive contempt:

- It is meant to be coercive, not punitive, though it certainly is going to feel like punishment to someone sitting in jail for refusing to comply with a court order.
- The contemnor (the term we use for the person who has been found in contempt) has "the keys to the jailhouse door in his pocket." By complying with the court order, the contemnor can go free. The contempt lasts for an indefinite duration.[1]

1. In certain jurisdictions, including at the federal level as illustrated by the Chelsea Manning case described above, contempt for refusing to testify must end when the 18-month term of the grand jury expires, 28 U.S.C. §1826, though contempt could begin again with a newly

- Sometimes jail is not a practical means of coercion, because the defendant must be free in order to do certain things. For instance, if Pnina is refusing to manufacture the widget, and her presence is necessary for its manufacture, her imprisonment for contempt hardly seems a productive way to coerce compliance. In such a case, the use of fines may be a more productive means to coerce Pnina's compliance. Jail time might work if Pnina has manufactured the widget, but has hidden it and refuses to turn it over to Oscar.

Two main legal issues may arise in the context of civil coercive contempt. The first arises when the defendant is unable or has proven unwilling to comply with the court's order. The second concerns civil coercive cases in which courts require protections usually afforded only in criminal proceedings.

Imprisonment Without Coercion. In some circumstances, coercive contempt has lost (or never had) the power to coerce the contemnor and must be halted as improper punishment. *Acceturo, supra*, 576 A.2d at 903. This standard creates a difficult situation for the court, because defendants always have an incentive to lie and say that imprisonment has lost its coercive power. A hearing on the matter gives contemnors a chance to convince the court to lift the contempt order because further incarceration will prove futile.

The question becomes one of credibility. "Since a prediction is involved and since that prediction concerns such uncertain matters as the likely effect of continued confinement upon a particular individual, we think a district judge has virtually unreviewable discretion both as to the procedure he will use to reach his conclusion, and as to the merits of his conclusion." *Simkin v. United States*, 715 F.2d 34, 38 (2d Cir. 1983). Other courts require that there be some hearing at which a judge determines credibility.

An interesting case study is *Catena v. Seidl*, 343 A.2d 744 (N.J. 1975). Gerardo Catena refused to testify regarding organized crime activities despite being granted immunity from prosecution for his testimony. Catena had been held for nearly 5 years. He was 73 years old and in ill health, and he moved for release on grounds that coercive contempt had failed and confinement had become punitive.

At first, the trial court summarily decided that Catena had to remain imprisoned until he agreed to testify. The New Jersey Supreme Court,

---

empaneled grand jury. *See also Matter of State Grand Jury Investigation re Acceturo v. Zelinski*, 576 A.2d 900, 904 (N.J. Super. 1990) ("We have no doubt that as a matter of due process, [a hearing on whether contempt is still coercive] should without question be provided no later than the expiration of 18 months of incarceration, as that is the maximum sentence which a court may impose for criminal contempt. . . .").

however, then required a hearing on Catena's motion for release to determine "whether or not there was a substantial likelihood that continued commitment of Catena would accomplish the purpose of the order upon which the commitment was based." *Id.* at 746.

On remand, "[t]he trial court noted Catena's age (73 years old), state of health and confinement since March 1970. It reviewed the reason given by Catena for remaining silent (essentially Catena testified that he believed he had a right of privacy which could not be taken away from him), and while it did not believe him in that regard, concluded that no matter what Catena's real reason was, he had demonstrated such total obstinacy that the trial court was satisfied that he would never answer any questions." *Id.* at 746-747. The New Jersey Supreme Court upheld the trial court's judgment to release Catena, deferring to that court's credibility determination.

The dissent contended that the majority was rewarding an organized crime Code of Silence, and believed that Catena's consistent legal efforts to win release—along with the absence of any psychiatric testimony—meant Catena had not met his burden of proving he was no longer subject to coercion through continued incarceration.

Of course, Catena's case gives hope to others being held in contempt that by holding out long enough, the courts might eventually grant their release. It appears that Catena lived a long life after release, quietly retiring to Boca Raton, Florida, and dying of natural causes at age 98.[2] But waiting for the court is a big gamble for many contemnors, and it could be years before a court would seriously entertain the argument for release. Indeed, some judges may agree with the view of the dissent here: the more often the contemnor brings legal proceedings to win release, the more it shows that the contemnor cares about the incarceration and could be motivated to comply with the court's order to win release from prison.

Criminal-like Protections in Civil Contempt Proceedings. In cases of criminal contempt, a full array of procedural protections apply; when the fine is large enough or the jail time long enough, for example, the defendant gets the right to a jury trial. These protections generally do not apply in the context of civil coercive contempt, but the Supreme Court held that sometimes they do. In *International Union, United Mine Workers v. Bagwell*, 512 U.S. 821 (1994), a union involved in a labor dispute faced an order from the court to stop certain activities. The court held a hearing, determined that the union had violated its injunction 72 times, and fined it for the violations. It then announced a set of future fines of up to $100,000 per violent breach of the injunction. The trial court later held a contempt hearing where the

2. Thanks to Loyola Law School librarian Lisa Schultz for tracking down what appears to be Catena's death record.

court required proof beyond a reasonable doubt, but it did not give a jury trial, holding the union liable for $64 million in fines, with part payable to the companies and part payable to the state. Though the union and companies settled, the state still wanted its $52 million.

The Supreme Court held that the procedure the court used to assess the contempt fines violated due process, because the union was not given full criminal protections. In a confusing opinion that never fully explained the factors the Court used to reach its result—though the Court placed emphasis on the "complex fact finding" involved and the large amount of the fines—it characterized the fines as "criminal" and therefore improperly imposed by the court without adequate criminal procedure protections. (A simpler standard, proposed by Justice Ginsburg in her concurrence, would have found the fines criminal because they were paid to the state, and not to the plaintiff.)

The Supreme Court's *Bagwell* decision means that in certain cases involving *civil* contempt, courts are going to have to give criminal procedure protections to defendants. But which cases? The United States Court of Appeals for the Tenth Circuit gave its answer to that question in *F.T.C. v. Kuykendall*, 371 F.3d 745 (10th Cir. 2004) (en banc). The en banc court rejected the idea that "high-end" civil contempt awards or complex facts triggered additional criminal procedure protections for defendants charged with civil contempt. The case itself involved civil *compensatory* contempt, not civil *coercive* contempt, but its language applies to both types of contempt. Stating that the main question after *Bagwell* was "whether the contempt of which the defendants were accused is criminal or civil in nature" (how helpful is that?), the court declined to set forth a general explanation of *Bagwell*'s test. Instead, the Tenth Circuit announced a bright-line rule that "where the sanctions sought in contempt proceedings are solely to be used to compensate injured consumers, the proceedings are civil in nature." *Id.* at 752. And in the civil contempt hearing, "because this case was one for civil, compensatory sanctions, the burden of proof is clear and convincing evidence as to liability and preponderance of the evidence as to damages. We affirm the district court's resolution of evidentiary issues." *Id.* at 767.

After *Bagwell* and *Kuykendall*, many open questions remain about which "civil" contempt proceedings are really "criminal" and which protections apply in such cases.

EXAMPLE

Example 2

Carrie and Donald are divorced, and have a child, Emily. The court had awarded custody of Emily to Carrie; Donald had weekend visitation rights. The divorce was very bitter. At the end of one weekend, Donald did not show up to return Emily to Carrie. The court orders Donald to disclose the location of Emily. Donald later states that he does not know where Emily is, though airline records show he visited Canada over the weekend when Emily went missing. May the court use civil coercive contempt to get Donald to reveal Emily's location?

Explanation

The court must first make a credibility determination that Donald in fact knows Emily's location and is lying about not knowing it. If the court makes such a determination, it certainly can try to use civil coercive contempt to get Donald to reveal the location. Whether or not he can be coerced is unclear.

Sometimes a contemnor's cooperation is not required. If there is information about where Emily is located outside the United States, an international convention to which the United States is a signatory and federal law provide for the return of children improperly taken across international boundaries. *See* Scott M. Smith, *Construction and Application of International Child Abduction Remedies Act* (42 U.S.C. §§11601 *et seq.*), 125 A.L.R. Fed. 217 (1995).

What if Donald honestly does not know where Emily is? In that case, of course, he would be *unable* (rather than *unwilling*) to comply with the court's order. If Donald does not know Emily's location, he cannot legally be held by the court. The question is whether Donald can convince the court of that fact. The example shows that in these circumstances, we place a great deal of confidence in the trial court's ability to make a credibility determination—staking a defendant's personal freedom on it.

Example 3

Jake operated an adult business featuring nude dancing. The City of Coates passed a zoning ordinance barring its operation. Jake filed a declaratory judgment action (see Chapter 16) asking the court for a declaration that the zoning ordinance violated the First Amendment. The City counterclaimed, requesting an injunction barring Jake from operating the business in violation of zoning laws. The court held the ordinance was constitutional and issued the injunction barring Jake from operating a "sexually oriented business" in violation of the zoning ordinance, and requiring that Jake pay $1,000 per day for violating the injunction going forward. Jake closed his nude dancing business and reopened it a few days later with "lap dancers" who were fully clothed. Jake operated the business for 68 days, and the court at a contempt hearing fined him $68,000. Assume the court found that this conduct violated the terms of the injunction. Is this fine civil coercive contempt or criminal contempt (in which case Jake was entitled to criminal procedure protections, including the right to a jury trial)?

Explanation

This example is based upon *Jake's, Ltd. v. City of Coates*, 356 F.3d 896 (8th Cir. 2004). Though the fine was intended to coerce Jake's compliance—making it appear to be *civil* coercive contempt—the Eighth Circuit read *Bagwell* as requiring the court to give Jake's additional criminal procedure protections, including the right to a jury trial. "First, the injunction was complex, in that it enjoined Jake's from conducting any type of sexually-oriented business prohibited by the ordinances, not just the live nude dancing that Jake's had admitted was a sexually-oriented business in raising its First Amendment challenge." *Id.* at 902-903. Second, "the $68,000 fine imposed by the second contempt order was far different from this type of coercive remedy. The fine was substantial, it was payable into court, rather than to compensate the City, and it was 'determinate and unconditional,' that is, not capable of being purged."[3] *Id.* at 903.

Though the court was purportedly applying the two factors of *Bagwell*, the second part of its analysis is odd. After all, isn't what the court says about the fines applicable to any fines imposed to coerce compliance, when looked at after the fact?

It is unclear whether this case, and *Kuykendall*, ultimately will require all coercive contempt fines paid to the court to be governed by criminal procedure protections.

10.3 CRIMINAL CONTEMPT

Criminal contempt punishes the contemnor for past actions. This, too, is the stuff of the movies. Think of the classic movie *My Cousin Vinny* and the judge holding Vinny in contempt for being disrespectful to the judge:

Judge Haller: I don't like your attitude.
Vinny: So what else is new?
Judge Haller: I'm holding you in contempt of court.
Vinny [to Bill]: Now there's a f***ing surprise.
Judge Haller: What did you say? What did you just say?
Vinny: Huh? What did I say?[4]

---

3. The court suggested that Jake's may have had a good argument that the injunction was unconstitutionally vague, an argument that Jake's did not raise below and the court therefore did not address. It also suggested the injunction violated Fed. R. Civ. P. 65's prohibition on incorporating other documents—in this case, the zoning ordinance.

4. MY COUSIN VINNY (20th Century–Fox 1992).

Not much process is due when a court punishes for such "petty contempt": when committed in the presence of the court, it can be punished summarily. As the Supreme Court explained in *Bagwell*, "The necessity justification for the contempt authority is at its pinnacle, of course, where contumacious conduct threatens a court's immediate ability to conduct its proceedings, such as where a witness refuses to testify, or a party disrupts the court. . . . Thus, petty, direct contempts in the presence of the court traditionally have been subject to summary adjudication, 'to maintain order in the courtroom and the integrity of the trial process' in the face of an 'actual obstruction of justice.'. . . In light of the court's substantial interest in rapidly coercing compliance and restoring order, and because the contempt's occurrence before the court reduces the need for extensive factfinding and the likelihood of an erroneous deprivation, summary proceedings have been tolerated." *Bagwell*, 512 U.S. at 832.

When the court uses contempt to punish a defendant for alleged violations outside the court's presence,[5] criminal procedure protections are required. *See* Dobbs & Roberts §2.8(4). Often, an independent prosecutor will be appointed to prosecute the case, where the prosecution will have to prove *beyond a reasonable doubt* that the defendant *willfully violated* the court's order.[6]

In cases involving jail time of over six months, or large enough fines, defendants accused of criminal contempt have the right to a trial by jury. How large must the fine be? In footnote 5 of *Bagwell*, the Court wrote that a jury trial was required for "serious criminal contempt fines." It noted that it had held in an earlier case that no jury trial was necessary in a case imposing a $10,000 fine on a union, and that a federal statute defining "petty offenses" required a jury trial for amounts over $5,000. The precise amount triggering the right to a jury trial remains uncertain.

Civil coercive contempt and criminal contempt are not mutually exclusive. A contemnor such as Gerardo Catena who is released from civil coercive contempt after a finding that imprisonment was no longer coercive could later face *criminal contempt* as punishment for willfully violating the court's order.

5. *Bagwell* requires additional procedure even for some petty contempts: "If a court delays punishing a direct contempt until the completion of trial, for example, due process requires that the contemnor's rights to notice and a hearing be respected."

6. Dobbs & Roberts explain: "criminal as distinct from civil cases, the burden of proof is upon the prosecution to show beyond a reasonable doubt that the defendant was guilty. Guilt requires an intent to violate the order and an ability to comply, so the prosecution must also show that the defendant had the ability to comply and that he willfully violated the decree." Dobbs & Roberts, §2.8(4).

Example 4

After a hearing on the merits in the Oscar-Pnina dispute, the court determines that Pnina breached the contract, that Oscar is suffering irreparable injury by Pnina's failure to deliver the widget, and that Oscar is therefore entitled to an order of specific performance. The trial court orders Pnina to produce the widget for Oscar no later than January 1. Pnina does not produce the widget. On January 10, the court holds another hearing, and threatens Pnina with fines of $100 for the first day she is late after January 10 in producing the widget for Oscar, with fines doubling each day thereafter, until she produces the widget. Suppose Pnina comes to court on January 15, having not produced the widget. The judge fines her $3,100 for the first five days ($100 + $200 + $400 + $800 + $1,600). He then gives her five more days to produce the widget. He tells her that if she does not, the court will impose an additional fine, this time a punishment for noncompliance. On January 20, Pnina comes back to court. She tells the judge she is trying to produce the widget as fast as she can, but she does not have it ready yet. The court then finds beyond a reasonable doubt that Pnina failed to produce the widget as she promised in the contract and fines her an additional $7,000. How may Pnina defend herself against the second fine? Does she have a defense to imposition of the first fine? If the fines are upheld and she later produces the widget, does she get her money back?

Explanation

Pnina probably has some good arguments against imposition of the second fine. This fine ($7,000) looks to be punitive (though certainly it was aimed in part at coercing Pnina's compliance). If the fine is criminal, it is necessary to find beyond a reasonable doubt that Pnina *willfully* disobeyed the court's order. Note, however, that the court did not make such a finding. Instead, the finding was only that Pnina had disobeyed the court's order beyond a reasonable doubt. Without willfulness, Pnina cannot face a criminal punishment. Moreover, because of the size of the fine involved, she could be entitled to a jury trial if the court determines that a "serious" fine is involved. A $7,000 fine against an individual may or may not be a large enough criminal fine to trigger the right to a jury trial.

The first fine ($3,100) looks like an amount intended to coerce performance rather than to punish. A court would likely conclude it is coercive, not punitive, and therefore criminal procedures likely would not apply. The standard is not proof beyond a reasonable doubt, but is instead a lower, "clear and convincing evidence" standard.

But if Pnina can prove that she was *unable* to comply with the court's order (because she was trying to produce the widget but simply could not do so), the coercive fine appears improper. This will require a credibility determination by the court. However, if Pnina inadvertently violated the injunction—imagine that she negligently failed to have the widget, which had been completed, delivered on time—she could be liable for civil contempt, which does not require willfulness.

Pnina cannot get her money back if she eventually complies with the court's order. But note that the payment of a civil coercive contempt fine after compliance is no longer motivating future compliance. On the back end, the civil coercive contempt fine looks as much like punishment as a criminal contempt fine imposed by the court.

EXAMPLE

Example 5

Judy, a newspaper reporter, refuses to reveal to the federal grand jury the "source" who leaked confidential information to her. She is jailed for civil coercive contempt until she reveals the source. She tells the judge she will never reveal the source, and demands a jury trial on grounds that she is going to remain in jail for more than 6 months. (Recall that in federal court, the coercive contempt for failing to testify before a grand jury can last for only 18 months.) Does she get the right to a jury trial?

EXPLANATION

Explanation

Judy does not get the right to a jury trial. Remember that this is coercive contempt aimed at getting Judy to comply with the court order to testify; it is not about punishing her. Judy "holds the keys to the jailhouse door" in her pocket, meaning she can be out in less than 6 months if she agrees to testify.

This again points out some of the ironies of distinguishing among the types of contempt. Judy may spend up to 18 months in jail, without getting all the criminal protections such as the right to a jury trial. But someone who faces only 6 months in jail for *criminal* contempt gets full criminal procedures, including the right to a jury trial. For Judy to be in jail for 18 months will feel like punishment even if the court's purpose is to coerce her testimony.

10.4 CIVIL COMPENSATORY CONTEMPT

"Compensatory contempt is a money reward for the plaintiff when the defendant has injured the plaintiff by violating the injunction." Doug Rendleman, *Compensatory Contempt: Plaintiff's Remedy When a Defendant Violates an Injunction*, 1980 U. Ill. L. F. 971 (1980). In this way, compensatory contempt is more like damages than like an injunction. As Rendleman explains,

"Courts utilize compensatory contempt to restore the plaintiff as nearly as possible to his original position." *Id.* at 972. If that sounds familiar, it is because it mirrors the purpose of compensatory damages discussed in Part I of this book. The difference is that civil compensatory contempt looks at a more limited time frame, awarding only the measurable damages occurring between the time the court enters the injunction and the time the defendant complies with the injunction.

In a civil contempt action, federal courts apply an objective standard to determining if defendant had the requisite state of mind to merit a finding of contempt. *Taggart v. Lorenzen*, 139 S. Ct. 1795 (2019). In *Taggart*, defendant argued he acted in his subjective good faith in interpreting the injunction, believing he was complying, and he therefore could not be liable for violating it, but the Supreme Court said that the standard is that there is "*no fair ground of doubt* as to whether the order" barred defendant's conduct. Failure to meet an objective standard—what a reasonable person in defendant's position would have thought the injunction meant—is enough to merit contempt. Acting in bad faith would be enough to merit civil contempt as well, but acting in good faith is no defense.

Thus, if Pnina fails to comply with the specific performance order and her delay in complying with the injunction costs Oscar $40,000 in lost profits, compensatory contempt allows Oscar to recover those lost profits. Unlike the other forms of contempt, the money here goes to the plaintiff, *not* to the court. It is also retrospective, based upon damages for the finite period between the time of the injunction and the contempt finding. It does not apply to damages incurred prior to the issuance of the injunction.

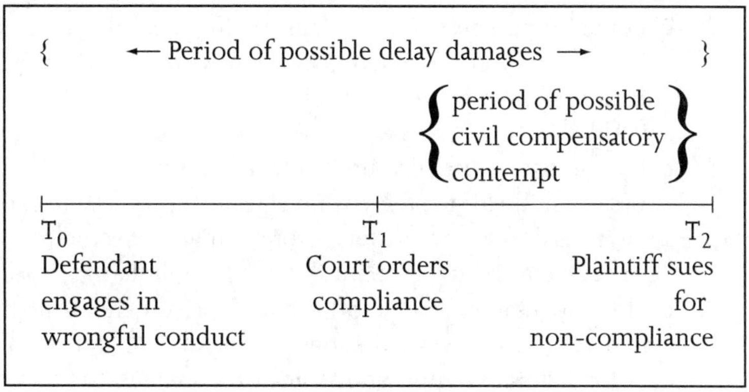

Figure 10.1

Figure 10.1 contrasts civil compensatory contempt with delay damages. At T_0, the defendant engages in the wrongful conduct. In our current example, this is the time when Pnina fails to deliver the widget at the time promised. At time T_1, the court issues an order of specific performance requiring the defendant to comply. In this case, the court orders Pnina to deliver the widget. At time T_2, plaintiff sues for non-compliance. In jurisdictions allowing for civil compensatory contempt, Oscar can seek damages that accrued during the T_1-T_2 period (but he cannot seek damages for the T_0-T_1 period).

In jurisdictions in which civil compensatory contempt is unavailable, Oscar can seek delay damages for the T_0-T_2 period.[7] From the entire period of T_0 to T_2, Oscar has suffered additional damages because of Pnina's delay in complying.

Rendleman has noted the "irony" of civil compensatory contempt: the court has awarded an injunction because, under the irreparable injury rule, it has determined that damages are not an adequate remedy for the plaintiff. Yet the injunction did not work to keep the plaintiff in the rightful position, and so damages are awarded for that purpose.

The way of resolving the irony is recognizing that the monetary award through civil compensatory contempt is a second-best solution. The plaintiff's first choice is compliance with the injunction. Plaintiff's second choice is this set of damages.

Finally, awarding such damages does not mean that the injunction issued was not necessary. To see this point, let's say that when Pnina fails to deliver the widget as promised (a widget that was not available from another seller for some time), Oscar had to close his factory, sustaining $30,000 in losses. At that point, the court could issue a judgment holding Pnina liable for $30,000 in damages for the delay and ordering Pnina to turn the widget over to Oscar immediately. When Pnina has not done so a week later, Oscar suffers another $40,000 in damages. The civil compensatory contempt remedy allows Oscar to recover those damages. But that still does not put Oscar in the rightful position. Pnina must turn over the widget, or Oscar will continue to pile on damages. Thus, the injunction, which ultimately forces Pnina to turn over the widget, working with delay damages and civil compensatory contempt, keeps Oscar in the rightful position.

Although civil compensatory contempt is no different in concept from delay damages (just measured in a narrower time period after the court issues the injunction), there is no right to a jury trial to recover these damages; instead, they are proven before a judge, in some jurisdictions using a "clear and convincing evidence" standard. Rendleman, *supra*, at 978. Because civil compensatory contempt would deprive defendants of a jury trial to seek damages, some jurisdictions do not allow plaintiffs to seek such damages through contempt, and instead require a separate action for further delay damages. *Id.* at 983-984.

---

7. As a matter of civil procedure, a request for delay damages may need to accompany the demand for specific performance; res judicata principles may preclude a later demand for such damages. *See Mycogen Corp. v. Monsanto Co.*, 51 P.3d 297 (Cal. 2002).

Plaintiff does get one advantage in some jurisdictions by using the contempt route to collect these damages: the court can use coercive techniques such as threats of imprisonment or additional fines to require compliance with the order. In contrast, as we shall see in Chapter 17, ordinary money judgments generally are not collectible through a court order.[8]

EXAMPLE

Example 6

A slight variation on the Oscar-Pnina example: Pnina fails to deliver the widget as promised (a widget that would not be available to Oscar from another seller for some time), causing Oscar to close his factory and sustain $30,000 in losses. His lawyer sues, asking only for an injunction ordering Pnina to turn over the widget. After trial, the court orders Pnina to turn over the widget, and Pnina does so immediately. Can Oscar recover the $30,000 as civil compensatory contempt?

EXPLANATION

Explanation

No. Oscar cannot recover these damages because Oscar did not sustain them because Pnina violated the injunction. These were damages from the delay in performance that occurred *before* the issuance of the injunction. Pnina turned over the widget immediately after it issued, so there are *no* damages that Oscar may recover through civil compensatory contempt.

Oscar should be entitled to the $30,000 in delay damages (to bring him back to the rightful position, along with the injunction), but not through a contempt proceeding. In many jurisdictions, however, Oscar's request for delay damages needs to be brought as part of his underlying suit for breach of contract against Pnina. Under civil procedure principles of *res judicata*, an action for delay damages must accompany a request for specific performance. A lawyer who fails to sue for delay damages along with a request for specific performance could be committing malpractice.

EXAMPLE

Example 7

You are Oscar's lawyer. In addition to the losses in Example 6, Oscar has suffered $40,000 in delay damages because of Pnina's failure to comply with the injunction. In your jurisdiction, you have a choice between bringing an ancillary action for civil compensatory contempt to collect these damages or initiating a separate damages proceeding. Which do you prefer?

8. Some courts allow plaintiffs to recover defendants' gains—a restitutionary measure, not a compensatory measure—through civil compensatory contempt.

EXPLANATION

Explanation

The answer to this question will turn on any salient differences between the two procedures in the jurisdiction. For example, if you believe Oscar would benefit from a jury trial and a lower "preponderance of the evidence" standard, you might be better off with a separate damages action. On the other hand, if you believe the additional money would be difficult to collect through usual damage collection measures, you could well prefer the contempt route. Another factor to consider is any state law or contractual provision in the Oscar-Pnina contract governing the availability of attorney's fees.

10.5 THE COLLATERAL BAR RULE (MORE ON CRIMINAL CONTEMPT)

Recall Example 3, in which Jake seeks a declaratory judgment that the city's zoning law prohibiting his operation of an adult business is unconstitutional. If Jake violates the city's zoning law and the law is in fact struck down as unconstitutional, Jake cannot be lawfully prosecuted for violating the zoning law. Indeed, if Jake were criminally prosecuted for violating the zoning, he could defend himself against that criminal prosecution by raising the unconstitutionality of the law as a defense.[9]

In contrast, imagine that the trial court declares the zoning law *constitutional*, and it issues an injunction barring Jake from operating his business in violation of the injunction. Jake appeals the trial court's issuance of the injunction to the appellate court. If he disobeys the trial court's order while the appeal is pending, thereby violating the injunction, he can be found liable and punished for *criminal contempt*. Suppose the appellate court later holds that the trial court erred, and in fact the injunction violated the Constitution. Can Jake defend himself in the criminal contempt prosecution by raising the unconstitutionality of the injunction as a defense?

The answer is no, and the doctrine used to explain this concept is the *collateral bar rule:* "One who disobeys an injunctive order that is later reversed on appeal for error may be held in criminal contempt for the disobedience in spite of the reversal." DOBBS & ROBERTS, §2.8(6), p. 155. It is called the *collateral* bar rule because the rule prevents a litigant from attacking the validity of an injunction in the collateral matter of a defense to a criminal

9. Though Jake could go to state or federal court seeking a declaratory judgment that the city's zoning law is unconstitutional, federal courts will not entertain such suits once the state has begun a criminal prosecution. *See Younger v. Harris*, 401 U.S. 37 (1971). More on this issue in Chapter 16.3.

prosecution. The appropriate course of action suggested by the collateral bar rule is a *direct appeal* of the order granting the injunction. Jake should have waited for the outcome of the appeal.

Note the contrast between the first and second of these scenarios. In the first scenario, Jake's claim of unconstitutionality trumps a legislatively enacted law. In the second, Jake's claim of unconstitutionality *does not trump* a court-issued injunction. Why the difference?

The Supreme Court explained and defended the collateral bar rule in *Walker v. City of Birmingham*, 388 U.S. 307 (1967), a case arising out of a civil rights march (including Dr. Martin Luther King, Jr.) planned for Good Friday in Birmingham, Alabama. A state court issued an *ex parte* order (an order without giving notice to the protesters of the right to be heard in opposition) barring the demonstration, but the marchers marched anyway. When they were later put on trial for criminal contempt, the marchers raised the unconstitutionality of the court's order. The courts held that the collateral bar rule prevented raising the defense.

The Supreme Court justified the rule as one that preserved the power of the courts and indeed civilization itself:

> The rule of law that Alabama followed in this case reflects a belief that in the fair administration of justice no man can be judge in his own case, however exalted his station, however righteous his motives, and irrespective of his race, color, politics, or religion. This Court cannot hold that the petitioners were constitutionally free to ignore all the procedures of the law and carry their battle to the streets. One may sympathize with the petitioners' impatient commitment to their cause. But respect for judicial process is a small price to pay for the civilizing hand of law, which alone can give abiding meaning to constitutional freedom.

Id. at 320-321. The Court suggested the more appropriate procedure would have been for the protesters to obey the injunction and seek immediate appellate relief in the Alabama courts. Indeed, the court suggested that if such a claim had been met with "delay or frustration," the protesters perhaps could have violated the injunction without facing criminal penalties.

The Supreme Court in dicta also mentioned two other possible exceptions to the collateral bar rule beyond "delay or frustration" in attacking the underlying injunction:

- *Court lacks jurisdiction over controversy*. If a court lacks jurisdiction over a controversy, the collateral bar rule does not apply. But a court has jurisdiction to check its own jurisdiction, and an order issued while the court is determining its own jurisdiction is valid.
- *Injunction is transparently invalid or has only a "frivolous pretense to validity."* When a court issues an order that is obviously invalid, it may be ignored.

In theory, but not in practice, this may be a large loophole. The order issued in *Walker* looked to be blatantly unconstitutional (the *Walker* Court itself noted that "[t]he breadth and vagueness of the injunction itself would also unquestionably be subject to substantial constitutional question"). But the Court did not apply the "transparently invalid" exception to the injunction in *Walker*. If it did not apply there, it is not clear when it would apply.

Some have criticized the collateral bar rule and its exceptions as being inconsistent in preserving the integrity of the courts and not sufficiently protective of other constitutional values.[10] Why, for example, should the collateral bar rule apply when the court issues an unconstitutional (but not transparently invalid) order but not apply when the court is without jurisdiction to issue its order? Is jurisdiction more important than preserving the First Amendment?

EXAMPLE

Example 8

In the Oscar-Pnina case, a court orders Pnina to produce the widget for Oscar by January 1. Pnina does not do so, and on January 15 the court determines that Pnina's delay in complying with the court's order has cost Oscar $10,000 in additional damages. The court awards Oscar $10,000 in civil compensatory contempt. Pnina does not pay, arguing that the court was wrong in the first place in ordering specific performance. An appellate court then reverses in the underlying case, holding that Oscar, not Pnina, breached the contract, and that therefore Pnina does not have to produce the widget. Can Oscar still collect the $10,000 under the collateral bar rule?

EXPLANATION

Explanation

No. The collateral bar rule applies only to criminal contempt, and Oscar's award comes from civil compensatory contempt. The purpose of the rule is to protect the integrity of the courts, and allowing Oscar to recover would be giving a private plaintiff the benefit of an erroneously issued injunction rather than protecting that integrity.

10. For an early critical view, see Doug Rendleman, *More on Void Orders*, 7 GA. L. REV. 246 (1973).

Example 9

BigCorp sues MegaCorp in federal court for an injunction blocking MegaCorp from selling its handheld "Blueberry" cell phone, which BigCorp alleges violates certain patents that it holds. MegaCorp makes a special appearance in court arguing that the court never acquired personal jurisdiction over the company. The court issues a temporary restraining order enjoining MegaCorp from selling the "Blueberry" while the court examines the jurisdictional question. MegaCorp violates the order by selling the "Blueberry," and is charged with criminal contempt. The court then holds that indeed it has no personal jurisdiction over MegaCorp and dismisses BigCorp's suit. Can MegaCorp defend itself at the criminal contempt trial on grounds that the trial court lacked personal jurisdiction over it?

Explanation

No. As noted, a court always has jurisdiction to determine jurisdiction. MegaCorp had to obey the trial court's order or seek an emergency ruling from the appellate courts on the jurisdictional question, perhaps through appeal of a motion to dissolve the TRO.

Example 10

A group of medical facilities and doctors who provide reproductive health care services commenced suit on March 22, 2012, against 68 defendants, including Gerald and Michael, for various state and federal charges related to blocking access to abortion clinics. The plaintiffs sought a TRO and preliminary injunction to establish limited buffer zones around abortion facilities to prevent the defendants from engaging in illegal activities designed to disrupt access to those abortion facilities. On April 15, the trial court issued a TRO against the 68 defendants barring them from being present within a "buffer zone" around certain reproductive health clinics. At an April 29 status conference, the court, over the objection of the defendants, extended the TRO pending a trial on a preliminary injunction. On May 18, Gerald and Michael protested within one of the "buffer zones" around a protected clinic. They believed the TRO was unconstitutionally vague and a violation of their First Amendment rights. If Gerald and Michael are charged with criminal contempt for violating the TRO, do they have any defense?

EXPLANATION

Explanation

This example is based upon *In re Criminal Contempt Proceedings Against Gerald Crawford and Michael Warren*, 329 F.3d 131 (2d Cir. 2003). The collateral bar rule appears to bar Gerald and Michael's defense. A TRO is a kind of injunction. Parties must obey it in the same way that they would have to obey a preliminary or permanent injunction. It is no defense that Gerald and Michael believe the TRO violates their constitutional rights. Unless the order is "transparently invalid" or issued with only a "frivolous pretense of validity" (which did not apply to the apparently invalid order in *Walker*), litigants must obey it. Nor is there a question about the court's jurisdiction over Gerald and Michael. Finally, nothing indicates that they were met by "delay and frustration" in getting a ruling on the merits dissolving the TRO. The strongest argument Gerald and Michael could make against contempt is that the TRO dissolved after (at most) 28 days under Fed. R. Civ. P. 65, meaning they were not violating any order at the time they acted.

As mentioned in Chapter 9.4, though there is a Supreme Court case that supports this view, *Granny Goose Foods, Inc. v. Brotherhood of Teamsters and Auto Truck Drivers Local No. 70*, 415 U.S. 423, 442-443 (1974) (suggesting that TROs of undisclosed duration dissolve after the 28-day [then a 20-day] period), most courts now appear to follow the Supreme Court's view in *Sampson v. Murray*, 415 U.S. 61 (1974), that TROs lasting more than 20 days [now 28 days] morph into appealable preliminary injunctions. In the actual case that this example illustrates, it was significant to the Second Circuit that in *Sampson* and in the case before it, but not in *Granny Goose Foods*, the defendants had notice that the TRO was being extended and had the opportunity to move to dissolve the TRO. In the actual case, the Second Circuit held it was proper to try Gerald and Michael for violating the TRO.

10.6 CONTEMPT AND THIRD PARTIES

We have already seen in Chapter 8.3 that courts may direct only "minor and ancillary" orders against third parties (that is, non-parties to the lawsuit or parties to the lawsuit who have not been adjudicated as wrongdoers).[11] But can a third party be held in contempt for violating a minor and ancillary order? Fed. R. Civ. P. 65(d)(2) provides that injunctions may be binding only on people with *actual notice of the court's order*[12] who are either parties,

11. Third parties may be *burdened* by injunctions somewhat more substantially, as Chapter 8.3 discussed.

12. Notice of the *order* here is in contrast to notice of the *hearing* at which the court issues the order. We consider the latter point below.

parties' officers, agents, servants, employees, attorneys, or persons who are in active concert or participation with parties or their agents. Thus, at least some third parties may be held in contempt for violating a court order.

Even without the express statutory provision, notice seems required as a matter of constitutional due process; otherwise, someone could be charged with contempt for violating an order she knew nothing about. Second, notice is required as an element of proof of the criminal contempt: one cannot be held criminally liable for contempt without proof of a *willful* violation of a court's order; one cannot willfully disobey an order one knows nothing about.

A somewhat more difficult question is whether a court may hold a third party in contempt for violating a court order if that person was not an officer, agent, employee, or attorney of a party, or in active concert or participation with a party. The leading case in the affirmative is *United States v. Hall*, 472 F.2d 261 (5th Cir. 1972). In *Hall*, a federal district court enjoined everyone from entering the grounds of a certain high school except for limited purposes listed in the order. This order was part of a larger desegregation suit. Eric Hall was not a party to the lawsuit, but he was served with the court order, and charged with criminal contempt when he entered the school grounds apparently to "prevent the normal operation of [the school] through student boycotts and other activities." *Id.* at 263.

The Fifth Circuit held that Hall could be charged with contempt even though he did not meet any of the criteria of Fed. R. Civ. P. 65(d). The *Hall* court held that the court had an inherent power to issue the order against Hall, because his activities "imperiled the court's fundamental power to make a binding adjudication between the parties properly before it." *Id.* at 265. The court also supported its ruling by noting the power of courts to issue *in rem* injunctions: "Federal courts have issued injunctions binding on all persons, regardless of notice, who come into contact with property which is the subject of a judicial decree." *Id.* at 265-266. *In rem* jurisdiction is not mentioned in Rule 65, but it existed before Rule 65 and the *Hall* court held that courts retained the inherent power to issue such injunctions.

The Fifth Circuit sidestepped a due process argument raised by Hall. As we saw in Chapter 9.4, constitutional due process requires that notice *of the hearing* at which a TRO is to be issued be given to the adverse party, absent some good excuse for not giving notice. Though Hall had notice of the court's *order* after it issued and before he violated it, he was not given notice of the court's *hearing* at which the order was issued (nor was there any reason offered why Hall was not given notice so as to satisfy Rule 65(b)). The court held that the order was properly classified as a TRO without notice because it was violated within four days of its issuance.[13] That may well be true, but

13. As we saw in the last chapter, Rule 65(b) limits the length of TROs issued without notice to 14 days, though such an order may be extended for an additional 14 days in appropriate circumstances.

it did not answer the constitutional objection to binding Hall to the order without giving him a chance to be heard before the order issued.

Hall's reach is unclear. Some courts have expressed skepticism about holding third parties not named in Rule 65(d) in criminal contempt for violating court orders. *See, e.g., Planned Parenthood Golden Gate v. Garibaldi*, 132 Cal. Rptr. 2d 46 (App. 2003); *Doctor's Associates, Inc. v. Reinert & Duree, P.C.*, 191 F.3d 297 (2d Cir. 1999). But *Hall* continues to be cited by courts for the principle that in certain cases third parties may be held in contempt for violating court orders.

Example 11

EXAMPLE

Same facts as in the *Hall* case, but imagine that Hall's friend, Oates, was neither named in the trial court's order nor served with a copy of it. Oates heard about the order of the district court (which prohibited everyone from entering school grounds except for limited, enumerated purposes) from Hall. Oates too went onto campus to arrange student protests and was charged with criminal contempt for violating the court's order. Can Oates be held liable for criminal contempt?

Explanation

EXPLANATION

Oates may raise two arguments against holding him in contempt. First, he may argue that the court must single him out for treatment by either giving him notice of the hearing, listing him as bound in the order, or personally serving him with the order. That line of argument divided a panel of the Second Circuit in *U.S. v. Paccione*, 964 F.2d 1269 (2d Cir. 1992). A majority held that a third party could be held liable for criminal contempt so long as he had actual notice of the order; it was not necessary that the third party be listed on the order or served with it. A dissenting judge disagreed, holding that at the very least the order by its terms had to apply to non-parties or that the non-party had to be acting in concert with defendants in the lawsuit. In the Hall and Oates example, it is possible that they were acting in active concert. If the court has authority to bind Hall, even if he is a third party, perhaps it could bind Oates as well, though that appears to be beyond what the text of Rule 65 allows.

The other argument Oates may raise is that he needed to receive some kind of *official* notice of the court's order, rather than informally hearing about it from his friend, Hall. That argument is likely to fail. Fed. R. Civ. P. 65(d)(2) provides for actual notice "by personal service *or otherwise*" (emphasis added).

EXAMPLE

Example 12

Nina, Pnina's sister, learns that Pnina has been ordered to turn over the widget to Oscar immediately. Nina knows Pnina does not want to do so. Without talking to Pnina about it but knowing her sister would likely approve, Nina sneaks into Pnina's factory and hides the widget. She won't tell Pnina where it is, and Pnina honestly tells the judge that she does not know where the widget is, and therefore she cannot turn it over. Can Nina be held for criminal contempt?

EXPLANATION

Explanation

The order is binding on Pnina, as well as upon her agents and those in active concert or participation with Pnina who have actual notice of the court's order. In this case, Nina has actual notice of the court's order: she knows that the court has ordered Pnina to turn over the widget. The case turns on whether the court could call Nina an "agent" or someone working in "active concert" with Pnina. In this case, it appears that Nina was working independently of Pnina to save Pnina from complying with the court's order. But the court may not believe it; it may be tempting to ask your sibling to help you out of a jam, and that's just what it looks like here (even if that is not in fact what happened). Even if Nina is working independently, perhaps the court, following *Hall*, could also order Nina to turn over the widget in order to effectuate its judgment and hold Nina in contempt if she fails to do so.

In any case, even if the court could not punish Nina criminally for contempt, it arguably could require Nina to appear in court to reveal the location of the widget. That appears to be a "minor and ancillary" order to a third party. Nina, of course, would have to receive notice of both the hearing and the order. If at that point Nina refuses to comply, she could be held in civil coercive contempt until she agreed to reveal the location of the widget. Recall that Gerardo Catena was a witness who was held in contempt for five years for refusing to testify with his grant of immunity.

PART III

Restitution

CHAPTER 11

No Gain, No Pain: Restitution and the Unjust Enrichment Principle

11.1 INTRODUCTION TO RESTITUTION

Restitution is different from damages and injunctions covered in the first two parts of this book. Both damages and injunctions are exclusively *remedies*. In contrast, restitution functions as both a *substantive area* of the law (much like torts and contracts) in cases in which a plaintiff would have no other remedy, and as an alternative *remedy* for certain tort and contract breaches. In this way, it is unlike any of the other remedies we consider in this book. And it is what makes the material tricky for students. *See* Restatement of the Law Third: Restitution and Unjust Enrichment (RTR), Ch. 7, Introductory Note ("The awkwardness of using the word 'restitution' to identify both a claim based on unjust enrichment and the corresponding remedy means that this simple division of the overall subject matter is not always apparent from its terminology.").

What do I mean by cases in which a plaintiff would have no other remedy? Consider this true example. A friend of mine—a law professor—went to close a bank account that held $1,250. When the bank gave her the check for the balance of her account, a bank employee made an error (most likely hitting the "00" rather than the "0" key), and the check arrived for $125,000. My friend naturally returned the check (wouldn't you?), asking for the bank to cut a new check in the proper amount. But suppose she had not returned the $125,000 check, and had instead cashed it and put the $125,000 in her safe. The bank could not sue my friend for breach of contract (there was no contractual obligation to return mistakenly paid monies) and perhaps not for tort (her actions may not meet the state's substantive test for conversion or any other tort). Whether or not a tort claim would work, restitution provides the *substantive basis* for the bank's suit to seek return of the excess paid ($125,000 paid less the $1,250 it actually owed). To allow my friend to keep the extra $123,750 would *unjustly enrich* her at the expense of the bank.

This bank check example shows how restitution can provide a cause of action when there is no other as a means of preventing unjust enrichment. Additionally, restitution can also provide a basis for a remedy measured by defendant's gain in a torts or contracts suit *when damages are also available as an alternative*. Suppose Anita steals Brianna's digital camera, worth $200. Anita sells it to a pawnshop for $150, and she bets the money at the racetrack. Anita wins at the track, and the $150 is now worth $1,000. When Brianna sues Anita for the tort of conversion (the appropriate tort for this kind of theft), she would ask for damages of around $200.[1]

The law, however, would allow Brianna the alternative restitutionary remedy measured by Anita's gains: $1,000. Naturally, Brianna would prefer this remedy to a claim for damages. As we will see in Chapter 13, the law will allow Brianna to trace "her" property, from the camera to the cash from the pawnshop to the winning tickets at the racetrack to the cash Anita got from the track in exchange for her winning tickets.

If you learn nothing else from this part of the book, you should know the following two basic points about restitution:

- Restitution is about *unjust enrichment*. Generally speaking, there will be no recovery in restitution absent proof that a defendant has been unjustly enriched. We will need to consider both what it means for a defendant to be *enriched* and when the law terms such enrichment *unjust*.
- As a matter of remedy, restitution gives plaintiff an award based on *defendant's gains* rather than plaintiff's losses. When defendant has no gains, restitution is an inappropriate remedy. When defendant has gains, there may be alternative ways of calculating and awarding the gains that sometimes will be subject to dispute between the parties. Whether a plaintiff may recover a defendant's gains gets complicated when defendant has other creditors and defendant is bankrupt.

There is a great deal of fundamental disagreement over precisely what restitution is and how it works. For example, among Remedies scholars, there is a debate over whether suits brought to recover defendants' gains in torts or contracts cases are properly considered suits brought under the substantive law of restitution or, rather, are suits in torts or contracts in which restitution is one of a number of possible remedies. *See* James S. Rogers, *Restitution*

1. Part I of this book explains the complications involved in computing Brianna's damages.

for *Wrongs and the Restatement (Third) of the Law of Restitution and Unjust Enrichment*, 42 Wake Forest L. Rev. 55 (2007). This debate is not about substance; for example, the two sides would agree that Brianna can recover $1,000 from Anita as a restitutionary recovery. But there is a practical significance to naming the cause of action: depending upon how one answers the question in the jurisdiction, the case either would be pled as an action for conversion, where the plaintiff "waives the tort and sues in *assumpsit*,"[2] or it would be pled as an action under the substantive law of restitution. The characterization could affect the applicable statute of limitations period as well.

There are also debates over other fundamental questions in the field, such as whether the contractual remedies of rescission and reformation are properly considered part of the law of restitution, whether there can ever be a restitutionary remedy without defendant's unjust enrichment, and even over what the field should be named.[3] There's also criminal "restitution," but that is a form of compensation awarded in criminal proceedings that we will ignore in this book. *See* RTR §1, cmt. *e*.

Part of the reason for the confusion and disagreement is that restitution as a field did not exist historically as a unified substantive body of law (like torts and contracts) or remedy (like damages and injunctions). Instead, courts of law and equity developed a number of doctrines and remedies we would now consider "restitution" across a broad array of categories. You may recall one of these concepts, *quantum meruit*, from your Contracts class. This doctrine allowed those workers who provided labor under an unenforceable contract to recover the reasonable value of their services.

Because these doctrines developed in both law courts and equity courts before the merger of law and equity, some restitutionary remedies are legal while some are equitable. This distinction will matter in a subset of restitution cases, especially when it comes to "tracing" remedies in Chapter 13. In some cases, a plaintiff will seek *specific* restitution in terms of the return of the very thing that was taken from him or her. In other circumstances, the result of a restitution claim might be a money judgment. Finally, in some circumstances, defendant gets a legal interest in some kind of property.

The modern field of restitution traces its evolution to the first Restatement of Restitution, published in 1937 by the American Law Institute. The second Restatement of Restitution project began in the 1980s, but it was never completed. Drafting of the Third Restatement of Restitution and Unjust Enrichment is now complete, and it is likely to be very influential in how courts approach the topic. This chapter uses as illustrations a number of examples from the new Third Restatement. The examples are useful even if your

---

2. This is simply arcane language pointing to the old writ for a restitutionary recovery stating that plaintiff wants to recover defendant's gains, not plaintiff's losses.

3. For some criticism on some of the basic points at issue, *see* Peter B.H. Birks, *A Letter to America: The New Restatement of Restitution*, 3 Global Jurist Frontiers (Issue 2) (2003).

professor does not cover the Third Restatement. I've put some details about the Third Restatement's treatment of issues into footnotes, which you might wish to skim or to ignore if your professor does not cover the Third Restatement.

The remainder of this chapter focuses on the substantive law of restitution. When is a defendant *unjustly* enriched to allow for a restitutionary remedy? Why is it that the law sometimes allows a plaintiff to recover more than her losses in apparent violation of the rightful position principle first set forth in Chapter 1? Finally, in which torts and contracts cases is it most advantageous for plaintiffs to pursue a restitutionary recovery rather than recover compensatory damages?

Chapters 12 and 13 focus on measuring the extent of defendants' gains in an unjust enrichment action. Chapter 12 considers fundamental issues of measuring gain—such as from whose perspective do we measure defendants' gains? Consider, for example, whether in a *quantum meruit* claim we use the reasonable value of plaintiff's services or the value added to defendant's property. What if the defendant mixes a misappropriated item of plaintiff's with his own to produce something of value? Should there be an apportionment of profits? If so, how should the apportionment be done?

Chapter 13 turns to constructive trusts, equitable liens, and other restitutionary remedies aimed at getting defendants' gains into the hands of plaintiffs. How can equitable restitutionary remedies help plaintiffs to capture gains and to gain a preference when the defendant is bankrupt? This chapter includes materials on "tracing" defendants' gains. Finally, Chapter 14 considers the contractual remedies of rescission and reformation, which, as noted above, are viewed by some scholars as part of the law of restitution.

EXAMPLE

Example 1

Same facts as in our Anita-Brianna hypothetical, but this time assume that Anita took the $150 and lost all but $50 at the racetrack. Would Brianna prefer a compensatory damages remedy or a restitutionary remedy?

EXPLANATION

Explanation

Okay, the field of restitution is hard, so I thought I would start out with an easy question. Of course, Brianna would prefer the damages remedy because under these facts, the gains to the defendant are smaller than the losses to the plaintiff. But the example is meant to hammer home a basic idea early on: where restitution is potentially available as a remedy, plaintiffs will prefer it to damages only when the amount of defendant's gain exceeds plaintiff's loss.

EXAMPLE

Example 2

Same facts as in our law professor–bank hypothetical, but this time, assume that the law professor took all the funds and put the funds in a safe. That safe, along with all of the law professor's other worldly possessions, are destroyed in a fire. Would the bank prefer a damages remedy or a restitutionary remedy?

EXPLANATION

Explanation

Trick question. Recall that in the bank hypothetical, there is likely *no* tort or contract cause of action that the bank could use to recover any damages. The *only* choice is a restitutionary remedy. The fact that all of the law professor's property is destroyed means that it is going to be very difficult for the bank to *collect* anything in restitution from the law professor. Still, the bank should at least be able to get a money judgment for $123,750, collectible from the law professor should she have any assets.

EXAMPLE

Example 3

Carmen steals $1,000 out of Diego's wallet. Carmen has held on to the cash. Does Diego prefer a remedy of tort damages for conversion, or a restitutionary remedy?

EXPLANATION

Explanation

In these circumstances, Diego is likely indifferent between a damages remedy and a restitutionary remedy because defendant's gains are equal to plaintiff's losses. In some jurisdictions, there may be reasons to prefer one remedy over another. For example, punitive damages generally may not be awarded unless there is also an award of compensatory damages. (See Chapter 15.) In some jurisdictions, punitive damages are not available for a restitutionary claim. If Diego has a strong punitive damages claim, he would likely prefer the remedy of damages in those jurisdictions. In addition, there may be different statutes of limitation applicable to the claims. Depending on the timing of the suit, Diego may prefer one cause of action over the other if one of the claims is time-barred.

EXAMPLE

Example 4

Test your intuition on *unjust* enrichment: Ella goes into sudden cardiac arrest while dining at a restaurant. She is unconscious and alone.

(a) Dr. Felice, a prominent cardiac surgeon, is at the next table. Dr. Felice performs CPR, saving Ella's life. Dr. Felice later sends Ella a bill for $1,000. Should Dr. Felice be able to recover the $1,000, or anything, in restitution?

(b) Same facts as (a), but Felice is not a doctor. She is instead an accountant who took a CPR class a few years back. Should Felice be able to recover the $1,000, or anything, in restitution?

EXPLANATION

Explanation

The law provides a "right answer" to these questions (as we will see in the next section) in that, generally speaking, the doctor but not the accountant would get to recover for the "reasonable value" of professional emergency services rendered. It is, however, more important for you now to focus on what you think is right. Would it be "unjust" for Ella not to pay anything to Felice the doctor? Should it matter that she is a doctor and not an accountant? If money should be paid in restitution, how should it be valued? Based on Dr. Felice's usual charges? The usual charges in the area? The value to Ella of having her life saved?

Note that we cannot get around these questions through contract law. Because Ella was unconscious, she could not have consented to assistance from Dr. Felice (nor was there anyone there, such as a spouse, who could consent on her behalf). You might be tempted to say (if you remember something from your Contracts class) the law should treat Ella and Felice *as though* they had a contract. We might call it a *quasi-contract*. Congratulations if you remembered this terminology—but it doesn't solve the problem of defining "unjust" enrichment. "Quasi-contract" is just another term for a restitutionary claim. If the law concludes that Ella should be treated *as though* she had a contract with Felice, it is because of a judgment that it would be unjust enrichment for Ella not to pay anything to Felice. More on these issues in the coming chapters.

11.2 THE MEANING OF "UNJUST ENRICHMENT": WHEN IS RESTITUTION AVAILABLE?

11.2.1 Introduction

Not every wrong by a defendant involves a gain to the defendant. Consider, for example, when Gwen accidentally runs over Horatio's foot with her Maserati, causing Horatio to suffer $10,000 in damages. Gwen's conduct might be sufficiently wrongful to qualify as negligence for purposes of tort law, but Horatio would not consider trying to recover in restitution from

Gwen, for the simple reason that Gwen has had no gain from their interaction. No enrichment, no valid claim in restitution.

Similarly, not every gain to a defendant involves unjust conduct. Ivan is drowning in the water and Jane throws him a life preserver, saving Ivan's life. Ivan has gained a great deal, but if Jane sues Ivan for compensation based upon Ivan's gain, Jane's going to lose. As we will see, the law generally provides that good Samaritans do not get compensation for coming to the assistance of a stranger. No *unjust* enrichment, no valid claim in restitution.

The Gwen-Horatio hypothetical is an easier one to understand because it is usually not a problem to ascertain whether or not a defendant has been enriched. In the Ivan-Jane hypothetical, in contrast, courts are going to need to make a *judgment* about when a defendant's enrichment at plaintiff's expense is unjust. That judgment about justice is at the heart of the substantive law of restitution.

This section explores some of the basics of that substantive law. Courses in Remedies vary in their coverage of the substantive law of restitution, with some focusing only on the restitutionary remedies described and analyzed in Chapters 12-14. But this section should be useful even in those courses emphasizing only the remedial aspects of restitution because the available remedies sometimes turn upon understanding the nature of the injustice forming the basis for plaintiff's restitutionary claim.

Putting aside some detail, the next few subsections explain the major types of cases in which courts will find *unjust enrichment* allowing the plaintiffs to recover in restitution.

11.2.2 Benefits Conferred by Mistake

Claims for a restitutionary remedy often result from a mistaken payment or benefit conferred by the plaintiff to the defendant. The bank–law professor hypothetical fits into this category: the law professor had no rightful claim to the money (in excess of the $1,250 owed by the bank), and it would be an easy call for the courts to decide that the law professor would have to return the bank's money.

We would not want to allow *all* mistaken transactions to result in a claim for restitution. The Restatement offers the following simple example of a mistake that would not allow a restitutionary claim: "Believing that her nephew would make good use of it, Donor makes him a gift of Blackacre. Nephew mismanages the property, causing Donor intense regret." RTR §5, cmt. *b*, illus. 7. The Restatement, consistent with the approach of the courts, would deny Donor the right to undo the transaction under some restitutionary theory.

In deciding which mistakes should provide the basis for a restitutionary claim, the Restatement takes the position that the person transferring the property must make a mistake of fact or law that caused the transfer to take place, and that the transferor does not bear the risk of the mistake. RTR §5. It is this last term—who bears the risk of the mistake—that allows for applications of principles of justice.

Why does the law professor have to return the money but the nephew gets to keep Blackacre? The doctrinal answer is that the bank did not bear the risk of the mistake while the donor/aunt did bear the risk. That, of course, simply postpones the question of injustice to the risk-bearing question.[4]

In making the determination of who bears the risk of the mistake, part of the answer depends upon the transferor's *fault* in making the mistake. But it is more complicated than that. The bank was somewhat at fault in giving the law professor too much money. But carelessness, as in the bank–law professor hypothetical, isn't enough to defeat the bank's claim for restitution. In contrast, Donor's *conscious bad judgment* in making the gift of Blackacre is enough to defeat the restitutionary claim.

The issue may turn upon the *relative* culpability of the parties. If Chauncey the gardener comes to mow Peter's lawn but mistakenly mows Paul's lawn, a court decision whether to allow Chauncey's claim against Paul for restitution (based on the value of the mowing services) could turn on whether Paul knew Chauncey was making a mistake and stood by without letting Chauncey know of the mistake. If Paul knew, restitution for the reasonable value of the mowing services could well be available; if Paul did not, a court is more likely to say Chauncey is out of luck.

Assessing relative culpability of the parties appears to matter most in mistake cases involving improvement of real estate. Consider this hypothetical: Ken and Liam are neighbors in a rural area. Making a negligent mistake about their property line, Ken builds a barn on Liam's land—intending to put it on his own land. The barn cost $10,000 to build, and it has increased the value of Liam's property by at least that amount, if not more.

As in the bank–law professor hypothetical, the plaintiff (Ken) has mistakenly conferred a benefit on the defendant (Liam). If it is unjust for the law professor to keep the cash, it seems unjust for Liam to keep the barn. The real estate context, however, creates two problems that do not exist in the law professor–bank hypothetical: problems of *valuation* and problems of *liquidity*.[5]

---

4. The Restatement takes the position that this risk could be allocated by an agreement of the parties (express or implied), or to the transferor when the transferor acts "in conscious ignorance of the relevant circumstances." RTR §5, cmt. *b*(2). Presumably the donor/aunt assumed the risk of the mistake, because she transferred Blackacre without adequately assuring herself that nephew would manage it well.

5. As the Restatement explains:

> Valuation is a problem because there is no necessary correlation between the objectively measurable value of an improvement to property and the value actually realized by the owner, which may be limited by subjective factors. Even if the value of an improvement

As to valuation, there may be a gap between objective and subjective valuation. If Ken mistakenly builds a barn on Liam's property, it might increase the property value, but it may have no immediate subjective value to Liam, who has no intention to use the barn or to sell the property in the foreseeable future. As to illiquidity, it could be that the barn adds $20,000 in value to the property, but if Liam has no assets besides the house, it would be quite harsh to force the owner to move to pay for the barn he never wanted.

Because of these problems common to the real estate context, in mistaken improvement cases, the courts may fashion remedies to ensure fairness. For example, a court could delay Ken's compensation for the barn, requiring payment for it only when Liam sells the house.[6]

EXAMPLE

Example 5

Adam's life is insured with Beta Company for $5,000. Carrie is the named beneficiary. The body of a shipwreck victim is identified as that of Adam. Neither Beta Company nor Carrie questions the accuracy of the identification. On receipt of formal proof of Adam's death, Beta Company pays Carrie $5,000. Adam is later discovered alive. May Beta obtain restitution from Carrie for the $5,000 payment?

EXPLANATION

Explanation

This example appears in RTR §5, cmt. *a*, illus. 1. Courts could well reach different conclusions in this case, depending upon how the court decides who should "bear the risk of the mistake" or whose conduct is more culpable. The court also might be swayed by liquidity concerns. At this point, does Carrie still have the money to pay back the insurance company?

---

can be stipulated, its relative illiquidity—by comparison to monetary benefits—means that an award of restitution may require the payment of money the owner does not have or would not have chosen to spend.

RTR §10, cmt. *a*.

6. The Restatement provides that a person who improves the real or personal property of another by mistake may obtain restitution "as necessary to prevent unjust enrichment. A remedy for mistaken improvement that subjects the owner to a forced exchange will be qualified or limited to avoid undue prejudice to the owner." RTR §10.

As with the "risk of loss" question discussed above, the Restatement test gives courts a great deal of discretion. In this case, courts may look at relative culpability and other factors in deciding whether restitution is "necessary" to prevent "unjust" enrichment. In this context, the Restatement takes the position that good faith, notice, and negligence of the parties are relevant in determining "what constitutes undue prejudice to the owner and substantial justice to the parties." RTR §10, cmt. *e*. Section 10 also gives courts the ability to fashion a remedy, such as barring plaintiff from forcing the sale of property.

For what it's worth, the Restatement takes the position in Illustration 5 that this kind of error results from the kind of mistake that allows for restitution, and we can see that it is much like the payment by the bank to the law professor. Yet this stands in contrast to Illustration 4 in the same Restatement section, involving a similar payment after Adam disappears without explanation. Illustration 4 assumes that the insurer "decides to pay the claim in view of (i) the perceived likelihood that A[dam] is in fact dead, and (ii) the small amount of the policy as compared to the anticipated cost of further investigation and litigation." As in Illustration 5, the insurer pays, and then Adam turns up alive. The Restatement takes the position that in Illustration 7 the insurer acted "in conscious ignorance of the relevant circumstances" and therefore assumed the risk of mistake, thereby taking away the insurer's claim to restitution. It is not clear why the Restatement treats the two cases differently, and the contrast illustrates how courts may well treat similar kinds of cases in very different ways.

Example 6

EXAMPLE

Maria contracts with Nancy to build a shed on what Maria believes to be Nancy's property. Maria builds the shed at a cost of $5,000, and Nancy has not paid. In fact, Otto is the real owner of the property, and he did not give Nancy permission to have the shed constructed. Otto evicts Nancy, tears down the shed, and sells the land to Penelope. The land contract price was unaffected by the razed shed. May Maria recover the $5,000, or perhaps some other amount, in restitution from Otto?

Explanation

EXPLANATION

This example too is based upon an illustration in the Restatement, and the answer is no under both the common law and the Restatement. RTR §10, cmt. *g*, illus. 17. Remember one of our earliest rules: no restitution without enrichment. In this case, Otto was not enriched by Maria's actions. Otto did not receive any additional funds from Penelope in the sale of the property because of Maria's actions. Maria might have a contractual claim or a claim in restitution against Nancy, but not against Otto.

If Otto had not razed the shed and in fact received additional consideration from Penelope because of the shed, it appears that Maria in this case would be able to get restitution from Otto for the value added by the shed. If Otto had neither razed the shed nor sold his property, the court would have had to decide whether Otto in fact gained by the presence of the shed. If he did receive a benefit, the court would then have to decide both how to value that benefit and whether Otto should be forced to make a payment now. It could be that Maria would get an interest that would allow her to receive the proceeds only upon the eventual sale of Otto's property.

11.2.3 Benefits Conferred by Transferor with Defective Consent or Authority

The preceding section discussed mistaken transfers and the possibility of a restitutionary remedy. The remedies we focused on there concerned monetary damages or the transfer of property. In certain cases of mistakes involving *contracts*, a mistake may provide the basis for the contract's rescission (or cancellation). For example, if Uncle intends to convey to Niece a life estate in Whiteacre but he mistakenly conveys a fee simple, a court may allow the restitutionary remedy of canceling the action.

We'll discuss rescission of contracts in more detail in Chapter 14. For now, though, it is worth looking at the *kinds* of defective consent or authority that may provide grounds for rescission. These include claims of fraud, innocent material misrepresentation, duress, undue influence, and incapacity.

First, consider *fraud*. For example, suppose Niece tells Uncle he is signing a promissory note guaranteeing a loan to Niece to pay for schooling expenses. Uncle is in fact signing away his fee interest in Whiteacre. A court will rescind the transaction upon discovery of the fraud, returning Whiteacre to Uncle. If Niece has already sold Whiteacre, Uncle will be able to use restitution to get the proceeds from the sale from Niece. Alternatively, under some circumstances, he might be able to get Whiteacre back from the new purchaser. RTR §13.

Some courts will even allow restitution in cases of *innocent material misrepresentations*. *Id*. So if Niece honestly believes (and tells Uncle) that Uncle's loan guarantee "isn't binding" on Uncle, the contract might be rescinded because of this innocent, though material (important), misstatement of fact.

Alternatively, suppose Niece tells Uncle he must sign over his property interest in Whiteacre or she will break Uncle's legs. A court will rescind the transaction upon proof that Uncle made the promise under *duress*. RTR §14. Similarly, if Niece takes care of Uncle and uses *undue influence* to get him to sign over his property interest in Whiteacre, a court could rescind the transaction. RTR §15.[7]

Finally, if Niece secures Uncle's signature transferring Whiteacre to her at a time when Uncle is mentally incompetent, the court will rescind the transaction on grounds of *incapacity* unless the transferor has regained legal capacity before the transfer and ratified the transaction. RTR §16(1).[8]

---

7. The Restatement defines "undue influence" as "excessive and unfair persuasion" between parties in a "confidential relation" or "relation of dominance on one side and subservience on the other" and in which "the free will of the transferor is overcome by the will of the person exerting undue influence." RTR §15(1).

8. Minors too can rescind their transactions, and a transfer by a municipal corporation acting wholly beyond its powers is void. RTR §16(2)(a); RTR §16 (2)(c).

Example 7

Quincy and Rita are brother and sister, the sole, equal heirs of their mother's estate. Sonia, a friend of Quincy and Rita's late mother, tells Quincy that his mother had very little personal property. Quincy then disclaims any interest in his mother's personal property in favor of his sister. It turns out that—unbeknownst to Sonia, Quincy, or Rita—Quincy and Rita's mother had a safe deposit box filled with diamonds worth millions of dollars. Sonia finds the key, retrieves the diamonds, and sells them for $2 million. Can Quincy recover half the value of the diamonds from Sonia?

Explanation

The case does not appear to involve either intentional fraud or misrepresentation. Whether we consider this a mistake case or an innocent material misrepresentation case (by Sonia), the result is the same: a court is likely to allow Quincy to recover in restitution. RTR §13 covers both fraud and innocent material misrepresentations. *See* RTR §13, cmt. c, illus. 3. The best argument for Sonia is that this should be treated as a mistake case, and that Quincy disclaimed his interest in conscious disregard of his rights (see Example and Explanation 5), and he should therefore be allocated the risk of his mistake.

11.2.4 Benefits Conferred Intentionally in Emergency and by Officious Intermeddlers

The first two types of cases in which courts allow restitution involve transfers occurring by mistake or through some lack of full consent or authority. We now turn to cases where the transferor intends to transfer a benefit and then later asks for compensation in restitution for the benefit conferred.

We certainly would not want a rule that lets anyone confer a "benefit" without your consent and then charge you for it. Just think of someone who mails you return address labels and then asks for payment. We call people who try to throw benefits at you in exchange for compensation "officious intermeddlers." The rationale for denying restitution to such persons is simple: if I want to buy return address labels, I can enter a voluntary transaction. Otherwise, we would always have to be on our guard to prevent benefits from being forced upon us.

That said, there are situations where someone intentionally (and with full capacity and authority) confers benefits on another and is able to recover restitution for the benefits conferred. Think back to the Ella-Felice hypothetical in this chapter's Example 4. Ella goes into sudden cardiac arrest while dining at a restaurant. She is unconscious and alone. Dr. Felice, a prominent cardiac surgeon, is at the next table. Dr. Felice performs CPR, saving Ella's life. Dr. Felice later sends Ella a bill for $1,000.

A professional who confers benefits in an emergency is eligible for compensation through restitution. *Cotnam v. Wisdom*, 104 S.W. 164 (Ark. 1907); RTR §20. Unlike the officious intermeddler who bypasses a voluntary transaction by foisting benefits on you, the professional acting in an emergency cannot negotiate with the person in need of emergency assistance. If there were a possibility of bargaining, the bargain would be so one-sided and unfair as to be voidable under duress or other principles of contract law.

Though professionals may be able to obtain the reasonable value of their services in restitution, nonprofessionals cannot get the same benefit. It is not that nonprofessionals are all "officious intermeddlers"; any one of us would be grateful if a stranger gave us life-saving CPR when we needed it. Instead, the law presumes that benefits conferred by Good Samaritans are conferred gratuitously (that is, as a gift), and therefore there is no expectation or requirement of restitution.[9]

Though the officious intermeddler is denied recovery, not all self-interested transactions are considered "intermeddling." For example, restitution might be allowed when one spares a neighbor an expense by taking an action to preserve one's own property. For example, Uri owns an easement consisting of a road over Victor's adjoining property. The road is used by Uri 60% of the time and Victor 40% of the time. Both Uri and Victor have a legal right to make necessary repairs to the road. If Uri makes the repairs, he will have an action in restitution against Victor for 40% of the reasonable cost of the repairs. *See* RTR §26, cmt. *b*, illus. 12.[10]

A more common example of this type of claim arises in the case of unmarried cohabitants. Wilma and Xavier lived together like a married couple. Wilma owns some land and Xavier contributes some of his funds for the building of a house upon the land. The house benefits them both. When the couple splits, Xavier may be entitled to restitution for the value he contributed to the house on Wilma's land, at least if a court does not view the payments as a gift to Wilma. *See* RTR §28.

---

9. The Restatement goes so far as to say that the Good Samaritan rescuer should not receive restitution even if the rescuer suffers "crippling injuries" as a result of the rescue, unless the rescued party has made a promise to pay the rescuer. (Such a promise, as you may remember from your first-year Contracts class, would be voidable because it is made under duress.) RTR §20, cmt. *a*, illus. 7. The Restatement's explanation for denying restitution to Good Samaritans is unpersuasive. *See* RTR §20, cmt. *b*. The Restatement writes that "[s]ervices of physicians, hospitals, and ambulance drivers are readily valued, while emergency rescue by a bystander is literally priceless." It is difficult to see why the law should assign something that is so highly valued (such as CPR) a value of zero. The Restatement seems to suggest that allowing recovery would somehow deter altruistic rescue, a point I have refuted. *See* Richard L. Hasen, *The Efficient Duty to Rescue*, 15 INT'L REV. L. & ECON. 141 (1995).

10. Indemnity and equitable subrogation fit into this category as well. These claims are discussed in detail in Chapter 13.

EXAMPLE

Example 8

Shana finds a boat floating near her lake house. She repairs the boat and stores it until its rightful owner comes to claim it. Two years later, Tammy discovers that Shana has been holding her boat and retakes it, refusing to pay for its repair or storage. Does Shana have a right to restitution? Should it matter whether she expected compensation from the boat's owner?

EXPLANATION

Explanation

The facts do not tell us whether or not Shana is a professional in handling boats—which could be required by some courts in order to allow her recovery; otherwise, courts could adopt the presumption applied in other "Good Samaritan" situations that Shana intended to offer her services as a gift to the boat owner. The Restatement provides that when someone comes to the protection of another's property (unlike when rendering emergency aid to a person), restitution is available if "the circumstances justify the claimant's decision to intervene without request" and "it is reasonable to assume the owner would wish the action performed." RTR §21. This is a very reasonable rule, and perhaps the Restatement should have extended it to cases involving the rendering of emergency aid to a person by a Good Samaritan.

EXAMPLE

Example 9

"Mother tells Son that if he constructs an addition to her house, she will allow him to live in it and will convey the property to him before her death. Son makes the requested improvements at a cost of $35,000, increasing the value of the property by a like amount. Repudiating her promise to Son, Mother sells the house to Daughter for one dollar. Daughter evicts son from the premises. Mother's promise to convey to Son is unenforceable." RTR §27, cut. *e*, illus. 12. Does Son have a claim in restitution against Daughter?

EXPLANATION

Explanation

Yes. Son conferred the benefit to benefit both himself and his mother. Now Daughter has benefited through the increased value of the property, and it would be unjust to allow her to keep this benefit. Because the benefit is attached to the land and raises questions of valuation and liquidity, a court might not give Son the right to an immediate money judgment. Instead, Son may end up with an equitable lien (discussed in Chapter 13) against Daughter's interest in the property.

11.2.5 Benefits Conferred in Contractual Settings, Including the Case of "Opportunistic Breach"

People often confer benefits on another and raise a claim in restitution in one of three contractual settings.

11.2.5.1 Restitution for Unenforceable Contracts

First, *restitution may be available when the contract is unenforceable*. For example, imagine Yolanda and Zena make an oral contract for the sale of Yolanda's land to Zena. Zena makes improvements on the property, and Yolanda then successfully claims the contract is unenforceable because it fails to satisfy the statute of frauds. In many jurisdictions, despite the statute of frauds, Zena may assert a restitutionary claim for the value of the improvements.

Restitution also might be available when a contract fails for: indefiniteness or lack of formality, RTR §31; illegality, RTR §32; incapacity of recipient, RTR §33; or mistake or supervening change of circumstances, RTR §34.

11.2.5.2 Restitution as an Alternative Measure of Recovery, Including in Cases of Opportunistic Breach

Second, *restitution may be an alternative measure of recovery by a non-breaching party for breach of an enforceable contract*. Suppose Alexa signs a contract to work for Betty for $30,000 for one year, payable in equal monthly installments. After six months, Betty breaches the enforceable contract by wrongfully terminating Alexa, having paid Alexa only $15,000. Both parties know that the first six months of the contract is the "hard season" in Alexa's line of work, and the reasonable value of Alexa's services during that period was $3,500 per month. *See* RTR §38, cmt. c, illus. 12.

Alexa might choose to sue for damages. As Part I of this book shows, assuming she can prove her damages with "reasonable certainty," Alexa would be able to recover damages for the breach for the remaining portion of the contract, plus incidental and consequential damages (such as the cost to find another job), but she must *mitigate* by trying to find reasonable alternative employment. Suppose she easily finds another job that pays the same salary. In that case, she might have no damages.

As an alternative, Alexa should be able to raise a restitutionary claim based on the reasonable value of what she provided to Betty during those six months. Recall she was paid $2,500 per month for work that was worth $3,500 per month, a difference of $1,000 per month. She should be able to obtain restitution for the $6,000 worth of value she gave Betty during those first six months.[11]

As we will see in section 11.4, restitution as an alternative basis of recovery for breach of contract is especially attractive in the case of "losing" contracts, but in some jurisdictions, it is subject to an important limit: the restitutionary measure cannot exceed the amount of compensatory damages for breach of contract. Consider the following example.

> A promises B to build a barn for $60,000. A is wrongfully discharged after completing part of the work and receiving $20,000 in progress payments. The court finds that the cost reasonably incurred by A in partial performance has been $30,000, and that the reasonable cost of completion (by A or anyone else) will be $45,000. From these facts the court determines that A has performed 40 percent of the work covered by the contract; the price of this work at the contract rate is $24,000. A's claim to restitutionary damages is limited to $4000 (representing the ratable portion of the contract price less $20,000 already paid).

RTR §38, cmt. *c*, illus. 11.

The first thing to note about this example is that it was a losing contract. If A had completed the contract, A would have spent $75,000 (the $30,000 already incurred plus an additional $45,000 in performance) to complete the performance. But A would have received only $60,000 for the project, with a projected loss of $15,000. Damages therefore do not look like an attractive option for A. Restitution looks more promising: A conferred a benefit on B worth $30,000 and received only $20,000, leading to a potential restitutionary recovery of $10,000. But some courts (and the Restatement) cap restitution at the amount of contract damages, meaning restitutionary recovery would be reduced to $4,000 (the pro rata portion of the contract was $24,000, less the $20,000 that had already been paid).

This raises the question why Alexa was able to recover more than the $15,000 contract price given that she had worked for half the time of the contract and received half the contract price. Shouldn't the $15,000 have capped the recovery? The answer is no, because the value of Alexa's performance during the first six months (the "hard season") was more than half the value of the contract.

Consider a harder variation on the Alexa-Betty contract, which raises a question under an important Restatement provision, Restatement §39,

11. The Restatement adopts the terminology of referring to this restitutionary recovery as "performance based damages." *See* RTR §38, cmt. *a* (explaining relationship between damages and restitution claim). I prefer to call the $6,000 a recovery "in restitution" as an alternative to contract damages. This terminology makes it easier to separate the concept of restitution from the concept of compensatory damages. The Restatement also allows the recovery of "incidental or consequential loss" on top of the recovery in restitution. RTR §38.

on "opportunistic breach" of contract. One clause of the contract provides that if Alexa's work for Betty increases Betty's overall profits by $1,000,000, Alexa would be entitled to a $100,000 bonus provided that she was not fired for good cause during the one-year term of the contract. Alexa in fact increased Betty's profits by over $1,000,000, but Betty dismisses Alexa to avoid paying the money (claiming, without merit, that she has good cause to fire Alexa). Alexa should have a good claim for the $100,000 in damages—but might she try to go after Betty's $1,000,000 in profits?

Ordinarily, the answer would be no, but the Restatement includes a section that might allow Alexa to recover those profits. Breaching parties who engage in "opportunistic breach" may have to pay their profits in restitution. RTR §39. The section is quite complex, but it is likely to be very influential in the future in defining the kinds of cases in which restitution will be denied to breaching parties.

Someone like Alexa would have to prove all the following:

- The breaching party's breach was material (that is, sufficiently important to the contracting parties).
- The breaching party's breach was opportunistic in that it was deliberate and profitable (meaning that the gains are greater than the breaching party would have received from performance of the contract).
- Damages would afford inadequate protection to the non-breaching party's contractual entitlement.

The Restatement says that such cases will be "infrequently available" because "a breach of contract that satisfies the cumulative tests of §39 is rare." RTR §39, cmt. *a*. It looks like Alexa's claim would fail because a contract damages remedy that would award Alexa the $100,000 bonus would be sufficient.

So if Alexa could not recover all of Betty's gains in such circumstances, precisely when would §39 apply? The Restatement offers the example of a landlord who leases Blackacre to a tenant. Tenant subleases the property without the landlord's consent in violation of the contract. Landlord learns of the sublease after its term has expired. The Restatement takes the position that the landlord can recover the profits Tenant earned on the sublease even though Landlord could prove no damages. RTR §39, cmt. *e*, illus. 8.

Expect more courts to apply Restatement §39 thanks to a recent Supreme Court case, *Kansas v. Nebraska*, 574 U.S. 445 (2015). The case was an unusual one under the Supreme Court's original jurisdiction, deciding a dispute between two states over water rights to the Republican River. The Supreme Court referred the case to a Special Master (the ordinary way that the Court first resolves interstate disputes). The Special Master found that Nebraska had taken too much water per an earlier agreement between Nebraska and

Kansas, and that Kansas suffered $3.7 million in damages because of the diversion. It also found the diversion was profitable to Nebraska, and that the gain to Nebraska from the diversion exceeded Kansas's loss. Relying on Restatement §39, It ordered "disgorgement" of some of the Nebraska's profits, $1.8 million.

A divided Supreme Court agreed with the Special Master's disgorgement remedy and reliance on §39. The Court held that in this context it had broad equitable discretion, and that disgorgement seemed fair under the circumstance: "whatever is true of a private contract action, the case for disgorgement becomes still stronger when one State gambles with another State's rights to a scarce natural resource." *Kansas*, 574 U.S. at 462.

Three Justices dissented on this point. Justice Thomas wrote that disgorgement was not traditionally available under the common law for breaches of contract:

> This Court, however, has never before relied on §39 nor adopted its proposed theory of disgorgement. And for good reason: It lacks support in the law. One reviewer of §39 has described it as a "novel extension" of restitution principles that "will alter the doctrinal landscape of contract law." Caprice L. Roberts, *Restitutionary Disgorgement for Opportunistic Breach of Contract and Mitigation of Damages*, 42 Loyola (LA) L. Rev. 131, 134 (2008). And few courts have ever relied on §39. The sheer novelty of this proposed remedy counsels against applying it here.
>
> In any event, §39 opines that disgorgement should be available only when a party *deliberately* breaches a contract. This makes sense. If disgorgement is an antidote for "efficient breach," then it need only be administered when "conscious advantage-taking" and "opportunistic calculation" are present. But as noted above, the Master expressly found that no deliberate breach occurred. The Master's reliance on §39 was accordingly misplaced.

Kansas, 574 U.S. at 483 (Thomas, J., concurring in part and dissenting in part). Justice Scalia, in a separate opinion, took a swipe at the Restatement drafting process and the value of the Restatements: "The object of the original Restatements was 'to present an orderly statement of the general common law.' Restatement of Conflict of Laws, Introduction, p. viii (1934). Over time, the Restatements' authors have abandoned the mission of describing the law and have chosen instead to set forth their aspirations for what the law ought to be." *Kansas*, 574 U.S. at 475 (Scalia, J., concurring in part and dissenting in part).

11.2.5.3 Restitution for Breaching Parties

Third, *restitution may be available to a breaching party of an enforceable contract to obtain benefits provided to the non-breaching party*. Imagine that A had promised to build the barn for B at a cost of $60,000, and that B had not yet paid anything to A for the performance. After A had completed 40% of the construction at a cost of $30,000, A breached the contract, refusing to do any more work. B hired another contractor to complete the performance for $45,000, the reasonable value of the services. A and B sue each other.

B makes a claim for breach of contract, claiming as damages the extra amount she had to pay for performance (plus any costs associated with finding a new contractor). There was 60% of the contract left to be performed, and the pro rata cost to B under the contract was $36,000 (60% of the $60,000 contract price). B had to pay $45,000 for that performance, leaving her with damages of $9,000.

A, however, has conferred the benefit of a 40% completed barn on B without receiving any payment. It would be unjust for B to be able to keep this value without paying anything, even though A breached the contract. A court would likely allow A to recover the reasonable value in restitution (perhaps the $30,000), but *capped* at the contract price (in this case, as in a previous A-B example, at $24,000, for 40% of the $60,000 contract price). In the end, a court would likely order B to pay A $15,000 in restitution, which represents the (capped) restitutionary value of what A conferred on B, $24,000, less the $9,000 in damages that A owes B for the breach of contract.

Some jurisdictions would not allow A to recover anything for breach of this contract, at least if A's breach was "willful." This standard is difficult to apply, and seems to be in tension with the "efficient breach" concept discussed in Chapter 4.2.[12]

Example 10

Carol signs a written contract to buy a used car from Dino for a purchase price of $5,000. The fair market value of the car is $4,000. Carol pays $5,000, and promptly crashes the car, destroying it. Carol is 16, and the law in Carol's state allows minors to rescind contracts for sale, receiving back the purchase price. Can Dino recover anything in restitution?

Explanation

Yes. Restitution often is available when a contract is unenforceable, including for reasons of incapacity. In this case, Dino would bring a claim for the reasonable value of the car, $4,000, not the contract price. Had the car not been destroyed, the restitutionary remedy of rescission would have required Carol to return the car. She can't do so in this case because the car has been destroyed. If Dino brings his counterclaim at the time Carol asks

12. The Restatement does not embrace the "willfulness" exception as a whole, but does note that in certain circumstances, such as those involving fraud or inequitable conduct, a breaching party may be denied the opportunity for restitution. RTR §36, cmt. *b*.

for rescission, the court is likely to offset the $5,000 Dino must pay Carol (refund of the purchase price) against the reasonable value of what Dino provided Carol (a car worth $4,000). The end result would be that Dino would pay Carol $1,000 and keep $4,000 as restitution.

Example 11

Bill promises to sell Amy his car for $5,000. The fair market value of the car at the time of the sale is $6,000. After they agree to the sale, but before title and money changes hands, Kevin offers Bill $9,000 for the car. Amy sues Bill for breach of contract. Rather than seeking $1,000 in contract damages, Amy wants to get $3,000 representing Bill's profits on the sale. Can Amy get this remedy in a jurisdiction that has adopted RTR §39?

Explanation

No. Amy likely cannot disgorge Bill's $3,000 profit by claiming he engaged in an opportunistic breach under RTR §39. To begin with, Amy cannot show that damages would not protect her contractual entitlement. If she gets $1,000 in expectation damages, she will still be able to buy a car worth $6,000 for $5,000 plus the damages she received. Further, if a court counts this as a willful or deliberate breach of contract, then it looks like that would undermine the ability to make an efficient breach. Why would one ever sell to a higher-valued user and pay damages if the additional profits will be disgorged? The deliberate standard probably requires some kind of bad faith showing or else §39 would go from a rare remedy to a common remedy.

11.2.6 Benefits Obtained Through Tortious or Otherwise Wrongful Conduct

The final common type of case in which plaintiffs claim restitutionary remedies arises from a defendant's tortious (or otherwise wrongful) conduct. Recall the example from the beginning of the chapter: Anita steals Brianna's digital camera, worth $200. She sells it to a pawnshop for $150 and bets the money at the racetrack. Anita does well at the track, and the $150 is now worth $1,000.

Brianna has a cause of action in tort for conversion. She can sue Anita for conversion, and recover her tort damages of about $200, or Brianna could decide to pursue a restitutionary remedy based on Anita's larger gains. Each jurisdiction has its own rules regulating how and when Brianna must decide whether to seek tort damages or to go for restitution.[13]

The Restatement lists the most common types of tort cases in which plaintiffs may seek a restitutionary remedy: (1) cases involving trespass, conversion, and comparable wrongs, RTR §40, (2) misappropriation of financial assets, RTR §41, (3) interference with intellectual property and similar rights, RTR §42, and (4) breach of fiduciary duties or confidential relations, RTR §43. The Restatement also includes a catchall provision for other wrongs. RTR §44.

Suppose that Shrek has gone onto Fiona's land to cut down some trees. He hauls off the trees and converts them to timber, yielding a nice profit. Under substantive tort law, Shrek committed a tort when he entered Fiona's land. His state of mind is irrelevant; if Fiona wants damages for the reasonable value of her trees, she can get it.

But if Fiona prefers a restitutionary recovery based upon the profits that Shrek received, Shrek's state of mind may be relevant. Consider these alternatives: (1) Shrek entered the land, innocently and reasonably believing that it was his own land (and his own timber), not Fiona's. (2) Shrek negligently thought the land (and timber) was his. (3) Shrek knew it was Fiona's land (and Fiona's timber), and he consciously chose to steal her timber.

Most courts (as well as the Restatement) would likely agree that in all three scenarios, Fiona would have the option of suing for damages or recovering Shrek's profits under a restitutionary recovery. But the measure of restitutionary recovery will differ depending upon Shrek's culpability. If Shrek acted innocently or negligently (the first two scenarios), Fiona is entitled only to the direct benefits received by Shrek (which in appropriate cases could be the reasonable rental or license value). In contrast, if he acted as a "conscious wrongdoer," Shrek "will be required to disgorge all gains (including consequential gains) derived from the wrongful transaction." RTR §40 cmt. *b*.

To make this a bit more concrete, let's apply some numbers to these concepts. Suppose that the market value of the unfinished trees taken from Fiona's land is $1,000. Shrek invests another $500 to process the trees into lumber, yielding lumber with a market value of $2,100. If Shrek is a conscious wrongdoer, he could have to pay the entire $2,100 gain to Fiona. In contrast, if Shrek was an innocent or negligent trespasser, a court could well give him a $500 credit for his costs in processing the lumber. He might even get credit for one-third of the $600 profit because he added one-third of

13. Recall that the language some jurisdictions use to describe this election of restitution: Brianna would "waive the tort" and sue in assumpsit. This is misleading because Brianna must prove the conversion by Anita: she's not waiving the tort at all. Instead, Brianna is *electing* to sue to recover Anita's gain rather than Brianna's loss.

the inputs ($500 processing cost divided by $1,500 in inputs to production) to produce the finished lumber. That one-third figure here is $200, meaning that Fiona might be able to obtain in restitution:

$2,100	(Shrek's profit)
− $ 500	(cost to Shrek for processing)
− $ 200	(portion of profits attributable to Shrek's inputs)
= $1,400[14]	

Either way, you can see that Fiona would prefer the restitutionary remedy. Damages get her only $1,000; restitution gets her either $2,000 or some lower amount of at least $1,400 depending upon the apportionment rules in the jurisdiction. There is one caveat to this point: if Shrek has acted as a conscious wrongdoer, his conduct might make him liable for punitive damages (discussed in Chapter 15). Punitive damages would be available if Fiona received compensatory damages; some jurisdictions would not allow punitive damages to be coupled with a claim in restitution. In making the election, Fiona (and her lawyers) will have to decide which looks like a more lucrative recovery for her.

Example 12

EXAMPLE

Kaavya writes her first novel. It sells well, earning her $100,000 in profits. Megan discovers that several the passages in the book have been copied from Megan's earlier novels. When confronted with the copied passages, Kaavya claims that the copying was innocent and done without the conscious intent to do so. She says she is a great fan of Megan's works and must have inadvertently copied the material. Is Megan entitled to Kaavya's profits, looking at the common law (and not the Copyright Act)?

Explanation

EXPLANATION

This hypothetical is based on a controversy surrounding the work of Kaavya Viswanathan. *See* Motoko Rich & Dinitia Smith, *Publisher to Recall Harvard Student's Novel*, N.Y. Times, Apr. 28, 2006. This is a case involving misappropriation of intellectual property, and because it is a copyright claim, in real life it is going to be governed by copyright law. Copyright law is strange in that it allows for the recovery of both actual damages and the profits of the infringer in some circumstances. *See* 17 U.S.C. §504(b); RTR §42, cmt. *d* (noting the potential for a double recovery if a plaintiff whose written work has been misappropriated could recover both damages and restitution).

14. We will look further at these issues of accounting and apportionment in the next chapter.

But the question asked you to consider this case only as a matter of the common law rules. Under the common law, the amount of restitution available to Megan could well depend upon whether Kaavya was a conscious wrongdoer. If she innocently copied the passages as claimed, the profits might be the value of a license to use the copyrighted material. Expert testimony on the cost of obtaining such a license appears necessary. To the extent it was conscious stealing of intellectual property, however, Kaavya might have to give up her entire $100,000 profit.

11.3 WHY ALLOW FOR THE RECOVERY OF DEFENDANT'S GAINS IN CASES OF UNJUST ENRICHMENT?

What explains why the law allows some plaintiffs to recover in restitution? There is no single answer because, as we saw in section 11.2, restitution is available for a variety of different claims.

In those cases involving mistaken payments and improvements, the rationale for restitution appears to approximate the *rightful position standard*: the position the plaintiff would have been in but for the wrong.[15] Restitution can serve in some cases to put plaintiff back in the position she would have been in before the plaintiff conferred a benefit on defendant.

Figure 11.1 illustrates this idea in connection with the law professor–bank hypothetical from the beginning of the chapter:

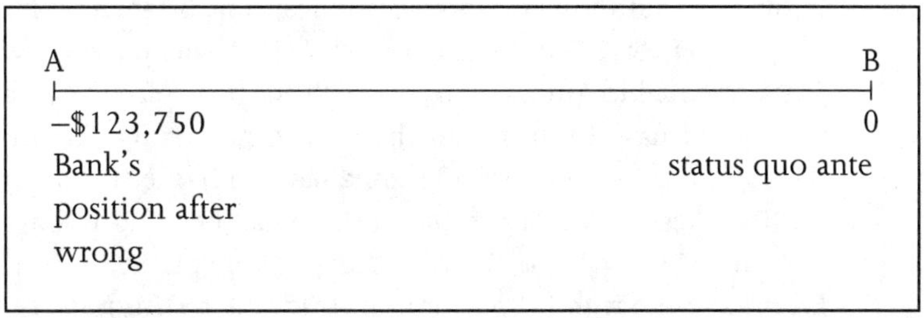

Figure 11.1

Recall that the bank owed the law professor $1,250 but paid the law professor $125,000 instead. Return of the excess $123,750 is necessary to put the parties back to the status quo ante position.

It is important to note that the analysis in Figure 11.1 *assumes* that there has been a wrong. That, of course, is what the substantive law of restitution needs to determine. Recall the Ella-Felice example, where Felice performs

15. The rightful position standard is discussed in the introduction and in Parts I and II as the main organizing principle for both compensatory damages and injunctions.

CPR on Ella, saving her life. If Felice is a doctor, the law allows her to recover the reasonable value of her services in restitution. We can conceive of that payment as moving Felice from position A (where she has conferred a benefit on Ella that has a reasonable value) back to B, the status quo ante. But recall that if Felice is a nonprofessional who gives CPR, she gets nothing *even though she still has conferred a benefit on Ella that has the same reasonable value*. So we must invoke the substantive law of restitution before we can use the rightful position standard as a justification for a payment for benefits conferred.

Though the rightful position standard can explain *some* restitution cases, it cannot explain *all* of them. Think again about Brianna, whose digital camera with a $200 value was stolen by Anita. Anita pawns the camera for $150, bets that money at a racetrack, and ends up with $1,000. Because Anita is a conscious wrongdoer, Brianna has a strong claim to recover the full $1,000 in restitution.

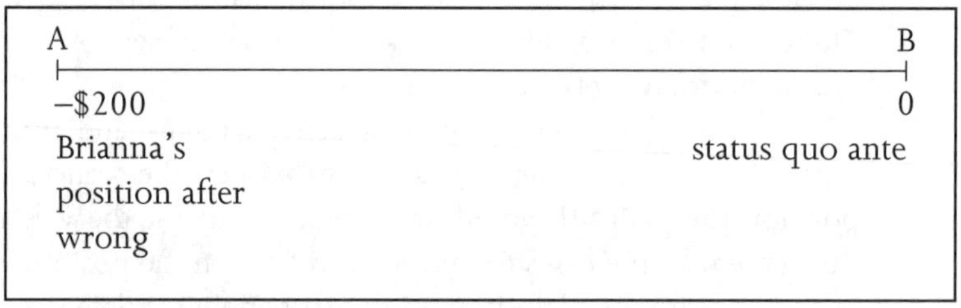

Figure 11.2

For those of you who have already reviewed Part I of this book, you know that, putting aside some complications, Brianna's tort damages would be (B – A), or $200. See Figure 11.2. If the jury could award Brianna an amount equal to Anita's gains of $1,000, she is placed in a *better position* than she would have been in had there been no wrong. The first $200 of that $1,000 award would bring Brianna back to B, the status quo ante. The next $800 makes her better off than if there had been no wrong.

The $800 gain to Brianna cannot be explained as an attempt to put Brianna in the rightful position. Instead, the restitutionary measure may be justified for two reasons: deterrence and punishment. We don't want conscious wrongdoers like Anita going around and taking things without permission. When these wrongdoers "bypass the market," they interfere with property rights in a way that offends both principles of justice (because people should not take what belongs to someone else) and principles of economics (because there would be a great deal of societal loss if we had to invest resources into protecting what we have rather than into new, productive activity). The potential for disgorgement of defendants' gains can deter wrongful activity and punish wrongdoers (serving a similar function to punitive damages that are potentially available only when a plaintiff seeks compensatory damages, not restitution).

This idea that restitution can serve deterrent and punitive functions is underlined by the fact that there are different measures of restitution in the case of conscious wrongdoers compared to innocent or negligent ones. When Shrek innocently converts Fiona's timber, the measure of restitution is one that comes closer to the rightful position standard: Fiona gets the value of her timber and a reasonable share of Shrek's profits. In contrast, when Shrek intentionally converts the timber, he must disgorge *all* his profits, even if he added substantial value to the timber before it was sold. In that case, restitution looks more like a deterrent and punishment.

EXAMPLE

Example 13

The rightful position standard arguably justifies allowing restitution for someone who confers a benefit in the course of performing under an unenforceable contract. What is the justification for allowing (a) non-breaching parties to recover restitution rather than contract damages in some cases, and (b) breaching parties to recover in restitution under certain circumstances?

EXPLANATION

Explanation

(a) The ability of non-breaching parties to choose restitution can be justified under the rightful position standard to the extent the non-breaching party would have difficulty proving contract damages, and the gains to the defendant and losses to the plaintiff are substantially equivalent. See RTR §38, cmts. *a*, *b*. To the extent that a non-breaching party can capture a breaching party's gains even when they exceed the value of the contract, restitution appears to serve a deterrent and punitive function.

(b) As far as breaching parties seeking restitution goes, the rationale appears to be to restore *the breaching party* to the rightful position, after the plaintiff has been put in that position. If anything, the rule giving the breaching party the right to restitution might create situations of underdeterrence.

11.4 MORE ON LOSING CONTRACTS: SHOULD THE CONTRACT PRICE BE THE CAP?

Recall the example discussed in section 11.2.5:

> A promises B to build a barn for $60,000. A is wrongfully discharged after completing part of the work and receiving $20,000 in progress payments. The court finds that the cost reasonably incurred by A in partial performance has been $30,000, and that the reasonable cost of completion (by A or anyone else) will be $45,000. From these facts the court determines that A has

performed 40 percent of the work covered by the contract: the price of this work at the contract rate is $24,000. A's claim to restitutionary damages is limited to $4,000 (representing the ratable portion of the contract price less $20,000 already paid).

As the example explains, the Restatement of Restitution takes the position that a non-breaching party's recovery in restitution should be capped by the amount of contract damages. (The exception here is for opportunistic breaches of contract, discussed above in 11.2.5.2.) That puts the Restatement position at odds with that taken by the Restatement of Contracts. RESTATEMENT (SECOND) OF CONTRACTS §373, cmt. *d* (1981). Under the alternative position, non-breaching plaintiffs in losing contracts are not limited by the contract price, and person A in the last illustration may recover the $30,000 benefit conferred on the breaching party. The rule of some jurisdictions allowing a non-breaching party to recover restitution exceeding the contract price is subject to an important limit: restitution is not available when the non-breaching party has *completed performance*. RTR §38, cmt. *d*.

Courts are split on their approaches to whether restitutionary measures should be capped by the amount of contract damages in the case of losing contracts. *See* RICHARD A. LORD, 24 WILLISTON ON CONTRACTS §64:5 n.8 (4th ed. 2018).

Which rule is better? In other words, *should* non-breaching parties to losing contracts be limited in restitution to the contract price? Again, it depends upon the reason that these parties are entitled to restitution. From the perspective of the rightful position, allowing the non-breaching party to recover in restitution an amount exceeding the contract price puts the party in a *better position* than had there been no contract. In our hypothetical, A is better off with B's breach than had B performed: A may recover $30,000, more than if there would have been no breach. In this way, the cap could be justified as keeping contracting parties in the rightful position. On the other hand, from the perspective of deterrence and punishment, it may be better to have no cap. But that might upset the expectations of contracting parties.

Example 14

EXAMPLE

Gerry is a contractor who has substantially completed a major remodel of Harry's kitchen. The contract price is $40,000, and Harry paid half in advance. Harry tells Gerry that he won't pay the $20,000 remaining because he believes Gerry's work is shoddy. In fact, Gerry's work has been perfect, and it is Harry who has breached the contract under applicable contract law. Gerry has spent $50,000 so far on remodeling, which is the reasonable value of the contracting work, and needs to put in about another $500 to complete the project. What, if anything, can Gerry recover in restitution?

Explanation

Gerry is a party to a losing contract. He agreed to remodel Harry's kitchen for a contract price of $40,000, and complete performance is going to cost $50,500. For those of you who have completed Part I, you know that Gerry's contract damages would be $20,000, the remainder of the contract price, which Harry has not paid. Gerry, however, would like to recover $30,000 in restitution, the difference between the reasonable value of what he has provided ($50,000) and what he has received ($20,000).

In some jurisdictions following the Restatement, Gerry's restitutionary recovery would be capped at $20,000, the amount of contract damages. In other jurisdictions, restitution may exceed the contract price, meaning Gerry has a chance to recover the $30,000. Harry, however, would argue that restitution should not be available because Gerry has completed performance, leaving Gerry only with contract damages. There are just a few odds and ends to fix up (worth $500): is Gerry's performance really completed? In a jurisdiction without a cap, but with the rule barring restitution when there is completed performance, the court will have to decide whether or not Gerry's performance was really complete. Such a ruling could in fact turn on the relative culpability of the parties, especially the reason why Harry breached, though a court might not discuss culpability as the legal basis for the ruling.

CHAPTER 12

Unjust Enrichment: Measuring Ill-Gotten Gains and Apportioning Profits

12.1 MEASURING ILL-GOTTEN GAINS

The previous chapter explained the circumstances under which a plaintiff may recover a defendant's gain through restitution. It dealt with the "unjust" aspect of the "unjust enrichment" principle. This chapter and the next explore the meaning of "enrichment," specifically, how courts identify and measure the defendant's gains. As we shall see, in some circumstances, the extent of the defendant's "injustice" (or culpability) sometimes can affect how courts measure "enrichment."

Consider the following scenarios in which a plaintiff might seek a restitutionary remedy, some of which are drawn from the discussion in the preceding chapter. Ask yourself how courts should measure the defendant's gain, if any:

- Gwen accidentally runs over Horatio's foot with her Maserati, causing Horatio to suffer $10,000 in damages.
- The bank, owing the law professor $1,250 from a bank account, mistakenly pays the professor $125,000.
- Dr. Felice, a cardiac surgeon, performs emergency CPR on an unconscious Ella, saving Ella's life. Dr. Felice normally charges $5,000 for a consultation. A reasonable fee for a professional performing CPR is $700. Ella's life is insured for $3 million.
- Anita steals Brianna's digital camera, worth $200. She sells it to a pawnshop for $150 and bets the money at the racetrack. Anita does well at the track, and the $150 is now worth $1,000. Anita is bankrupt.

- Shrek enters onto Fiona's land, taking timber with a market value of $1,000. Shrek invests another $500 to process the trees into lumber, which he sells on the market for $2,100.

By the time you are done with this chapter and the next, you should be comfortable answering the question of how courts are likely to measure the defendant's gain in these and other scenarios. For now, notice the following kinds of questions that these hypotheticals raise about restitutionary remedies: Do we measure value based upon the market? Should we measure the value of the gain to the defendant or the plaintiff's cost of providing the gain? If a defendant takes a misappropriated item and mixes it with his own labor or materials, must the defendant give up all of his gains, or just a portion? If a portion, which portion? If a defendant sells or exchanges a misappropriated item for something else, can the plaintiff get that new item? Should it matter if the defendant is bankrupt and there are other creditors who want the new item? These questions form the core of issues surrounding restitutionary measures of recovery.

We begin with two basic principles for measuring defendants' gains. The first principle, noted in the last chapter, is that *restitution is not available when a defendant has no gains*. Horatio may be able to sue Gwen successfully for negligence for running over his foot, but the remedy will be the remedy of tort damages, not restitution.

Second, *the measurement issue is easy when the transfer from plaintiff to defendant involves cash or another easily valued item*, at least when the defendant is not bankrupt, and the defendant has not traded the cash for a different item. *See* RTR §49(2) ("Enrichment from a money payment is measured by the amount of the payment or the resulting increase in the defendant's net assets, whichever is less."). Consider again the law professor–bank hypothetical: here, it is hard to argue for any measure of gain besides the difference between the amount paid to the law professor ($125,000) and the amount the professor was owed ($1,250), a total of $123,750.

In a case such as the law professor–bank hypothetical, the restitutionary award usually would be *embodied in a money judgment, enforceable in the same way as a money judgment for damages.*[1] If the law professor is insolvent, or if the money has been used to purchase another asset, the bank would likely prefer an equitable restitutionary remedy, such as a constructive trust or an equitable lien. These additional restitutionary remedies are discussed in the next chapter.

Measurement problems arise when (1) the transfer from plaintiff to defendant does not involve an easily quantifiable gain (think Dr. Felice–Ella) or (2) the defendant has mixed the item misappropriated from plaintiff with other items to produce an integrated product that yields profits to the

---

1. Chapter 17.1 discusses the rules for enforcement of money judgments.

defendant (think Shrek-Fiona). We'll deal with that first kind of problem now, and with the second problem in the next part of this chapter.

Consider Dr. Felice and Ella. Suppose the reasonable market value of a doctor's services is $700. Dr. Felice, however, is a famous (and expensive) cardiac surgeon who charges $5,000 for a consultation. These measurements reflect the market cost of the services. From the defendant's perspective, the gain is much more. Consider the immense benefit to Ella, whose life is saved. Though measuring the value of her life is fraught with difficulties (see the discussion in Chapter 4 on the problem in the context of tort damages), one piece of evidence of the value of Ella's life is her life insurance, which is set at $3 million.

Generally speaking, Dr. Felice is entitled to recover only the reasonable value of defendant's services, measured by a competitive market and not the idiosyncrasies of the plaintiff or defendant. The leading case on point is *Cotnam v. Wisdom*, 104 S.W. 164 (Ark. 1907). A doctor came to the aid of a person thrown from a streetcar. The doctor rendered emergency aid, but the person died. The doctor sued to recover from the estate. The Arkansas Supreme Court held that the doctor could successfully state a cause of action in *quasi-contract*.[2]

As to the *amount* of recovery, the court rejected the idea that the plaintiff could introduce evidence that the person aided by the doctor was wealthy even though the evidence showed that doctors at the time set their fees in part based upon a patient's ability to pay:

> In order to admit such testimony, it must be assumed that the surgeon and patient each had in contemplation that the means of the patient would be one factor in determining the amount of the charge for the services rendered. While the law may admit such evidence as throwing light upon the contract and indicating what was really in contemplation when it was made, yet a different question is presented when there is no contract to be ascertained or construed, but a mere fiction of law creating a contract where none existed in order that there might be a remedy for a right. *This fiction merely requires a reasonable*

2. *Quasi-contract* is another term for restitution that uses the fiction that the parties had a contract. Sometimes this will be referred to as a contract "implied in law." Don't be confused by the contractual terminology. There could be no valid contract between the parties, as one of the parties was unconscious. Under either the old, subjective "meeting of the minds" test or the modern, objective theory of contract, there is no way that any court would say that the parties entered into a voluntary transaction that formed the basis for a valid contract. Instead, the court allows recovery through the fiction of an "implied" or "quasi" contract to allow the suit in restitution.

Here is how the Arkansas Supreme Court explained *quasi-contract* in *Cotnam*: "A contract implied by law . . . rests upon no evidence. It has no actual existence. It is simply a mythical creation of the law. The law says it shall be taken that there was a promise, when in point of fact, there was none. Of course this is not good logic, for the obvious and sufficient reason that it is not true. It is a legal fiction, resting wholly for its support on a plain legal obligation, and a plain legal right. If it were true, it would not be a fiction."

> *compensation for the services rendered.* The services are the same be the patient prince or pauper, and for them the surgeon is entitled to fair compensation for his time, service, and skill. It was therefore error to admit this evidence, and to instruct the jury in the second instruction that in determining what was a reasonable charge they could consider the "ability to pay of the person operated upon." (Emphasis added.)

Cotnam certainly is authority for the principle that courts should use the reasonable value of the plaintiff's services rather than the benefit to the defendant in assessing the amount of restitution. *See also* LAYCOCK & HASEN p. 656 ("The benefit in these cases is measured by the market value of the treatment, whether or not successful, and not by the value of the life saved or the pain and suffering avoided."). But *Cotnam* does not directly say the reasonable value should either be set at the $700 reasonable market value for a medical professional's giving of CPR or the $5,000 typical fee of the doctor. The better argument is that the $700 fee is more appropriate because the $5,000 typical fee is likely imposed for rendering more complex diagnosis and treatment by the cardiac surgeon than for rendering services roughly equivalent to giving CPR. Indeed, if a lawyer who earns $500 an hour gives up her time to give Ella CPR, the lawyer gets nothing because it is presumed that good Samaritans render services gratuitously (without expectation of payment); the lawyer does not get her usual hourly rate.

In a situation such as that involving an unconscious patient, the law's measure of recovery is a moderate one. It is a measure that makes sense if you think about the kind of transaction the parties likely would have entered into had they been able to freely bargain (but for prohibitive transaction costs). In a free market, the patient would have expected to pay for the reasonable value of a doctor's services. Though Dr. Felice, the cardiac surgeon, might not have been interested in work that would pay her only $700 instead of her $5,000 fee, she would reasonably understand that if she agreed to do work worth $700, a patient would likely pay her only that amount.

The unconscious patient such as Ella who receives gains is innocent; there was nothing wrongful about her conduct (except perhaps her unwillingness to pay the doctor after she rendered CPR). When the defendant is more culpable, however, courts allow plaintiffs more generous measures of a defendant's gains. Consider Shrek again. Recall that he enters onto Fiona's land, taking timber with a market value of $1,000. He invests another $500 to process the trees into lumber, which he sells on the market for $2,100. As noted in the last chapter, the Third Restatement of Restitution and Unjust Enrichment takes the position that if the defendant is a conscious wrongdoer—here, if Shrek knew the trees belonged to Fiona and he took them anyway—he could have to give up *all* of his profits, even those that are attributable to the $500 worth of processing that he put into the lumber.[3] Shrek, the conscious wrongdoer, has enrichment measured in a pro-plaintiff manner because he has engaged in especially unjust behavior.[4]

The famous case of *Olwell v. Nye & Nissen Co.*, 173 P.2d 652 (Wash. 1946) is another example of a court using a tough—indeed punitive—measure of defendant's gains in a case of a defendant deliberately bypassing the market. In *Olwell*, plaintiff sold his interest in an egg packing business, but not an egg washing machine, to defendant. The plaintiff's machine was stored next to defendant's leased property, but not on the defendant's property. The defendant's treasurer, without seeking permission of the plaintiff, had the egg washing machine taken out of storage; apparently the defendant needed the machine because of a labor shortage during World War II. Defendant used the machine for about three years before the plaintiff learned of its use. When plaintiff found out, plaintiff offered to sell defendant the machine for $600; defendant countered with a $50 counteroffer, which plaintiff rejected. Plaintiff then sued for conversion, "waived the tort," and sued in assumpsit for restitution. The court awarded plaintiff a money judgment for $1,560, representing the labor cost saved by defendant of $10 per week for the period of 156 weeks. The appellate court upheld this measure of restitution.

In understanding the case, it is important to begin with what is *not* at issue. First, there is no question that the plaintiff, who owned the egg washing machine, was wronged. Defendant took and used plaintiff's property without permission. Nor does there seem any doubt that under substantive principles of restitution, the plaintiff could elect to receive a restitutionary remedy based upon defendant's gain rather than the plaintiff's loss. The question is how to *measure* the defendant's gain. Here, there are at least three options:

1. *The reasonable value of the machine.* The plaintiff offered to sell the machine for $600, which is pretty good evidence of (the upper value) of the machine.
2. *The reasonable rental value.* The Defendant argued for the reasonable rental value of the machine, which was probably somewhere at or below the $600 figure for owning the machine. (If the amount were higher

3. In the next section, we'll talk about how to apportion those profits if a court believes they should be apportioned.

4. As a "conscious wrongdoer," Shrek "will be stripped of gains from unauthorized interference with another's property." RTR §40 cmt. *b*. "However, courts are sometimes visibly reluctant to measure the unjust enrichment of a conscious trespasser by the full cost of making alternative arrangements, or by the full extent of consequential gains that an intentional trespass may have facilitated. Even against a conscious wrongdoer, restitution may be limited to avoid a liability for gains that are unduly remote (§51(5)(a)) or disproportionate to the loss on which liability is based (§58(3)(c))." *Id.*

to rent the machine for three years, a rational buyer would choose to buy the machine rather than rent it.)

3. *The profits defendant received from using the machine.* In this case, the court determined that the defendant saved $10 per week by not having to pay workers to wash the eggs in a less labor-efficient way, leading to savings of over $1,500.

The award of $1,500 gives a generous benefit to plaintiff, but at a high cost to defendant. The court in *Olwell* appeared to justify this measure by pointing to the defendant's "consciously tortious" actions, and so it might be that the higher measure is necessary to punish the defendant for willfully bypassing what could have been a voluntary market transaction, and to deter similar actions by others in the future. The Third Restatement endorses the principle that the measure of unjust enrichment depends in part on culpability. RTR §40, cmt. *b*.[5]

If you don't see the deterrence point, ask yourself this question: if the measure of restitution was the reasonable rental value that plaintiff would have charged defendant, what incentive would an unscrupulous defendant have to negotiate for the rental of the egg washing machine? If defendant is caught, the defendant pays what it should have paid in a fair transaction. If defendant is not caught, the defendant pays nothing.[6]

To understand how the measure of market gain might fluctuate depending upon the defendant's culpability, consider whether the court would have upheld the $1,560 award if the defendant's treasurer, who ordered the machine taken out of storage, did not know (and perhaps reasonably could

---

5. The Restatement provides that innocent recipients of enrichment generally pay "by the standard that yields the smallest liability in restitution" for unrequested benefits, but "[u]njust enrichment from requested benefits is measured by their reasonable value to the recipient. Reasonable value is normally the lesser of market value and a price the recipient has expressed a willingness to pay." RTR §50. For those enriched by misconduct, unjust enrichment is "not less than their market value." RTR §51. For "conscious wrongdoers," "the unjust enrichment . . . is the net profit attributable to the underlying wrong. The object of restitution in such cases is to eliminate profit from wrongdoing while avoiding, so far as possible, the imposition of a penalty." *Id.* Finally, the Restatement offers a third, middle category of recipients of enrichment who are not wrongdoers, but who are enriched for other reasons, such as their own negligence. These recipients in appropriate cases may be liable for greater liability in restitution than innocent wrongdoers. RTR §52 (They "may be subject to a greater liability in restitution than an innocent recipient of the same benefits, in order that the defendant rather than the claimant bear the costs of the transaction.").

6. This analysis suggests that if society wishes to deter those who infringe in the market, the measure of the gains should be substantial. Consider this example. Suppose that the reasonable rental value in *Olwell* is $600 and the profits to defendant are $1,560. Defendant knows that there is only a 25% chance the plaintiff will sue the defendant for conversion and recover in restitution for $1,560. That means the expected loss to the defendant of breaking the law is $390 (25% chance of paying $1,560), compared to a sure payment of $600 for the honest rental of the machine. An unscrupulous, risk-neutral defendant would still decide to bypass the market and take the chance on being caught.

not have known) that the machine belonged to the plaintiff. It seems more likely the court would have chosen a lower rental or sale value.

There is one important caveat to the principles set forth in this chapter. To the extent that a defendant misappropriates intellectual property (for example, infringes on copyrighted material or a patent), the measure of recovery is dictated primarily by federal statutory law and not general restitutionary principles. Infringers of patents, for example, are liable only for damages (and may be penalized up to three times the amount of damages). 35 U.S.C. §284 (2000). But an alternative restitutionary measure is not allowed. *See* RTR §42, cmt. *c* ("The Patent Act of 1946 has been interpreted (though only since 1964) to foreclose a claim by the patentee to disgorgement of the infringer's profits. Were it not for this statutory bar, the rule of this section would authorize such a claim against a conscious infringer—as did previous versions of the Patent Act, and as did the current version as previously interpreted.").

Copyright law provides another interesting remedy. 17 U.S.C. §504(b) (2004) allows recovery of a plaintiff's "actual damages" along with "profits of the infringer that are attributable to the infringement and are not taken into account in computing the actual damages."[7] The Restatement notes the risk of "double counting" from this formula that could lead to "a recovery exceeding *both* the claimant's loss and the infringer's profit." It calls such an outcome "strictly anomalous in restitution terms." RTR §42, cmt. *d*.

State statutes in appropriate circumstances also may alter or augment the common law for particular types of claims. It is always worth checking relevant state statutes.

EXAMPLE

Example 1

Andy's tire blows out while he's driving on State Route 5 in a remote area during a cold winter. There is no cell phone reception. He has no spare tire and does not know how to change a spare tire. After three hours with no one on the road, he spots Betty, a retired accountant who is driving down the road. He's very happy because if Betty had not come by, he would have suffered from hypothermia or worse. He stops Betty's car and asks her for help. Betty says: "I'm no good Samaritan, but I've got a tire that would fit on your car. I'll sell you the tire and put it on for $1,000." (A towing company would have charged Andy $150 for the service call and $100 for the tire.) Andy reluctantly agrees, promising to send Betty a check for $1,000 when he gets back home. Betty puts the tire on Andy's car, and Andy safely goes on his way. Andy does not send Betty the check. Betty sues Andy for breach of contract or, in the event the contract is unenforceable, for restitution.

7. Section 504(c) gives plaintiff an alternative to elect "statutory damages," which may be more advantageous for plaintiffs in certain circumstances.

Assume a court would hold the contract void on grounds of duress. To what amount, if any, is Betty entitled in restitution?

Explanation

Assuming the contract is void for duress, Betty should be able to recover the reasonable value of what she provided Andy, at least as to the tire. Betty will *not* be able to obtain the value to Andy of being saved from hypothermia, or worse. The best evidence of the tire's value is the $100 that a towing company would have charged Andy, though Betty could have other evidence. The $1,000 bargain was struck during conditions of bilateral monopoly (where there is only one buyer and one seller, meaning an efficient price won't emerge through competition) and duress, and is likely not good evidence of the value of the transaction.

Under the substantive law of restitution, there's a question of whether Betty is entitled to recover anything in restitution for the value of her services in putting on the tire (as opposed to the value of the tire itself). Betty is not a professional, and the presumption is that non-professionals who render emergency services do so gratuitously. In this case, Betty can likely overcome that presumption because she told Andy up front that she was "no Good Samaritan" and would not help him except for a fee. For this reason, a court could well allow Betty to recover the $150 reasonable value of the services provided. This is analogous to the "necessity" issue discussed in the next example. It seems only fair that a person who has benefited in times of emergency pay the reasonable costs of rescue after the emergency is over.

Example 2

The *S.S. Minnow* was a tourist boat out at sea for a three-hour tour. The weather started getting rough; the tiny ship was tossed. Thanks to the courage of the fearless Skipper and his first mate, Gilligan, the ship was brought safely into Davy Jones's dock as the storm was raging. Though Jones protested, Skipper and Gilligan kept the ship tied to the dock, to prevent the loss of life and property damage that would have resulted had the *S.S. Minnow* remained at sea. The dock suffered $500 in damages. Had the ship not remained at the dock, it is likely that there would have been $50,000 in personal injury and property damage. A reasonable fee to dock the boat under normal circumstances would have been $50.

Tort law provides that under conditions of "necessity," a person may use another's private property even without permission. *See Ploof v. Putnam*, 71 A. 188 (Vt. 1908). But the plaintiff whose property has been damaged should be able to recover damages or restitution. If plaintiff Jones seeks restitution, how should it be measured?

EXPLANATION

Explanation

Arguably, the amount of restitution should be $50, the normal dock fee that Jones would have charged in normal conditions. If Jones could show that he charged additional docking fees during inclement weather—perhaps to compensate for the increased risk of dock damage during such conditions—he perhaps could be entitled to those additional fees as well. If all Jones could get in restitution is $50 (or a bit more if additional fees are allowed), he could well prefer to sue for damages, possibly recovering the $500 worth of damage to the dock.

Wait a minute, you might say. In *Olwell*, the defendant chose not to enter into a voluntary transaction, and consciously chose to bypass the market. The penalty was that the defendant had to give up all those consequential gains, the labor savings equal to $1,560. Why doesn't that same reasoning apply here? Skipper and Gilligan docked the ship against the owner's wishes, again bypassing the market. Maybe they should have to pay the consequential gains of $50,000.

That reasoning is likely flawed, because Skipper and Gilligan did not bypass the market in the way that the defendant did in *Olwell*. In *Olwell*, there was presumably a functioning market for egg washing machines. The plaintiff could have rented his egg washing machine to defendant or refused to do so; the defendant could have agreed to rent the machine from plaintiff or refused to do so. There was no emergency.

In contrast, in the emergency *S.S. Minnow* hypothetical, there was no possibility of free bargaining. It is true that Skipper tried to get permission from Jones, who refused, but this was under the conditions of a non-working market. Again, we have a bilateral monopoly: there is only one buyer (Skipper and Gilligan) and only one seller (Jones). In such circumstances, parties are not expected to bargain to efficient results. It is just like a bargain struck under duress, which a court would void had they entered into a one-sided bargain under these conditions.

The lack of a well-functioning market means that the court would likely excuse defendants' bypassing of the market. Moreover, Skipper and Gilligan are not "conscious wrongdoers" in the way the *Olwell* defendant was; in other words, a court would likely say that the *S.S. Minnow* "needed" the dock more than the *Olwell* defendant "needed" the egg washing machine.

12.2 APPORTIONING PROFITS

In cases where a misappropriated item has been mixed with other items to create a benefit for the misappropriator, courts have to determine a method for calculating the appropriate amount of profits to award to the plaintiff whose item has been misappropriated. To get a handle on these issues of *apportioning profits*, let's look at my favorite case to teach in Remedies, *Gaste v. Kaiserman*, 863 F.2d 1061 (2d Cir. 1988).

Gaste involves an awful musical hit from the 1970s called "Feelings."[8] Here's a sample of the song's lyrics:

Feelings, wo-o-o feelings
wo-o-o, feel you again in my arms.

Though "Feelings" was a hit in the 1970s, it turns out that the song's author, Morris Albert, wrote the lyrics but stole the melody from a 1956 French song, "Pour toi," written by a Frenchman named Louis Gaste. Gaste sued Albert (whose real last name was Kaiserman) as well as Albert's publisher, Fermata, for copyright infringement. The jury determined that Albert had indeed misappropriated the music from Gaste. Gaste did not claim credit for the words.

From the perspective of a Remedies course, the interesting question is what a court should do once it has been determined that a misappropriated item was mixed with other items to produce something profiting defendant. Here we have a typical example of a mixture of an appropriated item (in this case, the infringed melody—a protected intellectual property right) with non-appropriated inputs (most importantly, in this case, the words to the song, "Feelings"). Individuals were buying the "package" of words and melody together, and Albert and Fermata had expenses associated with selling the package. The question becomes how these costs and revenues should be disentangled.

Let me assign some (fictional) numbers to this case to illustrate the choices facing the court. Assume the following numbers:

\$300,000	Gross receipts from the sale of the song "Feelings" for the year in question
\$50,000	Fermata's variable costs for creating the song and marketing it (these are costs that Fermata would not have incurred had the song "Feelings" not been sold)
\$500,000	Fermata's fixed costs for overhead during the relevant period (Fermata marketed 100 songs for the relevant period; revenues from "Feelings" made up 25% of its total revenue)

8. My Remedies students are subjected to my singing of the song *a cappella* to introduce this case. It is an experience they will never forget (even with years of therapy)'!

$60,000	Royalties for "Feelings" paid by Fermata to Albert, who spent 50 hours writing, working on, and recording the song
$10,000, plus 10% of Albert's profits	A reasonable royalty that the parties would have negotiated but for Albert's stealing of the music from Gaste

The reasonable royalty figure ($10,000 plus 10% of Albert's profits) might be a reasonable approximation of Gaste's damages. This is the loss that Gaste incurred but for Albert's misappropriation of his music. Under the principles of Part I of this book, awarding this royalty figure arguably puts Gaste back into the rightful position—the position Gaste would have been in but for Albert's wrong.

Let's turn to the "infringer's profits," however, which copyright law says that Gaste is entitled to as well (from both Albert and Fermata). The amount due to Gaste is not immediately obvious, which is why a court will order an *accounting for profits* to determine the appropriate amount of profits payable to plaintiffs in restitution cases like this one.

Turning first to Fermata, it seems clear that $300,000 does not represent Fermata's *profits*. This number instead represents the *income* that Fermata has received from sales of the song "Feelings." To get to Fermata's profits, we need to subtract the $50,000 in variable costs Fermata had in marketing and selling the song, and the $60,000 it paid Albert in royalties. That brings us from $300,000 down to $190,000.

Fermata also has an argument that a portion of its $500,000 in "fixed costs" (utility bills, rent, salaries), which it must pay regardless of the sales of "Feelings," should be deducted. A stingy allocation might give Fermata just $5,000 for this overhead, because "Feelings" was just 1 of 100 songs (or 1% of the $500,000 costs). A more generous measure would allocate a whopping $125,000 for this overhead because "Feelings'" sales made up 25% of the revenues for the company (and 25% of $500,000 is $125,000).

The courts vary in how they treat the question of subtracting out portions of overhead. The Second Circuit has said that infringers must demonstrate a "direct and valid nexus between each claimed overhead expense category and the production of" the infringing product. Then the infringer must propose a "fair and acceptable [allocation] formula." *Hamil America, Inc. v. GFI*, 193 F.3d 92 (2d Cir. 1999). The Ninth Circuit has suggested that willful infringers cannot deduct any fixed costs for overhead. *Frank Music Corp. v. Metro-Goldwyn-Mayer, Inc.*, 772 F.2d 505 (9th Cir. 1985). A good rule of thumb in those jurisdictions which allow deductions for fixed costs is that the more culpable the infringer, the likelier the court is going to be stingy about deducting expenses for overhead.

The Restatement rejects what it terms "punitive accounting" that would "disallow a provable deduction, logically relevant to a determination of the net profit attributable to the infringement" in the case of conscious wrongdoers. RTR §42, cmt. i. It recognizes, however, that the infringer "bears the burden of proof and the risk of uncertainty," and that "a court may properly adjust the stringency of the defendant's evidentiary burden in response to the character of the defendant's wrongdoing." *Id.* It further provides that when it comes to conscious wrongdoers, "the court may apply such tests of causation and remoteness, may make such apportionments, may recognize such credits or deductions, and may assign such evidentiary burdens, as reason and fairness dictate, consistent with the object of restitution as specified in subsection (4)." RTR §51(5).

Suppose the court determines that Fermata was not a conscious wrongdoer (Fermata did not know that Albert had stolen the music for the song from Gaste), and the court allows the deduction of $125,000 in fixed costs,[9] bringing the total profits down to $65,000:

$300,000	(receipts)
– $ 50,000	(variable costs)
– $ 60,000	(royalty payments)
– $125,000	(portion of fixed costs)
= $ 65,000	

Some courts might allow Gaste to recover this full $65,000 amount from Fermata. *See, e.g.*, *Maier Brewing Co. v. Fleischmann Distilling Corp.*, 390 F.2d 117 (9th Cir. 1968) (awarding all profits from infringing product to plaintiff without apportioning portion of profits due to infringement).

Other courts, however, would say that it is appropriate to apportion the $65,000 in profits to account for the fact the success of the song was attributable in part to the (misappropriated) melody of "Feelings" and in part to the (non-appropriated) words. In the actual *Gaste* case, the jury was asked to come up with such an apportionment, and it determined that 80% of the song's value came from the music and only 20% from the words.

Indeed, my favorite fact from *Gaste* is the following: "[Albert's expert] testified that he 'loved' the song 'Feelings' and that he believed the title and lyrics were 'far better' than the music itself. Nonetheless, he was unable to recall the words to the song on the stand and yet was able to sing the opening tune." (Talk about not adequately preparing an expert witness!)

9. In the actual *Gaste* case, the court rejected Fermata's argument that it should get to deduct 90% of its overhead because "Feelings" contributed to 90% of Fermata's profits.

Under this 80/20 allocation, Gaste would be entitled to $52,000 from Fermata, representing 80% of its $65,000 profits. (The entitlement would obviously be higher if a court allowed a smaller—or no—deduction to Fermata for the portion of its fixed costs.)

So to summarize our first-cut analysis on how to account for—and apportion—profits in cases of misappropriated items, follow these steps:

1. Identify revenues from misappropriated/mixed item;
   then
2. Deduct variable costs;
   then
3. Deduct appropriate portion of fixed costs if allowed by court (evidentiary burden and method of allocation may depend upon culpability of infringer);
   and finally,
4. Apportion profits attributable to misappropriated item in mixed item cases using some reasonable method of apportionment, except that some courts will refuse to apportion and will award *all* profits to the plaintiff.

When it comes to Albert (as opposed to Fermata), the analysis has a few more twists. Recall in our example we said that Albert earned $60,000 in royalties from Fermata for the sale of the song "Feelings." Like Fermata, Albert wants to be able to deduct his expenses, and like Fermata, Albert wants to have as much of the allocation as possible for the song's profits attributable to anything besides the misappropriated item.

Some courts will put two roadblocks in Albert's path. First, they won't allow Albert to deduct the value of his own labor. Even if Albert spent 50 hours writing the song (and suppose we could place an hourly value on that 50 hours), some courts hold that a wrongdoer cannot deduct the cost of his own labor; he can only deduct things he has *bought and paid for. See* Laycock & Hasen, p. 699. In addition, some courts reason that in performing the allocation of profits for the infringing and non-infringing portions of the work, the infringer could not get credit for the extent of profits attributable to the infringer's general reputation. *See Sheldon v. Metro-Goldwyn Pictures Corp.*, 309 U.S. 390, 407 (1940) (affirming the trial court's ruling that infringing defendants "could not count the effect of 'their standing and reputation in the industry'" in apportioning profits.).

In the actual *Gaste* case, the court said there was no percentage of profits attributable to Albert's reputation because he was unknown. But the court referred to a similar dispute involving one of the Beatles, George Harrison. Harrison had written a song called "My Sweet Lord," which infringed on the music from an earlier hit, "She's So Fine." The court in *ABKCO Music, Inc. v. Harrisongs Music, Ltd.*, 508 F. Supp. 798 (S.D.N.Y. 1981), found that 75% of the song's profitability came from the value of the lyrics of "My Sweet Lord" *and* George Harrison's general reputation.[10]

Suppose that of that 75%, a jury would determine that 40% of the value came from the lyrics and 35% from Harrison's general reputation—some people would just buy whatever song Harrison recorded. In some jurisdictions, then, Harrison, as a wrongdoer, could not get the allocation for the 35% of the profits attributable to his reputation; that percentage of the profits would go to the plaintiff, whose song was infringed. Note that in *ABKCO* itself, the court gave the infringer credit for profits attributable to Harrison's own reputation.

Adding in these complications, we now have a more complete picture of the means of apportioning profits in these mixed misappropriation cases:

1. Identify revenues from misappropriated/mixed item;
   then
2. Deduct variable costs, *but (in some courts) not costs associated with the infringer's own labor;*
   then
3. Deduct appropriate portion of fixed costs, if allowed by court (evidentiary burden and method of allocation may depend upon culpability of infringer);
   and finally,
4. Apportion profits attributable to misappropriated item in mixed item cases using some reasonable method of apportionment, except that some courts will refuse to apportion, awarding *all* profits to the plaintiff; *some courts that will allocate do not give the infringer any credit for profits attributable to the infringer's reputation.*

To bring this back to the apportionment in *Gaste*, in some courts Albert would have very little by way of deductions from his $60,000 in profits. He would have to point to any variable costs associated with producing the song "Feelings," along with a portion of his fixed costs if allowed by the court. Then the court would award a percentage based

10. Unlike *Sheldon*, the *ABKCO* court did not seem to have a problem with counting the value of Harrison's reputation, though it noted that had the court found that Harrison deliberately plagiarized the music, it would have awarded *all* the profits of "My Sweet Lord" to the plaintiffs.

upon the jury's allocation of the profitability of the songs, in some places, not considering any profit as a result of Albert's reputation. It could be that Albert would have to pay 80% of the full $60,000, or $48,000, to Gaste. Even worse for Albert: a court could refuse to apportion, awarding Gaste $60,000.

Example 3

Shrek enters onto Fiona's land, taking timber with a market value of $1,000. Shrek invests another $500 to process the trees into lumber, which he sells on the market for $2,100. How much should a court award Fiona in restitution?

Explanation

This is a mixed misappropriation example, just like the *Gaste* case discussed in the text. Here, Shrek has mixed Fiona's misappropriated lumber with his $500 investment to yield the finished lumber. Let's work our way through the four steps.

1. Identify revenues from misappropriated/mixed item.

In this case, it is easy to identify the revenues. Shrek sold the finished lumber for $2,100.

2. Deduct variable costs, but (in some courts) not costs associated with the infringer's own labor.

The facts tell us that Shrek invested $500 to finish the lumber. To the extent these represent variable costs that Shrek "bought and paid for," a court is likely to deduct the full $500, bringing the amount down to $1,600. If this $500 includes the value of Shrek's own labor, that is likely to be excluded (at least if Shrek is a willful infringer) on grounds that courts don't want to give infringers credit for the time they spend misappropriating items from others or using misappropriated items for their own profits.

3. Deduct appropriate portion of fixed costs, if allowed by court (evidentiary burden and method of allocation may depend upon culpability of infringer).

Shrek will have the burden of proving any of his fixed costs. The facts don't tell us about any fixed costs. We are still at $1,600.

4. Apportion profits attributable to misappropriated item in mixed item cases using some reasonable method of apportionment. However, some courts will refuse to apportion, awarding *all* profits to the plaintiff; some courts that will allocate do not give the infringer any credit for profits attributable to the infringer's reputation.

It seems unlikely that the price of the finished lumber was in any way enhanced by Shrek's reputation. If Shrek was a conscious wrongdoer (i.e., he entered Fiona's land with the intent to steal her lumber), a court might award Fiona the full $1,600. If Shrek was not a conscious wrongdoer (and even if he was one, in certain courts), the court might allow an allocation between Shrek and Fiona's contribution to the profit. Fiona's contribution was worth $1,000, or two-thirds of the total value of the inputs. Shrek's contribution was $500, or one-third of the total value of the inputs. A court might award Fiona two-thirds of $1,600, or $1,067. A somewhat more generous approach would be to award Fiona the $1,000 value of her stolen timber, along with two-thirds of the $600 in real profits on the transaction (remember, there was a $2,100 sale price after Fiona's forced contribution of $1,000 worth of timber and Shrek's $500 in expenses). That allocation would give Fiona $1,400 and leave Shrek (after taking his $500 expense into account) with $200. If a court refused to apportion, Fiona could get everything.

Whether Fiona could get $1,600, $1,067, or $1,400, the choice of restitution appears to make sense for Fiona, who could get only $1,000 if she chose damages as her remedy rather than restitution. The only benefit to Fiona of seeking damages is if she could get punitive damages as an additional remedy, a remedy which, as noted in the last chapter, is not available in some jurisdictions to a plaintiff who elects restitution over punitive damages.

One other point on choice of remedies questions here: state statutes might provide for more generous damages remedies, such as a trebling of actual damages in stolen lumber cases. Fiona's lawyer will need to determine if statutory law displaces the common law.

EXAMPLE

Example 4

Producer negotiates with Writer to buy the movie rights to Writer's fictionalized novel about George Washington's life. The two parties were close to a deal for the rights at $50,000, but the deal fell apart. Producer made a movie about George Washington anyway, using a script written by someone else. Unbeknownst to anyone but Producer, Producer inserted a few pages of dialogue into the script lifted directly from Writer's novel. The movie was a great success. The lead role of George Washington was played by Movie Star, an actor who recently starred in a string of hit movies. Producer made

$10 million in royalties from Studio, devoting two years of his time exclusively to the production of the movie, and spending $200,000 for assistants and office space. Writer seeks restitution from Producer (in addition to any actual damages allowed under the Copyright Act). How much, if any, of the $10 million in profits should Writer receive? What else would you need to know to answer this question fully?

EXPLANATION

Explanation

These facts are based roughly on the *Sheldon* case discussed above, 309 U.S. 390 (1940). Beyond the Copyright Act damages (which could be close to $50,000 if the evidence of that negotiation shows the reasonable royalty figure), Writer is going to want as much of the $10 million in restitution as possible. Consider again our four-step process.

1. **Identify revenues from misappropriated/mixed item.**

In this case, Producer's revenues from the film are $10 million.

2. **Deduct variable costs, but (in some courts) not costs associated with the infringer's own labor.**

From that $10 million, Producer should be able to subtract a good portion, if not all, of the $200,000 in assistant costs and office space. Ordinarily speaking, these are fixed costs (so we could discuss them under Step 3 next). But the facts tell us that Producer worked *exclusively* on the George Washington movie for two years, so it could be that *all* of his costs are attributable to the movie.

Producer cannot subtract the value of his own labor, which in this case is worth a significant amount of money. After all, he used his labor to produce a very valuable product, one that earned him a $10 million royalty.

3. **Deduct an appropriate portion of fixed costs, if allowed by court (evidentiary burden and method of allocation may depend upon culpability of infringer).**

See the discussion under Step 2 above. Best-case scenario for Producer is a deduction of $200,000 for his costs during the production of the movie.

4. **Apportion profits attributable to misappropriated item in mixed item cases using some reasonable method of apportionment. However, some courts will refuse to apportion, awarding *all* profits to the plaintiff; some courts that will allocate do not give**

the infringer any credit for profits attributable to the infringer's reputation.

Here is where Producer may stand to lose most of that $9.8 million (or worse, all of the profits in courts (such as *ABKCO*) that allow no deductions for willful infringers).

A jury is going to have to decide what portion of Producer's hefty profit is attributable to the stolen lines from the novel and what portion is attributable to everything else (besides the profits attributable to the reputation of Producer, if applicable). Likely the few lines of dialogue contributed only a negligible amount to the profit of the movie. People likely went to this movie because they like Movie Star, they like movies about historical figures, or for numerous other reasons. Realistically speaking, it is likely that the profits of the movie would have been the same had Producer not stolen the dialogue from Writer. (In this way, this case is fundamentally different from *Gaste* or the Shrek-Fiona hypothetical, both cases in which the misappropriated item added a great deal of value to the mixed product, creating its profitability).

Sheldon demonstrates that especially in cases of willful infringements, courts may be lax in apportioning for the benefit of plaintiffs. A holding that the stolen lines were worth 5% of the movie's profitability would give Writer in this case $490,000 in profits, but it is likely based on a gross overestimate about the importance of those stolen lines. Still, when it comes to deliberate infringers, evidentiary doubts are going to go against the infringer.

CHAPTER 13

Advanced Topics in Restitution: Constructive Trusts, Equitable Liens, and Other Restitutionary Remedies

13.1 CONSTRUCTIVE TRUSTS

13.1.1 Constructive Trusts: The Basics

The previous chapter described how plaintiffs who seek a restitutionary remedy may measure (and then collect) defendants' gains. In all but the simplest real-world cases, the measurement process requires courts to disentangle defendants' finances. How much revenue did plaintiffs' misappropriated item produce? Did defendant add something to the misappropriated item to produce value? If so, how much credit should defendant get for defendant's contribution? Courts will order an accounting for profits to determine the relevant dollar figures.

After the court conducts an accounting for profits and reaches a final dollar total, the amount may be embodied in a money judgment, collectible under the rules described in Chapter 17. If defendant is solvent and has assets that are easy to find and not protected by law, a money judgment will be an adequate way to ensure that plaintiff can collect defendant's gains. If defendant is bankrupt, however, a money judgment would be an inadequate remedy: plaintiff would have to stand in line with the defendant's other creditors and might only receive a small portion of the judgment as defendant's assets are divided up among the creditors. So, if Mr. Gaste (from Chapter 12) has obtained a six-figure money judgment from Fermata, but Fermata is insolvent, a money judgment won't be worth much to Mr. Gaste.

Additionally, if the defendant has taken plaintiff's misappropriated item and used it to purchase other assets that have appreciated in value, a money judgment may not fully capture that appreciation. Recall, for example, the case of Anita from the preceding chapter. Anita stole Brianna's digital camera and sold it to a pawnshop for $150. Anita then bet the money at the racetrack. She did well at the racetrack, and the $150 is now worth $1,000. Brianna would prefer the $1,000 in track winnings to the camera's $200 value or the pawnshop value of $150.

A money judgment may also not be a good remedy for plaintiff when defendant has transferred plaintiff's property to a third party. If Anita, for example, has given Brianna's digital camera as a gift to her friend David, Anita may wish to go after David for return of the camera (rather than sue Anita for damages).

The *equitable* restitutionary remedy of a *constructive trust* can be more beneficial to a plaintiff than a simple money judgment in at least three situations:

1. Defendant is bankrupt, and plaintiff can trace his or her property to an identifiable asset.
2. Defendant has purchased an identifiable asset with plaintiff's property, and this asset has appreciated in value.
3. Defendant has transferred plaintiff's property to a third person, and plaintiff wants the third person to return the item.

A word about equitable remedies before explaining what a constructive trust is: Part II of this book discussed equitable remedies in great detail (but some of you may be reading this part of the book before Part II). The most important equitable remedy is the injunction, but it is not the only one. To recap from Part II (or remind readers who have forgotten), an equitable remedy is one that was traditionally available in England in the courts of equity, and it requires the plaintiff to show that a traditional legal remedy—such as damages—is "inadequate" (the "irreparable injury rule"). (The new Restatement, however, takes the position that proof of irreparable injury should not be required to get any restitutionary remedy. RTR §4(2).) Equitable remedies are backed by the court's contempt power, meaning that the court can coerce a reluctant defendant to comply and can punish willful disobedience of the court's order.

A constructive trust is an equitable restitutionary remedy that in some circumstances (1) gives plaintiff seeking restitution a preference in bankruptcy, (2) allows plaintiffs to "trace" defendant's gains from plaintiff's misappropriated item into an item purchased by defendant that has appreciated in value, or (3) allows plaintiffs to "trace" plaintiff's item from defendant to a third person. There is a technical requirement (owing to the remedy's equitable origins) that plaintiffs seeking constructive trusts demonstrate irreparable injury, but many courts ignore this requirement.

A constructive trust is not a real trust: instead, the law engages in the *fiction* that the defendant was holding the plaintiff's property in trust, and that transactions involving the plaintiff's property were transactions defendant entered into with the intent to benefit the plaintiff. The constructive trust is a fiction because the defendant need not have had the intent to hold the property for the benefit of the plaintiff: rather, the law treats the defendant *as if* he or she had this intent.[1] *See Wadlington v. Edwards*, 92 So. 2d 629, 631 (Fla. 1957) ("[A] constructive trust is a relationship adjudicated to exist by a court of equity based on particular factual situations created by one or the other of the parties. The element of intent or agreement either oral or written to create the trust relationship is totally lacking. The trust is 'constructed' by equity to prevent an unjust enrichment of one person at the expense of another as the result of fraud, undue influence, abuse of confidence or mistake in the transaction that originates the problem.").

Thus, when Anita steals Brianna's camera, hocks it at the pawnshop, and bets the money at the track, you can be sure that Anita is not doing all these things to benefit Brianna as Brianna's "trustee." But if the court imposes a constructive trust, Brianna can recover the entire $1,000 winnings at the racetrack (assuming she can identify those funds—more about this point coming up) under the constructive trust fiction: it is *as though* Anita was holding the property in trust for Brianna.

A court acting in equity has discretion to impose a constructive trust or not depending upon whether justice requires doing so.[2] As the quotation from the *Wadlington* case shows, some courts will impose a constructive trust not only in cases of fraud or theft, but also in cases of mistake, such as when the bank mistakenly overpaid the professor upon closing her bank account.

In some other states, and everywhere in the bankruptcy context, however, courts will not impose a constructive trust for mere mistakes. The plaintiff must prove fraud, theft, or similarly bad conduct and be able to identify specific assets. *In re North American Coin & Currency, Ltd.*, 767 F.2d 1573 (9th Cir. 1985).[3]

Why these limits? The issue in bankruptcy is not just about the fairness of dividing goods or money between the plaintiff and the defendant; third parties are involved as well. Consider, for example, Anita's other creditors, such as her landlord, the bank holding her car loan, and other people Anita

---

1. The constructive trust is no more of a real trust than a quasi-contract (or "contract implied in law") is a real contract. See Chapter 11 for more on quasi-contract claims.

2. The Restatement generally follows the common law tracing rules, RTR §59(2), but it does not allow plaintiffs to trace into the gains of *innocent* recipients of unjust enrichment. Id., §59(3). It includes detailed rules on priority of competing claims, beginning with §60. See especially §§66-67, on bona fide purchasers.

3. Some courts do not allow the use of a constructive trust in bankruptcy. See *In re Omegas Group, Inc.*, 16 F.3d 1443 (6th Cir. 1994). But some courts have rejected *Omegas*. *In re Leitner*, 236 B.R. 420 (Bank. D. Kan. 1999); Laycock & Hasen, pp. 734-737 (rounding up cases on both sides and describing the controversy).

has wronged. Bankruptcy law sets up a system of priorities to determine which classes of creditors get to collect money first and how much each creditor obtains. Those at the bottom of the list often will get nothing. The constructive trust, using the fiction that the money is really the "plaintiff's money," in effect gives the plaintiff a preference in bankruptcy over other creditors who would have priority to collect from defendant's assets.

One way of limiting the plaintiff's preference in bankruptcy obtained through a constructive trust is to grant the preference to plaintiff *only to the extent of plaintiff's losses*. For example, recall that Brianna lost a camera worth $200. A court could well say that in the bankruptcy context, Anita held in constructive trust $200 of the $1,000 racetrack winnings for Brianna, allowing Brianna to use the constructive trust to recover through a preference *only to the extent of her losses*. Without the constructive trust giving Brianna a preference in bankruptcy, Brianna might get a judgment for $200 but no realistic possibility of collecting that amount. Instead, Brianna would stand in line with other creditors to receive only a small portion of her $200 loss (or nothing at all). With the constructive trust, Brianna gets priority against other creditors over $200 of Anita's winnings (but not the full $1,000).

Recall that in bankruptcy, the plaintiff must not only show fraud, theft, or similar wrongdoing; the plaintiff must also point to *identifiable assets*. Indeed, this *identification requirement* is a prerequisite to court imposition of a constructive trust in or out of bankruptcy. RTR §55 cmt. *a* ("A transaction in which the defendant (i) has been unjustly enriched (ii) by acquiring legal title to specifically identifiable property (iii) at the expense of the claimant or in violation of the claimant's rights is one in which—by the traditional formula—the defendant's title to the property is subject to the claimant's equitable interest.").[4]

To understand the identification requirement, consider three variations on the Anita-Brianna hypothetical. Anita steals the camera and hocks it at the pawnshop for $150. After that, one of the following three scenarios occurs:

1. Anita takes the $150 and bets it at the track. She loses all the money.
2. Anita takes the $150 and deposits it into her bank account, which had a balance of $500. She later withdraws $150 and bets it at the track, winning $1,000.

4. The Restatement offers the example of a son who works in his father's business for a nominal salary, upon an oral promise that at the father's 75th birthday, the son will receive a 50% share of the business. The father repudiates the promise, which is unenforceable under the Statute of Frauds. Though the son has a claim in restitution, and possibly a claim for an equitable lien (discussed below), he cannot get a constructive trust "because the transaction by which Father was unjustly enriched was not the source of Father's title to identifiable property." *Id.*, illus. 14 & 15.

3. Anita takes the $150 and deposits it into one of her bank accounts, which had a balance of $500. She then withdraws $150 from a *different* bank account and bets it at the track, winning $1,000.

In hypotheticals 1 and 3, Brianna will not be able to use the constructive trust remedy, whether or not Anita is in bankruptcy. The problem for Brianna is that she cannot point to an *identifiable asset* of hers that Anita used to realize a gain.

In hypothetical 1, there simply was no gain, and therefore no assets to trace. Brianna's best bet is to seek damages for the $200 loss of her camera, and hope that the damages (or at least part of them) will be collectible from Anita in bankruptcy.

In hypothetical 3, there was a gain, but it is not traceable to Brianna's loss. Figure 13.1 contrasts the original hypothetical with hypothetical 3, showing traceability only in the original hypothetical. In the original hypothetical, we can say that the digital camera was Brianna's. Anita turned that camera into $150 cash at the pawnshop, which she later converted to winning racetrack tickets and finally to cash. In hypothetical 3, in contrast, Anita turned Brianna's camera into $150 cash at the pawnshop, and that money then stayed in bank account 1. The track winnings came from separate money in bank account 2. Because Brianna cannot trace her assets to the track winnings in hypothetical 3, she cannot trace to Anita's gains in a constructive trust either to realize a greater gain or, in the case of bankruptcy, to gain a preference in bankruptcy.

Original hypothetical

Digital camera → $150 from pawnshop → racetrack tickets → $1,000 track winnings

Hypothetical 3

Digital camera → $150 from pawnshop → bank account 1

Bank account 2 → racetrack tickets → $1,000 track winnings

Figure 13.1

Note the odd happenstance of hypothetical 3. Anita could just as easily have taken the $150 she bet at the track from bank account 1 rather than bank account 2. If she had done so, then Brianna would have been able to trace to the track winnings. See Figure 13.2.

Hypothetical 3: Variation with money taken from same bank

Digital camera → \$150 from pawnshop → bank account 1 → racetrack tickets → \$1,000 track winnings

Figure 13.2

If you reexamine the three hypotheticals, you will notice that this last variation is actually hypothetical 2. Courts facing a situation like hypothetical 2 will allow Brianna to trace the digital camera to the pawnshop money to the bank account to the track winnings—either to allow Brianna to capture Anita's gain at the track or, if Anita is bankrupt, to give Brianna a preference in bankruptcy.

Consider, however, for a while longer the tracing illustrated in Figure 13.2. It does not seem farfetched to say either that Anita transformed Brianna's camera into \$150 or to say that the \$150 Anita took from the bank was transformed into winning tickets that allowed her to receive \$1,000. But in the middle of that transaction was the bank deposit. Let's suppose the pawnbroker gave Anita a \$100 bill and a \$50 bill. When Anita brought those bills to the bank and "deposited them" in her account, the bank did not keep the two particular bills for Anita. Instead, the bank simply noted on Anita's account a credit in the amount of \$150, payable on demand to Anita either in new bills or in some other financial instrument such as a check. It took the \$100 and \$50 bills and used them for other bank purposes, such as giving the bills to another bank customer.

When Anita withdrew \$150 in cash, did the money really come "from" Brianna's camera, or was it from Anita's own \$500 funds or from somewhere else? Despite the reality that the \$150 deposited into the bank account is gone, courts routinely will treat plaintiff's money that goes into a bank account (or similar financial account) as traceable to plaintiff (at plaintiff's option) when it is removed—at least when it is advantageous for plaintiff to so treat the money (it would not be advantageous if, for example, Anita lost all of her bets with that \$150). In the next subpart of this chapter, I address the details on fictions related to tracing—particularly when the defendant has commingled her assets with plaintiff's assets. The bottom line here is that courts will engage in a fiction that monies deposited in a bank account remain identifiable for tracing purposes, even though the actual dollars are exchanged for a bank's promise to pay the depositor later when depositor demands the money.

What if, instead of winning \$1,000 with the proceeds of Brianna's camera, Anita won \$1 million? Or used the \$150 to buy Powerball lottery tickets, one of which yielded a payoff of \$250 million? There are few real cases with such extreme facts. An Illinois court allowed the state of Illinois to recover the value of a $35,000 lottery ticket that was bought with illegal drug proceeds of $200. The case was not one in restitution but under a state drug forfeiture law. *People v. $35,315.00 in United States Currency*, 64 N.E.3d 754 (Ill. App. Ct. 2016).

The Restatement would not allow the windfall recovery. "When property from which a claimant is entitled to restitution is exchanged for a more valuable product, the claimant's rights may be limited . . . (c) to prevent a recovery that is grossly disproportionate to any loss on which the claimant's right to restitution is based." RTR §58(3). It offers an example of an artist who steals art supplies to paint a painting that sells for $250,000. "The fact that $250,000 may be identified in Artist's bank account as the traceable product of Supplier's materials does not permit Supplier to take these funds if the resulting recovery would be grossly disproportionate to Artist's wrongful act." *Id.*, illus. 26.

Finally, a constructive trust is useful when plaintiff's asset (or something the defendant converted the asset into) has fallen into the hands of third parties. The example again is David, who obtains Brianna's stolen digital camera as a gift from Anita. So long as David is not a bona fide purchaser—that is, someone who paid fair market value for the item without actual or constructive ("reasonably should have known") knowledge that the seller did not possess good title to the item (*see* RTR §§66, 67)—Brianna will be in a position to ask for return of the item as a form of specific restitution (or replevin, see section 13.3.1 below) under the fiction that David was holding the camera for Brianna in a constructive trust. *See* RTR §58(2). Brianna can trace even further. For example, if David took the gift camera from Anita, sold it for $150 at the pawnshop and went to the track, winning $1,000 with the money, Brianna should be able to get a constructive trust over that $1,000, though it again would be limited to $200 if David were insolvent. If David, unaware of the theft, adversely changed his position after receiving the camera, the Restatement gives room for courts to limit Brianna's remedies. RTR §65.

Example 1

Defendants sold rare coins over the Internet. The business was not doing very well. It looked as though the business might fail. Defendants took all the orders that arrived during the week of January 1 and put the payments for those orders in a special bank account. Defendants knew there was a risk that they could not fulfill the orders and wanted to protect their newest customers. Defendants did not fill the orders, and a week later, Defendants went bankrupt. Rather than receive only pennies on the dollar in the bankruptcy court, a group of plaintiffs whose orders arrived during the week of January 1 asked the court to grant them a constructive trust over the assets in that separate bank account. Should the court grant the constructive trust remedy, giving the January 1 plaintiffs a preference in bankruptcy?

Explanation

EXPLANATION

This hypothetical is based on *North American Coin*, a case cited earlier in the chapter. In that case, state law provided that plaintiffs in the position of the January 1 plaintiffs should be entitled to a constructive trust. That, of course, stretches the identifiability requirement somewhat. We already engage in the fiction that when a defendant deposits plaintiff's money in an account, that money remains identifiable in that account. Here, we have a commingling of a number of plaintiffs' assets, and so a court granting a constructive trust to the class engages in the fiction that the bank is holding this set of plaintiffs' funds separately for each plaintiff.

There is a further problem here, however, concerning the application of the constructive trust in the bankruptcy context. Though the assets are (arguably) identifiable, a court will not impose a constructive trust in *bankruptcy* in the absence of fraud, theft, or similar bad conduct. In this case, defendants were not guilty of fraud. (It is not fraud to continue to solicit orders for your company even if the company faces a risk of bankruptcy.) Were this not a bankruptcy case, some courts in equity might have imposed a constructive trust.

This example is good for thinking about whether the fraud and identifiability requirements are sensible criteria for determining when certain plaintiffs should obtain a benefit in bankruptcy. Let's analyze the fraud requirement first. Imagine that, in the coin case, Defendants were committing fraud on all their clients. They promised to send them rare gold coins, but they were sending counterfeits. Someone at the company, however, segregated the money coming in the week of January 1 out of fear that the company was going to go under soon.

If a court would grant the January 1 plaintiffs a preference in bankruptcy under these conditions, it would mean that those plaintiffs who were lucky enough to be defrauded last would have a preference over those customers of Defendants who were defrauded earlier. It is not clear why these later-defrauded plaintiffs should get such a preference from the court.

Now vary the hypothetical a bit. Suppose only the January 1 plaintiffs were victims of fraud by Defendants. (For all pre–January 1 orders, Defendants had every intention of filling the orders; for the January 1 plaintiffs, Defendants knew the company was going to go bankrupt, and they committed fraud by soliciting sales they knew they could not fulfill.) Defendants took the money from all plaintiffs and deposited it into an account with money from all sources, including pre–January 1 order payments. Under these circumstances, plaintiffs can prove the requisite fraud, but they cannot identify their assets—because their money went into a larger bank account with income from a variety of sources. It is not clear why this fact, either should be dispositive in the decision whether or not to grant plaintiffs a preference in bankruptcy.

Example 2

Back to our Anita-Brianna hypothetical, with a new twist. This time, after Anita steals the camera, she sells it to the pawnshop for $200, its fair market value. The owner of the pawnshop is a bona fide purchaser and later sells the camera to another person (who cannot be located) for $225. Anita deposits the $200 into her bank account. Anita is not bankrupt; indeed, she has many assets. Should the court impose a constructive trust on the $200 in Anita's bank account?

Explanation

At first glance, this looks like a no-brainer. Brianna's asset is still identifiable: Anita transformed the camera into $200 that is now in Anita's bank account. Moreover, Anita's conduct in stealing the camera likely would be sufficiently bad to convince most courts that a constructive trust is warranted in the court's discretion.

The complication here is that a constructive trust is an *equitable* remedy, and at least formally, courts are not supposed to grant an equitable remedy unless the plaintiff can demonstrate that there is no adequate remedy at law. (Much more about this "irreparable injury" requirement can be found in Part II of the book.) Here, Anita could argue that damages are just as good a remedy as a constructive trust because Anita is not bankrupt, and therefore Brianna will be able to collect her money with a money judgment. The measure of Brianna's loss is the same as the measure of Anita's gain: $200.

Anita might prefer that Brianna seek a legal remedy so that she can have a jury trial—not available when a plaintiff seeks equitable relief—and because court enforcement of legal remedies is not backed by the court's power of contempt. Still, it appears that many courts do not take the irreparable injury requirement seriously in the context of equitable restitutionary remedies such as constructive trusts. In some courts, however, it will be necessary to show that damages are not as good a remedy as the constructive trust remedy would be.

13.1.2 Advanced Tracing Problems

We have now seen the constructive trust concept applied to allow for tracing into defendant's assets or even into the hands of third parties who are not bona fide purchasers. In this section, we consider some additional complications that arise in tracing, particularly when there has been a mingling of plaintiff's assets and defendant's (or a third party's) assets.

Let's begin with a straightforward example to illustrate the problem, continuing with variations on our Anita-Brianna hypothetical. Again Anita steals Brianna's camera and sells it to the pawnshop for $150. Anita takes the $150 and deposits it into her bank account, which had a balance of $150, so the new balance is now $300. Anita withdraws the full $300, bets $150 on red at the roulette wheel, and loses it all. She then bets $150 on the horses, winning $1,000. See Figure 13.3.

Digital camera → $150 from pawnshop →
bank account (prior $150 balance, new $300 total)
→ $150 → roulette wheel → 0
→ $150 → racetrack → $1,000

Figure 13.3 Anita's Commingled Funds

A look at Figure 13.3 reveals the problem. Anita would want to argue that she spent Brianna's $150 on the roulette wheel (the bad investment) and Anita's own $150 at the racetrack (the good investment that yielded a $1,000 payoff). If that were the case, Brianna's attempt to trace would fail because the assets from the camera fell to zero. Brianna, in contrast, would want to argue that Anita's money went to the bad investment and Brianna's to the track winnings. Maybe the fairest thing to do would be to say that $75 of Brianna's money and $75 of Anita's money went into the good investment, meaning Brianna would be able to trace to $1,000.

Fortunately for those who like simplicity, the law lets the plaintiff engage in whatever fictions yield the best result for her, *determined with perfect hindsight*. This is a key point, but it is rather counter-intuitive: when a plaintiff uses a constructive trust for tracing in the case of commingled assets, the plaintiff gets to use two fictions to identify the most advantageous means of tracing:

1. The wrongdoer spends his own money first on *bad* investments.
2. The wrongdoer spends plaintiff's money first on *good* investments.

In the case illustrated in Figure 13.3, Brianna gets to use the fiction that Anita spent Anita's money first on bad investments, and spent Brianna's money first on good investments. The question is *not* one of Anita's intent. Her intent is irrelevant.

The fictions have their limits however. Consider this further variation on the Anita-Brianna hypothetical. Again Anita steals Brianna's camera and sells it to the pawnshop for $150. Anita takes the $150 and deposits it into her bank account, which had a balance of $0. Anita withdraws the $150 and bets the $150 on red at the roulette wheel and loses it all. Anita then deposits $150 of her own money in her account, then withdraws it and bets $150 on the horses, winning $1,000. See Figure 13.4.

Digital camera → $150 from pawnshop →
bank account (prior $0 balance, new $150) →
$150 → roulette wheel → 0
Anita's own $150 → bank account →
$150 → racetrack → $1,000

Figure 13.4 Anita's Non-commingled Funds

A court will not allow Brianna to trace in this situation because her asset went down to zero: it went from the camera to the pawnshop to the bank account to the cash to the loss at the roulette wheel. The winnings at the track indisputably came from money that was not Brianna's. "Once plaintiffs trace their money into a commingled account, anything that was possible is presumed in their favor, however unlikely, but the impossible is not presumed." LAYCOCK & HASEN p. 742. In other words, the plaintiff can never trace more than that which originated from the *lowest intermediate balance* in the bank account.

While there is some logic to the rule that prevents tracing where chronology makes it impossible to do so, it does show the limits of the fictions and the serendipity of tracing. Comparing Figures 13.3 and 13.4, Anita committed exactly the same wrong and had exactly the same gains and losses with exactly the same bets. The only difference between the two examples is that in Figure 13.4, Brianna was unlucky that Anita did not commingle her own $150 in her bank account before Anita withdrew the money for the two investments.

The fictions themselves are not difficult to apply with enough practice. The key is to work backward, keeping some kind of ledger as to which funds and assets should be attributable to plaintiff and which to defendant.

Consider the following example. Larry takes care of his old aunt Gertrude's finances. Unbeknownst to Gertrude, Larry cashes a $100,000 certificate of deposit belonging to Gertrude and deposits it in his own account, which had a balance of $50,000 in it. Larry takes $75,000 out of his account and buys 7,500 shares of Loserco stock. He takes another $25,000 out of his account and buys 2,500 shares of Winnerco stock. He then takes $40,000 from his bank account, losing it in Las Vegas. Gertrude discovers the fraud and sues for restitution. At this point, Loserco stock had fallen to $30,000 and Winnerco stock had gone up to $100,000. Larry is not bankrupt. How can Gertrude trace most advantageously in this case?

Let's begin by making a ledger showing Larry's bank account and transactions:

Bank account total	Action/explanation
$50,000	Larry's initial balance
$150,000	Addition of Gertrude's $100,000
$75,000	Withdrawal of $75,000 to buy Loserco stock
$50,000	Withdrawal of $25,000 to buy Winnerco stock
$10,000	Withdrawal of $40,000 for Vegas losses

Looking at this with hindsight (as Gertrude's lawyer can and should do), one thing that's for sure is that Gertrude wants to use the fiction that she bought the Winnerco stock for $25,000 that went up to $100,000. After tracing $25,000 to the Winnerco Stock, Gertrude has $75,000 more of her money to allocate. She could simply use the fiction that she spent this $75,000 on Loserco stock. That would mean the total value of her recovery would be the Winnerco and Loserco stock, currently worth a total of $130,000.

That's not bad for Gertrude, because she would be getting $30,000 more than the return of her $100,000 loss. But there's something she can do that's even more advantageous. The Loserco stock has declined in value by more than half (it was bought for $75,000 and has fallen to $30,000). But there is $10,000 in the account that has not declined in value at all. Gertrude can therefore do the following:

1. Allocate $25,000 of her funds for the purchase of Winnerco stock.
2. Allocate $10,000 of her funds to remain in the bank account.
3. Allocate the remaining amount of the funds ($65,000) to buy Loserco stock.

If Gertrude takes these steps, she maximizes her recovery:

1. Her purchase of Winnerco stock is now worth $100,000.
2. Her $10,000 bank account allocation is still worth $10,000.
3. Her purchase of $65,000/$75,000 worth of the Loserco stock means that she now has stock worth $26,000. (This is a 65/75, or 13/15, interest in stock worth a total of $30,000.)

$100,000 + 10,000 + 26,000 = $136,000, which is better than if Gertrude had taken all of the Loserco stock.

The lesson: from the plaintiff's perspective in tracing, watch the bottom line, looking for the most advantageous way to allocate money used by defendant. Work backward and look at options to maximize plaintiff's recovery.

EXAMPLE

Example 3

Same facts as in the Larry-Gertrude example just given, but assume that Larry's bank account started with nothing, and that Larry deposited his own $50,000 in the account after he purchased the Loserco stock. How, if at all, does that change Gertrude's tracing options?

EXPLANATION

Explanation

Let's begin by making a ledger so we can keep these transactions straight:

Bank account total	Action/explanation
$0	Larry's initial balance
$100,000	Addition of Gertrude's $100,000
$25,000	Withdrawal of $75,000 to buy Loserco stock
$75,000	Addition of Larry's $50,000
$50,000	Withdrawal of $25,000 to buy Winnerco stock
$10,000	Withdrawal of $40,000 for Vegas losses

As this sequence indicates, Gertrude has no choice but to allocate to herself the purchase of the Loserco stock for $75,000. Larry *had no money of his own in the account at the time*, so a court will not allocate any Loserco stock to him. This is an application of the lowest intermediate balance rule. This leaves Gertrude with $25,000 remaining to allocate. She could allocate some or all of it for the purchase of the Winnerco stock. One possibility is that she allocates all of it to the Winnerco stock. Another possibility is that she allocates $15,000 to the Winnerco stock and $10,000 to the money remaining in the bank account. The former allocation is more advantageous for Gertrude. If she buys all the Winnerco stock, she gets stock now worth $100,000. If she allocates only $15,000, she gets $15,000/$25,000 (3/5) of the stock now worth $100,000, for $60,000. This $60,000 plus the $10,000 in the bank account gives Gertrude a total of $70,000.

Gertrude's best allocation under these facts is to take all the Loserco stock, now worth $30,000, plus all the Winnerco stock, now worth $100,000, for a total of $130,000. The example shows that Gertrude gets $6,000 less than she would have gotten in the original hypothetical because of the timing of Larry's $50,000 deposit into his own account.

EXAMPLE

Example 4

Hilda steals Ike's car and sells it for $25,000 cash to a buyer, who has disappeared with the car. Hilda gives $10,000 of the cash to her boyfriend, Jake. Jake deposits the money into his bank account, which had a balance of $1,000. Jake then withdraws $100 from his account and uses it to buy groceries and a lottery ticket. The lottery ticket is a winner, and Jake wins $1,000,000. Meanwhile, Hilda takes the $15,000 remaining and goes on a shopping spree, buying a plasma television set and nice new furniture. What, if anything, can Ike recover from Hilda and/or Jake?

EXPLANATION

Explanation

Let's consider tracing to Jake first. Jake received the $10,000 as a gift, so Ike can trace his assets to Jake. (In the common legal jargon, we would call Jake a gratuitous donee, rather than a bona fide purchaser for value.) Let's begin again with a ledger:

Bank account total	Action/explanation
$1,000	Jake's initial balance
$11,000	Jake's balance after the addition of Ike's $10,000
$10,900	Jake's balance after the $100 withdrawal

To maximize Ike's recovery, he should trace $9,999 of his $10,000 into Jake's bank account. He would argue that one of his dollars was part of the $100 withdrawn by Jake and used to purchase the lottery ticket worth $1,000,000. This gives him a restitutionary recovery from Jake of $1,009,999.

Hilda has taken Ike's $15,000 and converted it into specific household goods. Ike may recover these goods—in addition to his recovery from Jake—in restitution.

EXAMPLE

Example 5

Same facts as in Example 4, except Hilda has sold her car to Karen, who buys it knowing that it is stolen. Also, Jake did not win the lottery. How does this change Ike's options?

EXPLANATION

Explanation

Like Jake in the preceding example, Karen is not a bona fide purchaser for value. For this reason, Ike can trace to get back the car itself from Karen. He does not have to do so, however. He could instead choose to trace the funds that Hilda gave to Jake (there's still Ike's $10,000 in Jake's account) and to the household goods Hilda has purchased. The choice is Ike's. The significant point is that Ike *must choose*. He can't trace to both the car and the proceeds of the car: to do so would violate the fiction that one is tracing the assets.

In this case, it is not clear that one choice is better than the other for Ike. It depends on the values as discovered by Ike's lawyer. If, however, Jake had won the lottery, it would certainly make sense to trace the money and not the car.

13.2 EQUITABLE LIENS

An *equitable lien* is another restitutionary remedy that can give plaintiffs seeking restitution an advantage in certain situations. Like a constructive trust, an equitable lien is an *equitable* remedy that is subject to the requirements and benefits of equitable relief discussed earlier.

Before describing how an *equitable* lien works, it is important first to understand how a *lien* works. "A lien is a charge against property that makes the property stand as security for a debt owed. A creditor who has a lien upon property of the debtor is entitled at a proper time to have the property sold and the proceeds used for payment of the debt. The lien creditor thus stands in a better position than a general, unsecured creditor of the same debtor, because he has a priority: the property subject to his lien is in effect set aside for the satisfaction of his claim first." DOBBS & ROBERTS §4.3(3), at 407-408. So, for example, my car loan with my bank is subject to a lien. If I don't pay my debt, the bank can repossess my car and get priority over the car even if I am in bankruptcy and have other creditors. This repossession occurs instead of the bankruptcy trustee's selling the car, putting the proceeds into the rest of the pot of my money, and paying off creditors in the order set by bankruptcy law. Similarly, if I don't pay my home mortgage, the holder of the mortgage can force a sale of my house ("foreclosure"), using the proceeds first to pay the debt I owe, then turning the rest of the money over to me (or to other creditors who may have a secured interest in the house).

An equitable lien "is a money judgment secured by a lien on specific property." LAYCOCK & HASEN p. 756. It creates a real lien on property that (in most circumstances) can be subject to foreclosure. The lien that is created is real, but it is not created through any agreement of the parties (as when the bank and

I agreed on the conditions of my car loan); instead, it is created by the court to prevent unjust enrichment. Dobbs & Roberts §4.3(3), pp. 408-409.

For example, suppose that Mona owns land adjacent to Ned's land. Mona builds a shed on Ned's land, mistakenly believing that it is on Mona's land. Ned realizes that Mona is making this mistake as she builds the shed, and he does nothing to correct the error. Under the substantive law of restitution (as described in Chapter 11), Ned has been unjustly enriched. If Mona can move the shed off Ned's property, a court will allow Mona access to remove it. But if it cannot be removed, an equitable lien may be an appropriate remedy. Suppose the shed has increased the value of Ned's land by $20,000. A court can award Mona a money judgment in the amount of $20,000, backed up by the equitable lien. If Ned does not pay up, Mona can foreclose on Ned's land, keep the first $20,000 of the proceeds for herself, and give the rest of the money to Ned.

As the Mona-Ned example shows, an equitable lien can be a powerful remedy. There is the danger that in some cases, however, it is too powerful a remedy. Suppose, for example, that Ned is poor and old, and cannot afford to pay Mona the $20,000. A foreclosure would force him out of his modest house. For this reason, a court in equity might award Mona the equitable lien, but not allow her to foreclose on the property until Ned transfers ownership of his property to someone else or dies. RTR §10, cmt. *g*, illus. 19. Whether a court would delay the possibility of foreclosure is a question of fairness the court would address; Ned's case for a delay in foreclosure would be even stronger if he did not learn of Mona's mistake until after she built the shed.

The Mona-Ned hypothetical illustrates the flexibility that courts can employ in difficult cases such as those involving mistaken improvements to land.[5]

---

5. The RTR's general position on remedies in mistaken improver cases states, "A remedy for mistaken improvement that subjects the owner to a forced exchange will be qualified or limited to avoid undue prejudice to the owner." RTR §10.

The Restatement notes the range of options for courts in mistaken improver cases:

> The remedy for a given instance of mistaken improvement will be fashioned by the court in the interest of substantial justice. Possible remedies available for use in an appropriate case include:
>
> (1) an order permitting the improver to remove all or part of the improvement, on condition that the owner be indemnified against damage to the property;
>
> (2) a money judgment for the increased value of the property resulting from the improvement, or for the cost of the improvement to the improver, whichever is less, payable on such terms as the court may specify;
>
> (3) an equitable lien securing the improver's allowable money claim, subject to such limitations (concerning the time of foreclosure and otherwise) as the court may specify;
>
> (4) an order allowing the improver to remain in temporary possession of the improvements, subject to appropriate limitations regarding the extent and nature of such possession, on payment to owner of the value thereof;
>
> (5) an order giving the owner an option either (i) to pay the improver for the increased value of the property attributable to the improvement or for the cost of the improvement, whichever is less, or (ii) to sell the improved property to the improver at its unimproved value;

Delaying the timing for foreclosure can sometimes work to ensure a fair remedy in appropriate cases.

An equitable lien is typically used in real property disputes (though it is not limited to such applications), and when it is, the dispute must be connected to the real property. When Anita steals Brianna's camera worth $200, for example, Brianna may be entitled to restitution for any gains Anita receives from the theft. But Brianna cannot get an equitable lien for the value of these gains over Anita's home. *The wrong must be connected to the property itself. See* RTR §56(1)(b).

In some circumstances, it might appear that either a constructive trust or an equitable lien would be an appropriate restitutionary remedy. Suppose, for example, that Olivia is Pauline's lawyer. Olivia is holding Pauline's money in a client trust account to pay future legal bills. Olivia steals $20,000 of Pauline's money from the account and uses the money to remodel her kitchen. One possible remedy for Olivia's tort is that the court will impose an equitable lien in the amount of $20,000, forcing Olivia to either pay up or face Pauline's foreclosure. An alternative remedy a court might impose is a constructive trust made up of an interest in Olivia's house equal to the $20,000 increased value. For example, a court could award a constructive trust over 5% of Olivia's $400,000 home.

Which remedy should Pauline prefer? The answer may depend upon whether the property is increasing or decreasing in value. An equitable lien defines the remedy in set dollar amounts (here $20,000), a good choice for *declining assets*. A constructive trust defines the remedy as a percentage interest in the property (here 5% of Olivia's home), a good choice for *assets appreciating in value*.

Thus, if Olivia's house decreases in value from the time of the wrong (value of $400,000) to the time of trial (value of $300,000), an equitable lien preserves Pauline's right to $20,000. Conversely, if Olivia's house increases in value from the time of the wrong (value of $400,000) to the time of trial (value of $500,000), a constructive trust gives Pauline a chance to share in that appreciation. Rather than getting only $20,000 (5% of

---

(6) an order giving the owner an option either (i) to pay the improver for the increased value of the property attributable to the improvement or for the cost of the improvement, whichever is less, or (ii) to exchange the improved property for a specified tract, substantially equivalent to the improved property in its unimproved state; and

(7) an order directing that the improved property be sold, as on partition, the improver to receive the increased amount of the net proceeds attributable to the improvement or the cost of the improvement, whichever is less.

RTR §10, cmt. *g*; *see also* RTR §56(2) ("An equitable lien secures the obligation of the defendant to pay the claimant the amount of the defendant's unjust enrichment as separately determined. Foreclosure of an equitable lien is subject to such conditions as the court may direct.").

the $400,000 value), Pauline will be able to get $25,000 (5% of the new $500,000 value).

Note that not all courts will allow Pauline to obtain a constructive trust in these circumstances. Dobbs and Roberts take the view that "if defendant merely uses plaintiff's money to add a house on a lot he already owns, it is clear that plaintiff has no claim to a constructive trust on the house and lot because his money did not go into the lot. She is entitled instead to an equitable lien on the house and lot for the amount of money embezzled from him." DOBBS & ROBERTS §4.3(3), p. 409. Whether courts allow constructive trusts, equitable liens, or a choice between the two in appropriate cases depends upon each state's case law as well as the judge's views of the equities of the particular case. The Restatement's position is that anyone who meets the requirements for a constructive trust may, at her option, choose an equitable lien instead. RTR §56(3).

EXAMPLE

Example 6

"A dies, leaving a tract of unimproved land by will to B. B sells the land to C, a bona fide purchaser, who clears the land and builds a house which he occupies. The will is found to be invalid, with the result that the title to the land passes to D, A's heir. D intends to sell the property as soon as title can be cleared." RTR §10, cmt. *g*, illus. 14. (a) Can C get an equitable lien over the value of the improvements he made to D's property? (b) What if D did not intend to sell the property but instead intended to build a house and live there?

EXPLANATION

Explanation

(a) The Restatement says that D should be given an election between paying C the portion of the sale attributable to C's improvements or selling to C at the property's unimproved value. To secure C's right to one of the remedies, the court should grant C an equitable lien on the property until D decides.

(b) The Restatement illustration does not pose (or answer) the second question, but it is considerably harder as a matter of justice. In the original example, the tract of land had value to D only for its sale value. Under the alternative scenario, D intends to use the land to build a home; perhaps the land has sentimental value to D that exceeds the market value. Perhaps D does not have the funds to pay C for the extensive improvements C has made to the property; D perhaps planned to build a more modest home. The Restatement gives courts the power to be flexible with remedies in the interest of justice. In this case, a court likely would have a difficult time deciding whether to give C the right to foreclose on an equitable lien for the value of the improvements he made to the property.

Example 7

Quentin steals $1,000 from Rana, his employer. Quentin uses the $1,000 to buy a gold necklace for his girlfriend, Samantha. Can Rana get an equitable lien against the necklace?

Explanation

An equitable lien may not appear to be the appropriate remedy in this case. Although the necklace is property, it is not real property, and some courts will limit the remedy to real property claims. Further, recall that the equitable lien would give Rana the right to a money judgment secured by the property. Though that's a possible remedy, the more straightforward thing for Rana to do is to use the constructive trust remedy to gain the necklace itself, which Rana could then sell or keep. A constructive trust would be especially attractive if the necklace appreciated in value between the time of the wrong and the time of judgment.

Example 8

Shrek steals lumber from Fiona's property and uses it to build a house on his land. The lot alone was worth $50,000; the lot and house together are worth $150,000. The market value of the lumber that Shrek stole from Fiona's property and used to build his house is $10,000. The other building materials cost Shrek $40,000. Is Fiona entitled to an equitable lien? If so, for how much? If Fiona is entitled to an equitable lien, would she prefer a constructive trust (if allowed by a court) over that remedy?

Explanation

Fiona should be entitled to an equitable lien. Shrek has stolen her lumber, giving Fiona a right either to damages or to restitution. An equitable lien appears to be an appropriate remedy here, given that Shrek has used Fiona's property to add value to his home.

The amount of the equitable lien presents an interesting question. At the very least, Fiona should be entitled to an equitable lien for the fair market value of the lumber, or $10,000. She might, however, also claim a higher amount based upon her share of the appreciation under an apportionment of profits. As explained in the previous chapter, when a defendant mixes a misappropriated item with other items the defendant bought and paid for to produce something of value, courts will sometimes allow an apportionment of profits between plaintiff and defendant based upon each of their contributions. Here, Shrek combined his $50,000 in land with Fiona's $10,000 worth of lumber and with $40,000 in additional materials, to equal $100,000 in total costs to produce the house and land worth $150,000. Of the $100,000 in costs, Fiona's lumber represented 10% ($10,000/$100,000). Arguably, she should be entitled to 10% of the $50,000 profit, or an additional $5,000, meaning that Fiona should get an equitable lien of $15,000. Some courts could give Fiona an even greater recovery, allowing her the *full* $50,000 profit in addition to the $10,000 value of lumber because Shrek was a conscious wrongdoer. Whatever the value—$10,000, $15,000, or $60,000—the money judgment against Shrek will be backed up by the equitable lien, giving Fiona the ability to force the sale of the house if Shrek does not pay.

A court may give Fiona the option of a constructive trust instead. (Not all courts would do so in these circumstances.) Recall that a constructive trust is expressed not as a dollar amount (the way an equitable lien is), but rather as a percentage interest in property. Fiona could argue that her $10,000 contribution toward the total $100,000 cost entitles her to a 10% interest in Shrek's home and land. With the house now worth $150,000, her interest would be worth $15,000. If the house is appreciating in value, a constructive trust could be a good choice—though if a court would give Fiona an equitable lien in the amount of $60,000, that might be a better choice.

13.3 OTHER RESTITUTIONARY REMEDIES

13.3.1 Replevin and Ejectment

Most of the restitutionary remedies we have considered are *substitutionary remedies*. As defined in Chapter 1, substitutionary remedies are those in which the court awards plaintiff a sum of money rather than the very thing that was lost or has the potential to be lost. Considering Example 8 above, Fiona's equitable lien (or possible constructive trust) is substitutionary in that she gets a sum of money representing Shrek's gain at her expense; she does not get her lumber back.

The other type of remedy discussed in Chapter 1 was *specific relief*. Specific relief gives the plaintiff the very thing that was lost or has the potential to be lost. The remedy of specific performance in contract, for example, gives plaintiff the performance that defendant promised to deliver under the contract.

Replevin is an example of specific restitution for the return of plaintiff's personal property. It is a *legal remedy*, meaning there is no requirement to prove irreparable injury.[6] It requires defendant to return to the plaintiff the very thing that was lost and pay any additional damages for loss of use during the time that plaintiff was deprived of possession. Until recent times, courts did not consider replevin as a restitutionary remedy; historically in England, it was a writ that was distinct from the writs used to obtain forms of restitution. LAYCOCK & HASEN p. 783. Today, however, some scholars (with courts likely to follow) consider replevin restitutionary because the remedy takes away defendant's gain: defendant gives up plaintiff's property (which defendant presumably kept because it had some value). The Restatement seems to allow for this remedy, referring to it generally as a type of "specific restitution" rather than "replevin." *See* RTR §4, cmt. *e*.

Replevin has a compensatory aspect as well. Plaintiff gets back the thing that was lost, which serves as compensation for plaintiff's loss. Plaintiff can recover additional compensation in damages for the value of the loss of use of the item during the time defendant possessed it. In rare circumstances, courts have also allowed a plaintiff to recover damages for any loss in value of the item caused by defendant's mishandling of plaintiff's property. *E.g.*, *Welch v. Kosasky*, 509 N.E.2d 919 (Mass. App. Ct. 1987); LAYCOCK & HASEN pp. 783-784.

In *Welch*, defendant stole plaintiff's property that at the time of the theft was worth $7,500. By the time plaintiff recovered the property 13 years later, it would have appreciated in value to $25,000, but it did not because defendant damaged it, making it worth only $3,000. In addition to the return of the property, plaintiff was awarded $10,000 for the loss of use of the property for 13 years and $22,000 for the diminution in value of the property.[7]

Replevin is not always available as a remedy. Consider Shrek's theft of Fiona's lumber in Example 8. Shrek has used the lumber in construction, and it cannot be removed in any useful way from the finished home. But when

---

6. See Chapter 7.2, comparing the legal remedy of replevin with the equitable remedy of injunction for the return of personal property. Some courts also recognize a cause of action for "equitable replevin." *See Desiderio v. D'Ambrosio*, 463 A.2d 986, 988 n.3 (N.J. Super. 1983) ("An equitable replevin, as distinct from a legal replevin, is an action for return of an item which has a special value apart from its intrinsic value and for which, therefore, there can be no measure of money damages."). In those jurisdictions recognizing the cause of action, equitable replevin, as an equitable remedy, presumably is subject to the same irreparable injury rule as an injunction.

7. The court also allowed plaintiff to recover consequential damages of $5,000, representing costs to find and recover the property that had fallen into the hands of third parties.

Not all courts would grant plaintiff the right to recover these additional damages for the diminution in value of the property. Some courts would give plaintiff the choice between (1) replevin plus damages for loss of use and (2) damages for conversion (damages through an action for theft of personal property traditionally called "trover"), which would be measured at the time of loss, plus interest since the time of loss. Though the interest on the $7,500 would be considerable for a 13-year loss, an award of market value plus interest likely would yield a smaller recovery for plaintiff than the remedy the court allowed in *Welch*.

the personal property is still available, whether in the hands of defendants or in the hands of third parties who are not bona fide purchasers, replevin can be an attractive option. It is especially attractive for certain personal property, such as property with sentimental value to the plaintiff, where plaintiff's subjective valuation exceeds the market valuation of the property.

Ejectment is a form of specific restitution for *real property*, paralleling replevin's remedy for personal property. Thus, if Shrek had come onto Fiona's land as a trespasser and hoped to gain title by adverse possession, ejectment was the common law writ Fiona would have used to force Shrek to leave her property.

Ejectment has been replaced by statutory remedies in a number of states; a common type of claim (brought under these statutory successors to the writ of ejectment) involves landlords and tenants who have not paid their rent. Ejectment was not used as a remedy in cases involving genuine disputes about the title of property. These disputes were more commonly resolved through an action to quiet title, similar to a declaratory judgment action, discussed in Chapter 16.

EXAMPLE

Example 9

Sandy and Tom were law school classmates. Sandy stole Tom's state-of-the-art laptop computer. At the time it was stolen, the laptop was worth $2,000. Tom promptly went to the store and bought an identical laptop as a replacement for the same $2,000 price. Three years later at a graduation party, Tom noticed his computer in Sandy's house. Sandy refuses to give it back but offers to pay Tom $400, the reasonable value of a three-year-old laptop (which was no longer state-of-the-art) given falling prices for laptops and advances in technology.

Is Tom entitled to replevin? If so, to what else should he be entitled? Should Tom prefer a damages remedy to replevin? Why or why not?

EXPLANATION

Explanation

Tom is entitled to replevin if he wants it. Replevin is a legal remedy, not an equitable one. Tom does not have to prove irreparable injury as he would if he wanted to obtain an injunction. He does not have to accept Sandy's $400 offer.

If Tom opts for replevin, a court will award Tom possession of the laptop. (He'll have to send the sheriffs to seize it; if he wants a court order requiring Sandy to turn over the laptop, he will need to get an injunction or other equitable remedy backed by the power of contempt.) In addition to the return of the laptop, Tom should be entitled to damages for loss of use. Because Tom went out and covered by buying a substitute item, a court may find that Tom suffered no damages for the loss of use.

(This is unlike personal, sentimental property for which there is no substitute. In that case, there are real damages for loss of use, though they are difficult to measure for reasons explained in Part I of this book.) For this reason, Tom may use replevin to get his three-year-old laptop and nothing else.

Tom likely would prefer a damages remedy for Sandy's conversion of the laptop, which would be measured by the market value of the laptop at the time of theft plus interest. (See Part I of this book.) Because the laptop is an item that has depreciated in value, Tom would be better off with a remedy measuring value at the time of the loss (when the value was higher).

The damages remedy also does a better job of putting Tom back into the rightful position. Recall that Tom immediately went out after the theft and bought a replacement computer for $2,000. An award of $2,000 plus interest from the time of the theft appears likely to put the plaintiff in the position he would have been in but for the theft.

Example 10

Albert steals the melody from Gaste's hit song in France to write the hit song "Feelings." Albert uses the proceeds to buy a fancy television set and a piece of land, Blackacre. Can Gaste use replevin to obtain the television set? Can he use ejectment to obtain Blackacre? Alternatively, can Gaste use any other restitutionary remedies to obtain the television and/or Blackacre?

Explanation

Gaste cannot use replevin to obtain the television and he cannot use ejectment to obtain the land. Replevin is a remedy for the return of *plaintiff's personal property*. In this case, the television was never Gaste's property. It might have been bought with proceeds from Albert's misuse of Gaste's music, but that does not give Gaste a right to replevin. A parallel analysis applies to Gaste's use of ejectment: because Blackacre is not *real property to which Gaste holds title*, ejectment is not available. The point of this part of the question is to make you realize that you should not use replevin or ejectment simply because you see that there has been unjust enrichment and defendant is holding personal or real property.

It is still possible that Gaste could end up with the television set and/or Blackacre. First, if Gaste seeks restitution through a money judgment (such as after a successful claim for quasi-contract or accounting for profits), he might be able to force a sale of the television or Blackacre to collect his winnings. The details on collection appear in Chapter 17.

In addition, Gaste may attempt an accounting for profits and tracing into a constructive trust to obtain an interest in either the real or personal property. If Albert, for example, took his royalty check for "Feelings" and used it in a traceable way to buy the television set or Blackacre, Gaste may be able to get a constructive trust over all or a partial interest in the items. This is a restitutionary recovery, but it is not recovery through replevin or ejectment.

13.3.2 Subrogation, Contribution, and Indemnity

The final set of restitutionary remedies we consider in this chapter are subrogation, contribution, and indemnity. We begin with subrogation.

Subrogation is a remedy that prevents a defendant from being unjustly enriched when the plaintiff pays a sum to a third party to settle a liability or debt owed to that third party by the defendant. Subrogation can arise through a contractual agreement, in which case it is termed *conventional subrogation*, or it can arise in the absence of agreement through court creation, termed *equitable (or legal) subrogation*.

Consider this example of conventional subrogation: Ursula negligently causes an automobile accident, injuring Vicki. Vicki has health insurance with Worldwide Insurance. Worldwide pays all of Vicki's health bills. Vicki does not sue Ursula for her personal injury damages, because Vicki's contract with Worldwide has a "subrogation clause" stating that any monies Vicki receives from third parties to compensate for personal injuries must be paid over to Worldwide to compensate for the expenses Worldwide incurs in providing health care to Vicki for her personal injuries.[8] Subrogation gives Worldwide the right to "step into Vicki's shoes" and recover from Ursula the medical expenses incurred by Worldwide in bringing Vicki back to the rightful position. *See* RTR §57 cmt. f ("Subrogation . . . yields a claim against the recipient that is strictly derivative.").

Figure 13.5 illustrates the concept of subrogation. Subrogation involves a triangle consisting of the party that caused the loss (the defendant), the party that suffered the loss (the subrogor), and the party paying the defendant's debt to the subrogor (the subrogee). In the absence of a subrogee, the defendant would be responsible to pay damages directly to the party suffering loss. Once the subrogee has paid the party suffering loss (the subrogor), the defendant no longer has an obligation to pay the subrogor (because the subrogor has already received satisfaction for her losses). After the subrogee pays the subrogor (see Step 1 in Figure 13.5), defendant would be unjustly enriched if defendant did not have to pay the subrogee. Under subrogation, defendant pays the subrogee (see Step 2 in Figure 13.5).

8. Without such a subrogation clause, Vicki would be able to receive both the health care from Worldwide *and* tort damages from Ursula under the collateral source rule. The collateral source rule is an exception to the rule barring plaintiff from recovering compensatory damages that exceed plaintiff's losses. See Chapter 4.

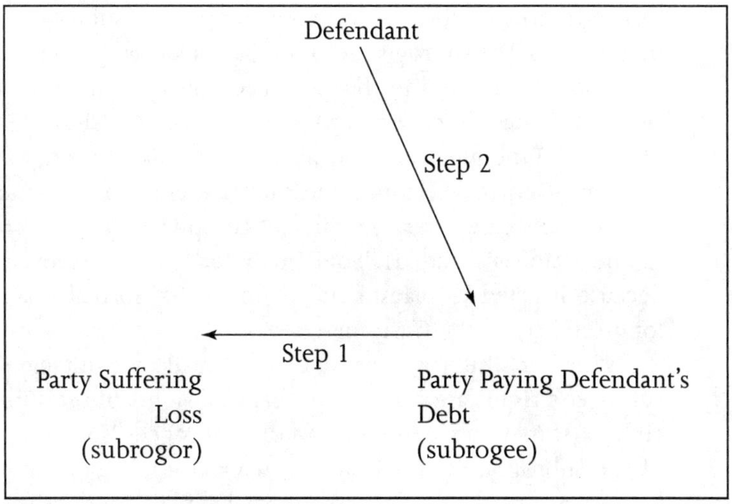

Figure 13.5 Flow of Payments in Subrogation

Equitable (or legal) subrogation[9] works similarly to conventional subrogation, in that a subrogee pays a debt that defendant owes to the subrogor and then demands payment from the defendant, who caused the loss to the subrogor. For example, Distributor is a widget distributor for a number of manufacturers, including Manufacturerco. Distributor delivers widgets from Manufacturerco to Customerco, one of Distributor's best customers. The widgets are defective. Though Distributor has no liability for the defective widgets to Customerco, Distributor buys replacement widgets for Customerco as an accommodation to keep the customer happy. Distributor then turns around and sues Manufacturerco for the cost of the replacement widgets.

You should see that this subrogation suit parallels the earlier, conventional subrogation hypothetical. In Step 1, Distributor makes Customerco whole, thereby relieving Manufacturerco of the obligation to do so. In Step 2, Distributor sues Manufacturerco to obtain the costs it expended in making Customerco whole.

There is an important limitation on equitable (or legal) subrogation: the subrogee cannot be a "volunteer." The non-volunteer requirement echoes the rules discussed in Chapter 11 depriving "officious intermeddlers" of the right to restitution.

What does it mean to be a "volunteer," a status precluding the right to subrogation? A volunteer makes the payment even though it has no business

9. Though some courts refer to this type of subrogation as "legal subrogation," it is in fact an equitable remedy and subject to the rules discussed earlier in this chapter and in Part II for equitable remedies.

reason to do so. Subrogees, in contrast, pay the subrogor for rational business reasons. The subrogee need not have a *legal obligation* to pay the subrogor; it is enough that it is in the subrogee's business interests to do so. *See Am. Nat'l Bank & Trust Co. of Chicago v. Weyerhaeuser Co.*, 692 F.2d 455, 463 (7th Cir. 1982) ("[T]he *potential* for legal liability *to the subrogor*, as well as the disruption of normal relations and the frustration of reasonable expectations can, in many cases, supply sufficient compulsion to support subrogation.") (some emphasis added). So Distributor gets to recover in subrogation because it acted to placate and maintain its normal relationship with its long-time customer, Customerco.

Whether a subrogee seeks conventional or equitable subrogation, the subrogee's rights are no broader than the rights of the subrogor. This principle is sometimes expressed as the subrogee "stepping into the shoes" of the subrogor. So, for example, if Vicki could not recover from Ursula because a jury would determine that Ursula's conduct was not negligent, Worldwide Insurance would not be able to recover from Ursula through subrogation after paying Vicki's medical expenses. Similarly, if Customerco's claims against Manufacturerco would be barred because of the statute of limitations, Distributor's claims would be similarly barred.

The tort doctrines of *contribution* and *equitable indemnity* work in a way that is similar to subrogation but involve joint tortfeasors. So, imagine that Allie and Betty both drive negligently, causing injury to Curt. Curt sues Allie only, and obtains a complete recovery from Allie.[10] Under the state's applicable tort doctrine, Allie may have a right to sue Betty to obtain *all* of the money she paid Curt (under traditional principles of equitable indemnity), a *pro rata share* of the money she paid Curt (under traditional principles of contribution), or a *share based on a percentage of the defendant's relative share of responsibility or fault* of the money she paid Curt (under modern principles of comparative equitable indemnity). *See Am. Motorcycle Ass'n v. Super. Ct. of Los Angeles County*, 578 P.2d 899 (Cal. 1978).

Figure 13.6 illustrates the concepts of contribution and indemnity. Like subrogation, contribution and indemnity involve a three-party triangle. Here, there are two defendants, Defendant 1 and Defendant 2, who jointly caused injury to plaintiff. Under principles of joint and several liability, either defendant could be required to pay the total amount of plaintiff's loss. If Defendant 1 pays the entire amount of plaintiff's loss, Defendant 2 could be unjustly enriched if he too caused injury to plaintiff but did not have to pay. Under joint and several liability, however,

10. Under the traditional tort principle of joint and several liability, a plaintiff injured by multiple defendants has the right to collect all or part of his damages from any or all plaintiffs. Though many states have modified this principle, these modifications are not important for the remedies issues discussed in the text.

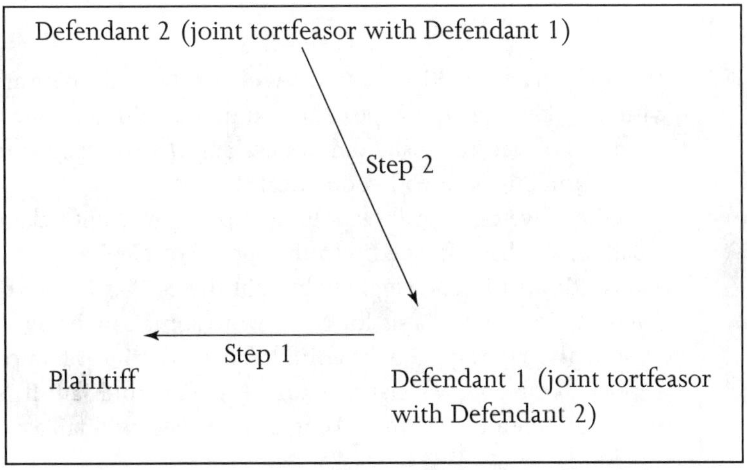

Figure 13.6 Flow of Payments in Contribution/Equitable Indemnity/Partial Equitable Indemnity

Defendant 2 has to pay nothing on account of Defendant 1's payment. Once Defendant 1 satisfies the judgment to the plaintiff in Step 1, contribution or indemnity works in Step 2 to require Defendant 2 to partially or completely reimburse (the amount depending upon the state's applicable tort law doctrine) Defendant 1 for Defendant 1's payment to plaintiff.

When is subrogation appropriate, and when is contribution or indemnity appropriate? According to the Restatement, contribution or indemnity is appropriate when there are joint tortfeasors, and subrogation is appropriate when there are no joint tortfeasors. *See* RTR §§23, 24. Neither Worldwide Insurance and Ursula nor Distributor and Manufacturerco were joint tortfeasors; in these cases, subrogation was the appropriate remedy. If Distributor and Manufacturerco *were* in fact jointly liable for Customerco's losses, it would appear that contribution or indemnity would have been the appropriate remedy under the Restatement.

Example 11

Nephew buys a used car from Ripoff Motors for $5,000 "as is," with no warranties. The car is a lemon, and its fair market value is only $2,000. Aunt feels sorry for Nephew, and agrees to take the lemon from Nephew and to buy him a good used car for $5,000. After she buys Nephew the replacement car and takes title to the lemon, she sues Ripoff Motors, claiming subrogation. Will Aunt's subrogation claim succeed?

EXPLANATION

Explanation

Aunt's claim against Ripoff Motors will not succeed. There are two problems with this claim. First, it appears that Aunt is a volunteer. She acted out of the goodness of her heart; she did not act out of any business reason, as in the Distributor-Customerco hypothetical.[11]

Even if we disregard the volunteer problem, Aunt's claim appears likely to fail, as she has "stepped into the shoes" of Nephew in asserting a claim against Ripoff Motors. Nephew bought the car "as is," with no warranties. Unless there is some basis for Nephew to somehow bring a damages claim or void the contract (such as under the doctrine of unconscionability), it looks like Nephew's claim against Ripoff would fail. If Nephew's claim would fail, then the claim of Aunt, as subrogee, will fail as well.

EXAMPLE

Example 12

Patient sues Doctor and Nurse for medical malpractice in connection with a colonoscopy done negligently, leading to Patient's infection and hospitalization. The jury determines that Patient incurred $10,000 in medical expenses and suffered $20,000 of emotional distress damages. It also determines that both Doctor and Nurse were negligent, Doctor being 60% at fault and Nurse being 40% at fault. Patient's hospitalization was covered by insurance and paid for by Insurco. The Patient-Insurco contract contained no subrogation clause. Patient collects $30,000 from Doctor. The state uses comparative equitable indemnity for joint tortfeasors. (a) What, if anything, can Doctor recover from Nurse? (b) What, if anything, can Insurco recover from Patient?

EXPLANATION

Explanation

(a) Doctor and Nurse are joint tortfeasors in a state that has adopted comparative equitable indemnity. Doctor has fully satisfied the judgment to Patient in the amount of $30,000. The jury found Nurse 40% at fault, and therefore Doctor can recover 40% of the $30,000 judgment, or $12,000, from Nurse through a comparative equitable indemnity action.

(b) At issue here is the $10,000 in medical expenses; the $20,000 in emotional distress damages is not at issue. Ordinarily, a plaintiff cannot obtain a double recovery, as appears to occur here: plaintiff's $10,000 in medical bills are picked up by Insurco, and Patient recovers another $10,000

---

11. As an aside, we might ask why the law bars volunteers from pursuing these kinds of claims. If Nephew, after all, had a valid claim, Ripoff Motors would have been unjustly enriched if it were lucky enough to have Aunt pay the claim. If the idea is that courts are trying to prevent volunteers from reviving stale claims, it is difficult to see the gain to the volunteer: at best, the volunteer recovers no more than the amount volunteer paid to the subrogor.

in damages from Doctor and Nurse. But the collateral source rule allows plaintiff to recover both amounts, and some insurance companies do not seek subrogation in such circumstances. In this case, the contract contains no subrogation clause; for this reason, conventional subrogation will not be available. However, there may be a claim for equitable (or legal) subrogation here, with a twist. Instead of going after Doctor and Nurse, Insurco goes after Patient to prevent *Patient's unjust enrichment*. Some courts may allow the case to go forward on this basis. But Insurco should be smart if it wants to pursue such remedies in the future by including a subrogation clause in the contract. A court may find that the failure to do so should bar Insurco's right to seek equitable subrogation.

CHAPTER 14

Rescission and Reformation

14.1 INTRODUCTION: ARE RESCISSION AND REFORMATION RESTITUTIONARY REMEDIES?

This chapter, the last of Part III, addresses two additional remedies that arise out of contract disputes: rescission and reformation. *Rescission* is a remedy giving a plaintiff the right to cancel a contract, and it is often followed by restitution, whereby each side returns the consideration it has received under the contract. *Reformation* is a judicial rewriting of the parties' contract.

Some remedies scholars view these remedies as falling in the "restitution" category because they can be used to prevent unjust enrichment. *See, e.g.*, RTR §1, *cmt. c*; LAYCOCK & HASEN p. 722 (calling rescission "the quintessential restitutionary remedy"). *But see* DOBBS & ROBERTS §4.3(6), p. 422-423 (calling rescission "less a remedy and more a matter of the conceptual apparatus that leads to the remedy . . ." and stating that "rescission is not the restitution that follows and it is the restitution that follows that is remedially important."); LAYCOCK & HASEN p. 635 (noting disagreement with other scholars' treatment of reformation as restitutionary, and calling the remedy "declaratory"[1]).

---

1. Chapter 16 covers declaratory remedies. Laycock and Hasen call reformation declaratory "because it can be brought to resolve the potential claims created by the mistaken writing before those claims give rise to any other justiciable dispute." *Id.*

What is the connection between these remedies and restitution? Consider these examples: (1) Child sells Dealer a baseball card worth $1,000 for $20. Rescission by Child prevents Dealer's unjust enrichment. (2) Smith signs a contract to buy Blackacre from the seller, Jones. Both parties believe that the contract contains a clause giving Jones the right to remain on Blackacre for one year after the sale, and the negotiations over the purchase price made it clear that Jones agreed to a lower purchase price to have the right to stay for a year incorporated into the contract. The contract as written mistakenly does not provide Jones with the right to remain. If Smith seeks to force Jones to leave before one year, a court would likely reform (rewrite) the contract to give Jones the right to remain. By reforming the contract, the court prevents Smith's unjust enrichment; the bargain gave Jones the right to be on the land for a year, yet the contract as written did not accurately summarize the bargain.

Though it may be appropriate to classify these remedies as restitutionary because they often prevent unjust enrichment, rescission and reformation can occur even when there is no unjust enrichment. Thus, when Child sells baseball card to Dealer for a fair $1,000 price, Child still has the right to rescind under substantive contract law, which makes contracts with minors voidable at the minor's option. Rescission would not prevent unjust enrichment in that case. Similarly, if a court reforms the Jones-Smith contract to specify that the land contract covers a certain 500 acres of Jones' land rather than an equivalent other 500 acres of Jones' land, the correction of the error might not prevent any unjust enrichment; it would just ensure that the contract accurately reflected the parties' deal.

The remaining sections of this chapter consider the contours of rescission claims, the contours of reformation claims, and a small group of cases in which a plaintiff may have a choice between rescission and reformation. For most students, the question of how to classify these remedies is unimportant; most students will care about this categorization only if their instructors care about such issues.

Example 1

Dealer sells Child a baseball card for $20 that Dealer falsely and intentionally misrepresents as worth $300. The card in fact is worthless. Child pays $20 and is in possession of the baseball card. You are Child's lawyer. Assume the law allows Child to seek rescission of the contract. How would the court grant rescission? Is it restitutionary? Is rescission a good remedy for Child? What other remedies might you as Child's lawyer want to consider to maximize Child's recovery?

EXPLANATION

Explanation

The court would rescind the contract by declaring it void, and then order the parties to each return the consideration received to the other. Under this order, Child gives the baseball card back to Dealer and Dealer gives the $20 back to the Child. Dealer would be unjustly enriched in the absence of rescission (or some other remedy); Dealer would be receiving $20 for a baseball card worth nothing.

While rescission is a better remedy for Child than no remedy at all, it may not be the best remedy under these facts. Child, for example, might seek to affirm the contract (that is, not void the contract but enforce it) and sue for damages for breach of contract. Dealer promised a card worth $300 and delivered a worthless card. In some jurisdictions, this contractual fraud claim would allow Child to receive the difference between what was promised (a card worth $300) and what was received (a card worth nothing), for damages of $300. See Chapter 5.2.

14.2 THE REMEDY OF RESCISSION

Rescission is a remedy for canceling the contract (a process sometimes termed "avoidance" or "termination"[2]). When a court grants rescission, it requires an undoing of the contract to the extent possible, a step necessary to prevent unjust enrichment. Undoing can sometimes be complicated, and the longer a party waits to claim rescission, the harder the undoing might be.

We now consider five major points about rescission.

1. *Contract necessary.* First and foremost, for rescission to be available, the parties must have entered into a *contract*; it is insufficient that there be only unjust enrichment. When Albert steals Gaste's music to write the song "Feelings" (see Chapter 12), for example, Gaste has a valid claim in restitution for Albert's profits. But he could *not* seek rescission, because there is no contract to be canceled or undone.

2. *Rescission available for void or voidable contracts.* Second, rescission is available when contract law provides that a contract is void or voidable. Chapter 11.2, discussing the various grounds for restitution, raised a number of circumstances in which rescission is available for void or voidable contracts. A void contract is one that courts will not enforce (such as a contract to engage in illegal activity); a voidable contract is one that may be terminated at the

2. Dobbs and Roberts and some courts draw some minor distinctions among these terms, Dobbs & Roberts §4.3(6), but many lawyers will use these terms interchangeably.

option of one party, but may be enforced at that party's election. Here are some circumstances involving void or voidable contracts in which rescission appears to be an appropriate remedy:

- Uncle intended to sell Niece his inexpensive but reliable old watch for a fair price. In fact, neither Uncle nor Niece knew that the watch was a very valuable antique. Some courts would allow this *mutual mistake of fact* to render the contract voidable, allowing for rescission and restitution. Rescission also might be available in some cases of *unilateral mistake of fact*, where the non-mistaken party did not rely on the mistake at all. *See* LAYCOCK & HASEN p. 633.
- Niece tells Uncle he is signing a promissory note guaranteeing a loan to Niece to pay for schooling expenses. Uncle is, in fact, signing away his fee interest in Whiteacre. This *fraudulent conduct* renders the contract voidable, allowing for rescission and restitution.
- Niece tells Uncle he must sign over his property interest in Whiteacre or she will break Uncle's legs. This *promise under duress* renders the contract voidable, allowing for rescission and restitution.
- Niece takes care of Uncle and uses "undue influence" to get him to sign over his property interest in Whiteacre. This *undue influence* renders the contract voidable, allowing for rescission and restitution.
- Niece secures Uncle's signature transferring Whiteacre to her at a time when Uncle is mentally incompetent. Unless Uncle ratifies the sale at a time when he is judged competent, his *lack of capacity* renders the contract voidable, allowing for rescission and restitution. The Child-Dealer hypothetical falls into this same category.
- Yolanda and Zena make an oral contract for the sale of Yolanda's land to Zena. Zena makes improvements on the property, and Yolanda then successfully claims the contract is unenforceable because it fails to satisfy the statute of frauds. The *failure to comply with the statute of frauds* renders the contract voidable, allowing for rescission and restitution.

3. *Rescission sometimes available for breach of enforceable contract, when there has been a substantial breach of contract.* Courts will sometimes allow the non-breaching party to an enforceable contract to cancel it when the breaching party has committed a substantial (as opposed to minor) breach of contract. In *O.C.T. Equipment, Inc. v. Shepherd Mach. Co.*, 95 P.3d 197 (Okla. Civ. App. 2004), for example, Buyer paid $42,000 to seller for delivery of a farming tractor. The tractor arrived without antifreeze in it, and because the delivery person drove the tractor without antifreeze (before the risk of loss passed to the buyer), the engine burned up and was ruined. The court held that under

Oklahoma's version of U.C.C. §2-711(1),[3] Buyer had the right to reject the goods, cancel (rescind) the contract, and receive back its $42,000 purchase price.

4. *Undoing of contracts can be complicated.* As noted, once a court cancels a contract, it has to undo any performance that has already taken place. Sometimes such undoing is straightforward. In the Child-Dealer example, Child returns the card and Dealer returns the money. But other situations are much more complicated. In the Yolanda-Zena hypothetical, suppose that Zena made $10,000 worth of improvements to the land over the course of a month before Yolanda brings suit to void the contract on statute of frauds grounds. To undo the contract, it is inadequate for Yolanda to return the consideration Zena paid for the contract and cancel the deed to Zena. In order to *put the parties in the same position they would have been in had there been no contract*, a court would likely order Yolanda to pay Zena for the value of the improvements and require Zena to pay Yolanda a reasonable rent for the one-month Zena was in possession.

The court is going to have to figure out how to value the improvements and the rent. On top of that, complications may arise if one of the parties does not have the money to pay the other. If Yolanda, for example, cannot afford to pay Zena for the improvements, a court may grant Zena a money judgment for the amount of improvements (offset by the value of the rent Zena paid Yolanda), backed up by an equitable lien (see Chapter 13.2). In the interest of justice, a court might delay Zena's ability to foreclose on the property through the equitable lien to satisfy the judgment.

There's a certain unfairness in Yolanda's waiting a month (until after Zena has invested significant costs in reliance) before seeking to rescind the land contract. Some courts will say that, as a matter of substantive contract law, contracts voidable under the statute of frauds become enforceable once a party has relied on the contract. *See* Restatement (Second) of Contracts §139(1) (1981). Even in those jurisdictions rejecting reliance as a means of overcoming a statute of frauds objection, a court could hold that Yolanda's claim should be barred because she waited too long to sue, prejudicing Zena. This is a defense referred to as *laches*, discussed in Chapter 18. *See also* RTR §70(2)(a).

---

3. This section provides:

> (1) Where the seller fails to make delivery or repudiates or the buyer rightfully rejects or justifiably revokes acceptance then with respect to any goods involved, and with respect to the whole if the breach goes to the whole contract (§2-612), *the buyer may cancel* and whether or not he has done so may in addition to recovering so much of the price as has been paid
>
> (a) "cover" and have damages under the next section as to all the goods affected whether or not they have been identified to the contract; or
>
> (b) recover damages for nondelivery as provided in this article (§2-713).

U.C.C. §2-711(1) (emphasis added).

5. *Plaintiffs sometimes have the choice between (a) voiding a contract and suing for rescission and (b) standing on the contract and suing for compensatory damages.* When a contract is void—as opposed to merely voidable—rescission may be one of the only remedies available to a plaintiff. In contrast, when the contract is merely *voidable*, the law gives the plaintiff an option between voiding the contract and suing for rescission or standing on the contract and suing for compensatory damages.

Which choice the plaintiff should make depends upon the facts of the particular case. Consider one of my favorite contracts cases, *Stambovsky v. Ackley*, 572 N.Y.S.2d 672 (N.Y. App. Div. 1991). Buyer contracted to buy a house from Seller. Seller failed to disclose that the house had a reputation for being haunted. The fact that the house had this reputation had a negative impact on its market value. The *Stambovsky* court held that Buyer could rescind the contract, receiving back its contract price (though Buyer would need to pay a reasonable rent for the period of time Buyer remained in the house).

This failure to disclose a material fact provided a basis for rescission. Though New York (like many other states) held that mere non-disclosure ordinarily would not provide the basis for rescission, "[w]here a condition which has been created by the seller materially impairs the value of the contract and is peculiarly within the knowledge of the seller or unlikely to be discovered by a prudent purchaser exercising due care with respect to the subject transaction, nondisclosure constitutes a basis for rescission as a matter of equity." *Id.* at 676.

New York law did not give Buyer the option to sue for damages arising out of a nondisclosure, *id.* at 675, but other states might give Buyer the option to do so. And in cases of affirmative fraud by Seller, even New York courts should give Buyer the option of rescission or standing on the contract and suing for damages.

Assuming the jurisdiction gave plaintiff a choice of remedy, which remedy is better for Buyer? Imagine that the purchase price of the house was $200,000. The house's "haunted" reputation "greatly impair[ed] both the value of the property and its potential for resale." *Id.* at 674. Suppose the fair market value of the house with the haunted reputation was only $150,000. Buyer discovers the reputation the day escrow closes on the house.

If Buyer asks for rescission, Buyer gets back the $200,000 consideration and Seller keeps the house. Buyer could then turn around and buy another house worth $200,000. Alternatively, Buyer could keep the house, really worth $150,000, and get $50,000 in damages. From here, Buyer could either keep the house and the damages or sell the house for $150,000 and use the proceeds plus the damages to buy another house worth $200,000.

Framed this way, the rescission and damages options look equivalent: both put Buyer back in the rightful position of having a house (or the equivalent in house and money); both put Buyer in the same position as if there had been no wrong. But there may be reasons why Buyer would prefer rescission over damages:

- Buyer may have lost confidence in Seller, questioning what else might be wrong in the house and thus preferring the chance to "start over."
- Buyer may not trust the court to accurately estimate the difference between the purchase price and the house's true market value.
- The market may have changed during the period between the close of the deal and the trial, and plaintiff might want to use rescission to get out of a bad bargain.

The last point is worth emphasizing. Suppose, for example, that the purchase price of the house was $200,000 but market values have dropped in the interim by $25,000. Rescission gives Buyer back the purchase price of $200,000, allowing Buyer to buy a new house equivalent to the old one (without the bad reputation) for only $175,000, saving $25,000. In contrast, if Buyer sues for damages, the damages would be measured at the time of the wrong, meaning Buyer would get only $50,000, not $75,000, in damages.

This point can be generalized: when it comes to losing contracts, rescission presents an enticing opportunity. Rather than sticking to the bad deal and take damages (if there are any), plaintiff can undo the deal and cut her losses.[4] Consider this powerful example: an insurance company that insured a man's life under non-smoking rates gets to rescind the contract (returning premiums paid and interest) after the man dies and an investigation revealed the man lied about being a non-smoker. The insurance company did not have to pay substantial benefits under the contract. *See* LAYCOCK & HASEN p. 722 (citing *Mut. Benefit Life Ins. Co. v. JMR Elecs. Corp.*, 848 F.2d 30 (2d Cir. 1988)). Note that U.C.C. §2-711(1) (quoted in footnote 3 of this chapter, and applicable to contracts for the sale of goods) gives plaintiff the right both to rescind a contract *and* to obtain damages for the cost of cover when appropriate. Thus, using the tractor example, Buyer gets back its $42,000 purchase price and returns the tractor to Seller. If Buyer's reasonable substitute price for a similar tractor is $45,000, Buyer is entitled to receive the $3,000 in damages as well as the right to rescission.

---

4. The Restatement hedges a bit on the propriety of such a move: "The fact that rescission permits the claimant to escape from an unfavorable bargain does not by itself make rescission inequitable, but rescission will be denied it if its effect could be the unjust enrichment of the claimant at the expense of the other party. The potential for unjust enrichment is obvious when one party seeks rescission to pursue opportunistic gain, or as a means of speculating at the other's expense." RTR §54, cmt. f.

EXAMPLE

Example 2

Seller promises to sell Buyer 50 tons of carrots for $20/ton. Buyer sends $1,000 to Seller, but Seller fails to deliver the carrots. At this time, the price of carrots had fallen to $15/ton. What is the best remedy for Buyer?

EXPLANATION

Explanation

Buyer will want to rescind the contract and receive back his $1,000 payment. With the price falling to $15/ton, Buyer will be able to get the 50 of carrots for $750, saving $250. This was a lucky break for Buyer, because Seller breached what would have been a losing contract for Buyer. This is a sale of goods contract governed by U.C.C. §2-711. In addition to rescinding the contract, Buyer would have the right to damages under §2-711, but Buyer has suffered no damages because he can cover for less than the contract price. For more on this damages point, see Chapter 4.

EXAMPLE

Example 3

Owner makes a contract with Contractor to remodel Owner's kitchen for $40,000. The contract specifies that Contractor will use "Cohoe" brand copper pipes in the remodel. Contractor inadvertently uses "Reading" brand copper pipes instead. The quality of the pipes is identical. Owner would like to rescind the contract because Owner believes the fair market value of the remodel is $30,000. Will a court allow Owner to rescind the contract and pay Contractor in restitution?

EXPLANATION

Explanation

The facts of this hypothetical are loosely based upon *Jacob & Youngs, Inc. v. Kent*, 129 N.E. 889 (N.Y. 1921). It appears that Owner would like to use a minor breach of contract by Contractor to get out of a bad contract, paying a lower price than the contract price. A court is unlikely to allow Owner to rescind the contract based on a minor breach; under substantive contract law, as the *Jacob & Youngs* case establishes, the inconsequential breach here does not count as a "substantial breach" that courts would require for rescission.

EXAMPLE

Example 4

Alberto is on a small pleasure boat (worth $50,000) that is sinking during a storm. Bill is on a larger pleasure boat that is passing by. Alberto asks Bill for his help. Bill agrees to tow Alberto and his boat to safety, but only if Alberto agrees to let Bill keep the boat. Alberto, fearing for his life, reluctantly agrees. Bill tows the boat to shore, saving Alberto's life but keeping the boat. Alberto sues to rescind the contract. What result? Explain.

EXPLANATION

Explanation

A court is likely to void this contract on grounds of duress because Alberto entered into it without free choice. Rescission would allow Alberto to receive his boat back. That might leave Alberto unjustly enriched, however: Bill rescued him without receiving any compensation. The fact that Bill demanded compensation should serve to refute the presumption that Bill was rendering his services gratuitously. (See Chapter 11.) A court will need to determine the reasonable value of Bill's services, perhaps considering the amount that a professional rescuer would have charged under the circumstances.

EXAMPLE

Example 5

Carmen sells his home to Deborah for $250,000. Before the sale, Deborah asked about termite damage. Carmen lied, saying there was no damage. In fact, there was damage that Carmen took active steps to hide and that will cost $20,000 to repair. Deborah discovers the damage shortly after she moves in. The house is appreciating in value and is now worth $300,000 (once the termite damage is repaired). Should Deborah rescind the contract? Why or why not?

EXPLANATION

Explanation

Rescission is certainly a possibility: Deborah would receive back her $250,000 purchase price, and Carmen would get back the deed to the home (plus a reasonable rental value for the period that Deborah lived in the house). Deborah could then go out and buy a new house without the damage. The problem with this remedy for Deborah is that prices are appreciating, and a new home of similar quality will cost her more, perhaps $300,000.

A more desirable alternative, if it is available, is for Deborah to affirm the contract and sue for the $20,000 in damages. If Carmen pays for that repair, Deborah gets to keep the house for the $250,000 contract price (which turns out to be a good deal given the home's appreciation), paying nothing for the termite repair.

14.3 THE REFORMATION REMEDY

Reformation is an equitable remedy that gives courts the power to rewrite a contract of the parties.[5] "When parties come to an agreement, but by fraud or mistake write it down in some fashion that does not truly reflect their contract, equity will reform the writing to make it reflect the parties' true intention." DOBBS & ROBERTS, §4.3(7), p. 425.

To take a typical example, A and B sign a land contract that they both believe covers a sale of the property at 123 Elm Street. In fact, because of a typographical error that no one notices, the contract describes property at 124 Elm Street. The parties may simply agree to rewrite their contract to correct the error. In the event there is a disagreement (for example, if A owned both 123 Elm Street and 124 Elm Street, and B prefers buying 124 over 123), the reformation matter may end up in court. Assuming the party seeking reformation can prove that the parties' intent was not accurately reflected in the written contract, a court will order the contract reformed so that it covers the correct property.

Note that the mistake in the A-B contract is one that goes to *the content of the writing*. If the parties make a mistake as to the contract's *substance*, reformation will not be available. If, for example, A believes the contract is for the sale of 123 Elm Street and B believes the contract is for the sale of 124 Elm Street, reformation is not an appropriate remedy: to see why, ask yourself how the court would rewrite the contract (not for 123.5 Elm Street!). Rescission may be a more appropriate option in such circumstances.

Fraud as to the content of the writing—leading to the other party's unilateral mistake—can also be a basis for reformation of a contract. Thus, if A and B agree to the sale of 123 Elm Street, but B, desiring 124 Elm Street (which A also owns), has the contract written to state the contract as covering 124 Elm Street, a court will allow the contract to be rewritten for the sale of 123 Elm Street.[6]

---

5. Despite reformation's status as an equitable remedy, "[t]here does not seem to be any ripeness or irreparable injury requirement for reformation, although not many cases are filed in which these issues could plausibly be raised." LAYCOCK & HASEN p. 635.

6. If it seems odd to you that the court will rewrite a contract when there has been no "meeting of the minds" regarding the sale of 123 Elm Street, remember that under modern substantive contract law, it is not the parties' subjective desires that count. In this case, both A and B outwardly indicated their intent to enter into a contract for the sale of 123 Elm Street. Under the objective theory of contract, that should be sufficient to allow such a sale to go through. If you don't like that theory, it is also possible to see the reformation remedy as a kind of punishment for B's fraud. If B pretended to be interested in buying 123 Elm Street (when B secretly desired 124 Elm Street), reformation would make B stick with the deal to which B pretended to agree.

Reformation may be accompanied by a plea for another remedy, such as damages for breach of contract. Thus, suppose Eddy is renting a retail site from Francesca for one year. Their lease contract was supposed to include a provision requiring Francesca to have the windows washed twice per week. Because of a typographical error, the contract states the requirement that the windows are to be washed twice per *year*. Francesca refuses to wash the windows for four months, so Eddy has them washed twice per week at a cost of $300 per week. Eddy may go to court to have the contract reformed to reflect the "twice per week" agreement. He may then seek damages for breach of contract, based upon Francesca's failure to wash the windows twice weekly as promised by the reformed contract. If the $300 per week was a reasonable cost for the service, a court is likely to award the value of those expenses to Eddy. Additionally, if Eddy is convinced that Francesca will not wash the windows twice a week for the remaining portion of the contract, he might seek an order of *specific performance* requiring that she do so.[7]

EXAMPLE

Example 6

Restaurant enters into an insurance contract with Insurer covering certain liability related to the operation of the restaurant. Restaurant accurately told Insurer that it served alcohol, but Insurer erroneously classified Restaurant as not serving alcohol. Had Insurer known that Restaurant served alcohol, it would have included a provision in the insurance contract excluding liability for alcohol-related incidents. After the insurance policy drafted by Insurer arrived at Restaurant, Restaurant's manager noticed that the policy incorrectly described Restaurant as not serving alcohol. Restaurant sent Insurer a letter pointing out the error, but Insurer did nothing about it. A few months later, while the policy was in effect, one patron stabbed another patron in Restaurant's parking lot in an alcohol-related incident. May Insurer, in order to avoid paying damages arising out of the stabbing, bring suit to reform the contract to correctly classify Restaurant as an establishment that serves alcohol and to exclude liability for alcohol-related incidents? Can Insurer alternatively seek rescission of the contract on the grounds of mutual mistake?

7. Specific performance is a kind of injunction requiring that a party perform as promised in a contract. For more on specific performance, see the discussion in Chapter 7.

EXPLANATION

Explanation

This example is based loosely on *Alea London Ltd. v. Bono-Soltysiak Enter.*, 186 S.W.3d 403 (Mo. Ct. App. 2006). This case involves no mistake as to the writing or as to fraud related to the writing. The court is likely to reject reformation for this reason. It is also likely to reject rescission, as the case involves neither a mutual mistake of fact nor a unilateral mistake of fact accompanied by fraud. As the Missouri court wrote in rejecting the claim: "[Insurer] adduced absolutely no evidence, let alone clear and convincing evidence, that [Restaurant] acted in bad faith, committed fraud or deceived [Insurer]. Moreover [Restaurant] did nothing to hinder [Insurer] in the discovery of its error. It is well settled that '[e]quity will not relieve against mistake when the complaining party had within his reach the true state of facts, and, without being induced by the other party, neglected to avail himself of his opportunities of information.'" *Id.* at 416 (citation omitted).

Note that because reformation is an equitable remedy, a court may be especially disinclined to grant reformation given these facts. Not only was this a unilateral mistake for which the party seeking reformation was totally responsible; the other party told the mistaken party of the mistake, and the mistaken party did nothing to correct it until the positions of the parties had changed dramatically with the stabbing. See also Chapter 18, discussing the equitable defenses of *waiver*, *estoppel*, and *laches*, which could come into play here to bar the reformation claim based on the delay even if there *were* initially a mutual mistake.

14.4 THE CHOICE BETWEEN RESCISSION AND REFORMATION

In rare circumstances, a party may have the choice between rescission and reformation. Consider the case of *Hand v. Dayton-Hudson*, 775 F.2d 757 (6th Cir. 1985). Hand worked as an attorney for Dayton-Hudson Corporation. The company decided to lay off Hand. He was offered $38,000 in exchange for his agreement to release all claims he might have against the company. After initially refusing the offer, Hand took the proposed contract offering the $38,000 and copied it using the same typewriter,[8] so that it appeared to be the company's offer. He secretly changed the language of the release to exclude claims for age discrimination (leaving him the right to sue for age discrimination). Both parties then signed the contract, but Dayton-Hudson did not know Hand had altered it. Hand then turned around and sued Dayton-Hudson for age discrimination.

8. Some of you may be old enough to remember what a typewriter is. Hand's fraud would likely be much easier today with computer-based word processing.

The *Hand* case nicely illustrates the choice that Dayton-Hudson faced. As should be clear from the previous two sections, Hand's conduct entitled the company to seek either rescission of the contract or reformation. Rescission was appropriate because the parties had a voidable contract as a result of Hand's fraud; the company could rescind the contract if it chose to do so. Alternatively, *Hand* is a classic case of unilateral mistake in the writing procured by fraud. Reformation is appropriate to make the contract reflect a full release in exchange for the $38,000 payment.

In this circumstance, reformation was a much better option for the company than rescission. (Before reading on, see if you can answer why.) As Laycock and Hasen explain, "Reformation leaves the release in effect as reformed. Hand gets to keep the $38,000; Dayton-Hudson is still released; Hand cannot sue for breach of contract or age discrimination. . . . Rescission would reverse the transaction. Dayton-Hudson would get its $38,000 back, Hand would get the release back, and Hand could sue for breach of contract and age discrimination." LAYCOCK & HASEN p. 633.

Though *Hand* is a unilateral mistake with fraud case, *mutual mistake as to a writing* also could provide a choice between rescission and reformation in appropriate cases. If Hand and Dayton-Hudson both thought, for example, that they were signing a release that excluded age discrimination claims, but the contract was drafted without the exclusion, Hand might either seek to reform the contract to put back in the exclusion or seek to rescind the contract on grounds of mutual mistake. However, if the court finds that it was clear what both parties thought they were contracting for, the court could deny rescission and grant only reformation.

Example 7

If you were Hand in the mutual mistake variation described immediately above (as opposed to the actual fraud case), would you prefer the remedy of reformation or rescission?

Explanation

The answer to this question will depend upon the facts of the case. If Hand believes he has viable claims besides age discrimination, he might ask a court to rescind the contract, allowing him to sue for various claims beyond age discrimination. In doing so, he would need to return the $38,000 he received as consideration for giving up these claims. In contrast, if Hand believes his only viable claim is one for age discrimination, he is better off asking for reformation so that he can have both the payment and the right to sue for age discrimination.

Again, a court might not be willing to give Hand the choice of remedies in such circumstances. But if the court gives the choice, it is important for Hand (and for Hand's lawyer) to carefully consider the costs and benefits of the various choices.

Example 8

In another variation on the Hand–Dayton-Hudson hypothetical, the parties sign a contract paying Hand $38,000 and releasing Dayton-Hudson from all of Hand's claims against it *except* for age discrimination claims. Dayton-Hudson claims that Hand committed fraud by altering the contract. Hand says that the parties agreed to include the age discrimination exclusion as a condition for him to sign the contract. Is Dayton-Hudson entitled to reformation to exclude the release from the age discrimination claim? Is it entitled to rescind the contract?

Explanation

The answer will depend upon what the judge as fact finder believes about the case. (Because these are equitable remedies, they will be tried before a judge, not a jury.) Reformation usually requires that the party seeking reformation prove by clear and convincing evidence what the parties intended the written contract to say. If Dayton-Hudson can prove that this was a case of fraud under the strict evidentiary standards, it will be entitled to reformation. The same goes for rescission. The issue may come down to a swearing contest between the parties, and the right of Dayton-Hudson to any remedy is going to depend upon what it can prove to the court. (In the actual *Hand* case, attorney Hand admitted to altering the document without informing Dayton-Hudson!)

PART IV

Other Important Remedies Concepts

CHAPTER 15

Dishing It Out: Punitive Damages and Their Constitutional Limits

15.1 INTRODUCTION TO PUNITIVE DAMAGES

In Part I, especially Chapter 3, we considered the rightful position standard and tort damages. Tort damages are *compensatory*; they aim to put the plaintiff back in the "rightful position," the position that plaintiff would have been in but for the defendant's wrong. Consider Figure 15.1.

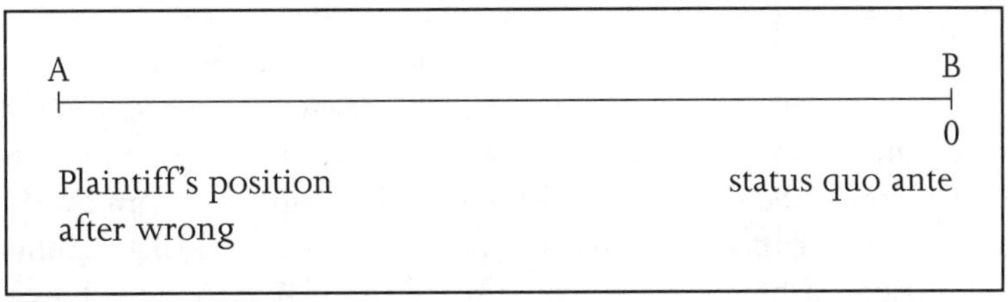

Figure 15.1

At least in theory, an award of damages equal to (B – A) puts the plaintiff back in the position she would have been in but for the wrong. For example, if Adam steals Beverly's new phone valued at $300, Beverly is at –$300 after the theft (putting aside some additional damages for the delay and for the costs of obtaining the new phone, which we will ignore for the rest of this discussion). As Figure 15.2 shows, Beverly started at B (or 0, the status quo ante) before the theft. The theft moved Beverly to A, at –$300. Compensatory tort damages would be (B – A), or (0 – (–300)), or $300, an award which will, at least in theory, put Beverly in the same position as if there had not been a theft. In this way, Beverly has been *compensated* for the loss of her phone.

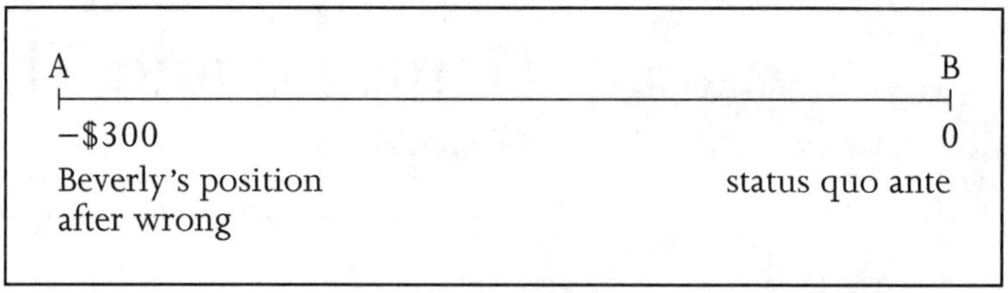

Figure 15.2 Adam and Beverly

Economists have long noted that compensatory damages may serve a *deterrent* function as well. The fact that Adam would have to pay Beverly for the cost of the phone may make him less likely to steal it, and Adam's payment may make others think twice before engaging in the same tortious activity.

But compensatory damages may not be enough to deter Adam and others who otherwise might have no moral qualms about taking someone else's property. Adam might not be found, and if he is found, Beverly may have difficulty proving one or more elements of her tort case against Adam. Indeed, given that only $300 is at stake, Beverly would have a tough time finding a lawyer who would take her case; would *you* put in many hours of your time to get a 30% contingent recovery on a $300 claim?

Punitive damages may serve that deterrent function. Punitive damages are damages awarded *in addition to* compensatory damages that are aimed at *punishing and making an example* out of the defendant.

Imagine if, in addition to the $300 that Beverly could receive in compensatory damages, a jury has the discretion to award her another $3,000 in punitive damages. The possibility of that larger punitive damage award could deter Adam and those like him. Suppose Adam thinks there is only a 20% chance he would be located, served, and successfully sued for damages. If he thinks he would pay $300 if Beverly finds him and successfully sues him, his expected loss is 20% of $300, or $60. But if he expects to pay $3,300 if a judgment is issued against him ($300 in compensatory damages and $3,000 in punitive damages), his expected loss is 20% of $3,300, or $660. There will be some thieves, perhaps including Adam, who would be deterred by a $660 expected loss but not a $60 expected loss. After all, even if the phone is not worth $300 to Adam, it is likely worth more than $60 but less than $660.

The possibility of punitive damages also may make the case more appealing to lawyers who would work for a contingency fee: better to have 30% of $3,300 than 30% of $300. Punitive damages therefore make some suits economically viable for plaintiffs when they otherwise would not be viable.

Punitive damages are sometimes referred to as *exemplary* damages because they make an example out of the defendant. This name stresses a *corrective justice* feature of these damages unconnected with the economic deterrence argument. A $3,300 damage judgment is going to hurt Adam a lot more than a $300 award, and the fact that a jury has awarded a large punitive award tells the community that Adam has done something worthy of their condemnation.

With all of these pluses for punitive damages, perhaps they should be available in every case as a way of making up for the fact that a number of lawsuits that should be successful are not successful because of procedural barriers or other problems.[1] But this would create some problems. Consider the case of Carla, who is engaged in the abnormally dangerous activity of dynamite blasting. Carla uses all reasonable care to avoid causing any damage while demolishing a building, but flying debris still busts the window on David's car. Blasting is a strict liability tort offense, so Carla will be paying even though she is not at fault. *See* RESTATEMENT (THIRD) OF TORTS—LIABILITY FOR PHYSICAL AND EMOTIONAL HARM §20.

Economic theory suggests we might want to allow punitive damages against Carla for the same reason as we might want them available for Beverly's suit against Adam: to create additional incentives for people like Carla not to injure others. But Carla likely is already using a high level of care to avoid paying damages in a strict liability system. Creating additional incentives for Carla to take care might lead to *overdeterrence*: she might become too careful, and not engage in the risky but useful activity of blasting.

In addition, there are justice problems with holding Carla liable for punitive damages. If she has done nothing wrong, corrective justice might still support requiring her to *compensate* David.[2] But even if the law says Carla should compensate David, why should we also make an example out of Carla and punish her? And if we are going to punish her, is it right to do so through the *civil justice* (as opposed to the criminal justice) system? In the civil justice system, we generally require proof by only a preponderance of the evidence (just more likely than not), and not proof beyond a reasonable doubt. Think if you were in Carla's place, acting as carefully as you could while engaging in a dangerous but useful activity. The threat of punitive

1. Economists would think of punitive damages simply as serving as a "multiplier" of the compensatory damages. These damages would be calibrated somehow to make up for the underdeterrence caused by failures of the tort system to make every defendant pay who should pay under the applicable legal rule.

2. Corrective justice theorists have long debated whether a rule of negligence or a rule of strict liability is the appropriate one for unintended conduct that causes injury to persons. But this debate concerns the question of compensation, not punishment.

damages, imposed under a preponderance standard, just might drive you out of business.

Just as compensatory damages may serve a *deterrent* purpose, punitive damages may serve a *compensatory* purpose because plaintiff gets to collect the punitive damages as well. But they can *over*compensate. Even in the Adam-Beverly hypothetical, there is the windfall feature of punitive damages that some people find troubling. Consider Figure 15.3.

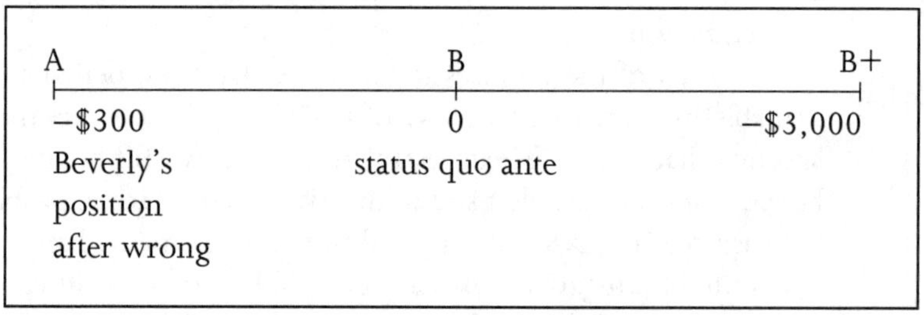

Figure 15.3 The Windfall Aspect of Punitive Damages in the Adam-Beverly Hypothetical

When Adam steals Beverly's phone, she moves from B, the status quo ante, to A, −$300. Putting aside search and other incidental costs, a compensatory award of $300 moves her back to B, the rightful position in a typical tort damages suit. But with the addition of punitive damages, she ends up at B+, a gain of $3,000. If the first $300 of the award truly compensated her, Beverly *is now better off* than had there been no theft; a $3,300 award makes her $3,000 richer than she would have been had there been no theft. This is why punitive damages are so appealing to plaintiffs (and plaintiffs' lawyers).

Recognizing both the potential benefits of punitive damages as well as the concerns raised in the last few paragraphs, courts (and legislatures) have created special rules for punitive damages:

- *Conduct*. The conduct that merits the award of punitive damages must be quite bad. Though states use different language to express this idea (such as "malice" (Tex. Civil Prac. & Remedies Code §41.001(7)) or acting with an "evil mind" (*Linthicum v. Nationwide Life Ins. Co.*, 723 P.2d 675, 679 (Ariz. 1986)), one general point is that the conduct must be *worse than negligence*.[3] Defendant's intent to injure is an easy case for imposition of punitive damages, but such an intent is not required; in some states recklessness as to injury may be enough. In determining

3. How much worse? It depends upon the jurisdiction. Certainly, all states allow punitive damages when a defendant has been proven to have an intent to harm a plaintiff. The harder cases are when the defendant acts with something like recklessness, ignoring a substantial probability of serious harm to others.

if the conduct merits the award of punitive damages, you should not focus on the name of the cause of action, but rather on the nature of the conduct. For example, the fact that the tort raised against Carla for blasting is a strict liability tort does not prevent an award of punitive damages against her if, for example, she acted recklessly by not taking any steps to minimize injury from blasting.

- *Burden of proof.* Many states raise the burden of proof for a plaintiff to be eligible to collect punitive damages. Rather than proving the requisite bad conduct by a preponderance of the evidence, a plaintiff might have to prove it by a higher standard, such as California's "clear and convincing evidence" standard (a standard greater than the preponderance standard but less than the criminal standard of proof beyond a reasonable doubt). *See* CAL. CIV. CODE §3294.
- *Need for award of compensatory damages.* A majority of states require that a jury must first find plaintiff entitled to *compensatory damages* before the jury may award punitive damages. Among those states, most allow nominal damages to qualify,[4] and plaintiffs sometimes seek nominal damages precisely because they want to use such damages as a hook to get punitive damages. Historically, equity courts would not award punitive damages in; today more courts will allow plaintiff to couple a punitive damages claim with equitable relief,[5] such as when an injunction prevents a defendant from engaging in a bad act. In some jurisdictions, a plaintiff can couple a restitutionary remedy with a claim for punitive damages. *Compare Thomas Auto Co., Inc. v. Craft*, 763 S.W.2d 651, 654 (Ark. 1989) ("We can think of no reason why punitive damages should not accompany a restitutionary award if there is proof of the elements of deceit as a basis of revocation of acceptance or extrajudicial rescission.") *with Merritt v. Craig*, 746 A.2d 923, 931 (Md. Ct. Spec. App. 2000) (plaintiff cannot couple rescission claim with claim for punitive damages); *Hong v. Kong*, 683 P.2d 833, 841 (Haw. Ct. App. 1984) (punitive damages not awardable in an action for restitution).
- *More state-specific rules.* Some states have statutes that limit the ability to sue certain defendants for punitive damages without a preliminary showing of wrongdoing. Some states require that some of the

---

4. *See* Richard C. Tinney, *Sufficiency of Showing of Actual Damages to Support Award of Punitive Damages—Modern Cases*, 40 A.L.R 4th 11 §§6-9 (1985 & 2023 Supp.) (collecting cases on both sides of issue); *but see* N.J. STAT. ANN. 2A:15-5.13(c) (nominal damages cannot support the award of punitive damages). The reporters' notes in the forthcoming Restatement (Third) Torts: Remedies section on liability for punitive damages will give a list and count of states.
5. DOBBS & ROBERTS §3.11 p. 317 ("Though this rule [against awarding punitive damages in equity] is rejected by contemporary decisions that have addressed it as a serious issues, there are still cases that still repeat it"). Chapter 7 discusses the distinction between legal and equitable remedies in some detail. See also Chapter 13's discussion of how some restitutionary remedies are legal and some are equitable.

punitive award go to the state rather than to the plaintiff. And states are split over whether an employer may be *vicariously liable* for punitive damages based on the actions of its employees.[6] In some states, vicarious liability is available as a matter of course. In other states, for the employer to be liable the employee must have exercised managerial discretion or approved or participated in the tort of the employee. *See* RESTATEMENT (SECOND) OF TORTS §909 (1979).

- *Punitive damages in contract actions.* As we will see in the next section of this chapter, courts make it very difficult to recover punitive damages in *contract* actions.
- *Constitutionality of high damage awards.* Finally, as we will see in the last section of this chapter, many courts impose limits on and strict judicial review of the *amount* of punitive damages. In recent years, the United States Supreme Court has imposed limits on the amount of punitive damages under the Due Process Clause of the Fourteenth Amendment to the United States Constitution.

EXAMPLE

Example 1

Ellen is driving down the street, paying more attention to her cell phone conversation than to the road conditions. Because of her carelessness, she strikes Frank, who is crossing the street, causing him serious personal injuries. A jury finds that Ellen was negligent and caused Frank economic and noneconomic losses of $10,000. May the jury also award Frank punitive damages?

EXPLANATION

Explanation

Probably not. The answer will depend upon each state's standard for the award of punitive damages, but this looks like a garden-variety negligence case, for which punitive damages will *not* be available. Her conduct would have to be worse than carelessness.

6. Under *vicarious liability*, one person is strictly liable for the tort of another. Most states hold employers strictly liable for the torts of their employees, requiring the employer to pay damages to a person injured by an employee. The doctrine applied in the tort context is sometimes referred to by the Latin term *respondeat superior*.

Example 2

After Ellen hit Frank and gave information to the police, she got back into her car and resumed driving. Again, she picked up her cell phone, and she became so engrossed in a conversation that she did not notice the large flashing sign stating that she was entering a school zone and that children were present. As she tried to hold the cell phone with one hand and roll down her car window with the other, she ran over Gina, Harry, and Ivan, three schoolchildren who were on the sidewalk waiting for the school bus to take them home. A jury finds that Ellen was negligent and caused the children each $25,000 in economic and noneconomic losses. May the jury also award the children punitive damages? If Ellen was driving in the course and scope of her employment, may her employer be vicariously liable for any punitive damages?

Explanation

Ellen likely will be liable for punitive damages. Again, the answer will depend upon each state's standard for the award of punitive damages and the jury's assessment of blameworthiness, but this case looks like Ellen engaged in worse conduct than in Example 1. Although she did not have an intent to injure, a jury could well conclude that Ellen acted with substantial disregard of the high probability of causing injury to others, a form of reckless conduct. She had just been in an accident after using her cell phone while driving, yet she continued the practice. She ignored the flashing warning lights and took both hands off the steering wheel simultaneously for non-emergency reasons. She was so inattentive that she let her car go onto the sidewalk in a school zone. Although Ellen did not have an intent to injure, this kind of bad conduct is likely to merit an award of punitive damages in most states.

Note that the cause of action here is negligence, but the cause of action alone does *not* dictate whether or not punitive damages are available. Focus on the *conduct*, not the *name of the tort*.

Jurisdictions are split over whether Ellen's employer may be vicariously liable for Ellen's tort. In some states, it depends upon whether the bad conduct meriting punitive damages was an exercise of managerial discretion. In this case, her driving habits were not a managerial decision, so in those jurisdictions Ellen's employer would *not* be vicariously liable for punitive damages. Some states require that the employer approve of or participate in the tort of the employee. Under these facts (without more) there would be no punitive damages available against Ellen's employer unless the state automatically held an employer vicariously liable for the employee's torts.

EXAMPLE

Example 3

Suppose in Example 2 the jury agreed that it was more likely than not that Ellen engaged in bad conduct required for the award of punitive damages in the state, but they do not agree that she engaged in such conduct beyond a reasonable doubt. May the jury award punitive damages?

EXPLANATION

Explanation

You would need more information to answer the question. First, you would need to know the burden of proof in the jurisdiction for proving the conduct relevant for an award of punitive damages. Suppose the standard is one of "clear and convincing evidence." Even knowing the standard, you would need more information. Because the "clear and convincing" standard falls somewhere between the preponderance standard and the reasonable doubt standard, we do not know how the jury would conclude under the correct standard: was there in fact clear and convincing evidence that she engaged in the bad conduct?

EXAMPLE

Example 4

Jared spits in Ken's face, deliberately, with no one else present, to express his disgust at the style of shoes that Ken is wearing. In his tort suit, Ken successfully proves the elements of an offensive battery, but he suffers no damages. The jury awards Ken $1 in nominal damages and finds by clear and convincing evidence (the right standard under state law) that Jared engaged in his actions with malicious intent, meeting the state's punitive damages standard. May the jury award punitive damages?

EXPLANATION

Explanation

Yes, if (as in many states) nominal damages count as compensatory damages. As we saw in Chapter 2.4, nominal damages serve a *declaratory* rather than a compensatory function: they tell the world the respective rights of plaintiff and defendant rather than compensating the plaintiff. Nonetheless, many courts will allow an award of punitive damages to piggyback on a nominal damages award. Without this rule, many dignitary harms that do not cause actual damage could be difficult to deter.

EXAMPLE

Example 5

Anita steals Brianna's digital camera worth $200, hocks the camera at a pawnshop for $150, and bets the $150 at the racetrack, winning $1,000. Brianna brings suit in restitution, and the court awards a constructive trust over the $1,000 winnings. (A constructive trust is an equitable restitutionary remedy discussed in detail in Chapter 13.) (a) May the court also award punitive damages? (b) Should the court allow the jury to consider awarding punitive damages? (Note this second part asks for your opinion; there is no correct answer.)

EXPLANATION

Explanation

(a) The court may allow the jury to award punitive damages. Historically, punitive damages were not available when a plaintiff sought an equitable remedy rather than a remedy at law. In this case, the constructive trust is an equitable remedy. Courts were split too on whether punitive damages could be awarded in a case seeking restitution. Today, more courts allow punitive damages in appropriate cases even for those plaintiffs seeking a remedy in equity and those seeking restitution.

(b) The normative question whether the law should allow punitive damages is an interesting one. The purpose of the constructive trust is to take away the defendant's ill-gotten gains. In this hypothetical, Anita never would have been able to get the $1,000 winnings if she did not steal Brianna's digital camera. This "disgorgement principle," which is central to certain restitutionary claims, has a punitive element to it. Certainly, it would feel more like punishment for Anita to pay $1,000 as part of a restitutionary remedy than $200 (or so) in damages. But should Anita be on the hook for additional punitive damages?

Consider this first from the perspective of justice. On the one hand, perhaps the disgorgement of profits punishes Anita enough. On the other hand, if Anita's conduct is particularly bad (and we would all agree that theft is bad conduct), perhaps a jury should decide whether Anita should have to pay more than the $1,000. After all, think of *Anita's* position before and after the wrong: if a court forced Anita to pay the $1,000 gain back and nothing else, Anita would be left in the same position as if she had not engaged in the wrong. In other words, disgorgement puts Anita financially in no worse a position than had she not stolen Brianna's camera. See Figure 15.4. Anita steals the camera and bets the money, leaving her at C, up $1,000. The restitution measure forces her to pay this money back, moving her to down to B, the status quo ante. In other words, she is no worse off than had she not engaged in the theft. It would take additional punitive damages to move Anita into negative territory.

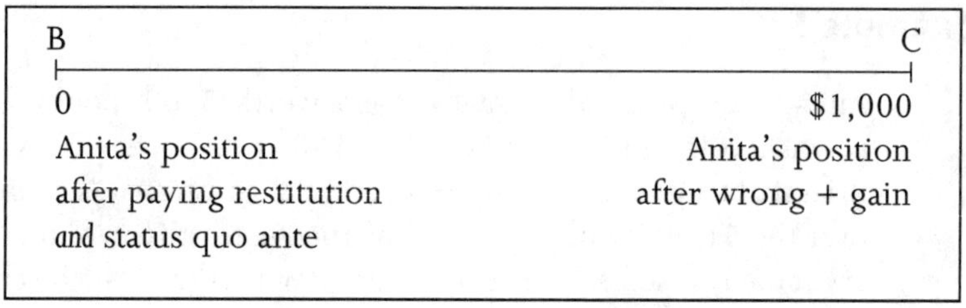

Figure 15.4 Wrongdoer's Position After Disgorgement in Anita-Brianna Hypothetical

Of course, allowing Brianna to recover *both* Anita's gains through the constructive trust *and* punitive damages gives Brianna something of a double windfall. Brianna ultimately would be in a much better position than she would have been in had she not suffered the $200 loss of her camera. To illustrate, suppose the court awards Brianna $1,000 in restitution and another $1,000 in punitive damages. As shown in Figure 15.5, after the wrong Brianna is at A, −$200. An award of $2,000 moves her to C: the first $200 compensates Brianna for the wrong, and the remaining $1,800 counts as gain. Is that fair to Anita and Brianna? Perhaps it is, given the wrongful nature of Anita's conduct.

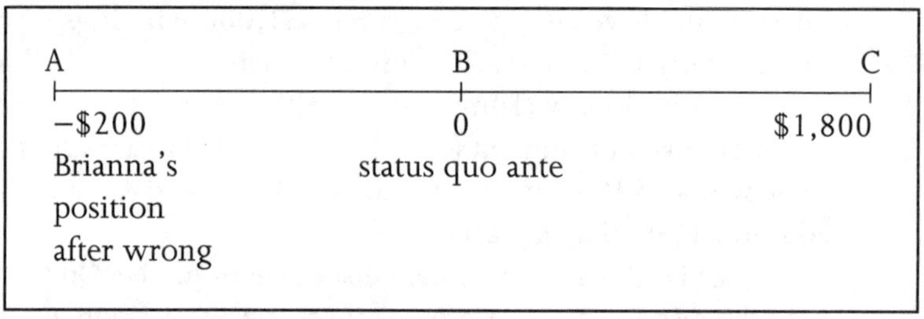

Figure 15.5 The Windfall Aspect of Punitive Damages and Restitution in Anita-Brianna Hypothetical

As for economic arguments, the same arguments for punitive damages in the context of compensatory damages might apply here as well. That is, a court might want to allow punitive damages to make up for the underdeterrence that comes from imperfections in the tort system. If there is only a 10% chance that Anita is going to have to pay the $1,000 in restitution, the expected loss is $100, and the camera is worth at least $150 to her (the value she can obtain from the pawnshop). Adding the possibility of punitive damages could cure the problem of underdeterrence.

15.2 PUNITIVE DAMAGES AND CONTRACT

It is sometimes said that punitive damages are not available in a claim arising out of a contract, but this is an oversimplification. Consider these three scenarios:

Scenario 1: Lawrence, a professional photographer, promises to take pictures at Marvin and Naomi's wedding for a price of $2,000. Lawrence fails to show up as promised because he was home drunk, and Marvin and Naomi are left without any professional photographs of their wedding. They sue Lawrence for breach of contract and also want punitive damages.

Scenario 2: Ophelia promises to deliver widgets to Polonius for $15 per widget. Ophelia breaches, selling the widgets instead to another buyer, who pays $18 per widget. Polonius sues for breach of contract and punitive damages.

Scenario 3: Dr. Quinn negligently treats Roger for an ailment. Roger sues Dr. Quinn for breach of contract, alleging and proving that Dr. Quinn breached an implied term of their contract for medical care to use reasonable care. Roger also asks for punitive damages.

A court would likely hold that punitive damages would not be available in either *Scenario 1* or *Scenario 2* because punitive damages are generally unavailable for breach of contract. A court could treat plaintiffs in *Scenario 1* more generously than plaintiff in *Scenario 2* by allowing the recovery of *emotional distress damages*. Usually, emotional distress damages are not recoverable in breach of contract actions either, but courts occasionally allow such damages when such losses are particularly foreseeable. *Compare Lewis v. Holmes*, 34 So. 66 (La. 1903) (allowing emotional distress damages for failure to deliver promised wedding dress), *with Carpel v. Saget Studios, Inc.*, 326 F. Supp. 1331 (E.D. Pa. 1971) (barring emotional distress damages for photographer's breach of promise to take wedding pictures). To the extent that emotional distress damages *are* available in *Scenario 1*, they can increase the amount of the plaintiffs' damages award in the way that punitive damages do, potentially creating greater deterrence for defendants like Lawrence. Unlike punitive damages, however, emotional distress damages, at least in theory, are designed to serve a compensatory function.

Scenario 3 is a different story. A court is quite likely to allow Roger to recover punitive damages for Dr. Quinn's conduct. Doctrinally, the reason Roger gets to recover punitive damages (while Marvin, Naomi, and Polonius do not) is that Dr. Quinn did more than breach a contract; she has also *committed an independent tort*, the tort of negligence. But this doctrinal answer is an unsatisfying one. It does not explain *why* breach of the medical contract is a tort, while breach of the widget contract or the photography contract is not.

There seems widespread consensus that certain breaches of contract also constitute an independent tort, allowing for the award of punitive damages. *This is essentially a policy determination that courts make in each jurisdiction.* Besides the medical malpractice context already discussed, one of the most important areas where breaches of contract are also torts is in the insurance context. When an insurer denies an insured's claim in "bad faith," many states will treat that as a tort, allowing not only for the award of emotional distress and other tort damages, but also the possibility of punitive damages.

For example, consider the facts of *State Farm v. Campbell*, 538 U.S. 408 (2003), a very important case for the constitutional questions we consider in the next section. In *Campbell*, two drivers sued a third driver, Campbell, for negligent driving leading to personal injuries and wrongful death. Campbell had an insurance policy with State Farm. The two drivers offered to settle for Campbell's policy limits—$25,000 each. State Farm's own investigation showed that Campbell was completely at fault.

Under applicable insurance law, State Farm had the obligation not to put its interest over that of the insured. The only reasonable conclusion on the facts as read most favorably to the plaintiff is that State Farm should have settled this case for the policy limits. With liability clear for its insured and the injured parties ready to settle for the policy limits (having sustained serious injuries), the insurer's job was to settle. If the case were not settled, then Campbell would have been on the hook personally for any of the damages over the limit. Rather than settle, State Farm fought the claims. It put false facts in the file (for example, falsely alleging that one of the other drivers had a pregnant girlfriend), and there was evidence that its handling of the case was part of a nationwide practice of rejecting good offers to settle.

The tort case against Campbell went to trial. The jury found Campbell 100% liable and ordered damages in the amount of $185,000. State Farm refused to pay the extra $135,000 and told Campbell to start putting his assets up for sale. Eventually, State Farm agreed to pay the entire damages award, but by then Campbell had sued State Farm for bad faith (fraud) and intentional infliction of emotional distress.[7] In Campbell's bad faith claim against State Farm, the jury found Campbell suffered $2.6 million in compensatory damages (primarily for emotional distress, an amount the trial court reduced to $1 million) and an additional $145 million in punitive

7. To settle his claim with the other two drivers, he assigned 90% of his bad faith claim against State Farm to the other two drivers.

damages, an amount the United States Supreme Court later reduced for reasons discussed in the next section.

It is easy to see why on policy grounds courts would decide that breaches of an insurance contract like the one in *Campbell* should constitute a tort. The possibility of tort damages can serve to deter bad behavior such as that of State Farm in contracts where consumers are trying to buy peace of mind and reduce risk through the purchase of insurance.

But not all breaches of insurance contracts create an independent tort and raise the possibility of punitive damages. For example, suppose in the *Campbell* case that State Farm refused to pay because it had a reasonable argument that the policy did not cover these kinds of accidents. Suppose further that a court later determines that State Farm's argument about what the policy covered, though reasonable, was wrong. Then State Farm's failure to pay would constitute a breach of contract, but not a tort (and, for this reason, not a kind of action allowing Campbell to recover punitive damages for the failure to pay).

In the end, the question of what kind of breach of contract also counts as an independent tort (allowing for punitive damages) comes down to a balancing of policy considerations. On the one hand, courts may want to deter certain bad conduct, especially in cases involving vulnerable plaintiffs. On the other hand, allowing punitive damages routinely in contract cases would upset parties' expectations. Parties would be wary of entering into a contract if they did not know what their total exposure was for breach of that contract. Indeed, for those who subscribe to the theory of "efficient breach" described in Chapter 4, allowing for punitive damages would upset the theory of efficient breach.

To understand why punitive damages in a typical contract case would upset the theory of efficient breach, consider *Scenario* 2 above. The theory of efficient breach says that Ophelia *should* breach the contract for the sale of widgets at $15 per widget and pay Polonius compensatory damages when Ophelia would make a profit in doing so *after compensating Polonius for his damages*.[8] Doing so moves the widgets to the highest-valued user and does not make Polonius worse off (assuming he is compensated for his loss). But punitive damages upset this calculation. Both the possibility that Ophelia might have to pay punitive damages for breach and the amount of such damages, if awarded, are highly uncertain. The uncertainty alone may deter the efficient breach. More significantly, if the punitive damages amount to

8. For example, suppose that the fair market value of the widgets is $16 per widget, but Ophelia could sell them to another buyer (who perhaps has a special need for the widgets) at $18 per widget. The Ophelia-Polonius contract was for $15 per widget, so (we know from Chapter 4 that) an award of $1 per widget (plus incidental and consequential damages, less expenses saved) would compensate Polonius. Ophelia could breach the contract, compensate Polonius for the loss, and still pocket an extra $2 per widget by selling to the user who values the goods more highly.

an additional $3 per widget, these damages might deter Ophelia's breach of contract even if it would have been efficient for her to have breached.

In striking this balance, courts have generally rejected arguments to create independent torts (allowing for punitive damages) out of typical breach of contract cases. For a time, some jurisdictions (including California) allowed punitive damages when a party to a contract in bad faith denied the contract's existence. But courts have pulled back from recognizing this tort. *See Freeman & Mills, Inc. v. Belcher Oil Co.*, 900 P.2d 669 (Cal. 1995).

Still there is a temptation in certain contract cases to continue to find the independent tort to allow for punitive damages. California Supreme Court Justice Mosk, concurring and dissenting in the *Freeman & Mills* case, listed three categories of contract breaches for which tort damages (including punitive damages) should be awarded:

1. Breach accompanied by a traditional common law tort, such as fraud or conversion;
2. Tortious means used by one contracting party to coerce or deceive another party into forgoing its contractual rights; and
3. The case where one party breaches the contract intending or knowing that such a breach will cause severe, unmitigable harm in the form of mental anguish, personal hardship, or substantial consequential damages.

Of Justice Mosk's three proposed categories, the third is the most controversial. It suggests that in a number of consumer *and* business contracts, where one contracting party uses sharp practices along with breaching the contract, punitive damages should be available. Many courts would likely reject such an extension on grounds that it would interfere with contractual expectations. (Query whether Justice Mosk's third proposed category would apply to Lawrence, the drunk photographer in *Scenario 1*.)

EXAMPLE

Example 6

Sally is a dog sitter. She agrees to come twice a day for one week to Tabitha's house to walk, feed, and take care of Tabitha's dog while Tabitha is on vacation. In exchange Tabitha agrees to pay Sally $200. Sally is lazy, and she neglects to visit Tabitha's dog for two days. During that time, Tabitha's dog became quite ill and died. When Tabitha confronted Sally about her conduct, Sally lied and said she had in fact shown up twice a day to feed the dog. Tabitha's security camera tapes conclusively proved otherwise at trial. Expert testimony established that if Sally had performed as promised and obtained prompt veterinary attention, Tabitha's dog would have survived. In Tabitha's suit against Sally, may Tabitha recover punitive damages? If so, does it matter that Sally lied about her conduct?

Explanation

Tabitha certainly has a strong case for breach of contract. Sally promised to show up twice a day to walk, feed, and take care of Tabitha's dog during the week Tabitha was on vacation. Sally indisputably failed to do so. In addition to return of the contract price, Tabitha may be able to get consequential damages given how foreseeable they were. (See Chapter 4.)

The question of punitive damages, however, turns upon whether there is an independent tort. Arguably, Sally committed the independent tort of fraud when she lied about whether or not she performed under the contract. It is not clear that lying about performance itself should be enough to turn the breach of contract into a tort. Compare the majority and dissenting opinions in *Robinson Helicopter Co., Inc. v. Dana Corp.*, 102 P.3d 268 (Cal. 2004).

Without the lie, there's still a potential argument to treat this like a tort, to the extent a court accepts Justice Mosk's third category of contract breaches where punitive damages should be available: a situation in which one party breaches the contract intending or knowing that such a breach will cause severe, unmitigable harm in the form of mental anguish, personal hardship, or substantial consequential damages.

If you were the judge presiding over this case, would you allow the jury to consider the award of punitive damages? If so, to what degree is your answer driven by your view of the relationship between people and their pets? To test that sentiment, imagine that Sally had promised instead simply to house-sit for Tabitha (with no pets involved), and because of Sally's failure to check on the house as promised, she did not catch in time a leak in the laundry room which caused serious property damage to Tabitha's house. Sally then lied about her performance. If you would award lower (or no) punitive damages in this situation, but would in the former situation, your views are probably being driven in part by the pet factor.

Example 7

Universal Insurance Company receives a claim from its insured, Vicki, related to an automobile injury caused by Vicki that seriously injured Walter. Walter is prepared to settle the case with Vicki for $100,000, Vicki's policy limits. Universal employees perform an investigation to determine whether or not Vicki was negligent in causing the accident. But the employees themselves were negligent in the investigation. Because of their carelessness, they overlook evidence that makes it very clear that Vicki was negligent in causing Walter's injuries. Universal refuses to settle and the case goes to trial, leading to a jury verdict in Walter's favor of $250,000. Because Vicki's policy limits were $100,000, Vicki is personally liable for the additional $150,000.

Vicki then sues Universal for breach of contract in handling the claim, alleging that Universal breached the contract and acted in bad faith when they negligently evaluated her claim. Assume that a jury would agree that this conduct constituted a breach of the contract and would conclude that to compensate Vicki, Universal must compensate Vicki for the additional $150,000 she paid out to Walter. May Vicki also recover *punitive* damages in her suit against Universal?

EXPLANATION

Explanation

Vicki likely will not be able to recover punitive damages in this case. Recall that the *conduct* which allows for the award of punitive damages must be worse than negligence. In this case, it does not appear that Universal's conduct was anything worse than negligent. So even if Universal's negligent claims handling constituted both a breach of the insurance contract and a tort, it likely is not bad enough conduct to merit the imposition of punitive damages.

15.3 CONSTITUTIONAL LIMITS ON THE *AMOUNT* OF PUNITIVE DAMAGES

Thus far, this chapter has focused on the question *whether* or not punitive damages would be available in particular lawsuits and the standards for courts and juries to determine their appropriateness. Though this is an important question in the law of punitive damages, equally important is the question of how juries determine (and courts review) the *amount* of punitive damages if such damages are to be awarded. Consider the rules from New Jersey on the amount of punitive damages:

> If the trier of fact determines that punitive damages should be awarded, the trier of fact shall then determine the amount of those damages. In making that determination, the trier of fact shall consider all relevant evidence, including, but not limited to, the following:
>
> (1) All relevant evidence relating to the factors [used to determine whether punitive damages are to be awarded];[9]

9. The factors include the following:

> (1) The likelihood, at the relevant time, that serious harm would arise from the defendant's conduct;
> (2) The defendant's awareness o[r] reckless disregard of the likelihood that the serious harm at issue would arise from the defendant's conduct;
> (3) The conduct of the defendant upon learning that its initial conduct would likely cause harm; and
> (4) The duration of the conduct or any concealment of it by the defendant.

N.J. Stat. Ann. §2A:15-5.12b.

(2) The profitability of the misconduct to the defendant;
(3) When the misconduct was terminated; and
(4) The financial condition of the defendant.

N.J. STAT. ANN. §2A:15-5.12c.

When faced with instructions such as these, a jury could well choose a very high amount for the punitive damages. This is true in part because a jury considering the "financial condition of the defendant" is going to pick a large amount to punish a wealthy defendant. After all, a $100,000 punitive damage award would feel different to you compared to how it would feel to a very wealthy person such as Bill Gates. Moreover, the awards are going to be high because of the very conduct involved. "The purposes of the award—the deterrence of egregious misconduct and the punishment of the offender—when mixed with a finding that the defendant is malicious, can readily inflame an otherwise-dispassionate jury." *Lockley v. State of New Jersey Dep't of Corrections*, 828 A.2d 869, 878 (N.J. 2003).

For these reasons and others (notably a push by business entities for "tort reform" to reduce their potential liability), many states either cap the amount of damages or provide for courts to lower the amount of damages in certain circumstances. In New Jersey, for example, the *maximum* amount of punitive damages that may be assessed against a defendant is "five times the liability of that defendant for compensatory damages or $350,000, whichever is greater." N.J. STAT. ANN. §2A:15-5.14b. According to one count, "five states either prohibit punitive damages or severely restrict their use. Statutory caps in at least in some form exist in half the states. Limits tied to the amount of actual or economic damages exist in 14 states." Joseph Sanders, *Punitive Damages in Consumer Actions*, 8 J. TEX. CONSUMER L. 22 (2004) (footnotes omitted).

Some states, however, provided no meaningful review of punitive damage awards. In *Honda Motor Co. v. Oberg*, 512 U.S. 415 (1994), the U.S. Supreme Court held that some kind of review of the amount of a punitive damage award was necessary to comply with the U.S. Constitution.

You might reasonably ask what the U.S. Constitution has to do with *state* awards of punitive damages. This is a fair question, and one that turns out to be quite controversial. For those of you who have not yet taken a Constitutional Law course, you should know that the U.S. Constitution provides in the Fourteenth Amendment that no state may deprive any person of life, liberty, or property "without due process of law." The meaning of this "Due Process Clause" consumes quite a bit of time in the typical Constitutional Law course, and one of the major questions is whether the clause guarantees only fair *procedures* (so-called "procedural due process") or also fair *outcomes* (so-called "substantive due process").

The U.S. Supreme Court began its examination of the constitutionality of large punitive damage awards in 1989, when it rejected the idea that the

Constitution's Eighth Amendment, prohibiting excessive fines, served as a limit on punitive damages awards. *Browning-Ferris Industries of Vermont, Inc. v. Kelco Disposal Inc.*, 492 U.S. 257 (1989). But two years later, in *Pacific Mutual Life Insurance Co. v. Haslip*, 499 U.S. 1 (1991), the Court first suggested that a high punitive damages award could violate substantive due process; the Court talked about punitive damages that "run wild" and said that an award of punitive damages that was four times the amount of compensatory damages was "close to the line" of constitutional excessiveness. The Court next refused to overturn a punitive damages award with a 500:1 ratio of punitive to compensatory damages (*TXO Production Corp. v. Alliance Resources Corp.*, 509 U.S. 443 (1993)), leading some to wonder whether the Court was serious about reining in the amount of large punitive damages awards.

The breakthrough for defendants came in the 1996 case *BMW v. Gore*, 517 U.S. 559 (1996). If you were on the Supreme Court and looking for a case to rein in punitive damages, this case was a good one because it featured a relatively unsympathetic plaintiff, a relatively non-culpable defendant, and involved a very large damages award for little injury.

In *BMW*, Dr. Gore purchased a $40,000 BMW sports sedan in Alabama. After driving it for nine months, he took it to "Slick Finish" to make the car look "snazzier." The owner, Mr. Slick (I'm *not* making this up), informed Gore that his car had been repainted by the dealership before Gore purchased it. It turns out that the car had suffered some damage from acid rain before it arrived at the dealership. BMW's policy was to repaint new cars with minor damage, without disclosing the practice. In Alabama, the non-disclosure counted as a fraud, though in other states it did not.

The jury determined that Gore's compensatory damages were $4,000, based upon expert testimony that the repainting reduced the value of the car by about 10%. It then assessed $4 million (!) in punitive damages, finding the non-disclosure policy to be "gross, oppressive or malicious fraud." The Alabama Supreme Court reduced the award to $2 million, on grounds that acts that occurred in other jurisdictions should not be the basis for punishment. BMW further appealed to the U.S. Supreme Court, which struck down the award on substantive due process grounds.

The *BMW v. Gore* opinion was quite tentative, suggesting three "guideposts" for courts to consider in determining whether the amount of punitive damages was constitutionally excessive:

1. *The degree of reprehensibility of the conduct.* The more reprehensible the conduct, the higher the punitive award should be.
2. *The ratio of punitive damages to actual damages.* The higher the ratio, the more constitutionally suspect the punitive award.
3. *Sanctions for comparable misconduct.* If civil or criminal penalties for similar conduct are low, then a punitive award should be low as well,

because those penalties signal that the state does not consider the conduct to be highly blameworthy.

The first factor, of course, seems relevant in any discussion of the proper amount of punitive damages: certainly BMW should not be punished as harshly as someone who intentionally causes physical injury to another person. The ratio factor is somewhat less defensible; the Court did not explain why ratio should matter so much, and it issued some caveats related to the use of the ratio. First, the comparison is between punitive damages and the amount of actual *and potential* damages that a defendant could have caused had he not been stopped from acting. Moreover, the Court suggested there was no "simple mathematical formula" to determine the constitutionality of a punitive damage award. (Keep this language in mind.) The Court gave the example of "a particularly egregious act [that] has resulted in only a small amount of economic damages," which would justify a high ratio. It also noted that a higher ratio "may be justified in cases where the injury is hard to detect or the monetary value of noneconomic harm might have been difficult to determine."

The last factor, sanctions for comparable misconduct, sends a somewhat perverse message. Punitive damages may be *most useful* when the state does not have other civil or criminal sanctions in place to deter bad conduct.

Four Justices (Chief Justice Rehnquist, the liberal Justice Ginsburg, and the conservative Justices Thomas and Scalia) dissented, stating that the amount of punitive damages should be determined by state law, and not federalized in this way.

After *BMW v. Gore*, courts began to review awards of punitive damages for constitutional excessiveness. In states without great limits on punitive awards, the case had the potential for greater impact than in those states that already conducted some kind of excessiveness review. But because *BMW* imposed a squishy multifactor "guideposts" test, it did not appear likely to lead to great changes in the law. But then along came the *State Farm v. Campbell* case, described in the last section *Campbell* put "the *BMW* guideposts on steroids." LAYCOCK & HASEN p. 246.

You've already read the *Campbell* case's facts. Here is how the Supreme Court in *Campbell* changed the *BMW* guideposts related to constitutional review of the amount of the awards in striking down the $145 million punitive award.

1. *The Court has limited the evidence that may be considered for purposes of judging reprehensibility*. The majority said that State Farm's conduct "merits no praise," quite an understatement if one accepts the plaintiff's view of the conduct (as the Court ordinarily does on appeal). More importantly, the Court said that in judging reprehensibility for purposes of

determining the amount of punitive damages, a jury may consider only similar conduct that has a *close nexus* to the kind of bad conduct at issue in the case itself. So, defendants will be able to exclude much evidence of a pattern of similar bad conduct.

2. *The Court is now using mathematical formulas to limit the ratio of punitive and compensatory damages.* Though the *Campbell* Court said that there are "no rigid benchmarks," it suggested that it would be the rare case where damages could exceed a 9:1 ratio of punitive damages to actual and potential compensatory damages: "Single-digit multipliers are more likely to comport with due process, while still achieving the State's goals of deterrence and retribution, than awards with ratios in the range of 500 to 1 or, in this case, 145 to 1." Indeed, in cases like this one, with "substantial" compensatory awards (recall the $1 million in damages plaintiff was awarded for emotional distress), "then a lesser ratio, perhaps only equal to compensatory damages, can reach the outermost limit of the due process guarantee."
3. *The wealth of the defendant cannot be used as a reason to increase the award of punitive damages.* This is perhaps the biggest and most important change coming from *Campbell*. "The wealth of a defendant cannot justify an otherwise unconstitutional punitive damage award." While absence of wealth might be a reason to *lower* the amount of damages, the presence of great wealth cannot be a reason to *raise* the amount.

Arguably, the treatment of defendant's wealth is the most indefensible part of the *Campbell* test. Note the New Jersey factors for the award of punitive damages listed earlier in this section. Of course, the New Jersey courts (like the courts in many other states) consider the wealth of the defendant to be a relevant factor in assessing the amount of the award, for the reasons discussed above in relation to wealthy people such as Bill Gates: it takes a lot more money to deter a rich person (or corporate management) than a poor person. How this factor is supposed to square with the deterrent purpose of punitive damages is yet to be explained.

On remand in *Campbell* the Utah Supreme Court reduced the punitive award to $9 million. *State Farm Mutual Insurance Co. v. Campbell*, 98 P.3d 409 (Utah 2004). Not coincidentally, that created a 9:1 ratio between punitive damages and compensatory damages. The U.S. Supreme Court declined to hear the case a second time.

Campbell is not the last word from the Supreme Court on policing the amount of punitive damages. A more recent Supreme Court case has created added confusion about constitutional standards. In *Philip Morris USA v. Williams*, 549 U.S. 346 (2007), the Court held on a 5-4 vote that a jury cannot consider the defendant's similar conduct toward other in-state residents for purposes of punishing the defendant through punitive damages. But the Court added that a jury *could* consider that similar conduct for purposes of determining reprehensibility (which in turn is a factor to consider when juries determine the amount of punitive damages). The dissenters thought this distinction "elus[ive]" (Justice Stevens) and the opinion's logic "inexplicable" (Justice Ginsburg).

Philip Morris was followed by yet another Supreme Court punitive damages case. In *Exxon Shipping Co. v. Baker*, 554 U.S. 471 (2008), the Court reviewed a $2.5 billion punitive damages award (on top of $500 million in compensatory damages) arising out of the infamous Exxon Valdez oil spill. Sitting *as a common law court* (and therefore not making a constitutional pronouncement) considering the propriety of a punitive damages award under federal admiralty law, the Supreme Court held that the punitive award had to be limited to a 1:1 ratio of punitive to compensatory damages. The opinion is likely to be influential, though its reach is far from clear; technically speaking, this was the Supreme Court deciding a case in admiralty, and its ruling is not binding on state courts reviewing the amount of punitive damages under state law.

The Court in *Exxon Shipping Co.* limited the scope of its holding, explaining that the 1:1 ratio applies to "this particular type of case." *Id.* at 511. It is not clear if cases involving wrongs motivated by the hope of financial gain, or those leading to more serious personal injuries, would be subject to a different ratio. Despite the limiting language, the fact that the Supreme Court of the United States put its stamp of approval on a 1:1 ratio in such a high-profile case could well lead state courts to follow *Exxon Shipping Co.* in review of punitive damages award amounts under state law.

In the meantime, every justice in the majority *BMW* and *Campbell* has since left the Supreme Court, and only Justice Thomas remains among the dissenters. It is unclear where the new Justices stand on the question of constitutional analysis of punitive damages. It is possible that the Court could reverse this entire line of cases should someone seek to have them overturned.

EXAMPLE

Example 8

Defendant ran a hotel that was infested with bedbugs. Though hotel guests complained about the bedbugs, the hotel did nothing serious to correct the problem and misrepresented its rooms as clean. Bedbug bites are uncomfortable and unsightly, though not life-threatening. A group of hotel guests sue the hotel in tort for fraud and other torts. A jury awards $5,000 in compensatory damages and $186,000 in punitive damages. The defendant is quite wealthy. May the *amount* of the punitive award stand?

EXPLANATION

Explanation

This hypothetical is based upon *Mathias v. Accor Economy Lodging, Inc.*, 347 F.3d 672 (7th Cir. 2003). In an opinion written by the influential Judge Richard A. Posner, the court upheld the punitive award against a challenge that it was unconstitutionally high. The ratio of the award was quite high, 37.2:1, but the court held it did not violate the rules of *Campbell*, arguing it fit into an exception for cases involving egregious facts but low compensatory damages: "The defendant's behavior was outrageous but the compensable harm done was slight and at the same time difficult to quantify because a large element of it was emotional. And the defendant may well have profited from its misconduct because by concealing the infestation it was able to keep renting rooms."

Perhaps most interesting about *Mathias* is what Judge Posner said about the defendant wealth issue:

> Finally, if the total stakes in the case were capped at $50,000 . . . , the plaintiffs might well have had difficulty financing this lawsuit. It is here that the defendant's aggregate net worth of $1.6 billion becomes relevant. A defendant's wealth is not a sufficient basis for awarding punitive damages. *Campbell; BMW* (concurring opinion); *Zazu Designs v. L'Oreal, S.A.*, 979 F.2d 499, 508-09 (7th Cir. 1992). That would be discriminatory and would violate the rule of law . . . by making punishment depend on status rather than conduct. Where wealth in the sense of resources enters is in enabling the defendant to mount an extremely aggressive defense against suits such as this and by doing so to make litigating against it very costly, which in turn may make it difficult for the plaintiffs to find a lawyer willing to handle their case, involving as it does only modest stakes, for the usual 33-40 percent contingent fee.
>
> In other words, the defendant is investing in developing a reputation intended to deter plaintiffs. It is difficult otherwise to explain the great stubbornness with which it has defended this case, making a host of frivolous evidentiary arguments despite the very modest stakes even when the punitive damages awarded by the jury are included.

One of my former students has written a law review note arguing, I think correctly, that *Mathias* is in fact inconsistent with *Campbell* in considering the wealth of the defendant. It seems that Judge Posner is trying to get defendant's wealth information into the case through the back door. My student further argues that *Mathias* is right and that *Campbell* is wrong on the role of the wealth of the defendant in punitive damages cases. Leila C. Orr, Note, *Making a Case for Wealth-Calibrated Punitive Damages*, 37 Loy. L.A. L. Rev. 1739 (2004).

Following *Campbell*'s pronouncement about the role of wealth in assessing the amount of punitive damages, it is not clear that jury instructions such as those used in New Jersey (allowing the jury to consider the wealth of the defendant) remain constitutional.

EXAMPLE

Example 9

Acting with malicious intent, X shoots Y, causing Y to become permanently disabled and in constant pain. X is convicted criminally for attempted murder, receiving a 25-years-to-life sentence, and then Y sues X in tort for a number of torts, including battery. A jury determines that Y suffered $1 million in compensatory damages for past and future medical care, past and future lost wages, and emotional distress. It then awards an additional $2 million in punitive damages. X has very few assets. May the *amount* of the punitive award stand under U.S. constitutional standards?

EXPLANATION

Explanation

Certainly X's conduct is reprehensible; indeed, it is probably among the most reprehensible conduct juries likely would see in a punitive damages case. The ratio here is 2:1, which is relatively low. Recall that in *Campbell*, the Court discussed how, in cases involving "substantial" compensatory damages, a ratio of 1:1 might be the most appropriate. Still, it is difficult to imagine a court reducing the punitive damages on this basis in this case; unlike the $1 million award in *Campbell*, which was exclusively for emotional distress damages, here the $1 million award is compensating in great part for medical expenses and lost wages—which a court may see as serving a greater compensatory purpose. In addition, criminal sanctions are severe; X has received a serious criminal sentence.

Even though all three of the *BMW/Campbell* guideposts support upholding the amount of punitive damages in this case, it is likely a court would reduce the award because of the defendant's *lack of wealth*. Courts sometimes say that a punitive award cannot bankrupt or destroy the defendant, and someone with few assets facing a $2 million punitive award (on top of a $1 million compensatory award) would indeed face the possibility of bankruptcy.

The Supreme Court's opinion in *Campbell* does not say it is improper to *reduce* a large award to take into account defendant's lack of wealth. It says only that it is improper to *increase* a punitive award to take into account defendant's great wealth.

CHAPTER 16

Declaratory Judgments and Related Remedies

16.1 INTRODUCTION: WHY DECLARATORY JUDGMENTS?

Federal law gives federal courts the power in most cases to "declare the rights and other legal relations of any interested party seeking such declaration, whether or not further relief is or could be sought." 28 U.S.C. §2201. An earlier uniform act that served as a model for federal law, the Uniform Declaratory Judgments Act (1922), adopted by many states, gives state courts the power to grant similar relief.

When would a party want a declaratory judgment from a court, as opposed to seeking another kind of remedy? Consider the following scenarios, and ask yourself whether a declaration of the parties' respective rights is the best solution, or a different remedy might be better:

- Zelda and Alex are neighbors. Alex wants to build a shed on his land, but Zelda objects because she believes that Alex's plans would go over the property line, putting part of the shed on her property.
- Barbara owns a patent on an espresso maker. She has been threatening to sue Carrie, the manufacturer of a different espresso maker, for patent infringement unless Carrie pays a royalty. Carrie does not believe her patent is infringing.
- Marchers wish to stage a protest in the city square, protesting the city's treatment of the homeless. City leaders tell Marchers that if

> they march, they would be violating a city ordinance prohibiting any public assembly without the posting of a $100,000 bond for any damage that may be caused. Marchers believe the city law is unconstitutional under the First Amendment.

In each of these cases, a declaratory judgment may be the best, or one of the best, remedies. In the first example, Alex might not want to build his shed while there is a dispute over the boundary line; a court might force Alex later to pay damages for trespass, or even possibly to remove the structure after it has been built. A declaration of rights would save Alex money and both parties possible further inconvenience.

From Zelda's perspective, a declaration would be useful as well to determine the parties' respective rights. Assuming Zelda believes that her neighbor Alex is likely to abide by a court's determination of the boundary line, a declaration may be all that Zelda needs and may be cheaper than obtaining other remedies, such as an injunction. In contrast, if there's a chance that Alex might build anyway, despite a declaration of rights, Zelda might prefer an injunction barring Alex from building over the (now determined) property line. (See Part II of this book for more on the rules related to injunctions.) As we shall see, it is procedurally easier to get a declaratory judgment compared to an injunction.

The contrast between injunctions and declaratory judgments reveals an important fact about declaratory judgments: they are *implicitly coercive*. When a court declares the parties' respective rights, a violation of those rights is not the same as violating a court injunction. In other words, a party who ignores a declaratory judgment cannot be held in contempt of court (the way a party can be for violating a court injunction). But once a court has declared the parties' respective rights, a court will be quite receptive to the option of later issuing an injunction, should it be necessary in case one of the parties fails to respect those rights. Knowing this, most parties will simply obey declaratory judgments *as if* they were coercive.

The Zelda-Alex hypothetical demonstrates that declaratory judgments are useful because they *reduce uncertainty* and can be *implicitly coercive*, like injunctions. The reduction of uncertainty is especially useful in two contexts.

First, *declaratory judgments can be used to eliminate frivolous threats of litigation*. In the patent context, Barbara may have a "scarecrow patent," one that is used to intimidate others to pay royalties for a patent that may be invalid or not infringing. The declaratory judgment ends Barbara's ability to threaten Carrie with a patent infringement suit. In this regard, consider *Cardinal Chemical Co. v. Morton International, Inc.*, 508 U.S. 83 (1993), a case that shows the true economic value of declaratory judgments in appropriate cases.

Morton International sued Cardinal Chemical Co. for patent infringement related to some chemical compounds. Cardinal denied infringement and filed a counterclaim for declaratory relief, asking the court to declare Morton's patents invalid. A trial court had determined that Cardinal had not infringed on Morton's copyright and issued a declaration that Morton's patent was invalid. The United States Court of Appeals for the Federal Circuit (which handles such patent disputes) affirmed the holding on patent infringement, but vacated the declaration on grounds that the question was moot. Indeed, the Federal Circuit had a per se rule dismissing all declaratory judgment requests as moot upon a finding of no infringement. The Supreme Court reversed the Federal Circuit on the declaratory judgment point, noting that the circuit's rule denied patentees meaningful appellate review. Moreover, the Supreme Court said, the Federal Circuit's refusal to issue declaratory judgments in these circumstances "prolongs the life of invalid patents [and] encourages endless litigation (or at least uncertainty) over the validity of outstanding patents." Once such a case is brought for a declaratory judgment, the burden of proof follows the substantive law. For example, in a declaratory judgment action seeking a declaration that a plaintiff is not infringing the defendant's patent, the burden of proof is on the defendant patent holder to prove infringement. *Medtronic, Inc. v. Mirowski Family Ventures*, LLC, 571 U.S. 191 (2014).

Second, *declaratory judgments can serve to vindicate important constitutional rights*. In some circumstances, a group might decide to schedule a march (or engage in other political activities) precisely to test a law that the group believes is unconstitutional. This is a variation on eliminating uncertainty in the very important context of protecting the right to free speech and assembly (along with other constitutional rights).

Though declaratory judgments can serve useful social purposes, they can be abused as well. A party might try to use a declaratory judgment for tactical reasons, such as forum shopping. *See* LAYCOCK & HASEN p. 605. For this reason, courts have wide discretion whether or not to entertain declaratory judgment suits.

For example, consider a case between Xoxide, Inc. and Ford Motor Company. *Xoxide, Inc. v. Ford Motor Co.*, 448 F. Supp. 2d 1188 (C.D. Cal. 2006). Xoxide operated a business that manufactured accessories for Ford Mustangs, advertising its accessories on a website. Ford sent a letter to Xoxide claiming that some of the company's activities violated Ford's trademarks.[1] The parties exchanged more letters but reached no resolution. Xoxide, anticipating trademark infringement litigation brought by Ford in

---

1. "Ford specifically alleged that Xoxide: (1) had allegedly "misappropriated the world-famous trademark Mustang® in the internet domain name MustangTuning.com" in violation of the Anticybersquatting Consumer Protection Act (ACPA); (2) misappropriated the Mustang trademark in its business name, MustangTuning; (3) wrongfully incorporated Ford's Mustang trademark or a variation thereof into Xoxide's vanity phone number, 1-888-STANG-GT; and (4) was 'manufacturing, marketing, advertising, and/or distributing wheels bearing a confusingly similar variation of Ford's registered' trademarks." *Id.* at 1190.

Michigan, filed a declaratory judgment action in federal district court in California seeking a declaration that Xoxide was *not* infringing on Ford's trademarks.[2] The court, citing a rule against anticipatory suits and forum shopping, refused to allow Xoxide's suit to go forward. Xoxide had to settle Ford's claims or defend itself in a Michigan suit.

Declaratory judgments do present some risk to parties in terms of issue preclusion and claim preclusion (collateral estoppel and res judicata). As to issue preclusion (collateral estoppel), suppose Zelda asks for and obtains declaratory relief regarding the boundary between her land and Alex's land. Alex ignores the declaration and builds over his property line and onto Zelda's land. Zelda sues for a court order requiring Alex to remove his new construction. In that later suit, Alex cannot litigate the boundary line question again. So long as Alex had a fair opportunity to make his case in the declaratory judgment action, that issue is now closed.

As to claim preclusion (res judicata), a party is certainly allowed to couple a claim for declaratory relief with a claim for additional relief, such as an injunction or damages for past conduct. *See* 28 U.S.C. §2201 (a party may obtain declaratory relief "whether or not further relief is or could be sought"). Moreover, a party can ask for additional relief in an action after first requesting declaratory relief. *See* 28 U.S.C. §2202 ("Further necessary or proper relief based on a declaratory judgment or decree may be granted, after reasonable notice and hearing, against any adverse party whose rights have been determined by such judgment.").

Here's the tricky part. If a plaintiff *couples* declaratory relief with a request for *any other relief* (such as an injunction or damages), the plaintiff is barred from asking for additional relief in a later case. This may seem like an arcane point (and it is), but the point was worth a quarter of a *billion* dollars in a California Supreme Court case, *Mycogen Corp. v. Monsanto Co.*, 51 P.3d 297 (Cal. 2002).[3] Two parties to a complex license agreement disputed if and how it applied. The licensee successfully sought a declaration that the licensor had an obligation to license its technology to the licensee; it also asked for an order of specific performance requiring the licensor to do so. In subsequent litigation, the licensee sought damages for the licensor's delay in licensing the technology. A lower court allowed the delay damages case to go forward, leading to a $175 million judgment (plus interest).

---

2. Why would Xoxide prefer a California court over a Michigan court? One possibility is Xoxide's fear that a Michigan court would be too sympathetic to Ford, a powerful corporation in Michigan. In addition, Xoxide's lawyers are likely based in California, and they would be more familiar with California judges and procedure. It is also cheaper to engage in litigation locally than halfway across the country.

3. Disclosure: I consulted for one of the parties in this case.

The California Supreme Court held that the later case should not have gone forward,[4] citing the reasons given by a federal district court in *Christe v. City of Steamboat Springs*, 122 F. Supp. 2d 1183, 1189 (D. Colo. 2000):

> First, to allow the exception to extend beyond purely declaratory relief would run counter to the purpose of declaratory actions, which is "to provide a remedy that is simpler and less harsh than coercive relief." [Citation.] Perhaps more importantly, to permit some but not other coercive actions to accompany a request for declaratory relief would open the door to uncertainty and potential claim splitting. The Court sees no justification, for example, for applying ordinary claim preclusion rules to cases where the plaintiff seeks declaratory and damage relief, but a different set of rules to cases where the plaintiff seeks declaratory and injunctive relief. Moreover, if courts were to apply a more lenient set of rules to the latter situation, this would encourage parties to split their causes of action to gain a second bite at the apple if not successful in the first lawsuit. To avoid uncertainty, application of preclusion rules must be clear. Once a party seeks and obtains coercive relief, the basis for applying the declaratory judgment exception evaporates, and ordinary rules of claim preclusion must apply.

Bottom line: either bring suit *solely* for pure declaratory relief or, if you couple declaratory relief with requests for other forms of relief, make sure that you've asked for *everything* you'll ever want to ask for from this defendant for this series of transactions.

Example 1

Darcy and Eunice got into a traffic collision in Texas in which Eunice sustained serious personal injuries. Eunice is a resident of Arkansas; Darcy is a resident of Texas. Anticipating that Eunice would file a suit for negligence in Arkansas, Darcy filed suit against Eunice first, asking for a declaration from a Texas court that Darcy was not driving negligently. Should the Texas court hear the declaratory judgment suit?

Explanation

The Texas court is likely to decline to hear Darcy's declaratory judgment suit. Like the Ford Mustang case described above, this looks like an anticipatory suit and forum shopping. Darcy presumably expects to get a more favorable

4. In other words, the licensee should have sought the delay damages in the same suit as that for specific performance and a declaratory judgment. Such damages would not have given the licensee a double recovery. The specific performance prevented future harm from the failure to perform under the contract. The delay damages compensated for the *past harm* caused by the failure to comply with the contract. For more on specific performance, see Chapter 8.

reception from courts in her own state, which is likely why she is engaging in this forum shopping. Laycock and Hasen report that "[t]here is an especially strong presumption that personal injury plaintiffs are entitled to choose their forum." Laycock & Hasen p. 606.

Example 2

Same facts as in Example 1. Only this time, Eunice files the suit first. Her lawyer files suit asking only for a declaration that Darcy was negligent. The lawyer figures that if the court finds Darcy was negligent, he can later sue for damages. In the meantime, seeking only a declaratory judgment can save some time and money. Did Eunice's lawyer make a wise choice?

Explanation

No. There is no good reason for Eunice's lawyer to seek a declaratory judgment in this case. There is no benefit to reducing uncertainty so as to avoid any future litigation: Eunice has been injured, and if Darcy has been negligent in causing Eunice's injuries, Darcy is going to have to pay damages. Such a piecemeal approach to litigation serves no useful purpose. Besides the delay, such a tactic could work against Eunice's interests. Declaratory judgments are determined by *courts*, not juries. Having a court make a determination of negligence would end up depriving Eunice of the chance to have her case heard by a jury, and a jury could well be more sympathetic (and generous, when it comes to damages) than the trial judge. If Eunice's lawyer files a suit only for a declaratory judgment Eunice could have a strong cause of action—against her own lawyer for attorney malpractice!

Example 3

Variation on the Zelda-Alex hypothetical: Alex begins building his shed on what Zelda believes is Zelda's land. Zelda seeks a declaratory judgment that Alex is building on her land. She asks for no other relief. The court issues the declaration that Alex is building on Zelda's land. Alex refuses to remove the shed. (a) Can Zelda go back to court to have Alex held in contempt of court? (b) Does claim preclusion or issue preclusion prevent Zelda from obtaining an injunction ordering Alex to remove the property and pay damages for the past trespass?

Explanation

(a) Alex cannot be held in contempt of court. The declaration addressed *only* the parties' rights; it did not impose any obligation upon Alex to remove his structure or to compensate Zelda. Subject to a few exceptions not applicable here (see Chapter 10), a party cannot be held in contempt absent a valid injunction that the party disobeys. Zelda can go back to court and ask for an injunction, and Alex could be held in contempt *at that point* if he fails to abide by the court's order.

(b) Because Zelda brought a suit for *pure* declaratory relief (i.e., a request for a declaratory judgment with no other relief requested), Zelda may bring a follow-up lawsuit asking for an injunction, damages, or both. (Thus, this situation is unlike *Mycogen v. Monsanto*.) The question of where the parties' property line is, however, has already been settled in the declaratory judgment action. Both parties should be precluded from re-litigating that issue.

16.2 RIPENESS REQUIREMENTS FOR DECLARATORY JUDGMENTS

Declaratory judgments are different from some other kinds of remedies in that a plaintiff usually seeks the remedy *before* there has been an injury. This feature of declaratory judgments makes them like injunctions and raises the same problem that the remedy may be brought *before* there is an actual, live controversy between the parties. As we saw in Chapter 7, the "propensity" requirement a plaintiff must meet to get injunctive relief deals with this problem in the context of injunctions. (Plaintiffs seeking injunctions also must prove "irreparable injury," something not required when plaintiffs seek declaratory judgments.)

In the context of declaratory relief, courts impose a "ripeness" requirement on declaratory judgment actions. If a court holds that a case is "unripe," it will not consider a claim for declaratory relief. This section considers how much of a controversy there must be before a claim is considered ripe enough for courts to consider it.

In the federal courts, ripeness has a *constitutional* dimension. Article III of the United States Constitution grants federal courts jurisdiction only to hear "cases" or "controversies." In *Nashville, Chattanooga & St. Louis Railway v. Wallace*, 288 U.S. 249 (1933), the United States Supreme Court held it had Article III jurisdiction to hear an appeal of a declaratory judgment action brought in a Tennessee state court. The Supreme Court held a declaratory judgment case may be heard under Article III "so long as the case retains the essentials of an adversary proceeding, involving a real, not a hypothetical, controversy, which is finally determined by the judgment below." More recently, in *Susan B. Anthony List v. Driehaus*, 573 U.S. 149 (2014), the Court held that a political organization, which had been subjected in the past to claims it violated an Ohio law by making false political statements could bring a declaratory judgment action to have courts hold the law a violation of the First Amendment. Given a "credible threat" the law would be enforced again against the group, the Court held the case was ripe.

In *California v. Texas*, 141 S. Ct. 2104, 2116 (2021), the Supreme Court suggested that a plaintiff has no standing for Article III purposes to seek a declaratory judgment if plaintiff would not be entitled to other relief (whether or not such relief is actually sought). That determination seems to refute the idea that declaratory judgments have a lower standard of constitutional ripeness than claims for injunctions. It is at odds with the statute, which authorizes declaratory judgments "whether or not further relief is or could be sought." The statement was dicta, not a court holding, but it still may affect what lower courts do in considering declaratory judgments.

Although state courts are not limited in their jurisdiction by Article III of the United States Constitution, some also impose ripeness requirements on declaratory judgment claims. (Other state courts are more willing to issue purely advisory opinions.) Another example out of Texas is instructive. In *Save Our Springs Alliance v. City of Austin*, 149 S.W.3d 674 (Tex. Ct. App. 2004, no pet.), an environmental group sought a declaration that the City of Austin's approval of a land use project violated a city ordinance.[5] The court held the claim was unripe because the City had not yet approved the project; it had only been approved by a land-use committee, and not the agency with the final power to approve the project. It was possible that the city would never approve the project. If it ever did, the dismissal of the original suit without prejudice would allow a new suit to be filed once there was a riper controversy.

The court opinion gave some reasons in favor of the ripeness doctrine. "The doctrine has a pragmatic, prudential aspect that is directed toward '[conserving] judicial time and resources for real and current controversies, rather than abstract, hypothetical, or remote disputes.' [Citation.] Moreover, avoiding premature litigation prevents courts from entangling themselves in abstract disagreements, while allowing other branches of government and governmental agencies to perform their functions unimpeded."

Example 4

EXAMPLE

Professors F and G have a heated argument over an arcane but important point of state insurance law. The disagreement is so intense that the two of them

5. The group also sought an injunction barring development of different property in the same area that had already been approved by the city. The court held that this claim was moot for reasons that do not concern us here.

refuse to speak to each other or work together on faculty committees. They agree to jointly petition the state supreme court to resolve the issue "once and for all" through a declaratory judgment. They prepare and file briefs with the court presenting well-researched and written arguments on the two sides of this issue. Should the court agree to the request for a declaratory judgment?

EXPLANATION

Explanation

"[C]ourts shouldn't grant declaratory judgments to resolve law professors' hypotheticals." LAYCOCK & HASEN p. 594. The *Save Our Springs Alliance* case provides some rationales for the ripeness doctrine, and they seem to apply here: it would be a waste of judicial resources for courts to decide hypothetical questions where there is nothing of substance at stake. Though the question posits that the law professors care passionately about the question and have prepared good briefs on the topic, that's not the kind of "real controversy" that courts care about. If the question presented in the petition is really an important one about state insurance law, it will eventually arise in a real controversy, where someone's property interests (at the least) are at stake. Putting aside bad feelings between two law professors, there's no good reason to gear up the machinery of the state supreme court to involve itself in a case like this, and it is difficult to imagine any court that would do so—even in jurisdictions where courts issue advisory opinions. These professors would be better off designing a "moot court question" judged by state supreme court justices to get some feedback on their dispute.

EXAMPLE

Example 5

Same facts as in the original Zelda-Alex hypothetical about building the shed, except Alex files papers with the court saying he has no intention of building the shed, either on his property or across the property line. Zelda counters by showing pictures she took of Alex outside near her property with a surveyor. Should the court issue a declaratory judgment regarding the property boundary between the two parties?

EXPLANATION

Explanation

This case comes down to a credibility issue for the court. If the court believes there is a live controversy between the parties, then the court is likely to decide the matter through a declaratory judgment. If the court does not believe that a dispute is likely to arise, then the court will not decide the case.

If a court declines to hear a declaratory judgment motion, then the case is dismissed without prejudice. This dismissal would allow Zelda to file a later suit (perhaps for an injunction and/or for damages) in the event that Alex actually begins construction of the shed on what Zelda believes to be her land. Of course, in this variation on the hypothetical, Alex has represented to the court that he has no intention of building a shed either on his land or on Zelda's land. If Alex actually builds such a shed and then faces new litigation from Zelda (especially before the same judge), a court is likely to be very unfavorable to Alex's position in this case.

16.3 DECLARATORY JUDGMENTS AND FEDERALISM

Consider again the example of Marchers and the city from earlier in this chapter. Marchers believe that the city's bond requirement unconstitutionally burdens their First Amendment rights to free speech and assembly. City officials believe the law is constitutional, and plan to arrest Marchers if they in fact march.

Marchers have a few options (besides complying with the law by posting a bond). First, they could decide to break the law and, if arrested for violating it, defend themselves on the ground that the law is unconstitutional. Such a prosecution would take place in state court. If the suit is successful, the prosecution will be dismissed. If it is unsuccessful, Marchers can be punished under criminal law. This strategy therefore is risky unless Marchers are quite confident that the courts will strike down the law as unconstitutional.

Second, Marchers could seek an injunction from a court barring the city from enforcing its law against Marchers. Provided Marchers can prove irreparable injury and propensity (see Chapter 7), the court will consider whether to bar enforcement of the law. This suit could be brought in either federal or state court; both courts have the power to enjoin enforcement of a law that violates the U.S. Constitution. In *Ex parte Young*, 209 U.S. 123 (1908), the Supreme Court approved of an injunction to eliminate the tough choice to obey an arguably unconstitutional law or violate it and risk prosecution.

Third, Marchers could seek a declaration from a court that the city's law is unconstitutional, at least as applied to Marchers. Marchers would need to show that the claim was ripe, as noted in the previous section of this chapter. The declaration would not hold the power of contempt, but the city would be expected not to prosecute Marchers following a declaration that the bond provision is unconstitutional; if the city did prosecute, the issue of the provision's unconstitutionality should be collaterally estopped in any future criminal prosecution, thereby barring that prosecution. This suit could be brought in either federal or state court; assuming state law allows for declaratory judgments, both courts have the power to declare a law in violation of the U.S. Constitution. *See Steffel v. Thompson*, 415 U.S. 452 (1974).

To this point, everything should seem straightforward. The complication arises if Marchers violate the law, get prosecuted in state court for violating the city provision, and *then* go to *federal court* seeking a *declaration* that the city provision is unconstitutional. Once a state prosecution is pending, a federal court will abstain from hearing the case requesting a declaration that the city provision is unconstitutional; nor will a federal court issue an injunction barring state prosecution. *Younger v. Harris*, 401 U.S. 37 (1971); *Samuels v. Mackell*, 401 U.S. 66 (1971). Federal courts abstain out of federalism concerns; it would be a big deal for federal courts to interfere with ongoing state criminal law prosecutions.

Here are three important details about these issues. First, given that both federal and state courts have the power to declare laws in violation of the U.S. Constitution, it may not be clear what is at stake; after all, Marchers can simply defend themselves in the state court prosecution on grounds that the law is unconstitutional. The answer is that historically—though perhaps no longer true today—many litigants (particularly those involved in civil rights struggles) saw federal courts as more protective of federal constitutional rights than state courts.

Second, timing is everything in these cases, and the rules are complicated. Once state prosecutors take formal steps to begin criminal prosecution (such as filing an indictment), *Younger* abstention applies. However, even if a would-be criminal defendant files a declaratory relief action in federal court *first*, *Younger* abstention still applies if the state commences a prosecution "before any proceedings of substance on the merits" takes place in the federal court. *Hicks v. Miranda*, 422 U.S. 332, 349 (1975). The *Hicks* rule bars criminal defendants who go to federal court too late as plaintiffs seeking a declaratory judgment. Of course, the would-be criminal defendant cannot file the suit too *early* either, or else the suit may not be ripe. *See* LAYCOCK & HASEN p. 615.

Third, assuming no state prosecution has commenced, there still must be a *ripe controversy* for a federal court to declare a state or local law unconstitutional. *See Steffel* ("[R]egardless of whether injunctive relief may be appropriate, federal declaratory relief is not precluded when no state prosecution is pending and a federal plaintiff demonstrates a genuine threat of enforcement of a disputed state criminal statute, whether an attack is made on the constitutionality of the statute on its face or as applied."). In *Steffel*, the lower court had held that injunctive relief was inappropriate because the plaintiff could not show irreparable injury.[6] *Steffel* then firmly established the right to a declaration of unconstitutionality even absent proof of irreparable injury, so long as the case was ripe.

6. The plaintiff in *Steffel* abandoned his request for injunctive relief in the Supreme Court. The Court therefore did not rule on whether the lower court was right in concluding that plaintiff could not prove irreparable injury.

EXAMPLE

Example 6

A city passes an ordinance barring topless dancing. The three clubs in the city that produced topless dancing shows ceased the practice and went to federal court seeking a declaration that the ordinance was unconstitutional and an injunction barring its enforcement. Right after filing suit but before any court rulings, one of the three clubs then began featuring topless dancing again. Before the federal court considered the request for a declaratory judgment and injunction on the merits, the state commenced prosecution of the club that resumed the topless dancing. (a) Should the state be held in contempt for prosecuting the club that began the topless dancing again? (b) Does the federal court have the power to declare the law unconstitutional and enjoin its enforcement?

EXPLANATION

Explanation

(a) The state cannot be held in contempt for prosecuting the club. Although the three clubs filed a complaint seeking a declaratory judgment and an injunction, the court had not yet granted these requests. Indeed, it had not done anything on the merits in the case. Without an injunction issued, a federal court would not hold the state in contempt for commencing prosecution of the clubs for violating the ordinance.

(b) The facts of this problem are based upon *Doran v. Salem Inn, Inc.*, 422 U.S. 922 (1975). To begin with, the three plaintiff clubs in the federal suit are not in the same situation. The two clubs that ceased their activities and did not restart the topless dancing should be entitled to declaratory relief under *Steffel* and, if they can prove irreparable injury, to an injunction in the event the federal court determines that the ordinance is unconstitutional. However, the third club, which continued the topless dancing, cannot get the benefit of declaratory relief or injunction. The state began its prosecution of the third club before there had been any proceeding of substance on the merits, meaning the state prosecution was commenced first for purposes of *Younger* abstention. (*See Hicks*.)

This ruling creates an anomaly: three similarly situated defendants are going to be treated differently even though all three were at one point engaging in activities violating the local ordinance, which may be unconstitutional. In *Doran*, the Supreme Court recognized the anomaly but held that "each of the [clubs] should be placed in the position required by our cases as if that [club] stood alone."

EXAMPLE

Example 7

The state of Pacifica has a long-standing statute on the books declaring the practice of oral or anal sex between men to be illegal. Harry, a gay rights activist, thinks the law is unconstitutional under the U.S. Supreme Court's opinion in *Lawrence v. Texas*, 539 U.S. 558 (2003). (a) No one has been prosecuted under this statute for 80 years. May a federal court declare it unconstitutional? (b) Harry calls a press conference covered by the local television news in which he announces that next week he plans to invite police to his home to arrest him for engaging in activity that violates the statute. He then goes to federal court seeking a declaration that the statute is unconstitutional. May the federal court declare it unconstitutional?

Explanation

EXPLANATION

(a) Even though this law appears to violate the applicable Supreme Court precedent of *Lawrence*, it is possible the court would refuse to declare the law unconstitutional on grounds that the case is not ripe. The state has not prosecuted anyone for violating the statute for 80 years, and absent evidence of a new prosecution, it may not be worth gearing up the judicial machinery if only to make a symbolic point. On the other hand, the law remains on the books, and we do not know how many people might be deterred from engaging in likely legal conduct because of this statute. To the extent that Harry can demonstrate that the law would chill him (or others, who might be joined as plaintiffs) from engaging in constitutionally protected conduct, there is a chance the court would agree to decide the declaratory judgment case.

(b) Harry's conduct here seems aimed at creating a "test case" to avoid the possibility that the challenge to the law will be declared unripe. The federal court might well intervene, particularly if Pacifica officials give some indication they actually intend to arrest Harry for violating the law. On the other hand, if this law is unquestionably unconstitutional under *Lawrence*, perhaps the federal court will decide it is better to let the unconstitutionality of the statute be determined in state court as part of Harry's defense should he be prosecuted for violating the statute.

Arguably, Harry does not like either of these scenarios; he would prefer that any negative publicity generated by his opposition to the statute will cause the legislature to repeal it, as the statute appears to be unconstitutional. Legislative action would remove any of the reasons for either a declaratory judgment or a prosecution.

16.4 OTHER DECLARATORY REMEDIES

Though declaratory judgments are a relatively new judicial remedy (having found acceptance in many courts only within the last century or so), courts have for a much longer time given other remedies that serve a similar declaratory purpose.

We have already seen two of these remedies earlier in this book. First, in Part I we considered *nominal damages*. To illustrate the declaratory nature of this remedy, let's return to our Zelda-Alex hypothetical. Suppose that Alex is out surveying the land where he intends to build his new shed. In doing so, he crosses what Zelda believes to be the line dividing their properties. Zelda could, at least in theory, sue Alex for trespass. (The tort does not require knowledge that defendant is on plaintiff's land, just an intent to enter that land.) Zelda suffered no damages by Alex's trifling trespass. But a jury determination that Alex indeed trespassed and must pay $1 to Zelda in nominal damages could serve a function like a declaratory judgment in having a court determine the boundary line between the parties.

Today, with declaratory judgments easier to get, it is less likely that a party would need to use nominal damages to achieve the declaratory result.

Second, the contract remedy of reformation is declaratory, at least in form. As we saw in Chapter 14, reformation is a court rewriting of the parties' contract, especially in cases where the writing does not conform to the parties' outward manifestations of the intentions they held when entering into the contract. Reformation may be considered declaratory because the court declares what the parties' contract now contains. But reformation is more than a declaration of the parties' rights: it imposes new obligations on the parties to a contract. Indeed, as noted in Chapter 14, some scholars consider reformation to be more restitutionary rather than declaratory, because it puts the parties in the position they would have been in had there been no error in the recording of their intentions in the written contract.

Besides nominal damages and reformation, a traditional declaratory remedy predating many courts' adoption of a Declaratory Judgment Act is the equitable *bill to remove cloud on title* (also referred to in some jurisdictions as a bill to quiet title or a bill to determine adverse claims). This declaratory-type remedy was (and in some states remains) useful in dealing with disputes over ownership of real property, particularly if those disputes concern the validity of any document related to title.[7] In some states this equitable remedy has been replaced with a statutory one, and today in many jurisdictions a declaratory judgment action can serve the same purpose as a bill to remove cloud on title.

The rules on when to use this remedy for property disputes have varied from state to state. One question concerns the overlap of the remedy with the remedy of *ejectment*. In some states, "[i]f defendant is in possession, the action is still called ejectment, or analogized to ejectment, and either party can demand a jury; if not, the action is analogized to removing a cloud on

---

7. As early as 1936, some courts were allowing the remedy to be used to resolve disputes involving personal property as well. *See Right to Quiet Title or Remove Cloud on Title to Personal Property by Suit in Equity or under Declaratory Judgment Act*, 105 A.L.R. 291 (1936).

title and is said to be equitable." LAYCOCK & HASEN p. 627. When an action is equitable, it is decided by a court rather than a jury.

The rules for what to call your cause of action can be a malpractice trap in certain states. Especially if you are handling a land dispute in a different state from the one you ordinarily practice in, it is prudent to consult local sources to determine the proper form for your action. And you should always consider whether to couple your request for relief under a traditional form of remedy with a request for a declaratory judgment.

As to the labels used for remedies to declare rights in property disputes, consider an Indiana case, *Wetherald v. Jackson*, 855 N.E.2d 624 (Ind. Ct. App. 2006). The Jacksons and Strahls had adjoining lots on lakefront property. The Jacksons used their lot on Sundays for recreational purposes. The lot had a boat dock. "There was also a sandy beach area which the Jacksons believed was situated on their lot. On the side of the beach area nearest to Lot 66, a wooden board jutted out into the water. James Strahl told the Jacksons that the board was the boundary line between the two properties." In fact, the property was on Strahl's side of the line.

The Jacksons replaced the dock and built a deck and gazebo. The Strahls sold their property to Wetherald, who then installed a Jet Ski dock near the Jacksons' beach area. The Jacksons objected, claiming the dock was on their side of the property line, and asked Wetherald to remove it. Wetherald filed a complaint to quiet title alleging that the Jacksons had no legitimate claim to the transfer area and that they were interfering with his use of the property. In response, the Jacksons filed a counterclaim for declaratory judgment of adverse possession.

Note that Wetherald filed the complaint as an action to "quiet title" because he alleged he was the rightful owner of the property as recorded by the deeds to the properties. In response, the Jacksons sought a declaratory judgment that they had acquired the disputed property through adverse possession. (It does not appear that a claim for adverse possession could be resolved through a quiet title action in the jurisdiction.) The claims were tried before a trial court, which determined that the Jacksons had acquired the property through adverse possession. Though this procedure for resolving this garden-variety property dispute appears correct under Indiana law, the proper procedure in other jurisdictions may differ and will require some research.

Example 8

EXAMPLE

Wife dies as the separate owner of some real property. Wife's siblings claim that the property belongs to them, not to Husband. Husband brings a declaratory judgment action asking the court to declare that Wife's siblings have no interest in the real property. Should the court consider Husband's claim in a declaratory judgment action?

EXPLANATION

Explanation

It would appear that this dispute would be a fine candidate for a declaratory judgment action, so long as the claim was ripe. If Husband can present evidence that there is a genuine dispute over the ownership of the land between him and Wife's siblings, a declaratory judgment action can remove uncertainty and allow all parties to move forward knowing their rights.

But appearances can be deceiving. As noted in the text, the rule here about the proper form of action to bring in land disputes is quite jurisdiction-specific. In *Porter v. Houghton*, 542 S.E.2d 491 (Ga. 2001), the Georgia Supreme Court held that a declaratory judgment action was *not* the proper method for resolving this controversy, because "a party must establish that it is necessary to relieve himself of the risk of taking some future action that, without direction, would jeopardize his interests." (It is not clear why he could not make this showing if he planned to use or dispose of Wife's real property and Wife's siblings would oppose such action.) The court held that, under Georgia law, the statutory action to quiet title would be appropriate. GA. CODE. ANN. §23-3-60. According to the *Porter* court, the purpose of that statute is for "readily and conclusively establishing that certain named persons are the owners of all the interests in land defined by a decree entered in such proceeding." Again, beware of the malpractice trap.

CHAPTER 17

Help! I Need Somebody: Ancillary Remedies

17.1 COLLECTING MONEY JUDGMENTS

Ancillary remedies are helping remedies—that is, they are remedies that help other remedies work properly. We have already considered the most important ancillary remedy in Chapter 10: contempt. The contempt power gives injunctions their bite. When a party fails to follow an injunction, the contempt power allows for coercion, punishment, and, in some cases, compensation.

Unfortunately for prevailing plaintiffs in suits seeking a legal remedy such as compensatory damages, the contempt power is generally unavailable, except in some family law cases, as discussed below. The practical effect of this distinction is enormous. In some cases a damages judgment isn't worth anything because it is uncollectible.

Consider a very famous, albeit dated, damages judgment: the O.J. Simpson civil case. O.J. Simpson, a former football star and sports broadcaster, was acquitted in 1995 in a criminal trial of killing his ex-wife, Nicole Brown Simpson, and her friend, Ron Goldman in 1994. Families of the victims then sued Simpson in civil court for the tort of wrongful death. The jury concluded that Simpson was liable for their deaths in the amount of $8.5 million in compensatory damages and $25 million in punitive damages.[1]

1. You might wonder why the first trial did not have an issue-preclusive effect in the second trial; that is, if jurors in the first trial found Simpson not guilty of murder, how could a second jury find him liable for Brown Simpson and Goldman's deaths? The answer turns on the different evidentiary standards in the case. Jurors in the first trial considered whether

Simpson refused to pay the judgment voluntarily, as happens with a number of defendants (called "judgment debtors," after judgment against them) who are found liable for damages. In cases where defendants do not voluntarily pay, plaintiffs (called "judgment creditors," after judgment in their favor) have three ways to try to collect. First, a judgment creditor may place *a judgment lien on the judgment debtor's non-exempt real property.* Second, the judgment creditor may *execute on the judgment debtor's non-exempt personal property.* Third, a judgment creditor may *garnish the judgment debtor's wages or bank accounts.*

Judgment Lien. If the judgment debtor owns real property, the judgment creditor may file a lien on that property, eventually forcing a sale to pay for at least some of the judgment. The judgment creditor, however, does not take before other lenders with priority, such as the bank that holds a secured mortgage on the property. For example, suppose Simpson owned some real property as an investment worth $300,000 and subject to a $200,000 mortgage. The judgment creditors could force the sale of the house, with the first $200,000 going to pay the mortgage holder and the rest of the money going toward paying the judgment.

The possibility of a judgment lien is subject to a very large exception, however. States have instituted so-called "homestead exemptions," which prevent a creditor's executing on a judgment debtor's home, or at least protect a *portion* of that home's value; as a result, if judgment creditors do force a sale, a judgment debtor will have a way to find other living accommodations through the proceeds from the value protected by the homestead exemption. In some circumstances, the exemption prevents the judgment lien altogether. For example, during the Simpson controversy, O.J. Simpson moved to Florida and purchased an expensive home in which to live. Florida has an unlimited homestead exemption, meaning that Simpson's home could not have been sold to satisfy the judgment.[2]

Execution. The first step that the judgment creditors in the Simpson case tried to take after judgment was "execution": having sheriffs seize some

---

Simpson was guilty of murder *beyond a reasonable doubt* (the applicable criminal standard). But in the civil trial, for purposes of liability and compensatory damages, the jurors used the easier-to-meet *preponderance of the evidence* standard in determining that Simpson was responsible for the murders. Regarding the punitive damages, the jurors used a *clear and convincing evidence* standard in judging whether Simpson acted with fraud, oppression, or malice. *See* CAL. CIV. CODE §3294. The *clear and convincing evidence* standard is harder to meet than the *preponderance of the evidence* standard, but still weaker than the criminal standard. Accordingly, the jurors' conclusion in the first trial under the very difficult criminal standard did not preclude the possibility they would have found Simpson liable (and worthy of punishment) under the civil court standards. As a result, the criminal trial did not have a preclusive effect on the civil claim.

2. Under federal law a person in bankruptcy usually may not protect more than $189,050 in a home's value from creditors even if state law, like Florida's, allows for an unlimited homestead exemption. 11 U.S.C. §522(p)(1).

of Simpson's personal property and then sell it to satisfy the judgment. Judgment creditors face two major hurdles when they execute on a judgment debtor's property. First, they must find the property. If the defendant has been successful in hiding his assets during trial, a plaintiff will have little to go after once there is a judgment.[3] The sheriff will *not* investigate to find the property; instead, the judgment creditor needs to tell the sheriff where and when to go to collect the property. More importantly, not all assets can be seized. We have already considered the homestead exemption. State law and federal law provide exemptions from execution on other property as well. For example, federal law prevents execution on money in certain pension funds. Thus, creditors could not touch Simpson's $25,000-per-month draw from his $4 million pension. Anne McDermott, *The O.J. Simpson Case + 5 Years: Where Are They Now?*, CNN, June 11, 1999. Despite the huge judgment, Simpson said in an interview with *People* magazine that "a lot of guys would like to be in my position, raising my kids and playing golf." Alex Tresniowski, Meg Grant, Lorenzo Benet, Lyndon Stabler, Kelly Carter, Ana Figueroa, Ron Arias and Johnny Dodd, *Playing Through*, People, June 21, 1999 at 59.

Exemptions from execution have left the judgment creditors in the Simpson case with few options. In 1997, Simpson's lawyers were fighting attempts by the judgment creditors to seize his $40,000 Ford Expedition and a baby grand piano Simpson claimed was a gift to his mother. *Simpson's Vehicle, Piano Focus of Court Battle*, CNN, Aug. 7, 1997, http://www.cnn.com/US/9708/07/simpson.hearing/index.html. Twelve years later, the battles continued. By 2022, Goldman's family had collected only $123,000 from Simpson. He owed over $96 million with interest. Mike Florio, *O.J. Simpson Currently Owes Ron Goldman's Estate $96 Million*, NBC Sports, June 26, 2022, https://www.nbcsports.com/nfl/profootballtalk/rumor-mill/news/o-j-simpson-currently-owes-ron-goldmans-estate-96-million

Garnishment. "Garnishment is an independent action against a third party who owes money to the judgment debtor. The most common garnishees are banks and employers." LAYCOCK & HASEN p. 874. Thus, if Simpson had a regular job or money in bank accounts that could be located, the judgment creditors could go to the employer or bank and have at least some of that money diverted to them. State law can limit the amount that may be garnished from wages, and on top of any state limits, federal law limits the percentage of a worker's wages that can be garnished, again to prevent the judgment creditor from being able to force the judgment debtor onto the street. *See* 15 U.S.C. §1673. Outside the family law context, where percentages are higher, garnishment is limited to 25% of the worker's take-home pay, or 30 times the minimum wage, whichever is less.

3. If a plaintiff suspects that a defendant is hiding assets to avoid paying a judgment, a plaintiff might seek a prejudgment freeze order, the topic of the next section of this chapter.

In 2006, Simpson agreed to write a book called "If I Did It," in which he said how he would have committed the murders if he were the killer. The publisher of the book, Judith Regan, called it a confession. Amidst the controversy, the book deal was canceled and Regan was fired. Before the deal was canceled, Regan claimed that Simpson himself would not receive the reported $3.5 million advance; the money would go through a third party to his children. *Raw Data: Judith Regan Statement:* "Why I Did It," FOX News, Nov. 17, 2006, http://www.foxnews.com/story/2006/11/17/raw-data-judith-regan-statement-why-did-it.html. Depending upon state law, such an attempt to avoid creditors through a third party would fail, and the advance would be obtainable through execution (once Simpson received it) or through a garnishment order to the publisher. (The book was eventually published for the benefit of the judgment creditors, with the word "If" in the title printed in very small print, so that it appeared to read "I Did It" by O.J. Simpson.)

Because of the possibility of execution or garnishment, wealthy judgment debtors with easily seized assets will tend to pay to avoid execution. Consider one case involving this author and a major national company. Plaintiffs obtained a multimillion-dollar punitive damages verdict against the company, and the company filed a petition in the U.S. Supreme Court to reverse the judgment. A petition for certiorari to the Supreme Court does not stay execution of a judgment automatically; the company moved for a stay with a Supreme Court Justice, and plaintiffs voluntarily agreed not to execute until the Supreme Court had ruled. When the Justice denied the stay, the company (as was its right) filed a stay petition with another Justice. At that point, the plaintiffs told the company that it would not wait any longer. If the second stay was denied, the sheriff would be at one of the company's offices seizing office equipment. The company quickly had the checks cut to the plaintiff to avoid this result. (The second Supreme Court Justice quickly denied the stay, and the full Court later declined to hear this case.)

The nitty-gritty details on how to accomplish execution or garnishment differ from state to state and are not covered here. There are some general rules, however, on execution, as summarized by Professor Moringiello:

> In most states, if the property is real estate, a judgment creates a lien on the property when it is docketed or recorded in the records specified in the applicable statute. The resulting lien is known as a "judgment lien." . . .
>
> If a judgment creditor cannot perfect a lien against the debtor's property by recording a document, the judgment creditor must seize or otherwise gain control over the property in order to obtain and perfect the lien. A judgment creditor has no right to use self-help to seize a debtor's property to satisfy the

> judgment, but instead must enlist the help of the sheriff. After winning a judgment, a creditor has the right to a writ of execution, originally known and still known in some places as a writ of *fieri facias*. . . .
>
> The creditor must deliver the writ to a sheriff and it is the sheriff's job to execute the writ. The sheriff does so by way of a levy. When the property is easily movable, to "levy" means to take actual physical possession of the property. At common law, a sheriff could execute the writ of fieri facias only by physical seizure of tangible property. When the property cannot be moved easily, constructive possession can result in a levy. Whether the seizure is actual or constructive, notice is key. So long as the owner of the property and third parties have notice that the property is levied upon and will be sold, the levy is effective.

Juliet M. Moringiello, *Seizing Domain Names to Enforce Judgments: Looking Back to Look to the Future*, 72 U. Cinn. L. Rev. 95, 130-131 (2003) (footnotes omitted). Professor Moringiello notes that these rules have not traditionally applied to intangible property rights, such as intellectual property.

One complication with levying on goods is that other creditors may have an interest in the same good. In such circumstances, state statutes will set the order of priority. This priority often depends upon who filed first, but not always. For example, secured creditors who properly noticed their security interest in property have a right in property that is superior to that of the judgment creditor.

As payment methods change, garnishment orders must change too. Journalist Yashar Ali owed hundreds of thousands of dollars in unpaid loans to a Getty heir. "The debt collector is asking L.A. Superior Court for the power to seize funds sent to Ali on various online platforms, including PayPal, Venmo, Zelle, GoFundMe and Square. The debt collector also wants 'all rights to future payments' that Ali may get from his newsletter on Substack; income he derives from Twitter, where he has more than 700,000 followers; as well as future payments he may get from freelance journalism he publishes at Huffpost, MSNBC News or New York magazine, according to the filing." Matt Hamilton, *Twitter Star Yashar Ali Still Owes $230,000 to Getty Heir; A Debt Collector Now Wants His Income*, L.A. Times (Apr. 24, 2023)

Regarding the nitty-gritty of garnishment, let's begin with a hypothetical and some terminology. Eric runs over Frannie, injuring her. Frannie obtains a judgment against Eric for $20,000, and Eric refuses to pay. Eric is employed by G-Corp. Frannie can go to G-Corp and get an order of garnishment requiring G-Corp to pay a portion of Eric's wages directly to Frannie (subject to state and federal limits on the amount of garnishment). In this situation, Eric is the defendant and judgment debtor. Frannie is the plaintiff, judgment creditor, and garnishor. G-Corp is the garnishee. See Figure 17.1.

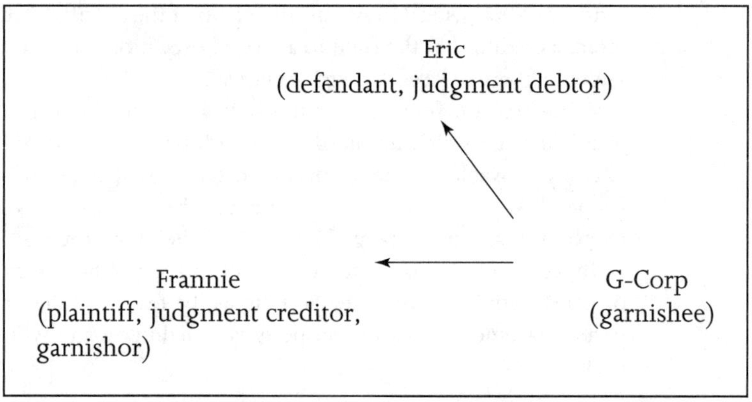

Figure 17.1. The Three-Sided Relationship in Garnishment

In Figure 17.1, garnishment causes G-Corp (the garnishee) to divert some of the wages it would be paying to Eric over to Frannie (the garnishor). Though this looks like it poses no big deal to the garnishee (besides the accounting hassle of writing two checks), garnishment imposes a risk on the garnishee. If G-Corp, the garnishee, makes a mistake and pays all the money to Eric rather than to Frannie, a court is going to require G-Corp to pay Frannie as well. *See Lakeshore Bank & Trust Co. v. United Farm Bureau Mut. Ins. Co., Inc.*, 474 N.E.2d 1024, 1027 (Ind. Ct. App. 1985) ("It is said that by commencement of the proceedings and service of the summons the creditor acquires an equitable lien on the credit or funds due to the debtor. . . . Thus, if the garnishee transfers the funds to the debtor after the equitable lien attaches, he will still be liable to the creditor in the garnishment proceedings and is treated as still having the funds in his possession. The court may order the garnishee to make payment a second time, this time to the creditor.").

The rules on execution and garnishment show that successful plaintiffs often have to jump through a lot of hoops to become successful judgment creditors. To put it another way, for plaintiffs (and the lawyers who work for them, often for a percentage of the recovery—see section 17.3), getting a judgment is not much good if the defendant is likely to be "judgment proof"—i.e., without the ability to pay a money judgment. That factor must be considered when one is deciding who to sue and how much effort to expend on such suits. It is what motivates plaintiffs in civil lawsuits to join "deep pocket" defendants with other defendants, when possible.

We could instead have a system that allows money judgments to be backed by the power of contempt. With a few exceptions that appear not to be used routinely, coercive collection of money judgments is not available outside the family law context. It is routinely available in child support situations and, less typically, in spousal support (alimony) contexts. *See In re McCarty*, 98 P. 540 (Cal. 1908) (allowing use of contempt power for failure to pay alimony).

So, if Henrietta fails to pay her child support obligations to support her son Isaiah, a court can order her to pay or risk jail time if she does not. Some judgment debtors owing child support are certainly motivated to pay by that kind of coercion, which accompanies the contempt power. But this kind of coercion raises new problems, primarily questions over a judgment debtor's inability to comply.

As Chapter 10 explains in detail, a court may not use contempt if it has no ability to coerce a party into complying with a court order. Thus, if Henrietta is homeless and destitute, with no possibility of paying her child support obligations for the foreseeable future, a court cannot use the contempt power: such a power would cease to be coercive, and it would only be punitive. This rule means that courts must inquire into the *ability* of judgment debtors to pay, and that raises additional questions as to how much money is necessary to support oneself.

Suppose, for example, that Henrietta lives in an apartment in a nice, but not the nicest, part of town, paying $1,500 per month rent. Should a court say she could afford to pay at least $500 more a month in child support, upon proof that in less nice parts of town, Henrietta should be able to rent a somewhat dilapidated apartment for $1,000 per month?

And what if Henrietta was capable of holding a job she could use to pay child support, but refused to work? The California Supreme Court held that a judgment debtor owing back child support could be held in contempt for failing to find and keep a job. *See Moss v. Superior Court*, 950 P.2d 59 (Cal. 1998).

Given the importance of child support, perhaps society has made the best choice by allowing the contempt power to be used in that context but not in the general context of judgments. From the position of judgment creditors, however, perhaps the child support example shows that it is possible to have a workable system for coercing the payment of money. Certainly O.J. Simpson has some earning capacity, and his choice not to use it to pay his debts is one that society may think Simpson should not have the freedom to make. Would you support the extension of the contempt power to the collection of ordinary judgments? From the point of view of the additional burden on the courts, would such a change be worth the administrative hassle in the general case?

EXAMPLE

Example 1

Umbro International, a company that sells popular soccer clothing and other merchandise in England and elsewhere, sued 3263851 Canada, Inc. for its use of the web domain name "umbro.com." Umbro obtained a declaratory judgment that Umbro had the right to use the "umbro.com" domain name, an injunction barring 3263851 Canada, Inc. from use of the name, and a $24,000 judgment. 3263851 Canada, Inc. did not have easily seized assets, but it did own the rights to 38 other web domain names. Umbro brought a garnishment action against Network Solutions, Inc., which held the domain names for 3263851 Canada. Umbro wanted to auction off the right to these domain names (some of which are valuable) to satisfy its judgment. Should the court allow Umbro to do so?

Explanation

The Virginia Supreme Court said that Umbro could not force Network Solutions to give Umbro the power to sell these domain names. *Network Solutions, Inc. v. Umbro Int'l, Inc.*, 529 S.E.2d 80, 87-88 (Va. 2000). The court construed Virginia statutes as not applying to these new technologies. Professor Moringiello, in the article cited earlier in this chapter, argued that the Virginia Supreme Court got it wrong:

> Many garnishment and execution statutes have not been amended in decades and state legislatures could not have anticipated the new types of property that technology would create. It is unquestioned that a domain name registrant can receive the benefits of a domain name. The name leads people to his business and when the registrant no longer wants the name, he is entitled to the potentially enormous proceeds of its sale. The holder of a domain name should also be forced to bear the corresponding burdens of holding valuable rights. Allowing creditors to enforce money judgments by seizing and selling domain names would force domain name registrants to bear those burdens.

Moringiello, *supra*, at 149-150.

Example 2

Back to the Eric-Frannie hypothetical. Eric refuses to pay Frannie, and Frannie discovers that Eric has a bank account with $10,000 in it at Happy Bank. Frannie properly files a demand for garnishment of this bank account with Happy Bank. Before Happy Bank makes a notation in its computer system, Eric walks into a bank branch and removes his $10,000, closing the account. Is Happy Bank liable to Frannie?

Explanation

Yes. Once Happy Bank received notice of the garnishment, it was the bank's responsibility to direct payment to Frannie, not Eric. The bank can try to go after Eric in restitution for return of the money, but whether it is successful in doing so or not does not affect Frannie's ability to obtain the $10,000 from the bank.

EXAMPLE

Example 3

Here's another variation on the Eric-Frannie hypothetical. After Frannie files a garnishment order against Eric requiring his employer to turn over 25% of his wages to Frannie, Eric quits his job and moves back in with his parents. Eric tells Frannie: "I'd rather not work than work for you!" Can Frannie get an order requiring Eric to go back to work to pay off the judgment?

EXPLANATION

Explanation

In most jurisdictions, the answer is no. Outside the context of family law cases, a court will not use the power of contempt to force Eric to work to pay off his debt. Some judgment debtors hope that if they stall long enough, the judgment creditor will go away (and some will do so). But the O.J. Simpson case shows that this is not always the case. Indeed, sometimes it is not even about the money. The father of the deceased Ron Goldman in the O.J. Simpson case promised to give up his right to Simpson's assets if Simpson gave a full written confession to the crime. In the Simpson case, as in others, the judgment may be about much more than money, or about issues besides money. But when it is primarily about money, as in the Eric-Frannie case, coercive contempt is not an option.

17.2 PREJUDGMENT FREEZE ORDERS, ATTACHMENTS, AND RECEIVERSHIPS

In the first section of this chapter, we saw just how difficult it is for judgment creditors to collect from judgment debtors who are unwilling, or unable, to pay after judgment. Defendants in civil cases will often be tempted to try to hide or transfer their assets before judgment, in an effort to prevent the judgment creditors from collecting. Under applicable state laws, a defendant may not hide assets or transfer them in an attempt to defraud creditors or prevent enforcement of a valid judgment. But what can a plaintiff do to prevent such conduct?

When fraudulent transfers are discovered after a judgment, a court can reverse the transaction and order the asset sold to pay the creditors. Thus, if a court believed O.J. Simpson had not really made a gift of the baby grand piano to his mother before judgment, but did so to protect his assets, the court could have ordered the gift returned and sold to pay the judgment creditors.

But sometimes plaintiffs want to take steps *before* judgment to prevent defendants from hiding and dissipating assets in anticipation of a verdict against them. Plaintiffs have three potential tools to help them before judgment.

1. *Freeze orders.* A freeze order is a kind of preliminary injunction that prevents a defendant from transferring specific assets pending judgment. Chapter 9 details the requirements for a preliminary injunction; to understand how freeze orders work, one must first understand the workings of preliminary injunctions. In brief, a plaintiff seeking a freeze order must show a likelihood of success on the merits of the underlying suit, as well as the irreparable harm that would come from denial of the order. In deciding on whether to grant the freeze order, the court must balance the harm to the plaintiff if the court errs in failing to grant the freeze order against the harm to the defendant if the court errs in granting the freeze order. A court may require the plaintiff to post a bond to cover costs associated with an erroneously granted freeze order.

Consider the facts of *In re Estate of Ramlose*, 801 N.E.2d 76 (Ill. App. Ct. 2003). Mr. Haneberg was a trustee of the Ramlose Trust. The trust's beneficiary, Alexander Ramlose, filed a suit for breach of fiduciary duty against Haneberg. He alleged that Haneberg was diverting funds from the trust for personal use. Eventually, the Public Guardian successfully petitioned to represent Ramlose's interests, on grounds that Ramlose, who was 95 years old, was suffering from dementia. The Public Guardian alleged that Haneberg transferred over $700,000 from the Ramlose Trust to the Haneberg Trust soon after Ramlose was diagnosed with dementia. Haneberg resisted discovery requests, eventually being held in contempt for failing to appear, and during the litigation, Ramlose died, with the Public Guardian then representing the estate.

The Public Guardian, fearing that Haneberg would dissipate assets during trial, asked the trial court for a freeze order over certain bank accounts and real property owned by Haneberg. The court, without holding an evidentiary hearing, issued an order as follows: "All of the assets and accounts, whether involving real or personal property of Elmer Haneberg, including all such assets and accounts held individually or jointly with any person or held in a trust wherein he is named as a trustee for any family member, including himself, his wife, *** his mother, *** and his children *** or any trust in which Elmer Haneberg has any beneficial interest are hereby frozen and may not be accessed for any reason without further order of Court."

The appellate court reversed the order to give Haneberg a chance for a hearing on whether or not the order was appropriate. The appellate court further noted that the freeze order, which included freezing sale of a Park City, Utah, time-share, went too far in covering more of Haneberg's property than requested by the Public Guardian. Finally, the appellate court saw a potential due process problem: "no nexus was ever established between the Ramlose Trust funds and Haneberg's bank accounts, assets and real estate properties and those of his family, who are not and have never been parties to these proceedings." The lesson from this case is that even when a defendant appears to be engaging in bad conduct, it is important to carefully craft a freeze order that complies with due process and delineates both the property to be frozen and the reasons for it to be frozen.

2. *Attachments.* An attachment "generally refers to a preliminary garnishment or seizure before judgment." LAYCOCK & HASEN p. 906. It is a more extreme order than a simple freeze order, which prevents a defendant from dissipating assets pending judgment; it puts the defendant's assets into the hands of the plaintiff before there has been a final judgment on the merits.

States differ on the standard for obtaining an attachment. In New York, for example, a plaintiff must show that the defendant has an "intent to defraud his creditors or frustrate the enforcement of a judgment that might be rendered in plaintiff's favor" and that the defendant has "assigned, disposed of, encumbered or secreted property, or removed it from the state or is about to do these acts." N.Y. C.P.L.R. §6201(3). In Connecticut, in contrast, it is enough to show "that there is probable cause that a judgment in the amount of the prejudgment remedy sought, or in an amount greater than the amount of the prejudgment remedy sought, taking into account any known defenses, counterclaims or set-offs, will be rendered in the matter in favor of the plaintiff." CONN. GEN. STAT. ANN. §52-278c(a)(2). The defendant has the right to a hearing to contest the attachment. *Id.* at §52-278c(g).[4]

Consider a Connecticut case illustrating how the Connecticut scheme works, again from the "truth is stranger than fiction" department. Two neighbors, the A Family and the B Family, had an ongoing series of disputes. When the A Family put two homes it owned up for sale, the B Family caused several inoperable Jeep vehicles and a trailer to be placed on their property. The Jeeps looked like they had come from a junkyard. The trailer parked on the street right next to [one of the for-sale properties and] had bumper stickers that stated, "Bambi makes cute sandwiches," and, "I'd Rather Be Loading My Muzzle." [The A family] erected a six foot high fence between their property and that of the defendants, and [the B family] thereafter constructed a ten foot high structure that consisted of two wooden posts with several rusty cylinders hanging on a wire between the posts. The [B Family] also put up "No Trespassing" signs on their property and targets in their windows.

See Kinsale, L.L.C. v. Tombari, 897 A.2d 646, 647 (Conn. App. Ct. 2006) (internal quotations omitted).

The A Family sued for nuisance and raised a separate libel claim. On the nuisance point, the A family argued that the sale of their property was

4. The Connecticut legislature added this right to a hearing after lawsuits successfully arguing that granting the plaintiff the right to an attachment in the absence of a hearing violated due process rights guaranteed by the U.S. Constitution. *See Kinsale*, 897 A.2d at 651 (dissenting opinion).

decreased by $250,000 because of the junk in the B Family's yard (which the B Family defended as art protected by the First Amendment). The A Family also asked for an attachment for $250,000, arguing that it would obtain that much money in its suit on the merits. The trial court granted an attachment in the amount of $100,000, finding that the A Family was likely to prevail on its nuisance claim and to prove $100,000 in damages. A Connecticut appellate court, over a dissent, upheld the attachment, holding that the trial court's factual findings were not clearly erroneous.

What is to stop the A Family from now dissipating the $100,000, making it unavailable, if after a trial on the merits the court finds for the B Family? CONN. GEN. STAT. ANN. §52-278d(d) provides in pertinent part that "the defendant may request that the plaintiff post a bond, with surety, in an amount determined by the court to be sufficient to reasonably protect the defendant's interest in the property that is subject to the prejudgment remedy against damages that may be caused by the prejudgment remedy." In deciding on whether a bond is appropriate and, if so, the right amount, "the court shall consider the nature of the property subject to the prejudgment remedy, the methods of retention or storage of the property[,] and the potential harm to the defendant's interest in the property that the prejudgment remedy might cause." *Id.* at §52-278d(e). The court can also waive the bond requirement for indigent plaintiffs. *Id.* at §52-278d(f).

3. *Receiverships.* A receivership is a kind of preliminary injunction like an attachment, but one that allows a neutral third party to run an ongoing business, or take steps to wind it down, during a dispute involving the business. Thus, if shareholders or business partners end up in litigation, a neutral third party might be required to run the business during litigation to prevent fraud or mismanagement.

A Texas statute, Texas Civil Practice and Remedies Code §64.001, sets out the reasons why a court might want to grant a receivership:

> (a) A court of competent jurisdiction may appoint a receiver:
>
> (1) in an action by a vendor to vacate a fraudulent purchase of property;
>
> (2) in an action by a creditor to subject any property or fund to his claim;
>
> (3) in an action between partners or others jointly owning or interested in any property or fund;
>
> (4) in an action by a mortgagee for the foreclosure of the mortgage and sale of the mortgaged property;
>
> (5) for a corporation that is insolvent, is in imminent danger of insolvency, has been dissolved, or has forfeited its corporate rights; or
>
> (6) in any other case in which a receiver may be appointed under the rules of equity.

Further, the Legislature has set forth the receiver's powers and duties in §64.031:

> Subject to the control of the court, a receiver may:
> (1) take charge and keep possession of the property;
> (2) receive rents;
> (3) collect and compromise demands;
> (4) make transfers; and
> (5) perform other acts in regard to the property as authorized by the court.

Example 4

Greta is injured seriously when Horace punches her in the face in a barroom fight, causing serious damage to her nose that will require corrective surgery. Greta is poor and has no health insurance. She sustains $25,000 in damages and is facing possible bankruptcy before her tort case for battery against Horace will be going to trial. Horace will be claiming self-defense as an affirmative defense at trial. Horace is quite wealthy and has a number of easily found assets that could be used to satisfy any judgment that Greta might receive. Might Greta use a freeze order, attachment, or receivership to obtain money from Horace before trial?

Explanation

A freeze order does not appear to be an appropriate remedy in this case. There are no specific assets Greta can point to that Horace is planning on dissipating before trial. Indeed, the fact that he has many assets that could be found after judgment suggests any freeze order would be unnecessary to satisfy the judgment. In any case, a freeze order does not put any money into Greta's hands before judgment.

Attachment is a better possibility here, depending on the jurisdiction. In a jurisdiction like New York, attachment would be difficult to obtain absent proof of some kind of attempt at fraud or waste of Horace's assets. Greta would have an easier time in a jurisdiction like Connecticut, if she could prove she is more likely than not to succeed at trial. The decision by the court would require taking a peek at the merits to see if Greta's claim of battery is likely to succeed in the face of Horace's claim of self-defense. This kind of swearing contest might not be easily resolvable before trial.

If a court would grant an attachment, Horace might demand a bond. If the court gives Greta her $25,000 and she uses it to pay medical bills, it would not be available to pay Horace back in the event Horace prevails in the actual trial. Under Connecticut law, a court would have discretion to waive the bond requirement because of Greta's indigence.

Finally, a receivership is not an appropriate remedy here. There is no business that Horace is running in which Greta has some interest, nor is there fear of Horace hiding or dissipating any business assets.

17.3 ATTORNEY'S FEES AND LITIGATION EXPENSES

Lawyers, like law students, need to eat, and—aside from some pro bono assignments—few attorneys work for free. In addition to legal fees, litigation brings additional expenses: court costs, expert witness fees, and other expenses. Under the *American rule*, in the absence of a provision in a contract or as provided by statute, each side to a lawsuit bears its own attorney's fees.[5] (The contrasting rule used in England, the unsurprisingly named *English rule*, has the loser pay the winner's attorney's fees.)

The fact that a plaintiff must bear her own attorney's fees affects the rightful position standard. Recall an example from Chapter 2: Alex carelessly burns down Barbara's house, causing Barbara $100,000 in damages. As illustrated in Figure 17.2, we would calculate Barbara's damages as (B – A), or $100,000.

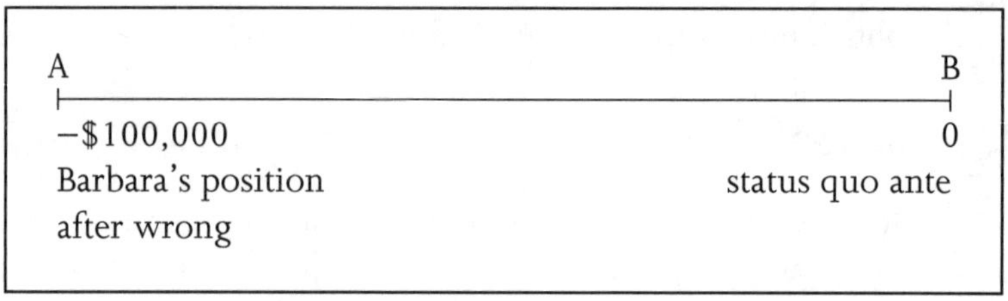

Figure 17.2

As Chapter 2 noted, calculating $100,000 as the amount to put Barbara in the rightful position masks a number of complications, and we now focus on one of them: attorney's fees. Suppose Carla is Barbara's attorney. The Barbara-Carla contract might require Barbara to pay Carla by the hour, or it might have some other financial arrangement, such as a *contingency fee*. With a contingency fee, Barbara would pay nothing to Carla if the suit is unsuccessful, but Carla would receive a *percentage of the recovery* in the event that the suit is successful.

5. Attorney's fees also may be available as a penalty for bad faith litigation, as a sanction for contempt of court, in family law cases, when a private plaintiff sues as a private attorney general, and in common fund cases such as class action suits. *See* Rest. (Third) Torts: Remedies § 16 (Am. Law Inst. Tent. Draft No. 2, 2023) (listing potential bases for the award of attorney's fees in a torts lawsuit).

Suppose that Carla successfully obtained a $100,000 verdict for Barbara against Alex, and was able to collect from Alex. Suppose Carla's fee, whether by the hour or through a contingency fee, is $25,000. In that case, Barbara is not really brought back to the rightful position by the $100,000 verdict. (See Figure 17.3.) Barbara instead is brought to B–, equal to –$25,000. In other words, Barbara has $25,000 less wealth than she would had there been no wrong, leaving her short of the rightful position.

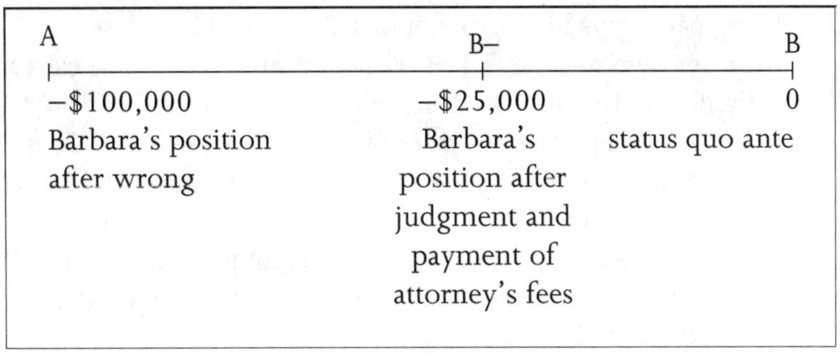

Figure 17.3

Society can deal with the undercompensation of plaintiffs caused by the American rule in a few ways. One way is to switch to the English rule. It is not clear, however, that switching to the English rule would result in a net gain for plaintiffs. For plaintiffs with strong suits, the English rule looks like a good idea. But for plaintiffs with suits that may be harder to prove, the English rule can be a deterrent. A contingency fee allows the plaintiff to shift the risk of paying *her own* attorney's fees to the plaintiff's attorney, but it does nothing to shift the risk of having to pay the *defense* attorney's fees.[6]

A second way to deal with the undercompensation problem is to allow only *one-way fee shifting*, in which the plaintiff gets attorney's fees if she wins, but does not pay defendant's attorney's fees if she loses. That system, of course is a great benefit to plaintiffs (and a burden on defendants). Such fee shifting has been adopted in particular areas by statute, as we'll see, but it is not the general rule.

Third, rules like the collateral source rule and the possibility of punitive damages in particular cases could increase the return to plaintiffs, thereby making up for some of the compensation that is lost through the payment of attorney's fees. These rules work in a haphazard way to solve the general problem, however.

Finally, juries—which likely will contain jurors who understand the American rule—might *overcompensate* plaintiffs so that plaintiffs are really put in the rightful position *after* plaintiff's attorney is paid.

6. Some proof that the English rule is not necessarily a good thing for plaintiffs is that change to the English rule has been advocated by defense-oriented "tort reform" groups.

Recall the earlier statement of the American rule: *in the absence of a provision in a contract or as provided by statute*, each side to a lawsuit bears its own attorney's fees. Consider first the *contractual* exception to the American rule. It is very common that parties to a contract will include a contractual provision providing that if a dispute arises between the parties over the contract, the losing party shall pay the winner's attorney's fees.

If you were a clever lawyer, you might try to draft a one-way fee shifting provision in the contract. If my client is sued and wins, the other contracting party pays his attorney's fees. But if my client loses, each party bears his or her own attorney's fees. That drafting may be too clever by half. Under California law, for example, courts construe such one-sided provisions to apply *reciprocally* to both sides of the contract. CAL. CIV. CODE §1717(a).

Attorney's fees may also be provided by *statute*. "More than 200 federal statutes and 4,000 state statutes authorize awards of attorney's fees." LAYCOCK & HASEN p. 925. For example, under the Copyright Act, the prevailing party—plaintiff or defendant—is entitled to reasonable attorney's fees. 17 U.S.C. §505.

Some statutory attorney's fees provisions expressly impose one-way fee shifting. *See, e.g.*, 15 U.S.C. §1640(a)(3) (allowing prevailing plaintiffs suing for federal truth-in-lending violations to recover reasonable attorney's fees). Sometimes the courts read *facially evenhanded* attorney's fees provisions as applying in ways that primarily help plaintiffs. Certainly, one of the most important attorney's fees provisions on the federal level, 42 U.S.C. §1988(b), allows prevailing plaintiffs who succeed in civil rights litigation to recover attorney's fees in most cases in which plaintiff prevails. However, a prevailing defendant may recover fees under the statute from the plaintiff only if the plaintiff brought the suit frivolously or with intent to harass the defendant. *See Hensley v. Eckerhart*, 461 U.S. 424, 429 n.2 (1983).

Once a court determines that a party is entitled to reasonable attorney's fees for whatever reason,[7] it must determine what a reasonable fee is.[8] Typically, the party entitled to fees will put in a request for fees, itemizing the attorney expenses. The losing party will then argue that the fees are excessive, and the court, sometimes going line by line over the attorney's bills, will decide on what would be a reasonable fee.

Courts sometimes use the "lodestar" method to calculate reasonable attorney's fees: "the number of hours reasonably expended on the litigation multiplied by a reasonable hourly rate" *Id.* at 433; *see also City of Riverside v. Rivera*, 477 U.S. 561, 568 (1986). As explained in *Rivera*, though

---

7. First the court will have to determine who the "prevailing party" is, which is sometimes difficult to do when a plaintiff has received some of the relief requested, but not most of it.
8. The timing for filing a fee application is a malpractice trap. Check the rules carefully, and know that a pending motion for attorney's fees, at least on the federal level, does not delay the time to file an appeal from the underlying judgment.

the lodestar is the starting point in calculating reasonable fees, it is not the whole story. In enacting the Civil Rights Attorney's Fees Awards Act of 1976, 42 U.S.C. §1988, Congress did not define the method for calculating reasonable attorney's fees. But House and Senate reports accompanying the legislation endorsed a 12-factor test set forth in *Johnson v. Georgia Highway Express, Inc.*, 488 F.2d 714 (5th Cir. 1974). These factors are (1) the time and labor required, (2) the novelty and difficulty of the questions, (3) the skill requisite to perform the legal service properly, (4) the preclusion of employment by the attorney due to acceptance of the case, (5) the customary fee, (6) whether the fee is fixed or contingent, (7) time limitations imposed by the client or the circumstances, (8) the amount involved and the results obtained, (9) the experience, reputation, and ability of the attorneys; (10) the "undesirability" of the case, (11) the nature and length of the professional relationship with the client, and (12) awards in similar cases. *Id.* at 717-719.

In civil rights litigation, where a court awards only nominal damages, the reasonable fee is often zero. *See Farrar v. Hobby*, 506 U.S. 103, 115 (1992). Even though the precedent created by such cases may be valuable, a lawyer who wants to recover fees should therefore seek more than nominal damages; for example, the lawyer might want to seek an injunction barring defendants from engaging in certain proscribed conduct in the future. The lawyer can then point the court to the injunction as a benefit of the litigation that should entitle the lawyer to higher attorney's fees. Even without the injunction, some courts will still grant fees, relying on Justice O'Connor's concurring opinion in *Farrar* noting that fees might be permissible if the litigation, in addition to earning plaintiff nominal damages, "also accomplished some public goal other than occupying the time and energy of counsel, court, and client." *Id.* at 121-122.

One of the most contentious areas for dispute over reasonable attorney's fees has been class action lawsuits, particularly those involving cases in which the plaintiffs each receive awards with small value—sometimes including nothing more than a coupon for a discount on a future purchase from the wrongdoer! In some of these cases, each plaintiff has little at stake, and therefore little reason to police the plaintiff class attorneys for self-dealing. In such cases, the plaintiffs' attorneys may have economic interests that line up with the defendants' interests; for example, attorneys might be willing to settle each plaintiff's claim for less than the claims are worth (such as a coupon instead of a small monetary award) in exchange for defendant agreeing to an acceptable amount of attorney's fees.

The details of attorney's fees issues in class actions are better left for a treatise on class actions or advanced civil procedure. Suffice it to say here that there has been a great deal of both litigation and legislation to deal with these problems. Some courts have tried to resort to "reverse auctions," whereby plaintiffs' attorneys bid against each other for the right to represent the plaintiffs' class for the lowest fee. There has also been much debate over whether these lawyers' fees should be calculated on an hourly rate or as a percentage of the total recovery.

Congress also made some changes in this area in the Class Action Fairness Act of 2005. Pub. L. No. 109-2, 119 Stat. 4 (codified as amended at 28 U.S.C. §§1711 *et seq.*). For example, to stop the coupon abuse, §1712(a) of the Act provides:

> If a proposed settlement in a class action provides for a recovery of coupons to a class member, the portion of any attorney's fee award to class counsel that is attributable to the award of the coupons shall be based on the value to class members of the coupons that are redeemed.

For a detailed analysis of the Act, *see Class Action Fairness Act of 2005, With Commentary and Analysis by Georgene M. Vairo of the Moore's Federal Practice Board of Editors, in* MOORE'S FEDERAL PRACTICE (Daniel R. Coquillette et al. eds., 2005).

Finally, a word about litigation costs, such as court reporter costs. These costs are generally recoverable by the prevailing party in both state and federal court. But, absent special mention in a statute, costs generally do not include expert witness fees, which can be quite expensive in complex cases involving such witnesses.

Example 5

If you were drafting a contract for a client, would you want to include an attorney's fees provision? What are the costs and benefits of its inclusion?

Explanation

There is, of course, no right or wrong answer to the first part of this question. As a matter of practice, most commercial contracts do include such provisions. Especially in consumer contracts, the provisions might discourage litigation brought by consumers against the companies whose lawyers draft the contracts. Besides discouraging litigation, these clauses reduce some uncertainty about the cost of contracting.

It is also possible that attorney's fees provisions increase the chance of settlement of disputes by raising the costs to both sides of failing to settle in the face of a possible losing case. Thus, if there is a contract dispute worth $100,000 and each side expects to incur $25,000 in attorney's fees in litigation, the parties deciding whether or not to settle or litigate will consider the fact that the costs of litigating are increased by an additional $25,000 when the contract contains an attorney's fees provision, making settlement more attractive.[9]

The major downside of including such an agreement is that your client might be on the wrong end of litigation, losing in court and now saddled with additional attorney's fees. A party believing that there is a fair chance that she will lose in court (whether rightfully or not) in the event of a contract dispute would likely not be enthusiastic about an attorney's fee provision. But parties tend to overestimate their chances of winning in the event of a dispute, so it is hard to imagine a large number of contracting parties deciding to exclude the attorney's fee provision on this basis.

EXAMPLE

Example 6

> Jarius Piphus was a freshman at Chicago Vocational High School. During school hours, the school principal saw Piphus and another student standing outdoors on school property passing back and forth what the principal described as an irregularly shaped cigarette. The principal approached the students unnoticed and smelled what he believed was the strong odor of burning mari[j]uana. He also saw Piphus try to pass a packet of cigarette papers to the other student. When the students became aware of the principal's presence, they threw the cigarette into a nearby hedge. The principal took the students to the school's disciplinary office and directed the assistant principal to impose the "usual" 20-day suspension for violation of the school rule against the use of drugs. The students protested that they had not been smoking mari[j]uana, but to no avail. Piphus was allowed to remain at school, although not in class, for the remainder of the school day while the assistant principal tried, without success, to reach his mother.

The above quotation comes from *Carey v. Piphus*, 435 U.S. 247, 248-249 (1978). In *Piphus*, the student sued under §1983, alleging that his right to procedural due process was violated because he was not given a hearing where he could have defended himself. The Court held that the failure to hold a hearing was a due process violation, but absent proof of emotional distress damages stemming from the failure to grant a hearing, Piphus could receive only nominal damages. The case did establish that the failure to provide a hearing in this school context constituted a denial of due process.

If Piphus's lawyer sought attorney's fees under 42 U.S.C. §1988, could he get them? What could his lawyer have done to maximize the chances of recovery?

---

9. Unsurprisingly, there is a rich literature in the law and economics field on how attorney's fees provisions affect settlement. For an introduction to the issue in the context of principal-agent problems, *see* Geoffrey P. Miller, *Some Agency Problems in Settlement*, 16 J. LEGAL STUD. 189 (1987).

EXPLANATION

Explanation

Generally speaking, the reasonable attorney's fee in a case resulting in only nominal damages for plaintiff is zero. However, if Piphus's lawyer could show some other public purpose for the litigation, attorney's fees might be available. It would strengthen the case if Piphus's lawyer could couple the nominal damages claim with another remedy, such as an injunction barring future school suspensions without a hearing, that accomplishes such a public purpose.

CHAPTER 18

Remedial Defenses

18.1 PLAINTIFF'S BAD CONDUCT: UNCONSCIONABILITY, UNCLEAN HANDS, AND *IN PARI DELICTO*

In a typical civil suit, for the plaintiff to win, she will have to prove a prima facie case by a preponderance of the evidence. If plaintiff succeeds in proving all the elements, plaintiff wins, unless the defendant can prove an affirmative defense by a preponderance of the evidence. For example, in a typical tort suit for battery, the plaintiff will have to prove that the defendant engaged in a nonconsensual, intentional touching, as well as proving the elements of actual cause, proximate cause, and damages. The defendant wins if the plaintiff cannot prove one of these elements—for example, if the jury believes that it is more likely than not that plaintiff consented to the touching, or if the defendant can prove an affirmative defense, such as self-defense.

Typically, defenses taught in first-year law courses are substantive: defendant wins by presenting a substantive defense (e.g., "I wasn't the person who touched the plaintiff" or "I win because it was self-defense"). But there are other defenses that do not depend upon substantive law, and typically these defenses are available in a variety of substantive law areas—from battery, to breach of contract, to a property dispute.[1] Many of these defenses were developed in the equity courts before the merger of the

1. Of the defenses discussed in this chapter, unconscionability is a defense that arises only in the context of contract disputes. The defenses considered in the remainder of this chapter apply in a variety of contexts.

courts of law and equity,[2] and some remain available only when the plaintiff seeks equitable relief, such as an injunction. This chapter examines these remedies—typically, but not exclusively, equitable remedies—available across a variety of civil cases. We begin with a cluster of defenses concerning plaintiff's bad conduct.

18.1.1 Unconscionability

Consider the case of *Campbell Soup Company v. Wentz*, 172 F.2d 80 (3d Cir. 1948). Campbell's entered into a contract with the Wentzes, who were farmers in Pennsylvania, for delivery "by the Wentzes to Campbell of all the Chantenay red cored carrots to be grown on fifteen acres of the Wentz farm during the 1947 season" at a price of $23-$30 per ton, depending upon the time of delivery. This kind of carrot had special commercial value to Campbell's: "Its blunt shape makes it easier to handle in processing. And its color and texture differ from other varieties. The color is brighter than other carrots. . . . It also appeared that [Campbell's] uses these Chantenay carrots diced in some of [its soups] and that the appearance is uniform." *Id.* at 82.

The contract contained a number of provisions that were especially beneficial to Campbell's. The court singled out one provision that was so one-sided that the court described the provision as "a good joke [carried] too far . . .":

> . . . Campbell is excused from accepting carrots under certain circumstances. But even under such circumstances the grower, while he cannot say Campbell is liable for failure to take the carrots, is not permitted to sell them elsewhere unless Campbell agrees. . . . What the grower may do with his product under the circumstances set out is not clear. He has covenanted not to store it anywhere except on his own farm and also not to sell to anybody else.

Id. at 83. The Wentzes breached the contract to Campbell's at a time when Chantenay carrots were in short supply and the market price of the carrots had skyrocketed to $90 per ton. The Wentzes sold 62 tons of carrots to a neighboring farmer, who turned around and sold 58 tons of them on the open market, half of them to Campbell's.

Viewing the original deal between Campbell's and the Wentzes as unconscionably one-sided, the court refused to order specific performance (an injunction ordering the Wentzes to deliver the carrots as promised).[3]

---

2. See Part II, especially Chapter 7, for background on the courts of law and equity.
3. The Wentzes had sold their carrots, but presumably, under the contract, they would have had to go out on the open market and buy carrots at the new market price to supply to Campbell's.

The court decided that "a party who has offered and succeeded in getting an agreement as tough as this one is, should not come to a chancellor and ask court help in the enforcement of its terms. That equity does not enforce unconscionable bargains is too well established to require elaborate citation." *Id.*

Wentz is an illustration of the principle that courts may refuse to grant specific performance or other equitable remedies in the face of an unconscionable contract. The ruling would not prevent Campbell's from suing the Wentzes for contract damages, which in this case would have been quite large,[4] except for the fact that the contract contained a liquidated damages clause providing the meager remedy of $50 *per acre* of crops planted.[5]

It is not clear what benefit the classic rule had for defendants who entered into unconscionable contracts with plaintiffs. If the Wentzes were not protected by the liquidated damages clause, they would have had to fork over as much in damages as they would have lost had they had to sell the carrots to Campbell's at the contract price. Probably for this reason, some modern courts, including those following the U.C.C. for sales contracts, now allow unconscionability to be a defense for both equitable relief *and* legal relief. *See* U.C.C. §2-302. Indeed, the U.C.C. gives courts great *flexibility* in crafting an appropriate legal remedy in the face of an unconscionable contract. Section 2-302 gives the court the power in essence to *rewrite* the parties' contract to avoid an unconscionable result, allowing the court to split the difference between the parties in appropriate cases. The fact that unconscionability has become more generally available as a defense does *not* mean, however, that it has become a cause of action: someone cannot sue another for "unconscionability."

The *Wentz* court determined that the contract at issue was so one-sided as to be unconscionable, barring an equitable remedy by the contract's drafter. This decision appears to be one based upon the *substantive unfairness* of the contract. You may recall from your Contracts class that some courts are skeptical of substantive unconscionability claims, believing that if two parties freely enter into a contract knowing its terms, courts should enforce the contract even if it appears one-sided. But even in those skeptical jurisdictions, defects in the bargaining process, such as onerous terms being written in dense language or buried in the fine print, can lead to successful

---

4. Using the rules for U.C.C. buyers' damages set forth in Chapter 4.5, it appears that if Campbell's was entitled to damages, such damages would be measured by the difference between the market price and the contract price at the time of breach (which is a difference of $60-$67 per ton multiplied by the number of tons produced by the Wentzes), plus any incidental and consequential damages in making the cover purchase, less expenses saved. These would have been considerable damages, especially for 1949.

5. Why would Campbell's have included such a meager liquidated damages figure? Perhaps Campbell's figured that it was the party more likely to breach, and it was trying to keep its exposure for damages low.

defenses of *procedural unconscionability*. Some courts say that procedural and substantive unconscionability should be considered together; the more of one type of unconscionability that is present, the less the defendant needs to show the other type.

Unconscionability and related doctrines have been very important for consumer laws, which are often enforced by private lawyers bringing class actions against companies allegedly engaging in bad practices. The U.S. Supreme Court dealt a major blow to consumer class actions in *AT&T Mobility LLC v. Concepcion*, 563 U.S. 333 (2011). California law barred companies like the wireless mobile company AT&T from blocking class actions against it in arbitration agreements signed by consumers. California recognized that such class actions are often the only way to make such litigation economically feasible. The U.S. Supreme Court, however, held that California's rule was preempted by the Federal Arbitration Act. Thus, states cannot prevent companies from requiring arbitration of disputes and banning the use of class actions to resolve them.

18.1.2 Unclean Hands

Unclean hands is an equitable defense in which the defendant claims that plaintiff's bad conduct should bar plaintiff from obtaining equitable relief such as an injunction. Many courts require that defendant demonstrate not only that the plaintiff's conduct is inequitable, but also that "the conduct relates to the subject matter of its claims." *Fuddruckers, Inc. v. Doc's B.R. Others, Inc.*, 826 F.2d 837, 847 (9th Cir. 1987). How bad does the conduct have to be? "Almost any kind of conduct the chancellor may consider to be unethical or improper might suffice to bar the plaintiff's claim, even if the conduct is not actually illegal." DOBBS & ROBERTS §2.4(2) at p. 67.

What better case to discuss "unclean hands" than one involving Häagen-Dazs ice cream bars? In *Häagen-Dazs, Inc. v. Frusen Glädje Ltd.*, 493 F. Supp. 73 (S.D.N.Y. 1980), the Häagen-Dazs ice cream company found itself it in a sticky situation. (Groan!) It brought a claim against an ice cream competitor for unfair competition under the Lanham Act. Among the claims made by Häagen-Dazs was that the competitor Frusen Glädje sought to confuse customers into thinking its ice cream was related to the Häagen-Dazs line by:

> (i) the phraseology used in reciting the ingredients of the product in issue; (ii) a recitation of the artificial ingredients not contained in the product; (iii) the manner in which the product is to be eaten in order to enhance its flavor; (iv) a two-word germanic-sounding name having an umlaut (ä) over the letter "a" and, (v) a map of Scandinavia.

Id. at 74. Nevertheless, the district court refused to grant a preliminary injunction against the competitor. It gave three reasons. First, Häagen-Dazs failed to demonstrate that the competitor's marketing would confuse members of the public. Second, there was no proof of irreparable harm. Finally, the court held that Häagen-Dazs itself had unclean hands.

> I turn finally to consider plaintiff's allegations that defendants' container is intended to deceive the public into believing that their product is made and/or sold in Sweden. In particular, plaintiff charges:
>
>> defendants claim their ice cream is manufactured "under the authority" of a Swedish corporation, although Frusen Glädje is produced in Pennsylvania by an American company and is not sold in Sweden at all; defendants fail to reveal the actual manufacturer, packer or distributor, all of which are American companies, which violates the applicable statutory labelling requirements; defendants also employ three lines of Swedish language on their container to add to the false impression that their product is sold or made in Sweden; and the English translation appearing beneath the Swedish language states that the recipe for Frusen Glädje comes "From Old Sweden," whereas, in fact, the recipe is American.
>
> Although defendants dispute the accuracy of these charges, even if true[,] they simply do not advance plaintiff's case at all. On the contrary, since plaintiff itself has attempted to package its product in such a way as to give the impression that it is of Scandinavian origin, although it too is, in fact, of domestic origin, [plaintiff] is guilty of the same deceptive trade practices of which it accuses defendants. In short, since plaintiff's hands are similarly unclean, they may not secure equitable relief simply because defendants' hands may be a shade or two less clean.

Id. at 75-76. The unclean hands rule no doubt has some appeal. After all, why should a court, especially one that is charged with "doing justice" like an equity court, be in the business of helping a wrongdoer? The classic case illustrating this principle is one involving a group of robbers who have a dispute over how to divide up their loot and want the court to help—a remedy the court declines to impose. *Highwayman's Case*, 9 L.Q.R. 197 (1893). But there are at least three important criticisms raised against the unclean hands doctrine:

- First, because it is not clear exactly what conduct is bad enough for the doctrine to apply, it could be used unfairly by judges, turning the right to sue into a mere privilege. DOBBS & ROBERTS §2.4(2) at p. 68.
- Second, if plaintiff has been guilty of bad conduct in relation to the subject matter of the lawsuit, it is not clear why that conduct should bar only equitable relief and not a claim for legal relief, such

as damages, as well. *See* LAYCOCK & HASEN p. 989 ("Is there any reason to deny injunctive relief for plaintiff misconduct that would not be sufficient to deny damages or rescission?").

- Third, if plaintiff has engaged in bad conduct, but defendant has engaged in worse conduct, unclean hands does not (at least in theory) allow for courts to balance the equities between the two parties. That can be unfair to plaintiffs and can hurt the public when the plaintiff's suit cannot stop the defendant's bad conduct. *But see* LAYCOCK & HASEN p. 992 (stating that courts in "most unclean hands cases" engage in balancing and citing some cases where courts engage in balancing, such as illegal gambling cases involving defendants who cheated at gambling).

The third (failure to balance) argument may not be as serious as first appears. In some cases, a court can engage in de facto balancing by determining that the plaintiff has not engaged in bad conduct (when in fact the plaintiff has engaged in such conduct, but it is not nearly as bad as defendant's conduct) or that the conduct does not relate sufficiently to the defendant's wrong. Thus, the first criticism of the doctrine, that the term "unclean hands" is not easily defined, may help deal with the third criticism about the lack of balancing under the doctrine.

18.1.3 *In Pari Delicto*

The defense of *in pari delicto* (literally "in equal fault") "is rooted in the common-law notion that a plaintiff's recovery may be barred by his own wrongful conduct." *Pinter v. Dahl*, 486 U.S. 622, 632 (1988). This definition makes *in pari delicto* sound like unclean hands, and the two are often raised at the same time. However, there are two major differences between the two defenses:

- First, *in pari delicto* can apply to bar suits in equity *or law*, while unclean hands (at least traditionally) applies only to suits in equity.
- Second, *in pari delicto* requires balancing. A defendant *must* prove that plaintiff's conduct was *at least as bad as defendant's conduct* for the *in pari delicto* defense to apply.

As with the common understanding of unclean hands, the *in pari delicto* defense requires that the wrongful conduct of the plaintiff and defendant arise from the same bad act.

Consider the case of *Parente v. Pirozzoli*, 866 A.2d 629 (Conn. App. Ct. 2005). Defendant approached Plaintiff about the opportunity to run a restaurant Defendant owned. Plaintiff agreed to do so, but because Plaintiff was a convicted felon, he could not obtain a liquor license. Defendant agreed to become a partner with Plaintiff and to keep all the business records in Defendant's name in order to get the license. After a while, Defendant forced Plaintiff out of the business, and Plaintiff sued for breach of contract, recovering $138,000 in damages.

The Connecticut appellate court reversed. The contract between Plaintiff and Defendant was an illegal one, because the parties hid the true identity of one of the partners in order to obtain a liquor license. Plaintiff therefore could not get damages. The court acknowledged that its ruling would give Defendant a windfall, but noted:

> . . . in the case of a contract whose inherent purpose is to violate the law, 'if both parties [thereto] are in pari delicto, the law will leave them where it finds them.' 'Knowing that they will receive no help from the courts and must trust completely to each other's good faith, the parties are less likely to enter an illegal arrangement in the first place.'

Id. at 639 (internal quotations and citations omitted).

EXAMPLE

Example 1

A made a deal to sell Blackacre to B for $100,000. A then refused to deliver the deed to Blackacre. B brought an action for specific performance. A raised the defense of unclean hands, pointing to B's conviction 10 years earlier for attempted armed robbery. (a) Should the court deny B the right to specific performance on grounds of unclean hands? (b) If B instead seeks damages, should the court deny the right to damages on grounds of either unclean hands or *in pari delicto?*

EXPLANATION

Explanation

(a) No. *See Morey v. Sings*, 570 N.Y.S.2d 864, 872-873 (N.Y. App. Div. 1991). There seems to be no question that attempted armed robbery is bad conduct and that the plaintiff is seeking equitable relief (specific performance). Nonetheless, there is absolutely no connection between B's prior wrong and this contract. To allow A to raise an unclean hands defense would mean that anyone convicted of a crime, such as attempted armed robbery, would never be able to use the courts to obtain equitable relief, a result that most people would probably think is an unfair kind of punishment.

(b) No. Besides the reasons for denying unclean hands listed in the answer to part (a) of this question, traditionally unclean hands has been available as a defense only when the defendant sought *equitable relief*. If B is seeking damages, this is a form of legal relief, not equitable relief, and therefore unclean hands is not available as a remedy. *In pari delicto* also should be unavailable. Although B's conduct in life might be worse than A's (we have no evidence A has engaged in violent crime like B has), the comparison involves conduct *in relation to the transaction at issue in the case*. Because the armed robbery is unconnected to the real estate sale, *in pari delicto* should not bar a suit for damages for breach of the land contract.

EXAMPLE

Example 2

Wisconsin Auto Loans (WAL) entered into an agreement with Jones for an auto loan. Jones borrowed $900 toward the purchase of an automobile, signing a standard form contract prepared by WAL. The contract contained many terms in fine print, including a number establishing finance charges and fees that were not readily understandable to the average consumer. The contract also contained an arbitration clause requiring that disputes over the contract be subject to binding arbitration, except for any claims by WAL against a borrower to enforce the lender agreement. Jones defaulted on his auto loan and WAL brought an action for replevin (see Chapters 7.2 and 13.3.1) to force Jones to return the car. Jones brought counterclaims for himself and a class of other WAL borrowers, alleging that the contract transaction violated various state consumer protection laws. In response, WAL moved for the court to dismiss the counterclaims and issue an order to compel Jones to arbitrate those claims pursuant to the contract. How should the court rule on that motion in the face of Jones' claim that the clause is unconscionable? If the court agrees the clause is unconscionable, what is the remedy?

EXPLANATION

Explanation

The Wisconsin Supreme Court faced these facts in *Wisconsin Auto Title Loans, Inc. v. Jones*, 714 N.W.2d 155 (Wis. 2006). The court held that the arbitration provision was unconscionable and, thus, unenforceable. It therefore denied the company's motion to compel arbitration of the counterclaims. The majority found both procedural and substantive unconscionability in the contract, particularly the arbitration clause. On the substantive unconscionability point, the majority wrote:

> The exception to the arbitration provision is far too broad and one-sided, granting Wisconsin Auto Title Loans a choice of forum—arbitration or the circuit court—for its claims, while permitting the borrower to raise claims only before an arbitrator. The doctrine of substantive unconscionability limits the extent to which a stronger party to a contract may impose arbitration on the weaker party without accepting the arbitration forum for itself.

Id. at 173.

Once the court found the clause unconscionable, it had the option under modern views of unconscionability doctrine to enforce the contract without the objectionable clause. In the context of this case, this meant that the arbitration clause was unenforceable, and the court could consider WAL's claim for replevin as well as the defendant's counterclaims.

The dissenting judge would have upheld the arbitration provision. The judge agreed that the clause was substantively unconscionable as a matter of law but held that there was no evidence of procedural unconscionability as well. The dissenting judge said that both kinds of unconscionability were required in Wisconsin before a court could decline to enforce a contractual provision on unconscionability grounds. *Id.*

18.2 ESTOPPEL AND WAIVER

If you've already read Chapter 16, you will remember the series of hypotheticals involving two neighbors with a property dispute. Alex is building a shed near the property line with his neighbor Zelda. Zelda believes the shed is over the property line and either brings a declaratory judgment action, to have the court determine the property line, or seeks an injunction barring Alex from building the shed on grounds that part of the structure extends onto Zelda's land. Chapter 16 considered the merits of these alternative approaches for Zelda.

But suppose we add the following facts. Before Alex undertakes the building of his shed, he asks Zelda where the property line is. Zelda tells him where she believes the property line is, and it turns out that she gives him wrong information: she erroneously indicates that a portion of her land belongs to Alex. Alex then builds about half of the shed before Zelda seeks the declaratory judgment or injunction.

You can easily see why these additional facts could change the entire course of the case. Though Zelda could well meet the elements of her prima facie case showing that Alex is trespassing on her land, Alex has a good affirmative defense: *Alex relied on a statement of Zelda's to his detriment, causing him damage.* This indeed is the essence of the defense of *equitable estoppel.*

Note the three requirements for estoppel: (1) a misstatement or action by plaintiff, (2) reliance by the defendant, and (3) injury to the defendant. So if Zelda gave Alex the wrong information about the property line, but she then corrected it before Alex incurred any costs in building over the property line, estoppel would not defeat Zelda's claim.

Though estoppel is an equitable doctrine, it can be used to defeat a claim for either equitable relief or legal relief. Thus, if Alex completed building the shed and Zelda sued later for damages, then her misstatement, Alex's reliance, and his subsequent injury should bar Zelda's case.

Equitable estoppel is an interesting doctrine in that it can be used as an affirmative defense by a defendant against a plaintiff, as in the Zelda-Alex hypothetical, or *as a way of defeating an affirmative defense* by a plaintiff against a defendant. This is a tricky point to understand, so consider this example: Montel and Norine get into an automobile accident in which Montel sustains serious personal injuries. Montel wants to sue Norine for negligence. Norine is a lawyer, and Norine tells Montel that he should not rush to sue because Montel has five years to sue under the applicable statute of limitations (statutes of limitation are considered in the next section of this chapter). In fact, the statute of limitations in the jurisdiction is only two years. Montel waits until nearly five years to sue. Watch what happens next:

1. Montel sues Norine for negligence.
2. Norine raises the statute of limitations as an affirmative defense.
3. Montel *defeats* Norine's affirmative defense by raising equitable estoppel.

Norine made a misstatement about the applicable statute of limitations period, Montel relied on it by suing later, and he suffered injury (because his suit would be barred). As you can see, in the Montel-Norine hypothetical the plaintiff uses estoppel to defeat the defendant's affirmative defense.

Closely related to the doctrine of equitable estoppel is the doctrine of *waiver*. Waiver is the *intentional relinquishment of a known right*. To begin with some easy examples, if Zelda signed a quitclaim deed covering the land where Alex was building his shed, or if Montel signed a release of liability stating that he would not sue Norine for any damages resulting from their automobile accident, the court is likely to accept an affirmative defense of waiver by Alex or Norine to defeat any claims against them. It is likely that Zelda or Montel would not sign such documents, absent some compensation in settlement of their claims. But once that sign-off does occur, a court is likely to use waiver to say that the sign-off ends the matter, unless there is some evidence that Zelda or Montel did not intentionally relinquish their rights to sue through these documents.

Note one important difference between waiver and estoppel: for waiver, the defendant need not prove reliance. It is puzzling that reliance is unnecessary for waiver defenses but required for estoppel; perhaps in cases of waiver, reliance is usually easy to find. Thus, the waiver doctrine avoids "litigation over attenuated reliance questions." LAYCOCK & HASEN p. 1004.

How does a party show that the other party intentionally relinquished a known right? When that relinquishment is express, as in the quitclaim deed or release of liability described above, proof may be rather easy. In contrast, sometimes a party will claim an *implied* waiver based upon conduct, and courts may require proof of an implied waiver by *clear and convincing evidence*.

For example, consider *Baumann v. Capozio*, 611 S.E.2d 597 (Va. 2005). Tyler was injured in a fight with Allen when Tyler was 17 years old. Tyler's parents initially brought suit against Allen on Tyler's behalf in tort. In response to an interrogatory, Tyler's parents listed about $20,000 in medical expenses incurred to take care of Tyler's injuries. When Tyler turned 18, he took control of the litigation and settled the case against Allen for $75,000. Under Virginia law involving injury to minors, the child has one cause of action for his pain and suffering, for any permanent injury, and for impairment of earning capacity after attaining majority. The parents have a separate cause of action for loss of services during minority and necessary expenses incurred for treating the minor. Tyler's parents then sought to recover their medical expenses in a separate suit; Allen argued that the parents impliedly waived that suit by listing their medical expenses in the interrogatory and having the son settle his suit afterward.

The trial court held that the parents impliedly waived their right to seek medical expenses in a second suit, but the Virginia Supreme Court, applying a clear and convincing evidence standard to implied waiver claims, reversed:

> Even though Tyler[']s mother signed an interrogatory in her capacity as next friend that identified medical bills as damages that Tyler's parents had incurred while he was an infant, the parents lost control of that litigation when their son reached the age of majority and signed a release that resulted in the settlement of that lawsuit. Plaintiffs in this appeal were not parties to the release, and they had not filed a lawsuit in their own name to recover damages that they had incurred. We hold that [Allen] failed to prove by clear and convincing evidence that the plaintiffs impliedly waived their right to recover any medical expenses that they incurred for the treatment of their son proximately caused by [Allen's] alleged tortious conduct.

Id. at 600.

It is common for parties to raise waiver and estoppel as alternative claims in a single pleading. The more proof there is of the intentional relinquishment of a right, the stronger the waiver claim will be. The more reliance that a party can show, the stronger the case for estoppel. But the claims are not completely interchangeable. In *Baumann*, there was no misstatement that Allen could point to by Tyler's parents that could meet the first element of equitable estoppel.

One final point: generally speaking, one may not raise an estoppel argument against the government. For example, Smith calls the Social Security office and receives incorrect advice on how to apply for benefits. As a result of the incorrect advice, Smith files the wrong papers and loses the ability to receive certain benefits. The Supreme Court has held that in a suit to recover such benefits, the government cannot be estopped from denying the benefits on grounds of erroneous advice. *Schweiker v. Hansen*, 450 U.S. 785 (1981).

Though this rule certainly seems unfair to plaintiffs who innocently rely on erroneous government advice, some have defended it on grounds that it protects against "misconduct by the executive" or permitting "the executive to effectively override legislation." LAYCOCK & HASEN p. 998-999. It is also possible that allowing estoppel claims against the government would cause the government to give less advice. *Id.*[6]

EXAMPLE

Example 3

Jane Doe brings a tort action against the Archdiocese of Cincinnati alleging that when she was a teenager, she became pregnant following an alleged sexual relationship with a priest. The Archdiocese raises the affirmative defense of the statute of limitations because it has been many years since the event took place. Doe responds by arguing equitable estoppel, stating that Archdiocese employees told her that her pregnancy was solely her fault; that a teacher at her Catholic school pressured her to give the child up for adoption and remain silent about the priest's identity; and that the teacher told her that her child would not be baptized and, therefore, not cleansed of original sin if she did not consent. How should the court rule on Doe's attempt to use equitable estoppel to defeat the limitations period?

EXPLANATION

Explanation

This hypothetical is based upon *Doe v. Archdiocese of Cincinnati*, 855 N.E.2d 894 (Ohio Ct. App. 2006). This case is difficult because, unlike the Montel-Norine hypothetical, which involved a misstatement about the limitations period itself, this case involves alleged statements of opinion, particularly religious opinion, about the effect of revealing the priest's actions. The appeals court nonetheless would have allowed the issue of estoppel to be presented to a jury:

> Doe's complaint asserts that the statements made to her by various representatives of the Archdiocese were "made with the sole purpose and intent to coerce Ms. Doe to forgo the best legal interests of her and of her child." It further alleges that the conduct of, and the actions taken by, the Archdiocese "were calculated to, and resulted in, Ms. Doe's relinquishment of her parental rights and the forbearance from any legal action." After reviewing Doe's complaint, we conclude that these statements adequately allege that the Archdiocese's conduct was motivated by a desire to prevent Doe from bringing suit. Again, we

6. In contrast to estoppel, it is easier to raise waiver arguments against the government, at least if the official who waived the government's rights had the authority to do so.

> emphasize that we pass no judgment as to whether the Archdiocese was actually motivated by such a desire; rather, our conclusion is based on the well-pleaded allegations in Doe's complaint.

Id. at 899 (footnotes omitted).

The state Supreme Court reversed, siding with the Archdiocese:

> To be sure, Father Heil and Sister Mary Patrick did not want the identity of the father of Doe's baby to become public knowledge, and a lawsuit would have revealed his identity. But to infer from the acts alleged in the complaint an intent to prevent Doe from filing suit requires a leap of logic that we are not prepared to take. The complaint contains many statements attributed to Father Heil and Sister Mary Patrick, but none of them address, even implicitly, the general subject of a lawsuit or litigation, and none of them reflect or imply an effort to discourage Doe from filing a lawsuit. The purpose of equitable estoppel is to prevent fraud, and none of the statements or threats constitute an actual or constructive fraud. . . .The passage of nearly 40 years, at the time the case was filed, is likely to have obscured the recollection of witnesses associated with the events, assuming they are still living and can be located, and judicial inquiry would be, at best, "difficult and uncertain." Further, assuming the truth of Doe's allegations of mental anguish, hospitalization, and years of psychotherapy stemming from the 1965 events, there is no indication why 2004 was the first time in nearly 40 years that Doe was able to file suit.

Doe v. Archdiocese of Cincinnati, 880 N.E.2d 892, 895-896 (Ohio 2008).

EXAMPLE

Example 4

From the "truth is stranger than fiction" department: Crystal Lovely contracted with Dr. Percy, a plastic surgeon, for breast augmentation surgery. Lovely claims that Percy orally promised the surgery would increase her breast size to at least a "34C." Dr. Percy denied making such a promise. Dr. Percy performed the surgery, but Lovely alleges her breast size after surgery was a smaller, "34B" size. She sued the doctor for breaching his promise regarding breast size and for other causes of action. The jurisdiction's statute of frauds provides in pertinent part that "[n]o action shall be brought to charge a person licensed by [the code] to practice medicine or surgery . . . in this state, upon any promise or agreement relating to a medical prognosis unless the promise or agreement is in writing and signed by the party to be charged therewith." Statute of frauds is to be pled in the state as an affirmative defense, but Dr. Percy failed to plead it. Can Lovely use waiver or estoppel to block Dr. Percy's affirmative defense? *Lovely v. Percy*, 826 N.E.2d 909 (Ohio Ct. App. 2005).

EXPLANATION

Explanation

The *Lovely* court held that the doctor waived the defense by not listing it as an affirmative defense in the answer to the complaint. It looks like poor lawyering on both sides of the case; the court raised the issue *sua sponte* and noted: "We mention this issue only because it does make available to physicians a legal defense against claims of oral promises concerning outcomes should a physician desire to avail himself or herself of the defense."

Estoppel would not work as a defense here because Dr. Percy made no statement to Lovely such as one that he would not rely upon a statute of frauds defense in the suit (nor was there any proof of reliance by Lovely on such a statement).

18.3 LACHES AND STATUTES OF LIMITATION

18.3.1 Laches

Laches is an affirmative defense that applies only when the plaintiff seeks an equitable remedy. The defendant must show that *the plaintiff unreasonably delayed bringing suit against the defendant and that the defendant suffered prejudice because of the unreasonable delay.*

The first part of the defense requires not only delay in suing, but *unreasonable* delay in suing. Consider in this regard the facts of *Emery v. Smith*, 603 S.E.2d 598 (S.C. Ct. App. 2004). Ex-Husband and Ex-Wife get a divorce, and as part of the divorce decree, Ex-Husband promises Ex-Wife 25% of his retirement benefits when he retires from the military. He also agrees, among other provisions, to provide "any and all information necessary" for Ex-Wife to get the 25% share of the benefits.

Ex-Husband retires from the military and does not tell Ex-Wife for 10 years. When Ex-Wife discovers that Ex-Husband had retired, she sues for an order requiring Ex-Husband to pay her share of the benefits, and Ex-Husband asserts laches as an affirmative defense. There is no question that Ex-Wife delayed for a long period before asking for the court order to the pension. But the reason she delayed is that she did not know, and had no reason to know, that Ex-Husband had retired. The trial court and appellate court rejected the laches argument:

> [Ex-Wife]'s ten-year delay in enforcing her rights came as a result of [Ex-Husband]'s own failure to comport with the court decree. [Ex-Husband] admitted that he did not inform his ex-wife of his retirement, and the family court found credible [Ex-Wife's] testimony that she did not know [Ex-Husband] had

> retired. Thus, it was [Ex-Husband] who acted unreasonably by failing to honor his duty to [Ex-Wife].

Id. at 604. The court further held that Ex-Husband was barred from asserting laches because of his own "unclean hands."

In addition to showing *unreasonable* delay, a defendant asserting laches must show reliance. On this point, consider *National Association for the Advancement of Colored People v. N.A.A.C.P. Legal Defense & Education Fund*, 753 F.2d 131 (D.C. Cir. 1985). The NAACP and the NAACP Legal Defense and Education Fund (LDF) were once affiliated, with the LDF group created for tax purposes. The NAACP granted permission to the LDF to use "NAACP" as part of its name. Eventually the groups split, and tension arose between them, with NAACP withdrawing permission to use its name and threatening litigation to get the LDF to change its name.

Though the NAACP *threatened* litigation, it has never brought litigation in the 13 years since the threat. In the meantime, the LDF continued to build name recognition and goodwill using the NAACP name. For this reason, the court accepted the laches claim of the LDF, barring the NAACP from suing the LDF for infringement.

Note that because a laches claim may be brought only to defeat a plaintiff's claim *for equitable relief*, laches-like conduct in a suit in which plaintiff seeks *damages or other legal relief* must be recast as some kind of estoppel or waiver. Thus, in the *NAACP* case, if the NAACP sought some kind of damages from the LDF, the LDF would need to argue either (1) estoppel—with the act being the failure to sue after threatening to do so—reliance, and injury, or (2) waiver—that the NAACP's failure to sue after asserting a right to do so 13 years earlier constituted the intentional relinquishment of a known right. This analysis should show you that plaintiff's conduct can sometimes be recast to fit into more than one of these remedial defenses. But it is a bit tricky here because it requires a finding of estoppel or waiver primarily by a party's *failure to act*.

Example 5

Jerry is running against Chuck for state attorney general. Jerry is the Democrats' nominee; Chuck is the Republican nominee. About two weeks before the election, supporters of Chuck file a lawsuit claiming that Jerry is ineligible to run for the office of attorney general. State law requires that candidates for the office be admitted to the state bar for the five years immediately preceding the election. Jerry had been admitted to the bar for many decades, but he was on "inactive" status while he served as mayor of one of the state's cities. Should the suit be dismissed on laches grounds?

EXPLANATION

Explanation

This question is based upon the facts surrounding the 2006 race in California between Democrat Jerry Brown and Republican Chuck Poochigian. My view, which I've set out most fully in Richard L. Hasen, *Beyond the Margin of Litigation: Reforming U.S. Election Administration to Avoid Electoral Meltdown*, 62 WASH. & LEE L. REV. 937 (2005), is that courts should aggressively use laches to prevent election lawsuits that easily could have been brought at an earlier date.

Think about this from the perspective of the election system. Suppose that opponents of Brown knew for a long time about the bar membership issue. Without an aggressive application of laches, you would be giving these opponents an option: if Brown does poorly in the polls before the election, don't sue and let your favored candidate win. On the other hand, if Brown does well, bring suit at the last minute so that the other side won't have time to come up with a viable replacement candidate. This shows the prejudice that could be caused by unreasonable delay. Strong application of laches in the election system helps to ensure that candidates, parties, and other agents don't try to manipulate election outcomes through the court system.

18.3.2 Statutes of Limitation

Statutes of limitation are also about time limits, but they differ in substantial ways from laches. Whereas the defense of laches applies only in cases where plaintiff seeks equitable relief, statutes of limitation bar suits brought for either legal relief or equitable relief.[7] In addition, while the doctrine of laches is flexible and depends upon a case-by-case analysis, the time limits for statutes of limitation are set by statute and are usually inflexible.

To use an easy illustration first, let's return to the Zelda-Alex hypothetical. Let's suppose that Alex builds over his property line and Zelda considers a suit for trespass. The jurisdiction will have a set of statutes imposing time limitations for different causes of action. Suppose the statute of limitations for trespass in the jurisdiction is two years from the date of injury. Generally speaking, if Zelda does not sue within two years from the date when Alex trespassed on her property, her claim will be barred by the statute of limitations.

---

7. The only exception to this rule is suits for causes of action where the *only* kind of relief a plaintiff may seek is equitable relief. "Breach of trust was the most important example, but most states now apply statutes of limitations to claims for breach of trust." LAYCOCK & HASEN p. 1013. In suits such as those historically for breach of trust, the only time limit would be set by a laches defense, not a statute of limitations.

Now on to some complications:

- As we have already noted, in some circumstances a defendant may be *estopped* from asserting the statute of limitations, such as when the defendant gives the plaintiff false information about the length of the limitations period.
- One particular circumstance of estoppel occurs when defendant *fraudulently conceals* the existence of a cause of action. Suppose Doctor operates on plaintiff while plaintiff is unconscious. Doctor commits malpractice, injuring plaintiff during surgery. When plaintiff complains of symptoms caused by Doctor's malpractice, Doctor falsely claims the symptoms are a normal side effect of surgery. In such circumstances, courts are likely to hold that the statute of limitations is "tolled" (that is, suspended) by Doctor's fraudulent concealment, until the plaintiff discovers, or reasonably should have discovered, that Doctor concealed the cause of plaintiff's injury.
- In a certain class of cases—those involving injuries with long latency periods, such as an individual who contracts cancer from prolonged exposure to chemicals at a nearby factory—the statute of limitations presents a major obstacle to a successful suit. In some jurisdictions, the statute begins to "accrue" (that is, run) when the plaintiff suffers injury, regardless of whether plaintiff knows she's been injured or who caused the injury. Thus, in some circumstances, a plaintiff's recovery could be barred before the plaintiff even knew about it.

To illustrate this last point, consider the timeline in Figure 18.1. Suppose that plaintiff is exposed to defendant's chemicals from 1990 through 2000. By 2000, plaintiff has cancer that is detectable, but it is not detected. In 2004 plaintiff detects the cancer, and in 2006 plaintiff learns that defendant is responsible for the cancer through the factory pollution. The applicable statute of limitations is one year.

1990	2000	2004	2006
Exposure to cancer	Cancer detectable	Plaintiff diagnosed	Plaintiff discovers Defendant is cause

Figure 18.1

In some jurisdictions, plaintiff's cause of action would begin running in 2000, at the time plaintiff's injury *could have been discovered*, even if the injury was not actually discovered until 2004 and the cause of injury discovered until 2006. In that circumstance plaintiff's action would be time-barred because it was not filed within one year of 2000, or 2001. The statute of limitations will be measured to the day. So, if the court determines that the cause of action accrued on May 5, 2000, the action would be barred if not brought by May 5, 2001. Therefore, a suit brought on May 6, 2001, or later would be time-barred.

In other jurisdictions, the cause of action would accrue at the time plaintiff *actually discovered the injury*, in this case 2004. Plaintiff would have only until 2005 to sue, which means that the suit would again be too late under these facts.

Some jurisdictions have a *discovery rule*, which either delays accrual or tolls the statute of limitation (functionally the same thing) until plaintiff discovers, or reasonably could have discovered (with due diligence), both her injury and that the defendant is a cause of the injury. In those jurisdictions with the discovery rule, it is unnecessary for a plaintiff to prove fraudulent concealment; any reasonable basis for not discovering the injury or the cause of plaintiff's injury is enough. In the present example the one-year period would run from 2006.

There's one final complication for us to consider regarding statutes of limitation. How should courts deal with statutes of limitation in cases of *continuing violations*? Consider again the *NAACP* case. If the LDF indeed was infringing on the NAACP name, it was doing so continuously. Assuming the NAACP sued for damages (making laches an unavailable defense) and assuming no other defenses such as estoppel applied, how should the statute of limitations deal with this kind of continuous conduct?

The majority approach appears to be, for cases of continuous violations, to award damages for the period of injury that accrues during the limitations period. Thus, consider Figure 18.2. Assume a 3-year statute of limitations. The LDF has been infringing for 13 years and has continued to infringe during the entire 13-year period. But the NAACP can get damages only for the final 3-year period (from year 10 to year 13), looking at the date of the suit and counting back from the limitations period.

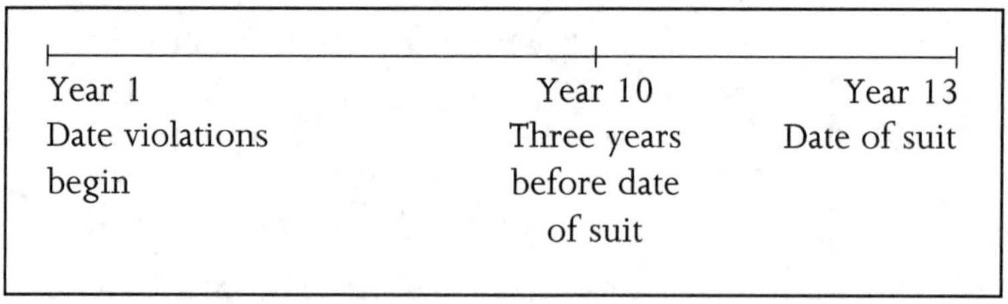

Figure 18.2

Note that it is not enough that *harm* continues. Take the Montel-Norine case again, where Norine injures Montel in an automobile accident. Assume a 3-year statute of limitations. Suppose the injury occurs in year 1 and

Montel continues to suffer harm from the accident through year 13. He cannot sue in year 13 to recover damages he sustained from year 10 to year 13. The statute of limitations would completely bar the suit in year 13 because there must be *continuing violations* that *cause harm* during the period of limitations.

Issues of continuing violations and statutes of limitation gained national prominence thanks to a Supreme Court case and subsequent federal legislation at the beginning of President Obama's first term. In *Ledbetter v. Goodyear Tire & Rubber Co.*, 550 U.S. 618 (2007), Lilly Ledbetter, who worked as a production supervisor at a Goodyear plant, sued her employer for sex discrimination under Title VII of the Civil Rights Act of 1964. Among her claims was an argument that she was paid less than male workers doing similar jobs. Title VII imposed a short, 180-day limitation period to sue, and there was no dispute that the decision to pay her less because of her gender had been made years before. Goodyear took the position that because Ledbetter filed her claim more than 180 days after it made its discriminatory pay decision her claim was time-barred. Ledbetter argued that her claim was not barred, because each paycheck, including her recent ones, reflected the past discrimination: she received raises based upon an earlier discriminatory pay scale.

By a 5-4 vote, the Supreme Court sided with Goodyear. The Court rejected both a discovery rule and a continuing violation argument raised by Ledbetter. In dissent, Justice Ginsburg wrote that under the majority's decision, "Any annual pay decision not contested immediately (within 180 days) . . . becomes grandfathered, a *fait accompli* beyond the province of Title VII ever to repair." She urged Congress to rewrite the statute.

Congress did revisit the question, and the first bill Barack Obama signed as President was the Lilly Ledbetter Fair Pay Act of 2009, Public Law No. 111-2, 123 Stat. 5 (2009). The Act explicitly rejected the *Ledbetter* interpretation and provided that for discrimination claims under Title VII, the Age Discrimination in Employment Act, the Americans with Disabilities Act, and the Rehabilitation Act, a cause of action for pay discrimination occurs, among other times, "when an individual is affected by application of a discriminatory compensation decision or other practice, including each time wages, benefits, or other compensation is paid, resulting in whole or in part from such a decision or other practice." *Id.* §3.

Example 6

EXAMPLE

From *Burns v. McClinton*, 143 P.3d 630, 631 (Wash. Ct. App. 2006):

> For many years Dennis Burns, a wealthy inventor and investor, used the professional accounting services of David McClinton. Burns gave McClinton carte blanche over his personal finances in 1995. They orally agreed to an indefinite

retainer agreement pegging McClinton's monthly fee at $1,500. Burns fired McClinton in 2001 after discovering that McClinton had long been paying himself at the rate of $2,500 per month, as well as additional sums for special projects.

Burns had not agreed to the fee increase. Burns sued McClinton in 2003 for breach of an oral contract, whose applicable statute of limitations is three years. Should the statute of limitations bar any or all of Burns' claims?

EXPLANATION

Explanation

It appears that Burns could, at most, get damages for the period going back three years from the date of suit. This is a case with a continuing violation, in which the defendant is committing the wrong each month by taking out the money.

If the jurisdiction has a discovery rule, Burns might try to argue that the statute of limitations should have been tolled, and he should be able to recover damages during the entire period, because he did not discover the breach of contract before 2001. But the question is not only what the plaintiff *actually discovered*, but what he *reasonably could have discovered with due diligence*. In the actual case, the court said there was nothing that would have prevented Burns from looking at the books to discover the defendant's breach of contract. Indeed, the fact that the defendant did not conceal the payments prevents any claim of fraudulent concealment from tolling the statute of limitations.

The *Burns* court did note an exception for the case of attorney malpractice claims in which an attorney's *continuous representation of a client* tolls the statute of limitations. The doctrine is meant to prevent disruption of the attorney-client relationship that could result if the client always had to be looking over the shoulder of the attorney. But the court held that this exception did not apply to the accountant's breach of contract in this case, even if it might apply to certain accountant malpractice cases:

> The wrong occurred during the general course of an ongoing professional relationship, not in continued representation with respect to a particular undertaking or specific transaction in which McClinton had committed a professional error. Burns did not have to choose between engaging in speculative litigation and waiting to see if things might turn out all right after all in some specific matter. . . .

Burns, 143 P.3d at 636.

18.3.3 Relationship of Laches to Statutes of Limitations

The Supreme Court weighed in on the relationship between laches and statutes of limitations in the context of the Copyright Act in *Petrella v. Metro-Goldwyn-Mayer, Inc.* 572 U.S. 663 (2014). The Copyright Act provides that "[n]o civil action shall be maintained under the [Act] unless it is commenced within three years after the claim accrued." 17 U.S.C. §507(b). Frank Petrella assigned the screenplay rights used in the famous movie *Raging Bull* about the life of boxer Jake LaMotta in the 1970s. Petrella died in 1981. A Supreme Court case established that heirs of copyright holders had the right to renew copyrights, even those that had been already assigned. In 1991, upon learning of this holding, Frank Petrella's daughter Paula renewed the copyright. In 1998, her lawyer notified MGM, which made the film, that she held copyright, and in 2009 she sued for copyright infringement, claiming damages and injunctive relief for the period going back three years to 2006, and the period going forward. Lower courts had held her entire claim barred by laches.

The Supreme Court, in an opinion by Justice Ginsburg, reversed. The Court held that MGM engaged in a continuing copyright violation by continuing to distribute the film. Each new distribution was a new violation, and under §507(b) of the Copyright Act she could look backwards to damages for three years. It held that laches could not bar legal relief such as damages, as Congress had already determined with the statute of limitations how long was too long to seek damages. "As to equitable relief, in extraordinary circumstances, laches may bar at the very threshold the particular relief requested by the plaintiff. And a plaintiff's delay can always be brought to bear at the remedial stage, in determining appropriate injunctive relief, and in assessing the 'profits of the infringer . . . attributable to the infringement.' §504(b)." *Petrella*, 572 U.S. at 667-668. The Court treated the restitutionary remedy of accounting for profits as equitable. *Id.* at 668 n.1. Three dissenters, led by Justice Breyer, would have allowed laches to be asserted even in an action seeking damages. He thought that modern litigation should no longer draw distinctions between law and equity in this context since the merger. *Id.* at 696-697 (Breyer, J., dissenting).

EXAMPLE

Example 7

Should courts allow laches defenses in cases of continuing violations where plaintiffs claim damages? Why or why not?

EXPLANATION

Explanation

There is no right answer to this question, but the *Petrella* case presents a nice test case. On the one hand, when a legislative body such as Congress passes a statute of limitations, it sets a boundary on when a claim is generally too late. But that idea gets stressed when it comes to continuing violations, as claims may be made many years after the initial violation and after a defendant may have relied upon the plaintiff's failure to act as evidence that there is no violation.

On the other hand, there is something odd about letting the dead hand of history get its way here, too. Why should it be that the damages claims may be brought no matter how much delay and prejudice, but that equitable claims may be barred under the laches doctrine, even for continuing violations, upon a balancing of all relevant considerations? If courts have the power to engage in such balancing for some remedies, perhaps courts should have that power for all remedies.

CHAPTER 19

Putting It All Together: Taking a Remedies Exam

19.1 HOW TO PREPARE FOR A REMEDIES EXAM

If you have worked your way diligently through the chapters of this book, including the Examples and Explanations, you are well on your way toward mastering the basic concepts across the variety of issues discussed in most Remedies courses. This body of knowledge is *necessary* to do well on Remedies exams, but it is not going to be *sufficient* in many courses. This final chapter is aimed at giving you practice with the two other components you will need for success: *issue spotting* and *comparing remedies*.

Issue spotting is important for successfully answering many essay questions. It is also a valuable real-life lawyering skill. In earlier chapters, you did not have to guess what issue would be tested in the Examples; the Examples are designed to test the ideas in the immediately preceding text. But in many essays, as in real life, Remedies questions don't come in nicely labeled packages. Instead, you will see a fact pattern and you will need to decide which issues are viable enough to be worth considering.

Comparing remedies is another skill valuable for both essays and real life. For example, a client could come into your office complaining about some kind of misappropriation tort, and you might be able to draft a beautiful complaint for damages and recover those damages. But you would be committing malpractice if you did not consider the possibility of a restitutionary alternative based upon defendant's gains. On Remedies exams, as in real life, think of the various remedies in this book as a toolbox, a menu, or whatever metaphor works to help you remember that you may have *choices* about how to proceed, and existing law makes some choices better (more lucrative, appropriate, or in line with your client's goals) than others.

Unfortunately, learning how to spot issues and compare remedies is harder than learning the black letter law and its exceptions. The learning comes not from memorization but from sustained practice of the skill. The essay questions in the rest of this chapter will give you that opportunity to practice, though the best set of practice questions are your own professor's old exams. (We professors tend to recycle ideas, so past exams are often a good predictor of future exam style and coverage.) Some professors emphasize issue spotting and comparing remedies skills; other professors expect more in-depth treatment of easily identified issues.

The following are real essay questions I have included on past examinations, along with my answer keys. Of course, I have no guarantee that your instructor will give questions or answers that are similar to mine, but I hope these will help you nonetheless.

When writing a good Remedies essay examination answer, make sure you:

- *Write clearly and understandably*, underlining or otherwise emphasizing key terms;
- Look at the *call of the question* to figure out what the professor wants you to do;
- *Consider the range of potential options* for the plaintiff in choosing a remedy;
- *Evaluate the strength of plaintiff's arguments for each remedy* and in light of defendant's (likely) counterarguments;
- When appropriate, *reach conclusions* about the call of the question; you might need to explain
  - what is *plaintiff's best remedy* and why,
  - how much could plaintiff *recover*,
  - what are the *best counterarguments or defenses* a defendant may raise, and/or
  - whether a particular remedies claim is likely to be *successful* and why.

Of the above elements, it is most important that you be sure that you are answering the question the professor wants you to answer. Again, look at the call of the question.

Finally, be organized and logical in your answer. Make it easy for the professor to follow your argument and reasoning. While you may be fatigued when completing your exam, keep in mind that your professor will probably be fatigued when reading your exam. Make it easy for the professor to give you points.

19.2 SAMPLE REMEDIES ESSAY EXAMINATION QUESTIONS AND ANSWER KEYS

Each of these is a 60-minute question. If your professor gives a closed-book examination, answer these with a closed book. If it is an open-book examination, feel free to use whatever materials the teacher will allow you to consult.

Many of these questions are loosely based on some real-world cases, but I have altered the facts to make them better for testing certain concepts. Nothing in these questions should be taken as reflecting any real-world events; they are for pedagogical purposes only.

Here are the instructions I give my students on typical Remedies exams:

> Subparts within questions are not equally weighted. Be sure to follow any special instructions and to answer only the questions asked. Do not identify yourself on your examination by name or in any other way that sacrifices anonymity until after you have received your grade in this course.
>
> Use the parties' initials; don't write out their names. Don't write on the backs of the pages.
>
> Assume each question takes place in the state of Pacifica, a state in the United States that applies the common law and its own statutes.
>
> Please note that I do not intend to call for any detailed discussions of the underlying *substantive* law involved in any of these questions, except as you deem necessary for a complete analysis of the *remedial* aspects of the questions.
>
> If you feel any additional facts are required, indicate what facts, explain why they are important, and make reasonable assumptions. I will not respond to questions about ambiguities during the exam. Good luck!

The answer keys below are *not* what I expect student answers to look like. Instead, they are my guide to grading the exam, noting the key points and the areas requiring more extensive discussion.

Examples

EXAMPLES

1. In the Bag. BagCo manufactures a heavy-duty polyethylene bag known as the "Model Oscar." The bag design is protected by various patents and trademarks. The Model Oscar incorporates a heavy-duty handle with a snap-style closure across the top of the bag, and the bag is typically resold at retail as a durable shopping bag.

FunCo runs a major amusement park, and it was interested in purchasing 300,000 Model Oscar bags for resale at its park. Each bag would feature a picture of "Ricky the Rat," the FunCo mascot.

BagCo and FunCo signed a contract for the purchase of the 300,000 bags at the price of $1 per bag, provided that BagCo produced a bag "to the satisfaction of FunCo" using artwork provided by FunCo. Among the other provisions of the contract were the following:

1. BagCo shall provide a prototype bag using FunCo's artwork for FunCo's approval within one month of the signing of the contract.
2. All designs, which may be submitted in whatever form to FunCo, or copies or derivatives of such designs, remain the exclusive property of BagCo. It is prohibited to reproduce, use, or remit to third parties such designs, artwork, etc., without BagCo's express written consent.
3. In the event of a dispute arising out of this contract leading to a court determination that either BagCo or FunCo breached the contract, damages shall be set at 10 cents per bag.

Two weeks after the parties signed the contract, BagCo produced a prototype "Ricky the Rat" Model Oscar bag for FunCo's approval. The head of FunCo's marketing department, Jane, sent an email message to Mike, the FunCo employee working on the BagCo contract: "These bags look perfect, but the price is way too high. See if you can find an overseas supplier who could make these bags cheaper."

Mike sent the BagCo prototype bag to CheapCo, along with a copy of the BagCo-FunCo contract. CheapCo promised to manufacture 300,000 bags for 50 cents per bag. It promised FunCo that the bags would be "identical in quality and appearance" to the BagCo prototype. FunCo paid $150,000 to CheapCo to deliver the bags. It cost CheapCo $50,000 to make the 300,000 bags.

Mike sent a note to BagCo reading: "Sorry, but we don't like the quality of the bags. Accordingly, since you have not made bags to our satisfaction, we are under no obligation to buy any bags from you. We have no binding contract." FunCo had not sent BagCo any money.

BagCo executives had been counting on the money from FunCo, and they missed a mortgage payment to the bank, costing them a late fee of $10,000. They had no other work at the moment, despite looking hard for new projects. BagCo executives had expected to make a profit of 40 cents per bag, and they were disappointed. The president of the company sent back a note to Mike reading: "We really tried hard, and we are sorry that the bags disappointed you. Maybe next time."

Despite the email, BagCo executives later decided to sue FunCo over the dispute. In discovery, BagCo executives learned from the email that the bags actually were satisfactory to FunCo.

The bags from CheapCo arrived at FunCo's amusement park. They were inferior in terms of both the quality and strength of the bag and the artwork. FunCo will not sell the lousy bags to its customers; they are a total loss.

Assume that FunCo breached its contract with BagCo and that CheapCo breached its contract with FunCo.

A. What remedy or remedies, if any, may BagCo pursue against FunCo and/or CheapCo? Explain and be specific. Do *not* discuss ancillary remedies and do *not* discuss any federal statutory remedies (for example, under patent or trademark law).
B. What remedy or remedies, if any, may FunCo pursue against CheapCo? Explain and be specific. Do *not* discuss ancillary remedies.

2. Occupy Pacificana! The "Occupy Pacificana" movement was very active in Pacificana City. The movement protested against what its supporters saw as too much influence of corporate wealth over the political process and unacceptably high rates of unemployment. About 100 Occupy Pacificana supporters had been camped at a Pacificana park across from City Hall for the last month, many sleeping at the park in tents. The group has no official leaders or official membership. Although the overnight protesters violated a city ordinance banning sleeping in city parks or remaining in a city park after sunset, the police had not moved to evict the protesters.

Pacificana City officials were worried about sanitation and health in the park, as well as occasional violence perpetrated against others who had come to visit the park. Pacificana City's mayor, Mayor McCheese, also was "tired of all the bellyaching" by the Occupy Movement. He told his aides: "I can hardly concentrate on improving my putting game in my office with this racket across the street!"

City attorneys went to Pacifica state judge Jones and sought a temporary restraining order requiring members of Occupy Pacificana to exit the park and to be there only during the park's normal hours of sunrise to sunset. When city attorneys appeared before Judge Jones at an *ex parte* hearing, Judge Jones asked where the attorney for the Occupy Pacificana movement was. The city attorney said: "The group has no official leaders. We did not know whom to serve regarding this hearing, so we served no one."

Judge Jones then issued the following order. "It is hereby ordered that all members of 'Occupy Pacificana' and their agents and those acting in concert with them shall immediately leave Pacificana Park to allow for park cleaning. Following that, no one may enter the park for any reason without permission from the city police for a period of 20 days following the issuance of this order. Following the 20-day period, everyone must obey the 'sunrise to sundown' time restrictions on entering the park. Anyone violating this order shall be subject to imprisonment, fines, or both under the contempt power of this Court. It is so ordered."

Police went to Pacificana Park and used bullhorns to repeatedly read Judge Jones's orders to the crowd in the park. The police posted prominent signs stating that no one may enter the park for any reason for the next 20 days.

A. Amy is one of the people who had camped out in the park during the Occupy Pacificana protest. She refused to leave the park after hearing the judge's order over the bullhorn. Police forcibly removed her from the park and she was charged with criminal contempt. What result? Explain.

B. Three days after Judge Jones issued her order, members of the Social Freedom Party, which has no official ties to the Occupy Pacificana movement, held a silent vigil in Pacificana Park running from 5 p.m. to midnight. They held signs reading, "Mayor McCheese is a Capitalist Tool." Police removed Gayle, a member of the Social Freedom Party, from the protest and charged her with violating the city ordinance and with contempt of Judge Jones' order. She was released on bail, and at the bail hearing Judge Jones told her: "Stay out of Pacificana Park or I will fine you $1,000." Fifteen days after Judge Jones issued her original order, Gayle attended another protest in the park and was charged again with violating the ordinance and with civil and criminal contempt. May Gayle raise the First Amendment as a defense against any of these charges? Explain. (Do *not* evaluate the *merits* of the First Amendment argument.) What other arguments may Gayle raise against any of the contempt charges, and how likely is each argument to succeed?

C. Tom, who is a homeless 40-year-old man and has been unemployed for many years, was asleep on a park bench in Pacificana Park 25 days after Judge Jones issued her order. At midnight, police entered the park and told Tom he had to leave or he would be violating a city ordinance and thus be in contempt of court. Tom, who had been drinking heavily, arose very slowly in an attempt to get up. Police officers, who felt Tom was not moving quickly enough to satisfy their desire to go on break, sprayed pepper spray in Tom's eyes. Tom, reacting to the pain of the pepper spray, fell off the park bench and injured his spinal cord. He will never be able to walk again. Tom sued the police department for damages in tort. If Tom proves the police acted tortiously and the police can raise no defenses successfully, to what damages, if any, will Tom be entitled? Explain. What remedial defenses, if any, may the police department raise against Tom? Explain. Do *not* discuss substantive tort defenses, such as comparative negligence.

3. Fit-for-Life. The Fit-for-Life Corporation sells a number of dietary supplements, including Fit-for-Life 356, a supplement containing the drugs ephedra and caffeine, that the corporation promotes to reduce weight as well as to increase physical strength and endurance. Fit-for-Life 356 is the most widely sold supplement containing ephedra in the state of Pacifica.

In the five years that Fit-for-Life 356 has been on the market, the corporation has received 13,000 health-related complaints about the product from across the United States. Most complaints involved stomach ailments such as nausea or diarrhea, though there were more than 80 reports of heart attacks, strokes, and other serious ailments occurring after someone had used the product for an extended period. The product does appear to be effective in promoting weight loss in some users. The product package says that Fit-for-Life 356 is "safe and effective when used as directed."

Scientists have begun studying the safety of products containing ephedra. The Food and Drug Administration (FDA) has received 1,200 reports of serious reactions to ephedra. A recent preliminary FDA review of some 16,000 adverse event reports revealed two deaths, four heart attacks, nine strokes, one seizure, and five psychiatric cases involving ephedra in which the records appeared thorough and no other contributing factors were identified. The FDA called such cases "sentinel events," because they may indicate a safety problem but do not prove that ephedra caused the adverse event. On January 1, 2003, the FDA issued a press release on the potential problems with products containing ephedra. The ephedra issue has since received extensive media coverage.

Two recent studies of ephedra's safety were published too late to be included in the FDA's review, and each raises further concerns about ephedra. One study found that although ephedra products make up less than 1% of all dietary supplement sales, these products account for 64% of adverse events associated with dietary supplements. Another study concluded that the statistical rate of strokes among ephedra users was significantly higher than among non-users. Additional research continues.

The Fit-for-Life website links to the FDA report. In response to proposed legislation to ban the sale of products containing ephedra, the website contains the following statement: "In Fit-for-Life's opinion, there is no scientific basis for a ban, and we believe that our ephedra products are safe and effective when taken as directed on our product label." At this point, no federal or state laws or regulations prohibit or even regulate the sale of products containing ephedra.

A. Assume the following for purposes of *this subpart only*. You have just been retained as class counsel for Pacifica consumers who have used or currently use Fit-for-Life 356 and have suffered, or may suffer, strokes or heart attacks. You believe that a fact finder could well determine that Fit-for-Life violated applicable Pacifica tort law in selling Fit-for-Life 356. The issue will turn on questions of actual causation. Can you get *preliminary relief* (1) enjoining the sale of

Fit-for-Life 356? (2) enjoining Fit-for-Life from selling any of its products in Pacifica? Explain.

B. Assume the following for purposes of *this subpart only*. Percy took Fit-for-Life 356 every day over a period beginning Jan. 1, 1999, and ending Jan. 1, 2000, when Percy had a stroke. Percy sues Fit-for-Life on Feb. 1, 2003, for damages under Pacifica's applicable tort law, claiming the product caused Percy's injury. The statute of limitations for a tort suit in Pacifica is two years from the date of injury. Fit-for-Life argues that Percy's suit is time-barred. Evaluate the arguments both sides may make on the timeliness of Percy's filing.

C. Assume the following for purposes of *this subpart only*. Jane, a Pacifica resident, used Fit-for-Life 356 and then suffered a debilitating stroke. After Jane filed her tort suit, Fit-for-Life removed Fit-for-Life 356 from the Pacifica market, but it is still sold in other states. Jane was a 50-year-old unemployed janitor at the time of her stroke. The jury holds Fit-for-Life liable for negligence under Pacifica law, and awards Jane $10 million in compensatory damages, including $2 million for future lost wages, $3 million for past and future medical expenses, and $5 million for pain and suffering. The jury also awards Jane $60 million in punitive damages, which happens to equal the national profits of Fit-for-Life in the five years since it started selling Fit-for-Life 356. On appeal, Fit-for-Life attacks the damages awards but does not contest liability for negligence. What result? Explain.

4. Robert v. Therese. In early 1989, Robert explained to his sister Therese that he was suffering from financial and emotional difficulties relating to his job and a failed marriage. He was unable to make the mortgage payments on his home, and he was concerned that he would lose it through foreclosure. He had investigated selling the house, but he had no equity in the house, which meant that a sale would not generate sufficient proceeds to cover closing costs. He asked his sister if he could transfer the house to her, which would require her to assume the mortgage.

Therese agreed, even though the house was located in southern Pacifica, and she lived in the far north end of the state. Robert transferred the house (in which his ex-wife had no interest) to Therese. As part of the transaction, Therese assumed a $49,500 debt, which was secured by a mortgage on the property. Also, she was required to pay an assumption fee on the loan and to obtain hazard insurance for the house.

In 1990, the siblings executed a lease which provided that Robert was to pay $500 in monthly rent and was to provide an additional $200 per month in maintenance and services on the house. Robert has taken the position that the lease was not binding on either party, but was executed for the sole purpose of enabling Therese to obtain a loan. Therese, on the other hand, takes the position that she and Robert had a binding lease agreement.

From 1989 until 1997, Robert exercised control over the house. Therese executed a power of attorney giving him the authority to manage the property, make deposits into the rental account, and otherwise maintain and care for the property. Robert lived in the house, performed necessary maintenance and services on the house, and paid rent about half the time.

After Robert transferred the house to his sister, he applied for public assistance. In his initial and subsequent applications for public assistance, Robert represented that he rented the house from Therese—failing to disclose that he often did not pay rent on the home.

The siblings agreed that Robert transferred the house to Therese with the understanding that he could repurchase it. What they disagree about is the timing. Therese stated that Robert told her that the arrangement "would just be for a little while" until he could get his affairs in order. She further stated her belief that if Robert was unable to take back his house, it would belong to her, meaning that she could sell it to a third party and retain the proceeds. Robert disputes this characterization.

Therese began talking to her brother about taking the house back shortly after its initial transfer. However, Robert was never able to put his affairs in order so that he could accomplish the task. Finally, in 1993, she told her brother that he must either repurchase the house or the house would be sold to a third party. Robert continued living in the house, and continued paying rent about half the time, for four more years.

In October 1997, Therese sent Robert a letter informing him that his power of attorney was revoked. She further informed him that she was putting the house on the market. Robert moved out. Soon thereafter, Therese sold the house for $80,000, generating net proceeds of $30,000. She took half the proceeds and spent it on a trip around the world. She used the other half to pay off a car loan.

1. What remedy or remedies may Robert and Therese pursue against one another? What else might you need to know about the substantive law before you could fully answer this question? (Do *not* go on to analyze the substantive law questions in any depth.) Do *not* discuss preliminary or ancillary remedies. Assume the parties' claims are *not* barred by the statute of limitations.

2. Assume the following for purposes of *this subpart only*: During the course of the lawsuit, the trial judge orders Therese to turn over all records showing how much rent Robert paid to Therese from 1989 through 1997. Therese claims that her accountant, Juan, keeps all of her business records, and Juan has told Therese that the relevant information is lost. Juan has not testified in court and is not a party to the lawsuit.

The trial judge disbelieves Therese and then summarily issues the following order: "Therese and Juan are each fined $100,000 for willfully disobeying my court order. In addition, Therese and Juan each shall pay a $1,000 fine per day until the material is turned over." Therese and Juan each challenge the trial judge's order. What result? Explain.

5. FruityIce. The FruityIce Corporation manufactures frozen desserts sold in supermarkets. Its most popular dessert is a chocolate-covered dessert "pop" in strawberry and banana flavors. The pops have become very successful, in large part because FruityIce advertises the pops as "low fat." The dessert box's "Nutrition Facts" label lists the pops as having only 2 grams of fat per pop. It is a violation of federal statutes to knowingly or unknowingly provide inaccurate information in the "Nutrition Facts" box on a product.

Since its inception in 1998, FruityIce has made profits of $1 million per year, half of that from the sale of its chocolate-covered dessert pops in strawberry and banana flavors, and half from the sale of other products.

You are a plaintiff's lawyer. Bob comes into your office with the following story. Bob is very overweight and has been attending Weight Crushers, a diet support group. Bob tells you that at a number of support group meetings beginning in 1998, fellow support group members talked positively about these FruityIce pops. Bob reported that people at the meetings would say things like, "The pops really fill you up, and they are very low fat."

Bob has been eating a box of six pops each day, thinking he was getting only 12 grams of fat. But Bob has been gaining rather than losing weight. So he had the pops tested by a lab.

It turns out that each pop contains 10 grams of fat per serving, well exceeding the fat content classified as "low fat" under federal regulations. At this point, it is unclear why the labeling is incorrect: it may have been an honest mistake in calculating the fat content; it may be affirmative fraud to induce people concerned about fat content to buy the pops.

Assume any lawsuit you might bring would be timely.

A. What remedy or remedies might you pursue on Bob's behalf, and how likely are you to be successful pursuing each remedy? Do not discuss ancillary remedies or remedial defenses.
B. Assume the following facts for purposes of *this subpart only*. You bring suit on Bob's behalf. After you file suit, FruityIce changes the "Nutrition Facts" box on its pops so as to provide correct information. At the trial on the merits, the judge is outraged by the facts of the case. She enters the following order: "FruityIce is hereby enjoined from selling frozen dessert products in the United States for a period of three years." FruityIce appeals the issuance of the

injunction and continues to sell products after judgment, but while the appeal is pending. The trial judge holds a hearing and summarily fines FruityIce "$1 million for contempt." How successful may FruityIce be (1) in its appeal of the injunction and (2) in overturning the contempt fine? Explain.

6. Greg v. Phyllis. In 1990, Greg went to work as the only associate in a law firm owned by Phyllis. Greg had an "at will" employment contract with Phyllis, meaning that either Greg or Phyllis could terminate the agreement at any time for any reason. Greg never signed a covenant not to compete or any other documents governing the employment relationship. Phyllis promised to pay Greg an annual salary of $60,000 per year for as long as the employment relationship existed. (In law firms similar to Phyllis's, attorneys who work by the hour generally receive $100 per hour from their employers.) All revenue the firm received for work done by Greg and Phyllis went into Phyllis's business account.

Phyllis's law firm handled primarily personal injury cases, almost always on a contingency fee (meaning that they only earned a fee if the case was successful, in which case the firm received a percentage of the recovery). In 2000, Greg decided he would open up his own firm to handle personal injury cases. He told Phyllis of his decision; Phyllis responded, "Good luck. You've helped me for many years, and I won't do anything to prevent you from getting rich like me."

At the time Greg left the firm, he had put in 100 hours on the "Smith" personal injury case, and 50 hours on the "Jones" personal injury case. Phyllis had put in no time on these cases. Both cases were pending at the time Greg left.

After Greg left, Smith and Jones each decided to terminate their retainer agreements with Phyllis (as is their absolute right under the law) and to retain Greg to handle their cases. Smith and Jones told Phyllis of their decisions. Greg did nothing improper to solicit Smith and Jones, and the action did not constitute a tort or breach of the at-will contract between Greg and Phyllis.

Greg put an additional 100 hours into the Smith case and an additional 25 hours into the Jones case. Thereafter, Greg settled the Smith case for $300,000, taking his one-third contingency fee of $100,000 to buy Blackacre for his nephew, John. However, Blackacre may turn out to be a bad investment, because a new sewage treatment plant likely will be built nearby.

Greg won a $225,000 verdict in the Jones case, pocketing a $75,000 contingency fee. Greg kept that money in an account for one year, then took that $75,000 to Las Vegas and bet it all on roulette. He walked away with $75. He put that $75 back in an account with $50,000 that he had obtained from work unconnected with his immediately prior employment.

Phyllis decides to sue, and she files her suit two years after Greg left the firm, within the applicable limitations period. *Assume that the Model Rules of Professional Conduct provide no guidance on how to resolve this case.*

What remedy or remedies may Phyllis pursue against Greg and/or John, and how likely is Phyllis to prevail in obtaining these remedies, taking into account both remedial requirements and remedial defenses that may be raised? Explain. Do not discuss preliminary or ancillary remedies.

7. Victor's Secret. Victoria's Secret, Inc., is the owner of the "Victoria's Secret" trademark, which has been registered in the United States Patent and Trademark Office since 1981. Victoria's Secret sells a complete line of women's lingerie, as well as other clothing and accessories.

Victoria's Secret operates over 750 stores and distributes 400 million copies of the Victoria's Secret catalog each year, including 39,000 in Pacific Heights, Pacifica. Victoria's Secret products are also sold over the Internet. Victoria's Secret has two stores in Oceanville, Pacifica, within 60 miles of Pacific Heights. In 1998, Victoria's Secret spent over $55 million dollars on advertising its products. According to a recent survey, Victoria's Secret is rated as the ninth most famous brand in the apparel industry.

In February 1998, Victor Moseley opened "Victor's Secret," a store in a strip mall in Pacific Heights selling a wide variety of items, including men's and women's lingerie, adult videos, and other adult-oriented products. Although Victoria's Secret sells women's lingerie, it does not sell men's lingerie or adult products.

Attorneys for Victoria's Secret sent Moseley a letter in February 2001, two years after learning of the existence of Moseley's store, demanding that Moseley change the name of his store to a name unrelated to the Victoria's Secret mark. Moseley subsequently changed the name of the store to "Victor's Little Secret."

In 1998, Moseley's store made profits of $50,000. In 1999, the number reached $100,000. Since 2000, the store has averaged $250,000 per year in profits.

In March 2001, Victoria's Secret sued Moseley under a Pacifica statute regulating use of trademarks. Under the statute, Victoria's Secret must prove that Moseley's use of the "Victor's Secret" name "dilutes" the quality of the Victoria's Secret mark. *Assume that Victoria's Secret can prove such dilution.*

The Pacifica statute allows plaintiffs to obtain any remedy that otherwise would be available and appropriate under the common law. It imposes a one-year statute of limitations.

What remedy or remedies may Victoria's Secret pursue against Moseley, and how likely is Victoria's Secret to prevail in obtaining these remedies, taking into account both remedial requirements and remedial defenses Moseley may raise? Explain. Do not discuss preliminary or ancillary remedies.

8. Fixing the hospital. You have been appointed a federal district court judge, and you have just received your first big case, a class action lawsuit under 42 U.S.C. §1983 against the State of Pacifica by 400 developmentally disabled individuals residing or formerly residing in Pacifica's four psychiatric hospitals. The complaint seeks compensatory damages, injunctive relief, and any other appropriate relief. Pacifica has waived its right to a jury trial on any damage issues and has waived any sovereign immunity defense (that is, Pacifica consents to be sued for damages even though it is a state defendant).

After a trial on the merits, you determine the following facts:

Approximately half of the developmentally disabled class members currently at the hospitals have no diagnosis of mental illness. Developmental disability involves difficulty and slowness in learning and delayed development of intellectual functioning; mental illness, on the other hand, involves a mental disturbance of emotions or thinking, from whatever cause, which interferes with a person's ability to handle life situations. Individuals suffering from developmental disability can be trained and educated to function more independently, a process termed "habilitation."

Most of the class members who have developmental disabilities have been confined to the general psychiatric wards side-by-side with mentally ill patients; only one of the four hospitals has a separate unit for developmentally disabled people who are not mentally ill. There is a professional consensus that developmentally disabled people who are continuously exposed to mentally ill patients begin to "model" the dysfunctional behaviors of the mentally ill patients with whom they are confined. There is also a professional consensus that the developmentally disabled should receive habilitation and should not be housed with the mentally ill.

Conditions are otherwise deplorable for class members. Those class members confined with the mentally ill have been physically injured by the mentally ill. In addition, some class members have been seriously endangered and injured by the use of antipsychotic drugs, which are not appropriate to treat developmental disability in the absence of mental illness. Many of the class members also have been unnecessarily confined in locked wards of psychiatric hospitals.

You then examine the substantive law:

In *Youngsberg v. Romero* (1982), the Supreme Court held that a developmentally disabled individual in state custody "enjoys constitutionally protected interests in conditions of reasonable care and safety, reasonable nonrestrictive confinement conditions, and such training as may be required by those interests." You hold that Pacifica has violated the *Youngsberg* standard, and you ask the plaintiffs to propose appropriate remedies. Plaintiffs propose the following:

A. Each class member shall receive $10,000 per year spent in Pacifica hospitals in damages to compensate for past pain and suffering caused by Pacifica's unconstitutional treatment and for any loss of dignity.

B. Because plaintiffs would suffer irreparable injury, the court issues an injunction as follows:
   1. Pacifica shall take all reasonable steps to ensure that class members (1) do not suffer physical violence while in Pacifica's care; (2) do not receive antipsychotic drugs unless medically indicated; and (3) are not unnecessarily confined.
   2. Pacifica shall take all reasonable steps to ensure that developmentally disabled class members who are not mentally ill are separated from mentally ill hospital patients so that they may undergo habilitation during the period they remain at a Pacifica hospital. As used in this paragraph, "reasonable steps" means (i) housing the developmentally disabled class members who are not mentally ill in a segregated ward or (ii) building such a ward if no such ward is currently available.
   3. Pacifica, at its own expense, shall provide developmentally disabled class members who are no longer at a Pacifica hospital, and those class members later released from a Pacifica hospital, with habilitation and vouchers for food and shelter (in an amount sufficient to pay for reasonable food and shelter) for a period of 10 years from the date of this injunction or from the date of release, whichever is later.

C. If Pacifica violates the injunction set forth in B.2 above in any way, whether knowingly or not, it shall pay a $20,000 fine for each violation.

A. Evaluate Proposed Remedy A. Does the law permit you to grant this remedy if you choose to do so?

B. Evaluate the three parts of Proposed Remedy B. Does the law permit you to grant these remedies if you choose to do so? Discuss each part separately.

C. Evaluate Proposed Remedy C. Does the law permit you to grant this remedy if you choose to do so?

Explanations

1. *In the Bag*

A. BagCo v. FunCo: Remedies (CheapCo discussed in Section B)

1. Compensatory Damages **(0-15 points)**

[Preliminarily, let me note that while this contract is governed by Article 2 of the U.C.C. (because these bags are moveable goods), I told you that you were not responsible for the U.C.C. damages formulas. The analysis of the issues in this problem does not differ whether one uses those formulas or the general rules we learned in class.]

The facts tell us that F breached the contract with B (it did so by not acting in good faith under the "satisfaction" clause of the contract). One remedy that F might seek is expectation damages, which ordinarily would be the difference between what was promised and what was received. However, this contract contains a "liquidated damages" provision, and if that provision is enforceable, damages will be limited to the liquidated damages of $30,000 (300,000 bags @ 10 cents/bag).

It is not clear that the provision is enforceable and is not an unenforceable penalty. For such a provision to be enforceable, (1) it would have to be difficult to measure actual damages and (2) the liquidated damages figure must be a reasonable approximation of actual damages. It does not appear that it would be difficult to measure damages: this is a typical business dispute about which it would probably not be difficult to gather relevant information on costs of producing the bags and other particulars. More importantly, it does not appear that the 10 cents/bag figure is a good way of figuring loss. It applies to breach by either party, and the amounts don't appear to be tied to how much either party would actually suffer in the event of a breach (we know, for example, that B expected to make 40 cents per bag). If the court strikes the liquidated damages provision, then the regular expectation measure would apply.

Under the usual expectation damages, B would be entitled to the difference between what was promised and what was received, less any expenses saved in mitigation. We know what was promised ($300,000 contract price) and nothing was received. While we don't know the expenses B saved by not having to make the bags, we do know that B expected profits of 40 cents per bag, leading to damages of $120,000. While it might be possible to get incidental or consequential damages (we are not told of any limitation on such damages in the contract), the only ones listed are the $10,000 cost of missing the mortgage payment to the bank. In the first place, for contract damages, consequential damages must be foreseeable (*Hadley*). Arguably, these are not (no indication of any communication of the payment to the buyer). Further, under the *Meinrath* rule, consequential damages for failure to pay money are limited to interest at the legal rate. Thus, the $10K is not recoverable.

Credit is also given in this section for any discussion of whether the email from B to F promising to try harder next time creates an estoppel or waiver from suit. (It likely does not because it is not an unequivocal statement not to sue, and there is no evidence of prejudice.)

<u>2. Punitive Damages **(0-8 points)**</u>

It is possible that B will also be able to get punitive damages in this case. Ordinarily punitive damages are not available for breach of contract. But they are available when the breach of contract also includes an independent tort. Here, there are two theories, one weak and one stronger. The weak theory is that F committed the *Seaman's* tort, by denying in bad faith the existence of a contract. ("We have no binding contract.") The reason this is weak is that most, if not all, courts to have considered this possible tort have rejected it. The stronger theory is that the breach was accompanied by fraud: F lied about whether or not the bags were satisfactory in order to avoid its contractual obligations. This could provide a basis for an independent tort, as well as fraudulent conduct, which, as in California (we don't know Pacifica's precise law), would serve as a basis for punitive damages.

3. Specific Performance **(0-5 points)**

Specific performance is a theoretical alternative to damages in this case, but because the breaching party failed to pay money, an order of specific performance would have F paying the contract price and getting the bags from B—putting B in no better a position and costing F more money for performance it doesn't want. You also receive points here for any discussion of an injunction barring C from using B's intellectual property in its products.

4. Restitution **(0-6 points)**

One other possible option for B to pursue is to go after F (or perhaps C; see below) in restitution. The restitutionary claim would be based upon F taking B's intellectual property (in the form of the bag prototype) in violation of the B-F contract and using that prototype to produce a cheaper version of the bag. Had the F-C contract actually produced a successful set of bags, then perhaps B could get both F and C's profits on the contract. (C knew full well about the theft of the intellectual property, as it was supplied with a copy of the B-F contract barring the use of the prototype.) But the contract failed. So, although both F and C arguably were wrongdoers, it is hard to see where the profits would come from. (If F is successful in suing C, perhaps B can get some of those funds.) If you discussed apportionment correctly, you get some credit here.

Note that there do not appear to be any other claims that B could bring against C aside from the injunction and restitution. C did not breach a contract with B, though perhaps there could be some tort for interfering with an existing contract (not covered in this text).

B. FunCo v. Cheapco: Remedies

1. Compensatory Damages/Defenses **(0-10 points)**

Here, C breached the contract by not providing the goods as promised to F. The goods arrived, but they are worthless and not in conformance with the contract ("a total loss"). The amount of damages to which the buyer F here would be entitled is equal to the difference between what was promised and what was received, which in this case is the cost difference of substitute performance. Here, F contracted to get \$300,000 worth of performance (the cost for B to produce bags, though perhaps it is a bit lower) for \$150,000. So it needs \$150,000 to make up the difference. Plus it already paid $150,000 for the worthless bags. $150K − (−$150K) = $300,000 in damages. (The first $150K refunds the purchase price, and the second $150K represents the difference in value.) F would also be allowed to get any incidental/consequential damages, such as the cost of contracting performance.

C, however, may raise the defense of *in pari delicto*, claiming that F was just as much at fault in this contract as C was. Both conspired to steal the intellectual property of B for use in this contract. (*Unclean hands* would not be available as a defense in seeking a legal remedy.) Although it does seem that F is just as much at fault in using B's intellectual property, it is not clear that this wrong is closely enough connected to the contract to deprive C of a remedy.

2. Specific Performance **(0-5 points)**

Alternatively, F could ask for C to perform as promised under the contract, by producing higher-quality bags. First, it is not clear that F would want that (given the earlier shoddy work) or that C is even capable of providing it. Would damages not be as good? In this case, they might be better, by allowing F to get performance from B directly. If F seeks specific performance, the court might have to address an unclean hands defense (see above).

3. Rescission **(0-5 points)**

Since C did not fully perform under the contract (its bad performance does not count), F could seek to undo the contract, getting a return of its purchase price. This would seem a weaker remedy than damages, and it is not clear why F would pursue it. (There do not appear to be any other gains to serve as the basis for a restitutionary claim.)

2. *Occupy Pacificana!*

A. Amy in Criminal Contempt (0-12 points)

It appears A willfully disobeyed a court order, which she heard over the bullhorn. If a fact finder/jury believes beyond a reasonable doubt that A willfully violated the order, she will be in contempt of court.

Under the *collateral bar rule*, she would not be able to attack the validity of the injunction (including on First Amendment grounds) as a defense to a prosecution for criminal contempt. She would have had to raise the issue before violating the court order in a direct attack on the order.

A may make a few arguments as to why she cannot be bound by the order. First, she may argue that neither she nor Occupy Pacificana (OP) representatives were given notice of the court's hearing before the order was imposed. We are in state court, so Fed. R. Civ. P. 65 does not apply. Under the Supreme Court's decision in the *Princess Anne* case, it violates the Due Process Clause of the Fourteenth Amendment for a state to subject someone to a TRO without giving the person an opportunity to be heard. This may be subject to an exception when the person to serve cannot be found (or giving notice would allow the person to cause irreparable harm before notice can be issued). In this case, the city attorneys explained that because the group was amorphous, they did not know whom to serve. This seems like a stronger case than the facts of the *Princess Anne* case (where the leaders were easy to find), but not a very strong case, as they might have been able to serve all at the park or somehow get a representative to serve. If this was a due process violation, and the court had no jurisdiction over A, then the contempt charge likely would not stand.

A could also argue that she cannot be bound because the court has no jurisdiction over her, because she is not a "member" of OP, or an "agent" or someone "acting in concert" with the group. But the facts tell us that she is "one of the people who camped out in the park during the Occupy Pacificana protest." So, it would be hard for her to argue that she is not acting in concert with this group.

Finally, A might try to claim some of the possible exceptions to the collateral bar rule mentioned in the *Walker* case. But aside from the jurisdiction issue (discussed above), none of these exceptions seem to apply. For example, the order does not appear to be transparently invalid (there was a public health and safety reason to clear the park, even if the order raised First Amendment concerns), and there were no attempts to appeal that were frustrated by state courts.

B. Claims Against G

1. First Amendment Defense Against the Charges **(0-6 points)**

The collateral bar rule applies only to criminal contempt proceedings. It does not apply to any criminal proceeding for violating a city ordinance (as opposed to a court order), and it does not apply to any proceedings for civil contempt. So, G can raise a First Amendment defense for being charged (1) with violating the Pacificana ordinance and (2) in the civil contempt proceedings.

As to the criminal proceedings, the collateral bar rule will bar that defense. (As to the second criminal contempt charge, she could have raised the First Amendment issue at the bail hearing.)

2. Other Arguments G May Raise Against Contempt Charges **(0-10)**

As to the first criminal contempt charge, G has a strong argument that she cannot be bound by the order because she was not given notice of it as well as an opportunity to be heard. Note that the part of the order she violated was not the order to vacate the park (applicable only to OP and its agents and those acting in concert; see the *Planned Parenthood* case); instead, it was the order to the entire world, stating that "no one may enter the park for any reason without the permission of city police for period of 20 days following the issuance of the order." As noted above, on due process grounds generally people need an opportunity to be heard before an order can be made against them, and G had no opportunity to be heard before the order was imposed (nor did anyone acting in concert with her). Accordingly, the court never acquired jurisdiction over her.

However, the city is likely to point to the 5th Circuit's *Hall* case and argue either that the court had *in rem* jurisdiction over the park itself or that the order was needed to effectuate the court's judgment to keep the park open. How the *Hall* case gets resolved may depend in part upon what the state's statute governing TROs looks like, and how it compares to Rule 65 (which contains neither of these exceptions but which the court in *Hall* said existed in the common law before Rule 65 and survived Rule 65). Under either of these theories, G could be bound and held in criminal contempt.

One other possibility: if Pacificana's statute provides (like Rule 65) that TROs issued without notice expire after 14 days (unless renewed for a like period), then the order could be a nullity.

As to the second criminal contempt charge, the judge specifically ordered G to stay out of the park. She had a chance to be heard at the bail hearing, and to appeal that order if she did not like it. There seems little chance she could find some way of attacking the second criminal contempt charge collaterally.

There's no problem with G collaterally attacking the charge of civil coercive contempt and its penalty, in this case likely a fine for $1,000 for entering the park. If, for example, it violates the First Amendment, she would be able to raise that as a defense to the contempt charge. Aside from that, she will not have much of a defense as this looks like willful conduct.

C. T's Claims Against the City

1. T's Damages **(0-10 points)**

If T can prove the police acted tortiously and the police have no defenses, then he can get the following damages: (1) costs of past and expected future medical and health care, which are likely to be substantial given his permanent paralysis (with future damages reduced to present value) and (2) pain and suffering, although those costs will be difficult to measure given that we have no market to compare to (and these will include the current pain and suffering as well as the pain from the pepper spray). T likely will not get any past or expected future lost wages, as he has "been unemployed for many years" and he will have difficulty proving future lost wages with reasonable certainty.

T also may be able to recover *punitive damages*, in addition to the tort damages meant to compensate him for past (and likely future) harm. We do not know the precise language of Pacifica's statute, but if it is typical and anything like California's, the conduct here might constitute implied malice or oppression. The police decided to evict T from the park using pepper spray because T "was not moving quickly enough to satisfy their desire to go on break." This sounds like conduct showing a conscious disregard for the safety of others. The amount would be one appropriate to punish and deter, but the amount must comply with state standards as well as U.S. constitutional standards in cases such as *Campbell v. State Farm*.

2. The City's Possible Defense **(0-5 points)**

T was violating the city's ordinance when he was in the park, and he was also violating the court's order to stay out of the park between sundown and sunrise (if that order remained in effect 25 days after the order; see above). The city may point to T's violation of (at least) the ordinance as a basis for claiming the *in pari delicto* defense (unclean hands would not be available in an action for damages). It is hard to imagine a court saying that a person sleeping in the park was at least as blameworthy as the police who tortiously used pepper spray on a sleeping person they needed to evict from the park.

None of the other defenses (unconscionability, estoppel, waiver, laches) would seem to apply.

3. Fit-for-Life

A.1. Preliminary Relief to Enjoin Only the Sale of Product 356 **(0-10 points)**

The two kinds of preliminary relief the consumers may try to get are a *temporary restraining order* and a *preliminary injunction*. To get any injunctive relief, the plaintiff must prove *propensity*, that there is a substantial threat of a violation; and *irreparable injury*, that damages at law are not as complete, practical, and efficient as injunctive relief.

Because the relief is preliminary, however, there is an additional showing required here. Although there are many verbal formulations of the test, there are two central questions: (1) the plaintiff's *likelihood of success on the merits*, and (2) whether the *balance of the equities* favors plaintiff. This latter requirement takes into account that plaintiff suffers if the court fails to give preliminary relief when it should, and that defendant suffers if the court grants the preliminary relief when it shouldn't—in light of what comes out at trial. We look only at the period between the time the preliminary relief is requested and the time of final judgment. The courts also consider (3) the *public interest*, in appropriate cases.

In terms of *propensity*, there is no question that F is going to continue to sell the product. However, it is not clear that this is going to be a violation. It depends on whether the product violates the substantive law. On that point, we do not know yet whether there is a substantive violation.

In terms of the usual *irreparable injury* requirement, the threat here is that 356 causes a variety of serious physical ailments, including strokes and heart attacks. Certainly, a court would say that damages after the fact would not be so great.

The most vigorous dispute in seeking preliminary relief would turn on likelihood of success on the merits, balancing the hardships, and the public interest. It is very difficult to measure the *likelihood of success on the merits*. There's lots of evidence here showing some kind of link between people who used the product and serious ailments, but nothing has been definitively established yet. The court will need to take a sneak peek at the evidence and make an evaluation.

Balancing the hardships is also difficult. On the one hand, serious injury could occur to class members using 356 in the interim period. On the other hand, this looks like a major portion of F's business, and preliminary relief could lead to the business's closing. To the extent that the court views this as a public health issue, the public interest might favor granting the injunction.

If the court agrees to a preliminary injunction, it might require the plaintiffs to post an injunction bond in case the court turns out to have issued the relief in error. This could be in a very high amount, depending on the losses that F might suffer because of the granting of the injunction.

A.2. Preliminary Relief to Enjoin the Sale of All of F's Products **(0-3 points)**

It seems much less likely that the court would grant preliminary relief to prevent the sale of all of F's products. An injunction must be proper in *scope* and limited to the extent to which it has been shown that the defendant committed a violation. Absent any evidence that F's other products create any dangers, a court order would likely be limited to F's products containing ephedra or to 356 itself.

B. Timeliness Issue **(0-10 points)**

Is P's claim time-barred? The relevant Pacifica statute runs to two years from the date of injury. The injury probably occurred on January 1, 2000, when P suffered a stroke. It might be possible to argue that the injury occurred earlier, some time in 1999, when the ephedra did appreciable harm to the body, but that would depend upon what scientific evidence might show. Two years from January 1, 2000, is January 1, 2002. Because P did not sue until February 1, 2003, the claim appears to be time-barred unless P can make a good argument for *delayed accrual* or *tolling*.

This is not a case of a *continuing violation*. At the latest, the violation ended for P on January 1, 2000, when P stopped taking the ephedra. We do not know if Pacifica has a *discovery rule*. If Pacifica has such a rule, then the question would be whether the case was tolled until P reasonably discovered both her injury and the cause of injury. Here, P discovered the injury on January 1, 2000. The open question is when P discovered the cause of the injury. On these facts, P may argue that the statute of limitations was tolled until January 1, 2003, when the FDA issued its press release challenging the safety of ephedra. We are told that there were extensive media reports, but we do not know precisely when they began. This issue may turn out to be dispositive.

If the jurisdiction does not have a discovery rule, P may still win by claiming *fraudulent concealment*. P would have to prove everything proven for the discovery rule, plus that F had superior information about 356's safety (likely true here) and that F made affirmative misrepresentations relied upon by P (F is not a fiduciary, so there is no duty to disclose). Here, the website indicated as late as 2003 that F believed the product was "safe and effective." This may be enough. To show reliance, we would need some evidence that P relied upon the promises of safety included on the box or in advertisements.

Laches is another possible way to raise a problem with delay, but here P is seeking *legal relief* of damages, not equitable relief; thus, laches is not available.

Estoppel, because of delay, seems a stretch. Where is the prejudice to F?

C. Damages Issues

1. Challenge to Compensatory Damage Awards **(0-10 points)**

F can raise challenges to all three elements of J's compensatory damages award.

First, on the *$2 million for lost wages*, F may have a good argument that the damages are excessive given J's work history. It is hard to believe that a 50-year-old, unemployed janitor has $2 million in lost future wages as reduced to present value—to take into account that the money will be paid now and will earn interest to compensate for a loss in the future. Even putting present value aside and assuming another 20 years of work, J's lost wages award represents an average of $100,000 per year—well above the average annual salary of virtually any janitor in America. The court might remit such an award to a reasonable amount, or it might order a new trial on this damages issue.

Second, the *$3 million for past and future medical expenses* is much more difficult to judge. The facts tell us that J had a "debilitating stroke." We need to know more about how much it costs to care for her now, and what medical economists predict for the future in light of her prognosis. Any amount will have to be reduced to present value.

Third, the $5 *million for pain and suffering* is also going to be difficult to evaluate. Unlike lost wages or medical care, there is no functioning market in pain and suffering. When a court reviews these awards, it sometimes takes into account awards in like cases. While there is serious harm here, how is the court to draw the line? One might discuss how a court *should* evaluate whether such a figure is an appropriate measure of compensation, and how a plaintiff's lawyer might use a per diem argument to package such a large award in smaller chunks.

2. Challenges to the Punitive Damage Award

a. Challenges on Level of Conduct **(0-5 points)**

The first challenge F might bring to the punitive award is to argue that its conduct is not sufficiently reprehensible to merit the award of punitive damages. We know that F is not contesting the finding of negligence; but in no state is negligence enough for punitive damages. The question is what conduct the Pacifica statute uses to determine if punitive damages are available. If Pacifica's punitive standard is like the California standard, the question will be whether J can prove by clear and convincing evidence that F acted with fraud, oppression, or malice, express or implied. On these facts, one could argue that F consciously disregarded a high probability of harm to others. Evaluating whether the punitive damages standard would be met would require reviewing the testimony about what F's managerial personnel knew and when they knew it.

You need to also address the impermissibility of punishing F's conduct in other states, as well as the limited nature of the role of F's conduct directed toward others in Pacifica in determining whether the punitive award is appropriate.

b. Challenges to the Amount of the Award **(0-10 points)**

We do not know if there is any particular state statute that governs the review of the amount of punitive damages.

Under the *BMW/State Farm v. Campbell* factors, the U.S. Constitution's Due Process Clause provides some "guideposts" on whether the punitive damages amount is excessive.

First, *reprehensibility*: how bad is this conduct? The conduct here is potentially worse than the repainting in *BMW* or the bad claims handling in *Campbell* because this case involves human health. But it may be that F was only negligent. So, it is difficult to determine how reprehensible the conduct is. The jury is not supposed to consider conduct outside of Pacifica (such as continuing to sell the product), and it an only consider conduct in Pacifica if it can demonstrate some kind of causal nexus (such as that the product is dangerous, and F continues to market it).

Second, *ratio:* a ratio of 6:1 may be too high. The *Campbell* court suggested that a 1:1 ratio might be appropriate in cases, like this one, where there are significant compensatory damages. J might argue for a higher ratio, looking at potential harm that could be stopped by the suit (strokes that won't happen in Pacifica), thus helping the overall public health. The *wealth* of F cannot be considered as a reason to uphold an otherwise unconstitutionally high award (though its lack of wealth could be a reason to lower the award). What else is necessary for deterrence (note tension with the Posner *Mathias* opinion)?

Third, *sanctions for comparable conduct:* the higher these sanctions are, whatever their nature, the higher the amount that the courts will accept.

One should draw whatever conclusion one can about what the court will do with the $60 million punitive damages award.

4. *Robert v. Therese*

A.1.a. Contract Damages **(0-7 points)**

R may attempt to recover *contract damages* for breach of the agreement to reconvey the house to him. R would claim that T breached the promise by selling the house to someone else. We would need to know more about substantive contract law to know whether the contract is enforceable (for example, is it barred by the Statute of Frauds?) and what the terms (for example, the terms of the repurchase) would be. Would R simply assume the mortgage and pay T the amounts she had paid in the interim? Would he have to compensate her for the appreciation in value of the house? We would need to know such information to measure the contract damages as the difference between what was promised and what was received. It will be difficult to value the promised position.

Note: Specific performance is no longer possible, as T no longer owns the house, and there does not appear to be a way to go after the bona fide purchaser (BFP).

A.1.b. Restitution **(0-10 points)**

Rather than pursuing contract damages, which presents the problems of valuation described above, R might instead seek restitution for the gains that T received in selling the house. Restitution requires a showing of unjust enrichment. This can possibly be shown by the breach of contract. Alternatively, even if the contract were unenforceable, R might argue, under the substantive law of restitution, that it would be unjust for T to keep the gains from the house, because T had promised to reconvey the house to R at the appropriate time.

If the court allows restitution, the question will center on the proper *amount* of restitution. The question is: how much did T gain? R might argue that he is entitled to the $30,000 gain on the sale of the house, which shows how much T was enriched by not selling the house at its initial value back to R. The court might not agree that this measure is appropriate, given that T had made mortgage payments over the years and did not always receive rent to make up for it. Thus, it may be that T's gain overall (when she was not living in the house and R was) was lower than the $30,000 figure. Indeed, if courts take *relative culpability* into account, the court may choose a lower number. The transaction started out with T doing a favor for R so that R could avoid foreclosure, and for many years T let R live at the house even when he did not pay rent.

If the court allows some measure of restitution, the court would likely use something like an *accounting for profits* or *quasi-contract* theory to measure the value. This would lead to a money judgment that R could seek to enforce against T. Alternatively, R might try to seek a *constructive trust* over at least the $15,000 that he can still identify; this sum paid off the car loan and so the value can be traced to the car. The other $15,000 was dissipated, and therefore R cannot trace to it.

Note that even though this is a case involving a contract, *rescission* does not appear possible. Rescission would have each party return the consideration received from the other. Here, the property has been sold, presumably to a BFP, and therefore the contract cannot be undone.

A.1.c. Remedial Defenses **(0-10 points)**

T may be able to raise a number of remedial defenses.

First, to the extent that R is seeking any *equitable relief* (such as the constructive trust), T may argue *laches*. There likely was unreasonable delay in R seeking to get the house back. It had been eight years, after numerous warnings that he must leave. T could then argue prejudice in being forced to turn over money after she had already dissipated half of it. R may counter the *laches* argument by claiming that T *waived* it. She threatened to get rid of the house by 1993 and did not do so for four more years. So, she could be said to have intentionally relinquished her known right to sell to another.

Second, in opposing R's request for *legal relief* (such as damages and any legal forms of restitutionary relief), T may seek to recast her delay argument as an *estoppel argument* (as we talked about in connection with the *NAACP* case). With the failure to repurchase the house when he said he would do so a little while later, R's words or acts are arguably inconsistent with a right he later asserted. T detrimentally relied by selling to someone else, and she would be hurt now if she had to pay back the money. T may similarly argue *waiver* in that R intentionally relinquished his known right to buy back the house.

Finally, T may raise *unclean hands* or *in pari delicto*. R apparently lied when he applied for public assistance while he was paying rent (something he did only half the time). A court may find such conduct sufficiently blameworthy as to deny any *equitable relief* (though it is not clear that this conduct is sufficiently connected to the wrong). Although some courts won't balance under unclean hands, if a court does engage in balancing, it might look at R's conduct in possibly signing a false lease agreement in order to secure a loan. For *legal relief*, T may raise *in pari delicto*, and she will have to show that R's conduct is at least as bad as T's.

A.2.a. Damages or Restitution for Unpaid Rent **(0-7 points)**

T may seek to recover damages or restitution for the *unpaid rent*. The facts tell us that he paid rent about half the time. To the extent that there is an enforceable rental agreement (contract law will tell us that), or under the property principles of lessor-lessee, R breached the lease-contract when he failed to pay. Even if there is no enforceable lease-contract, for R to live in the house without paying anything probably would constitute *unjust enrichment* entitling T to the *reasonable rental value* of the property in restitution. (A counterargument is that this was a gift in a family relationship for which T should not expect consideration.) If restitution applies, we would measure the lost rent with the contract price (plus interest at the prevailing legal rate), and we would need more facts to know the reasonable rental value. How the court sets that amount may, again, depend upon the culpability of the parties.

A.2.b. Remedial Defenses **(0-5 points)**

R may not make a *laches* argument, as it appears any remedy here would be legal, not equitable. R's strongest defense is *waiver*: T knew she had a right to collect rent, never insisted on it, and let T live there for years paying the rent only half the time. Implicitly, then, T thereby intentionally relinquished her known right to rent. The same argument could be recast as an *estoppel argument:* T's act was not collecting the rent consistently, R detrimentally relied by continuing to live there, and R would suffer damage now if he had to pay all that rent back. Particularly given the family relationship, R may even have thought his no-rent residence was a gift. The same *unclean hands* and *in pari delicto* arguments enunciated above could also apply here.

B.1. The Trial Judge's Contempt Order Against Therese **(0-7 points)**

The trial judge appears to have issued an order that imposes a *criminal contempt* citation (for willful past violations) as well as threatening a *civil coercive contempt* citation (to get T to comply with the court's order).

In challenging the criminal contempt, T may argue that the judge failed to provide sufficient criminal procedure protections, given that the facts tell us that the judge summarily issued the order. The rights implicated include the right against self-incrimination, potentially the right to counsel, and given the high amount of the fine, the right to a jury trial. T may argue that there must be proof of a willful violation, and that willfulness needs to be proven beyond a reasonable doubt.

There is not much that T can do about the civil coercive contempt except convince the court that she is unable to comply. To the extent that the fine becomes large, she might be entitled to criminal procedure protections under *Bagwell*.

B.2. The Trial Judge's Contempt Order Against Juan **(0-7 points)**

J can raise all the arguments that T can raise for both kinds of contempt. He can also argue that he cannot be held in criminal contempt because he received no notice of the hearing at which to make his case. Under *Princess Anne* (*but see Hall*), he should have had a right to notice of the hearing. It is also not clear whether the court had jurisdiction over him, as he had never been in court. As to holding him in contempt, we do not need to use the *Hall* exceptions for *in rem* proceedings or to effectuate the judgment of the court, since J appears to be an agent of T under Fed. R. Civ. P. 65.

J may also argue that, as a non-party, he cannot be ordered to do anything more than "minor and ancillary" actions under the *General Service Contractors* case. But here he is being asked to turn over records, and that looks about as minor as you can get.

5. FruityIce

A. Remedy or Remedies

1. Preliminary Relief **(0-10 points)**

You could move in court for a *temporary restraining order* or a *preliminary injunction*—pursuant to Fed. R. Civ. P. 65(d), if you are in federal court. One would likely seek preliminary relief to enjoin F from mislabeling the boxes of its pops pending a trial on the merits. (One might also ask for the mislabeled boxes to be pulled from the shelves and/or for F to alert the public about past errors in labeling.)

A TRO is the fastest way to get relief. You could approach a judge even in the middle of the night for a TRO. However, this does not look like the kind of immediate relief case that would cry out for a TRO. If you seek a TRO under Rule 65 (and under the Constitution; *see Princess Anne*), you will have to either give notice to F or provide a reason why you couldn't/didn't give notice. However, no grounds for avoiding notice appear to be present here. If you go for the preliminary injunction, notice will be required, though the statute does not define the difference between a preliminary injunction and a TRO.

As a threshold matter, B will need to prove *propensity* and *irreparable injury*. *Propensity* means that there is a realistic threat that the defendant will engage in the prohibited conduct. Here, B has told us the results of the lab tests. There is no question that if the lab tests are reliable, F is committing prohibited conduct (it is a strict liability offense). But you will have to convince the judge that the tests are reliable. Right now, you just have B's word for it.

B will also need to show *irreparable injury*—that damages would not be as complete, practical, and efficient. Such an argument may not work in B's suit. If B tried to bring his suit as a class action for others, then damages would not be nearly as good (at least in part because a court may have a hard time valuing damages; see below). But B already knows the pops are mislabeled. So where's the harm to *him*?

Because this is a suit seeking *preliminary relief*, the court also will have to engage in balancing. Although we looked at several tests for balancing, the tests all look at the *probability of success on the merits* and *irreparable harm during the period until final judgment*. As for success on the merits, we are told of B's test, but again we don't know how reliable it is. The judge will need to determine reliability. The irreparable harm to B occurs if the goods continue to be mislabeled (maybe a stretch, for the reasons given above). The irreparable harm to F would come if the court forces the pops to be relabeled as containing 10 grams of fat when in fact they only contain 2 grams of fat. This could well hurt F's sales.

Note: You should give your opinion based upon the factors stated above regarding the likelihood that the court will grant such preliminary relief.

2. Compensatory Damages **(0-5 points)**

Moving on to the first of the permanent remedies, B could seek compensatory damages. Assuming he can prove the mislabeling, he is entitled to be put in the rightful position—i.e., the position he would have been in but for the wrong.

Where would B have been? He will argue that he would have eaten many fewer pops, and that he thus would have not gained as much weight and would have been healthier. Damages must be proven with reasonable certainty, and there are certainty problems here. (The problems do seem reasonably foreseeable, however—especially if the mislabeling was intentional.) Would he really have eaten healthier and not gained the weight? There's also a serious valuation problem here; how do we measure the cost of additional pounds to a person who is overweight? Could this be analogized to a dignitary harm? Given these factors, B may have a difficult time proving his damages. Getting some actual damages might be important as a hook for punitive damages, although nominal damages may serve that function. (See below.)

3. Injunction **(0-5 points)**

See the discussion of propensity and irreparable injury above—although with the permanent injunction, there would no question about whether F was engaging in prohibited conduct. The scope of the injunction would also be at issue here. The idea here would be to prevent future harm or future effects of past harm. Such prevention would be easier to argue if B brought this as a class action. Then an injunction would protect all those people who would otherwise buy the pops mistakenly believing they are low fat. (If you discussed declaratory judgments, you get points for that here as well.) Be sure to address the new standard.

4. Restitution **(0-5 points)**

Rather than attempt to recover his losses through damages, B might go after restitution, claiming that F was unjustly enriched by its conduct of mislabeling the items. This seems like a plausible claim. At least some of the people are buying the pops because the pops are advertised as low fat, with only 2 grams of fat per pop. Thus, F is enriched (getting money) and it is unjust (based upon the misstatement, which may be fraudulent). The issue would then become measuring the gains to F. Unless this is brought as a class action or other common fund claim, it is hard to see how B can claim half of the $1 million per year in profits for the pops. Perhaps he can claim all the profits that F made from selling pops to B. But how many pops did B buy, and how much did F make on those sales to B? This may be a relatively low number. (Again, the class action may be the only way to make this worthwhile to bring as a suit, from a recovery perspective.)

5. Punitive Damages **(0-5 points)**

Punitive damages are aimed at punishing and deterring. At this point, we do not have enough evidence to evaluate a punitive damages claim. First, we don't know what the Pacifica statute says is the requisite bad conduct. Second, we don't know yet why F engaged in this conduct. If it was affirmative fraud intended to induce people to buy the pops, then punitive damages seem in order. If it was mere negligence, that likely won't be enough to warrant punitive damages. One issue will be the amount of damages. If it will be hard to prove much actual damage, then the ratio of punitive damages to actual damages may be high, raising a potential constitutional problem (though *BMW v. Gore* and later cases contain some language that might limit such an argument).

B. Appeal of the Injunction/Contempt Order

1. Appeal of the Injunction **(0-10 points)**

F has strong grounds for appeal. First, F can argue mootness: no injunction should issue at all, because it has voluntarily ceased engaging in the prohibited conduct (*W.T. Grant*). The relevant question will then be whether F is likely to start engaging in the conduct again. The key here is credibility. Nothing would prevent F from engaging in the conduct again—that is, from reprinting the boxes with the incorrect labels. So, an injunction seems right; the case is probably not moot.

But a serious problem is the *scope* of the injunction. The court did not simply order F to use correct labeling. It told F that it could not sell its products in the United States for three years. This looks punitive. It seems very tough to argue that this injunction is consistent with the rightful position, or that this injunction is a prophylactic measure aimed at protecting the rightful position. The injunction goes well beyond preventing future harm to B.

2. Contempt Order **(0-10 points)**

F arguably committed criminal contempt when it defied the judge's order not to sell products in the United States for three years. Criminal contempt requires a *willful violation*, and it does not seem plausible for F to argue that this was an accidental violation. This looks like criminal contempt, not an attempt to coerce F into complying (no ability to purge) or to compensate B. F may wish to argue that it did not need to obey the order, because it was a wrongful order. However, under the collateral bar rule, a court order, even if erroneous, must be complied with. This is not a case where the court lacked jurisdiction. F could argue that the order is so wrong as to be transparently invalid; but if that did not work in the *Walker* case, it is difficult to see how it would work in this case.

F has a stronger argument that the court failed to follow the procedural requirements for finding contempt. Whether we call it criminal or not, F should be entitled to the full panoply of criminal protections, including the right to a jury trial (given the high fine amount). Under *Bagwell*, full criminal procedures apply in cases where violations take place outside the presence of the court (which is the case here) and where a large penalty is involved (this is a $1 million penalty). The facts say that the court summarily fined F this amount. At the least, a jury should make these decisions and other criminal protections should apply.

6. *Greg v. Phyllis*

A. No Cause of Action for Compensatory Damages, Injunction, or Punitive Damages **(0-5 points)**

G vs. P is one of those cases where the only viable cause of action is restitution. The facts tell us that there was an at-will contract and that G did not breach the contract and did not commit a tort when he took on the S or J work. Thus, there does not appear to be a breach of contract or tort entitling P to any damages. For similar reasons, there would be no injunction available. Correspondingly, there is no requisite bad conduct that would entitle P to punitive damages (and we would need at least nominal actual damages in order to get any punitive damages). Accordingly, nothing besides restitution has any reasonable chance of success. (You could consider a declaratory remedy, but that won't work because all the court could declare is a right to restitution. Thus, it would end up coupled with a restitutionary remedy anyway.)

B. Restitution Against G and Possibly Against the Nephew

1. Entitlement to Restitution **(0-5 points)**

P should be entitled to restitution under principles of unjust enrichment. Here, restitution is the substantive cause of action (as in the example of the professor and the check from the bank). G certainly was enriched: half the work (100 of 200 hours) that G put in on the Smith case and two-thirds of the work (50 of 75 hours) that G put in on the Jones case was performed while G *was an employee of* P. Under the former P-G arrangement, G got a set salary of $60,000 per year, and all the revenue received for G's work went into P's account. G thus earned the $175,000 in commissions with much of that work attributable to P's business. It would be unjust for G to keep all these funds when he did most of the work as an employee for P. If that does not seem clear to you, imagine that a totally new lawyer took over at this stage of the S or J cases; would it not be unjust for the new lawyer to keep all the contingent fees earned at the end of the successful case?

2. Form of Restitution **(0-5 points)**

The facts do not tell us that G is bankrupt, and the fact that he had $50,000 in his business account suggests that he has some assets. P might bring a claim simply to get a money judgment in *quasi-contract* (or perhaps called just "restitution," "accounting for profits," or some similar term in the jurisdiction) in an amount equal to the enrichment of G that was attributable to P. Alternatively, P may wish to use the equitable restitutionary device of a *constructive trust* or an *equitable lien*. Such a device will allow for recovery of additional gains through the fiction of tracing (more about the tracing fiction below) and allow the asset to be followed into the hands of a third-party donee (more about that issue below). For an equitable lien there will have to be some connection between the wrong and the property subject to the lien. With the equitable restitutionary remedy, P will have the power to enforce the judgment, perhaps by forcing a sale. To get this remedy, at least in theory, G will have to prove *irreparable injury*. P may be able to do so by showing that it is a hassle to try to recover funds from G; success will depend upon whether the court will insist on proof of irreparable injury and, if so, on how much proof is required by the court.

3. Amount of Restitution (Aside from Tracing) **(0-10 points)**

Putting aside tracing for the moment, there may be a few ways to value G's unjust enrichment. One way may be simply allocating the percentage of time spent by each firm on the case. For the Smith case, that would be a 50/50 allocation, meaning that restitution should be in the amount of $50,000 (50% of the $100,000 contingency fee) from G to P. For the Jones case, that would be a 50/25 allocation (or the two-thirds attributable to P), meaning that restitution should be in the amount of $50,000 (two-thirds of the $75,000 contingency fee) to P from G. So, P may simply seek a money judgment in the amount of $100,000 from G by way of aggregate time-share allocation.

An alternative way to measure restitution might be to use the average hourly rate paid to attorneys who work by the hour (i.e., $100 per hour). That would be $100 multiplied by 150 hours for both cases, which yields $15,000 total. This is a much stingier measure of restitution. The court could perhaps choose this measure if the relative culpability of the parties suggests that P should get a small recovery, but this seems unlikely.

Finally, G may make some arguments that the allocation on the basis of time percentage spent would be inappropriate because G did more important work on the cases during the time he handled the cases for his own firm. We would need more facts to evaluate such an approach. Again, it may depend upon the culpability of the parties. Neither party seems particularly culpable. Absent a compelling reason not to use such a measure, a court would likely use the allocation of percentage of time measure.

4. Tracing in the Smith Case: Blackacre/Nephew **(0-7 points)**

For purposes of a constructive trust (or equitable lien), the line for tracing is fairly straightforward. G took the $100,000 contingency fee and used it to purchase Blackacre for N. N looks like a gratuitous donee, rather than a good faith purchaser for value. We generally can trace to donees in such circumstances. Right now, P likely will be entitled to $50,000. She might try to get a constructive trust over half of Blackacre, or an equitable lien worth $50,000 against Blackacre. Because the property looks like it will decline in value, the equitable lien, if a court agrees to give it, would be a better bet because it preserves the full $50,000, rather than giving away half of whatever Blackacre is worth at the time P enforces the judgment.

5. Tracing in the Jones Case: Bank Account **(0-5 points)**

G put the $75,000 contingency fee from the Jones case into the account and he withdrew the money a year later. If the problem ended at this point, P could trace to nothing in the account under the "lowest intermediate balance" rule. G took all the money out; and then, after losing most of it in Las Vegas, he put $75 back in the account, along with $50,000 attributable to G. Only the $75 is attributable to P, and that is all that she could trace to in that account.

C. Possible Defenses to Restitution Action

Even if restitution would otherwise be proper, G (and perhaps N) may raise a few defenses.

1. Laches **(0-5 points)**

Although the case was filed within the applicable limitations period (and therefore there is no statute of limitations issue), laches may be a partial defense for G. P must have *unreasonably delayed* in bringing suit and G must have suffered *prejudice* as a result. Here, we know that P waited two years before bringing suit. The facts do not tell us how much time elapsed between settlement of the S and J cases and P's bringing suit, and it may be that the delay for a typical business dispute like this one is not too long. G has a stronger argument on prejudice. He held that $75,000 in the account for an entire year before blowing it in Vegas. If he knew he would owe $50,000 on it, then he likely would not have indulged in the gambling. (Depending on the timing of the house purchase for N, G may make the same argument for the Smith contingency fees.)

Laches works for only equitable remedies; to the extent that P seeks a legal form of restitution, this argument would have to be recast as an estoppel argument (see below).

2. Estoppel **(0-8 points)**

G has two potential estoppel arguments. First, G may argue that P's statement that she won't "do anything to prevent [G] from getting rich like [P]" was an act or statement inconsistent with suing, that P reasonably relied upon that statement in taking the work from S and J, and that G thereby suffered prejudice by having to pay the amounts of restitution. This argument is rather weak. Specifically, the statement is ambiguous; it also seems unreasonable for G to rely upon such a flimsy statement as an agreement not to sue.

Second, G could also make a laches-like argument cast as estoppel as a way to get around the use of laches only for equitable remedies. The act or statement would be failure to sue, the reasonable reliance would be shown by G's spending the money in Las Vegas, and the prejudice would be the same as above. For the same reason that the laches argument is weak, this pseudo-estoppel argument would likely fail as well.

3. Waiver **(0-5 points)**

Waiver is the intentional relinquishment of a known right. Here, G would argue that the same statement referred to above, under laches, amounted to intentionally giving up the right to obtain any money from the S or J case. This also seems a stretch. At the time P made the statement, she did not know that S or J would be taking their business to G. So, this does not look like a known right that is being intentionally relinquished. There is nothing in the equities here that militates in favor of accepting the waiver argument. This argument is also likely to fail.

7. *Victor's Secret*

VS can perhaps pursue an injunction, compensatory damages, restitution, and punitive damages (though not necessarily all of them). M has several possibly meritorious defenses.

A. Injunction **(0-10 points)**

A permanent injunction would be aimed here at future conduct (or perhaps as a reparative injunction, to prevent future bad effects of past harm) to prevent further trademark dilution of the VS trademark. VS would like an injunction to prevent future dilution by M of its mark. To get an injunction, VS must prove both *propensity* and *irreparable injury*.

Propensity poses somewhat of a problem here. It is true that M has diluted VS's trademark in the past. But now M has changed the name of the store to "Victor's Little Secret." The facts do not tell us whether the new name would be considered dilution under the law as well. If it would not, then there's a chance of *mootness*. If the new name constitutes a dilution as well, it looks like M is continuing the unlawful conduct, and propensity is likely shown thereby.

Irreparable injury would be easier to prove. It is hard to put a value on the losses that come to VS from the dilution of the mark. Certainly there could be some losses by causing people to think less of the VS mark because M sells items that might impugn the reputation of VS. But it will be hard to put a dollar value on such losses for damages purposes. Because damages are not as complete, practical, and efficient as equitable remedies, irreparable injury is probably shown.

M could perhaps argue that the injunction should not issue because of the hardship on the defendant. For example, M could lose some of his business if he must change the name. This argument probably won't succeed for at least two reasons. First, the hardship on the defendant does not seem very great; he has already changed the name once. Second, if (and we don't know) M chose the name in order to take advantage of the VS mark, he might be considered a wrongdoer, who thus cannot raise this argument.

B. Defenses to Injunction

Even if the injunction is otherwise proper, M may raise a few defenses.

1. Statute of Limitations **(0-5 points)**

The applicable statute of limitations is one year. In this case, M started diluting the VS trademark in February 1998, but suit was not brought by VS until March 2001. It may be that the entire case is barred by the statute of limitations. However, VS could argue for a continuing violation, through the continuing dilution on the trademark (as in the *NAACP* case, each infringement is a new violation). Here, every day that M is out there using the "Victor's Secret" name, he is further diluting the VS mark. Because M was diluting the mark within a year of the suit, the statute of limitations does not appear to be a problem. There could be a problem if the change to "Victor's Little Secret" means that the dilution has ended.

2. Laches **(0-5 points)**

Laches may be a stronger defense for M. VS must have *unreasonably delayed* and M must have suffered *prejudice* as a result. Here, we know that VS waited three years after learning of the infringement before bringing suit. There do not appear to be any excuses for the delay, such as settlement negotiations. This may well be too long to wait. M suffered prejudice (as in the *NAACP* case) because it continued to build up goodwill using the diluting name. Had VS brought suit earlier, M could have minimized the damage by choosing a new name in the early stages of promoting his new store. (This laches argument may also be cast as an estoppel argument, described below.)

C. Compensatory Damages **(0-10 points)**

In addition to an injunction to prevent future harm, VS may ask for compensatory damages *to compensate for past harm*. The goal of compensatory damages is to put the plaintiff back in the rightful position, the position that VS would have been in had M not diluted its trademark. That's very easy to state in theory, but it will be very difficult in fact to *prove* those damages. Damages to reputation are always difficult to prove (that's why in defamation cases court sometimes allow "presumed damages"). Perhaps through the use of focus groups or surveys, VS could try to prove its losses. But such proof may be very difficult to establish.

Even if VS can prove damages, under the *statute of limitations* those damages will be limited to the last year of loss for continuing violations. M could try to make a *laches-like* argument to prevent the suit for damages as well. Strictly speaking, laches does not apply to suits for damages (even though the *NAACP* court assumed it did). But the same argument could be recast as an *estoppel* argument: (1) VS, through its inaction over three years of knowing of the trademark dilution, did nothing about it, and it later took a position in the lawsuit that is inconsistent with its inaction; (2) M relied on the inaction by not changing the name (indeed, it is not clear that M was even aware of the VS trademark or of VS's potential infringement action); and (3) M suffers injury by paying damages in the lawsuit.

D. Restitution **(0-10 points)**

Instead of seeking compensatory damages, VS might try to get restitution (along with an injunction preventing future dilution of the trademark). A plaintiff can get restitution from a defendant when there is unjust enrichment. In this case, VS will argue that M was unjustly enriched because he used the VS trademark without permission. VS may make a claim for M's profits.

VS likely will not be able to get *all* of M's profits under restitution. An accounting for profits will show the amounts available; but because of the *statute of limitations* issue raised above, the profits would likely only be for the last year, or $250,000. M likely will argue that there should be an apportioning of profits, with some portion of the profits allocated to the value caused by the infringement and some portion to non-infringing activities. Not every court will so apportion. It may depend upon how bad M's conduct was: we don't know if he was a willful infringer.

The burden will be on M to prove the apportionment. In many (but not all) jurisdictions, M cannot attribute to himself any value that his own reputation brought to the store (there's no evidence in the facts on this point here). It is likely that most of the profits are attributable to factors other than use of the "Victor's Secret" name. A jury will make the determination.

Laches may apply if VS seeks an equitable form of restitution, such as a constructive trust. Otherwise, M may try to make an estoppel argument, as described above.

If the claim is successful, VS may try to get the profits delivered in the form of a *constructive trust* so that it is backed with the contempt power.

E. Punitive Damages **(0-5 Points)**

If VS succeeds in getting compensatory damages, it might seek punitive damages as well. Punitive damages may be available with restitution, depending on the state. The purpose of punitive damages is to punish and deter. We don't know Pacifica's specific punitive damages statute, but the statute will prescribe the requisite bad conduct for punitive damages. We also don't know much about M's conduct, such as whether he was a willful infringer. If the jury finds M's conduct sufficiently bad, it may award punitive damages, but the amount will be reviewed, possibly under state law and definitely under federal constitutional requirements (*BMW v. Gore*) to make sure they are not excessive. In this case, the compensatory damages may be low because they are difficult to measure, so the "ratio" guidepost may be less important.

8. *Fixing the Hospital*

A. $10,000 per year in pain and suffering and loss of dignity damages **(0-8 points)**

You are given the facts, which describe deplorable conditions at Pacifica mental hospitals, and you are given the *Youngsberg* standard. From the facts and the law, there appears no question that members of the plaintiff's class have been deprived of constitutional rights. The facts may support an award of damages for emotional distress, which is probably a more accurate term to use than "pain and suffering," usually associated with emotional damages stemming from physical injuries. Both emotional distress or pain and suffering awards are difficult to quantify in dollars; but we still allow juries (or factfinders) to do the best they can (and then courts police amounts that seem too high). But it does not appear that the court can simply choose the same number (here, $10,000 per year) and apply it across the board to class members. *Hatahley* stands for the proposition that one generally needs individualized, reasonably certain determinations of damages; group-based damage remedies generally are disallowed. Thus, to give such an award, there must be testimony or other evidence from each class member to substantiate each award. Each class member may have suffered different pain, and had different experiences. The award suggestion only partially deals with that by giving an amount per year. *Levka* suggests there should be rough parity among plaintiffs to make sure that awards are commensurate with relative suffering.

The fact that it is done per year provides some basis to say it is a more individualized determination. Also, some of the award is for loss of "dignity," and you could make arguments that each person's dignity is the same and the award can be done more across the board than through an individualized determination.

This is a bench trial, not a jury trial. So, discussion about instructing the jury on *per diem* amounts (*DeBus*) do not directly apply here.

B. Injunction (generally) **(0-4 points)**

There is no inconsistency (or double recovery) resulting from an award of damages for past harm and also an injunction to prevent future harm or the future bad effects of past harm. An injunction may be appropriate in this case because (1) propensity—there's no question that defendants will violate plaintiff class's constitutional rights; they have already done so; and (2) irreparable injury—the proposed judgment states that there's irreparable injury, and it looks like it is met here: damages after the fact would not be as good as preventing violence and failing to provide adequate habilitation for the class members who can benefit from it. Since we are in federal court, you should also be analyzing the injunction question using the *eBay* 4-part test.

B.1. Reasonable steps regarding safety and treatment **(0-6 points)**

There are two ways that courts can write injunctions; one is in line with the rightful position standard; try and keep the plaintiff in the same position but for the wrong. The other is more free-wheeling equitable discretion, and it represents an attempt to do overall justice without close connection between the defendant's wrong and plaintiff's injury. The Supreme Court's recent cases point to the rightful position as the correct standard. The B1 injunction appears to meet the rightful position standard; it aims to prevent physical violence, bad drug treatment, and unnecessary confinement. All of these factors are mentioned in the applicable substantive law standard of *Youngsberg*. Thus, this step looks particularly tailored to the rightful position. It is a typical kind of preventive injunction. One potential problem is the lack of specificity on how this is to be done. We are told that Pacifica is to take "all reasonable steps," and also that plaintiffs should not be "unnecessarily" confined. Under Rule 65, the injunction must be specific, and it could be argued this is not specific enough, particularly if plaintiffs later claim that defendant has violated the injunction and should be held in contempt.

B.2. Habilitation and new building **(0-6 points)**

Like the B.1 injunction, the B.2 injunction also is a preventive injunction, aimed at preventing future harm. There is no problem with the provision that Pacifica provide habilitation. The *Youngsberg* standard particularly mentions "training" as required by the constitutional interests of plaintiffs, and there is a professional consensus that habilitation is appropriate. Even the idea of separating the plaintiffs (or that subset of plaintiffs who are not mentally ill) from mentally ill patients appears to be consistent with the rightful position, because of the professional consensus that negative "modeling" could result without the separation. The difficulty is in defining the "reasonable steps" that must be taken to separate to undertake the separation. By defining "reasonable steps," the provision avoids claims that it is not specific enough. But it orders that there be a segregated ward, and that such a ward needs to be built if it is not currently available. Is that going too far? What if Pacifica finds another way to separate without building a ward? What if there is no money in the budget to pay for the ward? Does that mean that there needs to be a tax increase to pay for building the ward? Perhaps the requirement of building a separate ward is a prophylactic measure, aimed at the rightful position but going a bit beyond it in order to ensure that the rightful position is reached. Prophylactic injunctions are usually upheld. Or perhaps the separate ward/building requirement is more like a form of free-wheeling equitable discretion.

A good answer would compare the remedy here with *Brown v. Plata*, which required new health care facilities in prisons. *Plata* is governed by PLRA and this is not, but the question is whether the building of new buildings is really necessary to deal with the problem, especially given federalism concerns.

B.3. Outside training, food and shelter **(0-6 points)**

The B.3 provision stands the least chance of being upheld as legal. This appears to be a reparative injunction, aimed at preventing the future bad effects of past harm. The past harm is the failure to provide habilitation, and the housing of the developmentally disabled with the mentally ill which may have led to modeling. The future bad effects are that those developmentally disabled class members who are released from Pacifica hospitals will not be able to function as well as they would have had they received constitutional treatment in the hospitals. A reparative injunction seems appropriate here, provided it is aimed at the rightful position. Here, the part of the injunction that provides additional habilitation appears to be aimed at the rightful position; it is supplying the training that should have been given in the past, to prevent future bad effects (poor functioning) that will stem from the lack of training. The 10-year period seems arbitrary; shouldn't the period be tied to the period that each class member was in the hospital but did not receive habilitation? The food and shelter vouchers seem more suspect. Unless it can be shown that the lack of proper training in the hospital led to the released patients not being able to function to a point where they needed food or shelter, there does not appear to be a connection between the wrong and the remedy. (Indeed, if they were so dysfunctional, perhaps they should not have been released.) This will impose a great burden on the defendant, and it looks more like an effort at free-wheeling equitable discretion than an effort aimed at the rightful position. A judge who is outraged may go for the discretion to right a greater wrong, but there's a good chance an appellate court would reverse.

C, Contempt order **(0-10 points**

The final component of the proposed order is the threat of contempt order. What kind of contempt is it? It does not look like *civil compensatory contempt*; these are not damages going to the plaintiffs to compensate the plaintiffs for defendant's failure to abide by the injunction; indeed, the court orders no damages now. And it does not look like *criminal contempt*, because it is not punishment by the court for a past violation of a court order; indeed, the court orders nothing paid now to the court. Instead, it looks like *civil coercive contempt*, which is supposed to get the defendant to comply with the court order with a fine payable to the court. Usually, the threat comes in a separate proceeding after the injunction issues, but that is not required. There are a few potential problems with the order. First, there may be a large number of violations (especially given that the state can violate the order even by non-wilful conduct). Second, any violations are going to take place out of the presence of the court. *Bagwell* indicates that in those circumstances, a court might require that the civil coercive contempt be treated as a criminal contempt, meaning that full criminal procedure protections would be required. That means a trial by jury if the amount is above a requisite amount (though courts now differ on the exact amount necessary to invoke the jury trial right). It also means right to counsel, etc. Most importantly, it means no liability unless there is a *wilful violation*. *Taggart* suggests in the context of civil compensatory contempt a reasonable person standard, and perhaps that would apply if *Bagwell* did not. Either way, an order that says that Pacifica can be fined for an unknowing violation could violate these rules and due process requirements.

Regardless of the standard, the B.2 order language is problematic. There will potentially to be a lot of litigation over what constitutes a violation of the order because it requires taking "reasonable steps." How does the court know when this is violated? The measure defines reasonable steps at the end, and perhaps that helps, but it also requires constructing a building. How long should it take to construct the building before it would trigger contempt? These uncertainties further make this order unlikely to stand.

Table of Cases

Table of Books and Articles Cited

Abel, Richard, General Damages Are Incoherent, Incalculable, Incommensurable, and Inegalitarian (But Otherwise a Great Idea), 55 DePaul L. Rev. 253 (2006), 41

Akerlof, George, The Market for Lemons: Quality Uncertainty and the Market Mechanism, 84 Q.J. Econ. 488 (1970), 26

American Heritage Dictionary of the English Language (4th ed. 2000), 15

Atiyah, P.S., The Rise and Fall of Freedom of Contract (1979), 66

Birks, Peter B.H., A Letter to America: The New Restatement of Restitution, 3 Global Jurist Frontiers (Issue 2) (2003), http://www.bepress.com/gj/frontiers/vol3/iss2/art2/, 259

Black's Law Dictionary (8th ed. 2004), 52

Blanchard, Sadie, Nominal Damages as Vindication, 28 Geo. Mason L. Rev. 228 (2022), 28

Bray, Samuel, Multiple Chancellors: Reforming the National Injunction, 131 Harv. L. Rev. 417 (2017), 199

Calabresi, Guido & A. Douglas Melamed, Property Rules, Liability Rules and Inalienability: One View of the Cathedral, 85 Harv. L. Rev. 1089 (1972), 149

Chayes, Abram, The Role of the Judge in Public Law Litigation, 89 Harv. L. Rev. 1281 (1976), 181

Coase, Ronald H., The Problem of Social Cost, 3 J.L. & Econ. 1 (1960), 149

Dobbs, Dan B. & Caprice L. Roberts, The Law of Remedies: Damages, Equity, Restitution (3d ed. 2013), *passim*

Erickson, Edward E., The Right to a Jury Trial in Equitable Cases, 69 N.D. L. Rev. 559 (1993), 171

Farnsworth, Ward, Do Parties to Nuisance Cases Bargain After Judgment? A Glimpse Inside the Cathedral, 66 U. Chi. L. Rev. 373 (1999), 149

Final Report of the Special Master of the September 11 Victim Compensation Fund of 2001, 140

Fiss, Owen, Foreword—The Forms of Justice, 97 Harv. L. Rev. 1 (1979), 184

_________, Injunctions (1972), 171

_________, The Allure of Individualism, 78 Iowa L. Rev. 965 (1993), 180

_________, The Civil Rights Injunction (1978), 181

Fried, Charles, Contract as Promise (1981), 65

Gergen, Mark, John M. Golden & Henry E. Smith, The Supreme Court's Accidental Revolution? The Test for Permanent Injunctions, 112 Colum. L. Rev. 203 (2012), 166

Hasen, Richard L., Beyond the Margin of Litigation: Reforming U.S. Election Administration to Avoid Electoral Meltdown, 62 Wash. & Lee L. Rev. 937 (2005), 424

_________, The Efficient Duty to Rescue, 15 Int'l Rev. L. & Econ. 141 (1995), 269

_________, The Supreme Court and Election Law: Judging Equality from Baker v. Carr to Bush v. Gore (2003), 212

Knoll, Michael S., and Jeffrey M. Colon, The Calculation of Prejudgment Interest (May 31, 2005), http://ssrn.com/abstract=732765/, 30

Langevoort, Donald C., Agency Law Inside the Corporation: Problems of Candor and Knowledge, 71 U. Cinn. L. Rev. 1187 (2003), 73
Laycock, Douglas, The Death of the Irreparable Injury Rule (1991), 152, 168, 169, 175, 204
Laycock, Douglas & Richard L. Hasen, Modern American Remedies (5th ed. 2019), *passim*
Lord, Richard A., Williston on Contracts (4th ed. 2018), 66, 282

Maitland, F.W., Equity (1969), 150
McConnell, Michael W., Why Hold Elections? Using Consent Decrees to Insulate Policies from Political Change, 1995 U. Chi. L. Forum, 187
McCormick, Charles T., Handbook On The Law Of Damages (1935), 106
Miller, Geoffrey P., Some Agency Problems in Settlement, 16 J. Legal Stud. 189 (1987), 407
Miller, Marshall, Note, Police Brutality, 17 Yale L. & Pol'y Rev. 149 (1998), 180
Moore's Federal Practice, Class Action Fairness Act of 2005, With Commentary and Analysis by Georgene M. Vairo of the Moore's Federal Practice Board of Editors (Daniel R. Coquillette et al. eds., 2005), 406
Moringiello, Juliet M., Seizing Domain Names to Enforce Judgments: Looking Back to Look to the Future, 72 U. Cinn. L. Rev. (2003), 393, 396

Orr, Leila C., Note, Making a Case for Wealth-Calibrated Punitive Damages, 37 Loy. L.A. L. Rev. 1739 (2004), 370

Posner, Richard A., Breaking the Deadlock: The 2000 Election, the Constitution, and the Courts (2001), 212
_________, Economic Analysis of Law (9th ed. 2014), 19, 211
Pryor, Ellen Smith, The Tort Law Debate, Efficiency and the Kingdom of the Ill: A Critical Critique of the Insurance Theory of Compensation, 79 Va. L. Rev. 91 (1993), 41

Rasmussen, Robert K., The Uneasy Case Against the Uniform Commercial Code, 62 La. L. Rev. 1097 (2002), 83
Rendleman, Doug, Compensatory Contempt: Plaintiff's Remedy When a Defendant Has Violated an Injunction, 1980 U. Ill. L. Forum 971, 242
_________, More on Void Orders, 7 Ga. L. Rev. 246 (1973), 248
_________, The Trial Judge's Equitable Discretion Following eBay v. MercExchange, 27 Rev. Litig. 63 (2007), 166
Right to quiet title or remove cloud on title to personal property by suit in equity or under declaratory judgment act, 105 A.L.R. 291 (1936), 386
Rogers, James S., Restitution for Wrongs and the Restatement (Third) of the Law of Restitution, 42 Wake Forest L.R. 55 (2007), 258

Sanders, Joseph, Punitive Damages in Consumer Actions, 8 J. Tex. Consumer L. 22 (Fall 2004), 365
Schlanger, Margo, Beyond the Hero Judge: Institutional Reform Litigation as Litigation, 97 Mich. L. Rev. 1995 (1999), 189
_______, Civil Rights Injunctions Over Time: A Case Study of Jail and Prison Court Orders, 81 N.Y.U. L. Rev. 550 (2006), 190
Scott, Robert E., Contract Design and the Shading Problem, 99 Marquette L. Rev. 1 (2015), 71
Smith, Scott M., Construction and Application of International Child Abduction Remedies Act (42 U.S.C. §11601 et seq.), 125 A.L.R. Fed. 217 (1995), 238

Table of Statutes, Restatement Sections, and Uniform Commercial Code (UCC) Provisions

Uniform Commercial Code

Index